POWERLIFTING
THE **TOTAL** PACKAGE

WRITTEN BY PAUL SUTPHIN

authorHOUSE®

AuthorHouse™ LLC
1663 Liberty Drive
Bloomington, IN 47403
www.authorhouse.com
Phone: 1-800-839-8640

Published by AuthorHouse 08/08/2014

ISBN: 978-1-4918-6064-9 (sc)
ISBN: 978-1-4918-6063-2 (e)

Library of Congress Control Number: 2014902611

Dedication

The book *"Powerlifting : The TOTAL Package"* is dedicated
to Vince White who passed away April 29th, 2013.

Paul Sutphin
January, 2014

Acknowledgements

Appreciation is expressed to Frank White, Vince White, Don Hundley, Herb Fitzsimmons, Don Hall, John Messinger, and all others who inspired me to write the book, *"Powerlifting : The TOTAL Package."*

Disclaimer

I am not a practicing physician nor am I a certified athletic trainer or licensed physical therapist. Practicing the Squat, the Bench Press, and the Deadlift may be too strenuous or dangerous for some people. The reader should consult with a physician before engaging in an exercise program. The author or publisher is not responsible for any injury that may occur from the use or misuse of the information contained in the book, *Powerlifting : The TOTAL Package.*

Contents

Introduction

My chronological age in years on the date of this writing is fifty-nine (59). The lack of size and strength at the age of thirteen (13) prompted me to begin Weightlifting and Bodybuilding. Later, I chose Powerlifting as a competitive sport and lifetime activity. I entered my first Powerlifting competition in Atlanta, Georgia on February 5th, 1972 and won my 30th West Virginia Powerlifting Championship at the 38th Annual West Virginia State Powerlifting Championships on March 23rd, 2013.

Among the most significant contributions to the sport of Powerlifting through the 1970's, I was AAU Weightlifting Chairman (Weightlifting, Powerlifting, and Bodybuilding) of the West Virginia AAU Association from March, 1975 until June, 1977. Under my direction as West Virginia Powerlifting Chairman, the First Official AAU West Virginia State Powerlifting Championships were conducted on February 14th, 1976 in New Martinsville, West Virginia. The event was sponsored by *Luke's Gym* and the Meet Director was Luke Iams.

The sport of Weightlifting began in West Virginia with a few athletes as early as 1954. Beginning in 1960, many of the same Weightlifters in West Virginia participated in the first Powerlifting (a.k.a. "Odd-Lift") competitions. Prior to 1964, West Virginia Weightlifters were actually Powerlifting before the sport was officially recognized by the AAU (Amateur Athletic Union).

The early days of West Virginia Powerlifting included the accomplishments of the lifters from the *Charleston Barbell Club* (Charleston), *Herb's Gym* (Nitro-St. Albans), the *Mountianeer Barbell* (Parkersburg), *Nagy's Gym* (Weirton), *Slamick's Gym* (Fairmont), and *Luke's Gym* (New Martinsville). The events identified in the book are supplemented with contest results, specific to the dates when they occurred.

Powerlifting in the 1980's withstood a decade of change from within the sport at all levels. Throughout the 1980's, Powerlifting continued to grow at the state and national level in spite of the diversity which threatened the traditional existence of the sport during the 2nd half of the 1980's decade.

The number of Powerlifting organizations multiplied during the decade of the 1990's and into the 21st century. Due to the growing number of organizations after 1990, only major events and achievements significant to West Virginia Powerlifting are recognized in the book. Regardless of organizational affiliation, the highest Totals by West Virginia Powerlifters are recorded in, *"Powerlifting : The TOTAL Package."*

For the Record : The dates and titles of the Weightlifting championships identified within the book are referenced in the section, *Dates of Weightlifting Competitions : 1959 thru 1975.* The dates and titles of the Powerlifting championships identified within the book are referenced in the section, *Dates of Powerlifting Competitions : January 1ˢᵗ, 1960 thru September 30ᵗʰ, 2013.*

Why I Wrote the Book

"What is Powerlifting?" There appears to be a growing misconception among athletes, athletic coaches, and the general public specific to the true definition of Powerlifting. The sport of Powerlifting consists of three (3) lifts : The SQUAT, the BENCH PRESS, and the DEADLIFT along with a required TOTAL in official competition. Within the book, *"Powerlifting : The TOTAL Package,"* Powerlifting as a sport is clearly defined. The language of the definition orders a distinction between the competitive Powerlifter versus the individual who selectively participates in a "Single-Lift" category.

"What are the real Powerlifting Records?" A new Powerlifting organization will often advertise a newly established set of lifting records without credence to existing marks. For the purpose of education and history of the sport, the original Powerlifting Records from the state of West Virginia including several National, American, and World Powerlifting Records are highlighted. The categories of the Powerlifting Records are defined and specific dates are documented in the book, *"Powerlifting : The TOTAL Package."*

"What is strong?" There exists much debate about strength and how it should be defined. Strength training methods specific to "getting strong" may or may not originate from those who have performed at the highest level in competitive Powerlifting or Weightlifting. The records and achievements of several Powerlifters are identified within the book. The Powerlifting Records along with major Powerlifting Championships are highlighted for the purpose of *"Setting the Records Straight."*

Chapter One : Olympic Weightlifting – The Beginning

Before the Odd Lifts (Powerlifting), there was Olympic Weightlifting. The first lifting competitions in West Virginia were Olympic Weightlifting meets consisting of the Clean & Press, the Two Hands Snatch, and the Clean & Jerk. As early as 1958, the Weightlifters at the Charleston YMCA in Charleston, West Virginia hosted official AAU Weightlifting competitions.

Due to the active participation of the Charleston YMCA Weightlifters, official AAU Weightlifting Records were established and recorded for the state of West Virginia and the AAU West Virginia Association. Beginning in 1958, Kanawha Valley Open Weightlifting Records were established and recorded from 1958 thru 1961.

1958-1961
KANAWHA VALLEY OPEN WEIGHTLIFTING RECORDS

Wt. Class / Name		Press	Snatch	Clean & Jerk	Total
123	Vincent White	155	125	165	445
132	Frank White	175	145	195	515
148	Merle Kelly	225	205	265	695
165	Hank Rhodes	225	210	265	695
181	Doug Forth	240	215	290	740
198	Herb Fitzsimmons	250	240	320	810
HW	Herb Fitzsimmons	260	215	305	775
	Physique Competitors – Doug Forth, Frank White, Vincent White				

Conducting Olympic Weightlifting competitions at the Charleston, West Virginia YMCA became a regular practice by the *Charleston Barbell Club*. On February 24th, 1962 Bill March (Olympic Weightlifting Champion and member of the *York Barbell Club* of York, Pennsylvania) conducted a Weightlifting clinic at the 5th Annual Kanawha Valley Weightlifting Championships.   *Charleston Gazette / Mail*

1958 – 1972 West Virginia Olympic Weightlifting
Performance RANKINGS Determined by Total

Wt. Class / Name		Press	Snatch	Clean & Jerk	Total	Date
123	Vince White	155	140	185	480	3/31/1962
	Vince White	160	125	175	460	3/04/1961
	Vince White	165*	125	170	460	6/03/1961
	Vince White	155	125	165	445	2/11/1961
	Vince White	150	120	165	435	6/18/1961
	Vince White	140	110	165	415	5/07/1960
	Larry Wilson	125	115	150	390	2/1960
	Vince White	140	95	145	380	2/1960
	Vince White	110	85	125	320	2/14/1959
132	Frank White	170	145	205	520	5/14/1960
	Frank White	175	145	195	515	2/14/1959
	Vince White	185*	135	190	510	5/11/1963
	Vince White	170	145	185	500	2/24/1962
	Vince White	175	135	185	495	3/24/1962
	Frank White	175	130	180	485	2/1960
	Frank White	155	135	190	480	5/07/1960
	George Powell	145	145	190	480	3/31/1962
	George Powell	150	140	185	475	2/24/1962
	George Powell	145	145	175	465	3/24/1962
	Vince White	155	115	175	445	3/18/1961
	David Green	135	115	165	415	3/04/1961
	David Green	135	105	170	410	2/11/1961

* – West Virginia State Weightlifting Record

1958 – 1972 West Virginia Olympic Weightlifting
Performance RANKINGS Determined by Total

Wt. Class / Name		Press	Snatch	Clean & Jerk	Total	Date
148	Mickey Deitz	205	205	290	700	2/24/1962
	Charles Barker	225	195	265	685	2/11/1961
	Mickey Deitz	210	195	280	685	3/24/1962
	Frank White	230*AR	180	260	670	6/17/1961
	Mickey Deitz	200	205	260	665	6/17/1961
	Frank White	230	175	255	660	3/31/1962
	Mickey Deitz	195	195	265	655	6/03/1961
	Mickey Deitz	195	190	270	655	6/18/1961
	Charles Barker	200	185	255	640	1960
	Frank White	220	175	245	640	6/03/1961
	Frank White	215	175	245	635	3/18/1961
	Charles Barker	205	200	230	635	2/24/1962
	Frank White	220	170	240	630	3/04/1961
	Frank White	210	175	235	620	2/11/1961
	Joseph Taylor	200	175	230	605	2/14/1959
	Mickey Deitz	175	185	245	605	3/04/1961
	Joseph Taylor	190	170	240	600	2/1960
	Joe Firetti	165	160	215	540	2/1960
	Joe Firetti	145	180	205	530	1960

*AR – American Weightlifting Record (Teenage Division)

* – West Virginia State Weightlifting Record

1958 – 1972 West Virginia Olympic Weightlifting
Performance RANKINGS Determined by Total

Wt. Class / Name		Press	Snatch	Clean & Jerk	Total	Date
165	Frank White	270	210	295*	775	5/13/1967
	Frank White	265	205	300*	770	12/30/1967
	Frank White	270	215	275	760	9/16/1972
	Frank White (163)	270*	210	270	750	5/16/1964
	Frank White	265	210	275	750	11/20/1971
	Frank White	275*	210	260	745	4/06/1968
	Frank White	260	210	275	745	9/18/1971
	Frank White (162 ¾)	260	205	275*	740	3/14/1964
	Frank White	265	205	270	740	4/22/1967
	Frank White	265	200	275	740	3/20/1971
	Frank White	250	215*	270	735	4/03/1971
	Hank Rhodes	225	210	260	695	2/1960
	Frank White	245	190	260	695	2/24/1962
	Hank Rhodes	220	205	265	690	2/14/1959
	Hank Rhodes	210	200	260	670	5/14/1960
	Frank White	230	185	255	670	3/24/1962
	Hank Rhodes	205	195	255	655	3/18/1961
	Hank Rhodes	205	190	255	650	2/11/1961
	Joe Taylor	205	180	255	640	2/11/1961
	Joe Taylor	200	180	255	635	3/18/1961
	Mickey Deitz	185	190	245	620	2/11/1961
	Bob Bush	175	170	235	580	3/31/1962
	Byron Vaughn	160	165	215	540	2/1960
	Bob Bush	160	145	210	515	2/24/1962

* – West Virginia State Weightlifting Record

1958 – 1972 West Virginia Olympic Weightlifting
Performance RANKINGS Determined by Total

Wt. Class / Name		Press	Snatch	Clean & Jerk	Total	Date
181	Doug Forth	235	215	290	740	2/11/1961
	Doug Forth	240*	195	290	725	2/1960
	Doug Forth	230	210	285	725	1960
	Doug Forth	225	210	280	715	5/14/1960
	Hank Rhodes	230	210	260	700	2/24/1962
	Hank Rhodes	225	205	260	690	3/31/1962
	Doug Forth	220	195	265	680	2/14/1959
	Grover Litsinger	225	190	255	670	2/11/1961
	Wayne Upton	185	180	240	605	2/14/1959
	Charles Mullins	190	175	225	590	2/1960
	Byron Vaughn	190	155	225	570	2/14/1959
	Paul Allen	175	145	215	535	2/24/1962
	John Freeman	155	145	175	475	2/11/1961
	Bob Bush	----	----	280	Date Unnavailable	
198	Herb Fitzsimmons	250	240	330	820	3/18/1961
	Herb Fitzsimmons	250*	240	320	810	2/11/1961
	Herb Fitzsimmons	250	240	320	810	2/24/1962
	Herb Fitzsimmons	240	225	320	785	6/18/1961
	Doug Forth	250	225	300	775	3/24/1962
	Herb Fitzsimmons	240	220	310	770	5/14/1960
	Herb Fitzsimmons	245	220	290	755	1960
	Doug Forth (191)	235	220	300	755	6/03/1961
	Doug Forth (188)	230	225	300	755	6/18/1961
	Doug Forth	240	205	285	730	3/31/1962
	Ike Hartman	245	190	255	690	2/1960
	Wayne Upton	225	200	265	690	2/11/1961
	Ernie Nagy	220	205	250	675	1960
	Frank Hall	200	205	265	670	2/14/1959
	Wayne Upton	225	190	255	670	2/1960
	Ed Woodyard	170	170	230	570	3/31/1962
	Austin Miller	170	155	200	525	2/24/1962
	Edledge Turley	155	120	185	460	2/1960
	John Cook	250	Youngstown, Ohio		Date Unnavailable	

* - West Virginia State Weightlifting Record

1958 – 1972 West Virginia Olympic Weightlifting
Performance RANKINGS Determined by Total

Wt. Class / Name	Press	Snatch	Clean & Jerk	Total	Date
Heavyweight (HW)					
Herb Fitzsimmons (199 ¼)	245	235	330	810	6/03/1961
Doug Forth	250	230	300	780	2/24/1962
Herb Fitzsimmons	260*	210	305	775	2/1960
Herb Fitzsimmons	250	210	300	760	2/14/1959
Roy Hoblitzell (206)	235	190	250	675	2/11/1961
John Cook	180	155	210	545	2/24/1962

* – West Virginia State Weightlifting Record

John Cook's Press @ 198 at a Weightlifting meet in Youngstown, Ohio and Bob Bush's Clean & Jerk of 280 @ 181...Exact dates and Totals not available. Newspaper clippings as verification

Language and Performance

A complete review of the basic language defining the rules of the three (3) lifts before 1973 in AAU Weight Lifting is forthcoming. The source of the basic language of Olympic Weightlifting is referenced from the book, _Guide to Weight Lifting Competition_ written by Bob Hoffman. For the purpose of information, education, and introduction to the achievements of the first Weightlifters of West Virginia, a description of the performance of the lifts in AAU Weight Lifting is outlined. The text describes the three (3) lifts performed in official AAU Weightlifting competition before 1973.

Before 1973, the official lifts performed in sanctioned AAU Weight Lifting competitions included the Clean & Press (a.k.a. "Overhead Press with Two Hands"), Snatch (Two Hands), and the Clean & Jerk (Two Hands). All lifters were required to perform all three (3) lifts while competing in AAU Weightlifting competitions. Each lifter was granted three (3) attempts in the Clean & Press, three (3) attempts in the Snatch, and three (3) attempts in the Clean & Jerk. The lifter's best Press, best Snatch, and best Clean & Jerk were added together to get the Total which determined the winner for each weight class. The official weight classes recognized in official AAU Weight Lifting competion prior to 1967 were : 123lb., 132lb., 148lb., 165lb., 181lb., 198lb., and Heavyweight. In 1967, the 242lb. class was added.

The _Two Hands Clean and Press_ consisted of two parts. The first part of the Two Hands Clean & Press is the Clean. The language of the rules read, "The bar is placed horizontally in front of the lifter's legs. The bar is gripped with both hands with palms downward and brought to the shoulders in a single distinct movement while either bending or splitting the legs. The bar must be "cleaned" to the level of the shoulders or the clavicular bone."   _Guide to Weight Lifting Competition (pp 2-4)_

The second part of the _Two Hands Clean & Press_ is the "Press." Old Weight Lifting instruction manuals often identified the second part of the "Two Hands Clean & Press" as _"The Press Proper."_ The language of the rules read, "After the weight is "cleaned," the referee will give the lifter the signal to "press." After the referee has given the lifter the signal to "press", the bar shall be lifted until the arms are completely extended, without any jerk or sudden pause, bending of the legs, excessive backward bending of the body or displacement or movement of the feet. The final position will be held remaining motionless until the Referee gives the signal to return the bar to the ground" (a.k.a. platform).

Guide to Weight Lifting Competition (pp 2-4)

Prior to 1973, the second lift conducted in Official AAU Weightlifting competition was the _Two Hands Snatch_. The language of the rules read, "When performing the _Two_

Hands Snatch (a.k.a. "The Snatch"), the bar is placed horizontally in front of the lifter's legs. The bar is gripped with palms downward and pulled in one movement from the ground to the full extension of the arms, vertically above the head, while either splitting or bending the legs. The bar shall pass with a continuous movement along the body, of which no part other than the feet shall touch the ground during the execution of the movement. The weight which has been lifted must be held in the final position of immobility, the arms and legs extended, the feet on the same line, until the referee gives the signal to return the bar to the ground" (a.k.a. platform).

Guide to Weight Lifting Competition (pp 2-4)

Prior to 1973, the third lift conducted in Official AAU Weightlifting competition was the *Two Hands Clean & Jerk*. When performing the *Two Hands Clean and Jerk* (a.k.a. "Clean & Jerk"), the bar is "cleaned" to the level of the shoulders or the clavicular bone *[Refer to first part of the "Two Hands Clean & Press"]*. The language of the rules read, "After the bar is "cleaned" to the level of the shoulders or the clavicular bone, the feet shall be returned to the same line, legs straight, before the jerk is begun."

Guide to Weight Lifting Competition (pp 2-4)

During the second part of the *Two Hands Clean & Jerk*, the language of the rules read, "The lifter bends the legs and extends them, as well as the arms, so as to bring the bar to the full stretch of the arms, vertically extended. Return the feet to the same line, arms and legs extended and await the Referee's signal to return the bar to the ground. After the *Clean* and before the *Jerk*, the lifter is allowed to make sure of the position of the bar."

Guide to Weight Lifting Competition (pp 2-4) by Bob Hoffman
Copyright 1959 by STRENGTH AND HEALTH PUBLISHING COMPANY
York, Pennsylvania

Frank White : American Record Holder!

Frank White was one of the first athletes in West Virginia to begin serious weight-training with a goal to compete and win at competitive Weightlifting. According to Frank, he has specific dates which confirm that he began working out at the Charleston, West Virginia YMCA in 1954. Several years later, Frank placed 3rd at the 1961 Teenage National Weightlifting Championships held on June 17th, 1961 in York, Pennsylvania. While competing in the 148lb. class, Frank White broke the Teenage American Record in the Clean & Press with a lift of 230lbs!

Also competing at the *1961 Teenage National Weightlifting Championships* in York, Pennsylvania was Mickey Deitz. Deitz, a member of the *Charleston Barbell Club* and the Charleston YMCA, finished five (5) pounds behind Frank White with a Total of 665 which included a Clean & Jerk of 260lbs. Mickey Deitz officially placed 4th in the 148lb. class at the *1961 Teenage National Weightlifting Championships.*

The 1961 Mr. Teenage U.S.A. was held in conjunction with the *Teenage National Weightlifting Championships.* Frank White and Vince White competed in the *1961 Mr. Teenage U.S.A.* Frank White placed ½ point behind the legendary Frank Zane. Vince White (brother to Frank White), also placed in the *1961 Mr. Teenage U.S.A.* physique competition.

Immediately after the *1961 Teenage National Weightlifting Championships* in York, Frank White, Vince White, and Mickey Deitz drove across the state of Pennsylvania to Aliquippa and competed at the Steelworkers Open Weightlifting Meet on Sunday June 18th, 1961. By competing in two (2) consecutive Weightlifting competitions less than one day apart, members of the *Charleston Barbell Club* clarified the definition of "back-to-back" for Weightlifting events.

When Powerlifting began, many of the West Virginia Weightlifters participated in Powerlifting meets (a.k.a. "Odd Lift" events). Within the same time period, a few members of the *Charleston Barbell Club* also earned recognition in Bodybuilding. A photo of Vince White appeared in the "Success Stories" section of Strength & Health magazine (January, 1963). Exerpt from the section on page 21, *"Featherweight Vincent Joe White of Charleston, West Virginia, Totals 500 on the Olympic lifts, Bench Presses 240, Squats with 305, and Deadlifts 325."*   *Strength & Health magazine / January, 1963*

(Left to Right) : Weightlifters / Powerlifters - Vince White, Frank White (1962).
Joe Fazio photo contributed by Frank White

Chapter Two : An Introduction to Powerlifting

As a prerequisite to the history of Powerlifting and its origin in West Virginia, a brief description must be given regarding the difference between Weightlifting and Powerlifting. First, "What makes Powerlifting and Weightlifting different?" In Powerlifting, the weights are not lifted overhead. For the two (2) Olympic lifts, the Snatch and the Clean & Jerk, the weights are lifted over the head requiring not only absolute strength, but speed and agility. Unlike the Olympic lifts, Powerlifting requires more absolute strength in contrast to rapid, coordinated movements necessary for Olympic Weightlifting.

The three (3) lifts known as the Powerlifts are the Squat, the Bench Press, and the Deadlift. In a Powerlifting competition, each lifter is given a chance to perform three (3) Squats, three (3) Bench Presses, and three (3) Deadlifts. The lifter will attempt maximum lifts or lift as much weight as he (or she) can on each attempt of the Squat, the Bench Press, and the Deadlift.

Before January, 1973 the lifters in official Weightlifting competition were required to Total in three (3) Olympic lifts : The Clean & Press, the Snatch, and the Clean & Jerk. Following the 1972 Olympic Games, the elimination of the Clean & Press (a.k.a. "The Two-Hands (Standing) Barbell Press") likely contributed to the overwhelming growth of Powerlifting in the 1970's.

Prior to 1973, the sequence of the three (3) Powerlifts were different than today. The Bench Press was performed first, then the Squat, and each contest commenced with the Deadlift. Perhaps Powerlifting can best be described from the writing of an essay written in February, 1972 for a high school English class titled, *"Powerlifting."* *"Powerlifting is a sport that is gaining greater recognition day after day. It is a sport that specifically appeals to the real potential strong man as well as other athletes who seek greater strength for their athletic games. The three lifts involved in Powerlifting are the Bench Press, Squat or Deep Knee Bend, and the Deadlift. When lifting in an official Powerlifting competition, three (3) judges determine if the lift is legal. A white light indicates a good lift (the judge approves) and a red light indicates that the judges have declared "No lift." A lifter who fails in all three (3) attempts in either the Bench Press, the Squat, or the Deadlift is disqualified from the meet and not allowed to continue in the competition."*

The preceding text was copied from an essay written by a high school senior in 1972, Paul Sutphin. Although the sport has evolved over the past fifty (50) years, the basic lifts have not changed ; only the order of which they are performed and the authorization of personal equipment used by the athlete (Bench Press shirts, Squat suits, etc.) dependent upon the organization sanctioning the competition.

The rules which govern the sport of Powerlifting can be reviewed from the website domains of USAPL (USA Powerlifting), (International Powerlifting Association) IPA, (Southern Powerlifting Federation) SPF, (International Powerlifting Federation) IPF, (Revolution Powerlifting Syndicate) RPS, USPA (United States Powerlifting Association), and a number of other Powerlifting website internet addresses.

As late as 1960, the Powerlifts were called "Odd Lifts." At that time, the lifts were three (3) in number : Squat, Bench Press, and Deadlift. The first National Powerlifting Championship was held in York, Pennsylvania in 1964.

http://jva.ontariostrongman.ca/PLR.htm

Until 1967, the 242 ½ lb. class (110 kilos) did not exist and the 123lb. class was the lightest official weight division. The title of the 123lb. weight class was the bantamweight class. With the inclusion of the 242lb. class, the 198lb. class became known as the MHW (Middle-Heavyweights) and the 242lb. class became the HW (Heavyweight class). For lifters with a bodyweight greater than 242½, the SHW (Super-Heavyweight) class was created.

General Rules of Performance

The following narrative of the general rules of Powerlifting, synonymous in most organizations, defines the performance of Powerlifting and the "TOTAL Package." The lifts recognized in official Powerlifting competition are three (3) in number. In an official Powerlifting competition, each lifter is awarded three (3) Squats, three (3) Bench Presses, and three (3) Deadlifts. The lifter attempts to lift the most weight he (or she) possibly can in each one of the three (3) recognized lifts : The Squat, the Bench Press, and the Deadlift.

In the Squat, the lifter shall face the front of the platform. The bar is positioned horizontally and in front of the lifter, supported by Squat Racks or a Monolift (dependent on the organization conducting the meet). The bar shall be held horizontally across the shoulders, hands and fingers gripping the bar. The hands may be positioned anywhere on the bar inside and / or in contact with the inner collars. After removing the bar from the racks, the lifter must assume a starting position. After assuming the starting position with knees locked, the lifter will bend the knees and lower the body until the top surface of the legs at the hip joint is lower than the top of the knees. The lifter must recover at will to an upright position with knees locked. After the lifter has recovered at will and is in the apparent final position, the Chief Referee will give the signal to rack the bar. The lifter must stay under the bar during the process of "racking" the weight.

In the Bench Press, the bench shall be placed on the platform with the head facing the front. The lifter must lie on his (or her) back with head, shoulders, and buttocks in contact with the bench surface. The feet must be reasonably flat on the floor / platform. The hands and fingers of the lifter must grip the bar positioned in the rack stands of the bench. This position must be maintained throughout the lift. Foot movement is permissible but both feet must remain on the platform. The lifter may have assistance from the spotter / loaders when removing the bar from the racks of the bench. Refer to the familiar language of "taking a hand out" or "lift off."

In the Bench Press, the "hand out" or "lift off" given by the spotter / loaders must be taken at arms length by the lifter. The spacing of the hands shall not exceed a width of eighty-one (81) centimeters (cm) between the forefingers. After removing the bar from the racks with or without the help of the spotter / loaders, the lifter shall lock his (or her) elbows into the starting position. The lifter must lower the bar to the chest. After which the bar is motionless at the chest, the Chief Referee will signal the audible command, "Press." The lifter must then return the bar to arms length with elbows locked into the finished position. When held motionless in this position the audible command "Rack" shall be given.

In the Deadlift, the lifter shall face the front of the platform with the bar laid horizontally in front of the lifter's feet, gripped with an optional grip with both hands and lifted until the lifter is standing erect. On completion of the lift, the knees shall be locked in a straight position and the shoulders back. The Chief Referee's signal shall consist of a downward movement of the arm and the audible command, "Down." The signal will not be given until the bar is held motionless and the lifter is in the apparent finished position. Allowing the bar to return to the platform without maintaining control with both hands (i.e., releasing the bar from the palms of the hand) will result in the lift being disqualified.

Powerlifting "Clearly Defined"

An official Powerlifting competition requires each lifter to perform the Squat, the Bench Press, and the Deadlift. The Total of all three (3) lifts by the lifter determines the winner of each weight class in every category. Bench Press competitions, Bench Press / Deadlift (a.k.a. "Push and Pull"), are not complete Powerlifting competitions.

A Powerlifting event is an official Powerlifting competition *if and only if* all three (3) of the Powerlifts are performed by the lifters in the competition and the winners of each weight class are determined by a Total. The Total in an official Powerlifting competition is defined as a numerical sum by adding the weight lifted of the best singular attempt (pounds or kilos) in the Squat, the Bench Press, and the Deadlift. The Total weight lifted in the Squat, the Bench Press, and the Deadlift determines the winner in an official Powerlifting competition.

A lifter competing in an official Powerlifting competition shall not be granted more than three (3) attempts for the Squat, not more than three (3) attempts for the Bench Press, and not more than three (3) attempts for the Deadlift. The rule book in at least one (1) Powerlifting organization contains language of a "4ᵗʰ Attempt Rule" only for the purpose of breaking records. If the "Fourth (4ᵗʰ) Attempt Rule" is applied for any one of the three Powerlifts, *the fourth (4ᵗʰ) attempt will not count in the lifter's official Powerlifting Total.*

In recent years, Powerlifting has been defined in most federations as "Raw" or "Equipped." The definition of "Raw" means that lifters are not permitted to wear supportive equipment. Lifters competing in the "Raw" Division are allowed a non-supportive, one-piece lifting suit, lifting belt, and wrist wraps. The use of the "Bench Press Shirt" or a supportive suit for the Squat or the Deadlift is strictly prohibited in the RAW Division of Powerlifting. Recently, at least one (1) Powerlifting organization has identified the category of "Raw" Powerlifting as "Classic" Powerlifting.

When Powerlifting began, all lifting that took place would be eligible for the "Raw" or "Classic" category according to the standards of today defined in a number of Powerlifting organizations. In 1965, lifters were permitted to wrap only their knees and wrists with ace bandages.

The supportive suits and "Custom" lifting belts were not invented until 1976. In late 1976 and early 1977, supportive suits and the custom lifting belts were used by nearly all Powerlifters. Beginning in 1977 and ending in 1985, Powerlifting could be compared to the "Single-Ply" Division of Modern Powerlifting, <u>without</u> the use of a Bench Press shirt.

The "Bench Press Shirt" did not appear on the Powerlifting scene until early 1985 and was not allowed in IPF (International Powerlifting Federation) competitions until several years later. Most Powerlifters in the United States were using the Bench Press shirt after July, 1985. The implementation of the "Round System" and "Early Weigh-ins" did not take place at Powerlifting competitions until 1985.

The division of "Equipped" is sub-divided into two (2) categories to include "Single-Ply" and "Multi-Ply." Lifters competing in the "Single-Ply" category of the "Equipped

Division" are restricted to use a one-piece / single-ply supportive lifting suit, a single-ply "Bench Press shirt," a lifting belt, wrist wraps, and knee wraps.

At least three (3) major Powerlifting organizations recognize the "Equipped Multi-Ply" category as an optional division for lifters. Powerlifters competing in the "Multi-Ply" category of the "Equipped" Division may use a one-piece lifting suit of multiple-layer thickness in addition to Squat briefs. Competitors in the "Multi-Ply" Division may also use an open-back Bench Press shirt which may be more than a single layer in addition to a lifting belt, wrist wraps, and knee wraps of extended length.

Three "Eras" of Powerlifting

Era One (1960 thru 1976) – Powerlifting was governed by the AAU (Amateur Athletic Union). All lifting during the Era One time period met the criteria for what is now known as "RAW" Powerlifting. The only wraps allowed were ace bandages or a one (1) ply wrap with similar elasticity. In the early days of Powerlifting, there were specific regulations regarding the length of wrist wraps and knee wraps. Beginning January 1st, 1973 all wraps were declared illegal in Powerlifting competition. Knee wraps and wrist wraps were reinstated in late 1974. Throughout Era One, many Powerlifting meets were held in conjunction with physique competitions which took place after the Powerlifting was over.

Era Two (1977 thru 1984) – The lifting during Era Two met the criteria for what is now known as Powerlifting in the "Single-Ply" Division, *without the Bench Press shirt.* Era Two began with the introduction of the spandex suit, also known as the "Supersuit." In addition to supersuits, custom-made, suede belts were available. The "Superwraps" were introduced in 1977. The superwraps were equivalent to approximately twice the thickness of conventional ace bandages. The supersuits, superwraps, and custom-made belts, designed specifically for Powerlifting, changed the game in 1977. Powerlifting was governed by the AAU (Amateur Athletic Union) until 1980 when the USPF (United States Powerlifting Federation) became the unified government of Powerlifting. Until 1981, many Powerlifting meets were held in conjunction with physique shows.

Era Three (1985 to the present) – Era Three began with the introduction of "The Bench Press Shirt." Even though the IPF (International Powerlifting Federation) did not allow the Bench Press shirt in World Powerlifting competitions, the Bench Press shirt was universally accepted in America. Aside from the supportive shirt for the Bench Press came the adoption of the "Round System." The Round System prevented the lifter from having to wait for very long periods of time between each attempt and eliminated the situation of a Powerlifter following himself / herself between attempts.

In addition to the Round System, the practice of a "Twenty-Four (24) Hour Weigh-In" was adopted for Powerlifting by the USPF (United States Powerlifting Federation) in 1985. The 24-hour weigh-in replaced the rule which mandated "A Lifter must weigh-in *not before* 1 ½ hours prior to the beginning of his or her lifting session." The intervals for 24-hour weigh-ins vary as the scheduled times are the discretion of the Meet Director.

In 1989, the USPF began recognition of records in the "Single-Lift" category. The significance of the "Single-Lift" category embraced the concept that any lifter could enter a Bench Press competition and obtain recognition for a "Single-Lift Bench Press Record," versus the traditional ruling which required a Total from the Squat, the Bench Press, and the Deadlift. However, *the "Single-Lift Records" are not to be integrated with Powerlifting Records set or broken in a complete (3-lift) Powerlifting competition.*

In 1993, a very unique and innovative piece of equipment, known as a "Monolift" was introduced to the sport of Powerlifting. By 1994, the Monolift was accepted by at least three (3) Powerlifting organizations. In addition to multi-ply supportive suits, the Monolift revolutionized the Squat as well as the establishment of a new era of Squat Records. The special "Squat bars" (approximately 8 foot in length) and "Deadlift bars" have enabled many lifters in a number of Powerlifting organizations to Squat and Deadlift higher poundages.

In the 21st Century, the "Single-Ply" and traditional standards of Powerlifting have continued with a large segment of the lifting population. The resurgence of "Raw" Powerlifting (a.k.a. "Classic Powerlifting") initiated what many have perceived to be a new trend. Expanded opportunities for athletes in the sport of Powerlifting are supported by a variety of organizations of which to compete, earn recognition, and set new Powerlifting Records.

Chapter Three : Powerlifting Classification Program

On January 1st, 1971 the Classification Program for Powerlifting was inaugurated by the AAU. Totals were established in each weight class identifying each level of classification, beginning with Class III as the entry level and ending with the highest category identified as Master *(not to be confused with the Master Age Categories)*.

In 1971, the first Qualifying Totals for the Powerlifting Classification Standards were :

Weight Class	Class III	Class II	Class I	Master
123	740	850	960	1070
132	800	920	1030	1150
148	860	990	1110	1240
165	930	1070	1200	1340
181	1000	1150	1295	1440
198	1080	1230	1390	1545
242	1155	1320	1490	1655
Hvy	1260	1440	1625	1800

Reference A.A.U. Official Rules – Weightlifting Copyright, 1971

In 1973, the Powerlifting Classification Totals would be slightly changed to accommodate the new 220lb. class. In 1974, the Elite Classification Standards were added to the program and Qualifying Totals for the 114lb. class were included. In 1978, the Totals were modified once again as a new 275lb. class was accepted. Since 1985, a variety of Powerlifting classification standards and entry levels have been created among different lifting organizations. Currently, the USPF, USAPL, APF, IPA, SPF, USPA, and the RPS recognize a Classification Program for Powerlifters competing in their organization.

Definition of an Elite Powerlifter

The definition of Elite in terms of athletics refers to the best or most skilled members of a group. For Powerlifters, what is the standard for Elite and what does it mean? An Elite Powerlifter has achieved "Elite Powerlifting Classification" by lifting at least the minimum Total weight defined as the required Total for achieving Elite in his or her weight class.

An Elite Powerlifter has equaled or exceeded the minimum requirements for an Elite Total in his or her weight class with bonafide lifts made in official Powerlifting competition. The minimum requirements for Elite Powerlifter Classification may vary according to the Powerlifting organization sponsoring or sanctioning the Powerlifting meet.

Even though the Powerlifting Classification Program was established by the AAU in 1971, Elite Powerlifting Totals were not identified or recognized in the sport of Powerlifting until 1974. Whenever there was only one (1) Powerlifting organization in the United States, the AAU/USPF Elite standards were the only benchmarks for Powerlifter Elite Classification.

At the beginning of 2013, there were at least three (3) organizations that measure a lifter's standard of achievement by a Professional Total which represents a higher Total than the minimum Total for Elite. The same Powerlifting federations have went as far as establishing "Raw Elite" Totals for every weight class in the "Raw" category. Meanwhile, in 2011, the IPF (International Powerlifting Federation) changed their weight classes and the classification standards are in transition.   http://www.powerlifting-ipf.com/

In the AAU Official Handbook 1974-75 for Weightlifting and Powerlifting, the minimum requirements for a Total to earn Elite Classification status were :

AAU 1974–75 Elite Powerlifting Classification Standards
Total Weight in Pounds

123–1160, 132–1240, 148–1360, 165–1480, 181-1605, 198-1710,
220-1825, 242-1905, SHW-2100.

AAU Official Handbook 1974-75

Once the minimum Total for Elite status was achieved, Powerlifters could apply for Elite status with the AAU by completing the necessary paperwork as late as December, 1978 based on the above Totals.

The most widely accepted standards for Elite classifications are the modern USPF (United States Powerlifting) standards. The following Totals represent the minimum requirements by the USPF for Powerlifter Elite Classification for men :

USPF Elite Powerlifting Classification Standards
Total Weight in Pounds

114lb. class – 1064, 123lb. class – 1157,
132lb. class – 1246, 148lb. class – 1394, 165lb. class – 1527,
181lb. class – 1642, 198lb. class – 1731, 220lb. class – 1824,
242lb. class – 1890, 275lb. class – 1946, Superheavy – 2033

https://uspf.com/lifterclassification.htm
Powerlifting USA JAN/87 Vol.10 No. 6, pg.61

With the exception of the 148lb. class, traditional USPF Elite classification standards in comparison to the Modern USPF Elite classification standards for men are essentially the same. The traditional Elite standard for the 148lb. class was 1360lbs. Modern standards have increased the minimum requirement for Elite in the 148lb. class to a minimum Total of 1394.

The standards for Powerlifting Elite Classification in the American Powerlifting Federation were defined in 1985 and modified several years later to accommodate the standards of Modern Powerlifting. The Elite Powerlifting Classification Standards for men recognized by the American Powerlifting Federation (APF) include :

APF Elite Powerlifting Classification Standards
Total Weight in Pounds

114lb. class – 1085, 123lb. class – 1210, 132lb. class – 1300,
148lb. class – 1450, 165lb. class – 1580, 181lb. class – 1692,
198lb. class – 1780, 220lb. class – 1875, 242lb. class – 1940,
275lb. class – 2000, 308lb. class - 2040,
Superheavyweight (SHW) class – 2085.

http://www.worldpowerliftingcongress.com

The minimum Totals for Powerlifter Elite Classification in the International Powerlifting Association (IPA) were defined as early as 1992 and later modified to accommodate the standards of Modern Powerlifting. The standards for Powerlifting Pro Classification in the International Powerlifting Association (IPA) appear on the organization's website. The Pro / Equipped Powerlifting Classification Standards for men recognized by the International Powerlifting Association (IPA) include :

IPA Pro / Equipped Powerlifting Classification Standards
Weight Classes & Total Weight in Pounds

114lb. class – 1085, 123lb. class – 1210, 132lb. class – 1300,
148lb. class – 1450, 165lb. class – 1580, 181lb. class – 1692,
198lb. class – 1780, 220lb. class – 1875, 242lb. class – 1940,
275lb. class – 2000, 308lb. class - 2040,
Superheavyweight (SHW) class – 2085.   *http://www.ipapower.com*

The standards for Powerlifting Pro Classification in the International Powerlifting Association (IPA) for the Raw Division (a.k.a. Unequipped) have appeared on the IPA organization website. The Pro Powerlifting Unequipped Classification Standards for men recognized by the International Powerlifting Association (IPA) include :

IPA Pro / Unequipped Powerlifting Classification Standards
Weight Classes & Total Weight in Pounds

114lb. class – 904, 123lb. class – 984, 132lb. class – 1059,
148lb. class – 1185, 165lb. class – 1298, 181lb. class – 1396,
198lb. class – 1471, 220lb. class – 1551, 242lb. class – 1607,
275lb. class – 1654, 308lb. class - 1728,
Superheavyweight (SHW) class – 1748.   *http://www.ipapower.com*

The Powerlifting Classifications for Elite in the SPF (Southern Powerlifting Federation) are similar to the Elite Powerlifting standards in other Powerlifting organizations. The Elite Powerlifting Classification Standards for men recognized by the Southern Powerlifting Federation (SPF) include :

SPF Elite Powerlifting Classification Standards
Weight Classes & Total Weight in Pounds

114lb. class – 1064, 123lb. class – 1157, 132lb. class – 1246,

148lb. class – 1394, 165lb. class – 1527, 181lb. class – 1642,

198lb. class – 1731, 220lb. class – 1824, 242lb. class – 1890,

259lb. class - 1915, 275lb. class – 1946, 308lb. class - 1946,

Superheavyweight (SHW) class – 1990.   *http://www.southernpowerlifting.com*

With the availability of the multi-ply Squat suits and Bench Press shirts, the Pro Totals from the SPF (Southern Powerlifting Federation) and the RPS (Revolution Powerlifting Syndicate) are significant to all weight classes. For the purpose of identifying Powerlifters in the Professional category, the highest standards (Totals) have been acquired from the SPF (Southern Powerlifting Federation) and RPS (Revolution Powerlifting Syndicate) websites. All other references to Powerlifting's minimum standards for the Professional category are essentially the same.

Professional Powerlifing Classification Standards
Weight Classes & Total Weight in Pounds

114 – 1080, 123 – 1180, 132 – 1330, 148 – 1480, 165 – 1650,

181 – 1750, 198 – 1900, 220 – 2050, 242 - 2100, 275 – 2250,

308 – 2325, Superheavyweight (SHW) – 2450.   *http://www.rychlakpowersystems.com*
http://www.southernpowerlifting.com

According to the *Powerlifting Classification Program*, Powerlifters fall into a multiple area of classifications determined by their Total : Professional, Elite, Master, Class I, Class II, Class III, and Class IV. Lifters new to the sport of Powerlifting are referred to as novice. Most beginners or novice lifters fall into the classification category of Class II or below. In recent years, many support the premise that a "Professional Elite" Total represents the "New Elite." Relevant to the 21st century and Modern Powerlifting, the most recent TOP 100 Powerlifter Rankings published in *Powerlifting USA* magazine were analyzed to identify the number of Professional and Elite Powerlifters among the rankings.

Modern Powerlifting Classifications
Including the number of Professional and ELITE Powerlifters
(USA Lifters from Powerlifting Meet Results received from MAR 2010 thru FEB 2012)
Taken from USA TOP 100 Powerlifters published in Powerlifting USA magazine

T – Lifter Total

Weight Class	T # Pro	T # Elite	T # Master	T Class I	T Class II	T Class III
	Minimum	Minimum	Minimum	Minimum	Minimum	Minimum
114	(1080)	(1064)	(964)	(882)	(777)	(672)
#Lifters	1	---	3	16	42	38
123	(1180)	(1157)	(1064)	(953)	(838)	(733)
#Lifters	3	2	8	28	59	---
132	(1330)	(1246)	(1146)	(1025)	(934)	(788)
#Lifters	5	3	8	62	22	---
148	(1480)	(1394)	(1279)	(1152)	(1009)	(887)
#Lifters	6	4	16	53	21	---
165	(1650)	(1527)	(1400)	(1257)	(1102)	(965)
#Lifters	8	13	25	54	---	---
181	(1750)	(1642)	(1505)	(1350)	(1190)	(1036)
#Lifters	10	11	30	49	---	---
198	(1900)	(1731)	(1595)	(1422)	(1257)	(1097)
#Lifters	16	21	40	23	---	---
220	(2050)	(1824)	(1675)	(1505)	(1323)	(1157)
#Lifters	13	36	51	---	---	---
242	(2100)	(1890)	(1736)	(1554)	(1367)	(1196)
#Lifters	20	38	42	---	---	---
275	(2250)	(1946)	(1786)	(1598)	(1411)	(1229)
#Lifters	17	46	37	---	---	---
SHW	(2450)	(2033)	(1857)	(1670)	(1472)	(1279)
#Lifters	11	53	36	---	---	---
Classification	Pro	Elite	Master	Class I	Class II	Class III
# Lifters	110	227	296	285	144	38

The Modern Powerlifting Classifications Chart was created for the purpose of classifying the TOP 100 USA Powerlifters according to the meet results from *Powerlifting USA* magazine. Based on the categories listed, approximately thirty-one (31) percent of the TOP 100 Powerlifters have either achieved or exceeded the minimum standards for Elite Classification based on the United States Powerlifting Federation (USPF) Standards for Elite.

In addition, "Proposed Elite levels for each lift", submitted by Terry Unger appeared in the May, 1979 issue of *Powerlifting USA*. Elite Powerlifting levels include the Squat, the Bench Press, and the Deadlift for all eleven weight classes :

114lb. class – Squat 390, Bench Press 270, Deadlift 430
123lb. class – Squat 405, Bench Press 290, Deadlift 465
132lb. class – Squat 435, Bench Press 310, Deadlift 495
148lb. class – Squat 475, Bench Press 340, Deadlift 545
165lb. class – Squat 520, Bench Press 370, Deadlift 590
181lb. class – Squat 560, Bench Press 400, Deadlift 640
198lb. class – Squat 600, Bench Press 425, Deadlift 685
220lb. class – Squat 640, Bench Press 455, Deadlift 730
242lb. class – Squat 665, Bench Press 475, Deadlift 760
275lb. class – Squat 700, Bench Press 500, Deadlift 800
SuperHeavyWeight – Squat 735, Bench Press 525, Deadlift 840

Powerlifting USA Vol. 2, NO. 11, MAY/79

NOTE : Elite Powerlifting Classification in the 308lb. weight class could be the median between the 275's and the Superheavyweight's. For example, a Squat of 720, Bench Press of 515, Deadlift of 820, and a Total of 2155 would likely satisfy the minimum criteria for an Elite level of Powerlifting in the 308lb. weight class.

The "Proposed Elite levels for each lift" were relevant to Powerlifting in 1979. Adding approximately ten (10) percent to the proposed Elite level for the Bench Press would likely update the Bench Press standard in recognition of "The Bench Press Shirt." With exception to the Professional Powerlifting standards, the "Proposed Elite levels for each lift" are relevant to today's traditional standard of Powerlifting in the "Raw" or "Single-Ply" categories.

Chapter Four : Powerlifting in the 1960's

The first Powerlifting event recorded in the state of West Virginia was conducted at the Charleston YMCA on February 6th, 1960. The competition was titled <u>First Annual West Virginia Power Lift Championships</u>. The names of the lifters recorded in the official results of the premier event for Powerlifting are included in the first West Virginia Powerlifter Rankings. Following the event, a newspaper clipping from the *Charleston Gazette* read *"Fitzsimmons Wins Top Weightlifting Honors at YMCA"* and *"Fitzsimmons Has Top Weight Lift."* The article was referring to the lifting of Herb Fitzsimmons.

On December 17, 1960 the <u>Second Annual West Virginia Power Lift Championships</u> were held at the Charleston YMCA in Charleston, West Virginia. Newspaper coverage gave recognition to the individuals who participated in this commemorative event. The names of the lifters recorded in the official results of the second Powerlifting competition held in West Virginia are also included in the first West Virginia Powerlifter Rankings. Among the lifters were Mickey Deitz, Vincent White, Frank White, Austin Miller, Doug Forth, and Herb Fitzsimmons.

After 1961, many of the same lifters from the 1960 West Virginia Powerlifting competition competed in a Powerlifting meet held at the Boy's Club in Pittsburgh, Pennsylvania on January 27th, 1962. The copy of the official meet results listed a total of fifty-one (51) lifters, including several lifters from West Virginia. The West Virginia Powerlifters listed in the official results of the Powerlifting competition from the Boy's Club in Pittsburgh, Pennsylvania are Vincent White, George Powell, Frank White, Mickey Deitz, Doug Forth, and Eddie Woodyard ; all of which placed first or earned recognition for the Charleston, West Virginia YMCA.

Frank White was the only lifter from the *Charleston Barbell Club* that returned to Pittsburgh, Pennsylvania for the Annual Powerlifting "Odd Lift" Championships held at the Boy's Club in Pittsburgh, Pennsylvania on January 26th, 1963. Lifting at a bodyweight of 157, Frank White posted lifts of 310 in the Bench Press, 380 Squat, and a Deadlift of 425, finishing with a Total of 1115.

In 1963, Powerlifting became an official sport, recognized by the AAU, thanks to the successful efforts of the late Bob Hoffman, owner and founder of York Barbell Company. The first National Powerlifting event was conducted by Meet Director John Terlazzo. The <u>Powerlifting Tournament of America</u> was held on September 5th, 1964 in York, Pennsylvania. The weight classes were from 123 to Heavyweight. The weight classes (listed in pounds) included 123, 132, 148, 165, 181, 198, and Heavyweights. The 114lb. class and the 242lb. class did not exist in 1964. A lifter who weighed as light as

199 competed in the Heavyweight class among lifters with bodyweights that were often as much as 50 or 60lbs. heavier.

Among the winners of the *1964 Powerlifting Tournament of America* were Dave Moyer (1085 Total at 123), Larry Mintz (1225 Total at 148), and Nathan Harris (1350 Total at 165 including a 625 Deadlift). A 1455 Total won first place in the 181lb. class while 1425 won the 198's. Terry Todd won the Heavyweights with a 1780 Total that included a Deadlift of 710.

"You only win once"

Beginning in 1965, one of the most prestigious championship competitions in the history of Powerlifting began. The term "Junior" as associated with the Junior National Powerlifting competition had no meaning at all in regard to the age of the athlete, age groups, or categories. What made the Junior National Powerlifting Championship so unique was the fact that *a Powerlifter could only win the Junior National Powerlifting Championship title once.*

For the Junior National Powerlifting Champion, there was no such thing as a title defense. In addition, the Junior National Championship winner in a particular weight class was also prohibited from returning to the championship the following year and lifting in another weight class. In contrast, the Senior National Champion had the option of returning to the Senior National Powerlifting Championships for any number of title defenses. However, if a lifter entered the Juniors and did not win or skipped the Juniors and won the Seniors or the Worlds, he could return to the Junior National Powerlifting Championships and capture the title, once. Mike Lambert, founder of *Powerlifting USA* magazine, wrote in the AUG/84 issue, *"The Juniors is the "crossroads" meet of American Powerlifting."*   Mike Lambert, AUG/84 Powerlifting USA

The Junior National Powerlifting Championships was assumed to be a prerequisite to the Senior National Powerlifting Championships. The first Junior National Powerlifting Championships were held in August of 1965. As in Olympic Weightlifting, the official weight classes (listed in pounds) were official weight classes for Powerlifting competitions : Bantamweight (123lb. class), Flyweight (132lb. class), Lightweight (148lb. class), Middleweight (165lb. class), Lightheavyweight (181lb. class), Middleheavyweight (198lb. class), and Heavyweight (Over 198 pounds).

Highlights of the first Junior National Powerlifting Championships included the lifting of Dave Moyer, the 123lb. class winner. Dave Moyer's winning Total of 1145 included a 245 Bench Press, 455 Squat, and a 450 Deadlift, all Junior National Meet

Records. Moyer's Deadlift of 450 was an American Record in the 123lb. class. Terry Todd won the Heavyweights with lifts of 470 Bench Press, 710 Squat, 625 Deadlift, for an 1805 Total. The 1965 winner in the 148lb. class Totaled 1125 which included a Junior National Meet Record Deadlift of 505lbs. George Crawford placed 3rd in the 148lb. class at the 1965 Juniors with a Junior National Meet Record Squat of 405lbs.

The first Senior National Powerlifting Championships were held September 4th, 1965 in York, Pennsylvania. Junior National Champion Dave Moyer Totaled 1170 at 132 to win the 1965 Senior National Powerlifting title. Homer Brannum Totaled 1205 to win at 148 in a field of nine (9) competitors. George Crawford placed 5th in the 148lb. class with a Squat of 410, only 5 pounds less than the Squat made by the winner, Homer Brannum. *Powerlifting USA Vol. 19, NO. 8, MAR/96*

The 242lb. class was approved for Olympic Weightlifting and Powerlifting in 1967. The lifters at the 1967 Junior National Powerlifting Championships experienced the introduction of the new 242lb. weight class. Like the Junior Nationals, the 1967 Senior Nationals included the 242lb. class.

The fifth (1969) Junior National Powerlifting Championships were held during the weekend of August 10th, 1969. Jack Welch, whose name would later become familiar to me, won the 148lb. class with 1305 and Tom LaFontaine was 2nd in the 148's with 1250. Larry Pacifico won the 198 lb. Junior National Powerlifting Championship with a 1700 Total.

The 1969 Senior National Powerlifting Championships were held August 29th and 30th, 1969 in York, Pennsylvania. While competing for the 148lb. Senior National title, Jack Welch and Bill Spangler both Totaled 1290 with Jack Welch winning 1st Place on bodyweight. The 1969 Senior National Powerlifting Champion in the 165lb. class was Ron Hale with a 370 Bench Press, 500 Squat, 555 Deadlift, and a Total of 1425. In the SuperHeavyWeight (SHW) class, Don Cundy won the title over Jim Williams with a 2025 Total. Jim Williams' Total of 2005 at the 1969 Seniors included a Bench Press of 600 pounds! *Powerlifting USA Vol. 19, NO. 12.*

The Florida Connection

In 1967, Frank White relocated to the Sunshine State of Florida. While in Florida, Frank remained active in Weightlifting, winning state and regional titles. As a resident of Florida, Frank White was also active in Powerlifting. Frank won several Powerlifting competitions conducted in the Florida Association of the AAU during the late 1960's.

On April 22nd, 1967 Frank White lifted at the <u>Florida State Weightlifting Championships</u> held at Lakeland, Florida. Although Frank placed 2nd in the 165lb. weight class, he broke the Florida AAU Association Clean & Press Record with a lift of 265lbs. Frank's lifts at the 1967 Florida State Weightlifting Championships included a 265 Clean & Press, 205 Snatch, and 270 Clean & Jerk for a Total of 740lbs.

While lifting at the <u>Region III Weightlifting Championships</u> at Jacksonville Beach, Florida on May 13th, 1967 Frank White placed first in the 165lb. class with a 270 Clean & Press, 210 Snatch, and a 295 Clean & Jerk for a winning Total of 775lbs. Frank's Clean & Press of 270lbs. and Total of 775lbs. were new Florida State AAU Association Weightlifting Records.

Frank White closed out the year 1967 at Jacksonville Beach, Florida for the <u>10th Annual Weightlifting Tournament of Champions</u>. Lifting in the 165lb. class, Frank placed 2nd with a Total of 770lbs. At a bodyweight of 163lbs., Frank White's lifts on December 30th, 1967 included a 265 Clean & Press, 205 Snatch, and a 300lb. Clean & Jerk! As of December 31st, 1967 Frank held at least two (2) Weightlifting Records in the Florida Association of the AAU. Frank White's Clean & Press Record of 270lbs. and Total of 775lbs. remain intact for two (2) reasons :

1) After the *Two Hands Clean & Press* (a.k.a., Overhead Press) was eliminated from official Olympic Weightlifting competition, most AAU State and Regional Chairpersons began with a new set of Weightlifting Records requiring a Total from only two (2) lifts, the Snatch and the Clean & Jerk.
2) When the IWC (International Weightlifting Committee) changed the weight classes, another set of records were again recognized. A number of the Weightlifting Records broken by Frank White remain standing as a result of the restructuring that took place in the sport of Olympic Weightlifting.

On April 6th, 1968 Frank White lifted at the <u>1968 Florida State Weightlifting Championships</u> held at Jacksonville Beach, Florida. While competing in the 165lb. class, Frank White made lifts of 275 Clean & Press, 210 Snatch, and a 260 Clean & Jerk, for a Total of 745. Frank increased his Florida State Clean & Press Record to 275lbs. on 4/06/68 at the 1968 Florida State Weightlifting Championships.

While residing in the state of Florida, Frank White competed in the 1969 National Collegiate Powerlifting Championships before returning to West Virginia in 1970. The <u>1969 National Collegiate Powerlifting Championships</u> were held at Florida State University in Tallahassee, Florida on December 6th, 1969.

Wt. Class / Name	Bench Press	Squat	Deadlift	Total
165 Frank White (163 ¾)	315	380	420	1115

Representing Rollins C. Patrick AFB, Florida

Frank White placed 6th out of 12 MW lifters at the *1969 National Collegiate Powerlifting Championships.* The winning Totals among the Middleweight lifters were Vic Adlay (1st @ 1355), Art Johnson (2nd @ 1265), 3rd Place (1245), 4th Place (1165), and 5th Place (1120 Total). The winning Total in the 148lb. class at the 1969 National Collegiate Powerlifting Championships was 1200 and a 1085 Total placed second.

Muscular Development magazine / June, 1970 Vol. 7, No. 6., pg. 66.

1969 : "I Remember"

Beginning in 1969, I began training with weights and declared Weightlifting to be my lifestyle choice. I remember receiving a brand new set of cast iron weights on my 15th birthday. I remember attempting a Bench Press of 90lbs., only to have the weight pin me to the bench. Less than one (1) year after the incident, I remember performing a 210lb. "touch n' go" Bench Press at a bodyweight of 130 pounds.

I remember July, 1969 when the first man walked on the moon, even though I was more attentive to the July, 1969 issue of *Muscle Builder/Power.* I remember one of the first Powerlifters I read about was Jon Cole of Arizona. In the August, 1969 issue of *Muscle Builder/Power,* I remember the article written by Arnold Schwarzenegger titled, *"Jon...Of All Trades Master of All."* The article told about the lifting of Jon Cole at the *1968 Arizona State Powerlifting Championships* along with a photo of Cole performing a Bench Press of 485lbs.

Muscle Builder/Power Vol. 10, No. 10 August, 1969

I remember when Paul Anderson was recognized in 1969 as "World's Strongest Man", bar none! I remember Paul Anderson had actually performed a Squat exceeding 1100lbs. in at least one (1) strength exhibition during the 1960's. I remember Paul Anderson's visit to Bluefield, West Virginia in the Fall of 1969, making two (2) appearances on behalf of the Fellowship of Christian Athletes (FCA). I remember the first demonstration, which took place in the Bluefield High School Auditorium when Paul Anderson spoke at a school-wide assembly. At the same assembly, Anderson performed a back-lift with several members of the FCA (Fellowship of Christian Athletes) seated on top of a huge table constructed to withstand the stress of the event.

I remember the second demonstration by Paul Anderson during the evening hours at the FCA dinner. I remember when Paul Anderson secured a huge nail inside the palm of his hand and drove it (with one short strike) through a number of plywood boards, nailing them together. To this day, I remember and shall never forget the strength of Paul Anderson and his delivery of a Christian testimony of *Spiritual Strength* complimentary to the *Physical Strength* of "The World's Strongest Man."

I remember the argument, "Which sport has the strongest men? Olympic Weightlifting or Powerlifting?!" Several years after the debate, I remember that a few of the top Deadlifters from the 1960's and 1970's practiced the Olympic lifts and regularly performed pulling movements in some variation, such as the Clean & Press and the Power Clean. In contrast, a modern day strength training enthusiast may ask the question, "What should the Deadlifter's of today do for their training?" As for the 1960's, 1970's, and much of the 1980's, I recall the training routines and I remember!

Chapter Five : 1970 – 1972

There are no official records available for Powerlifting events conducted in the state of West Virginia between 1964 and 1970. According to training journals and personal interviews, Vince White, Frank White, Don Hundley, and Doug Forth trained together and competed in official Powerlifting competitions during 1970 and 1971. On December 5th, 1970 members of the *Charleston Barbell Club* competed at the Open Power Meet held at Norristown, Pennsylvania. *Strength & Health* magazine, May-June 1971

In the year 1971, the Powerlifting competitions attended by members of the *Charleston Barbell Club* were Open Powerlifting meets conducted at Youngstown, Kettering, and Franklin, Ohio. Thanks to Frank White, the official results of the Weightlifting and Powerlifting meets are available with rare photos from each event.

Frank White /June, 2011

Only a few athletes have competed "back-to-back" with Olympic Weightlifting and Powerlifting competitions. On March 20th, 1971 Frank lifted at the AAU Open Weightlifting Meet held in Kittaning, Pennsylvania. Lifting in the 165lb. class, Frank made the following lifts : 265 Clean & Press, 200 Snatch, and a 275 Clean & Jerk for a Total of 740lbs.

On April 3rd, 1971 Frank White traveled to Hampton, Virginia for the 1971 Chesapeake Bay Invitational Weightlifting Contest. The Chesapeake Bay Invitational was one of the biggest Weightlifting events in the Eastern United States with top caliber Weightlifters selected to compete by invitation only. Frank's Total of 735 in the 165lb. class included a 250 Clean & Press, a Snatch of 215, and a 270 Clean & Jerk. The official results of the 1971 Chesapeake Bay Invitational Weightlifting Contest were published in the August, 1971 issue of *Strength & Health* magazine.

Part I of the "Ohio Connection" for West Virginia Powerlifting occurred on May 7th, 1971 when Frank White, Vince White, and Don Hundley traveled to Youngstown for the Mahoning Valley Powerlift Championship. According to the official meet results, Frank White placed first and won the 165lb. class with a Total of 1200. The 1200 Total by Frank White on 5/07/71 included a Bench Press of 335, Squat of 420, and a Deadlift of 445.

Don Hundley placed first in the 181lb. class on 5/07/71 with a 1165 Total. Vince White entered the competition in Youngstown and Totaled 1175. Mistake or not, Vince White's lifts were scored in the Superheavyweight (SHW) class, representing 2nd Place in the official results.

Part II of the "Ohio Connection" took place on June 27th, 1971 at the 3rd Kettering Open Powerlift Championships in Kettering, Ohio. Frank White Bench Pressed 330, Squatted 430, and Deadlifted 440 for a 1200 Total in the 165lb. class. At 181, Don Hundley Bench Pressed 280, Squatted 440, and Deadlifted 475 for a 1195 Total. Vince White Bench Pressed 340, Squatted 450, and Deadlifted 400 for a Total of 1190. Doug Forth placed 2nd in the 242lb. class with a 360 Bench Press, 455 Squat, and a 550 Deadlift for a 1365 Total.

According to the official meet results from the *1971 Kettering Open Powerlift Championships*, Louie Simmons won 1st Place in the 181lb. class with a Total of 1500. The highlight of the 1971 Kettering Open Powerlifting Meet on 6/27/71 included the American Records by Larry Pacifico. Larry Pacifico broke two (2) American Records that included a 500 Bench Press and an 1815 Total at 198. Pacifico's Total also consisted of a 650 Squat and a 665 Deadlift. *Champion of Champions, 1986*

Frank White lifted at the 1971 AMA Weightlifting Contest in Butler, Pennsylvania on September 18th, 1971. At a bodyweight of 165, Frank Clean & Pressed 260, performed a Snatch with 210 and a Clean & Jerk of 275 for a 745 Total. Five (5) weeks later, it was Powerlifting once again for Frank White and the *Charleston Barbell Club*.

Part III of the "Ohio Connection" occurred when members of the *Charleston Barbell Club* attended the Miami Valley Open Powerlifting Meet in Franklin, Ohio on October 24th, 1971. The 1st Miami Valley Open Powerlifting Meet was sponsored by the *Miami Valley Weightlifting Club*. According to the official results of the 1st Annual Miami Valley Open Powerlift Meet, Frank White won first place in the 165lb. class with a Meet Record Total of 1200. Frank Bench Pressed 340, Squatted 425 for another Meet Record, and Deadlifted 435. Don Hundley finished 5th in the 181lb. class with a 300 Bench Press, 450 Squat, and a 500 Deadlift for a Total of 1250.

Only four (4) weeks after the Powerlifting meet in Ohio, Frank White took to the platform for another Weightlifting meet. On November 20th, 1971 Frank traveled to Butler, Pennsylvania for the Butler Open Weightlifting Meet. Frank Clean & Pressed 265, performed a Snatch of 210, Clean & Jerked 275, and Totaled 750lbs. in the 165lb. class for a first place victory. The official results of the 1971 Butler Open Weightlifting Meet were published in the June, 1972 issue of *Strength & Health* magazine.

The Rule Book

As late as 1971, the Clean & Press was the most familiar lift among athletes and the general public. The Bench Press was gaining in popularity, but the Clean & Press (a.k.a. Overhead Barbell Press) was king. If anyone became aware of the fact that an individual trained with weights, the question was often directed to them, "How much do you Press?"

After learning that the Clean & Press would probably be dropped from official Weightlifting competitions following the 1972 Olympics, I made the decision to concentrate on the three Powerlifts : the Bench Press, the Squat, and the Deadlift. As the workouts progressed, I realized that I preferred Powerlifting. In August of 1971, at a bodyweight of approximately 140 lbs., I unofficially Bench Pressed 240, Squatted 335, and Deadlifted 350. In spite of training alone and without the encouragement or assistance from workout partners, I was blessed with strength progression that remained consistent.

After reading cover-to-cover and page-by-page the issues of *Muscle/Builder Power* and *Mr. America,* it was not until I visited the periodicals section of a local pharmacy in Rockbridge County, Virginia when I discovered a copy of the York Barbell publication, *Strength & Health* magazine. When I returned home, I wasted no time in ordering a subscription to *Strength & Health* along with the newest York Barbell publication, *Muscular Development.*

During the Fall of 1971, I ordered an official Weightlifting and Powerlifting rulebook from the AAU National Office. According to the AAU Official Rules for Powerlifting in 1971, "Competition in Open or Team Power Lift Meets shall be restricted to competitors 17 years or older." I was excited that I had reached the minimum age of seventeen (17) in order to be eligible to compete in the sport of Powerlifting.

Reference A.A.U. Official Rules – Weightlifting Copyright, 1971

Since 1971, the minimum age for Powerlifting has been lowered to thirteen (13) in at least one (1) organization. Unlike the Junior Olympic Program that was in place during 1971 for Olympic Weightlifting, there were no age groups, categories, or sub-divisions for the sport of Powerlifting. An official AAU Powerlifting competition in 1971 had only one (1) division ; the <u>OPEN DIVISION</u>.

After reading the 1971 AAU Rule Book from cover to cover, I had numerous questions about AAU Registration and locating Powerlifting meets. I wrote a letter to Mr. Charlie Gschwind, AAU Region VI Powerlifting Chairman and Co-Chairman of Powerlifting in the USA. During the month of November, 1971 I remember the day

I returned home from school when my mother said, "You have received a letter from Ohio." Mr. Gschwind's written response guided me in the right direction to begin Powerlifting competition.

The Don Hundley Story

In November of 1971, my father shared with me a copy of the October, 1971 issue of a corporate publication from American Electric Power (AEP) titled, *The Illuminator.* Inside the pamphlet style magazine appeared an article with an action photo that told about a Powerlifter from West Virginia, Don Hundley. The article highlighted Hundley's current success in Powerlifting. Exerpts from the article read, *"Don Hundley, along with five other local weightlifters, is part of the Charleston YMCA's newly formed weightlifting team. The local team has to do a lot of traveling in order to find competition. Weighing only 175 pounds himself, Don has unofficially Bench Pressed 300 pounds, Squatted with 460, and Deadlifted 481 pounds."* Don Hundley was quoted within the article saying, *"West Virginia has very few serious weightlifting teams, so we must go to Ohio and Pennsylvania for most of our meets."* As the story revealed, Don Hundley competed in the 181lb. (Light-heavyweight) class.

After reading "The Don Hundley Story," I was excited about the fact that there were Powerlifters in Charleston, West Virginia who were active in official Powerlifting competitions. Learning that West Virginia had at least one (1) club of serious lifters prompted me to set a number of goals for 1972 which included winning Powerlifting competitions and breaking Powerlifting records. As for a long-term/short-term goal? Like the neighboring states of Ohio and Pennsylvania, I wanted organized Powerlifting in the state of West Virginia.

Due to the successful efforts and support of my father, I contacted Don Hundley. Don invited me to workout with him and other Powerlifters at the Charleston YMCA. It was during the first telephone conversation I had with Don Hundley when I acquired information for obtaining membership with the West Virginia Association of the Amateur Athletic Union (AAU). A couple of days following the conversation, I received an application in the mail from Don Hundley to apply for membership with the West Virginia Association of the AAU. For the record, the postage stamp on the letter was eight (8) cents.

In contrast to modern times, membership cards were not sold at Powerlifting or Weightlifting competitions. Before going to a Powerlifting meet, prior registration with the AAU (Amateur Athletic Union) was mandatory due to the fact that a valid

AAU card had to be presented to the officials during the weigh-in for each contest. In December of 1971, the cost of an annual membership in the AAU was $2.00. As an option, insurance was available to the athlete for an additional fee of $1.00.

Don Hundley - Deadlift - Steubenville, Ohio

"The Big Three"

Less than one (1) week after talking to Don Hundley, my parents and I made the trip to Charleston, West Virginia on a Saturday morning in January of 1972. It was at the Charleston YMCA where I met West Virginia's veterans of competitive Powerlifting and Olympic Weightlifting : Vince White, Don Hundley, and Frank White. Over the years, I have often referred to all three (3) men as "The Big Three" in West Virginia Powerlifting/Weightlifting.

After shaking hands at our initial introduction, the first question I asked Vince White was, "How long have you been Powerlifting?" Vince answered my question with the following statement, "I've been lifting since 1958!" Vince continued, "I'm Powerlifting now, but I started with Olympic Weightlifting : I've done it all."

On the day of our introduction, I had the most informative workout ever, learning in one mid-morning and early afternoon nearly as much lifting information as I had acquired in three (3) years. In less than two (2) hours, Vince White taught me several important concepts for the Bench Press, Squat, and the Deadlift. Don Hundley's specific instruction involved the initial set-up during the Squat, legal Squat depth, and the fundamentals of Deadlifting. When our workout was nearing completion, Frank White entered the Charleston YMCA's weightroom and Vince introduced him as, "This is my brother, Frank."

The first and most important facts that I learned about Frank White was that he had won major titles in Olympic Weightlifting while competing in the 148lb. and 165lb. weight classes during the 1960's, 1970 and 1971. Frank made it clear to me that he was also a Powerlifter and had won or placed in a number of Physique contests. In addition to Olympic Weightlifting and Powerlifting, Frank White was also a Racquetball Champion.

After our introduction, Frank White explained with clarity why he preferred the Olympic lifts to Powerlifting. Although, I soon learned that Frank, at a bodyweight of 165lbs., had done an unofficial Bench Press with more than 370lbs. In 1971, a Bench Press of 370lbs. at a bodyweight of 165 was close to the National Bench Press Record for the Middleweight (165lb. class).

On the day that I worked out at the Charleston YMCA with Don Hundley and Vince White, I told them about the plans I had to compete in my very first Powerlifting competition in Atlanta, Georgia scheduled for February 5th, 1972. I chose the Open Power Meet in Atlanta, Georgia because I had relatives in the region, making it easier for my parents to transport me to the contest. Based on the 1971 Powerlifting meet results reviewed from the lifting magazines, I declared to both Vince White and Don Hundley that I expected to "win or place" in Atlanta. After hearing me out, Vince stated, "If you don't win, don't be discouraged."

The 1972 Atlanta Open Powerlifting Meet was held February 5th, 1972 at the Allen Temple Gym in Atlanta, Georgia. I weighed-in at 146 ½ pounds and made lifts of 245 Bench Press, 330 Squat, and a 380 Deadlift for a 955 Total. It was on February 5th, 1972 when I met Ernesto Milian, one of my competitors in the 148lb. class. The real introduction came after the lifting started. Ernesto Milian Benched only 225lbs. and I felt no immediate threat as I had him by 20lbs., 245 versus 225. Suddenly, I remembered that Ernesto had placed 3rd at the 1967 Junior Nationals in the 123lb. class.

After the Bench Presses were over, I was literally "taken to school" by witnessing Ernesto's Squat of 455lbs., after I had finished with a mere 330. Ernesto won the 148lb. class with a Total of 1200. According to the official meet results from the 1972 Atlanta

Open Powerlifting Meet, Ernesto Milian's Squat of 455, Deadlift of 520, and Total of 1200 were all Georgia State Powerlifting Records in the 148lb. class.

I remembered what Vince White had told me about the first competition, "If you don't win, don't be discouraged." As it turned out, I did not win and I did not get discouraged. Even though the 7th Place finish and a Total of 955 was only Class III at 148, I was content to have officially made a Total in the competitive world of Powerlifting in the southern region of the U.S.A.

Powerlifting Behind Prison Walls

For West Virginia Powerlifting, a chapter of the "Pennsylvania Connection" was written on March 11th, 1972 at a Powerlifting meet held inside a state correctional facility in Pittsburgh, Pennsylvania. The contest was sponsored by an AAU registered club within the correctional facility and sanctioned by an AAU Association in the state of Pennsylvania.

In the 1970's, due to the efforts and goodwill of a few ambitious and benevolent promoters, many athletes who were serving time in the penitentiary were given the opportunity to participate in Powerlifting competitions. While lifting in the AAU sanctioned events, the same athletes enjoyed a rare privilege of breaking existing state and regional Powerlifting records while incarcerated. In order for the inmates to participate, the AAU sanctioned events were conducted inside the correctional facilities. Many of the competitions were open to any AAU registered athlete with a Qualifying Total in Powerlifting.

On the date of our introduction, Vince White and Don Hundley asked me to travel with them to Pittsburgh for the meet on March 11th, 1972. The decision was unanimous that the trip would not include overnight lodging. Instead, we would leave Charleston, West Virginia at approximately 2:00 am on 3/11/72, drive approximately five (5) hours, weigh-in, lift in the competition, and return home immediately following the awards presentation.

As a new lifter, I did not give a second thought that the next Powerlifting meet the *Charleston Barbell Club* was planning would be inside the confines of a prison. The potential risk factor did not enter my mind because I wanted to lift in another Powerlifting competition, any place, anywhere! Given the fact I was only seventeen (17) years of age, I had to share the plans to lift inside a prison with my parents. After much discussion, I was granted permission to lift at the Powerlifting meet in Pennsylvania on March 11th, 1972.

On Friday March 10th, 1972 I left Bluefield at about 11:30pm driving north on the West Virginia Turnpike (now I-77). When I arrived in Charleston, Vince White, Don Hundley, myself, and two (2) other lifters began the drive from Charleston to Pittsburgh in a 1970 Pontiac GTO, 4-Speed manual (400 CI / 350 horsepower) owned by Vince White. Vince was the only driver for the entire trip. We arrived at the meet site in Pittsburgh shortly before the process of checking into the correctional facility had begun.

What is now known as the "Equipment Check" was conducted by prison guards on the morning of 3/11/72. All lifters competing in the first and second session were required to submit to the equipment check. When entering the prison, our belongings and lifting gear was searched and scrutinized very carefully. Many lifters were not permitted to carry small glass containers of honey into the facility. Chewing gum was also prohibited. What made the situation unique was once admitted inside the prison, we were "locked in" until the entire Powerlifting meet was over.

The State Correctional Institution Open Powerlifting Meet was open to all AAU registered lifters (athletes) and the entry fee was $3.00. Late entries were not permitted. Vince White had taken care of our entry fees, sending them by U.S. Mail several days prior to the entry deadline. There were two (2) scheduled lifting sessions : a morning session and an afternoon session. The 123, 132, 148, and 165lb. weight classes were included in the first session. Lifters in the 181 thru the SuperHeavyWeight (SHW) classes competed in the second session. The official weigh-in for lifters competing in the first session began promptly at 9:00 am.

In 1972, the Bench Press was the first of the 3-lift sequence. During the Bench Press, I managed only a first attempt of 225lbs. on a bench with limited padding. Unlike one month earlier, the Bench Press of 245lbs. came to a dead stop between chest and lockout on both of my 2nd and 3rd attempts. With a Bench Press of only 225, I was excited to have beaten all but one of the lightweights ; *Charleston Barbell Club* teammate and competitor, Dave Hunt. Hunt finished the Bench Press with a lift of 270, out-lifting all of the 148lb'ers.

"System of Rotation"- Strategy for Winning

Perhaps I am in the minority as I have never been an advocate of the "Round System" which has radically changed Powerlifting competitions since the mid-1980's. I really miss the order of attempts determined by the systematic progression of the weight on the bar, better known as the System of Rotation. The System of Rotation is also known as "Standard Progressive Loading System."

Prior to the "Round System" (which did not exist until 1985), the bar was loaded to the first weight to begin the competition, which was the lightest poundage called for by the first lifter to begin the session of lifting. The weight would go up in a minimum of five (5) pound increments and, under no circumstances, be lowered. If a lifter, for whatever reason, missed his attempt, then he would be required to take another attempt at the same weight or at a heavier weight, if and only if, he had an attempt remaining. When a lifter missed a lift and was following himself, then the timekeeper allowed him a three (3) minute rest before his next attempt.

In the System of Rotation, a competitor had the option of calling for heavier attempts, whether he actually intended to attempt the poundage or not ; therefore, making a decision to "wait his opponent out." With such a strategy, it was possible for a lifter to actually witness all three lifts by his competitor before he made his first attempt. Before the lifter's name was called, he reserved the option of changing his attempt. Of course, any lifter had to make at least one of his attempts to avoid the "Bombout" and remain in the contest. With the old "System of Rotation," an effective strategy was as crucial as lifting the selected poundages necessary for victory. *I loved the "System of Rotation!"*

When the Bench Presses were over on 3/11/72, I had finished with 225lbs. Although I was trailing by 45lbs. after the Bench Press, I took the lead after making a solid Squat of 350lbs. Following the Bench Press and Squat, I had a Sub-Total of 575lbs. There were seven (7) lifters competing in the 148lb. class. Based on what my competitors had done, I knew that I would have to pull a PR Deadlift to place in the contest. How about all the sleep I was supposed to get ; driving, riding, etc., before the contest? As I learned, when it comes to time to Deadlift, you find the energy from somewhere!

The key components to win at Powerlifting are physical preparation, a "will to win," lifting experience, and coaching. Among the four (4) components, coaching is very important when determining strategy. I was most fortunate to have great coaches on March 11th, 1972. Vince White and Don Hundley selected my final Deadlift attempt of 390 that I successfully made, winning 2nd Place and actually having a chance to win first. But, the contest wasn't officially over.

After I had taken my final Deadlift attempt at 390, a few lifters attempting heavier weights were still Deadlifting. I had a five (5) pound lead going into the Deadlift only to have it wiped away by the eventual first place winner on his opening attempt. As it turned out, I had won 2nd Place with a Total of 965 over the nearest competitor who finished with a 380 Deadlift and a 960 Total. It appeared that the selected strategy had proven to be effective.

I had pulled my final Deadlift and was happy to have placed 2nd, according to calculations. It just so happened that there were twin brothers lifting in the competition

("*Twin 1*" *and* "*Twin 2*"). "Twin 1" was my competitor at 148 and his brother ("Twin 2") was competing in the 165lb. class. According to the scoring, I had beaten "Twin 1" for 2nd Place. At the time, I was not aware of the fact that my competitor had a twin brother ; only Don Hundley and Vince White had the full details.

It was obvious to those around me that I did not respond well to jokes and my new Powerlifting friends learned quickly. Don Hundley observed what a serious young man I was and chose to take advantage of the situation and have some fun. When "Twin 2" (competing in the 165lb. class) approached the platform for a 400lb. Deadlift attempt, Hundley pointed to me and declared, "Wait a minute! Who is this?" I believe that's "Twin 1" and he's lifting in the 148's!" After I witnessed "Twin 2" pull the 400 Deadlift with power to spare, I was disappointed for a moment. Immediately after my reaction, Don Hundley laughed and told me that the lifter who completed the 400 Deadlift attempt was "Twin 2", the 165lb'er and not the 148lb'er, "Twin 1." I breathed a sigh of relief after Hundley assured me that I had won 2nd Place while he enjoyed a moment of laughter.

Closing Arguments

It was afternoon on 3/11/72 and the lifting from the first session was over. Weigh-ins for the afternoon session were closed and the lifting for the second session had just begun. All visiting Powerlifters were instructed by the officials to avoid communication with spectators who were inmates. However, as a high school Senior, I did not always follow instructions.

The designated area for the inmates of whom were spectators at the Powerlifting meet was off limits to visiting lifters. As I walked by the restricted area, an individual asked me for chewing gum. I replied, "Sorry, I don't have any gum." Another individual said, "You did good today, man!" Before I could respond, a third person interrupted and proceeded with a question followed by a couple of statements, "Where are you from?" and "You know, you don't look strong! Too bad you didn't lift against me!"

The comment from the individual, "Too bad you didn't lift against me!" fired me up. I responded boldly and told the entire group in so many words, "Today was only my second Powerlifting contest, but I'll take on anybody, anywhere!" About that time, I heard Vince White shout from the warm-up area nearby, "Paul! Get over here!" Thinking that Vince needed immediate assistance with spotting or loading the bar, I rushed to the area where he was preparing for Bench Press warm-ups. Vince was stern with his commanding statement, "Don't talk to them guys!" I then asked, "Why?" Vince answered directly. "Because you're not supposed to!"

I provided direct assistance to Vince with his Bench Press warm-ups and learned first hand that he was a very strong Bench Presser. In the System of Rotation, the strongest lifters were usually the last lifters. At the end of the Bench Presses, Vince was credited with a lift of 345lbs., one of the highest Bench Presses made in the 198lb. class. Vince Squatted 465lbs. and finished with a 1180lb. Total at 198.

When the final results were tallied on 3/11/72, Don Hundley cleaned house at 181, winning first place by 10lbs. in a field of eleven (11) competitors. Don's lifting included a 310 Bench Press, 465 Squat, and a 490 Deadlift for a 1265 Total. When it was all said and done, the Powerlifting meet at the correctional institution was well organized and represented a carefully planned agenda by the Meet Director.

On Monday March 13th, 1972 the *Charleston Gazette* acknowledged the lifting achievements of Vince White, Don Hundley, Dave Hunt, Gaye Elmore, and Paul Sutphin within the article, *"Weightlifters Gain 5 Trophies."* In the aftermath, I wasted no time telling many of my relatives and friends about placing in an official Powerlifting competition in the state of Pennsylvania and predicted ultimate victories for future Powerlifting competitions.

The Virginia Connection

The Tri-City Open Powerlifting event marked the first chapter in the Virginia Connection for West Virginia Powerlifting. As a novice lifter, I seldom relied on extrinsic motivation. For a lesson in Driver's Education at the age of seventeen (17), I drove approximately 300 miles from Bluefield, West Virginia to Richmond, Virginia on April 21st, 1972 unsupervised and all alone ; specific to the purpose of competing in the *Tri-City Open Powerlifting Championships*.

The 1972 Tri-City Open Powerlifting Championships were held on April 22nd, 1972 in Hopewell, Virginia. Weighing in at 147 ¾, I Benched 245, Squatted 340, Deadlifted 385, and Totaled 970 for a 3rd Place finish in the 148lb. class. Ian Burgess, the 1971 Junior National Champion at 132, weighed in a few pounds over the limit and competed in the 148lb. class. Max Peek won the 148lb. class with a Total of 1200 which included a Deadlift of 500. Ian Burgess finished 2nd at 148 with a 1195 Total.

The toughest weight class on April 22nd, 1972 at Hopewell was the Middleweight class (165's). Joe Leonardis, American Record Holder in the Bench Press for the Middleweight (165lb. class), Totaled 1435 which included a new unofficial American Record Bench

Press of 415lbs.! A Total of 1325 placed 2nd at 165 while the 3rd Place winner Totaled 1320. Fourth place in the 165lb. class was a Total of 1280 while a 1205 Total finished 5th. When it was all over, the lifting for the 165lb. class at the 1972 Tri-City Open was equal to the caliber of the Junior Nationals!

A few days after returning home from the Tri-City Open Power Meet at Hopewell, Virginia, I was excited after reading the May, 1972 issue of *Muscular Development* magazine. Featured in the *"Young Strength Stars"* section was a photo of Paul Sutphin taken during the Summer of 1971. The 1972 featured narrative represents a minor detail among many years of Powerlifting, yet most significant at the time.

Muscular Development magazine – MAY/1972

5 – 5 and "No Weakling"

The 4th Kettering Open Powerlifting Championships were held on July 9th, 1972 at the Kettering YMCA in Kettering, Ohio. Frank White placed 2nd in the 165lb. class behind National Powerlifting Champion, Ron Hale. Frank Totaled 1240 with a 345 Bench Press, 450 Squat, and a 445 Deadlift. Frank White's Bench Press of 345 was the highest Bench Press in the 165lb. class at the 1972 Kettering Open as he and Ron Hale Benched the same weight.

On July 11th, 1972 the headline of the Sports section in the *Charleston Daily Mail* read, *"White only 5-5, But No Weakling."* The July, 1972 article in the *Charleston Daily Mail* could have been the first feature story to appear in a West Virginia newspaper about a competitive Weightlifter and a competitive Powerlifter. Based on the level of publicity received for the iron game in the year 1972, the feature article on Frank White was a big hit for Weightlifting, Powerlifting, and Bodybuilding.

Charleston Daily Mail / July 11th, 1972

A couple months following the article featured in the Charleston newspaper, Frank White returned to the Weightlifting platform again on 9/16/72 at Pittsburgh, Pennsylvania for the 1972 Open AMA Weightlifting Contest. Lifting in the 165lb. class, Frank Clean & Pressed 270, Snatched 215, and performed a Clean & Jerk of 275lbs. for a 760 Total.

POWERLIFTING NEWS Magazine

During the years prior to fax machines, pagers, the internet, cell phones, text messages, and smart phones, the Powerlifting world had to wait for official meet results to be published in printed media ; the lifting magazines. While acting on information provided to me by the National Powerlifting Chairman, I subscribed to *Powerlifting News* and received the September, 1972 issue. In the same issue of *Powerlifting News* magazine, I remember reading Mr. Gschwind's letter, "On the Move With the AAU." Among other articles featured in PN (Sept/72) were Pat Neve (468 BP @ 181) and inmate Richard Luckman's Junior National victory in the 148lb. class.

Powerlifting News magazine also featured in each issue a ranking list of the TOP TEN Powerlifters in the U.S.A., based on official meet results. In the *Powerlifting News* TOP TEN (Sept/72), Jack Welch was #1 in the 148lb. class with a 350 Bench Press and a 1365 Total. Also in the PN TOP TEN Rankings in the September, 1972 issue, Larry Pacifico was #1 in the 198's and 242's with the top spot in the Bench Press and Total.

Powerlifting News magazine included reports from State Correspondents. Each correspondent wrote a narrative / article about Powerlifting's current events in their state along with the latest activity from championship contenders, including the accomplishments of novice lifters. Soon, West Virginia Powerlifters would have a state correspondent to write about the highlights for publication in the pages of *Powerlifting News* and *Muscular Development* magazines.

Among the top articles written in the September, 1972 issue of *Powerlifting News* included the report of the 1972 Junior Nationals held on August 5th and 6th, 1972 in Cambridge, Wisconsin. Richard Luckman won the 148lb. class with a National Record Total of 1355 which included a Junior National Record Deadlift of 600! Tony Carpino won the 1972 Junior National Powerlifting Championship title in the 165lb. class on bodyweight over Tom LaFontaine. Carpino's lifts at the 1972 Junior Nationals included a 355 Bench Press, 520 Squat, 570 Deadlift, and a 1445 Total.

There were thirteen (13) competitors lifting in the 148lb. class at the 1972 Junior Nationals. Max Peek placed 6th with a 1270 Total. Lifting in the Superheavyweight class, Lyle Swartz (later famous for the *Swartz* Formula) won the title with an 1800 Total. Jim Taylor of Tennessee finished 3rd in the 242lb. class at the 1972 Junior Nationals with 1695 which included a 685lb. Deadlift.

2nd Annual Miami Valley Open

Prior to the Franklin, Ohio Powerlifting competition, Vince White had team shirts tailored for all lifters representing the *Charleston Barbell / Holley Health Club*. Each shirt was personalized and monogrammed in the upper left corner with our names in white cursive stitching. The shirts were black on the exterior with an orange inner lining.

For the *Charleston Barbell Club*, the 1972-73 Powerlifting Season began at the 2nd Annual Miami Valley Open Power Meet held Sunday October 22nd, 1972 in Franklin, Ohio. The 2nd Annual Miami Valley Open Power Meet had fifty-two (52) lifters and one (1) Guest lifter : World Powerlifting Champion, Larry Pacifico. The results of the 2nd Annual Miami Valley Open were published twice in *Powerlifting News* magazine. Lifting as a "Guest Lifter" in preparation for the *1972 World Powerlifting Championships*, Larry Pacifico completed lifts of 560 Bench Press, 710 Squat, and a 705 Deadlift for a Total of 1975 in the 242lb. class.

Prior to 10/22/72, Don Hundley had competed in the 181lb. class for all Powerlifting competitions. Don's lifts on 10/22/72 included a Total of 1125, good for 2nd Place in the 165lb. weight class. As for Paul Sutphin, a Total of 1010 was acceptable for an eighteen (18) year old. In reality, a 6th place finish in the 165lb. class behind Don Hundley and four (4) others culminated with a simple handshake at the awards presentation told the story. After the morning session, Vince White made it clear to me that I was not ready to compete in the 165lb. class and the 1010 Total should've been made while weighing within the limits of the 148lb. weight class.

I met Louie Simmons for the first time on 10/22/72. I had read about Louie's performance at the 1971 Junior National Powerlifting Championships held in West Paterson, New Jersey from the official results published in the November, 1971 issue of *Muscular Development* magazine. Louie Simmons' official lifts in the 181lb. class at the 1971 Junior Nationals included a 330 Bench Press, a 565 Squat (New Junior National Meet Record), and a 590 Deadlift for a Total of 1485!

Vince White had planned to compete in the 181lb. class for the 2nd Annual Miami Valley Open. Instead, Vince weighed-in on 10/22/72 at a bodyweight of 188 and competed in the 198lb. weight class. Vince White and Louie Simmons did battle on the Bench Press in the 198lb. class. After the Bench Presses were over, Vince finished with a Total of 1270. Louie Simmons had the highest Squat in the 198lb. class with a weight of 590lbs., sixty (60) pounds more than the 198lb. class winner.

The Tennessee Connection

Following the 2nd Annual Miami Valley Open Power Meet in Franklin, Ohio the next competition for the members of the *Charleston Barbell / Holley Health Club* was in Bristol, Tennessee. The 1972 Mountian Empire Powerlifting Meet became Part I of "The Tennessee Connection" for West Virginia Powerlifting. The <u>1972 Bristol YMCA Open Powerlifting Meet</u> was held December 9th, 1972 at the Bristol Family YMCA in Bristol, Tennessee. While competing in the 148lb. class at a bodyweight of 145, Paul Sutphin Totaled 1040 for a first place victory and achieved Class II in the 148lb. class. Don Hundley finished 2nd in the 165lb. class on 12/09/72 with a Total of 1110.

Vince White (lifting under the name of Vincenzo Bianco) Squatted, Benched, and Deadlifted his way to a fine Total and first place in the 181lb. weight class. When I told Vince that it was "Against the AAU Rules to lift under an assumed name" he declared, "According to my AAU card, Bianco *is* my original name." Vince White owned the highest Bench Press at 355 in the 181's. Only three (3) lifters Bench Pressed more than Vince White on December 9th, 1972 at Bristol, Tennessee and they were all heavyweights.

Vince Squatted with 455 and Deadlifted 425 for the winning Total of 1235 in the 181lb. class. Following the Powerlifting at Bristol, Tennessee on 12/09/72 was the Physique contest. Prior to December, 1972 it was nothing new for Vince White to compete with the best in the arena of Physique shows. After a first place victory in the Powerlifting competition, Vince White cruised to a respectable finish in the Physique contest, making Part I of "The Tennessee Connection" at Bristol, Tennessee a date to remember.

The First West Virginia Powerlifter Rankings
1960 – 1972 Performance Rankings for WV Powerlifters
RANKINGS Determined by Total

Wt. Class / Name		Bench Press	Squat	Deadlift	Total	Date
123	Vince White (122 ¼)	180	275* t	295* t	750* t	1/27/1962
	Vince White	200* t	255* t	275* t	730* t	12/17/1960
	Vince White	155* t	205* t	250* t	610* t	2/06/1960
132	George Powell (130 ¼)	175*	250	375*	800*	1/27/1962
	Larry Wilson	155	260*	360*	775	12/17/1960
	David Green	165	230	305	700	12/17/1960
148	Frank White (145)	285*	365	425	1075*	1/27/1962
	Mickey Deitz (148)	215	370*	465*	1050	1/27/1962
(145)	Paul Sutphin Age 18	255	370 t	415	1040 t	12/09/1972
	Frank White	260* t	320	400	980* t	12/17/1960
	Mickey Deitz	205	330* t	440* t	975	12/17/1960
	Paul Sutphin Age 17	245	340	385	970	4/22/1972
	Paul Sutphin Age 17	225	350 t	390	965	3/11/1972
(147 ½)	Paul Sutphin Age 17	245	330	380	955	2/05/1972
	Dave Hunt	265	275	375	915	3/11/1972
	Joe Taylor	220	280	400	900	2/06/1960
	Dave Hunt	250	235	370	855	10/24/1971
	Joe Firetti	180	310	330	820	2/06/1960
	Joe Firetti	185	275	350	810	12/17/1960
	Frank White	200* t	245* t	325* t	770* t	2/06/1960
165	Frank White	345*	450*	445	1240*	7/09/1972
	Frank White	335*	420*	445	1200*	5/07/1971
	Frank White	330	430*	440	1200	6/27/1971
	Frank White	340*	425	435	1200	10/24/1971
	Don Hundley	225	430	470	1125	10/22/1972
	Frank White (157)	310*	380*	425	1115*	1/26/1963
	Frank White (163 ¾)	315	380	420	1115	12/06/1969
	Don Hundley	240	445	425	1110	12/09/1972
	Don Hundley	260	360	415	1035	12/05/1970
	Paul Sutphin Age 18	260 t	360 t	390 t	1010 t	10/22/1972
	Byron Vaughn	205	375*	400	980*	2/06/1960
	Marshall Ferrell	235	265	450*	950	2/06/1960
	Bill Jackson	245*	255	425	925	2/06/1960

* - West Virginia State Powerlifting Record

t – West Virginia Teenage State Powerlifting Record

The First West Virginia Powerlifter Rankings
1960 – 1972 Performance Ranking for WV Powerlifters
RANKINGS Determined by Total

Wt. Class / Name		Bench Press	Squat	Deadlift	Total	Date
181	Don Hundley	310	465*	490	1265*	3/11/1972
	Don Hundley	300	450	500	1250*	10/24/1971
	Vince White	355*	455	425	1235	12/09/1972
	Don Hundley	280	440	475	1195*	6/27/1971
	Vince White	340*	450*	400	1190	6/27/1971
	Hank Rhodes	250*	420*	500*	1170*	2/06/1960
	Don Hundley	285	430*	450	1165	5/07/1971
	Wayne Upton	285*	405	435	1125	12/17/1960
	Vince White	325*	400	380	1105	12/05/1970
	Bud Carr	285	300	420	1005	12/17/1960
	Doug Forth	bp	sq	555*	tl	1/28/1961
198	Doug Forth (189 ¾)	325*	420*	570*	1315*	1/27/1962
	Vince White	370*	475*	425	1270	10/22/1972
	Doug Forth	305	405	530*	1240*	12/17/1960
	Vince White	345*	465*	370	1180	3/11/1972
	Wayne Upton	310*	415*	425*	1150*	2/06/1960
	Austin Miller	260	325	420	1005	12/17/1960
	Eddie Woodyard	175	350	475	1000	1/27/1962
242	Doug Forth	360*	455*	550	1365*	6/27/1971
	Herb Fitzsimmons	295	450*	525	1270*	12/17/1960
	Roy Hoblitzell	320*	365	550*	1235	12/17/1960
	Herb Fitzsimmons	275*	415*	485*	1175*	2/06/1960
SHW	Vince White	330*	445*	400*	1175*	5/07/1971

* - West Virginia State Powerlifting Record

Chapter Six : 1973

The month of January, 1973 marked the fourteenth (14th) month after the first World Powerlifting Championships held in November of 1971. Significant changes for Powerlifting included the "No Wrap Rule," the addition of a new weight class, and the change of the lifting sequence. Beginning in January, 1973 all Powerlifting meets would begin the competition with the Squat instead of the Bench Press.

For the year 1973, wraps were strictly prohibited in official AAU Powerlifting competitions. Being new to the sport, I was not exactly certain what impact the "No Wrap Rule" would have. I had used the rubber knee sleeves manufactured by York Barbell in the five (5) contests of which I had entered prior to January 1st, 1973. In comparison to modern Powerlifting, the "No Wrap Rule" mandated "Raw" lifting at all Powerlifting events for 1973 and most of 1974.

Wraps in 1972 were nothing more than standard ace bandages. The support from the ace bandage wrap was modest in comparison to the Superwraps that became available to Powerlifters in 1977. Nothwithstanding, the "No Wrap Rule," generated a high degree of interest among those who had used elbow wraps on the Bench Press and knee wraps for the Squat and Deadlift prior to 1973. The cover of the December, 1972 issue of *Powerlifting News* magazine read, "NO WRAPS" Rule Passed – 220 lb Class OK'ed.

Not since 1967 had another weight class been added to Weightlifting or Powerlifting. The supporting argument that athletes who weighed less than 220, but more than 200, were at a disadvantage to those who weighed the limit at 242½ pounds. As a result, the 220lb. class was created and included in all official AAU sanctioned Powerlifting competitions. For a few years following, the 220lb. class was referenced as "First Heavyweight" or the abbreviation, "1HW."

By 1973, Powerlifting was an International Sport recognized by the governing body of the newly formed IPF (International Powerlifting Federation). With the United States being the only exception, all of the participating countries performed the Squat first in official competitions rather than the Bench Press. Effective January 1st, 1973 the Squat would be performed first rather than the Bench Press at all AAU sanctioned Powerlifting competitions. Proponents of the change argued that the break between the Squat and the Deadlift would give the lifter's lower back a much needed rest. The transition occurred with minimal opposition.

During the final week of 1972, Vince White and I planned to lift at Youngstown, Ohio on February 10th, 1973 and again at Steubenville, Ohio on February 24th. However, an auto accident on New Year's Day (1/01/73) left me without a vehicle for several weeks. Vince told me, "Buddy, all you have to do is get to Charleston and we'll make it to the meets." On February 9th, 1973 the transportation I had from Bluefield to Charleston was a bus!

On the morning of February 10th, 1973 Vince White and I drove from Charleston, West Virginia to Youngstown, Ohio for the Youngstown Open Powerlifting competition. The sequence of lifts for Powerlifting competition was supposed to be changed. However, in Youngstown, Ohio on 2/10/73, the Meet Directors apparently were not receptive to the new rule and conducted the Bench Press first. I opened my Bench Press at 245lbs. and received one (1) red light. On the 2nd and 3rd attempts with 255, the weight would not go. Consequently, an off day for the Bench Press, but the Squat of 390 and Deadlift of 420 allowed for a PR Total of 1055 and a first place victory in the 148lb. class.

Vince White placed 3rd in the 198lb. class with a 365 Bench Press, 475 Squat, and a 420 Deadlift for a 1260 Total on 2/10/73. Only one (1) man lifted more weight on the Bench Press than Vince at Youngstown, Ohio on 2/10/73 ; a 242lb'er with a Bench Press of 370.

On February 23rd, 1973 it was "Take the bus and leave the driving to us." The advertising slogan said it all as to how I traveled from Bluefield to Charleston. Vince White, myself, and Don Hundley traveled from Charleston, West Virginia to Steubenville, Ohio in the early morning hours of February 24th, 1973 for the purpose of competing in the Steubenville Open Power Meet.

During the trip to Steubenville, Ohio on 2/24/73, we were delayed by construction work on the Ohio route. I became aggravated after seeing a familiar orange sign in the shape of a rhombus which read,"Road work ahead." Don Hundley then took advantage of another opportunity to tease Paul Sutphin. Hundley had me believing that we would probably miss the weigh-ins as a result of the delay. In response to Hundley's comments, I attempted to exit the vehicle. When Don Hundley realized I was preparing to approach the construction workers, he retracted the statement, laughed, and all was well. Later in the morning, we arrived at the Steubenville YMCA, a few minutes prior to the beginning of the official weigh-ins.

The Steubenville Open Power Meet was held February 24th, 1973 at the YMCA in Steubenville, Ohio. The competition was tough in the 148lb. class with eleven (11) lifters entered. At a bodyweight of 147, I won second place with a Total of 1085. Afterward, I had my first experience as an *Official* at the 2/24/73 Steubenville Open Power Meet during the afternoon session.

It was at the Steubenville YMCA in Steubenville, Ohio on 2/24/73 where I met Ernie Nagy. Ernie had lifted a couple of weeks earlier at Youngstown, Ohio. Shortly following our introduction, I recall Ernie telling someone that he been lifting weights for over twenty (20) years. The fact that Ernie Nagy was a resident of West Virginia made things interesting for future years. A few years after 1973, we all became friends through *the camaraderie of organized Powerlifting in West Virginia.*

The Discussion

Powerlifting was over in Steubenville, Ohio in the evening hours of Saturday February 24th, 1973. During the long drive back to Charleston, Vince White candidly delivered constructive criticism in regard to the "Officiating of Paul Sutphin." Vince informed me that I had passed more than a few Bench Presses that he felt should have been denied. My immediate thoughts were, in less than one (1) year, I had lifted in seven (7) Powerlifting meets, won or placed in five (5) of them and, at the age of eighteen (18), I was now a Powerlifting judge! Keeping my priorities straight, all I *really* wanted to do was lift! With all things considered, it was an honor to have been given the opportunity to adjudicate lifts and "give back" to the iron game.

A few miles later, Don Hundley stated, "What I would like to see are Powerlifting Meets held in Charleston, Huntington, Parkersburg, Morgantown, Beckley, and other towns in the state of West Virginia." I agreed with Don and told Vince White, "If we had meets in West Virginia, these long trips to neighboring states would not be necessary!" Vince replied to me with the question, "How much money do you have in the bank at Bluefield?" When I answered Vince's question, he stated, "Whenever you decide to hold a Powerlifting contest, we'll need all the money you got in the bank to have the meet." As a college student working part-time and earning about $2.10 per hour, I did not deliver a response to Vince's direct reference to fiscal reality.

It was during "The Discussion" on 2/24/73 when I learned about the Olympic Weightlifting Meets (Kanawha Valley Open Championships) and the "Odd Lift" (Powerlifting) Championships that Vince White and members of the *Charleston Barbell Club* had conducted from 1959 through 1962. However, since Powerlifting was not recognized as an official sport until 1963, the AAU had refused to recognize the individual lifts from the "Odd Lift" Meets held by the *Charleston Barbell Club* as official West Virginia State Powerlifting Records.

Another topic of "The Discussion" was the boundaries of the AAU West Virginia Association. On 2/24/73, I learned about how the state of West Virginia was divided in regard to Powerlifting, Weightlifting, and Bodybuilding. The AAU had the entire Northern Panhandle of West Virginia included in the Allegheny Mountain Association (AMA), which was predominately Pennsylvania.

Because of the AAU's territorial boundaries specific to the AAU West Virginia Association, Ernie Nagy and other lifters residing in the counties of the Northern Panhandle of West Virginia (a.k.a. "HBO" – the counties of Hancock, Brooke, and Ohio) were members of the Allegheny Mountian Association of the AAU. With a plan to organize Weightlifting, Powerlifting, and Bodybuilding for the entire state of West Virginia, I realized that the situation of having two (2) AAU Associations dividing the state of West Virginia presented a potential problem. Personally, I felt that a West Virginia AAU card should be just that ; a West Virginia AAU card. Following the February, 1973 Powerlifting meet at Steubenville, I had one (1) top priority among others : *Organize Powerlifting in the state of West Virginia.* According to the by-laws of the AAU (Amateur Athletic Union), a minimum of two (2) conditions had to be met in order for Powerlifting to be organized and governed as a sport within the boundaries of the West Virginia AAU Association.

In order to govern the sport of Powerlifting in accordance to the by-laws of the Amateur Athletic Union in the West Virginia AAU Association, a minimum of five (5) Teams (Powerlifting/Weightlifting/Bodybuilding) or clubs with valid AAU membership cardholders were required to register with the AAU West Virginia Association. The second requirement was to organize and conduct an official State Championship in order for Powerlifting Records to be officially recognized by the West Virginia Association of the AAU.

After arriving in Charleston (a.m.) on Sunday February 25th, 1973 it was the "bus ride" back to Bluefield. Remembering "The Discussion" and creating a Powerlifting program throughout the state of West Virginia dominated my thoughts. It was a fact that Vince White, Frank White, Don Hundley, and myself were setting West Virginia Powerlifting Records every time we competed in official competition. I was determined, above all else, to have our Weightlifting and Powerlifting Records entered as permanent marks into at least one (1) frequently referenced, historical archive.

The Workout Journal

In order to realize success in Powerlifting, all three (3) of the Powerlifts require extensive training and continued practice, preferably in some variation for each workout. The Powerlifting routines followed by most Powerlifters of the *Charleston Barbell Club* included all three (3) of the Powerlifts done three (3) times each week. The preferred days for working out were Monday, Wednesday, and Saturday. However, the same "3-day per week routine" can be modified to accommodate a variety of workout schedules performed on different days. For many years, I chose Monday, Wednesday, and Friday to complete the Powerlifting workout schedule.

With a few exceptions, most all of the Powerlifting Champions of the 1960's and 1970's followed a basic routine of three (3) workouts per week, performing all three (3) of the Powerlifts during each workout. The repetitions included 1 or 2 warm-up sets, then the pyramid of 5, 4, 3, 2, 1, 1, 1. The maximum weight was defined as the heaviest weight lifted in training or from the lifter's best official lift from a Powerlifting meet. Conclusively, the traditional Powerlifting routines represented a variation of the Pyramid, Progressive Resistance, Progressive Overload, and Training by Percents.

After learning that a "self report" or daily workout record was the practice of many top lifters and National Powerlifting Champions, I began keeping a written record of all workouts, beginning on Friday March 9th, 1973. The workout log began thirty-one (31) days prior to the *1973 Concord Invitational Power Meet*. For the first time, I achieved a Class I Total of 1110 in the 148lb. class (Raw Lifting). I had previously Totaled 1055 at Youngstown, Ohio and 1085 in Steubenville, Ohio in contests only two (2) weeks apart. The workouts prior to the 1973 Concord Power Meet are as follows :

Training Log #1
Paul Sutphin Workouts

Friday March 09, 1973
1. Squats – 175 x 5, 225 x 4, 280 x 3, 320 x 2, 345 x 1, 370 x 1.
2. Bench Presses – 135 x 5, 175 x 4, 200 x 3, 215 x2, 240 x 1, 240 x 2, 240 x 2, 240 x 2, 250 x 1.
3. Deadlifts – 245 x 5, 270 x 3, 345 x 1, 380 x 1, 400 x 1, missed 435, 405 x 1.
4. Incline Dumbell Presses – 60 x 7.
5. Standing Curls (EZ Bar) – 100 x 5.

Training Log #1
(Week 1)

Monday March 12, 1973
(Universal Machine Bench Press) – 140 x 3, 170 x 3, 220 x 1, 240 x 1.
1. Squats – 175 x 5, 225 x 4, 280 x 3, 320 x 2, 350 x 1, 370 x 1.
2. Bench Presses – 135 x 5, 175 x 4, 200 x 3, 225 x 2, 250 x 1, 250 x 1, 255 x 1, 260 x 1, 210 x 2.

3. Deadlifts – 245 x 5, 270 x 2, 345 x 1, 370 x 1.
4. Standing Curls (EZ Bar) – 100 x 5, 105 x 5.
5. Incline Dumbell Presses – 60 x 7, 60 x 6.

Wednesday March 14, 1973
1. Squats – 175 x 5, 225 x 4, 280 x 3, 320 x 2, 345 x 1, 360 x 1, 245 x 2.
2. Bench Presses – 135 x 5, 175 x 4, 200 x 3, 225 x 2, 245 x 3, 250 x 2, 230 x 5.
3. Deadlifts – 245 x 5, 295 x 2, 345 x 1, 365 x 1, 380 x 1.
4. Standing Curls (EZ Bar) – 105 x 5, 105 x 5.
5. Incline Dumbell Presses – 60 x 7, 60 x 6.

Friday March 16, 1973
1. Squats – 175 x 5, 225 x 4, 280 x 3, 320 x 2, 370 x 1.
2. Bench Presses – 135 x 5, 175 x 4, 200 x 3, 225 x 2, 250 x 1, 265 x 1, missed 290, 245 x 2, 215 x 8.
3. Deadlifts – 245 x 5, 295 x 2, 360 x 1, 390 x 1, 415 x 1.
4. Standing Curls (EZ Bar) – 105 x 5, 110 x 5.
5. Incline Dumbell Presses – 60 x 7, 60 x 6.

Training Log #1
(Week 2)

Monday March 19, 1973
1. Squats – 175 x 5, 225 x 4, 280 x 3, 320 x 2, 370 x 1, 390 x 1, 410 x 1.
2. Bench Presses – 135 x 5, 175 x 4, 200 x 3, 225 x 2, 240 x 2, 245 x 2, 255 x 1, 230 x 3.
3. Deadlifts – 245 x 5, 295 x 3, 350 x 1, 375 x 1, 400 x 1.
4. Standing Curls (EZ Bar) – 105 x 5, 110 x 5.
5. Incline Dumbell Presses – 60 x 7, 63 x 6.

Wednesday March 21, 1973
[(Universal Benches)] – 140 x 3, 170 x 1, 220 x 1, 240 x 1, 260 x 2, missed 280.
1. Squats – 175 x 5, 225 x 4, 280 x 3, 325 x 2, 370 x 1.
2. Bench Presses – 135 x 5, 175 x 4, 200 x 4, 235 x 4, 245 x 2.
3. Standing Curls (EZ Bar) – 105 x 5, 110 x 5.
4. Incline Dumbell Presses – 63 x 6, 63 x 6.

Friday March 23, 1973

[(Universal Benches)] – 140 x 3, 170 x 1, 220 x 1, 240 x 1, 240 x 3.

1. Squats – 180 x 5, 225 x 4, 280 x 3, 325 x 2, 370 x 1, 390 x 1.
2. Bench Presses – 135 x 5, 175 x 4, 200 x 3, 225 x 2, 255 x 1, 270 x 1, missed 290, 250 x 2, 230 x 6.
3. Standing Curls (EZ Bar) – 105 x 5, 110 x 5.
4. Incline Dumbell Presses – 63 x 6, 63 x 6.

Training Log #1
(Week 3)

Monday March 26, 1973

1. Squats – 180 x 5, 225 x 4, 280 x 3, 370 x 1, 395 x 1.
2. Bench Presses – 135 x 5, 175 x 4, 200 x 3, 225 x 2, 240 x 2, 225 x 3, 230 x 3, 245 x 2.
3. Deadlifts – 245 x 5, 270 x 3, 245 x 1, 385 x 1.
4. Standing Curls (EZ Bar) – 105 x 5, 110 x 5.
5. Incline Dumbell Presses – 63 x 7, 63 x 6.

Wednesday March 28, 1973

1. Squats – 175 x 5, 225 x 4, 280 x 3, 320 x 2, 375 x 1, 400 x 1, 420 x 1, 426 x 1.
2. Bench Presses – 135 x 5, 175 x 4, 200 x 3, 225 x 3, 250 x 2, 265 x 1, 240 x 5, 245 x 3.
3. Deadlifts (Standing on 4 inch platform) – 245 x 5, 275 x 3, 345 x 1, 370 x 1.
4. Standing Curls (EZ Bar) – 105 x 5, 110 x 5.
5. Incline Dumbell Presses – 63 x 7, 66 x 6.

Friday March 30, 1973

1. Squats – 180 x 5, 230 x 4, 280 x 3, 325 x 2, 370 x 1, 395 x 1.
2. Bench Presses – 135 x 5, 175 x 4, 200 x 3, 225 x 2, 255 x 1, 265 x 1, 240 x 3, 240 x 3.
3. Deadlifts – 245 x 5, 270 x 3, 350 x 1, 380 x 1, 400 x 1, missed 435.
4. Standing Curls (EZ Bar) – 110 x 5, 110 x 5.
5. Incline Dumbell Presses – 66 x 7, 66 x 6.

Training Log #1
(Week 4)

<u>Monday April 02, 1973</u>
1. Squats – 180 x 5, 230 x 4, 285 x 3, 325 x 2, 380 x 1, 410 x 1, 430 x 1.
2. Bench Presses – 135 x 5, 175 x 4, 205 x 3, 230 x 3, 250 x 1, 260 x 1, 250 x 5, 270 x 1.
3. Deadlifts – 245 x 5, 295 x 2, 345 x 1, 390 x 1, 405 x 1.
4. Standing Curls (EZ Bar) – 110 x 5, 110 x 5.
5. Incline Dumbell Presses – 66 x 7, 66 x 6.

<u>Thursday April 05, 1973</u>
1. Squats – 180 x 5, 230 x 4, 285 x 3, 325 x 2, 380 x 1, 400 x 1.
2. Bench Presses – 140 x 5, 180 x 4, 210 x 3, 235 x 2, 250 x 1, 260 x 1, 225 x 5.
3. Deadlifts – 245 x 5, 270 x 3, 345 x 1, 370 x 1, 385 x 1.
4. Standing Curls (EZ Bar) – 110 x 5, 115 x 5.
5. Incline Dumbell Presses – 66 x 7.

<u>Saturday April 07, 1973</u>
1. Squats – 180 x 5, 230 x 4, 285 x 3, 325 x 2, 375 x 1, 390 x 1.
2. Bench Presses – 135 x 5, 175 x 4, 205 x 3, 225 x 2, 250 x 1, 260 x 1, 270 x 1, 280 x 1, missed 290.
3. Deadlifts – 245 x 5, 270 x 3, 360 x 1, 400 x 1, missed 435, missed 420.
4. Standing Curls (EZ Bar) – 115 x 5, 115 x 5.
5. Incline Dumbell Presses – 66 x 7, 66 x 6.

Training Log #1
(Week 5 – Contest Week)

<u>Tuesday April 10, 1973</u>
1. Squats – 180 x 5, 230 x 4, 285 x 3, 325 x 2, 370 x 1, 400 x 1.
2. Bench Presses – 135 x 5, 175 x 4, 205 x 3, 225 x 2, 250 x 1, 275 x 1, missed 290, 255 x 2, 245 x 3.
3. Deadlifts – 245 x 5, 270 x 3, 345 x 1, 385 x 1, 405 x 1.
4. Standing Curls (EZ Bar) – 120 x 5, 120 x 5.
5. Incline Dumbell Presses – 66 x 7, 69 x 6.

Thursday April 12, 1973

1. Squats – 180 x 5, 230 x 4, 285 x 3, 325 x 2, 375 x 1, 390 x 1.
2. Bench Presses – 135 x 5, 175 x 4, 205 x 3, 225 x 2, 240 x 1, 250 x 1, 255 x 1.
3. Deadlifts – 245 x 5, 270 x 1, 345 x 1, 380 x 1.
4. Curls (EZ) – 120 x 5, 120 x 4.
5. Incline Dumbell Presses – 69 x 7, 69 x 6.

Training Log #1
(Powerlifting Competition)

Sunday April 15, 1973 (Contest Day)
Concord Invitational Power Meet
148lb. weight class

SQUAT – 410, BENCH PRESS – 260, DEADLIFT – 440,
TOTAL – 1110 – The first Class I Total.

Additional Training Notes : Nearly every day of training, I handled between 85% and 100% on the Squat, Bench Press, and the Deadlift. The percentages of the weights handled during the workouts prior to the 1973 Concord Powerlifting Meet are calculated from the maximum lifts made on April 15th, 1973. The workouts provide an example of Progressive Overload with Percentage of Maximum Effort Training.

Powerlifting : Class I

During the first week of March (1973) I talked to a high school alumni friend who happened to be a Freshman at Concord College. The topic of our conversation centered around the subject of official Powerlifting meets and the competitive lifting success I had experienced. I then learned from our conversation about a group of lifters on the campus of Concord College. The group had tentative plans to conduct a lifting event on the Concord College campus, yet the same individuals were somewhat reluctant to move forward with their agenda.

After a couple of meetings with the CWC leaders, the plans for a Powerlifting competition were confirmed. I assured the members of the *Concord Weightlifting Club* that a Powerlifting event conducted on the campus of Concord College would have the support of myself and the Powerlifters from the *Charleston Barbell / Holley Health*

Club. A Powerlifting meet was conducted in Athens, West Virginia during the weekend of April 14th, 1973.

The Concord Invitational Powerlifting Meet was held Sunday April 15th, 1973 in Athens, West Virginia. The Concord Invitational Powerlifting Meet was sponsored by the *Concord Power Club (a.k.a. Concord Weightlifting Club)*. The following lifters represented the *Holley Health Club* : Larry Wildman (132), Paul Sutphin (148), John Collias (165), Vince White (198), Doug Forth (220), and Gaye Elmore (242). Don Hundley could not compete due to an injury.

At the end of the day, the *Concord Weight Club* had a first place victory from Kevin Sheets (123lb. class), along with a number of second place finishers. Lee Shorter (SuperHeavyWeight winner), represented another collegiate Weightlifting club.

The 300 Deadlift by Kevin Sheets in the 123lb. class along with the 455 Squat, 525 Deadlift, and 1255lb. Total by Lee Shorter in the SHW's exceeded the existing Powerlifting Record marks in their respective weight classes for West Virginia Powerlifting. The Team Champions of the 1973 Concord Invitational were *Holley Health Club (Charleston Barbell Club)* captained by Vince White.

In the weeks leading up to the Concord Invitational, it was the "confidence of Vince White." On the day of the Concord Powerlifting Meet, it was "The lifting of Vince White." At the Concord Invitational Power Meet on 4/15/73, Vince White won the 198lb. class with a 500 Squat, 360 Bench Press, and a 440 Deadlift for a 1300 Total. The 500 Squat by Vince White at the Concord Invitational was recorded as a new West Virginia State Powerlifting Record in the 198lb. class.

Vince White – Preparing for a 500 Squat at the 1973 Concord Invitational

Doug Forth, lifting competitively for the first time since 1971, posted strong lifts in the new 220lb. weight class on 4/15/73. All of Doug Forth's lifts were recorded as new West Virginia State Powerlifting Records in the 220lb. class. The significance of the Concord Invitational Power Meet was that it was the last Powerlifting contest for Doug Forth. The lifting records set by Doug Forth on April 15th, 1973 have been retired as permanent marks, never to be broken!

At the *Concord Invitational Power Meet*, Paul Sutphin weighed in at 148 ¾ and Totaled 1110 for Class I in the 148lb. weight class. Sutphin's lifting included a Squat of 410lbs. a Bench Press of 260, and a Deadlift of 440 for a 1110 Total. The 440 Deadlift was the final lift of the morning session. When comparing Paul Sutphin's performance on April 15th, 1973 to Modern Powerlifting, *a "RAW" 1110 Total at 148 at the age of 18 is greater than or equal to many of the Teenage RAW/Classic American Powerlifting Records listed by a number of Powerlifting organizations during 2013!* Again, Powerlifting clearly defined.

The headline of the article which appeared in the *Bluefield Daily Telegraph (April, 1973)* read, *"Charleston Club Wins Power Meet."* The rare appearance of the *Charleston Barbell Club* in Southern West Virginia on April 15th, 1973 marked the beginning of organized Powerlifting in West Virginia.

9th Annual Midwest Open

The 9th Annual Midwest Open Powerlifting Championships were held on Sunday May 20th, 1973 at the Central Parkway Branch YMCA in Cincinnati, Ohio. Vince White and I made the trip to Cincinnati on Saturday May 19th and traveled through major thunderstorms, including tornado warnings. The real storm occurred on Sunday when the lifting began.

After looking at the roster of those who had entered in the 148lb. class, I knew that a first place victory was unlikely. I remained confident I would do well. I was so confident the morning of the 1973 Midwest Open that I told Vince, "My opening attempt in the Squat will be a weight of at least 400 pounds." After an assessment of the venue, the officials, and the roster of competitors, Vince said, "Paul, if you open with 400, then we'll be going back to Charleston early!"

I took Vince's advice and opened the Squats with a weight of 385 pounds. The 385 Squat, although successful, felt heavy. A 2nd attempt Squat of 405 was a strong lift, but a 3rd attempt at 415 received two (2) red lights from the officials. When the Squats were completed for the morning session, lifting veteran Bob Cortes had Squatted 410, only

5lbs. more than the weight I lifted. Jerry Bell and I were tied as both of us Squatted 405lbs. After the Squats, I felt that I was in a good competitive position.

I completed all three (3) Bench Press attempts and received all white lights with National Powerlifting Referees adjudicating each lift. Considering my level of strength at the time, a 270 Bench Press in the 148lb. class represented a PR for a lift done in official Powerlifting competition. However, when the Deadlifting began, I was literally given a "Deadlift clinic" by four (4) individuals with pulling capability that I had not seen in the 148lb. weight class.

Among the lifters competing in the 148lb. class at Cincinnati, Ohio was Jerry Bell. Jerry Bell, one of Ohio's top lightweight Powerlifters, was probably one of the first Powerlifters in the U.S.A. to adopt what became known as the "Sumo Style" of Deadlifting. *NOTE : In the "Sumo Style Deadlift," the lifter positions himself in a preferred stance (mostly wider) and assumes a grip on the bar with hands inside the legs.* Jerry Bell Deadlifted 545lbs. along with a Total of 1180 in the 148lb. class, winning 2nd place on bodyweight. The 545lb. Deadlift by Jerry Bell on 5/20/73 was a new Mid-West Open Powerlifting Championship Meet Record.

Jerry Bell was not the only man with a superior Deadlift at the 1973 Midwest Open in Cincinnati, Ohio. Competing in the 148lb. class was Hanley Olken (505 Deadlift - 1180 Total and 3rd Place) along with Bob Cortes and Fred Pfister. Fred Pfister pulled a Deadlift of 500 and placed 4th. Pfister's Total was 1115. Bob Cortes pulled 525 on the Deadlift to finish 1st Place in the 148lb. class with a Total of 1245. The 1245 Total by Bob Cortcs was a Master Classification Total according to the 1973 Powerlifting Classification Standards.

The most interesting part of the first session at the 9th Annual (1973) Midwest Open was the lifting of 165lb., 1971 World Powerlifting Champion, George Crawford. I first read about George Crawford from the pages of *Muscular Development* magazine in 1971. At the end of our session, I saw George Crawford easily Squat with over 600 pounds in the 165lb. class. *NOTE : National Referees were very strict at the 1973 Mid-West Open and the "No Wrap Rule" was in effect during 1973.*

When lifting at the *9th Annual Mid-West Open Powerlifting Championships* at Cincinnati, Ohio on 5/20/73, I was humbled quickly at the age of 18 while competing against some of the nation's best lightweight Powerlifters. At a bodyweight of 146 ¾, a Total of 1110 placed 5th out of eight (8) competitors. When comparing the Total of 1110 at Cincinnati to the first four (4) finishers at the 1973 Junior Nationals, a Total of 1320 finished 4th among the 148lb. class lifters at the 1973 Junior National Powerlifting Championships.

During the weeks that followed the Mid-West Open, I occasionally drove to Charleston for a workout with a few of the members of the *Charleston Barbell Club*. I met John Messinger for the first time while working out at the Charleston YMCA on July 23rd, 1973. John and I "maxed out" on the Bench Press. Afterward, I looked at the thermometer in the weight room and the reading was over ninety (90) degrees. After a heavy workout at the Charleston YMCA during the Summer of '73, it was a steak dinner at a favorite, established restaurant. I loved the Summer workouts at the Charleston, West Virginia YMCA!

Weightlifter and Powerlifter

Beginning in 1973, Olympic Weightlifting was a new game as the Clean & Press was gone from official Weightlifting competitions. Following the 1972 Olympic Games, the two (2) lifts contested in official Weightlifting competitions were : 1) The Snatch 2) The Clean & Jerk. Since returning to West Virginia from Florida, Frank White competed in both Powerlifting and Weightlifting throughout 1971 and 1972. The year 1973 was no exception. During the Summer of 1973, Frank White trained for three (3) Powerlifting meets : 1) Steubenville, Ohio (10/13/1973), 2) Munhall, Pennsylvania (11/17/1973), and 3) Durham, North Carolina (12/08/1973).

On April 14th, 1973 Frank White placed 1st at the Region III Weightlifting Championships in Savannah, Georgia while competing in the 165lb. class. Frank's lifts on 4/14/73 included a Snatch of 215 and a Clean & Jerk of 285 for a Total of 500. The official results of the Region III Weightlifting Championships held on April 14th, 1973 at Savannah, Georgia were published in the September, 1973 issue of *Strength & Health* magazine.

As a final chapter in the "Florida Connection," Frank White placed 2nd at the Region IV Weightlifting Championships held April 28th, 1973 at St. Petersburg, Florida. Franks lifts on 4/28/73 were 215 Snatch and a 280 Clean & Jerk for a Total of 495 in the 165lb. class. The official results of the Region IV Weightlifting Championships held on April 28th, 1973 at St. Petersburg, Florida were published in the September, 1973 issue of *Strength & Health* magazine.

On September 29th, 1973 at the AMA Open Olympic Weightlifting Contest in Pittsburgh, Pennsylvania, Frank White Snatched 205 and Clean & Jerked 270 for a 475 Total, placing 3rd among ten (10) lifters in the 165lb. class. For the Powerlifting Meet at Steubenville, Ohio on October 13th, 1973 Frank's strategy was to Total only enough for the win while conserving strength for the Beaver County Weightlifting Championships scheduled for Saturday October 27th at Butler, Pennsylvania. As it turned out, Frank competed as a Middleweight in the 165lb. class at Steubenville, Ohio and placed 2nd.

Following the Powerlifting meet on October 13th, Frank competed at the Beaver County Weightlifting meet on October 27th, 1973. Frank White won first place among five (5) Middleweight competitors at the *Beaver County Weightlifting Championships.* Frank's lifts at the 1973 Beaver County Weightlifting Championships were a 205 Snatch, 270 Clean & Jerk, and a Total of 475lbs in the 165lb. class. The official results of the 1973 Beaver County Weightlifting Meet at Butler, Pennsylvania were published in the March, 1974 issue of *Strength & Health* magazine.

Frank White – 205 Snatch – 165lb. class @ Butler, Pennsylvania

The <u>Steubenville Open Powerlifting Meet</u> was held at the Steubenville YMCA on Saturday October 13th, 1973 in Steubenville, Ohio. At a bodyweight of 148 ½, I managed a 415 Squat, a Bench Press of 260, and a Deadlift of 445 for a PR 1120 Total, good for 2nd Place. As it turned out, the Squat and Total were new West Virginia

State Powerlifting Records in the 148lb. class. An evaluation of six (6) months of Powerlifting competition had produced a mode of consistency at the Class I level ; three (3) consecutive Powerlifting competitions Totaling 1110, 1110, and 1120 while competing in the 148lb. class.

The lifting performance of Frank White fell just grams short of the ultimate first place victory. Frank Totaled 1205 to tie for 1st Place, yet was awarded the official 2nd Place victory as he was the heavier man. The rest of the story for the 165lb. class had Don Hundley with a Total of 1185 that locked him into a tie for 3rd Place.

Vince White was solid at 198 on 10/13/73 at Steubenville. The 198lb. class was extremely tough and Vince took 4th Place with a 1255 Total. Vince put together lifts of 480 Squat, 350 Bench Press, and a 425 Deadlift. Ernie Nagy produced some fine lifts at 198 with a 400 Squat, 310 Bench Press, 440 Deadlift, for a Total of 1150.

Frank White – Deadlift – Steubenville, Ohio

Powerlifting Records : November, 1973

Five (5) weeks after the Power Meet in Steubenville, Ohio on 10/13/73, members of the *Charleston Barbell Club* drove to Munhall, Pennsylvania for the <u>David Stoken Memorial Open Power Meet</u> held Saturday November 17th, 1973. Competing in the 148lb. class at a bodyweight of 148 ¼ pounds (age 19), I made a 420 Squat, 275 Bench Press, and a 450 Deadlift for a Personal Record (PR) Total of 1145. All three (3) lifts on 11/17/73 and the 1145 Total exceeded the existing West Virginia Powerlifting Records by a teenager.

On 11/17/73 in Munhall, Pennsylvania all of my lifts were done with power to spare ; a 9-for-9 day. The only problem I had in regard to winning first place was the fact that 148lb. Senior National Powerlifting Champion Jack Welch was lifting! Jack Welch had won both the Junior and Senior National Powerlifting Championships. On 11/17/73, Jack Welch secured an Elite Total for the win. Conclusively, lifting against the 148lb. National Champion was a great experience for a young Powerlifter. I hoped that someday, the lifts Jack Welch made I could eventually make myself.

Frank White and Don Hundley were winners in the 165lb. class at Munhall, PA. Frank White Squatted 450, Bench Pressed 345, and Deadlifted 465 for a Total of 1260. The Total of 1260 by Frank White was a new West Virginia Powerlifting Record in the 165lb. class. Placing 3rd at 165, Don Hundley Squatted 460, Bench Pressed 260, and Deadlifted 490 for a 1210 Total. Hundley's Squat and Deadlift were new West Virginia Powerlifting Records for the 165lb. class.

Vince White placed 2nd in the 220lb. class with lifts of 480 Squat, 340 Bench Press, and a 400 Deadlift for a Total of 1220 at the 1974 David Stoken Open Power Meet. Thanks to Vince White, the *Charleston Gazette* published the 11/17/73 accomplishments of the Powerlifters from West Virginia.

The North Carolina Connection

The "North Carolina Connection" to West Virginia Powerlifting began at the <u>All-South Powerlifting Championships</u> on Saturday December 8th, 1973. The venue for the 1973 All-South Powerlifting Championships was the Durham YMCA in Durham, North Carolina. Don Hundley, Frank White, and Paul Sutphin were the only West Virginia Powerlifters entered in the 1973 All-South Powerlifting Championships.

In 1973, all weigh-ins began 1½ hours prior to the beginning of the first session of lifting for all Powerlifting meets. Just before the 1973 All-South Powerlifting Championships, I weighed between 151 and 152lbs. for several days, in spite of watching my weight. I was given a break at the weigh-ins by North Carolina's Heavyweight Powerlifting Champion, one of the officials in charge at the meet.

At the official weigh-in, I weighed a few grams heavier than the limit of 148 ¾ pounds. The official scales used for the weigh-in were the old "balance act" scales. When I stepped onto the scales, the balance arm barely touched the metal at the top, indicating that my bodyweight was just about 149lbs. ; therefore, overweight.

I followed the advice given to me by the official when the scales would not balance at 148 ¾ lbs. Simultaneously, inhaling and exhaling, I took nine (9) deep breaths, exhaling completely between each maximum effort to fill my lungs with air. On the tenth (10th) deep breath, I held it and immediately stepped onto the scales. As a result, the balance arm did not touch metal. I was officially weighed-in at 148 ¾ pounds and exhaled a sigh of relief.

Prior to the 1973 All-South Powerlifting Championships, I was confident about my lifting and excited about competing again in the South. I Squatted 435lbs. and Bench Pressed 270, outpacing all of my competitors with an 805 Sub-Total and a lead of 25 pounds. I thought I had the situation covered and that a first place victory in Durham, North Carolina was imminent. However, the Deadlifting of the first and second place finisher represented some of the strongest pulls I had witnessed in the 148lb. class. Even though I placed 3rd at the 1973 All-South Powerlifting with a PR Total of 1135, I was "in the fight" until the end.

While competing at the 1973 All-South Powerlifting Championships, Frank White Totaled a solid 1255 in the 165lb. class, finishing 2nd behind the winner who Deadlifted 505 to take the Middleweight class with a Total of 1300. With a Bench Press of 350lbs., Frank White outlifted all eight (8) of his competitors, including the 165lb. class winner who Benched 345. Frank finished 50 pounds ahead of teammate Don Hundley who finished 3rd in the 165lb. class.

Don Hundley's lifting was impressive in Durham, North Carolina on December 8th, 1973 as he paced himself perfectly to place in the top three. Don gave up nearly 100lbs. on the Bench Press to the first place winner and Frank White, tied the first place winner on the Squat at 450, and beat teammate Frank White by 5lbs on the Squat. When it came time to pull the Deadlifts, only the first place winner beat Hundley, 505 vs. 500. Hundley pulled a 500 Deadlift, exactly what he needed to win 3rd place in the 165lb. class, beating the 4th Place finisher by five (5) pounds.

Chapter Seven : 1974

The lifters of the *Charleston Barbell Club* were determined to take West Virginia Powerlifting to a new level by "lifting more in '74." However, due to the fuel shortage that affected much of the nation, the year 1974 proved to be most challenging for the Champions of West Virginia Powerlifting. Beginning in January, 1974 many of the gas stations (a.k.a. service stations) frequently displayed signs, "Sorry, no gas!" The limited supply of petroleum was also linked to waiting lines at the pumps and higher fuel prices.

At the beginning of 1974, there were only a limited number of Open Powerlifting competitions on the calendar for the states bordering West Virginia. In spite of the problematic circumstances created by the fuel shortage in 1974, the members of the *Charleston Barbell Club* managed to drive to the neighboring states of Kentucky, Ohio, Virginia, Pennsylvania, and Tennessee to win at Powerlifting.

The <u>1974 Lexington Open Powerlifting Meet</u> was held in Lexington, Kentucky on January 12th, 1974. The 1974 Lexington (Kentucky) Open Powerlifting Meet became known as "The Kentucky Connection, Part I." The event was sponsored by the *Lexington Weightlifting Club.*

An introduction to National caliber Weightlifter and Powerlifter Tom LaFontaine took place at the 1974 Lexington Open. Tom did some spectacular lifting in the 148lb. class with a Total of 1335. With LaFontaine winning first place, the Deadlift of the 2nd place finisher put me in 3rd. Not having the best of days, I weighed in at 148 ½ pounds and Totaled 1120. I lost 2nd Place on bodyweight (tie) by virtue of the fact that I weighed in as the heavier man on 1/12/74.

It was at the 1974 Lexington Open Powerlifting competition where Herb Glossbrenner was competing. I did not introduce myself to Herb, nor did he make any effort to talk to me. I had a clear memory of reading about the achievements of Herb Glossbrenner when he competed in the 148lb. class at the Junior Nationals and at the 1971 Senior Nationals in Dallas, Texas. However, on 1/12/74, Herb was lifting in the 181lb. class. I overheard Herb make the comment to someone, "I'll never lift 148 again." Only one (1) year later, the opposite of Herb Glossbrenner's statement proved to be true.

During February of 1974, the gasoline shortage continued and so did Powerlifting. In an effort to protect low inventories of gasoline at the filling stations and distribution centers, the leadership in the state of West Virginia instructed all gas stations not to allow customers to purchase gasoline unless the gauge on the instrument panel of the customer's vehicle read *not more than* one quarter (1/4) of a tank. In lieu of the circumstances, a 1971 Volkswagen Super Beetle was very accommodating.

1974 Steubenville Open

The <u>1974 Steubenville Open Powerlifting Meet</u> was held on February 23rd, 1974 in Steubenville, Ohio. There were twelve (12) competitors in the 148lb. class, including Jerry Bell, Bob Cortes, and Tom LaFontaine. Back in those days, awards were only given to the top three (3) finishers. While competing in the 148lb. class at Steubenville on 2/23/74, I placed 4th.

Determination and physical preparedness fell short of a victory at Steubenville, Ohio as I took on Tom LaFontaine, Jerry Bell, and veteran Bob Cortes in the 148lb. class. The lifts that I made at the 1974 Steubenville Open included a 445 Squat, 265 Bench Press (missed 3rd attempt at 280), and a 440 Deadlift (missed 3rd attempt at 460) for a 1150 Total. I had the 2nd highest Squat with 445 in the 148lb. class. The highest Squat was made by Tom LaFontaine with an unofficial World Record of 530lbs.!

Topping it off, Jack Welch was Extra Lifter at the 1974 Steubenville Open Power Meet, weighing-in just over the 148 ¾ pound class limit. Jack Totaled 1380 with lifts of 480 Squat, 350 Bench Press, and three (3) reps with a final Deadlift attempt of 550lbs! Rather than wait for the "Down" signal from the head referee, Jack performed a second rep with the weight and then a third!

I set Personal Records (PR's) in all lifts at the 1974 Steubenville Open Power Meet. Placing 4th among Nationally ranked lifters and a National Champion in the lightweight class at Steubenville, Ohio on 2/23/74 was nothing to be ashamed of. Yet, in the days of "way back when", only the top three (3) of only one (1) division (the Open Division) received awards. The awards were often high quality, marble-based trophies.

Hopewell – Huntington - Parkersburg

The solid lifting at Steubenville continued seven (7) weeks later at the 1974 Hopewell Open Power Meet. On 4/12/74, Frank White and I traveled to Hopewell, Virginia for the 1974 Hopewell Open Powerlifting Meet. Rather than compete at the 1974 Hopewell Open, Frank White was "Coach" for Paul Sutphin at "The Virginia Connection" : Part II.

The <u>1974 Hopewell Open Powerlifting Meet</u> was held April 13th, 1974 at Hopewell, Virginia. The caliber of lifting was high with forty-five (45) lifters, five (5) competitors in the 148lb. class. I put together the highest Total to date of 1160 with lifts of 450 Squat, 270 Bench Press, and a Deadlift of 440 for a 2nd Place finish while Clyde Wright Totaled 1175 for first place in the 148lb. class on 4/13/74.

The gymnasium of Huntington East High School in Huntington, West Virginia was the site for two (2) lifting events during the Summer of 1974. Neither contest was AAU sanctioned. At the time, AAU sanctioned or not, my colleagues and I were finally given an opportunity to compete against someone from our home state for the first time in over a year. Highlights from the 1974 Huntington lifting events included the return of Herb Fitzsimmons and the Team title won by *Herb's Gym*.

The *"Almost Heaven" Weightlifting Championships* were held on Sunday June 30th, 1974 in Huntington, West Virginia. The lifts contested were the Clean & Jerk, the Bench Press, and the Deadlift. I met Herb Fitzsimmons for the first time on 6/30/74 along with veteran lifters, Bill Blankenship and Austin Miller. We all competed under the name of *Herb's Gym* for the Team Award at the *"Almost Heaven" Championships* and won it!

Approximately one (1) month later, the *West Virginia "Weight –Training" Championships* were conducted in Huntington, West Virginia at the same location. The lifts contested were the Clean & Jerk, the Bench Press, and the Deadlift. Once again, members of the *Charleston Barbell Club* and *Herb's Gym* worked together to win the Team Award at the July, 1974 Weightlifting / "Push – Pull" event.

The 1st Annual Mountianeer Open Championships were held Saturday October 26th, 1974 at the Parkersburg YMCA in Parkersburg, West Virginia. The First Annual Mountianeer Open included only the Bench Press. I weighed in at a bodyweight of 147 ¾ and opened with a lift of 260. The 2nd attempt of 275 was turned down as the weight shifted and started downward, even though I completed the lift. In a battle for first place, I had to select the weight of 280 for the final attempt as my competitor was also attempting 275. My competitor was the lighter man and, given the tie, would win the contest. When he missed his 3rd attempt, I took the 275lb. Bench Press on my 3rd attempt, made the lift, and won the contest.

Frank White took the win in the 165lb. class at the 1st Annual Mountianeer Open with a Bench Press of 345lbs. Vince White won the 198lb. class. The 1974 Mountianeer Open Team Champions, *Charleston Barbell / Herb's Gym* were led by veterans Vince White and Herb Fitzsimmons.

Wild Card System

In the early 1970's, Powerlifting endured much criticism regarding the length of time involved in a Powerlifting meet. Many people were of the consensus that the Powerlifting meets lasted too long. Meanwhile, there was much debate among Powerlifting's administrators to shorten the length of Powerlifting meets. As one Meet Director said in early 1974, "The contests last too long for the spectators." Whether or not those concerns were shared, not much could be done about the fact that every lifter was guaranteed his turn for the Squat, the Bench Press, and the Deadlift in as many as three (3) attempts per lift if he chose to take all three.

Among the few innovative proposals to shorten the length of Powerlifting meets, one method was identified as the "Wild Card System." Each lifter was granted only two (2) attempts on the Squat, Bench Press, and the Deadlift. An extra attempt (called the "Wild Card") could be used on any of the three lifts at the discretion of the lifter. Given the option of a third attempt (a.k.a. "Wild Card Attempt"), the total number of attempts from the Squat, the Bench Press, and the Deadlift by an individual lifter could not exceed seven (7).

During 1974, the "Wild Card System" was approved. Each lifter was allowed only two (2) attempts for the Squat, the Bench Press, and the Deadlift. A third lift (a.k.a., the "Wild Card") was available to the lifter if he decided to use it on one of the three Powerlifts of his choice (The Squat, or the Bench Press, or the Deadlift). The "Wild Card System" was not mandatory for Meet Directors. In late 1974, Meet Directors were encouraged, but not required, to conduct Powerlifting meets using the Wild Card System.

Another chapter in the "Pennsylvania Connection" took place for West Virginia Powerlifting in November of 1974. The *Charleston Barbell Club* considered the Newcastle, Pennsylvania Open Powerlifting Meet as the opener for the 1974-75 Powerlifting Season. The 1974 New Castle Open Powerlifting Meet was held Saturday November 16th, 1974 at the New Castle YMCA in New Castle, Pennsylvania. The 1974 New Castle Open Power Meet implemented the "Wild Card System." According to the official results, the 1974 New Castle Open Powerlifting Meet had fifty-nine (59) lifters.

During the rules briefing at the 1974 New Castle Open, the officials told everyone the rules for Squatting would be strictly enforced as "below parallel" had been re-defined once again. The good news of the day was that knee wraps were once again legal but I did not use knee wraps or wrist wraps at the time. I weighed-in at a bodyweight of 147 ½, competed in the 148lb. class, and placed 3rd among eight (8) competitors.

On 11/16/74, I lifted against Jack Welch, the 148lb. Senior and Junior National Powerlifting Champion for the 3rd time in twelve (12) months. Jack Welch made lifts of 470 Squat, 325 Bench Press, and a 565 Deadlift for a new (AMA) Allegheny Mountian Association Record. Jack Welch finished with an Elite Total of 1360 in the 148lb. class on 11/16/74.

Vince White, competed in the 198lb. class at the 1974 New Castle Open on 11/16/74 and placed 4th with a 1265 Total in a field of eight (8) competitors. Vince Squatted with

470 and Bench Pressed 380 for a new West Virginia State Bench Press Record in the 198lb. class. Only one (1) lifter at the 1974 New Castle Open Power Meet Bench Pressed more weight than Vince White (The 242lb. class winner on 11/16/74 in New Castle, Pennsylvania Bench Pressed 385).

Vince White – 380 Bench Press.
West Virginia State Bench Press Record of 380lbs. by Vince White was
recorded in the archives on 1/31/76. The 380 Bench Press mark in the 198lb.
class by Vince White on 11/16/74 was not exceeded until 5/21/77.

Power Rack Training

After I included partial exercises using the Power Rack, a Total of 1200 in the 148lb. class came in short order. In addition to selected movements from published articles available on "Rack Training," Vince White and Frank White suggested a number of routines with a variety of movements specific to both Powerlifting and Olympic Weightlifting. Favorable results from Power Rack training were evident on 12/14/74 at the Powerlifting meet in Bristol, Tennessee.

The <u>1974 Mountian Empire Powerlifting Meet</u> was held December 14th, 1974 at Bristol, Tennessee. Competing in the 148lb. weight class, I Totaled 1200 for the first time with a 460 Squat, 275 Bench Press, and a 465 Deadlift. Frank White competed in the 165lb. class and Totaled 1235 for a 2nd Place finish. Frank had the winning Squat by 15lbs. (435 to 420) and outlifted the winner on the Bench Press by 50lbs. (355 to 305). Frank White's 355 Bench Press in the 165lb. class stands as the "Raw" Bench Press Record for Era I in West Virginia Powerlifting.

Competing in the 198lb. class, Vince White Totaled 1315 at the 1974 Mountian Empire Powerlifting event. Vince Squatted 500, Bench Pressed 375, and Deadlifted 440. Vince had the winning Squat of 500 versus 415 done by the 2nd Place finisher. Vince's Bench Press of 375 was the 2nd highest Bench Press of the meet (the heaviest Bench Press of the 12/14/74 Powerlifting Meet at Bristol, TN was 400).

The 1974 Mountian Empire Powerlifting Meet became Part II of the Tennessee Connection for West Virginia Powerlifting. There were thirty-two (32) lifters competing at the event. The performance of Paul Sutphin (460 Squat – 148lb. class), and Frank White (355 Bench Press – 165lb. class), and Vince White's 380 Bench Press (11/16/74) earned TOP 10 spots in the Powerlifter rankings published in *POWERLIFTING NEWS* the following month. The members of the Bristol Powerlifting Team outscored Vince White, Frank White, and Paul Sutphin for the Team Award. As a result, the 1975 Mountian Empire Power Meet would have more lifters participating from West Virginia.

POWERLIFTING NEWS, Jan/1975

<u>From the 1970's to the 21st Century</u> : The use of a Power Rack and partial movements are essential for the purpose of implementing a serious and effective strength training program. Bench Presses, Lockouts, Squats, and Deadlifts from a variety of heights inside a Power Rack yield incredible results. The benefits of a Power Rack specific to only Squats and Deadlifts provide enough information for an entire book. Quarter Squats, partial lockouts for the Bench Press, and "Walkouts" ("setting up" for Squats with maximum weight) are best practiced inside a Power Rack.

For Modern Powerlifting, the use of a Monolift has all but eliminated the practice by most lifters of heavy "Walkouts." In place of "Walkouts," a variation of a "High Bar Good Morning" inside a Power Rack is recommended.

1973-1974 West Virginia Powerlifter Rankings
TOP RANKINGS Determined by Total
January 01, 1973 thru December 31, 1974

123 / Name	Squat	Bench Press	Deadlift	Total	Date
Kevin Sheets	200	170	300*	670	4/15/1973
Bob Black	181	151	251	583	6/28/1974
David Hall	141	121	201	463	6/28/1974
132 Larry Wildman	230	190*	360	780	1/12/1974
Larry Wildman	225	145	350	720	4/15/1973
Paul Muller	230	165	325	720	4/15/1973
Bob Patton	211	196*	286	693	6/28/1974
148 Paul Sutphin *Age 20*	460*	275	465	1200*	12/14/1974
Paul Sutphin *Age 19*	450* t	270	440	1160* t	4/13/1974
Paul Sutphin *Age 19*	445* t	265	440	1150* t	2/23/1974
Paul Sutphin *Age 20*	435	265	450	1150 wld	11/16/74
Paul Sutphin *Age 19*	420* t	275 t	450 t	1145* t	11/17/1973
Paul Sutphin *Age 19*	435* t	270	430	1135	12/08/1973
Paul Sutphin *Age 19*	415* t	260	445 t	1120* t	10/13/1973
Paul Sutphin *Age 19*	420	270	430	1120	1/12/1974
Paul Sutphin *Age 18*	410* t	260	440	1110* t	4/15/1973
Paul Sutphin *Age 18*	405	270 t	435	1110	5/20/1973
Paul Sutphin *Age 18*	400* t	255	430	1085* t	2/24/1973
Paul Sutphin *Age 18*	390* t	245	420	1055 t	2/10/1973
Dave Jeffrey	275	292*	401	968	6/28/1974
Dave Hunt	270	270	360	900	4/15/1973
Mark Shroeder	231	181	341	753	6/28/1974
Don Buttermore	231	201	311	743	6/28/1974

* - West Virginia State Powerlifting Record

t – West Virginia State Teenage Powerlifting Record

m – West Virginia State Master's Record

wld – Wild Card Meet

1973-1974 West Virginia Powerlifter Rankings
TOP RANKINGS Determined by Total
January 01, 1973 thru December 31, 1974

165 / Name	Squat	Bench Press	Deadlift	Total	Date
Frank White	450	345	465	1260*	11/17/1973
Frank White	440	350*	465	1255	12/08/1973
Frank White	450	350	455	1255	1/12/1974
Frank White	435	355*	445	1235	12/14/1974
Don Hundley	460*	260	490*	1210	11/17/1973
Frank White	440	310	455	1205	10/13/1973
Don Hundley	450	255	500*	1205	12/08/1973
Don Hundley	450	255	480*	1185	10/13/1973
Don Hundley	455	225	475	1155	1/12/1974
Don Hundley	465	240	465	1170	2/23/1974
Don Hundley	445	235	465	1145 wld	11/16/74
John Collias	415	205	435	1055	4/15/1973
Barry Barrows	286	281	426	993	6/28/1974
181 Don Hundley	445	270	425	1140	2/24/1973
Gary Clark	350	325	450	1125	PA/1973
Warren Knight	361	251	461	1073	6/28/1974
198 Vince White	500	375	440	1315	12/14/1974
Vince White	500*	360	440	1300	4/15/1973
Vince White	475	365	420	1260	2/10/1973
Vince White	480	350	425	1255	10/13/1973
Vince White	470	380*	415	1265 wld	11/16/1974
Vince White	480	360	405	1245	1/12/1974
Vince White	460	340	400	1200	2/23/1974
Ernie Nagy	400 m	310 m	440	1150 m	10/13/1973
Ernie Nagy	360 m	300 m	440 m	1100 m	PA/1973

* - West Virginia State Powerlifting Record

m – West Virginia State Master's Powerlifing Record

wld – Wild Card Meet

1973-1974 West Virginia Powerlifter Rankings
TOP RANKINGS Determined by Total
January 01, 1973 thru December 31, 1974

220 / Name		Squat	Bench Press	Deadlift	Total	Date
	Doug Forth	500*	385*	550*	1435*	4/15/1973
	Ernie Nagy	420m	340m	500m	1260m wld	11/16/1974
	Tom Barnes	470	270	500	1240	4/15/1973
	Vince White	480	340	400	1220	11/17/1973
	Ernie Nagy	375 m	320 m	440 m	1135 m	2/24/1973
242	Gaye Elmore	430	285	485	1200	4/15/1973
	Jerry Cromer	375	285	425	1085	4/15/1973
SHW	Lee Shorter	455*	275	525*	1255*	4/15/1973

* - West Virginia State Powerlifting Record

m – West Virginia State Master's Powerlifing Record

wld – Wild Card Meet

Chapter Eight : 1975

In January of 1975, the *POWERLIFTING NEWS* publication began printing once again in the form of a newsletter. The official results and highlights of the *1974 Mountian Empire Open Powerlifting Meet* appeared in the January, 1975 issue of *POWERLIFTING NEWS*. The *National TOP 10 Powerlifter Rankings* for all weight classes also appeared in the January, 1975 issue of PN. Included in the *National TOP 10 Powerlifter Rankings* for Middleweights was Frank White. Frank White ranked 6th in the *POWERLIFTING NEWS TOP TEN (10) Powerlifters* (Jan/75) for his Bench Press of 355 in the 165lb. class on 12/14/74.   *POWERLIFTING NEWS, Jan/1975*

It was not until 1974 that the AAU recognized the Elite status for Olympic Weightlifting and Powerlifting. Before the Elite category, the achievement of Master Classification earned major recognition for Powerlifters and Olympic lifters. In the *AAU Official Handbook 1974-75 for Weightlifting and Powerlifting*, the minimum requirements to earn an Elite Classification Total were :

123–1160, 132–1240, 148–1360, 165–1480, 181-1605, 198-1710, 220-1825,
242-1905, SHW-2100.

Once the minimum Total for Elite status was achieved, Powerlifters could apply for the official Elite Classification Patch as late as 1978 based on the Totals listed in the 1974-75 AAU handbook. Prior to the addition of the Elite status to the Powerlifting Classification System, the highest level was the Master Classification. *IMPORTANT NOTE : Master's Powerlifting Classification based on an achievement level of a required Total is NOT relevant to the lifter's chronological age.* From the 1974 AAU Rule Book, the minimum requirements for a Total to earn the Master's Powerlifting Classification status were :

123–1075, 132–1150, 148–1250, 165–1375, 181-1485,
198-1575, 220-1650, 242-1750, SHW-1900.

In order to meet the criteria for Class III, Class II, Class I, Master, or Elite, only Totals that were made in bonafide AAU sanctioned (3-lift) Powerlifting events were accepted. The Powerlifting Classification Program clearly defined Totals from below average to superior. In the first half of the 1970's, many lifters worked to attain goals based on achieving at the highest level of the Powerlifting Classification System. Once the required Total for the targeted level of classification was official, many of the same lifters were awarded classification patches. During the decade of the 1970's, it was very common at a Powerlifting meet to observe at least one-third to one-half of the competitors sporting classification patches on their lifting singlets or warm-up attire. The highest levels of the Powerlifting Classification Program often served as a baseline for determining the Qualifying Totals for the Junior and Senior Nationals.

West Virginia Weightlifting Chairman

The <u>1975 Lexington Open Powerlifting Championships</u> were held on January 18th, 1975 at the Lexington YMCA in Lexington, Kentucky sponsored by the *Lexington Weightlifting Club.* According to the official meet results, the contest had thirty-eight (38) lifters. The 1975 Lexington Open became Part II of the "Kentucky Connection" for West Virginia Powerlifting.

Vince White Bench Pressed 360 in the 198lb. class for a new Lexington Open Powerlifting Meet Record. John Messinger placed 2nd in the 220lb. class with a Total of 1220. The *Central Indiana Weightlifting Club* won the Team Trophy at the 1975 Lexington Open with the winners in every weight class but two (2). Perhaps what I remember most from 1/18/75 is that my friendship with Herb Glossbrenner (C.I.W.C.) actually began at the 1975 Lexington Open.

During the days of single platforms and the old "System of Rotation," Powerlifting meets often lasted a very long time. Prior to 1975, much work was done to generate external popularity for the sport of Powerlifting. As defined previously, "Wild Card Powerlifting" reduced the number of attempts for the Squat, the Bench Press, and the Deadlift from three (3) to only two (2). An extra attempt, defined as "The Wild Card," could be used at the discretion of the lifter on any one of the three Powerlifts : The Squat, the Bench Press, or the Deadlift.

The <u>2nd Annual N.C.S.U. (North Carolina State University) Open Powerlifting Meet</u> was held on March 1st, 1975 in Raleigh, North Carolina. The N.C.S.U. Open Powerlifting Meet was an official "Wild Card" Meet. According to the official meet results, the 1975 N.C.S.U. Open Powerlifting Meet had forty-four (44) lifters. I was happy to win 1st Place with a 1200 Total in a field of seven (7) competitors in the 148lb. class. The 1200 Total consisted of a 450 Squat, 280 Bench Press, and a 470 Deadlift. For the second time in less than a year, Frank White made the trip with me to provide assistance as "Powerlifting Coach." In summary, a great win and the end to the "Wild Card" while writing another chapter in the "North Carolina Connection" : Part II of West Virginia Powerlifting.

After a number of competitions held in West Virginia without an AAU sanction during the calendar year of 1974, events and situations were not proceeding in the direction of a bonafide program for Powerlifting. The first quarter of 1975 was over two-thirds history and West Virginia Powerlifting was still functioning "out of state" and "on the road." Determination and frustration prompted me to write a convincing letter to the President of the West Virginia Association of the AAU. On March 19th, 1975, I received an official letter of response from the President of the AAU West Virginia Association, appointing Paul Sutphin "Weightlifting Chairman for the West Virginia AAU Association for the 1974-1975 year."

During March of 1975, the West Virginia AAU Association President informed me that until there were a minimum of five (5) AAU registered Weightlifting clubs functioning in the state of West Virginia with an identified number of AAU members active in Weightlifting, Powerlifting, or Bodybuilding, the West Virginia AAU President would appoint a qualified individual to the position of West Virginia Weightlifting Chairman. In the Summer of 1975, I attended the AAU West Virginia annual meeting in Parkersburg and secured the appointment for another year.

State Powerlifting and Weightlifting Records are the responsibility of the State Chairperson; a familiar statement that I have heard for decades. As AAU Weightlifting Chairman of the West Virginia Association, I secured the existing West Virginia State Powerlifting and Weightlifting Records and continued with the process of establishing new records according to the requirements of the AAU. In an effort to effectively represent the lifting achievements and accomplishments of all West Virginia lifters, I submitted a list of established Powerlifting Records to the editor of *Powerlifting News* for publication and became the West Virginia State Correspondent for *Powerlifting News.*

Tennessee Connection : Part III

The workouts went exceptionally well during February and March of 1975. Vince White and I had weekly conversations leading up to the Powerlifting Meet on 4/12/75. In one of the conversations I told Vince, "I am definitely going to break the 500lb. barrier for the Squat in Johnson City." After hearing my comments, Vince declared, "I'm going to follow you with 560!"

The 1st Annual Johnson City Open Powerlifting Meet was held Saturday April 12th, 1975 in Johnson City, Tennessee with thirty-nine (39) lifters. I Totaled 1240 which included a Squat of 505, Bench Press of 285, and a Deadlift of 450, winning first place in the 148lb. class and the Outstanding Lifter Award. During numerous telephone conversations before the Powerlifting meet at Johnson City, Vince White had said, "Whatever you Squat, I'm going to follow you with the same weight." Action spoke louder than words as Vince Squatted with 505, Bench Pressed 360, and Deadlifted 435 for a 1300 Total to win the 198lb. class.

The lifting of John Messinger won a victory at Johnson City on 4/12/75. While competing in the 220lb. class, John Squatted 475, Bench Pressed 360, and made the highest Deadlift of the contest at 555lbs., winning first place by a margin of five (5) pounds with a Total of 1390. The lifters for the *Charleston Barbell Club (a.k.a. Holley Health Club)* at the 1st Annual Johnson City Open were Paul Sutphin (148), John Collias (181), Don Hall (181), Vince White (198), Wayne Dawson (198), and John Messinger (220).

The 505 Squat made by Paul Sutphin in Johnson City, Tennessee ranked among the TOP TEN 148lb. Powerlifters in the U.S.A., based on the *Powerlifting News* Powerlifter Rankings. In the June, 1975 issue of *Powerlifting News,* a computer printout using the Swartz Formula had Paul Sutphin ranked #22 among all Squats (1974-75) to date. Sutphin was also awarded a *National TOP Ten Certificate* in recognition of the 505 Squat (#4 Ranking among the TOP 10 148lb. Powerlifters) from the editor of *Powerlifting News.*

The Johnson City, Tennessee Powerlifting event became the third chapter of the Tennessee Connection in the history of West Virginia Powerlifting. The official contest results were published in *Powerlifting News, Powerman Magazine,* and *The Lifter.* The contest received newspaper coverage from the *Johnson City Press-Chronicle* (April 13th, 1975), the *Charleston Gazette,* and the *Bluefield Daily Telegraph.* The title of the article from the *Charleston Gazette-Mail* read *"Barbells Lead by Messinger, Sutphin, White."*

Paul Sutphin – Bench Press
Ambridge, Pennsylvania – 4/26/75

Powerlifting at Ambridge

On April 26, 1975, the <u>Jerrold S. Blum Open Powerlifting Meet</u> was conducted at the Ambridge VFW in Ambridge, Pennsylvania. The 1975 Jerrold Blum Powerlifting Meet had fifty-nine (59) competitors. Jack Welch, Senior and Junior National Champion (148lb. class), encouraged me to enter. Jack Welch won the 165lb. class on 4/26/75 with ease, lifting at a bodyweight of 155 and cruising to a 1340 Total. Vince White, lifting in the 198's, did a 470 Squat, 365 Bench Press, and a 415 Deadlift for a 1250 Total. Vince White owned the highest Bench Press in the 198lb. class by a margin of 30lbs.! I won a first place victory at the 1975 Jerrold Blum Open in the 148lb. class with a Total of 1190.

It was at the 1975 Jerrold Blum Powerlifting event that I met Jack Wilson and Roger Estep for the first time. Roger did not lift at the 1975 Jerrold Blum Open as he was coaching Jack Wilson, my competitor in the 148lb. class. Roger later earned the reputation as being the "Best Built Man in Powerlifting," validated over five (5) years later when he was pictured on the cover of the October, 1980 issue of *Muscular Development* magazine. During several brief discussions about Powerlifting and training on the day of 4/26/75, Roger emphasized Box Squats as the most effective method in preparation for maximum poundages and often mentioned the name of Powerlifting's West Coast legend, George Frenn. *Powerlifting USA (2005)*

One day later (Sunday 4/27/75) in Bedford Heights, Ohio (approximately 2 hours from Ambridge, Pennsylvania), another Powerlifting competition took place in the AAU Lake Erie District. After learning from Jack Wilson that he was entered in the event, Vincent White and myself decided that we would drive to Bedford Heights and check out the lifting at the Buckeye Open. Roger Estep was again present on 4/27/75 to assist Jack Wilson. Jack actually Totaled higher on Sunday (4/27/75 – 1175 Total) than on Saturday (4/26/75 – 1135 Total) : *Another success story for "Back-to-Back" Powerlifting competitions!*

The <u>1975 Buckeye Open Powerlifting Championships</u> had sixty-seven (67) lifters, all of whom had entered prior to the deadline. Excited after a victory the day before, I decided to enter the Buckeye Open the morning of the contest. The Meet Director informed me, "We do not accept late entries in the Lake Erie District." So, Vince White and I watched the contest during the first session until the Bench Presses were near completion and headed South, missing the evening session. What we did not find out until a later date was that several lifters from the "Ernie Nagy Powerlifting Team" and Luke Iams lifted at the 1975 Buckeye Open during the evening session. *Less than ten (10) months later, we were together at the first West Virginia State Powerlifting Championships.*

Bench Press – Deadlift – Physique

A "Push n' Pull" would be the modern description of the <u>Mid-Ohio Valley Open Bench Press and Deadlift Championships</u> conducted on June 7th, 1975 at the Parkersburg YMCA in Parkersburg, West Virginia. It was on 6/07/75 when I met Chuck Dunbar. During a 2009 interview by the late Ron Fernando (P/L USA FEB/2010), Chuck Dunbar mentioned the 1975 event and was quoted as saying that the event was "conducted by Paul Sutphin." As West Virginia Weightlifting Chairman, I approved the AAU sanction for the lifting and the physique competition, lifted and won the Bench Press / Deadlift and competed in the Mid-Ohio Valley Physique contest. For the record, the actual Meet Directors were affiliated with the Parkersburg YMCA.

Powerlifting USA / Vol. 33, No. 4 / February, 2010

I found out soon after becoming the West Virginia Weightlifting Chairman that physique competitions were very popular. During 1975 and in previous years, physique shows were held in conjunction with either Weightlifting or Powerlifting meets. Frank White, as he had done many times in years past, placed among the top finishers at the <u>1975 Mid-Ohio Valley Physique</u> competition conducted in Parkersburg on 6/07/75.

The 1975 Mid-Ohio Valley Bench Press and Deadlift Championship was one of the first lifting events that I approved for an AAU sanction as AAU West Virginia Weightlifting Chairman. The option to participate in the 1975 Mid-Ohio Valley Bench Press and Deadlift Championship did not include "either / or." Each lifter was required to do both the Bench Press and the Deadlift for a Total to determine the winner of each weight class. There was only one (1) division and that was the OPEN Division. As far as "Push n' Pull" events go, the meet was a very good one.

The *Charleston Barbell Club* "cleaned house" at the 1975 Mid-Ohio Valley Open Bench Press and Deadlift Championships. Chuck Dunbar owned the only first place win for *Luke's Gym* while lifting in the 114lb. class. Among the winners were : Paul Sutphin (148lb. class) – 270 Bench Press, 480 Deadlift ; Frank White (165lb. class) 305 Bench Press, 440 Deadlift ; Don Hall (181lb. class) 255 Bench Press, 455 Deadlift ; Vince White (198lb. class) 370 Bench Press, 425 Deadlift ; and John Messinger (220lb. class) 340 Bench Press, 555 Deadlift.

The summer of 1975 moved on and the progress of organizing Powerlifting in West Virginia continued. I attended the annual meeting of the AAU West Virginia Association on a sunny Sunday in Parkersburg. I was the only representative for Weightlifting-Powerlifting-Bodybuilding at the 1975 annual meeting.

Most everyone in attendance at the 1975 annual meeting of the AAU West Virginia Association represented the sport of Swimming. I gave the official report for Weightlifting, Bodybuilding, and Powerlifting through the month of June, 1975. In addition to a progress report, I presented to the West Virginia AAU Association Executive Committee an agenda which contained ambitious goals for the remainder of calendar year 1975 and throughout 1976. The final statement I gave to the West Virginia AAU Executive Committee *all but guaranteed* an official West Virginia State Powerlifting Championship for 1976 in addition to an official Mr. West Virginia Physique competition.

1975 Junior & Senior Nationals

Official meet results of Powerlifting competitions were appearing from all regions of the country in *POWERLIFTING NEWS*. Earning a spot in the National TOP TEN Powerlifter Rankings in the 148lb. class had me thinking more and more about lifting at the Junior National Powerlifting Championships. While achieving a respectable Total of 10lbs. less than the minimum (1250) requirement for Master Classification in the 148lb. class, Vince White talked me out of taking the trip to Nebraska for the 1975 Junior Nationals. An exerpt from Vince's diplomatic approach, "I would wait until the contest comes back East." The fact that a Total of less than 1300 at the Junior Nationals in the 148lb. class may not earn more than a handshake, coupled with the reality of spending the money and getting "worn out by the competition" factored in my decision to wait until 1976. A wise choice was made to skip the 1975 Juniors as a Total of 1250 would have been insignificant among the finishers in the 148lb. weight class at the 1975 Junior National Powerlifting Championships.

On July 26th & 27th, the 1975 Junior National Powerlifting Championships were held in Lincoln, Nebraska. The 1975 Juniors marked the first year in the United States that lifters had an opportunity to lift in the 114lb. weight class. Ernesto Milian was victorious with three (3) new Junior National Championship Meet Records and a Total of 885. The winner of the 148lb. class was Rickey Crain with a 1415 Junior National Meet Record Total. Included in the 1415 Total by Crain was a World Record 550lb. Squat!

On August 29th, 1975 I attended the annual meeting of the AAU National Committee for Powerlifting in York, Pennsylvania as a voting member for the AAU Association of West Virginia. After participating in the Referee's Clinic, I took the National Referee's test for Powerlifting for the first time, scoring 88%, two (2) points shy of the required ninety percent (90%) for passing. The examiner expressed moderate frustration with the fact that I had not succeeded and made the comment, "You missed a couple of easy questions, I thought!" It just so happened that in 1975, I was more concerned about lifting than obtaining a National Referee's Card. It would be nearly eight (8) years before I would take the National Referee's Exam again and obtain a National Powerlifting Referee's Card.

The *1975 Senior National Powerlifting Championships* were held August 30th & 31st, 1975 at William Penn High School in York, Pennsylvania. Among the winners were :

Enrique Hernandez (132 – 1289 Total),
Jack Welch (148 – 1422 Total),
Walter Thomas (165 – 1603 Total),
George Crawford (2nd @ 165 – 650 Squat, 1570 Total),
Dennis Wright (181 – 1631 Total),
Ed Ravenscroft (198 – 1824 Total),
Larry Pacifico (220 – 2000 Total),
Doug Young (242 – 1929 Total), and
Don Reinhoudt (SHW Winner – 2243 Total).

Powerlifting News / September, 1975

From the perspective of a college student, attending the 1975 Senior National Powerlifting Championships was like completing a semester course in Powerlifting. Witnessing some of the greatest lifts made in the sport of Powerlifting motivated me to train at a higher level. While observing lifters in the warm-up area, I witnessed a famous lifter handling maximum weight during Squat warm-ups. After backing out of the racks with a weight in excess of 600lbs., he loudly told the spotters, "Get out of the way!" The lifter proceeded to Squat the weight with ease. Evidently, the lifter did not trust the spotters to keep their hands off of the bar during the Squat or prior to re-racking the heavy load. From that moment on, I never worried about Squatting alone.

The Maryland Connection

The Powerlifting meet in Cumberland, Maryland was held on September 27th, 1975. According to the official Meet Results published in a section of *Powerlifting News* in late 1975, four (4) members of the *Charleston Barbell Club* competed at the event. Don

Hundley (165), Don Hall (181), Vince White (198), and Gaye Elmore (242). The top performer among the group on 9/27/75 was Vince White.

Vince White finished with a 1330 Total and placed 3rd in the 198lb. class. Vince White's lifts on 9/27/75 were 500 Squat, 380 Bench Press, and a 450 Deadlift for a Total of 1330. The 380 Bench Press on 9/27/75 by Vince White duplicated the same weight lifted at New Castle, Pennsylvania, ten (10) months earlier. The 1330 Total by Vince White on 9/27/75 broke the existing West Virginia State Total Record in the 198lb. class.

Vince White finished #1 in the West Virginia State Powerlifter Rankings for the year 1975 while competing in both the 198lb. class (380lb. Bench Press, 9/27/75) and 220lb. class (410 Bench Press, 12/13/75). Featured in the October, 1975 issue of *Powerlifting News* was a commentary and report about the Eastern USA Power Meet held on September 27th, 1975 in Maryland.

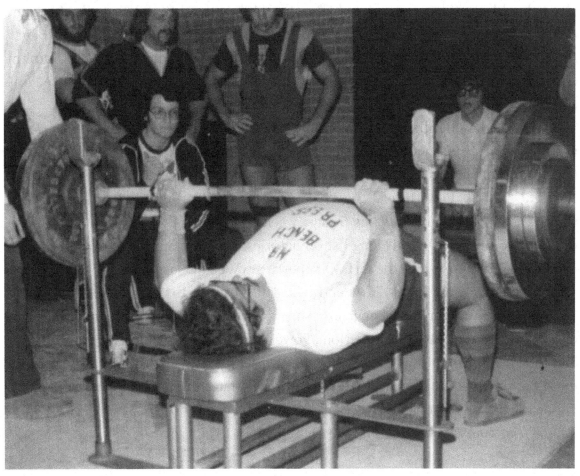

Vince White – Parkersburg, West Virginia – 10/25/75

"Mr. Bench Press"

The 2nd Annual Mountianeer Open Bench Press Championships were held in Parkersburg, West Virginia on October 25th, 1975 at the Parkersburg YMCA with forty-six (46) lifters. Based on the team scoring of 5 points for first place, 3 points for 2nd place, and 1 point for 3rd place, the WVU Bench Press Team won the Team Award (25 points) over *Charleston Barbell Club* (24 points) and *Luke's Gym* (23 points). In conjunction with the Bench Press contest, the 1975 Mr. Mountianeer physique contest and the 1975 Mr. Teenage Mountianeer were conducted following the lifting.

While competing at the 2nd Annual Mountianeer Open, Vince White earned the title of *"Mr. Bench Press,"* pushing an easy 395 Bench Press in the 220lb. class. Roger Estep was present to assist Jeff Jandik who Benched 435 at a bodyweight of 203. Roger also helped Jack Wilson who placed 5th in the 148's with a lift of 275 at a bodyweight of 142 ¼. Included among the winners of the *2nd Annual Mountianeer Open Bench Press Championships* were : Chuck Dunbar (114), Peery Reeder (123), Paul Sutphin (148), Frank White (165), Barry Barrows (181), Herb Fitzsimmons (242), and Luke Iams (SHW).

Leading the highlights of the *2nd Annual Mountianeer Open Bench Press Championships* was Chuck Dunbar. Chuck Dunbar, lifting in the 114lb. class, continued to improve with an easy lift of 235, good for a #1 ranking in the Bench Press among the 114 TOP TEN (10) Powerlifters! The 305 Bench Press by Paul Sutphin in the 148lb. class was the result of the "Jim Williams' 5-day a week Bench Press Routine." The Bench Press of Frank White added to his long list of victories. Herb Fitzsimmons won the 242lb. class while Luke Iams won the (SHW) SuperHeavyWeight class.

It was on October 25th, 1975 when I talked at great lengths with Luke Iams for the first time. After the brief exchange of resumes between Luke Iams and myself, it was clearly evident that Luke was a serious Powerlifter. After learning of his occupation and the Powerlifting team of *"Luke's Gym,"* I wasted no time in asking Luke Iams the question, "Will you conduct the 1976 West Virginia State Powerlifting Championships?" Following Luke's affirmative answer of "Yes!", plans for the *1976 West Virginia State Powerlifting Championships* began on October 25th, 1975.

Powerlifting Records at Huntington

John Messinger and Mike Houston ; the story of Powerlifting in 1975 at the Huntington YMCA, according to the Meet Director. On November 1st, 1975 at an <u>Open Powerlifting Meet</u> conducted at the Huntington YMCA in Huntington, West Virginia, John Messinger broke the 1400lb. Total barrier while competing in the 220lb. class. The 1420 Total by John Messinger on 11/01/75 included lifts of a 525 Squat, 355 Bench Press, and a Deadlift of 540!

John Messinger – 555lb. Deadlift – 220lb. class
West Virginia State Record

The "Deadlift to Win" Workout
Published in Powerlifting News Powerlift Forum / Submitted by Paul Sutphin

As an extension of the *POWERLIFTING NEWS* publication in late 1975, the *Powerlift Forum* was published with a number of lifters participating. I was a participant in the issue of *Powerlift Forum Vol. 1, Number 3 "Deadlift to Win."* An exerpt from the article read, *"Paul Sutphin spreads his Deadlift workout over the week, allowing for greater recovery time."*

The *"Deadlift to Win" Workout* submitted to *Powerlift Forum* in 1975 is as follows :

MONDAY
1) Deadlift in Power Rack (Bar positioned approximately five (5) inches below the knee). Sets performed in repetitions of 5, 4, 3, 2, 1, max.
2) Deadlift (Standing on 4 ½ inch platform) – Sets & Reps of 5, 4, 3, 2, 1, max.

WEDNESDAY
1) Deadlift Lockouts (Power Rack) – Sets performed in repetitions of 5, 3, 3, 2, 2, 2.

FRIDAY
1) Deadlifts (From floor or platform) – Sets & Reps of 10, 5, 4, 3, 2, 1, max.
2) Deadlift in Power Rack (Bar with 45lb. or 100lb. plates positioned approximately 2 inches above the floor or platform) – Sets & Reps of 5, 4, 3, 2, 1, max.

The routine featured in *Powerlift Forum "Deadlift to Win"* in late 1975 was one that I followed with some frequency beginning in October, 1974. During the late Spring and Summer of 1975, I did incorporate 5 sets of 5 repetitions for four (4) weeks and 5 sets of 3 repetitions for four (4) weeks using only the "Sumo" Deadlift style for the entire eight (8) weeks.

The *"Deadlift to Win" Workout* will produce results for lifters who prefer either the conventional style or the "Sumo" style of Deadlifting. It has been my experience over the decades to train both styles of Deadlifting during the workouts. The use of straps are not recommended. Although, one can benefit from the "Hook Grip" on occasion, if preferred.

"Team West Virginia"

The <u>1975 Mountian Empire Powerlifting Championships</u> were held on December 13th, 1975 at the Bristol Family YMCA in Bristol, Tennessee. The 1975 Mountian Empire Powerlifting Championships had thirty-four (34) lifters and became the Tennessee Connection : Part IV for West Virginia Powerlifting. Competing in the 123lb. class, Chuck Mooney beat Chuck Dunbar by five (5) pounds on Total, largely due in part to Mooney's Deadlift of 425lbs.! Mooney lifted the same weight in the 114lb. class for an American Record one month later (JAN/76) at Lexington, Kentucky.

Paul Sutphin captured 1st place in the 148lb. weight class with a 1300 Total and the Outstanding Lifter Award at the 1975 Mountian Empire Open Powerlifting Championships. The 1300 Total on 12/13/75 by Paul Sutphin included a 500 Squat, 305 Bench Press, and a 495 Deadlift. Sutphin's Total of 1300 in the 148lb. weight class on 12/13/75 represented a peak performance not surpassed until over two (2) years later.

Under the System of Rotation, my 2nd attempt Squat with 500 was good and I called for a poundage of 525 on 3rd attempt. Vince White needed only 525 to keep a lead over his competitor in the 220lb. class by 5lbs. Instead, Vince would have nothing to do with the possibility that I could actually beat him on the Squat. Like a true competitor, Vince White called for a 3rd attempt of 530 pounds.

After the bar was loaded and my name was called, I made the Squat of 525 easily, yet the lights from the officials were all red. Vince followed with one of the best Squats that I had ever seen him make with 530lbs. Vince White Bench Pressed an easy 410, Deadlifted 440, and Totaled 1380 for a 3rd place finish in the 220lb. class at Bristol. Among the heaviest Squats of the day (12/13/75) were Luke Iams (625), Ron Pillow (540), and Vince White (530).

I had talked to Luke Iams several weeks in advance about the 1975 Mountian Empire Powerlifting event. Luke agreed to bring a number of lifters from the *Luke's Gym Powerlifting Team* to the 1975 Mountian Empire Open. Also, we agreed to combine the lifters of the *Charleston Barbell Club* and *Luke's Gym* to create "Team West Virginia." The agreement for the arrangement was contingent upon the fact that Paul Sutphin would represent Luke's Gym in the very first Official West Virginia State Powerlifting Championships scheduled for February 14th, 1976. In conclusion, the Team Trophy for the 1975 Mountian Empire Powerlifting Championships was won by Charleston Barbell Club (a.k.a. "Team West Virginia") in Bristol, Tennessee on December 13th, 1975.

For Luke Iams and the lifters from *Luke's Gym*, the trip to Bristol, Tennessee from New Martinsville, West Virginia was approximately 350 miles. The 1975 Bristol,

Tennessee Powerlifting event was special as it was the first time that *Luke's Gym* and the *Charleston Barbell Club* teamed up for an out-of-state contest. On 12/13/75, the Powerlifting team of *Charleston Barbell Club* (a.k.a. "Team West Virginia") included Chuck Mooney (123), Chuck Dunbar (123), Chick Clegg (132), Paul Sutphin (148), Don Hundley (165), Bill Kyle (165), Don Hall (181), Chip Thomas (181), Vince White (220), and Luke Iams (SHW).

The first 1300 Total in the 148lb. class was only one of the highlights for me in Bristol, Tennessee on December 13th, 1975. The Deadlift of 495 and Total of 1300 at the 1975 Mountian Empire Powerlifting Meet were new West Virginia Powerlifting Records at 148. In celebration of the victory for "Team West Virginia," a photo was taken of the team with *the West Virginia State Flag in the background!* The official results of the 1975 Mountian Empire Powerlifting Championships were published in the May-June, 1976 issue of *Muscular Development* magazine. The newsletters, *Powerlifting News* and *The Lifter,* also published the official results of the 1975 Mountian Empire Open Powerlifting Meet.

During a meeting conducted on the night before the 1975 Mountian Empire Powerlifting contest, it was agreed by the West Virginia AAU Powerlifting club representatives from *Luke's Gym* and the *Charleston Barbell Club* that "Official Powerlifting Records" would begin at the *1976 (1st Annual) West Virginia State Powerlifting Championships* on the date of February 14th, 1976. Meanwhile, the West Virginia Powerlifting Records, recognized since 1960, would be "frozen" and given recognition in the archives of West Virginia Powerlifting. The old records would be "frozen" to the archives on January 31st, 1976.

From what began in January of 1973, the Totals from Olympic Weightlifting needed only two (2) lifts : The Snatch and the Clean & Jerk. Since the elimination of the Clean & Press from official Weightlifting competition, the Totals consisting of the Clean & Press, the Snatch, and the Clean & Jerk were history. The West Virginia Olympic Weightlifting Records consisting of the "Three (3) Lift" Totals would be "frozen to the archives" effective December 31st, 1975.

1975 West Virginia Powerlifter Rankings
RANKINGS Determined by Total
WV Powerlifters competing from January 1st, 1975 thru December 31st, 1975

123 / Name	Squat	Bench Press	Deadlift	Total	Date
Chuck Mooney	245	170	425*	840*	12/13/1975
Chuck Dunbar	300*	250*	285	835	12/13/1975
Peery Reeder	180	170	350	700	10/18/1975
132 Chick Clegg	240	230*	330	800	12/13/1975
Chick Clegg	200	225	300	725	10/18/1975
148 Paul Sutphin	500	305*	495*	1300*	12/13/1975
Paul Sutphin	505*	285	450	1240*	4/12/1975
Paul Sutphin	450	280	470*	1200 wld	3/01/1975
Paul Sutphin	455	280	455	1190	4/26/1975
Paul Sutphin	420	280	460	1160	1/18/1975
165 Frank White	430	340	450	1220	1/18/1975
Don Hundley	460	235	485	1180	12/13/1975
Don Hundley	440	245	470	1155	1/18/1975
Don Hundley	450	225	480	1155	9/27/1975
Don Hundley	445	225	475	1145	3/08/1975
Bill Kyle	310	290	425	1025	12/13/1975
Bill Kyle	325	275	400	1000	10/18/1975
181 Gary Clark	460	355	520	1335*	5/18/1975
Gary Clark	470*	330	510	1310*	4/27/1975
Gary Clark	430	360*	500	1290*	3/08/1975
Barry Barrows	365	310	500	1175	10/18/1975
John Collias	435	230	475	1140	4/12/1975
Don Hall	405	260	475	1140	12/13/1975
Don Hall	405	245	460	1110	9/27/1975
Don Hall	395	245	465	1105	4/12/1975
Don Hall	375	240	450	1065	3/08/1975
Chip Thomas	330	250	500	1080	12/13/1975
Don Hall	345	215	400	960	1/18/1975

* - Denotes West Virginia State Powerlifting Record

wld – Wild Card Meet

1975 West Virginia Powerlifter Rankings
RANKINGS Determined by Total
WV Powerlifters competing from January 1st, 1975 thru December 31st, 1975

198 / Name		Squat	Bench Press	Deadlift	Total	Date
	Vince White	500	380	450	1330*	9/27/1975
	Vince White	505*	360	435	1300	4/12/1975
	Pete Rocchio	450	300	540	1290	4/27/1975
	Vince White	490	360	400	1250	3/08/1975
	Vince White	470	365	415	1250	4/26/1975
	Pete Rocchio	435	275	525	1235	3/08/1975
	Vince White	400	360	400	1160	1/18/1975
	Wayne Dawson	300	230	330	860	4/12/1975
220	John Messinger	525*	355	540	1420	11/01/1975
	John Messinger	475	360	555*	1390	4/12/1975
	Vince White	530*	410*	440	1380	12/13/1975
	Ernie Nagy	480	360	520	1360	1/1975
	Ernie Nagy	460	365	515	1340	5/18/1975
	John Messinger	440	340	545	1325	3/08/1975
	Ernie Nagy	440	360	520	1320	3/08/1975
	Ernie Nagy	480	360	480	1320	1975 Grt Lakes
	Ernie Nagy	445	345	510	1300	4/27/1975
	Nick Busick	455	300	530	1285	4/27/1975
	Nick Busick	405	340	510	1255	3/08/1975
	John Messinger	400	320	500	1220	1/18/1975
242	Ernie Nagy	500* m	375*m	525 m	1400*m	10/18/1975
	Denny Cain	450	270	550	1270	4/27/1975
	Denny Cain	450	270	535	1255	5/18/1975
	Denny Cain	450	250	525	1225	3/08/1975
	Gaye Elmore	440	290	470	1200	9/27/1975
SHW	Luke Iams	625*	470*	515	1610*	12/13/1975
	Luke Iams	550*	450*	500	1500*	4/27/1975
	Phillip McClelland	480*	295	540*	1315*	3/08/1975
	Phillip McClelland	475	310	530	1315	5/18/1975
	Phillip McClelland	450	300	555*	1305	4/27/1975

* - Denotes West Virginia State Powerlifting Record

m – West Virginia State Master's Record

West Virginia Association AAU Olympic Weightlifting Records
As of December 31, 1975

LIFT	NAME	RECORDS
123lb. Class		
Snatch	Vince White	125
C & J	Vince White	175
Total	Vince White	300
132lb. Class		
Snatch	Frank White	145
C & J	Frank White	205
Total	Frank White	350
148lb. Class		
Snatch	Mickey Deitz	205
C & J	Mickey Deitz	290
Total	Mickey Deitz	495
165lb. Class		
Snatch	Frank White	215
C & J	Frank White	285
Total	Frank White	500
181lb. Class		
Snatch	Charles Litzsinger	220
C & J	Doug Forth	290
Total	Doug Forth	505
198lb. Class		
Snatch	Herb Fitzsimmons	240
C & J	Herb Fitzsimmons	320
Total	Herb Fitzsimmons	560
242lb. Class		
Snatch	Herb Fitzsimmons	235
C & J	Herb Fitzsimmons	330
Total	Herb Fitzsimmons	565
Super Hvywt. Class		
Snatch	Lee Shorter	242½
C & J	Lee Shorter	325
Total	Lee Shorter	562¼

West Virginia Association AAU Clean & Press Records
As of December 31, 1972

Weight Class	Name	Press
123lb. Class	Vince White	165
132lb. Class	Vince White	185
148lb. Class	Frank White	230 AR*
165lb. Class	Frank White	275
181lb. Class	Doug Forth	240
198lb. Class	Herb Fitzsimmons	250
242lb. Class	Herb Fitzsimmons	260
Super Heavy	-----------------------	-----

*AR – Teenage American Record

Chapter Nine : 1976

The year 1976 began with Part III of the Kentucky Connection. The 3ʳᵈ Annual Lexington Open Powerlifting Championships were held Saturday January 17th, 1976 at the Lexington YMCA in Lexington, Kentucky. The 1976 Lexington Open was sponsored by the *Lexington Weightlifting Club*. The 1976 Lexington Open had seventy-two (72) lifters. While competing in the 114lb. class at the 1976 Lexington Open, Chuck Mooney pulled a 425lb. Deadlift, officially breaking the American Record! The lifting of Chuck Mooney, Paul Sutphin, Don Hall, and Vince White on January 17th, 1976 enabled the *Charleston Barbell Club* to return to West Virginia with one of the team's most memorable performances.

Prior to 1976, the man responsible for most of Powerlifting's publicity from the local newspapers was Vince White. Vince believed, "getting your name with your lifts in the paper" was essential for promoting Powerlifting. Following the 1976 Lexington Open, the *Charleston Gazette* informed their readership that Chuck Mooney of Charleston was the new American Record Holder in the Deadlift for the 114lb. class.

A feature story in January, 1976 read *"Mooney's Desire for Body Strength Brings Lift Record."* Receiving publicity once again from *The Charleston Gazette*, Chuck Mooney's follow-up included a headline that read, *"Charleston Weightlifter Sets National Record."* Given the fact the Sportswriter referenced Chuck Mooney as a "Weightlifter" in the 1976 headline rather than correctly identifying him as a "Powerlifter" exemplified the depth of knowledge for the iron game among the most affluent members of the local news media. Regardless, the names of Vince White, Frank White, Don Hall, Don Hundley, Herb Fitzsimmons, John Messinger, Chuck Mooney, and Paul Sutphin frequently appeared in newsprint throughout the second half of the 1970's decade.

Vince White "got it right" in 1976 at the Lexington Open! Lifting in a field of sixteen (16) competitors in the 220lb. class, Vince placed 3ʳᵈ with a 1370 Total that included a 550 Squat, a 395 Bench Press for a *New* Lexington Open Bench Press Record, and a 475 Deadlift. In contrast, an air of controversy surrounded the aftermath of the 1975 Lexington Open Powerlifting event with an incident involving Vince White, a couple of officials, and the new Lexington Open Bench Press Record set by Vince in the 198lb. class. At the completion of the 1976 contest, Vince White owned the new official Powerlifting Meet Records in the Bench Press from the years of 1975 and 1976 while all issues were resolved.

Don Hall placed 7th among seventeen (17) competitors in the 181lb. class at the 1976 Lexington Open Powerlifting Meet with a 415 Squat, 250 Bench Press, 485 Deadlift, and a Total of 1150. While placing first among the lightweights, I Squatted 440, Bench Pressed 285, and Deadlifted 480. The Total of 1205 won the Outstanding Lifter Award at the 1976 Lexington Open for the morning session.

The Outstanding Lifters at the 1976 Lexington Open Powerlifting Meet were Paul Sutphin for the Lightweights and Louie Simmons for the Heavyweights. Louie won 1st Place at 198 with lifts of 530 Squat, 385 Bench Press, and a 645 Deadlift for a 1560 Total! All of Louie Simmons' lifts were Lexington Open Powerlifting Meet Records! The awards were gigantic, iron-posted and marble-based trophies. In addition, a gold Elgin wristwatch was part of the Outstanding Lifter Award at the 1976 Lexington Open Powerlifting Meet.

Official & Unofficial Powerlifting Records

It was decided at the meeting on 12/12/75 on the night before the Mountian Empire Powerlifting Meet in Bristol, Tennessee that all West Virginia State Powerlifting Records (thru 1/31/1976) be declared <u>Official / Unofficial Powerlifting Records</u> and *retired as permanent marks.* As an extension to the agreement, beginning February 14th, 1976 new Powerlifting Records would be set at the First Annual AAU West Virginia State Powerlifting Championships in New Martinsville.

As acting Chairman of West Virginia Powerlifting, I spoke in opposition to the proposal to "retire to the archives" the West Virginia Powerlifting Records from 1/01/1960 thru 1/31/1976. However, in a Democracy, everyone votes and due to the persuasion of Vince White and a few others, the "C word" known as compromise prevailed. As it turned out, many of the Official/Unofficial West Virginia Powerlifting Records were equaled or exceeded on February 14th, 1976 at the first official West Virginia State Powerlifting Championships.

Official & Unofficial West Virginia Powerlifting Records
West Virginia Powerlifting Records from January 1st, 1960 thru January 31st, 1976

Lift	Name	Record	Year	Location
114lb. class				
Squat	Chuck Dunbar	310	1976	National "Y"
Bench Press	Chuck Dunbar	230	1976	National "Y"
Deadlift	Chuck Mooney	425 AR*	1976	Lexington Open
Total	Chuck Dunbar	845	1976	National "Y"
123lb. class				
Squat	Chuck Dunbar	300	1975	Bristol Open
Bench Press	Chuck Dunbar	250	1975	Bristol Open
Deadlift	Chuck Mooney	425	1975	Bristol Open
Total	Chuck Mooney	840	1975	Bristol Open
132lb. class				
Squat	Larry Wilson	260	1962	WV Open
Bench Press	Chick Clegg	230	1975	Bristol Open
Deadlift	George Powell	375	1963	Pittsburgh, PA
Total	George Powell	800	1963	Pittsburgh, PA
148lb. class				
Squat	Paul Sutphin	505	1975	Johnson City Open
Bench Press	Paul Sutphin	305	1975	Bristol Open
Deadlift	Paul Sutphin	495	1975	Bristol Open
Total	Paul Sutphin	1300	1975	Bristol Open
165lb. class				
Squat	Don Hundley	465	1974	Steubenville Open
Bench Press	Frank White	355	1974	Bristol Open
Deadlift	Don Hundley	500	1973	Durham, NC
Total	Frank White	1260	1973	Munhall, PA

Lift	Name	Record	Year	Location
181lb. class				
Squat	Gary Clark	470	1975	Bedford, Ohio
Bench Press	Vince White	355	1972	Bristol Open
Deadlift	Doug Forth	555	1962	Pittsburgh, PA
Total	Gary Clark	1335	1975	Canton, Ohio
198lb. class				
Squat	Vince White	505	1975	Johnson City Open
Bench Press	Vince White	380	1974	Newcastle, PA
Deadlift	Doug Forth	570	1962	Pittsburgh, PA
Total	Vince White	1330	1975	Cumberland, MD
220lb. class				
Squat	Vincent White	530	1975	Bristol Open
Bench Press	Vincent White	410	1975	Bristol Open
Deadlift	John Messinger	555	1975	Johnson City Open
Total	Doug Forth	1435	1973	Concord Invitational
242lb. class				
Squat	Ernie Nagy	500	1975	Weirton, WV
Bench Press	Ernie Nagy	375	1975	Weirton, WV
Deadlift	Doug Forth	550	1971	Franklin, Ohio
Total	Ernie Nagy	1400	1975	Weirton, WV
Super Heavyweight Class				
Squat	Luke Iams	645	1976	Y – Nationals
Bench Press	Luke Iams	500	1976	Y – Nationals
Deadlift	Phillip McClelland	555	1975	Bedford, Ohio
Total	Luke Iams	1690	1976	Y – Nationals

1st Annual WV State Powerlifting Championships

The year 1976 marked a "New Beginning" for West Virginia Powerlifting. New Powerlifting Records were established at the First Official AAU West Virginia State Powerlifting Championships on February 14th, 1976 in New Martinsville, West Virginia. The West Virginia State Powerlifting Championships and the First Official Mr. West Virginia Physique competition were advertised in *Muscular Development* magazine.

The 1st Annual West Virginia State Powerlifting Championships were held February 14th, 1976 in New Martinsville, West Virginia. Meet Director Luke Iams and a network of sponsors in the township of New Martinsville and Wetzel County hosted the very first West Virginia State Powerlifting Championships with a total of forty-five (45) lifters from all regions of the Mountain State. The lifters represented five (5) different clubs and several lifters competed as unattached.

The lifters representing *Luke's Gym* included : Chuckie Dunbar (114lb. class), Peery Reeder (123lb. class), Charles (Chick) Clegg (132lb. class), Paul Sutphin (148lb. class), Frank Nicholas (165lb. class), William (Bill) Kyle (165), Scott Tusic (181lb. class), Mike Wolf (220lb. class), Tim Slamick (242lb. class), and SuperHeavyWeight (SHW) Luke Iams.

The lifters representing the *Charleston Barbell Club* included : Chuck Mooney (114lb. class), Fernando Aquilar (148lb. class), Frank White (165lb. class), Don Hundley (165), Don Hall (181lb. class), Warren Knight (198lb. class), Mitch Crislip (198), Vince White (220lb. class), and SuperHeavyWeight (SHW) Herb Fitzsimmons, weighing in at 243 ½ lbs.

Ernie Nagy brought a team of eight (8) competitors. The lifters representing *Nagy's Gym* included : Jim Jones (148lb. class), Michael Zinaich (165lb. class), Gary Clark (181lb. class), Pete Rocchio (198lb. class), Ernie Nagy (220lb. class), Nick Busick (220), Denny Cain (242lb. class), and SuperHeavyWeight (SHW) Phillip McClelland.

Lifting for the Powerlifting Team of the *Mountianeer's* were : Dennis Passantino (123lb. class), Ken Woodell (132lb. class), Tim Hill (148lb. class), Robert Canala (165lb. class), Barry Barrows (181lb. class), Steve Cvechko (198lb. class), and 242 lb. Bill Linger.

The lifting at the 1976 West Virginia State Powerlifting Championships began with Chuck Mooney (American Record Holder in the Deadlift), and Chuck Dunbar in the 114lb. weight class. Chuck Mooney set two (2) new West Virginia State Powerlifting Records in the Deadlift with 420 and a winning Total of 860lbs. in the 114lb. weight class.

Chuck Dunbar Squatted 320 for a new West Virginia State Powerlifting Record in the 114lb. class. In the 123lb. class, Peery Reeder set all four (4) records including a Total of 775. Competing in the 132lb. class, Don Giarletto broke the West Virginia State Powerlifting Record in the Squat on 2/14/76 with a lift of 280lbs. Chick Clegg Benched a new record with 240lbs. at 132 while Ken Woodell set the Deadlift and the winning Total.

In the 148lb. class, Paul Sutphin re-established three (3) West Virginia State Records in the Squat, the Deadlift, and the Total. Sutphin won the Outstanding Lifter Award (114 thru 165) and the Best Squat Award on 2/14/76. Tim Hill set the new Bench Press Record in the 148lb. class with a lift of 300.

In the 165lb. class, Frank White re-set two (2) West Virginia State Powerlifting Records with a Total of 1215 and Bench Press of 350. Don Hundley finished 2nd at 165 with re-established West Virginia State Powerlifting Records in the Squat and Deadlift.

Frank White – 350 Bench Press – 165lb. class – 2/14/76
West Virginia State Record

Gary Clark won the 181lb. class with three (3) new West Virginia State Powerlifting Records in the Squat, Bench Press and Total. Clark's Bench Press at 370 was an All-Time

West Virginia State Powerlifting Record for the Lightheavyweights. Finishing 3rd in the 181lb. class, Don Hall pulled a solid 500 Deadlift. Warren Knight won the 1976 West Virginia State Powerlifting Championship in the 198lb. class. Warren's State Record Total of 1270 included a West Virginia State Record Deadlift of 535.

The competition was toughest in the 220's as Vince White ended up 5th with a 1370 Total. Vince re-established the West Virginia State Squat Record in the 220's with a lift of 510lbs. While winning the 1976 West Virginia State Powerlifting Championship in the 220lb. class, Mike Wolf broke the Bench Press Record with a lift of 440lbs. and Total with 1455. Mike Houston, 2nd Place in the 220lb. class, set a new West Virginia State Record in the Deadlift at 625lbs.

In the 242lb. class, new West Virginia State Powerlifting Records were broken by the winner, Doug Horner. Horner Bench Pressed 410lbs., Deadlifted 600lbs., and Totaled 1510. All of Doug Horner's lifts were new West Virginia State Records in the 242lb. class at the 1976 West Virginia State Powerlifting Championships.

Herb Fitzsimmons, weighing 243 ½, competed in the SuperHeavyWeight Division. On February 14th, 1976 Herb Fitzsimmons began an assault on the Powerlifting Record books as he increased his Total by 700lbs. in only 38 months! Luke Iams won the 1976 West Virginia State Championship with a new West Virginia State Record in the Squat with 670lbs. and re-established his own records in the Bench Press and Total. Placing 2nd at the 1976 West Virginia State Powerlifting Championships, Phillip McClelland broke the SHW Deadlift Record with a lift of 560lbs.

The 1976 West Virginia State Powerlifting Championships had only one session which began at 8:30am with weigh-ins for all competitors. The Powerlifting and the Physique were over at approximately 9:00pm. The 1976 West Virginia State Powerlifting Championships had excellent coverage as *Powerlifting News* printed a comprehensive report along with several photos. The official results with photos of the 1976 West Virginia State Powerlifting Championships appeared in other lifting publications with photos including Mike Kennedy's newsletter, *"The Lifter."*

The NOV/DEC, 1976 issue of *Muscular Development* magazine published my team photo of the *Charleston Barbell Club* including Frank White, Mitch Crislip, Vince White, Chuck Mooney, Don Hundley, Don Hall, Herb Fitzsimmons and Paul Sutphin. Paul Sutphin was photographed with the *Charleston Barbell Club* and *Luke's Gym.*

1976 West Virginia State Powerlifting Championships

1ST OFFICIAL / AAU Mr. West Virginia Physique Contest

Held Saturday February 14, 1976
Magnolia High School
New Martinsville, W. VA

Wt. Class/Name	Club	Squat	Bench	Deadlift	Total
114 ½					
Chuck Mooney	Charleston	260	180	420*	860*
Chuck Dunbar	Luke's Gym	320*	225*	285	830
123 ½					
Perry Reeder	Luke's Gym	225*	200*	350*	775*
Dennis Passantino	Mountianeers	220	190	330	740
132 ¼					
Kenny Woodell	Mountianeers	240	235	360*	835*
Donald Giarlrtto	Unnattached	280*	190	360	830
Chick Clegg	Luke's Gym	270	240*	310	820
148 ¾					
Paul Sutphin	Luke's Gym	470*	290	485*	1245*
Tim Hill	Mountianeers	275	300*	360	935
Jim Jones	Nagy's PT	270	230	390	890
Doug Roberts	Unnattached	270	205	320	795
Fernando Aquilar	Charleston	225	225	340	790
Brian Williams	Unnattached	230	170	350	750
165 ¼					
Frank White	Charleston	425	350*	440	1215*
Don Hundley	Charleston	445*	230	500*	1175
Frank Nicholas	Luke's Gym	340	270	415	1025
Bill Kyle	Luke's Gym	305	290	400	995
Robert Canala	Mountianeers	305	280	400	985
Michael Zinaich	Nagy's PT	280	265	400	945
Bob Smith	Unnattached	230	255	375	860
Brian Phillips	Unnattached	250	200	325	775

Wt. Class/Name	Club	Squat	Bench	Deadlift	Total
181 ¾					
Gary Clark	Nagy's PT	470*	370*	490	1330*
Barry Barrows	Mountianeers	375	300	520*	1195
Don Hall	Charleston	425	265	500	1190
Bruce Cahill	Unnattached	365	280	500	1145
Mike Lorentz	Parkersburg	335	260	470	1065
Scott Tusic	Luke's Gym	340	315	400	1055
Mark Modesitt	Unnattached	325	290	350	965
198 ¼					
Warren Knight	Charleston	435	300	535*	1270*
Pete Rocchio	Nagy's PT	450*	300	500	1250
Steve Cvechko	Mountianeers	375	340*	440	1155
Gary Marks	Unnattached	325	300	450	1075
Mitchell Crislip	Charleston	340	280	425	1045
220 ½					
Mike Wolf	Luke's Gym	475	440*	540	1455*
Mike Houston	Unnattached	485	340	625*	1450
Ernie Nagy	Nagy's PT	480	380	525	1385
Nick Busick	Nagy's PT	470	380	530	1380
Vince White	Charleston	510*	395	465	1370
242 ½					
Doug Horner	Unnattached	500*	410*	600*	1510*
Tim Slamick	Luke's Gym	385	360	520	1265
Denny Cain	Nagy's PT	470	290	500	1260
Bill Linger	Mountianeers	340	220	400	960
Super Hvywt.					
Luke Iams	Luke's Gym	670*	500*	520	1690*
Phillip McClelland	Nagy's PT	525	330	560*	1415
Herb Fitzsimmons	Charleston	430	360	430	1220

* Indicates New Official State Record

Best Lifter (114 thru 165)	Paul Sutphin, 1245 Total
Best Lifter (181 thru SHW)	Gary Clark, 1330 Total
Best Squat Award	Paul Sutphin, 470
Best Bench Award	Mike Wolf, 440
Best Deadlift Award	Chuck Mooney, 420

Outstanding Team Award – Luke's Gym, New Martinsville, W. Va.

MR. WEST VIRGINIA PHYSIQUE CONTEST WINNERS

Jerry Potter	1st
Frank Nicholas	2nd
Frank White	3rd
Larry Robinson	4th
Charles Nagy	5th

The Charleston Barbell Club pictured after the 1st Annual West Virginia State Powerlifting Championships at New Martinsville, West Virginia on 2/14/76. *Left to Right* : Paul Sutphin, Frank White, Mitch Crislip, Vince White, Chuck Mooney, Don Hundley, Don Hall, Herb Fitzsimmons

1976 National Collegiate Powerlifting

The <u>1976 National Collegiate Powerlifting Championships</u> were held on April 3rd and 4th, 1976 at Ohio University in Athens, Ohio. The Meet Director was Jack Wilson. The Collegiate Powerlifting Team sponsoring the event was the *Ohio Barbell Club*. According to the official meet results, there were at least one-hundred twenty-two (122) lifters at the 1976 National Collegiate Powerlifting Championships. The official results of the 1976 National Collegiate Powerlifting Championships were published in the July-August, 1976 issue of *Muscular Development* magazine.

Paul Sutphin represented Bluefield College at the 1976 National Collegiate Powerlifting Championships. Among the winners at the 1976 National Collegiates were Enrique Hernandez from San Diego State in California. Hernandez's Total of 1185 in the 132lb. class was a National Collegiate Total Record. Roger Estep won the 198lb. Collegiate title with a Total of 1660. Wayne Bouvier won the Superheavyweight class with a Total of 2000!

In the 148lb. class, there were fourteen (14) competitors. Roger Wright, lifting in the 148lb. class, Squatted 490 and bombed out on the Bench Press. Afterward, it was Jack Wilson and myself battling for the Lightweight Collegiate Powerlifting title. I weighed in at 147 ¾ and Jack Wilson was the heavier man at 148 ¼. Both Jack Wilson and myself Squatted with 460lbs. I took the lead in the Bench Press with a lift of 290 versus 270 for Wilson. As it turned out, Wilson needed a 515 Deadlift to overcome a deficit of 20lbs. from a 730 Sub-Total. I managed only a 490 Deadlift and Wilson pulled 515 for the win in the 148lb. class with a 1245 Total. I finished 2nd in the 148's with a Total of 1240.

1976 Huntington Open Powerlifting

In April, 1976 lifters throughout West Virginia were competing in different competitions. Representing the *Charleston Barbell Club* on April 17th, 1976 at the *Buckeye Open Powerlifting Championships* were Vince White (198) and Herb Fitzsimmons (242). Vince White Totaled 1270 for 4th Place in the 198lb. class while Herb Fitzsimmons Totaled 1380 for 2nd Place in the 242lb. class. For the *Charleston Barbell Club*, the Buckeye Open was a preliminary to the Huntington Open Powerlifting Championships, one week later.

The <u>First Annual (1976) Huntington Open Powerlifting Championships</u> were held Saturday April 24th, 1976 at the Huntington YMCA in Huntington, West Virginia. The 1976 Huntington Open had thirty-two (32) lifters. Don Hall placed 3rd in the 181lb.

class with a Total of 1110. Warren Knight won the 198lb. class with a Total of 1255. In the 220lb. class, Mike Houston placed 1st with a Total of 1310 which included a 580 Deadlift. Vince White finished 2nd with a Total of 1300 in the 220lb. class. The Best Bench Press Award was won by Vince White for a Bench Press of 380 at a bodyweight of 200lbs. While winning the 242lb. class at the 1976 Huntington Open Powerlifting Championships with a Total of 1450, Herb Fitzsimmons broke the West Virginia State Record in the Squat with a lift of 550lbs. Weighing 244lbs., Austin Miller placed 2nd in the SuperHeavyWeight division while Bill Blankenship received honorable recognition for being the oldest competitor at the 1976 Huntington Open. The 1976 Huntington Open Powerlifting Championship Team Award was won by the *Charleston Barbell Club*, led by Vince White and Herb Fitzsimmons.

1976 Region VI Powerlifting & More

In the 1970's and the 1980's, a Regional Powerlifting Championship was a major title of which to win. The AAU divided the U.S.A. into Regions, with each Region including several states. The Region VI included Michigan, Illinois, Ohio, Kentucky, Indiana, and West Virginia. On June 12th, 1976 Herb Fitzsimmons, Vince White, and Paul Sutphin traveled to Lexington, Kentucky for the 1976 Region VI Powerlifting Championships. The 1976 Region VI marked the 4th Powerlifting event conducted in Lexington, Kentucky from January, 1974 until June, 1976.

The 1976 Region VI Powerlifting Championships had thirty-seven (37) lifters. The Meet Director of the 1976 Region VI Powerlifting Championships had earned himself the reputation for presenting the most elaborate awards to lifters. The trophies awarded at the Powerlifting Championships in Lexington, Kentucky were constructed of genuine marble, metal, and cast iron.

Although my Total of 1185 in the 148lb. class finished 2nd to Bob Cortes, I was more than pleased with breaking the Region VI Squat Record with a lift of 450lbs. The 450lb. Region VI Squat Record in the 148lb. class set on 6/12/76 by Paul Sutphin broke the previous record of 445lbs. held by Tom LaFontaine. Louie Simmons Totaled 1540 to win the 181lb. class at the 1976 Region VI Powerlifting Championships and also the Outstanding Lifter Award for the heavyweight classes.

Vince White finished 4th at the 1976 Region VI Powerlifting Championships in the 220's, yet he had the highest Bench in the 220lb. division with a lift of 385lbs. To compliment Vince's Bench Press and Total of 1310, Vince Squatted with 485 and Deadlifted 440. Herb Fitzsimmons won the 1976 Region VI Powerlifting title in the

242lb. class. Herb's winning Total of 1470 consisted of a 550lb. Squat, 360 Bench Press, and a Deadlift of 560.

The 1976 Junior National Powerlifting Championships were held July 11th and 12th, 1976 at the Southeast Area YMCA in Bedford, Ohio. The 1976 Junior Nationals was a good day for Chuck Dunbar. Chuck Dunbar of *Luke's Gym* won the Junior National Championship title in the 114lb. class. In the year 1976, Chuck Dunbar also won the *1976 Teenage National Powerlifting Championships* (18-19 Age Group).

Before the 1976 Juniors, my lifting was at a stalemate and literally going "South." As a result, I "bombed out," at the 1976 Junior Nationals. Afterward, I overheard a remark by one of the officials working the scorer's table, "Oh well, back to the gym." The statement replayed in my mind as I watched Clyde Wright win the 1976 Junior National Powerlifting Championship title in the 148lb. class with a Total of 1275. The 2nd day of the 1976 Juniors claimed Herb Fitzsimmons as a victim of the "Bombout." We would be back!

The Eastern U.S. Powerlifting Championships were conducted on October 17th, 1976 at Westernport, Maryland. According to the official meet roster, the contest had thirty-three (33) lifters. Among the lifters from West Virginia were Don Hundley, Don Hall, Vince White, Dave Snyder, and Herb Fitzsimmons. The 1976 Eastern U.S. Powerlifting Championship was sanctioned by the South Atlantic Association of the A.A.U. and became Part II of the "Maryland Connection" for West Virginia Powerlifting.

Don Hundley set a new West Virginia State Record in the Squat for the 165lb. class on 10/17/76 with a lift of 450lbs. Competing in the 220lb. class at Westernport, Maryland, Vince White set a new West Virginia State Powerlifting Record in the Squat with a lift of 515lbs. for the 220lb. class. Don Hall, Dave Snyder, and Herb Fitzsimmons all placed at the 1976 Eastern U.S. Powerlifting Championships on 10/17/76.

3rd Annual Mountianeer Open
An Official Powerlifting Championship

It was time for a major celebration as the 3rd Annual Mountianeer Open was now an official Powerlifting (3-lift) meet! The 3rd Annual (1976) Mountianeer Open Powerlifting Championships were held November 6th, 1976 in Parkersburg, West Virginia. The 1976 Mountianeer Open Powerlifting Championships had thirty-one (31) lifters. Seven (7) West Virginia State Powerlifting Records fell at the 3rd Annual Mountianeer Open Powerlifting Championships in Parkersburg.

Tim Hill Bench Pressed 310lbs. for a new West Virginia State Record in the 148lb. class. Don Hundley won the 165lb. class with a Total of 1200 that included a West Virginia State Record Squat of 470lbs. in the Middleweight class. Don Hall won the 181lb. class with a Total of 1215. Don Hall's 505 Deadlift gave him the victory by 5lbs. over Frank Nicholas' Total of 1210. Barry Barrows Totaled a West Virginia State Record of 1275 to win the 198lb. class.

Winning the 220lb. class at the 1976 Mountianeer Open was Mike Wolf of *Luke's Gym*. Mike Wolf Totaled a new West Virginia State Record of 1525lbs. Included in Wolf's Total was a West Virginia State Record Bench Press of 450lbs. in the 220lb. class.

Vince White Placed 2nd in the 220lb. class at the 1976 Mountianeer Open with a Total of 1355. Vince broke the West Virginia State Record in the Squat in the 220lb. class with a lift of 530lbs. Vince White Squatted more weight than anyone at the 1976 Mountianeer Open with the exception of Herb Fitzsimmons.

Herb Fitzsimmons weighed 246 ½ lbs. and won the SuperHeavyWeight class at the 1976 Mountianeer Open Powerlifting Championships with a Total of 1510lbs. Herb's 1510 Total on 11/06/76 included a Squat of 580lbs., Bench Press of 355lbs., and a West Virginia State Record Deadlift of 575lbs. Herb's Deadlift of 575 was the heaviest Deadlift of the competition.

Tennessee Connection : Part V

The <u>1976 Mountian Empire Powerlifting Meet</u> was held at the Bristol Family YMCA on December 11th, 1976 in Bristol, Tennessee. The 1976 Mountian Empire Open Power Meet had forty-three (43) lifters. Although members of *Luke's Gym* did not make the trip, "Team West Virginia" was formed once again.

The Powerlifting Team of *Herb's Gym / Charleston Barbell* was represented by nine (9) lifters at the 1976 Mountian Empire Powerlifting at Bristol, Tennessee. The team roster for *Herb's Gym / Charleston Barbell Club* at Bristol, Tennessee on 12/11/76 included : Ken Woodell (132 – 880 Total / 1st), Tom Plesich (148 – 1005 Total / 2nd), Paul Sutphin (165 – 1260 Total / 1st), Don Hundley (165 – 1210 Total / 2nd), Don Hall (181 – 1190 Total / 5th), Steve Brooks (181 – 1140 Total / 6th), Vince Crow (220 – 975 Total / 4th), Vince White (242 – 1400 Total / 1st), Herb Fitzsimmons (Superheavyweight – 1505 Total / 1st).

Ken Woodell competed in the 132lb. class, won 1st Place, and broke West Virginia State Records in the Squat and Total. Lifting in the 148lb. class and finishing 2nd with a Total of 1005 was Tom Plesich, also representing *Herb's Gym / Charleston Barbell Club*.

Paul Sutphin competed in the 165lb. class at the 1976 Mountian Empire Open and Squatted 460, Bench Pressed a competition PR of 310, and Deadlifted 490. Sutphin's lifts on 12/11/1976 represented a 1260 Total, a first place win in the Middleweight class, and four (4) new West Virginia Collegiate Powerlifting Records. Teammate Don Hundley (1210 Total) placed 2nd in the 165lb. class over the 3rd place finisher at 1205.

On December 11th, 1976 at Bristol, Tennessee Vince White Totaled 1400 in the 242lb. class with lifts of 525 Squat, 415 Bench Press, and a 460 Deadlift. Vince's bodyweight was less than 225lbs. Herb Fitzsimmons was the strongest man at the 1976 Mountian Empire Powerlifting contest at Bristol with lifts of 550 Squat, 355 Bench Press, and 600 Deadlift for a 1505 Total. Herb finished the contest with a Deadlift of 600lbs., a new West Virginia State Record, and the heaviest Deadlift of the day on 12/11/76.

1976 West Virginia Powerlifter Rankings
WV Powerlifters competing from January 1st, 1976 thru December 31st, 1976
TOP RANKINGS Determined by Total

114 / Name	Squat	Bench Press	Deadlift	Total	Date
Chuck Dunbar	345*	230	300	875*	4/17/76
Chuck Dunbar	335	250*	285	870*	3/27/76
Chuck Mooney	260	180	420*	860*	2/14/76
Chuck Dunbar	345 t	225 t	290 t	860 t	8/07/76
Chuck Dunbar	345 j	230	280	855	7/10/76
Chuck Dunbar	325	240	285	850	5/08/76
Chuck Dunbar	310	230	305	845	1/25/76
Chuck Mooney	235	170	425*AR	830	1/17/76
Chuck Dunbar	320*	225*	285	830	2/14/76
123 Ken Woodell	260*	215*	355*	830*	4/24/76
Perry Reeder	225*	200*	350*	775*	2/14/76
Dennis Passantino	220	190	330	740	2/14/76
132 Kenny Woodell	285	225	370	880	12/11/76
Kenny Woodell	240	235	360*	835*	2/14/76
Donald Giarletto	280*	190	360	830	2/14/76
Chick Clegg	270	240*	310	820	2/14/76
Perry Reeder	225	190	370	785	4/17/76
Scott Miller	250	195	340	785	4/24/76
David Hall	230	185	310	725	4/24/76
David Hall	240	175	300	715	11/06/76

* - Denotes New West Virginia State Powerlifting Record

t – West Virginia State Teenage Powerlifting Record

j – Junior National Meet Record

AR – American Powerlifting Record

1976 West Virginia Powerlifter Rankings
WV Powerlifters competing from January 1st, 1976 thru December 31st, 1976
TOP RANKINGS Determined by Total

148/ Name	Squat	Bench Press	Deadlift	Total	Date
Paul Sutphin	470*c	290 c	485*	1245*c	2/14/76
Paul Sutphin	460	290	490*c	1240	4/03/76
Paul Sutphin	440	285	480	1205	1/17/76
Paul Sutphin	450 R	275	460	1185	6/12/76
Tim Hill	330	310*	380	1020	11/06/76
Rich Stradtman	320	275	410	1005	11/06/76
Tom Plescish	310	255	440	1005	12/11/76
Tom Plescish	300	240	400	940	4/24/76
Tim Hill	275	300*	360	935	2/14/76
Fernando Aquilar	285	235	385	905	11/06/76
Jim Jones	270	230	390	890	2/14/76
Fernando Aquilar	275	230	380	885	4/24/76
Brian Williams	300	200	335	835	11/06/76
Doug Roberts	270	205	320	795	2/14/76
Fernando Aquilar	225	225	340	790	2/14/76
Brian Williams	230	170	350	750	2/14/76

165	Squat	Bench Press	Deadlift	Total	Date
Paul Sutphin	460 c	310 c	490 c	1260 c	12/11/76
Frank White	425	350*	440	1215*	2/14/76
Don Hundley	470	235	505	1210	12/11/76
Don Hundley	470*	240	490	1200	11/06/76
Don Hundley	445*	230	500*	1175	2/14/76
Don Hundley	450*	230	470	1150	10/17/76
Gene Underwood	365	305	455	1125	4/24/76
Dave Jeffrey	340	340	445	1125	4/24/76
Bill Kyle	360	295	425	1080	11/06/76
Stephen Brooks	320	250	465	1035	4/24/76
Frank Nicholas	345	265	420	1030	4/24/76
Frank Nicholas	340	270	415	1025	2/14/76
Robert Canala	305	280	400	985	2/14/76
Bob Smith	280	255	395	930	4/24/76
Bob Smith	300	250	370	920	11/06/76
Gary Park	315	250	350	915	11/06/76

* - Denotes New West Virginia State Powerlifting Record

c – West Virginia Collegiate Powerlifting Record

R – Region VI Powerlifting Record

1976 West Virginia Powerlifter Rankings
WV Powerlifters competing from January 1st, 1976 thru December 31st, 1976
TOP RANKINGS Determined by Total

181 / Name	Squat	Bench Press	Deadlift	Total	Date
Gary Clark	470*	370*	490	1330*	2/14/76
Barry Barrows	410 c	325 c	500	1235 c	4/03/76
Don Hall	445	265	510	1220	10/17/76
Don Hall	435	275	505	1215	11/06/76
Frank Nicholas	450	320	440	1210	11/06/76
Barry Barrows	375	300	520*c	1195	2/14/76
Don Hall	425	265	500	1190	2/14/76
Don Hall	435	275	480	1190	12/11/76
Don Hall	415	250	485	1150	1/17/76
Bruce Cahill	365	280	500	1145	2/14/76
Steve Brooks	360	280	500	1140	12/11/76
Don Hall	405	250	455	1110	4/24/76
John Francis	325	300	435	1060	11/06/76
Scott Tusic	340	315	400	1055	2/14/76
Don Ackerman	305	280	430	1015	11/06/76
Mark Modesitt	325	290	350	965	2/14/76
Ross Smith	355	215	380	950	11/06/76

198	Squat	Bench Press	Deadlift	Total	Date
Barry Barrows	425	355	495	1275*	11/06/76
Warren Knight	435	300	535*	1270*	2/14/76
Warren Knight	450 c	295 c	525 c	1270 c	4/03/76
Vince White	480*	365	425	1270	4/17/76
Warren Knight	440	290	525	1255	4/24/76
Pete Rocchio	450*	300	500	1250	2/14/76
Vince White	450	365*	435	1250	3/27/76
Vince White	460	365	420	1245	5/08/76
Steve Cvecho	375	340	500	1215	4/24/76
Bruce Cahill	370	290	520	1180	11/06/76
Steve Cvechko	375	340	440	1155	2/14/76
Gary Marks	320	310	450	1080	11/06/76
Gary Marks	325	300	450	1075	2/14/76
Gary Marks	330	295	445	1070	4/24/76
Mitch Crislip	340	280	425	1045	2/14/76
Steve Gilchrist	305	240	450	995	11/06/76
Bill Blankenship	265	250	300	815	4/24/76

* - West Virginia State Powerlifting Record

c – West Virginia Collegiate Powerlifting Record

1976 West Virginia Powerlifter Rankings
WV Powerlifters competing from January 1st, 1976 thru December 31st, 1976
TOP RANKINGS Determined by Total

220 / Name	Squat	Bench Press	Deadlift	Total	Date
Mike Wolf	525	450*	550	1525*	11/06/76
Mike Wolf	475	430	560	1465	4/17/76
Mike Wolf	475	440*	540	1455*	2/14/76
Mike Houston	485	340	625*	1450	2/14/76
Ernie Nagy	495	380	540 m	1415 m	3/27/76
Ernie Nagy	460	400 m	555 m	1415	5/08/76
Ernie Nagy	480	380 m	525 m	1385	2/14/76
Nick Busick	470	380	530	1380	2/14/76
Vince White	510*	395	465	1370	2/14/76
Vince White	500	395	475	1370	1/17/76
Vince White	515*	380	470	1365	10/17/76
Vince White	530*	370	455	1355	11/06/76
Mike Houston	405	325	580	1310	4/24/76
Vince White	485	385	440	1310	6/12/76
Vince White	480	380	440	1300	4/24/76
Steve Cvecho	420	350	455	1225	11/06/76
Dave Snyder	370	280	495	1145	10/17/76
Mitch Crislip	350	300	400	1050	4/24/76
Vince Crow	315	280	380	975	12/11/76

* - Denotes New West Virginia State Powerlifting Record

m – West Virginia State Master's Powerlifting Record

1976 West Virginia Powerlifter Rankings
WV Powerlifters competing from January 1st, 1976 thru December 31st, 1976
TOP RANKINGS Determined by Total

242 / Name	Squat	Bench Press	Deadlift	Total	Date
Doug Horner	500*	410*	600*	1510*	2/14/76
Herb Fitzsimmons	550	360	560	1470	6/12/76
James Goodnight	510	400	555	1465	11/06/76
Herb Fitzsimmons	550* m	345 m	555	1450 m	4/24/76
Herb Fitzsimmons	540	345	560	1445	5/08/76
Herb Fitzsimmons	550	330	550	1430	10/17/76
Herb Fitzsimmons	520 m	340 m	560 m	1420 m	3/27/76
Vince White	525	415*	460	1400	12/11/76
Herb Fitzsimmons	510	345 m	525	1380	4/17/76
Jim Goodnight	450	385	525	1360	4/24/76
Gregory Williams	385	340	550	1275	4/24/76
Tim Slamick	385	360	520	1265	2/14/76
Denny Cain	470	290	500	1260	2/14/76
Austin Miller	405	265	400	1070	4/24/76
Austin Miller	410	280	380	1070	11/06/76
Bill Linger	340	220	400	960	2/14/76
SHW Luke Iams	675*	500	525	1700*	7/11/76
Luke Iams	645	500	545	1690	1/25/76
Luke Iams	670*	500*	520	1690*	2/14/76
Luke Iams	650	500	525	1675	4/17/76
Luke Iams	640	480	500	1620	5/08/76
Jim Goodnight	530	430	585	1545	11/06/76
Herb Fitzsimmons	580 m	355 m	575*m	1510 m	11/06/76
Herb Fitzsimmons	550	355	600*m	1505	12/11/76
Tim Slamick	515	400	555	1470	11/06/76
Phillip McClelland	525	330	560*	1415	2/14/76
Phillip McClelland	525	325	540	1390	5/08/76
Herb Fitzsimmons	430	360	430	1220	2/14/76
Austin Miller	405	265	400	1070	4/24/76

* - Denotes New West Virginia State Powerlifting Record

m – West Virginia State Master's Powerlifting Record

Chapter Ten : Era I Powerlifting Records
(1960 – 1976) : West Virginia State "RAW" Powerlifting Records

The year 1976 marked the end of an "Era" in Powerlifting ; Era One. All lifting during the Era One time period of Powerlifting met the criteria for what is now known as "Modern RAW" Powerlifting. The following weight classes included in the Era One of Powerlifting are listed in pounds : 114, 123, 132, 148, 165, 181, 198, 220, 242, and Superheavyweight (SHW). The 114lb. class was not used by most Meet Directors until 1975. At the end of Powerlifting's Era One, the 275lb. class did not exist.

The Powerlifting Records of Era I for the state of West Virginia were finalized at the end of 1976 due to the introduction of supersuits, custom lifting belts, and superwraps. Therefore, the Powerlifting Records during Era I for the Squat, the Deadlift, and Total are identified as "RAW" Powerlifting Records. The Bench Press during the Era I of Powerlifting was also "RAW," even though the "RAW" Bench Press continued throughout the years of Powerlifting's Era II (1977 – 1984).

Most Powerlifters were using the supersuits and custom lifting belts at the beginning of 1977. Even though the Bench Press was virtually unaffected by the supportive gear, the Powerlifting Totals increased as a result of the supersuits, superwraps, and the custom lifting belts. Even though the Bench Press remained "RAW" until 1985, it's all about the Powerlifter's TOTAL.

Beginning with the Era I Powerlifting Records in the 114lb. class, Chuck Dunbar owns the West Virginia State "RAW" Powerlifting Records in the Squat, Bench Press, and Total. Chuck Mooney, former American Record Holder in the Deadlift, has the West Virginia State "RAW" Deadlift Record of 425lbs. in the 114lb. class.

Also in the 114lb. class, Chuck Dunbar became the owner of four (4) West Virginia State Teenage Powerlifting Records. Chuck Dunbar officially set four (4) West Virginia State Teenage Powerlifting Records while competing in the 1976 Teenage National Powerlifting Championships in the 114lb. class. Chuck Dunbar won the 1976 Teenage National Powerlifting Championship title (18-19 Age Group) with lifts of 345 Squat, 225 Bench Press, and a 290 Deadlift for a Total of 860. All of Chuck Dunbar's lifts at the 1976 Teenage National Powerlifting Championships were recorded as West Virginia State "RAW" Teenage Powerlifting Records.

During 1975 and 1976, Chuck Mooney and Chuck Dunbar competed in the 123lb. class. In the 123lb. class, all of the "RAW" Powerlifting Records are also held by both Chuck Dunbar and Chuck Mooney. Chuck Mooney's "RAW" Record Deadlift of 425lbs. also stands as the West Virginia State Deadlift Record in the 123lb. class.

Ken Woodell owns the West Virginia State "RAW" Squat Record of 285lbs. in the 132lb. class. The 1962 "RAW" Deadlift Record of 375lbs. in the 132lb. class by George Powell still stands. While competing in the 132lb. class at Bristol, Tennessee on December 11, 1976, Ken Woodell Totaled 880lbs. for the West Virginia State "RAW" Powerlifting Record. At the end of Era I, Chick Clegg had the "RAW" Bench Press Record in the 132lb. class with a lift of 240lbs. The Total by Chick (Charles) Clegg in the 132lb. class of 820lbs. included the 240 Bench Press made on 2/14/76 at the West Virginia State Powerlifting Championships.

Paul Sutphin owns the West Virginia State "RAW" Powerlifting Records from ERA I for the Squat, Deadlift, and Total for the 148lb. class. The "RAW" Bench Press Record in the 148lb. class at the end of Era I is 310 pounds by Tim Hill. The Tim Hill Total in the 148lb. class which included the 310 Bench Press was 1020lbs. on 11/06/76 at the Mountianeer Open Powerlifting Championships.

Frank White and Don Hundley own all of the "RAW" Powerlifting Records for ERA I in the 165lb. class. Frank White repetitively set and re-set the West Virginia State Bench Press Records in the Middleweight class and owns the Total Record at 1260 in the Open Division. The 470 Squat and 500 Deadlift by Don Hundley stand as "RAW" Powerlifting Records for the state of West Virginia.

In the 181lb. class, Gary Clark set the West Virginia State "RAW" Powerlifting Records for the Squat, Bench Press, and Total. Gary Clark's Squat of 470, Bench Press of 370, and Total of 1335 have survived in the "RAW" Powerlifting category. The 370 Bench Press Record by Gary Clark was included in a Total of 1330 set on 2/14/76 at the West Virginia State Powerlifting Championships. The "RAW" 555lb. West Virginia State Deadlift Record by Doug Forth in the 181lb. class is a "RAW Classic" Powerlifting Record yet to be broken!

Vince White owns the West Virginia State "RAW" Total Record of 1330 in the 198lb. class. The West Virginia "RAW" Powerlifting Record in the 198lb. class for the Deadlift was set by Doug Forth. The 570 Deadlift by Doug Forth has yet to be broken in the "RAW" Division of Powerlifting by a West Virginia Powerlifter while competing in the 198lb. weight class.

The very first West Virginia State Powerlifting Records in the 220lb. class were set on 4/15/73 at the *Concord Invitational Powerlifting Meet* by Doug Forth. The 500 Squat, 385 Bench Press, 550 Deadlift, and a 1435 Total by Doug Forth are frozen in the archives as permanent marks. In 1975, John Messinger pulled a 555 Deadlift in the 220lb. class for a "RAW" Deadlift Record on 4/12/75. Other West Virginia State "RAW" Powerlifting Records in the 220lb. weight class belong to Mike Wolf and Mike Houston.

112

The nationally ranked Bench Press by Mike Wolf and the "RAW" Deadlift Record in the 220lb. class by Mike Houston are "RAW" Classic marks for West Virginia Powerlifting.

In the 242lb. class, <u>Herb Fitzsimmons</u> and <u>Doug Horner</u> own the "RAW" Powerlifting Records for the Squat, Deadlift, and Total. While competing at the 1st Annual West Virginia State Powerlifting Championships, Doug Horner Bench Pressed 410lbs. on 2/14/76. Herb Fitzsimmons Squatted 550 in the 242lb. class on 4/24/76. <u>Vince White</u> intervened to break the "RAW" West Virginia State Bench Press Record of 415lbs. in the 242's on 12/11/76.

The West Virginia State "RAW" Powerlifting Records in the SuperHeavyWeight Class (SHW) belong to <u>Luke Iams</u> for the Squat, Bench Press, and Total. Luke Iams set the "RAW" Squat Record of 675lbs. in the SHW Division on 7/11/76. Luke Iams was the first West Virginia Powerlifter to officially Bench Press 500lbs. on 1/25/76, which was the "RAW" Bench Press Record at the end of Powerlifting's Era I. <u>Herb Fitzsimmons</u> owns the West Virginia State "RAW" Powerlifting Deadlift Record at 600lbs. among the Superheavyweights. Herb Deadlifted 600 at the Mountian Empire Powerlifting Championships on 12/11/76.

Powerlifting Records : Paul Sutphin – ERA I

The "RAW" West Virginia State Powerlifting Records in the 148lb. class from the Era I of Powerlifting belong to Paul Sutphin. Beginning at the age of seventeen (17), Paul set new West Virginia State Teenage Powerlifting Records on twelve (12) different occasions : 3/11/72 (350 Squat, 148lb. class), 10/22/72 (260 Bench Press, 360 Squat, and 390 Deadlift, 1010 Total – 165lb. class), 12/09/72 (370 Squat, 1040 Total – 148lb. class), 2/10/73 (390 Squat, 1055 Total – 148lb. class), 2/24/73 (400 Squat, 1085 Total – 148lb. class), 4/15/73 (410 Squat, 1110 Total – 148lb. class), 5/20/73 (270 Bench Press – 148lb. class), 10/13/73 (415 Squat, 1120 Total – 148lb. class), 11/17/73 (420 Squat, 275 Bench Press, 450 Deadlift, 1145 Total), 12/08/73 (435 Squat – 148lb. class), 2/23/74 (445 Squat, 1150 Total), and 4/13/74 (450 Squat, 1160 Total – 148lb. class).

<u>Paul Sutphin</u> owns the 148lb. West Virginia State Powerlifting Records in the Open "RAW" Division with a 505 Squat, 495 Deadlift, and a 1300 Total. Sutphin also has four (4) West Virginia State Collegiate "RAW" Powerlifting Records in the Collegiate Division with a 470 Squat, 290 Bench Press, and a 490 Deadlift, for a 1245 Total. Due to the fact that Sutphin was enrolled in college as a part-time student rather than a full-time student during the Spring Term of 1975 coupled with the decision of the West

Virginia AAU Powerlifting Committee to retire the West Virginia Powerlifting Records on 1/31/76, the 505 Squat, 305 Bench Press, 495 Deadlift, and 1300 Total made by Paul Sutphin are not recognized in the category of West Virginia Collegiate Powerlifting Records, 148lb. class.

In closing out the year 1976, <u>Paul Sutphin</u> set four (4) West Virginia State Collegiate "RAW" Powerlifting Records while competing in the 165lb. weight class at Bristol, Tennessee on December 11th, 1976.

Powerlifting Records : Don Hundley – ERA I

Don Hundley owns two (2) "RAW" Powerlifting Records from the Era I of Powerlifting : 1) 470 Squat - 165lb. class 2) 500 Deadlift - 165lb. class. From 5/07/71 thru 11/06/76, Don Hundley set eleven (11) West Virginia State Powerlifting Records on eight (8) different dates.

Beginning on May 7th, 1971, Don Hundley set a new West Virginia Squat Record of 430lbs. while competing in the 181lb. class. Ten (10) months later, Don Squatted 465 on 3/11/72 for another state record in the 181lb. class. Hundley's winning Total of 1265lbs. at Pittsburgh, Pennsylvania on March 11th, 1972 was a new West Virginia State Record in the 181lb. class.

As a competitor in the 165lb. class, Don Hundley broke the West Virginia Deadlift Record at Steubenville, Ohio on 10/13/73 with a lift of 480lbs. One (1) month later, Hundley set new marks in the 165lb. class in the Squat and Deadlift on 11/17/73. While competing at the Powerlifting meet in Munhall, Pennsylvania, Don's Squat of 460 and Deadlift of 490 were new West Virginia State Records in the 165lb. class. While competing at the 1973 All-South Powerlifting Championships in Durham, North Carolina on December 8th, 1973, Don Hundley broke his own Deadlift Record in the 165lb. class with a lift of 500lbs.

On February 14th, 1976 the West Virginia State Powerlifting Records had a new beginning. While competing in the 165lb. class at the 1st Annual (1976) West Virginia State Powerlifting Championships, Don Hundley re-set the Squat Record with a lift of 445lbs. and the Deadlift Record with 500lbs. On 10/17/76, Don Squatted 450lbs. for another West Virginia State Powerlifting Record. On 11/06/76, Don Hundley set a new West Virginia State Squat Record with 470lbs. in the 165lb. class while exceeding all previous marks. As a competitor in the 165lb. class at the 1976 Powerlifting meet at Bristol, Tennessee Hundley Squatted 470lbs. once again.

Powerlifting Records : Frank White

In addition to winning at Powerlifting, Frank White's record of achievements in official Weightlifting competition with the Clean & Press, the Snatch, and the Clean & Jerk placed him in a class by himself. From 1971 through 1976, the lifting of Frank White dominated the 165lb. class in West Virginia Powerlifting. With a style of lifting defined as "RAW," the Powerlifting Records of Frank White are forever.

For all of the Powerlifting Totals recorded from lifters competing in the 165lb. class in the state of West Virginia from January 1st, 1960 through December 31st, 1972, Frank White finished number one (1) in the rankings for the 148lb. weight class with a Total of 1075. The 1075 Total by Frank White on 1/27/62 while competing in the 148lb. weight class included a Bench Press of 285, Squat of 365, and a Deadlift of 425lbs.

Even though Powerlifting had not received the official nod from the AAU in 1960 and the fact that Teenage Powerlifting was not recognized, Frank White owns at least a few of the very first West Virginia Teenage Powerlifting Records. While competing in the 148lb. class on February 6th, 1960, Frank Bench Pressed 200, Squatted with 245, and Deadlifted 325 for a Total of 770. Frank's Bench Press, Squat, Deadlift, and Total were all West Virginia Teenage Powerlifting Records on 2/06/60. On 12/17/60, a 980 Total in the 148lb. class by Frank White included a 260 Bench Press, a Squat of 320, and a Deadlift of 400. The 260 Bench Press and 980 Total on 12/17/60 were West Virginia State Teenage Powerlifting Records in the 148lb. class.

In the first West Virginia Powerlifter Rankings (1960-1972), Frank White owns the top four (4) Totals in the 165lb. class. Frank White holds the number one (1) spot in the 165lb. class with a Total of 1240 set on 7/09/72. In addition to the Total of 1240, Frank made an official Total of 1200 while competing in the 165lb. class on three (3) different dates during 1971 : 5/07/71, 6/27/71, and 10/24/71.

Even though training for Olympic Weightlifting competition was a priority in 1973, Frank White managed to perform well at three (3) Powerlifting Meets from October 13th to December 8th, 1973. While competing at Steubenville, Ohio on 10/13/73, Frank managed a 1205 Total which included a 440 Squat, 310 Bench Press, and a 455 Deadlift. Five (5) weeks later at Munhall, Pennsylvania, Frank Totaled 1260 with a 450 Squat, Bench Press of 345, and a Deadlift of 465. Three (3) weeks later at Durham, North Carolina, a Total of 1255 by Frank White in the 165lb. class included a Squat of 440, Bench Press of 350, and a Deadlift of 465lbs.

While competing in the 165lb. class on 1/12/74, Frank White Totaled 1255 once again at the 1974 Lexington Open. The 1255 Total by Frank White on 1/12/74 included a Bench Press of 350. Eleven (11) months later, Frank Totaled 1235 on 12/14/74 which included a Bench Press of 355. The 355 Bench Press by Frank White on 12/14/74 was the highest Bench Press in the West Virginia Powerlifter Rankings for lifters competing in the 165lb. class from 1960 thru 1976.

For the year 1975, Frank White ranked number one among all of the West Virginia Powerlifters competing in the 165lb. class. Frank White's best Total of 1220 was made on 1/18/75. Frank's Total of 1220 at the 1975 Lexington Open Powerlifting Championships included a 430 Squat, 340 Bench Press, and a Deadlift of 450.

The Frank White Total in the 165lb. class which included the 355 Bench Press was 1235lbs. on 12/14/74 at the Mountian Empire Open at Bristol, Tennessee. Frank reset the West Virginia State Bench Press Record in the 165lb. class with a lift of 350 included in the winning Total of 1215 at the 1976 West Virginia State Powerlifting Championship.

Powerlifting Records : Vince White

The Weightlifting career of Vince White began in 1958. On February 6th, 1960 the first Powerlifting Records were recorded for the state of West Virginia. While competing in the 123lb. class, Vince White Bench Pressed 155, Squatted 205, and Deadlifted 250 for a Total of 610. All of the lifts made by Vince White on 2/06/60 were listed as the first West Virginia State Powerlifting Records in the 123lb. class. Due to the fact that Vince White was only sixteen (16) at the time, the records on 2/06/60 were among the first West Virginia State Teenage Powerlifting Records.

At another Powerlifting meet conducted by the *Charleston Barbell Club* on December 17th, 1960 Vince White Bench Pressed 200, Squatted with 255, and Deadlifted 275 for a Total of 730. On 12/17/60, Vince broke all of his own records from ten (10) months prior and set eight (8) new West Virginia State Powerlifting Records in both the Open and Teenage categories for the 123lb. class.

While competing in the 123lb. class at a bodyweight of 122¼ on 1/27/62, Vince White Bench Pressed 180, Squatted 275, and Deadlifted 295 for a 750 Total. The Squat of 275, Deadlift of 295, and Total of 750 by Vince White on 1/27/62 were recorded as new West Virginia State Powerlifting Records in the Open and Teenage categories.

Beginning in 1970, Vince White extended his portfolio of Powerlifting Records to the 181lb. weight class. While competing in the 181lb. class on 12/05/70, Vince Totaled 1105 with a new West Virginia State Bench Press Record of 325lbs. Additional Powerlifting Records were made by Vince White in June of 1971 while competing in the 181lb. class. Vince put together a Total of 1190 on 6/27/71 that included new West Virginia State Powerlifting Records in the Bench Press and Squat. While scoring PR's, Vince Bench Pressed a new West Virginia State Record of 340lbs. and Squatted a new West Virginia State Record in the 181lb. class with 450lbs.

On May 7th, 1971 a rare occurrence took place at a Powerlifting meet in Ohio attended by Vince White and several others from the *Charleston Barbell Club*. In order to spread the talent of the team to a number of weight classes, Vince intended to compete in a weight class heavier than the 181lb. division. The official at the weigh-in mistakenly placed Vince into the Superheavyweight (SHW) division. Vince White's lifts on 5/07/71 were recorded as the very first West Virginia State Powerlifting Records for the Superheavyweight division. Vince's Total on 5/07/71 was 1175 which included a 330 Bench Press, 445 Squat, and a 400 Deadlift.

Rolling into the year 1972, Vince White set West Virginia State Powerlifting Records in the Bench Press and Squat. While competing in the 198lb. class at the State Correctional Institution in Pennsylvania on 3/11/72, Vince Totaled 1180. The 1180 Total by Vince White on 3/11/72 included a Bench Press of 345lbs. and a Squat of 465, both recorded as new West Virginia State Powerlifting Records.

During October, 1972 Vince White began changing the Powerlifting Record books in the 198lb. class. While competing in the 198lb. class on 10/22/72, Vince put together a PR Total of 1270. The 1270 Total by Vince White on 10/22/72 included a new West Virginia State Bench Press Record of 370lbs. and a new West Virginia State Squat Record of 475lbs.

On December 9th, 1972 at Bristol, Tennessee Vince White returned to the 181lb. class and Totaled 1235. Included in the 1235 Total by Vince White on 12/09/72 was a new West Virginia State Record Bench Press of 355lbs. in the 181lb. class. The 355 Bench Press Record set by Vince White on 12/09/72 was not broken until March 8th, 1975.

During 1973, Vince White continued to produce higher Totals while competing in official Powerlifting competitions. At the Concord Invitational Powerlifting Meet on 4/15/73, Vince Totaled 1300 for the first time. The 1300 Total by Vince White on 4/15/73 included a 500 Squat which was recorded as a new West Virginia State Powerlifting Record in the 198lb. class.

In the 198lb. class, Vince White owns the West Virginia "RAW" Bench Press Record for Era I. The 380 Bench Press by Vince White on 11/16/74 stood as the West Virginia State Bench Press Record in the 198lb. class until 1977. Vince White also holds the 11/16/74 Total mark at 1265 in the 198lb. class for "Wild Card" Powerlifting.

During the year 1975, West Virginia Powerlifting Records continued to be re-written by Vince White. While competing in the 198lb. class at Johnson City, Tennessee on 4/12/75, Vince Totaled 1300 with a new West Virginia State Record Squat of 505lbs. On 9/27/75 at Cumberland, Maryland, Vince broke the existing Total Record in the 198lb. class with a new West Virginia State Powerlifting Record Total of 1330lbs. While competing in the 220lb. class on 12/13/75, Vince White set the West Virginia State Record in the Squat with a lift of 530lbs. and another record in the Bench Press with a lift of 410lbs.

A new slate of West Virginia State Powerlifting Records began on 2/14/76 at the First Annual West Virginia State Powerlifting Championships. Beginning in 1976, Vince White began setting the West Virginia State Powerlifting Records all over again. While competing in the 220lb. class at the 1976 West Virginia State Powerlifting Championships, Vince Totaled 1370 and re-set the West Virginia State Squat Record with a lift of 510lbs.

On 3/27/76, Vince White competed in the 198lb. class and broke the "Re-Set" West Virginia Bench Press Record with a lift of 365lbs. While lifting in Maryland on 10/17/76, Vince totaled 1365 and increased his West Virginia State Record in the Squat to a poundage of 515. Three weeks later on 11/06/76, Vince totaled 1355 in the 220lb. class which included a Squat of 530lbs. for another West Virginia State Powerlifting Record.

To close out the Era I of Powerlifting, Vince White competed in the 242lb. class at Bristol, Tennessee on December 11th, 1976. On 12/11/76, Vince put together a 1400 Total for the first time. Included in the 1400 Total by Vince White was a new West Virginia State Bench Press Record of 415lbs. During Era I, Vince finished #1 in the 198lb. class during 1973, 1974, and 1975 in the West Virginia Powerlifter Rankings.

Powerlifting Records : Herb Fitzsimmons – ERA I

Before Powerlifting was recognized by the AAU (Amateur Athletic Union) as an official sport, Herb Fitzsimmons was one of the first West Virginians to Powerlift and set records in what was once defined as "Odd-Lift" competitions. Due to professional and business commitments, Herb did not compete in official Weightlifting or Powerlifting competitions during the second half of the 1960's or the first half of the 1970's.

Herb Fitzsimmons officially returned to Powerlifting at the 1976 West Virginia State Powerlifting Championships on 2/14/76. On 3/27/76, while competing in the 242lb. class, Herb set West Virginia State Powerlifting Records in the Masters Division (Age 40 & Over) with a Deadlift of 560lbs. and a Total of 1420lbs. On 4/24/76, while competing in the 242lb. class, Herb Fitzsimmons broke the West Virginia State Record in the Squat with a lift of 550lbs. Herb's Total of 1450 on 4/24/76 set a new West Virginia Powerlifting Record in the Masters Division.

On 6/12/76 at the Region VI Powerlifting Championships, Herb Fitzsimmons set a new West Virginia State Record in the Total with 1470 in the 242lb. class. Herb set new Region VI Powerlifting Records while competing in the Masters Division at the 1976 Region VI Powerlifting Championships.

Herb Fitzsimmons set three (3) new West Virginia State Powerlifting Records in the Masters Division of the SHW class on 11/06/76 with a Squat of 580, Bench Press of 355, and a Total of 1510lbs. On 12/11/76, Herb officially weighed-in as a competitor in the SuperHeavyWeight (SHW) class and broke the West Virginia State Record in the Deadlift with a lift of 600lbs. The 600lb. Deadlift by Herb Fitzsimmons at Bristol, Tennessee on 12/11/76 was a West Virginia State Record for the Open and Masters Division.

The keys to reading the Era One (1960 – 1976) West Virginia Powerlifting Records include :

1) * - Indicates West Virginia State Powerlifting Record.
2) c – West Virginia State Collegiate Powerlifting Record
3) m – West Virginia State Masters Powerlifting Record
4) r – (re-set 2/14/76) West Virginia State Powerlifting Record
5) t – West Virginia State Teenage Powerlifting Record
6) ** - Record in Memory / Permanent Record
7) AR – American Powerlifting Record
8) wld – "Wild Card" Powerlifting

1960 – 1976 ALL-TIME TOP West Virginia Powerlifters
Powerlifting Records Ranked by Total
"RAW" Powerlifting

Beginning January 1, 1960 thru December 31, 1976

114 / Name	Squat	Bench Press	Deadlift	Total	Date
Chuck Dunbar	345*	230	300	875*	4/17/76
Chuck Dunbar	335	250*	285	870*	3/27/76
Chuck Mooney	260	180	420 r	860 r	2/14/76
Chuck Dunbar	345 t	225 t	290 t	860 t	8/07/76
Chuck Mooney	235	170	425*AR	830	1/17/76
Chuck Dunbar	320 r	225 r	285	830	2/14/76
123 Chuck Mooney	245	170	425*	840*	12/13/75
Chuck Dunbar	300*	250*	285	835	12/13/75
Ken Woodell	260*	215*	355*	830*	4/24/76
Perry Reeder	225 r	200 r	350 r	775 r	2/14/76
Vince White	275*t	180	295*t	750*t	1/27/62
Dennis Passantino	220	190	330	740	2/14/76
Vince White	255*t	200*t	275*t	730*t	12/17/60
Kevin Sheets	200	170	300*	670	4/15/73
132 Ken Woodell	285*	225	370	880*	12/11/76
Ken Woodell	240	235	360 r	835 r	2/14/76
Don Giarletto	280 r	190	360	830	2/14/76
Chick Clegg	270	240 r*	310	820	2/14/76
George Powell	250	175	375*	800	1/27/62
Perry Reeder	225	190	370	785	4/17/76
Larry Wildman	230	190	360	780	4/15/73
148 Paul Sutphin	500	305	495*	1300*	12/13/75
Paul Sutphin	470 rc	290 c	485 r	1245 rc	2/14/76
Paul Sutphin	505*	285	450	1240	4/12/75
Paul Sutphin	460	290	490 c	1240	4/03/76
Paul Sutphin	450 t	270	440	1160 t	4/13/74
Paul Sutphin	420	275 t	450	1145	11/17/73
Frank White	365	285	425	1075	1/27/62
Mickey Deitz	370	215	465	1050	1/27/62
Tim Hill	330	310*	380	1020	11/06/76

* - Indicates West Virginia State Powerlifting Record.
c – West Virginia State Collegiate Powerlifting Record
r – (Revised 2/14/76) West Virginia State Powerlifting Record
t – West Virginia State Teenage Powerlifting Record
AR – American Powerlifting Record

1960 – 1976 ALL-TIME TOP West Virginia Powerlifters
Powerlifting Records Ranked by Total
"RAW" Powerlifting

Beginning January 1, 1960 thru December 31, 1976

165 / Name	Squat	Bench Press	Deadlift	Total	Date
Frank White	450	345	465	1260*	11/17/73
Paul Sutphin	460 c	310 c	490 c	1260 c	12/11/76
Frank White	440	350	465	1255	12/08/73
Frank White	450	350	455	1255	1/12/74
Frank White	435	355*	445	1235	12/14/74
Frank White	425	350 r	440	1215 r	2/14/76
Don Hundley	460	260	490	1210	11/17/73
Don Hundley	450	255	500*	1205	12/08/73
Don Hundley	470*	240	490	1200	11/06/76
Don Hundley	465	240	465	1170	2/23/74
Don Hundley	445 r	230	500 r	1175	2/14/76
181 Gary Clark	460	355	520	1335*	5/18/75
Gary Clark	470 r	370 r*	490	1330 r	2/14/76
Gary Clark	470*	330	510	1310	4/27/75
Don Hundley	465	310	490	1265	3/11/72
Vince White	455	355*	425	1235	12/09/72
Barry Barrows	410 c	325 c	500	1235 c	4/03/76
Don Hall	435	275	505	1215	11/06/76
Frank Nicholas	450	320	440	1210	11/06/76
Barry Barrows	375	300	520 rc	1195	2/14/76
Doug Forth	sq	bp	555*	total	PA/1962
198 Vince White	500	380	450	1330*	9/27/75
Doug Forth (189 ¾)	420	325	570*	1315*	1/27/62
Vince White	500*	360	440	1300	4/15/73
Vince White	505*	360	435	1300	4/12/75
Pete Rocchio	450	300	540	1290	4/27/75
Barry Barrows	425	355	495	1275	11/06/76
Vince White	475*	370*	425	1270	10/22/72
Warren Knight	435	300	535 r	1270 r	2/14/76
Vince White	470	380*	415	1265 wld	11/16/74
Pete Rocchio	450 r	300	500	1250	2/14/76
Vince White	450	365*	435	1250	3/27/76

* - Indicates West Virginia State Powerlifting Record.
c – West Virginia State Collegiate Powerlifting Record
r – (re-set 2/14/76) West Virginia State Powerlifting Record
wld – "Wild Card" Powerlifting

1960 – 1976 ALL-TIME TOP West Virginia Powerlifters
Powerlifting Records Ranked by Total
"RAW" Powerlifting

Beginning January 1, 1960 thru December 31, 1976

220 / Name	Squat	Bench Press	Deadlift	Total	Date
Mike Wolf	525	450*	550	1525*	11/06/76
Mike Wolf	475	440*	540	1455*	2/14/76
Mike Houston	485	340	625*	1450	2/14/76
Doug Forth	500**	385**	550**	1435**	4/15/73
John Messinger	525*	355	540	1420	11/01/75
John Messinger	475	360	555*	1390	4/12/75
Ernie Nagy	480 r	380 m	525 m	1385	2/14/76
Vince White	530*	410*	440	1380	12/13/75
Nick Busick	470	380	530	1380	2/14/76
Vince White	510 r	395	465	1370	2/14/76
Vince White	515 r*	380	470	1365	10/17/76
Ernie Nagy	480 m	360	520	1360	1/1975
Vince White	530 r*	370	455	1355	11/06/76
Ernie Nagy	460	365 m	515	1340	5/18/75
242					
Doug Horner	500	410*	600*	1510*	2/14/76
Herb Fitzsimmons	550	360	560	1470 m	6/12/76
James Goodnight	510	400	555	1465	11/06/76
Herb Fitzsimmons	550* m	345	555	1450 m	4/24/76
Herb Fitzsimmons	520	340	560 m	1420 m	3/27/76
Ernie Nagy	500 m	375 m	525	1400	10/18/75
Vince White	525	415*	460	1400	12/11/76
Doug Forth	455	360	550*	1365	6/27/71
SHW					
Luke Iams	675*	500	525	1700*	7/11/76
Luke Iams	645*	500*	545	1690*	1/25/76
Luke Iams	670*	500 r	520	1690 r	2/14/76
Herb Fitzsimmons	580 m	355 m	575	1510 m	11/06/76
Herb Fitzsimmons	550	355	600* m	1505	12/11/76
Phillip McClelland	525	330	560*	1415	2/14/76
Phillip McClelland	450	300	555*	1305	4/27/75

* - Indicates West Virginia State Powerlifting Record.

M – West Virginia State Masters Powerlifting Record

r – (re-set 2/14/76) West Virginia State Powerlifting Record

** - Record in Memory / Permanent Record

Chapter Eleven : 1977

The year 1977 marked the first year of a new Era in Powerlifting : Era II. The year 1977 also began Phase II of the "Official New Beginning" for Powerlifting in West Virginia. In a series of phone calls between Luke Iams and myself, Luke shared with me part of a plan to reach his ultimate goal of winning a National Powerlifting Team Championship. Included in the plan were two (2) Elite Powerlifters, Jack Wilson and Roger Estep. By January, 1977 Jack Wilson and Roger Estep were active members of the *Luke's Gym Powerlifting Team*. Roger Estep and Jack Wilson proved to be an inspiration to serious lifters in the Mountain State and a welcomed addition to the new West Virginia Powerlifting program.

As West Virginia Powerlifting Chairman, monitoring the activity of the AAU registered clubs was an ongoing responsibility. In order to avoid potential controversy regarding "out of state" lifters who chose to relocate to the state of West Virginia, I directly addressed concerns from a number of registered athletes about the rules governing the legality of AAU membership, residency, and AAU club registration.

As the Weightlifting-Powerlifting-Bodybuilding Chairman of the AAU Association of West Virginia, I wrote a letter of inquiry to the National Powerlifting Chairman in regard to eligibility criteria. I received a response from the AAU National Powerlifting Chairman addressing the specific requirements for AAU registration and state residency. After reviewing the letter, major concerns specific to eligibility were alleviated.

On January 29, 1977 Herb Fitzsimmons, Vince White, and myself drove to Lynchburg, Virginia for the 1977 Lynchburg Open Powerlifting Meet. The 1977 Lynchburg Open Powerlifting Meet, referenced as the Virginia Connection : Part III, included West Virginia Powerlifters Ken Woodell, Paul Sutphin, Herb Fitzsimmons, and Vince White. Competing in the 165lb. class at the 1977 Lynchburg Open, I managed a Total of 1220 for 3rd Place and a West Virginia State Collegiate Deadlift Record of 505lbs. in the Middleweight class.

Finishing with a Total of 1425 in the 220lb. class on 1/29/77, Vince White Squatted with 525, a new *Official* West Virginia State Record in the 220lb. class. Herb Fitzsimmons finished with a Total of 1525 at the 1977 Lynchburg Open and a new West Virginia State Squat Record of 580lbs. in the 242lb. class. According to the official results, Ken Woodell placed in the 132lb. class at the 1977 Lynchburg Open Powerlifting Meet.

1st WV Collegiate Powerlifting Championships

The <u>1977 West Virginia State Collegiate Powerlifting Championships</u> were held March 12th, 1977 at Parkersburg Community College in Parkersburg, West Virginia. As a result, many of the first West Virginia State Collegiate Powerlifting Records were established. There were thirteen (13) entries for the 1977 West Virginia State Collegiate Powerlifting Championships on 3/12/77 with nine (9) colleges represented.

Aside from the fact that the athlete had to be registered with the West Virginia Association of the AAU, the eligibility requirements were two-fold :

1) The lifter was enrolled as a full-time college student in a college or university.
2) The lifter had to be a resident of West Virginia to set West Virginia State Collegiate Powerlifting Records. For Paul Sutphin, representing Bluefield College, winning first place in the 165lb. class along with three (3) West Virginia State Collegiate Records in the Squat, Deadlift, and Total are most memorable.

Tim Slamick won the SuperHeavyWeights (SHW's) with a 1400 Total on 3/12/77. Mike Wolf (not to be confused with Powerlifter Mike Wolf of 2010) represented Salem College at the 1977 West Virginia Collegiate Powerlifting Championships and also represented *Luke's Gym*. Mike Wolf was also one of the few West Virginia Powerlifters to Bench Press over 500lbs. during the 1970's. Mike Wolf won the 220lb. class with a 1610 Total.

After serving as the AAU West Virginia Chairman of Weightlifting, Powerlifting, and Bodybuilding for more than twenty-four (24) months, I was concerned about time constraints, job obligations, and commitments related to college graduation. Based on the facts, I contacted Luke Iams and informed him of the circumstances. During our conversation I told Luke, "I believe the time has come for you to become the Chairman of Weightlifting, Powerlifting, and Bodybuilding for the West Virginia Association." Soon after the 1977 West Virginia State Powerlifting Championships, Luke Iams became the new AAU Chairman of Weightlifting, Powerlifting, and Bodybuilding for the West Virginia Association.

"Postponed" Championship : The Report

The 2nd Annual (1977) West Virginia State Powerlifting Championships were originally scheduled for February, 1977 in New Martinsville, West Virginia. However, due to what may have been West Virginia's most severe winter on record, the contest was postponed until May 21st, 1977. Due to the conflict of dates between college graduation and the day of the 1977 West Virginia State Powerlifting Championship, I was unable to attend the event.

The 1977 West Virginia State Championship event had twenty-eight (28) lifters, down from a number of forty-five (45) in February of 1976. Elite Powerlifters, Jack Wilson and Roger Estep, established residence in West Virginia several months before May of 1977. Both Estep and Wilson broke most all of the Official West Virginia State Powerlifting Records in the 165lb. and 198lb. weight classes on 5/21/77. Ken Woodell, Ron Giarletto, Charles (Chick) Clegg, Gary Clark, Mike Wolf, Herb Fitzsimmons, Jim Goodnight, and Luke Iams all set new Powerlifting Records at the 1977 West Virginia State Powerlifting Championships.

At the beginning of the 1977 West Virginia State Powerlifting Championships, Ken Woodell Bench Pressed 230, Deadlifted 410, and Totaled 920 for three (3) West Virginia Powerlifting Records in the 123lb. class. At 132, Ron Giarletto Deadlifted 450 and Totaled 990 for new West Virginia State Powerlifting Records. Charles Clegg Benched 250 for a new West Virginia State Powerlifting Record in the 132lb. class. Jack Wilson Squatted 565, Deadlifted 605, and Totaled 1510 for new Middleweight (165lb. class records).

Gary Clark won the 1977 West Virginia State Powerlifting Championship title in the 181lb. class. Clark Squatted with 495 and Totaled 1400 for two (2) West Virginia State Powerlifting Records. Gary Clark finished first place over four (4) competitors at 181. Mike Wolf won the 1977 West Virginia State Championship title in the 220lb. class, breaking two (2) West Virginia State Powerlifting Records in the Squat with 590 and the Total at 1610.

Herb Fitzsimmons became the 1977 West Virginia State Powerlifting Champion with some very impressive lifting in the 242lb. class. In only fifteen (15) months, Herb increased his Total from the 1976 West Virginia State Championship meet by over 300 pounds! The victory for Herb also came with a new West Virginia State Record in the Deadlift for the 242lb. class with a lift of 630lbs.! Herb finished ahead of Jim Goodnight who broke the West Virginia State Powerlifting Record in the Bench Press with a lift of 425lbs in the 242lb. class. Members of the *Charleston Barbell Club / Herb's Gym* at the Second Annual (1977) West Virginia State Powerlifting Championships were : Don Hundley (165), Don Hall (181), Frank White (181), Vince White (198), Ross Smith (198), and Herb Fitzsimmons (242).

POWERLIFTING USA Magazine : Introduction

Among the primary sources of news for Powerlifting during the 1960's through 1971 were the publications from Bob Hoffman and the York Barbell Company. The York Barbell magazines were *Muscular Development* and *Strength and Health*. Among other sources of information and publications included *Iron Man,* published by Peary Rader. Iron Man magazine was an established source of news for Bodybuilding, Olympic Weightlifting, and also a voice for Powerlifting. Joe Weider's *Muscle Builder Power* published Powerlifting material from contributing writers including Bill "Peanuts" West and Powerlifter George Frenn.

With the exception of a few newsletters and *Powerlifting News, Muscular Development* and *Iron Man* magazines were the major publications for Powerlifting and Bodybuilding. In 1971, the *Weightlifting Journal* was published with superb photos from major Powerlifting and Olympic Weightlifting events. Other publications were short-lived while the athletes from the Squat – Bench Press – Deadlift sector of the iron game starved for a publication specific to Powerlifting.

An answer to the prayers of thousands of Powerlifters came in June, 1977 as the first issue of *Powerlifting USA* became available. The August, 1977 issue of *Powerlifting USA (Volume 1, Number 3)* published the complete results of the 2nd Annual (1977) West Virginia State Powerlifting Championships.

The first appearance for the *Luke's Gym Powerlifting Team* at a National Powerlifting event happened at the <u>1977 Senior National Powerlifting Championships</u> on August 20th and 21st, 1977 in Santa Monica, California. Luke Iams and *Luke's Gym* received major recognition on the National Powerlifting scene from their emergence as a team at the 1977 Seniors. Chuck Dunbar was victorious in the 114's over Kevin Meskew and John Redding. Jack Wilson bombed at 165 with a 573 Squat, Roger Estep was 2nd to Larry Pacifico in the 198's, and Luke Iams was 5th, lifting in the SuperHeavyWeight (SHW) Division.

In an article written about the 1977 Senior Nationals, featured in an issue of *Powerlifting USA* magazine, the author wrote *"Luke Iams, a WV mortician at 5'6" & 306, looked fearsome. With the ultimate in psyching preparation, he buried 799 SQ and punched 534 BP. He actually led going into the final lift. He ripped his hand on a 551 Deadlift and dropped out of the race."*   *Powerlifting USA /Herb Glossbrenner*

1977 West Virginia State Powerlifting Championships
Held Saturday May 21, 1977
New Martinsville, W. VA

Wt. Class/Name	Club	Squat	Bench	Deadlift	Total
114 ½					
Chuck Dunbar	Luke's Gym	380	260	305	945
123 ½					
Ken Woodell	----------------	280	230*	410*	920*
Peery Reeder	Luke's Gym	220	190	360	770
132 ¼					
Ron Giarletto	----------------	330	210	450*	990*
Chick Clegg	Luke's Gym	300	250*	340	890
148 ¾					
Jim Priest	Luke's Gym	400	260	435	1095
Brian Williams	----------------	300	225	375	900
165 ¼					
Jack Wilson	Luke's Gym	565*	340	605*	1510*
Don Hundley	Herb's Gym	475	260	480	1215
Bill Kyle	Luke's Gym	385	315	400	1100
181 ¾					
Gary Clark	Nagy's PT	495*	360	545	1400*
Frank Nicholas	Luke's Gym	470	325	475	1270
Don Hall	Herb's Gym	450	275	520	1245
John Francis	----------------	400	320	520	1240
Frank White	Herb's Gym	430	350	450	1230
198 ¼					
Roger Estep	Luke's Gym	705*	425*	645*	1775*
Vince White	Herb's Gym	480	350	440	1270
Gary Marks	----------------	360	320	485	1165
Ross Smith	Herb's Gym	425	280	460	1165
Dave Snyder	----------------	400	295	470	1165

Wt. Class/Name	Club	Squat	Bench	Deadlift	Total
220 ½					
Mike Wolf	Luke's Gym	560*	460	590	1610*
Ernie Nagy	Nagy's PT	430	375	460	1265
242 ½					
Herb Fitzsimmons	Herb's Gym	560	380	630*	1570
Jim Goodnight	----------------	550	425*	590	1565
Nick Busick	Nagy's PT	530	390	570	1490
Jeff Cook	Luke's Gym	335	225	555	1115
Super Hvywt.					
Luke Iams	Luke's Gym	750*	510*	585	1845*
Tim Slamick	----------------	550	440	600	1590

* - Indicates West Virginia State Powerlifting Record

Team Award – <u>Luke's Gym</u>, New Martinsville, W. Va.

National Master's Champions!
Herb Fitzsimmons, Don Hundley, Ernie Nagy

The <u>1977 Master's National Powerlifting Championships</u> were held in October, 1977 at Utica, Michigan. West Virginia was represented well with National Championship victories from Don Hundley (165lb. class / 45-49 Age Group), Herb Fitzsimmons (242lb. class / 40-44 Age Group), and Ernie Nagy (220lb. class / 50-54 Age Group). Bill Blankenship placed 2nd while competing in the 198lb. class (50-54 Age Group).

Prior to the 1977 Master's National Powerlifting Championships in Michigan, Herb Fitzsimmons established a few of the first Master's World Powerlifting Records at the 1977 Chattanooga Open Powerlifting Championships. According to the National Masters Newletter (6/05/77), Herb Fitzsimmons set two (2) National Masters Powerlifting Records in the 242lb. class at the 1977 Great Lakes Open Powerlifting Championships in Erie, Pennsylvania in April, 1977.

Herb's National Masters Record marks set at the 1977 Great Lakes Open Powerlifting Championships included a Squat of 580lbs. and a Total of 1540. Lifting in the 1977 Chattanooga Open Powerlifting Championships, Herb Fitzsimmons Squatted a National Masters Powerlifting Record in the 242lb. class of 610lbs., Bench Pressed 370, Deadlifted 600, and Totaled another National Masters Record of 1580!

National Masters Lifting Newletter, Vol. I, No. 6, June 5th, 1977

Parkersburg to Durham : Part I

Powerlifting "Back-to-Back"with the Mountianeer Open on Sunday and the All-South Powerlifting Championships the following Saturday : On Sunday November 6th, 1977 the <u>4th Annual Mountianeer Open Powerlifting Championships</u> were held in Parkersburg, West Virginia. The contest had fifty-six (56) lifters. John Black brought a team of lifters to Parkersburg on 11/06/77 and "steamrolled" the other teams competing for the Mountianeer Open Powerlifting Team Award. As a competitor in the 1977 Mountianeer Open Powerlifting Championships, John Black placed 3rd in the 181lb. class. Among others, the following first place winners represented <u>Black's Health World</u> : Gary Sanger (1525 @ 181), Jack Sideris (1850 Total @ 220), and John Florio (1700 Total @ 242).

As for *Luke's Gym* on the day of 11/06/77, Jack Wilson won the 165lb. class, breaking the West Virginia Squat, Deadlift, and Total Records. Chuck Dunbar won first place in the 123lb. class, Frank Nicholas was 5th in the 181's, and Jim Goodnight won the SuperHeavyWeight's.

I informed Vince White on 11/06/77 that I was going to return to the 148lb. class by December 17th, 1977 for the annual Mountian Empire Powerlifting Meet. Vince responded by saying, "You'll have your hands full." Realizing a tough task was at hand for the next few weeks, I wanted a higher Total while weighing less. Looking for redemption, I entered the All-South Powerlifting Championships held at the Durham YMCA on Saturday 11/12/77 in Durham, North Carolina. For West Virginia Powerlifting, the 1977 All-South Powerlifting Championships was the "North Carolina Connection": Part III.

On the morning of 11/12/77 at Durham, North Carolina, I weighed-in at 160 ¾, three (3) pounds less than what I officially weighed in Parkersburg. While competing at the 1977 All-South, I managed a 460 Squat, 275 Bench Press, and a 520 Deadlift for a 1255 Total. The 1255 Total on 11/12/77 was a modest increase from the 1240 Total at Parkersburg six (6) days earlier. Winning first place at the 1977 All-South Powerlifting Championships in the 242lb. class was Herb Fitzsimmons with a 1615 Total.

Tennessee Connection : Part VI

An evaluation of 1977 through the month of November indicated that most individual lifters were producing bigger Totals, yet my own lifting performance lacked motivation as well as enthusiasm with a progress score of zero. The primary reason was that academic commitments and career related issues had taken me out of the Powerlifting scene, at least as a viable competitor for major championships. It was clear that the 165lb. class was not for me, at least for the immediate future. Based on the phenomenal progress of Herb Fitzsimmons, I assured myself and others, beginning on December 17th, 1977 the approach would be different!

The 1977 Mountian Empire Open Powerlifting Championships were held at the Bristol Family YMCA in Bristol, Tennessee on December 17th, 1977. According to the official results, the 1977 Mountian Empire Powerlifting Meet at Bristol, Tennessee had forty (40) lifters. The 1977 Bristol Powerlifting competition marked the beginning of the journey to a Junior National Powerlifting Championship title in the Lightweight Division.

In preparation for the 12/17/77 event at Bristol, Tennessee, I lost seventeen (17) pounds in twenty-two (22) days. I officially weighed-in at a bodyweight of 144 ¾ lbs. on the morning of 12/17/77, four (4) pounds under the lightweight class bodyweight limit! A Total of 1215 for Paul Sutphin on 12/17/77 won first place in the 148lb. class which included a 505lb. West Virginia State Record Deadlift!

Vince White's Total of 1430 placed second at Bristol, Tennessee on 12/17/77. At a bodyweight of less than 225lbs., Vince White Squatted with 530, Bench Pressed 425, and Deadlifted 475 for a Total of 1430lbs. At a bodyweight of less than 250lbs., Herb Fitzsimmons won the SuperHeavyWeight division with a Total of 1700. Herb's lifting on December 17th, 1977 included a Squat of 650, Bench Press of 400, and a West Virginia State Deadlift Record of 650lbs. in the Superheavyweight (SHW) class!

On December 17th, 1977 I had the honor of meeting Bob Peoples. From what avid followers of the sport of Weightlifting and Powerlifting already know, Bob Peoples' accomplishments in the Deadlift are legendary. Bob was complimentary of the top performers at the 1977 Mountian Empire Powerlifting competition, specifically regarding the Deadlifts. Bob wrote the book, *Developing Physical Strength* which, I believe, is a must for anyone serious about increasing their strength on the Deadlift.

Herb Fitzsimmons – West Virginia State Record Deadlift
Bristol, Tennessee – 12-17-77

Herb Fitzsimmons set the West Virginia State Deadlift Record of 650lbs. on 12/17/77 weighing less than 250lbs., competing in the SuperHeavyWeight Class. Herb Fitzsimmons later set Masters (Over Age 40) American, World, and State Records in the Deadlift while competing in the 242lb. and 275lb. weight classes with lifts of 660, 680, 683, 700, 735, and 740lbs., in the Open and Masters Division of Powerlifting.

1977 West Virginia Powerlifter Rankings
WV Powerlifters competing from January 1st, 1977 thru December 31st, 1977
TOP RANKINGS Determined by Total

114 / Name	Squat	Bench Press	Deadlift	Total	Date
Chuck Dunbar	407	264*	292	964	8/20/77
Chuck Dunbar	380	260	305	945	5/21/77
123 Chuck Dunbar	405*	265*	315	985*	11/06/77
Ken Woodell	280	230*	410*	920*	5/21/77
Perry Reeder	220	190	360	770	5/21/77
Tom Lumadue	205 c	190 c	340 c	735 c	3/12/77
Mike Sarver	200	160	280	640	11/06/77
132 Ron Giarletto	330*	210	450*	990*	5/21/77
Ken Woodell	290	220	390	900	1/29/77
Chick Clegg	300	250*	340	890	5/21/77
David Miller	225 c	165 c	370 c	760 c	3/12/77
148 Paul Sutphin (144 ¾)	445	265	505*	1215	12/17/77
Jim Priest	400	260	435	1095	5/21/77
Fernando Aquilar	330	240	425	995	11/06/77
Harry Deitzler	290	290	395	975	11/06/77
Fernando Aquilar	315	240	390	945	3/12/77
Brian Williams	300	225	375	900	5/21/77
Brian Williams	250	200	365	815	3/12/77
165 Jack Wilson	565*	340	605*	1510* e	5/21/77
Jack Wilson	520	330	575	1425	11/06/77
Paul Sutphin (160 ¾)	460	275	520	1255	11/12/77
Paul Sutphin (163 ¾)	450	285	505	1240	11/06/77
Paul Sutphin	470 cm	280 cm	480 cm	1230 cm	3/12/77
Don Hundley	460	270	500	1230	11/06/77
Paul Sutphin	440	275	505 c	1220	1/29/77
Don Hundley	475	260	480	1215	5/21/77
Bill Kyle	430	310	460	1200	11/06/77
Don Hundley	455	245	495	1195	12/17/77
Frank White	405	345	445	1195	12/17/77
Don Hundley	440	260	450	1150	10/19/77
Bill Kyle	385	315	400	1100	5/21/77

* - West Virginia State Powerlifting Record
c – West Virginia State Collegiate Powerlifting Record
cm – West Virginia State Collegiate Powerlifting Meet Record
e – Elite Powerlifting Classification Total

1977 West Virginia Powerlifter Rankings
WV Powerlifters competing from January 1st, 1977 thru December 31st, 1977
TOP RANKINGS Determined by Total

181 / Name	Squat	Bench Press	Deadlift	Total	Date
Gary Clark	495*	360	545	1400*	5/21/77
Frank Nicholas	495	330	500	1325	11/06/77
Frank Nicholas	470	325	475	1270	5/21/77
Don Hall	450	275	520	1245	5/21/77
John Francis	400	320	520	1240	5/21/77
Don Hall	460	270	505	1235	11/06/77
Don Hall	465	270	500	1235	12/17/77
Frank White	430	350	450	1230	5/21/77
Steve Brooks	360	280	460	1100	3/12/77
Jim Carrico	380	250	460	1090	3/12/77
Gary Rexrode	325	290	440	1055	3/12/77
Mark Schroeder	350	260	400	1010	3/12/77
198 Roger Estep	694	440*	644	1780* e	8/21/77
Roger Estep	705*	425*	645*	1775* e	5/21/77
Warren Knight	470	310	615	1395	12/17/77
Gary Clark	500	360	525	1385	11/06/77
Warren Knight	460	290	550	1300	11/06/77
Vince White	480	350	440	1270	5/21/77
Ross Smith	460	295	480	1235	11/06/77
Gary Marks	360	320	485	1165	5/21/77
Ross Smith	425	280	460	1165	5/21/77
Dave Snyder	400	295	470	1165	5/21/77
Gary Marks	355	295	470	1120	11/06/77
Gary Marks	345	310	460	1115	3/12/77
Bill Blankenship	320	265	340	925	10/1977
Bill Blankenship	300	260	350	910	TN/1977
Greg Moodie	300	210	370	880	11/06/77

* - West Virginia State Powerlifting Record

c – West Virginia State Collegiate Powerlifting Record

e – Elite Powerlifting Classification Total

1977 West Virginia Powerlifter Rankings
WV Powerlifters competing from January 1st, 1977 thru December 31st, 1977
<u>TOP RANKINGS Determined by Total</u>

220 / Name		Squat	Bench Press	Deadlift	Total	Date
	Mike Wolf	605*	470*	625	1700*	11/06/77
	Mike Wolf	560c	450c	600c	1610 c	3/12/77
	Mike Wolf	560*	460	590	1610*	5/21/77
	Vince White	525	420	480	1425	1/29/77
	Vince White	520	400	460	1380	11/06/77
	Ernie Nagy	470	360	500	1330	10/1977
	Ernie Nagy	475	370	480	1325	4/17/77
	Bob Hill	470	300	520	1290	11/06/77
	Ernie Nagy	430	375	460	1265	5/21/77
242	Herb Fitzsimmons	635* nm	400 m	605	1640* nm	11/06/77
	Herb Fitzsimmons	610	400	605	1615	11/12/77
	Herb Fitzsimmons	610* nm	370	600 m	1580*nm	TN/1977
	Herb Fitzsimmons	560	380	630*m	1570	5/21/77
	Jim Goodnight	550	425*	590	1565	5/21/77
	Herb Fitzsimmons	580 nm	370	590	1540 nm	4/17/77
	Herb Fitzsimmons	580* m	365	580	1525	1/29/77
	Herb Fitzsimmons	540	370	610	1520	10/77
	Nick Busick	530	390	570	1490	5/21/77
	Nick Busick	535	385	535	1455	11/06/77
	Vince White	530	425	475	1430	12/17/77
	Vince White	540	400	470	1410	11/12/77
	Allen Johnson	360	325	500	1185	11/06/77
	Jeff Cook	335	225	555	1115	5/21/77
	Austin Miller	420	280	400	1100	TN/1977
SHW	Luke Iams	750*	510*	585	1845*	5/21/77
	Herb Fitzsimmons	650 m	400 m	650*m	1700 m	12/17/77
	Tim Slamick	550	440	600	1590	5/21/77
	Jim Goodnight	530	440	585	1555	11/06/77
	Tim Slamick	550	440	555	1545	11/06/77
	Tim Slamick	450	420	500	1370	3/12/77

* - West Virginia State Powerlifting Record   nm – National Masters Powerlifting Record

c – West Virginia State Collegiate Powerlifting Record   m – West Virginia State Master's Record

Chapter Twelve : 1978 – Part One
"The Journey to Elite"

The stage was set for what would be one of Powerlifting's greatest years, 1978! The 1977 World Powerlifting Championships conducted on November 3rd, 4th, and 5th, 1977 in Perth, Australia were aired on NBC TV's Sports World. The excitement generated by the 1978 World Powerlifting Championships on national television for the first time familiarized America with the three (3) Powerlifts : The Squat, the Bench Press, and the Deadlift.

The segmented features of the 1977 World Powerlifting Championships were shown by NBC over a period of two to three weeks. I have vivid memory recall of the television production highlighting the lifting of Larry Pacifico, the feature story of Doug Young, 148lb. World Champion Rick Gaugler, and Vince Anello's Squat and winning Deadlift.

In 1978, the addition of the 275lb. class along with official recognition in America of the 114lb. class presented a need for the addition and revision of the Powerlifting Classification System. With the addition of the Flyweight (114lb. class) and another Heavyweight (275lb. class) Division as an interval between the 242's and SHW (SuperHeavyWeight's), new minimum requirements for earning Elite Classification in Powerlifting were revised as follows :

114-1064, 123–1157, 132–1246, 148–1394, 165–1527, 181-1642,
198-1731, 220-1824, 242-1890, 275-1946, SHW-2033.

Although the original benchmarks would be acknowledged by lifters and the AAU for a long time to come, the 1978 changes involved the _addition_ of Totals to be used in determining the classification status for the 114lb. and 275lb. classes. The 1978 revised classification standards had actually _reduced the minimum_ classification Total for achieving Elite status in the Superheavyweight Division, _but increased the minimum Totals in most of the other classes._ When determining the criteria for lifters earning Elite classifications in the 114lb., 275lb., and Superheavyweight classes, the revised (reduced) Totals were recognized. For the weight classes of 123, 132, 148, 165, 181, 198, 220, and 242, _the minimum standards for Elite Classification in effect prior to 1978 were accepted throughout the 1970's._

The Elite Classification Standards recognized throughout the calendar year 1978 were :

114-1064, 123–1160, 132–1240, 148–1360, 165–1480, 181-1605, 198-1710,
220-1825, 242-1905, 275-1946, SHW-2033 (new) / 2100 (old).

YMCA National Powerlifting

One of the most high-caliber series of Powerlifting events began in 1974 with the YMCA Nationals. The 1974 YMCA National Powerlifting Championships were held in conjunction with the MR. YMCA America Physique Competition. According to the official meet results from the Jan-Feb, 1974 issue of *POWERMAN* magazine, there were thirty-three (33) competitors in the 1974 YMCA National Powerlifting event, including Vince Anello. Vince Anello won the 1974 YMCA National Powerlifting Championship title in the 181lb. class with a 1585 Total which included a Record Deadlift of 700lbs.!

Beginning in 1978, the YMCA National Powerlifting Championships were placed on the annual agenda for West Virginia Powerlifting. Prior to the 1978 YMCA National Powerlifting Championships, the 1978 Huntington Open Powerlifting Meet was conducted at the Huntington YMCA on January 14th, 1978 with Vince White as Meet Director. Among the lifters who did well at the 1978 Huntington Open were Ross Smith, Don Hall, and Gene Underwood. For Herb Fitzsimmons, Vince White, Warren Knight, and myself, the 1978 Huntington Open Powerlifting Meet served as a test for the 1978 YMCA Nationals held eight (8) days later.

The 5th Annual YMCA National Powerlifting Championships were held on Sunday January 22nd, 1978. The 1978 YMCA National Powerlifting Championships received a lot of publicity with forty (40) lifters listed in the official results. During the remainder of the 1970's and throughout the 1980's, a victory at the YMCA National Powerlifting Championships was perceived by the majority of lifters as one of the most prestigious Powerlifting titles.

For the sake of argument, I have been known to initiate discussion on the subject of dedication for the purpose of measuring one's commitment to their chosen sport. From my point of view, traveling to Powerlifting meets in adverse weather conditions demonstrates a determined effort separate from physical preparedness. Given an example, a few days prior to the 1978 YMCA National Powerlifting Championships, a Winter storm dumped a near record amount of snow in West Virginia. "Travel only if it is necessary!" was the advisory from state government officials. A YMCA National Powerlifting Championship was necessary, as far as I was concerned.

On January 21st, 1978 I drove North to Charleston on I-77, with over twenty (20) inches of snow on the shoulder of the interstate. After arriving in Charleston, Herb Fitzsimmons, Vince White and myself proceeded according to plan. In spite of treacherous road conditions, we arrived safely in Bedford Heights, Ohio during the early evening of 1/21/78 and rested well for a real battle in Powerlifting which took place the following day.

The Meet Director for the YMCA Nationals required each lifter to produce proof of membership from a YMCA in order to be eligible to compete at the YMCA National Powerlifting Championships. Although we were actually lifting for *Luke's Gym*, each individual member of the team had to be an affiliate of the same YMCA. A YMCA in West Virginia provided sponsorship and valid membership cards for the lifters of "Team West Virginia," competing as *Luke's Gym*.

Vince White had told me since 1974, "One day, you may want to lift in the YMCA Nationals." On January 22nd, 1978 that "one day" arrived. The lifts I made on 1/22/78 at the YMCA Nationals were mediocre, at best. Although eighty (80) pounds less than my PR Total of 1300, the 1220 Total in the 148lb. class included a new West Virginia State Deadlift Record of 510lbs.

Clyde Wright Squatted an easy 520 on 1/22/78 with only a traditional wrestling singlet! Clyde Wright won the 148's with his highest Total to date, 1390! Clyde's lifts included a 520 Squat, 550 Deadlift, and a 1390 Total for three (3) YMCA National Powerlifting Records.

Since the 1975 Seniors, Rickey Crain's performances of a 1495 Total at 148 and first place finish at the 1976 Senior Nationals were legendary. At the 1978 YMCA Nationals on 1/22/78, Rickey Crain made Powerlifting history at 165, Totaling an easy 1600 which included a 600 Squat, 355 Bench Press, and a 650 Deadlift. Rickey Crain's Squat, Deadlift, and Total on 1/22/78 were new YMCA National Powerlifting Records. Crain won the 165lb. class and Jack Wilson placed 2nd at 165 with a 1490 Total.

John Black Totaled 1550 in the 181lb. class for the win which included a YMCA National Bench Press Record of 415lbs. Warren Knight placed 4th at the 1978 YMCA Nationals in the 181lb. class with a 1345 Total. Warren Knight Deadlifted 570lbs. for a new West Virginia State Powerlifting Record in the 181lb. class.

Roger Estep was impressive on 1/22/78 in the 198's with a 710 Squat, 485 Bench Press, and a 620 Deadlift, for an 1815 Total. All of Roger's marks, except the 620 Deadlift, were YMCA National Records. Roger Estep's 710 Squat made the cover of the JAN/78 issue of *Powerlifting USA* magazine. The lifters pictured in the background of the *Powerlifting USA* cover shot are (your's truly) Paul Sutphin and Warren Knight.

Powerlifting USA magazine, Vol. 1, NO. 8, January, 1978

Vince White placed 3rd at the 1978 YMCA National Powerlifting Championships on 1/22/78 in the 220lb. class with a Total of 1445. John Florio won the 242's over Herb Fitzsimmons and Mike Wolf. On 1/22/78 Herb Fitzsimmons' Squat of 650 and Total of 1680 were new West Virginia State Powerlifting Records in the 242lb. class. Mike Wolf Bench Pressed 470 for a new West Virginia State Powerlifting Record in the 242lb. class.

In the SHW class (SuperHeavyWeight's) on 1/22/78, it was Dave Waddington over Luke Iams. Luke had the highest Squat of the contest with 805 and also the heaviest Bench Press of 535lbs. Luke Iams' Squat of 805, Bench Press of 535, and Total of 1860 were new West Virginia State Powerlifting Records.

Just five (5) days out of the YMCA Nationals, I hit the road again for another overnight trip, this time in the Eastern direction to Lynchburg, Virginia on Friday January 27th, 1978. The 1978 Lynchburg Open Power Meet was held Saturday January 28th, 1978 at the Lynchburg YMCA with ninety-four (94) lifters. The 1978 Lynchburg Open Power Meet became the Virginia Connection : Part IV to West Virginia Powerlifting.

The Total I put together for the first place win at the 1978 Lynchburg Open was 1250 in the 148lb. class which included a 515 Deadlift. The 1250 Total and 515 Deadlift on 1/28/78 were new West Virginia State Powerlifting Records in the 148lb. weight class. According to the official results of the 1978 Lynchburg Open Powerlifting meet, *not a single lifter totaled Elite.*

From what began on January 14th, 1978 in Huntington, West Virginia and ended on January 28th, 1978 at Lynchburg, Virginia, Sutphin improved on Total from 1190 to 1250, achieving Master Classification in the 148lb. class once again. On Monday January 30th, 1978 an article appeared in the *Bluefield Daily Telegraph* which read, *"Sutphin Wins Three Contests."* After a run of three (3) Powerlifting competitions over a period of fourteen (14) days, additional language was added to the definition of "Back-to-Back" Powerlifting competitions.

Friday Night Powerlifting

Following the Powerlifting meet at Lynchburg, it was the Southern Open in Raleigh, North Carolina on February 24th and 25th, 1978. The 1978 Southern Open Powerlifting Championships was one of the very first Powerlifting Meets conducted at a hotel venue. The venue for the *1978 Southern Open* was the Holiday Inn in downtown Raleigh, North Carolina.

The 1978 Southern Open Powerlifting Championships had eighty-nine (89) lifters competing in all sessions. For West Virginia Powerlifting, the 1978 Southern Open Powerlifting Championships was the North Carolina Connection : Part IV. The first session (114lb. thru the 148lb. classes), was conducted on Friday evening and finished at approximately 11:00 pm. Even though a couple of missed lifts on the Bench Press and the Deadlift resulted in a Total of only 1245, I won first place in the 148lb. class. The 455

Squat and 1245 Total by Sutphin were new Southern Open Powerlifting Championship Meet Records.

Herb Fitzsimmons, Warren Knight, Vince White, and Paul Sutphin were the only West Virginians who competed at the 1978 Southern Open. Herb Fitzsimmons Totaled 1740 for a first place victory in the 275lb. class. with lifts of 655 Squat, 425 Bench Press, and a 660 Deadlift. Herb's Squat, Deadlift, and Total were new West Virginia State Powerlifting Records in the 275lb. class. Herb Fitzsimmons' Squat, Bench Press, Deadlift, and Total on 2/25/78 were also new West Virginia State Masters Records in the 275lb. class.

While competing in the 181lb. class at the 1978 Southern Open Powerlifting Championships, Warren Knight pulled a 580 Deadlift for a new West Virginia State Record, breaking his old record of 570 set at the YMCA Nationals one (1) month earlier. Vince White was 4th in the 242lb. class with a 560 Squat, 395 Bench Press, and a 460 Deadlift, for a Total of 1415. Based on the Official Meet Results, *not one lifter at the 1978 Southern Open Powerlifting Championships Totaled Elite.*

3rd Annual WV State Powerlifting Championships

The 1978 West Virginia State Powerlifting Championships were held April 1st, 1978 at Magnolia High School in New Martinsville, West Virginia. The meet was sponsored by the *Luke's Gym Powerlifting Team* and the Meet Director was Luke Iams. The contest was conducted in two (2) sessions, morning and afternoon. The crowds present for both sessions at the 1978 West Virginia State Powerlifting Championships were large in number and actively involved.

The 1978 West Virginia State Powerlifting Championships had forty-eight (48) lifters. Twenty-two (22) of the lifters from the 1978 West Virginia States represented *Luke's Gym*. Due to the fact that Herb Fitzsimmons and Paul Sutphin were lifting for *Luke's Gym* in a few key events, "Herb's Gym" was not entered as a Team at the 1978 West Virginia Powerlifting Championships. The decision not to officially enter "Herb's Gym" as a Powerlifting Team and compete for the Team Award at the 1978 West Virginia States was in compliance with AAU Rules governing athletes switching teams within a certain timeframe.

The "Program" for the 1978 West Virginia State Powerlifting Championship was an improved version from the 1976 Championship Program. The official meet program of the 1978 West Virginia State Powerlifting Championships contained the roster of lifters, West Virginia State Powerlifting Records, and a few photos from previous West Virginia State Powerlifting Championship events.

During the first session of lifting on 4/01/78, Sutphin's 485 Squat, 550 Deadlift, and a PR Total of 1335 were new West Virginia State Powerlifting Records in the 148lb. class. After completing a 550lb. Deadlift to secure the 1978 West Virginia Championship with a Total of 1335, I went directly to the Scorer's table and told the Expeditor, "I'll take 600 for my final attempt!" When the Scorer/Expeditor told me without smiling that I did not have any attempts left, I then declared, "April Fool!"

At 165, Jack Wilson Totaled 1600. Wilson's lifts were 590 Squat, 375 Bench Press, and a 635 Deadlift. Jack Wilson's Squat, Bench Press, Deadlift, and Total on 4/01/78 were new West Virginia State Powerlifting Records. With a Total of 1600 in the 165lb. class, Jack won the Best Lifter Award for the first session. Wilson's Total also exceeded the Middleweight minimum standard for an Elite Total by 120lbs. In the 181lb. class, Bill Kyle's 1470 Total was a new West Virginia State Powerlifting Record.

In the 198's, Roger Estep totaled 1880 that included a 740 Squat, 470 Bench Press, and a 670 Deadlift. Estep's Squat, Deadlift, and Total were new West Virginia State Powerlifting Records. Roger's 1880 Total exceeded the MiddleHeavyWeight (198) standard for an Elite Total by 170lbs. Jack Wilson and Roger Estep were the only lifters to Total Elite at the 1978 West Virginia State Powerlifting Championships.

In the 220's, Vincent White won the 1978 West Virginia State Powerlifting Championship title. Mike Wolf Totaled 1770 at 242, including a West Virginia State Record 500lb. Bench Press and a new West Virginia State Record 645lb. Deadlift. Austin Miller finished 2nd at 242 at the 1978 West Virginia States.

While winning the 1978 West Virginia State Powerlifting Championships in the 275lb. class, Herb Fitzsimmons Totaled a West Virginia State Powerlifting Record of 1800lbs. which included another West Virginia State Record in the Deadlift of 700lbs.! Luke Iams Totaled 1900 easily to win the SuperHeavyWeight's. Luke Iams Bench Press of 550 and 1900 Total on 4/01/78 were new West Virginia State Powerlifting Records.

Herb Fitzsimmons : Outstanding Lifter!

At the age of forty-five (45) years plus, Herb Fitzsimmons was already the owner of several American and World Master's Powerlifting Records since 1976. In later years, the USPF defined Master Elite (Age 40+) Classification Standards. According to the criteria, a Total of 1791lbs. achieved minimum classification standard for an Elite Master's Total in the 275lb. class (Age 45-49). During the second half of the 1970's decade, Herb Fitzsimmons surpassed the Master's Elite Classification in both the 242lb. and 275lb. weight classes, many times!

At the 1978 West Virginia State Powerlifting Championships, Herb Fitzsimmons' official West Virginia State Record Total in the 275lb. class of 1800 included the final Deadlift of the day, 700 pounds! Herb's Deadlift of 700 was the heaviest Deadlift of the entire contest, capturing the attention of the huge crowd and all competitors during the 2nd Session of lifting.

During the official award's presentation following the conclusion of the second session of lifting at the 1978 West Virginia State Powerlifting Championships, I distinctly remember Roger Estep graciously accepting his awards and giving the Outstanding Lifter Award that he had won by formula to Herb Fitzsimmons. The voluntary act of sportsmanship demonstrated by Roger Estep was something that I have not seen in the sport of Powerlifting since that day. When Roger took the microphone and thanked everyone for their support, he acknowledged Herb Fitzsimmons' 700 Deadlift as one of the main reasons why Herb should be given the award in addition to Herb's 1800 Total in the 275lb. class!

The 1978 Mr. West Virginia Physique competition immediately followed the awards ceremony of the Powerlifting. Dave Jeffrey won the 1978 Title of Mr. West Virginia. Dave also captured Best Back, Best Chest, Best Legs, and the Best Abs Award at the 1978 Mr. West Virginia Physique competition. The 3rd Annual (1978) West Virginia State Powerlifting Championship results appeared in the April, 1978 issue of *Powerlifting USA* magazine. *Powerlifting USA, Volume 1, Number 11, April, 1978.*

Little-by-little, Powerlifting was beginning to receive proper recognition by local newspapers. A few days following the 1978 West Virginia State Powerlifting Championship victory, an article appeared in a local newspaper which read, *"Paul Sutphin Has Done it Again."* After reading the small paragraph, a man in my neighborhood met me on the street and said, "I don't know what you've done, but the paper said that you've done it again."

A very good article published in the April 26th, 1978 issue of the *The Charleston Gazette* on Herb Fitzsimmons revealed to the entire state of West Virginia the accomplishments of a World Record Holder and championship Powerlifter. Exerpts from the article, *"When Roger Estep won Best Lifter at the West Virginia Powerlifting Championships earlier this year at New Martinsville, the man who ranks second in the world in the 198-pound category handed the trophy to Fitzsimmons in deference to the ex-Rocket's outstanding Deadlift of 700 pounds."*

1978 West Virginia State Powerlifting Championships
Held Saturday April 1st, 1978
New Martinsville, W. VA

Wt. Class/Name	Club	Squat	Bench	Deadlift	Total
114 ½					
Chuck Dunbar	Luke's Gym	420*	275*	330	1025*
Cork Hall	Luke's Gym	200	120	315	635
John Deflorio	Nagy's Gym	145	120	215	480
123 ½					
Dave McCune	Luke's Gym	255	180	340	775
Dave Price	Luke's Gym	250	185	335	770
Mike Sarver	Luke's Gym	230	160	325	715
132 ¼					
Ron Giarletto	Nagy's Gym	360*	200	455*	1015*
David Conaway	Unattached	250	175	315	740
Wayne Anderson	Luke's Gym	225	150	350	725
Kenny Harmon	Unattached	240	180	300	720
148 ¾					
Paul Sutphin	Unattached	485*	300	550*	1335*
John Priest	Luke's Gym	450	270	475	1195
Tim Hill	Unattached	360	310	375	1045
Harry Deitzler	Dave's Gym	300	270	400	970
165 ¼					
Jack Wilson	Luke's Gym	590*	375*	635*	1600*
Gene Underwood	Unattached	420	340	530	1290
Don Hundley	Unattached	470	265	465	1200
Okey Clevenger	Unattached	365	255	510	1130
Matt Herrick	Luke's Gym	375	250	445	1070
Cary Wilson	Luke's Gym	325	265	400	990
Michael Fanary	Unattached	325	225	420	970
Al Anderson	Luke's Gym	385	195	385	965
Gary Park	Unattached	320	245	375	940

*- Indicates West Virginia State Powerlifting Record

Wt. Class/Name	Club	Squat	Bench	Deadlift	Total
181 ¾					
Bill Kyle	Luke's Gym	530	375	565	1470*
Frank Nicholas	Luke's Gym	540*	375*	550	1465
Gary Clark	Nagy's Gym	505	375	550	1430
Don Hall	Unattached	480	280	540	1300
Emmett Dalrymple	Luke's Gym	320	265	400	985
Terry Phillips	Unattached	300	240	385	925
198 ¼					
Roger Estep	Luke's Gym	740*	470	670*	1880*
Scott Tusic	Luke's Gym	500	390	510	1400
Robert Hill	Unattached	475	295	550	1320
Ross Smith	Unattached	480	320	500	1300
David Snyder	Unattached	425	310	500	1235
Steve Brooks	Unattached	420	290	500	1210
Dan Hall	Unattached	425	240	480	1145
Russell Stump	Fred's Gym	350	280	420	1050
220 ½					
Vince White	Unattached	570	400	480	1450
Ernie Nagy	Nagy's Gym	465	380	500	1345
Brian Tucker	Luke's Gym	490	270	500	1260
Tom Jones	Unattached	375	295	470	1140
242 ½					
Mike Wolf	Luke's Gym	625	500*	645*	1770*
Austin Miller	Unattached	390	280	405	1075
275					
Herb Fitzsimmons	Unattached	650	450	700*	1800*
Jim Goodnight	Luke's Gym	610	465*	600	1675
Jeff Cook	Luke's Gym	535	240	575	1350

*- Indicates West Virginia State Powerlifting Record

Wt. Class/Name	Club	Squat	Bench	Deadlift	Total
SHW					
Luke Iams	Luke's Gym	750	550*	600	1900*
Tim Slamick	Luke's Gym	560	480	425	1465

Best Lifters – Jack Wilson / First Session

                  Roger Estep / Second Session

NOTE : Roger Estep presented the Best Lifter Award to Herb Fitzsimmons During the Award's Presentation

Best Squat – Roger Estep

Best Bench Press – Roger Estep

Best Deadlift – Jack Wilson

Team Award – <u>Luke's Gym</u>, New Martinsville, W. Va.

1978 MR. WEST VIRGINIA PHYSIQUE CONTEST WINNER
Dave Jeffrey – 1978 Mr. West Virginia

*- Indicates West Virginia State Powerlifting Record

The Chattanooga Open

By the year 1978, the Chattanooga Open Powerlifting Championships had become one of the premier Powerlifting competitions in the eastern United States. Meet Director Jim Taylor elevated the "Chattanooga Open" to one of Powerlifting's most prestigious competitions. Citing a few examples beginning with the year 1975 :

1) Among the winners at the 1975 Chattanooga Open Powerlifting were Mike Cross (123), Bob Cortes (148), Larry Pacifico (220), and Don Reinhoudt (SuperHeavyWeight).

2) Don Reinhoudt's Total of 2345 at the 1975 Chattanooga Open included a Squat of 915, Bench Press of 580, and a Deadlift of 850!

3) It was at the 1975 Chattanooga Open when Larry Pacifico Totaled 2020 in the 220lb. class with a 760 Squat, 545 Bench Press, and a 715 Deadlift.

4) Herb Fitzsimmons broke National and World Master's Powerlifting Records at the 1977 Chattanooga Open.

In preparation for the 1978 Chattanooga Open Powerlifting Championships, I lifted at the Roanoke Valley Open Powerlifting Meet in Roanoke, Virginia on Saturday April 29th, 1978 ("The Virginia Connection : Part V"). While competing in the 148lb. class, I placed first and won the Outstanding Lifter Award. The 1978 Roanoke Open had forty-nine (49) lifters with no Elite Totals among the winners. While making the lifts of 480 Squat, 300 Bench Press, and a 540 Deadlift for a Total of 1320, the stage was set for Chattanooga, Tennessee seven (7) days later.

"The Journey to Elite" required traveling hundreds of miles to and from all major Powerlifting competitions, including the 1978 Chattanooga Open. Given that fact, I loved traveling with Herb Fitzsimmons. Aside from always being a gentleman with ultimate class, Herb Fitzsimmons lifted heavy weights and drove fast! Given the assistance of a radar detector, CB radio, and the stereo / 8-track tape recordings of several classic singers, we seldom looked in the rear view mirror. On Friday May 5th, 1978 the drive from Charleston, West Virginia to Chattanooga, Tennessee on I-64 West and I-75 South posted record time. The driver of the new 1978 Ford LTD was Herb Fitzsimmons for the entire trip.

The 9th Annual Chattanooga Open Powerlifting Championships were held on May 6th, 1978 at the Chattanooga YMCA in Chattanooga, Tennessee. Meet Director Jim Taylor reported the turnout to be a record number of lifters, possibly for any

Powerlifting competition. According to the May, 1978 issue of *Powerlifting USA* magazine, the original number of competitors entered at the 1978 Chattanooga Open included "204 lifters and 38 Physique contestants." Published in the official results of the 1978 Chattanooga Open Powerlifting Championships were one-hundred eighteen (118) lifters in the Novice Division and fifty-six (56) lifters in the Open Division.

The Chattanooga Open was one of the few Powerlifting competitions in the U.S.A. where American and World Records could be set or broken. The Meet Director spared no expense to acquire officials with the necessary credentials required for American and World Record certification. Lifting in the 123lb. class, Chuckie Dunbar did not win first place at the 1978 Chattanooga Open. Instead, veteran and former Senior National Champion Mike Cross with a 465 Deadlift, beat Dunbar's Total by 10lbs. for the victory. Chuck Dunbar did manage a World Record 4th attempt Squat of 460lbs. that made the cover of the MAY/78 issue of *Powerlifting USA* magazine with Herb Fitzsimmons in the background.

The morning session of the 1978 Chattanooga Open began with an enthusiastic group of lifters from several states. At a bodyweight of 148 ¾, I opened my Squats with 465, went to 490 for the 2nd attempt, and finished with a solid 3rd attempt at 500lbs. On the Bench Press, I made lifts of 285, 295, and 305lbs. With a Sub-Total of 805, I was "6 for 6," on attempts, getting all white lights from the officials. I was primed for a 555lb. Deadlift, the minimum poundage necessary to reach what had been an elusive mountaintop, an Elite Total of 1360lbs.

"Get that Elite!"

The time of day was late afternoon, the Deadlifts were in progress, and the bar was approaching a weight of 500lbs. After opening with an easy 515 to secure the victory in the 148lb. class, I called for a weight of 555 pounds for my 2nd attempt Deadlift, the lift that I needed to Total Elite! I missed the 2nd attempt Deadlift of 555lbs. as it rolled out of my left hand at the initial beginning of the pull. So, as it stood, *I had only one shot remaining to reach Elite status with a 3rd attempt Deadlift of 555!* I had a three (3) minute rest as I was following myself. I took most all of the three minutes and was ready to go again.

On the 3rd and final attempt Deadlift of 555, I approached the platform, facing one of the most enthusiastic crowds that I had ever seen at a Powerlifting event. The crowd was fired up, shouting and chanting encouragement, "Let's go, Paul! Get that Elite!!" I carefully gripped the 555 Deadlift and pulled the weight with power to spare! The result was a victory in the 148lb. class by 45lbs. over the 2nd Place finisher, the *Outstanding Lifter Award,* and an *Elite Total of 1360 at 148!*

Out of all the winners in the Open Division at the 1978 Chattanooga Open only the 165lb. class winner, Lloyd Wehunt (North Carolina), and the 148lb. class winner Paul Sutphin (West Virginia), Totaled Elite. Lloyd Wehunt Totaled 1480 (1978 Elite Total) for the win in the 165lb. class. SuperHeavyWeight Paul Wrenn (Tennessee), Extra Lifter at the 1978 Chattanooga Open, made a Squat of 850, Bench Press of 470, and a Deadlift of 710 for a Total of 2030! The fact that most of the officials at Chattanooga, Tennessee had National and International caliber credentials, the achievement of Powerlifting's Elite status at the 1978 Chattanooga Open left no doubt in the minds of our competitors.

In 1978, Master's (Age group of 40 years and over) Powerlifting was a unique category. The fact that Herb Fitzsimmons was forty-six (46) years young in 1978, while Totaling in excess of 1700 and 1800 pounds, placed him in a class by himself. According to the USPF Master's (Age 40+) Elite Classification Standards published nearly a decade later, Herb's Total in the 242lb. class far exceeded the minimum standard Total of 1741 for Master's Elite (Age 45-49).

While breaking World Master's Powerlifting Records at the 1978 Chattanooga Open, Herb Fitzsimmons won the 242lb. class in the Open Division with ease. Herb's lifts of 670 Squat, 425 Bench Press, and a Deadlift of 680 marked an incredible performance with a 1775 Total! Herb Fitzsimmons' lifts on May 6th, 1978 were all done with power to spare. Herb demonstrated stamina and endurance in addition to strength as he finished his final Deadlift at approximately 6:30 am, (Sunday May 7th, 1978)!

Herb Fitzsimmons broke American and World Masters Records in the 242lb. class at the 1978 Chattanooga Open, including six (6) new West Virginia State Powerlifting Records. Herb's Squat of 670, Deadlift of 680, and Total of 1775 were three (3) new West Virginia State Powerlifting Records in the Open Division and the Master's (Over 40 Age Group) category. Luke Iams won the (SHW) SuperHeavyWeight class at the 1978 Chattanooga Open with an 810 Squat, 550 Bench Press, and a 1945 Total. Other West Virginian's at the 1978 Chattanooga Open Powerlifting event were Ross Smith (Novice 198lb. class) and Master's Lifter / West Virginia State Record Holder Bill Blankenship (181lb. class).

The 1978 Chattanooga Open Powerlifting Championships lasted approximately twenty-two (22) hours! The spectacular event could be described as "A Powerlift Marathon" where battle-tested athletes demonstrated to the Powerlifting nation precisely what dedication and the spirit of competitiveness were all about!

West Virginia Powerlifters at the 1978 Chattanooga Open Powerlifting Championships completed Part VII of the Tennessee Connection to West Virginia

Powerlifting. The Team Title in the Open Division of the 1978 Chattanooga Open Powerlifting Championships went to *Luke's Gym*, as Chuck Dunbar (2nd at 123), Paul Sutphin (1st at 148), Herb Fitzsimmons (1st at 242), and Luke Iams (1st at SHW) earned eighteen (18) points on the 5 points for 1st, 3 points for 2nd, and 1 point for 3rd system of determining team scoring.

Chapter Thirteen : 1978 – Part Two
Championship Powerlifting

Three weeks after the 1978 Chattanooga Open on May 21st, 1978, *Luke's Gym*, represented by Jack Wilson, Roger Estep, and Luke Iams, was part of the USA Team in the North American Powerlifting Championships. Jack Wilson won the 1978 North American Powerlifting title at 165 with a 1587 Total. Roger Estep won the 198's with 1813, while Luke Iams cruised to a 1912 Total in winning the SHW's. The 1978 USA North American Powerlifting Team scored a victory, largely due to the success of the Powerlifters from *Luke's Gym* of New Martinsville, West Virginia.

Following the 1978 Chattanooga Open, I was excited for weeks about the upcoming trip to Arkansas and the 1978 National (Junior) Powerlifting Championships. My workouts were going well and so was the training of Herb Fitzsimmons. Phone conversations with Luke Iams on a regular basis indicated he would be ready. As the entry deadline for the 1978 Nationals approached, I phoned the Meet Director about every other day. During each conversation, he called out many of the names of individual lifters entered at the 1978 National Powerlifting Championships.

The <u>1978 Junior National Powerlifting Championships</u> were held July 8th & 9th, 1978 in Little Rock, Arkansas. The contest was later referred to in the pages of *Powerlifting USA* magazine as "Little Rock – Shell Shock" with approximately one-hundred twenty-five (125) lifters. The 1978 Junior Nationals was one of my favorites and John Orsini, my competitor, lifted exceptionally well.

John Orsini was a member of the 1977 USA Team to the IPF (International Powerlifting Federation) World Powerlifting Championships in Perth, Australia where he placed 5th for the USA and Totaled 1366 pounds (620 kilos), while competing in the 148lb. class. Consequently, John Orsini won a spot on the USA World Team before he won the Juniors, which was rare. Orsini had also placed 2nd behind Dr. Mauro DiPasquale at the 1978 Hawaii International. Realizing it would be a difficult task to defeat John Orsini, I felt I had developed an effective strategy for the 1978 Nationals at Little Rock.

When the lifting began on July 8th, 1978, I was credited with only one (1) Squat of 217.5 kilos (479 ½ lbs). The 1st attempt at 479 was missed as I failed to recover, losing my balance at the bottom position. The 2nd attempt with the same poundage was made with ease, earning three (3) white lights from the officials. My 3rd attempt at 227.5 kilos (501 ½ lbs.) was turned down, receiving only one white light from the judges.

After the Squats at Little Rock on 7/08/79, getting down to business for the remainder of the meet was easier because training for the Bench Press had gone exceptionally well and I knew that I could pull a Deadlift heavier than 555 lbs. After a 325lb. PR Bench Press, I pulled myself into 2ⁿᵈ Place in the 148's with a 573lb. PR Deadlift, Totaled 1377 lbs. (625 kilos) for 2ⁿᵈ Place, and made the resolution that I would return in 1979 to "win it all", which happened in California one year later!

Herb Fitzsimmons had a spectacular day on 7/09/78 at the 1978 National Powerlifting Championships, finishing with an 1868 Total at 275, placing 5ᵗʰ behind Bill Kazmaier, Dave Shaw, Bill Clayton, and Tom Hardman. Herb's 1868 Total (847.5 kilos) would earn the #12 spot in the *P/L USA TOP 100* in the 275lb. class for lifters competing from October, 1977 thru September, 1978.

Herb Fitzsimmons' 722 Squat at the 1978 Nationals finished #11 and the Fitzsimmons 700 Deadlift on 4/01/78 was #9! Placing 5ᵗʰ in the 275lb. class at the 1978 National Powerlifting Championships may not impress some, but there were nine (9) lifters who finished behind Herb Fitzsimmons. Fitzsimmons broke several Master's (45-49 Age Group) Records in the 275 lb. weight class with his lifting on July 9ᵗʰ, 1978 in Little Rock, Arkansas.

Luke Iams : National Powerlifting Champion!

Lifting at SuperHeavyWeight, Luke Iams broke the (Junior) National Bench Press Record at the 1978 Nationals in the Superheavyweight class with a lift of 260 kilos (573lbs) and Totaled 1973lbs. (895 kilos) for the SHW (SuperHeavyWeight) National Powerlifting Championship victory. The 573 Bench Press was ranked #2 in the Powerlifting USA TOP 100 SHW's for lifters competing from November, 1977 through October, 1978. A rare photo of Luke's National Meet Record Bench Press was published in the November, 1978 issue of *Iron Man* Magazine ; Vol. 38, No. 1.

Among the top performances at the 1978 National (Junior) Powerlifting Championships were Troy Hicks and Jerry Bell. Troy set a new Junior National Meet Record Deadlift of 606lbs in the 148lb. class. Jerry Bell finished 6ᵗʰ in the 165lb. class at Little Rock with an incredible opening Deadlift of 302.5 kilos (667 lbs)!

As of July 9ᵗʰ, 1978, the Total of 1377lbs. / 625 kilos by Paul Sutphin was the *fourth (4ᵗʰ) highest Total ever made in the 148lb. class at the Junior Nationals!* Leading the pack in the 148lb. weight class among the All-Time Best Performances at the Junior National Powerlifting Championships since 1965 was John Orsini (1449) followed by Mike Bridges (1445) and Rickey Crain (1415) in third.

In accordance with International Powerlifting Federation (IPF) regulations, the 1978 National Powerlifting Championships were conducted in kilo weights rather than pounds.

National (Junior) Powerlifting Championships
TOP TEN (10) Performance RANKINGS (1965 thru 1978)

114 / Name	Squat	Bench Press	Deadlift	Total	Year
Doug Heath	308	220	424*	953*	1978 W
B. Schlegel	325	175	390	890*	1977 W
Ernesto Milian	305*	190	390*	885*	1975 W
Joe Steinfield	281	248	347	876	1978
Chuck Dunbar	345*	230*	280	855	1976 W
Kevin Meskew	270	187	391	848	1978
B. Martin	286	209	347	843	1978
S. Walsh	275	195	340	810	1976
Kevin Meskew	285	165	355	805	1977
Kevin Meskew	250	185	365	800	1976
Mike Sauers	203	275*	303	782	1978
123 Dave Moyer	455*	245*	450**	1150*	1965 W
John Redding	440	215	460*	1115	1972 W
N. DeSantis	396	264	440	1102	1978 W
Bob Lech	395	255	430	1080	1976 W
J. Nunez	330	285**	440	1055	1977 W
Gerri Ringi	345	280*	425	1050	1971 W
John Redding	410	210	420	1040	1971
Roman Mielec	330	255	415	1000	1967 W
Milt McKinney	330	230	430	990	1968 W
Phil Trujillo	300	250	435	985	1970 W
132 Joe Grosson	468*	292	473	1234*	1978 W
Leroy Mabie	400	300	500	1200*	1974 W
Ernest Thayer	385	315*	485	1185*	1973 W
B. Haar	418	303	457	1179	1978
B. Benoit	400	260	510*	1170	1973
Bob Luna	402	314	451	1168	1978
Ian Burgess	385	275	505*	1165*	1971 W
M. Arthur	425	235	500	1160	1977 W
R. Beaudoin	440*	265	450	1155	1977
Frank Riley	405*	280	465	1150	1969 W

* Junior National Meet Record   **American Record   W – Winner

151

National (Junior) Powerlifting Championships
TOP TEN (10) Performance RANKINGS (1965 thru 1978)

148 / Name	Squat	Bench Press	Deadlift	Total	Year
Bdywt.					
John Orsini	523	347	578	1449*	1978 W
Mike Bridges	515	380*	550	1445*	1977 W
Rickey Crain	550**	310	555	1415*	1975 W
Paul Sutphin (148.59)	479	325	573	1377	1978 2nd
Mike Elliott	540	303	523	1366	1978
Danny Thompson	501	341	518	1361	1978
J. Phillips	496	380	479	1355 ¾	1978
Richard Luckman	455	300	600*	1355*	1972 W
Jim Krueger	500	295	560	1355	1972
Don Jones	530	270	545	1345	1977
Troy Hicks	440	286	606*	1333	1978 6th
165 Byron Wadie	600 ¾	336	633	1570	1978 W
Roger Bell	551	347	622	1521	1978
Ted Mossbarger	556	352	611	1521	1978
Larry Stone	570	370*	570	1510*	1977 W
Mike Zeilinski	595	325	589	1510	1978
George Crawford	605*	350	550	1505*	1971 W
Lloyd Wehunt	534	363	606	1504	1978
Jerry Bell	507	314	667	1488	1978
Mike Zielinski	565	315	605	1485	1977
Jim Lem	573	330	578	1482	1978
Jim Rouse	485	425*	545	1456	1978 8th
181 Dennis Wright	650*	440	575	1665*	1974 W
Jim Grudzien	573	413	661	1647	1978 W
Gary Sanger	584	418	617	1620	1978
Martin Joyce	550	355	685*	1590	1976 W
J. Dignan	580	360	650	1590	1976
Paul Woods	525	430	630	1585*	1972 W
Martin Joyce	550	360	675	1585	1972
B. Weber	525	420	630	1575	1974
F. Barefield	585	390	600	1575	1974
Vince Peterson	600	355	620	1575	1976

* Junior National Meet Record   **American Record   W – Winner

National (Junior) Powerlifting Championships
TOP TEN (10) Performance RANKINGS (1965 thru 1978)

198 / Name	Squat	Bench Press	Deadlift	Total	Year
Jim Cash	661	402	749*	1813*	1978 W
Sam Mangialardi	710*	407	688	1807	1978
Fred Hatfield	650	407	694	1752	1978
Steve Miller	625	465*	640	1730*	1977 W
Keith Boyer	589	440	683	1714	1978
L. Russell	625	430	655	1710*	1974 W
John Needham	606	446	655	1708	1978
Ed Ravenscroft	625*	460	620	1705*	1973 W
Larry Pacifico	610*	460*	630	1700*	1969 W
Ed Matz	570	370	730*	1670	1975 W
220 Dennis Reed	733*	418	733*	1884*	1978 W
Jack Sideris	699	473	688	1862	1978
Steve Wilson	640	460	715*	1815*	1977 W
Richard Keller	620	485*	675	1780	1977
Danny Moreates	655	440	672	1769	1978
Charlie Perkins	617	446	699	1763	1978
Richard Keller	628	512*	622	1763	1978
Mark Dimiduk	639	440	655	1736	1978
S. Sparr	650	435	650	1736	1978
Paul Ellering	600	425	700	1725*	1976 W
242 Hollie Evett	700*	480	725*	1905*	1977 W
R. Scott	670*	510*	700	1880*	1971 W
Ernie Steinkirchner	677 ¾	501	672	1851	1978 W
Mike MacDonald	655	540*	640	1835	1972 W
Larry Plumlee	677 ¾	468	677 ¾	1824	1978
Terry McCormick	655	470	690	1815	1973 W
Tom Paulucci	661	462	683	1807	1978
Ed Bodkin	645	455	705	1805	1975 W
Hollie Evett	670	480	650	1800	1973
Clay Patterson	660	470	670	1800	1975

* Junior National Meet Record   **American Record   W – Winner

National (Junior) Powerlifting Championships
TOP TEN (10) Performance RANKINGS (1965 thru 1978)

275_Name	Squat	Bench Press	Deadlift	Total	Year
Bill Kazmaier	749	512	771*	2033*	1978 W
Dave Shaw	760*	507	760	2028	1978
Bennett Clayton	727	485	744	1956	1978
Tom Hardman	622	556*	705	1884	1978
Herb Fitzsimmons	722	462	683	1868	1978
Barry Groves	699	490	655	1846	1978
John Hawbaker	699	479	633	1813	1978
Mike Stark	606	451	677	1736	1978
O. Muniz-Zacca	650	413	650	1714	1978
Garlon Collins	644	407	655	1708	1978
(SuperHeavyweights)					
Don Reinhoudt	900*	560*	780*	2240*	1973 W
Doyle Kenady	805	515	730	2050	1974 W
Paul Wrenn	840	440	730	2010	1975 W
Luke Iams	821	573	578	1973	1978 W
G. Roberson	730*	505*	735*	1970*	1966 W
T. Smith	700	510	730	1940	1975
T. Smith	700	510	730	1940	1976 W
Russ Fletcher	740*	435	760*	1935	1969 W
Wayne Bouvier	700	530	660	1890	1975
K. Reidy	738	512	628	1879	1978

* Junior National Meet Record   **American Record   W – Winner

154

Training Log #2
Paul Sutphin Workouts

For many of the WORKOUTS, only the exercise, sets, and repetitions are listed

From December 17th, 1977 until December 10th, 1978 I lifted in twelve (12) Powerlifting competitions. During this time, I competed in the 148lb. weight class and went from a 1215 Total (Class I) to a Total of 1425 (Elite Powerlifter Classification). As for the training routine, the workouts placed emphasis on percents of maximum weight lifted, tonnage, and maximum effort. The poundage of multiple sets of five (5) repetitions and three (3) repetitions were calculated from maximum lifts made at official Powerlifting competitions.

The loading and deloading phases often took place before and immediately after the Powerlifting competitions. The "No Fear" approach dominated. I would not hesitate to put the weight on the bar, and I never missed workouts.

A ton (not a metric ton) is 2000lbs. Formula for calculating Tonnage : $T = rw / 2000$. An example 5 sets of 5 repetitions with 400 on Squats : $r = 25$, $w = 400$. $25 \times 400 = 10000$ divided by 2000 equals 5 tons. Estimating the amount of tons (tonnage) for each of the Powerlifts must be adjusted according to the level of strength for each individual.

Other than handling maximum poundages, sometimes I took the conservative approach. There were absolutely no injuries during the weeks and months of 1978 or 1979. After reducing from a bodyweight of 175lbs. in August, 1977 to 144lbs. on December 17th, 1977 I could have allowed my bodyweight to increase again. However, due to the goals that were in place, the bodyweight was controlled with a strict, low-fat diet to remain as a lightweight (148lb. class) competitor for all official Powerlifting competitions during 1978.

Beginning on 11/06/77 through 7/08/78, Paul Sutphin competed in eleven (11) official Powerlifting meets. From 11/77 thru 7/78, Sutphin progressed from a Class I Total in the 165lb. class to an official *Elite Powerlifter Classification* in the 148lb. class. *There were no "high rep" schemes, no aerobic weight-training, circuit training, stopwatches, or "rep 'till you collapse" workouts.* An effective plan for becoming the strongest Lightweight Powerlifter in the USA along with the goal(s) of <u>winning major Powerlifting championships</u> remained in the forefront.

The beginning of the routine (Training Log #2) begins with the *1978 Southern Open Powerlifting Championships*, covering the time period from February 24th, 1978 at Raleigh, North Carolina to the *1978 Junior Nationals* (July 8th, 1978) at North Little Rock, Arkansas.

Friday February 24, 1978
Southern Open Powerlifting Championships
@ Raleigh, North Carolina

1. Squat – 455
2. Bench Press – 280
3. Deadlift – 510

TOTAL – 1245 @ 146 ½ Bodyweight

Tuesday 2/28/78
1. Bench Press – 135 x 5, 205 x 4, 255 x 3, 275 x 2, 255 x 4.
   Pausing with every repetition.
2. Hyper – Extensions – Bodyweight x 10 repetitions, 20lbs. x 8.
3. Performed a few hurdler stretches.

Saturday 3/04/78
1. Bench Press – 135 x 5, 180 x 4, 225 x 3, 255 x 2, 275 x 1, 295 x 1, 300 x 1, missed 305.
2. Incline Bench Press (shoulder width grip) – 135 x 5, 160 x 4, 185 x 3, 205 x 2, 225 x 1, 235 x 1, 240 x 1.
3. Lying Triceps Presses – 70 x 5, 85 x 4, then 100 x 3, 110 x 3, 110 x 3, 120 x 3, 120 x 3, 130 x 3, 130 x 3.

Sunday 3/05/78 - Squats – 180 x 5, 240 x 5, 290 x 5, 335 x 5, 335 x 5, 335 x 5.

Monday 3/06/78 - Deadlifts (Conventional Style) – 180 x 5, 255 x 5, 305 x 5, 355 x 5, 355 x 5, 355 x 5.

Wednesday 3/08/78 - Triceps Presses – 50x 5, 60 x 5, 70 x 5, 80 x 5, 90 x 5.

Friday 3/10/78
1. Squats – 180 x 5, 240 x 5, 290 x 5, 335 x 5, 360 x 5, 360 x 5.
2. Bench Presses – 135 x 5, 190 x 5, 230 x 4, 265 x 3, 265 x 3.

Sunday 3/12/78 – Squats – 180 x 5, 240 x 5, 290 x 5, 335 x 4, 360 x 3, 385 x 3, 410 x 3.

Monday 3/13/78
1. Deadlifts (Standing 4-inch Plaform)(Conventional Style)
   250 x 10, 300 x 5, 345 x 5, 380 x 3, 410 x 2, 410 x 2.
2. Deadlifts (Wide/Sumo Stance) 305 x 3, 365 x 3, 410 x 3.

Tuesday 3/14/78
1. Bench Presses – 135 x 5, 160 x 5, 185 x 5, 210 x 5, 210 x 5, 210 x 5, 210 x 5.
2. Incline Bench Presses – 135 x 5, 155 x 5, 170 x 5, 170 x 5, 170 x 5, 170 x 5.
3. Lying Triceps Presses – 70 x 5, 85 x 5, 100 x 5, 110 x 5, 110 x 5, 110 x 5.

Wednesday 3/15/78
Squats – 180 x 5, 240 x 5, 290 x 5, 335 x 4, 360 x 3, 385 x 2, 410 x 2, 430 x 2, 430 x 2, 435 x 2.

Thursday 3/16/78
1. Bench Presses – 135 x 5, 170 x 5, 200 x 5, 225 x 5, 225 x 5, 225 x 5, 225 x 5.
2. Incline Bench Presses – 135 x 5, 160 x 5, 180 x 5, 180 x 5, 180 x 5, 180 x 5.
3. Lying Triceps Presses (EZ Bar) – 70 x 5, 85 x 5, 100 x 5, 110 x 5, 115 x 5, 115 x 5.

Saturday 3/18/78
1. Power Rack Deadlifts (Conventional Style) / (Bar 5 inches below knee) –
   225 x 5, 265 x 5, 320 x 5, 375 x 4, 425 x 3 475 x 3, missed 505.
2. Power Rack Deadlifts (Wide Stance / Sumo Style) / (Bar 5 inches below knee)
   505 x 3, 505 x 3, 525 x 3, 550 x 3, 560 x 3, 565 x 3, 580 x 3, 600 x 3.
3. Bench Presses –
   135 x 5, 160 x 5, 185 x 5, 210 x 5, 210 x 5, 215 x 5, 220 x 5, 220 x 5, 225 x 5.
4. Incline Bench Presses –
   135 x 5, 155 x 5, 170 x 5, 170 x 5, 175 x 5, 180 x 5, 180 x 5, 180 x 5.
5. Lying Triceps Presses (EZ Bar) –
   70 x 5, 95 x 5, 115 x 5, 115 x 5, 115 x 5, 115 x 5, 120 x 5, 125 x 5.
6. Cheating Eccentric Curls (EZ Bar)/(Close-Grip) – 125 x 5, 135 x 5, 145 x 5, 155 x 5.
7. One Arm Dumbell Rowing – 60 x 5.

Monday 3/20/78
1. Squats – 180 x 5, 240 x 5, 290 x 5, 340 x 4, 380 x 3, 410 x 2, 440 x 1.
2. ½ Squats – 470 x 1.
3. ¼ Squats – 500 x 3, 550 x 3, 575 x 3, 605 x 3, 605 x 3.
4. Bench Presses – 135 x 5, 185 x 5, 225 x 5, 255 x 5, 255 x 5, 255 x 5, 255 x 5.
5. Incline Bench Presses – 135 x 5, 175 x 5, 205 x 5, 205 x 5, 205 x 5, 205 x 5.
6. Lying Triceps Presses – 80 x 5, 100 x 5, 100 x 5, 100 x 5, 105 x 5, 110 x 5.

Wednesday 3/22/78
1. Bench Presses – 135 x 5, 160 x 5, 185 x 5, 215 x 5, 215 x 5, 215 x 5, 215 x 5.
2. Incline Bench Presses – 135 x 5, 155 x 5, 170 x 5, 170 x 5, 170 x 5, 170 x 5, 170 x 5.
3. Lying Triceps Presses – 70 x 5, 90 x 5, 105 x 5, 110 x 5, 120 x 5, 130 x 5.

Thursday 3/23/78 – Squats – 255 x 10, 290 x 5, 360 x 4, 400 x 3, 440 x 2, 440 x 2, 315 x 10.

Friday 3/24/78
1. Deadlifts (Conventional Style) – 10, 5, 4, 3, 2, 2, 2.
2. Bench Presses – 135 x 5, 175 x 5, 215 x 5, 240 x 5, 240 x 5, 240 x 5, 240 x 5.
3. Incline Bench Presses – 135 x 5, 170 x 5, 190 x 5, 190 x 5, 195 x 5, 195 x 5.
4. Lying Triceps Presses – 70 x 5, 95 x 5, 110 x 5, 120 x 5, 130 x 5, 130 x 5.

Sunday 3/26/78
1. Squats (Knee Wraps) – 290 x 5, 350 x 4, 400 x 3, 430 x 2, 450 x 2, 450 x 2.
2. Bench Presses – 135 x 5, 200 x 4, 250 x 3, 275 x 3, 275 x 3, 275 x 3, 280 x 3.
3. Incline Bench Presses – 135 x 5, 180 x 4, 220 x 3, 220 x 3, 220 x 3, 220 x 3, 220 x 3.
4. Lying Triceps Presses – 70 x 5, 90 x 5, 105 x 5, 115 x 5, 115 x 5, 115 x 5.
5. Cheating Eccentric Curls (EZ Bar) – 130 x 5, 150 x 5, 165 x 5.

Tuesday 3/28/78
1. Bench Presses – 135 x 5, 170 x 4, 200 x 3, 225 x 3, 225 x 3, 225 x 3, 225 x 3.
2. Incline Bench Presses – 135 x 5, 160 x 4, 180 x 3, 180 x 3, 180 x 3, 180 x 3, 180 x 3, 180 x 3, 180 x 3.
3. Lying Triceps Presses – 70 x 5, 95 x 5, 110 x 5, 120 x 5, 120 x 5, 120 x 5.

Wednesday 3/29/78

1. Squats – 290 x 5, 340 x 4, 380 x 3, 410 x 2, 440 x 1.

   NOTE : Used knee wraps due to competition scheduled for Saturday April 1st, 1978.

2. Deadlifts (Conventional Style) – 290 x 5, 370 x 3, 435 x 2.

3. Deadlifts (Wide Stance / Sumo Style) – 290 x 5, 370 x 5, 435 x 3.

Thursday 3/30/78

1. Bench Presses – 135 x 5, 180 x 4, 220 x 4, 240 x 3, 250 x 3, 250 x 3, 250 x 3.

2. Lying Triceps Curls (EZ) – 70 x 5, 95 x 5, 115 x 5, 125 x 5, 125 x 5.

Saturday April 1st, 1978
1978 West Virginia State Powerlifting Championships
New Martinsville, West Virginia
Bodyweight of 146 ¾

SQUAT – 485* WV State Championship Record

BENCH PRESS – 300

DEADLIFT – 550* WV State Record

TOTAL – 1335* WV State Record

First place winner in the 148lb. class with three (3) WV State Powerlifting Records. A "9-for-9" day as all attempts were made with power to spare. With exception to the Deadlift, calculate percentages in workouts prior to 4/01/78 on the maximum weights listed : SQUAT @ 480 (100%), BENCH PRESS @ 300 (100%), and DEADLIFT @ 520 (100%). Prior to 4/01/78, the best Deadlift in competition was 520 (160lb. bodyweight) at the 1977 All-South Powerlifting Championships in Durham, North Carolina. At the previous meet in Raleigh, North Carolina, I missed a 3rd attempt 530lb. Deadlift.

Today's lifts represented the following percentage : SQUAT (485lbs. approximately 101.04% of 480lbs.), BENCH PRESS (300lbs. exactly 100% of 300), DEADLIFT (550 approximately 105.77% of 520)! Beginning the week of 4/03/78, the SQUAT percentage max is 500 (100%), BENCH PRESS @ 310 (100%), and DEADLIFT percentage max @ 550 (100%).

Wednesday 4/05/78 – Bench Presses – 135 x 5, 205 x 4, 255 x 3, 275 x 2, 255 x 5.

Thursday 4/06/78 – Squats – 200 x 5, 250 x 5, 300 x 5, 350 x 5, 375 x 5, 375 x 5, 385 x 5.

Saturday 4/08/78
1. Bench Presses – 135 x 5, 185 x 4, 230 x 3, 260 x 2, 280 x 1, 300 x 1, 310 x 1, missed 320.
2. Incline Bench Presses – 135 x 5, 165 x 4, 190 x 3, 210 x 2, 230 x 1, 240 x 1, 250 x 1.
3. Lying Triceps Presses – 70 x 6, 90 x 4, 110 x 3, 130 x 3, 140 x 3, 150 x 3, 150 x 3, 150 x 3.

Sunday 4/09/78 – Squats – 200 x 5, 255 x 5, 310 x 5, 360 x 4, 385 x 3, 410 x 3, 435 x 3, 435 x 3.

Monday 4/10/78
1. Deadlifts (Standing on a 4 inch Platform) / (Conventional Style) 250 x 10, 300 x 5, 345 x 4, 380 x 3, 410 x 2, 410 x 2.
2. Deadlifts (Floor)/(Wide Stance) – 305 x 3, 365 x 3, 425 x 3, 465 x 3.

Tuesday 4/11/78
1. Bench Presses – 135 x 5, 180 x 5, 215 x 5, 215 x 5, 220 x 5, 220 x 5, 220 x 5.
2. Incline Bench Presses – 135 x 5, 160 x 5, 175 x 5, 175 x 5, 175 x 5, 175 x 5.
3. Lying Triceps Presses – 80 x 5, 105 x 5, 125 x 5, 125 x 5, 135 x 5, 135 x 5.

Thursday 4/13/78
1. Squats – 180 x 5, 250 x 5, 300 x 5, 350 x 4, 375 x 3, 400 x 2, 425 x 2, 425 x 2.
2. Bench Presses – 135 x 6, 180 x 5, 210 x 5, 230 x 5, 230 x 5, 235 x 5, 235 x 5.
3. Incline Bench Presses – 135 x 5, 165 x 5, 185 x 5, 185 x 5, 190 x 5, 190 x 5.
4. Lying Triceps Presses – 85 x 5, 110 x 5, 130 x 5, 140 x 4 (missed 5th rep), 140 x 5, 140 x 5.

Saturday 4/15/78
1. Power Rack Deadlifts
   (Conventional Style)/(Bar 5 inches below knee)
   225 x 5, 275 x 5, 320 x 4, 375 x 4, 425 x 3, missed 475.
2. Power Rack Deadlifts
   (Wide Stance) / (Bar 5 inches below knee) –
   475 x 3, 505 x 3, 505 x 3, 525 x 3, 550 x 3, 560 x 3.

3. Bench Presses – 135 x 5, 180 x 5, 205 x 5, 220 x 5, 225 x 5, 225 x 5, 225 x 5, 230 x 5, 235 x 5.
4. Incline Bench Presses – 135 x 5, 160 x 5, 175 x 5, 175 x 5, 180 x 5, 190 x 5, 190 x 5.
5. Lying Triceps Presses – 90 x 5, 115 x 5, 130 x 5, 140 x 5, 140 x 5, 140 x 5.
6. Cheating Eccentric Curls (EZ Bar) – 130 x 5, 145 x 5, 160 x 5, 170 x 5.
7. Deadlifts (Floor)/(Conventional Style) 220 x 10, 265 x 10, 310 x 10.

Monday 4/17/78
1. Squats – 180 x 5, 240 x 5, 290 x 5, 340 x 4, 380 x 3, 410 x 2, 440 x 1, 470 x 1.
2. ¼ Squats – 500 x 3, 550 x 3, 575 x 3, 605 x 3, 605 x 3.
3. Bench Presses – 135 x 5, 190 x 5, 235 x 5, 265 x 5, 265 x 5, 265 x 5, 265 x 4 (missed 5th rep).
4. Incline Bench Presses – 135 x 5, 185 x 5, 210 x 5, 210 x 5, 215 x 5, 215 x 5.
5. Lying Triceps Presses – 90 x 5, 100 x 5, 105 x 5, 110 x 5, 115 x 5, 120 x 5.

Wednesday 4/19/78
1. Bench Presses – 135 x 5, 180 x 5,, 205 x 5, 220 x 5, 220 x 5, 220 x 5. 220 x 5.
2. Incline Bench Presses – 135 x 5, 160 x 5, 175 x 5, 175 x 5, 175 x 5, 175 x 5.
3. Lying Triceps Presses – 90 x 5, 100 x 5, 120 x 5, 125 x 5, 130 x 5, 130 x 5.

Thursday 4/20/78 – Squats – 255 x 10, 310 x 5, 360 x 4, 400 x 2, 400 x 3, 400 x 3, 315 x 10.

Friday 4/21/78
1. Deadlifts (Floor) / (Conventional) – 250 x 10, 310 x 1.
2. Bench Presses – 135 x 5, 185 x 5, 220 x 5, 250 x 5, 250 x 5, 250 x 5, 250 x 5.
3. Incline Bench Presses – 135 x 5, 175 x 5, 200 x 5, 200 x 5, 200 x 5, 200 x 5.
4. Lying Triceps Presses – 90 x 5, 110 x 5, 130 x 5, 135 x 5, 135 x 5, Declined to do a planned 6th set with 135lbs.
5. Deadlifts (Floor) / (Conventional) – 310 x 5, 365 x 4, 415 x 3.
   NOTE : Slightly overtrained ; indicated by lower back.

Sunday 4/23/78
1. Squats – 290 x 5, 350 x 4, 400 x 3, 430 x 2, 455 x 2, 470 x 2.
   NOTE : Put on knee wraps today for Squatting.
2. Bench Presses – 135 x 5, 205 x 4, 260 x 3, 285 x 3, 285 x 3, 290 x 3, 295 x 3.

3. Incline Bench Presses – 135 x 5, 205 x 4, 230 x 3, 230 x 3, 230 x 3, 230 x 3.
4. Lying Triceps Presses – 90 x 5, 110 x 5, 125 x 5, 135 x 5, 140 x 5, 145 x 5.
5. Cheating Eccentric Curls (EZ Bar) / (Close-grip) – 140 x 5, 160 x 5, 180 proved to be a bit heavy.

Tuesday 4/25/78
1. Bench Presses – 135 x 5, 190 x 4, 230 x 3, 235 x 3, 235 x 3, 240 x 3, 240 x 3.
2. Incline Bench Presses – 135 x 5, 165 x 4, 185 x 3, 185 x 3, 190 x 3, 190 x 3, 195 x 3, 195 x 3, 200 x 3.
3. Lying Triceps Presses – 90 x 5, 110 x 5, 120 x 5, 125 x 5, 130 x 5, 135 x 5.

Wednesday 4/26/78
1. Squats – 290 x 5, 340 x 4, 390 x 3, 420 x 2, 450 x 1.
   NOTE : Put on knee wraps for Squatting.
2. Deadlifts (Floor) / (Conventional Style) 290 x 5, 370 x 3, 435 x 2.
3. Deadlifts (Floor) / (Wide Stance / Sumo Style) 290 x 5, 370 x 5, 440 x 3.

Thursday 4/27/78
1. Bench Presses – 135 x 5, 190 x 4, 230 x 3, 250 x 3, 255 x 3, 260 x 3.
2. Lying Triceps Presses – 90 x 5, 110 x 5, 130 x 5, 140 x 5, 150 x 5.

Saturday April 29th, 1978
1978 Roanoke Open Powerlifting Championships
Roanoke, Virginia / Bodyweight of 148 ¼

SQUAT – 480,
BENCH PRESS – 300,
DEADLIFT – 540,
TOTAL – 1320

SQUAT of 480 (96%), BENCH PRESS of 300 (96.77%), DEADLIFT of 540 (98%)

NOTE : The Total of 1320 at the 1978 Roanoke Open Powerlifting was done on 2ⁿᵈ attempts. Only six (6) attempts were made in order to conserve strength for the Chattanooga Open scheduled for the following weekend. Continue calculations of percentage max's for the following week.

Tuesday 5/02/78
1. Bench Presses – 180 x 5, 230 x 2, 230 x 3, 230 x 3, 230 x 3, 230 x 3.
2. Lying Triceps Presses – 100 x 3, 120 x 3, 140 x 3, 150 x 3, 160 x 3.

Wednesday 5/03/78
1. Squats – 290 x 5, 340 x 4, 390 x 3, 420 x 2, 450 x 1.
   NOTE : Put on knee wraps for Squats.
2. Deadlifts (Floor) / (Conventional Style) 290 x 5, 370 x 3, 435 x 2.
3. Deadlifts (Floor) / (Wide Stance / Sumo Style) – 290 x 5, 370 x 5, 440 x 3.

Thursday 5/04/78
1. Bench Presses – 135 x 5, 190 x 4, 210 x 3, 220 x 3, 220 x 3, 220 x 3, 220 x 3.
2. Incline Bench Presses – 135 x 5, 160 x 4, 175 x 3, 175 x 3, 175 x 3, 175 x 3.
3. Lying Triceps Presses – 90 x 5, 115 x 4, 135 x 3, 150 x 3, 150 x 3.

Saturday May 6th, 1978
1978 Chattanooga Open Powerlifting Championships
Chattanooga, Tennessee
Bodyweight of 148 ¾

SQUAT – 500,

BENCH PRESS – 305,

DEADLIFT – 555* West Virginia State Record

TOTAL – 1360* West Virginia State Record

NOTE : First Official ELITE Total for Powerlifting.

1978 Chattanooga Open Powerlifting Championships

SQUAT @ 500 (100%),
BENCH PRESS @ 305 (98.39%),
DEADLIFT @ 555 (Approximately 101%).

-Following the Chattanooga Open, took a two(2) week rest-
-Resumed workouts in preparation for the 1978 Junior Nationals 5/21/78-
Continued the SQUAT maximum @ 500, the BENCH PRESS
max @ 325, and DEADLIFT maximum @ 560.

Sunday 5/21/78 – Squats – 180 x 10, 250 x 10, 300 x 5, 325 x 5, 350 x 5.

Monday 5/22/78
1. Bench Presses – 180 x 6, 205 x 6, 230 x 6, 230 x 6, 230 x 6.
2. Lying Dumbell Flyes – 30 x 10, 30 x 10, 30 x 10.

Wednesday 5/24/78 – Power Rack Deadlifts (75lb. York Plates – 2 inches off floor)
    225 x 5, 335 x 4, 385 x 3, 425 x 3, 425 x 3.

Thursday 5/25/78
1. Bench Presses – 180 x 8, 205 x 8, 220 x 8, 240 x 8.
2. Lying Dumbell Flyes – 30 x 10, 30 x 10.

Saturday 5/27/78
1. Seated Presses – 135 x 8, 155 x 5, 165 x 4, 175 x 3, 185 x 2, 195 x 2, 205 x 2.
2. Bench Presses – 135 x 10, 205 x 5, 230 x 3, 250 x 3, 260 x 3, 260 x 3, 260 x 3.
3. Dead Stop Bench Presses (5 second pause) – 230 x 1, 250 x 1.
4. Box Squats (Box @ 11 ½ inch height) – 135 x 5, 225 x 4, 335 x 3, 370 x 2.
5. Squats – 405 x 1.
6. Power Rack Deadlifts
   (Bar 5 inches below knee) / (Conventional Style) 225 x 5, 315 x 4, 385 x 3, 405 x 3.

<u>Tuesday 5/30/78</u>
1. Squats – 180 x 5, 250 x 5, 300 x 5, 325 x 5, 325 x 5, 345 x 5, 350 x 5.
2. Seated Presses – 135 x 5, 160 x 5, 160 x 5, 160 x 5, 160 x 5.

<u>Wednesday 5/31/78</u>
1. Bench Presses – 135 x 5, 190 x 4, 235 x 3, 260 x 3, 265 x 3, 270 x 3, 275 x 3, 280 x 3.
2. Dead Stop Bench Presses (5 second pause) – 250 x 1, 270 x 1.

<u>Sunday 6/04/78</u> – Squats – 180 x 5, 250 x 5, 300 x 5, 325 x 5, 325 x 5, 325 x 5.

<u>Monday 6/05/78</u>
1. Deadlifts (Standing on 4 inch Platform) –
2. Power Rack Deadlifts (Lockouts – Bar Positioned above knees)
(Wide Stance / Sumo Style) – 225 x 10, 445 x 5, 515 x 3, 565 x 3, 625 x 2, 675 x 2.
3. Seated Presses – 135 x 5, 160 x 5, 165 x 5, 170 x 5, 175 x 5, 180 x 5.

<u>Tuesday 6/06/78</u>
1. Bench Presses – 135 x 5, 190 x 4, 235 x 3, 260 x 3, 260 x 3, 260 x 3, 260 x 3.
2. Dead Stop Bench Presses (5 second pause) – 250 x 1, 270 x 1.

<u>Friday 6/09/78</u>
1. Lying Dumbell Flyes – 30 x 10, 30 x 10, 30 x 10, 30 x 10.
2. Bent Over Dumbells (Alternate w/Dumbells) – 30 x 10, 75 x 8, 75 x 8, 75 x 8.
3. Lying Triceps Extensions (EZ Bar) – 70 x 8, 70 x 8.
(Keeping elbows high and allowing bar to go behind head)

6/10/78 Workout at High Point, North Carolina w/Powerlifting Friends

<u>Saturday 6/10/78</u>
1. Squats – 135 x 10, 225 x 5, 315 x 5, 350 x 5, 360 x 5, 370 x 5, 370 x 5.
2. ¼ Squats – 505 x 3, 555 x 3.
3. Bench Presses – 135 x 5, 205 x 4, 255 x 3, 280 x 2, 300 x 1, 315 x 1, 320 x 1, missed 325, missed 325.
4. Dead Stop Bench Presses (5 second pause) – 250 x 1, 280 x 1.

Monday 6/12/78

1. Deadlifts (Floor) / (Conventional Style) –
   180 x 5, 255 x 5, 305 x 5, 355 x 5, 360 x 5, 365 x 5, 370 x 5.
2. Seated Presses (Slight Incline) – 135 x 5, 145 x 5, 155 x 5, 155 x 5, 155 x 5, 155 x 5.
3. Bench Presses – 135 x 5, 180 x 5, 205 x 5, 225 x 5, 225 x 5, 225 x 5, 225 x 5.
4. Lying Dumbell Presses (EZ Bar) – 70 x 6, 95 x 6, 95 x 5, 100 x 5, 105 x 5, 105 x 5.

Tuesday 6/13/78 Alternate Dumbell Rowing – 75 x 8, 75 x 8, 75 x 8.

Wednesday 6/14/78 (Session One)

1. Squats – 180 x 5, 240 x 5, 300 x 5, 350 x 5, 350 x 5.
2. Seated Presses – 135 x 5, 150 x 5, 165 x 5, 165 x 5, 165 x 5, 165 x 5.
3. Bench Presses – 135 x 5, 185 x 5, 215 x 5, 240 x 5, 240 x 5.

Wednesday 6/14/78 (Session Two)

1. Bench Presses – 240 x 5, 240 x 5.
2. Lying Triceps Presses – 70 x 5, 90 x 5, 110 x 5, 130 x 5, 130 x 5, 130 x 5.

6/17/78 Workout @ St. Albans, WV with Powerlifing Friends

Saturday 6/17/78

1. Seated Presses – 135 x 5, 155 x 4, 165 x 3, 175 x 2, 180 x 2, 180 x 2, 180 x 2.
2. Bench Presses – 135 x 5, 205 x 5, 240 x 5, 270 x 4 (missed 5th rep), 225 x 5, 225 x 5, 225 x 5.
3. Dead Stop Bench Press (5 second pause) – 260 x 1.
4. Squats – 135 x 5, 245 x 5, 335 x 4, 390 x 3, 405 x 3, 420 x 3, 430 x 3.

Monday 6/19/78

1. Squats – 180 x 10, 250 x 10, 310 x 10.
2. Deadlifts (Standing on 4 inch Platform) / (Conventional Style)
   250 x 10, 300 x 5, 345 x 4, 380 x 3, missed 410, 410 x 2, 410 x 2.
3. Deadlifts (Floor) / (Wide Stance / Sumo Style) –
   305 x 3, 370 x 3, missed 430, missed 430, 430 x 3.

Tuesday 6/20/78

1. Bench Presses – 135 x 5, 190 x 5, 240 x 5, 270 x 5, 270 x 5, 270 x 5, 270 x 5.

2. Incline Bench Presses – 135 x 5, 185 x 5, 220 x 3, 210 x 3, 195 x 5, 195 x 5.
3. Lying Triceps Presses – 85 x 5, 110 x 5, 130 x 5, 130 x 5, 130 x 5, 130 x 5.

Wednesday 6/21/78 – Squats – 180 x 5, 250 x 5, 300 x 5, 350 x 4, 400 x 3, 425 x 2, 440 x 2, 450 x 2, 450 x 2, 450 x 2.

NOTE : Calculating from a maximum weight of 500, worked up to 90% today with multiple sets of 2 reps with 450.

Thursday 6/22/78
1. Bench Presses – 135 x 5, 190 x 5, 210 x 5, 225 x 5, 225 x 5, 225 x 5, 225 x 5.
2. Incline Bench Presses – 135 x 5, 160 x 5, 180 x 5, 180 x 5, 185 x 5, 185 x 5.
3. Lying Triceps Presses – 85 x 5, 110 x 5, 130 x 5, 140 x 5, 145 x 5, 150 x 5.
4. Cheating Eccentric Curls (EZ Bar)(Close-grip) – 120 x 5, 130 x 5, 140 x 5.

Saturday 6/24/78
1. Power Rack Deadlifts (Bar 5 inches below knee) (Conventional Style) – 225 x 5, 275 x 5, 325 x 5, 375 x 4, 425 x 3, 475 x 3, missed 505, missed 505.
2. Power Rack Deadlifts (Bar 5 inches below knee) (Wide Stance / Sumo Style) – 505 x 3, 505 x 3, 530 x 3, 555 x 3, 580 x 3, 605 x 3, missed 605, 605 x 3.
3. Bench Presses – 135 x 5, 205 x 5, 235 x 5, 255 x 5, 255 x 5, 260 x 5, 260 x 5.
4. Incline Bench Presses – 135 x 5, 185 x 5, 205 x 5, 205 x 5, 185 x 5.
5. Lying Triceps Presses – 90 x 5, 115 x 5, 135 x 5, 145 x 5, 145 x 5.

Sunday 6/25/78
1. Squats – 180 x 5, 250 x 5, 310 x 5, 360 x 4, 400 x 3, 435 x 2, 465 x 1.
2. ¼ Squat – 500 x 3, 550 x 3, 600 x 3, 630 x 3, missed 660 (bar slid off of back / dropped w/no problem), Attempted 660 once again. Stood up with weight but concerned about the position / did not attempt, Finished with 585 x 5.

Monday 6/26/78 – Bench Presses – 135 x 5, 225 x 4, 275 x 3, 295 x 2, 295 x 1, 295 x 1.

Wednesday 6/28/78
1. Squats – 260 x 10, 310 x 5, 360 x 4, 410 x 3, 450 x 2, 450 x 2, 315 x 10.
2. Seated Presses – 135 x 5, 155 x 4, 170 x 3, 175 x 3, 180 x 3, 180 x 3.
3. Bench Presses – 135 x 5, 190 x 4, 225 x 3, 240 x 3, 240 x 3, 240 x 3, 240 x 3.

4. Lying Triceps Presses – 95 x 5, 120 x 5, 140 x 5, 140 x 5, 140 x 5, 140 x 5.
5. Cheating Eccentric Curls (EZ Bar)/(Close-grip) 140 x 5, 150 x 5, 150 x 5.

Thursday 6/29/78 – Deadlifts (Floor) / (Conventional Style) – 250 x 10, 310 x 5, 365 x 4, 420 x 3 460 x 2, 480 x 2, missed 490, missed 490.

Friday 6/30/78
1. Seated Presses – 135 x 5, 155 x 4, 175 x 3, 190 x 2, 200 x 2.
2. Bench Presses – 135 x 5, 205 x 4, 235 x 3, 255 x 3, 255 x 3, 255 x 3, 255 x 3.
3. Lying Triceps Presses – 95 x 5, 125 x 4, 145 x 3, 160 x 3.

Sunday 7/02/78
1. Squats – 290 x 5, 350 x 4, 400 x 3, 440 x 2, 465 x 2, 480 x 2, 490 x 2.
   NOTE : Put on knee wraps for Squats.
2. Bench Presses – 135 x 5, 225 x 4, 275 x 3, 300 x 2, 310 x 1, missed 320, missed 320.

Tuesday 7/04/78
1. Seated Presses – 135 x 5, 160 x 4, 180 x 3.
2. Bench Presses – 135 x 5, 190 x 4, 220 x 3, 240 x 3, 240 x 3, 245 x 3, 250 x 3.
3. Incline Bench Presses – 135 x 5, 165 x 4, 195 x 3, 195 x 3, 195 x 3.
4. Lying Triceps Presses – 90 x 6, 125 x 5, 150 x 5, 150 x 5, 150 x 5.
5. Lying Dumbell Flyes – 30 x 10, 30 x 10, 30 x 10.
6. Cheating Eccentric Curls (EZ Bar)(Close-grip) 150 x 5, 150 x 5.

Wednesday 7/05/78
1. Squats – 290 x 5, 350 x 4, 400 x 3, 440 x 1, 465 x 1.
   NOTE : Put on knee wraps for Squats.
2. Deadlifts (Floor)/(Conventional Style) – 290 x 5, 400 x 3, 460 x 2.
3. Deadlifts (Floor)/(Wide Stance / Sumo Style) – 290 x 5, 400 x 5, 465 x 3.

Thursday 7/06/78
1. Bench Presses – 135 x 5, 190 x 5, 230 x 3, 255 x 3, 255 x 3, 255 x 3, 260 x 3.
   The final set with 260 was selected as it is 80% of 325lbs.
2. Lying Triceps Presses – 100 x 5, 130 x 5, 150 x 5, 170 x 3.
   NOTE : Triceps Presses were performed with the EZ Curl Bar.

Traveled Friday 7/07/78 : Drove to Charleston, then by plane to Arkansas.

Saturday July 8th, 1978
1978 National (Junior) Powerlifting Championships
North Little Rock, Arkansas
Bodyweight at 67.4 kilos (148.59 lbs. or 148 ½)

SQUAT – 479 ½ lbs. (217.5 kilos)

BENCH PRESS – 325lbs. (147.5 kilos)*

WV State Record

DEADLIFT – 573lbs. (260 kilos)*

WV State Record

TOTAL – 1377 ¾ lbs. (625 kilos)*

WV State Record

Placed 2nd at the *1978 National (Junior) Powerlifting Championships*. Three PR's (Personal Records) and three (3) new West Virginia State Powerlifting Records in the 67.5 Kilo Weight Class (148lb. Class). For the percentages at the 1978 National Powerlifting Championships, the SQUAT of 479.5 is 95.9 % of 500, the BENCH PRESS of 325 was 100%, and the DEADLIFT was 102.32% of the maximum percentage calculations of 560lbs.

In summary, all the Deadlift workouts from the floor were done using conventional standard York Barbell cast iron plates and a 7-foot vanadium steel bar WITHOUT revolving sleeves. Also, 75lb. cast iron plates used are smaller in diameter than the 45lb. Olympic Barbell plates / discs or the 100lb. plates. Consequently, the pulls were equivalent to one standing on a 1 to 1 ½ inch platform.

During the workouts, most of the Deadlifts performed were conventional (regular) style. I used Sumo/Wide stance in official Powerlifting competitions. The Triceps Presses were performed with an EZ Bar, sometimes with grip variations. A belt was used on all sets of Squats and Deadlifts. When performing Deadlifts, I used a conventional Weightlifting belt rather than the thick suede belt used for Squatting.

After returning home from Little Rock, Arkansas, a feature story appeared in the *Bluefield Daily Telegraph* on 8/06/78 with a headline which read, *"Sutphin Would*

Rather Be First." In a spirit of humbleness, I was thankful that God blessed me with the opportunity to attend the 1978 Nationals and compete. However, unlike today, in order to be the best in Powerlifting, <u>one had to "OUTLIFT" the best!</u> *In 1978*, without the divisions and the various number of lifting federations of which to migrate, *<u>one either competed against the best or remained at home</u>!* For the record, there were a few of us that were not home very often.

The Team of *Luke's Gym* was represented at the 1978 National Powerlifting Championships in Little Rock, Arkansas by Paul Sutphin, Herb Fitzsimmons, and Luke Iams. Approximately six (6) weeks later at the 1978 Senior Nationals, *Luke's Gym* was represented by Chuck Dunbar (114), Jack Wilson (165), Roger Estep (198), and Luke Iams (SuperHeavyWeight).

Competing in the 148lb. weight class, Paul Sutphin's 1377 ¾ lb. Total at the 1978 Junior Nationals far exceeded the minimum Qualifying Total of 1300 for the 1978 Senior Nationals. Rather than attend the 1978 Senior Nationals, I made the decision to focus on the 1979 National Powerlifting Championships (scheduled for California in July, 1979) of which I was determined to win. Therefore, *I made the decision NOT to compete at the 1978 Senior National Powerlifting Championships, one of the few times that I elected to stay home.*

Chuck Dunbar became the 2nd West Virginia Powerlifter to officially achieve the Powerlifter Elite Classification at the 1978 Senior National Powerlifting Championships on August 25th, 1978 in California. Chuck Dunbar's 1096 Total in the 114lb. class included a 440 Squat, a World Record Bench Press of 281, and a Deadlift of 374.

The 1978 Seniors was not the best of contests for the *Luke's Gym Powerlifting Team* as Chuckie Dunbar placed 2nd to John Redding and Jack Wilson was 4th at 165 behind Rick Gaugler, Doc Rhodes, and Rickey Crain. Roger Estep was 4th behind Vince Anello, Steve Miller, and Jerry Jones. Luke Iams bombed out on Squats with a weight of 894lbs.

Don Hundley : Cover of Powerlifting USA!

The title or phrase, "On the Cover of a Rolling Stone" is well known among Rock n' Roll music fans. It has been my perception for over three (3) decades that it would have meant more to a Powerlifter to be "On the cover of *Powerlifting USA* magazine." The November, 1978 issue of *Powerlifting USA* magazine pictured West Virginia Powerlifter and National Masters Powerlifting Champion, Don Hundley on the cover!

On October 7th, 1978 the <u>Ohio Valley Open Powerlifting Championships</u> were held in New Cumberland, West Virginia under the direction of Ernie Nagy. The event hosted forty-four (44) lifters. Only a couple of lifters from *Luke's Gym* were there : Mike Sarver and Bill Kyle. The *St. Alban's Barbell Club* (a.k.a. "Herb's Gym") was well represented with Don Hundley (1st at 165 - 1305 Total), Ross Smith (2nd - Novice Division / 181lb. class), Bob Hill (1st at 198 - Novice Division with a 1340 Total including a 590 Deadlift), and Master's Lifter Austin Miller (1st at 242 / Novice Division).

The contest in New Cumberland, West Virginia was the second Powerlifting event at New Cumberland for the year 1978. Only four (4) months earlier, the New Cumberland Novice Powerlifting Meet was held on June 24th, 1978. The Meet Director was Ernie Nagy. The New Cumberland Meet in June of 1978 was for novice Powerlifters only and had seventy-six (76) lifters.

A rare photo from the 1978 Ohio Valley Open Powerlifting Championships at New Cumberland appeared on the cover of the November, 1978 issue of *Powerlifting USA* : Don Hundley! Also in the pages of the November, 1978 issue of *Powerlifting USA* magazine, an article written by Ron Giarletto appeared. The title of the article was *Luke and the Wild Bunch*. The caption at the top of the page read, *"If He Don't Get You Now… He'll Get You Later."* The article written by Ron Giarletto featured action photographs of Luke Iams, Scott Tusic, Chuck Dunbar, and Jack Wilson.

A photo of young Bill Kyle, another member of the *Luke's Gym Powerlifting Team*, also appeared in the NOV/78 issue of P/L USA adjacent to the official 1978 Ohio Valley Powerlifting Meet results. The article,*"Luke and the Wild Bunch"* along with the success of Herb Fitzsimmons, Don Hundley, and Ernie Nagy elevated West Virginia Powerlifting to a new level.

During 1978, the popularity of Professional Wrestling was on the rise. Prior to the 1978 Ohio Valley Open Powerlifting Meet at New Cumberland, Nick Busick had appeared on local television while wrestling some of the WWWF (World Wide Wrestling Federation) Professional Wrestling stars. Nick Busick won the Ohio Valley Open Powerlifting Meet with a Total of 1595 while competing in the 242lb. class. Nick's lifts on 10/07/78 included a 605 Squat, 410 Bench Press, and a 580 Deadlift.

The November, 1978 issue of *Powerlifting USA* magazine also published the official results of the 1978 National Masters Powerlifting Championships held October 29th, 1978 in Arlington, Texas. Ernie Nagy won the 220lb. class (55-59 Age Group) with a 1421 Total. Ernie's lifts at the 1978 National Masters included a Squat of 507, Bench Press of 385, and a Deadlift of 529.

Parkersburg to Durham – Part II

The 5<u>th</u> Annual 1978 Mountianeer Open Powerlifting Championships held November 4<u>th</u> and 5<u>th</u>, 1978 in Parkersburg, West Virginia was a huge success. Thanks to the hard work of the Meet Directors and support of the Powerlifters from West Virginia and Ohio, the Mountianeer Open evolved from a local Bench Press event to one of the major Powerlifting competitions in the eastern U.S.A.!

The 1978 Mountianeer Open Powerlifting Championships had forty-eight (48) lifters from several states. *Black's Health World* won the 1978 Mountianeer Open Powerlifting Team trophy as they did in 1977. Appearing in *Powerlifting USA* magazine, the official meet results of the 1978 Mountianeer Open Powerlifting Championships read :

BEST LIFTERS - <u>Paul Sutphin</u>, Lightweights

<u>Louie Simmons</u>, Heavyweights

While competing at the 1978 Mountianeer Open, Louie Simmons' lifts of 680 Squat, 435 Bench Press, and a 640 Deadlift comprised a 1755 Total, Elite Powerlifting Classification at 198! Louie attempted a 720 Deadlift which would've given him an 1825 Total! Louie Simmons 680 Squat, 640 Deadlift, and 1755 Total at the 1978 Mountianeer Open were new Mountianeer Open Powerlifting Championship Records.

For Paul Sutphin, the strategy implemented at the 1978 Mountianeer Open Powerlifting Championships was, "Take only the attempts necessary for the win." While taking only two (2) attempts per lift, the 490 Squat, 325 Bench Press, and 570 Deadlift for a PR Total of 1385 marked the achievement of a number of goals, including a West Virginia State Total Record and the Mountianeer Open Championship Meet Record in the 148lb. weight class.

Beginning in the 1970's, many Powerlifters often wore "talking shirts." At the 1975 Mountianeer Open, Vince White wore a shirt which read, "Mr. Bench Press." Three (3) years later, the shirt "talked" while Vince lifted. Vince White, weighing a few pounds over the limit for the 220lb. class, finished 2<u>nd</u> at the 1978 Mountianeer Open with a Mountianeer Open Powerlifting Championship Bench Press Record of 420lbs. in the 242lb. class.

Other noteable performances at the 1978 Mountianeer Open Powerlifting Championships included Doug Heath (1<u>st</u> at 114), Don Hundley (1<u>st</u> at 165), John Black (1<u>st</u> at 220), Bob Hill (3<u>rd</u> at 220… with a 600 Deadlift), John Florio (1<u>st</u> at 242), and Austin Miller (3<u>rd</u> at 242).

One week after the 1978 Mountianeer Open on November 5th, it was on to Durham, North Carolina for the All-South Powerlifting Championships held on November 11th, 1978. The 1978 All-South Powerlifting Championships became known as "North Carolina Connection" : Part V. The 1978 All-South Powerlifting Championships had seventy-three (73) lifters. Lifting in the 148lb. class, I made the following lifts : 520 Squat, 325 Bench Press, 560 Deadlift, and a Total of 1405, breaking the 1400lb. Total barrier for the first time.

A 1400 Total represents mediocrity in some weight classes, but how about the 148's? The 1405 Total on 11/11/78 exceeded the new minimum standard for an Elite Total of 1394 at 148. The 520 Squat and 1405 Total by Paul Sutphin at the 1978 All-South Powerlifting Championships were new West Virginia State Powerlifting Records in the 148lb. class.

In November of 1978, there were only a few contests in America or the world where a Total of 1405 in the 148lb. class would earn only a second place finish. For the Lightweight class, the 1978 All-South Powerlifting Championships was a continuation of "Little Rock, Shell Shock" without John Orsini. The lifting of Clyde Wright won first place on 11/11/78 with a 1435 Total. The place finishers at the 1978 All-South Powerlifting Championships in the 148lb. class were 1435, 1405, 1365, and 1360.

Vince White : YMCA National Champion!

On January 22nd, 1978 the YMCA National Powerlifting Championships were held in Ohio. Eleven (11) months later on December 10th, 1978 the YMCA Nationals were held in Sandusky, Ohio by Meet Director Dave Waddington. The 12/10/78 contest was originally scheduled for the month of January, 1979. However, due to the difficulty of securing a venue for that time period, the event was moved up to December 10th, 1978. The weather conditions, with exception to the extreme cold, were somewhat cooperative.

The victory of Vincent White was a major highlight of the December, 1978 YMCA National Powerlifting Championships. Vince White, weighing-in at approximately 224lbs., put together a 1460 Total to win one of the most coveted titles in Powerlifting, *a YMCA National Powerlifting Championship!* In the 114lb. class, it was Chuck Dunbar winning his 3rd consecutive YMCA National Powerlifting title. Chuck Dunbar Squatted an American Record of 445lbs. (actual weight @ 447lbs.). Dunbar met the Elite Powerlifting Classification requirement by more than twenty (20) pounds over the minimum Total for the 114lb. weight class.

173

Winning the YMCA National Powerlifting title at a bodyweight of 148 ½ was the mission on 12/10/78. After an easy 500lb. opener on the Squat, the 2nd attempt of 525 was a PR, a West Virginia State Record, and a new YMCA National Squat Record! Following myself, I had a three (3) minute rest. The 3rd attempt of 540 received three (3) red lights for lack of depth. Reason? I was too busy celebrating the successful attempt of 525 and forgot to remove the knee wraps.

When it came time to Bench Press on 12/10/78, I opened with 320 and missed 330 on a 2nd attempt. I repeated with 330 and it was a slow push, but a new PR and another West Virginia State Record at 148. Due to the fact that I did not have close competition, the 570 Deadlift was all I would get, as the 585 was not necessary for victory. For 12/10/78, Paul Sutphin's YMCA National Total Record in the 148lb. class was recorded at 1425lbs.

Jack Wilson Totaled 1605 and won the 165lb. class. One of the lifters I remember most from the December, 1978 YMCA Nationals was the legendary George Crawford. George Squatted 645 and Totaled 1520 for 2nd Place in the 165lb. class. George Crawford was also the 1971 World Powerlifting Champion.

At 181, Bill Kyle of *Luke's Gym* was 3rd with 1485 behind Tim Gallagher (2nd at 181) and New York's Vince Peterson who Totaled 1610 at 181 for the win. The cold day on 12/10/78 was one of Roger Estep's finest hours as the 769 ½ Squat and 1944 Total were World Powerlifting Records!

Roger Estep's 769 ½ Squat was #2 in the TOP 100 198's for lifters competing from June, 1978 through May, 1979 in the JUN/79 issue of Powerlifting USA. Roger's 490 Bench Press was #2 (2nd only to Mike MacDonald's 560), and his Total of 1944 was #1! Estep's 685 Deadlift was 17th. As of this writing, Roger Estep's 1944 Total still stands as the All-Time West Virginia State Total Record in the 198lb. class.

Louie Simmons did outstanding lifting in the 198lb. class on 12/10/78, beating Gary Sanger by 10lbs. (1770 to 1760) to win 2nd Place. John Black was 4th at 198 with a Total of 1725. Scott Tusic of *Luke's Gym* finished 6th in the 198's with 1630. Tom Farchione was impressive at 220 with an 1860 Total and a 745 Deadlift. John Florio won 2nd in the 220's with an 1825 Total followed by Dan Wohleber in 3rd with a Total of 1800 which included a 755 Deadlift.

The December, 1978 YMCA Nationals was good for Jeff Cook of *Luke's Gym*, finishing 3rd in the 275's. Luke Iams turned in a very conservative performance, spacing his attempts in order for Roger Estep to have extra time between attempts (an advantage of the "System of Rotation"). Consequently, it was a great day for West Virginia Powerlifting at the YMCA National Powerlifting Championships on December 10th, 1978 in Sandusky, Ohio.

The Team Champs for the 1978 YMCA Nationals on December 10ᵗʰ, 1978 were listed in the official reports as the Parkersburg YMCA, represented by "Luke's Gym" (a.k.a. "The Wild Bunch"). The 1978 YMCA Powerlifting Nationals was the last time that *Luke's Gym* was together as a team with Roger Estep and Jack Wilson.

Due to the lifting at the Dec/78 YMCA National Powerlifting Championships, Paul Sutphin scored well in the TOP 100 LW's (148lb. class). Appearing in the MAR/79 issue of *Powerlifting USA*, Paul Sutphin was ranked #6 with a 1425 Total for lightweights (148lb lifters competing from March, 1978 through February, 1979). The 525 Squat was #8, the 330 Bench was #27, and the 573 Deadlift was tied for 10ᵗʰ.

From the twenty-nine (29) lifters at the YMCA National Powerlifting Championships on 12/10/78, there were eleven (11) Elite Totals, based on the following minimum standards for determining Elite Powerlifting Classification :

114 – 1064, 123–1160, 132–1240, 148–1360, 165–1480, 181-1605, 198-1710, 220-1825, 242-1905, 275 – 1946, SHW-2033.

Chuck Dunbar Totaled 1085 in the 114lb. class. Paul Sutphin exceeded minimum standards for Elite Classification by 65lbs. with a 1425 Total in the 148lb. class. Other lifters Totaling Elite at the YMCA National Powerlifting Championships on 12/10/78 were Jack Wilson (1605 at 165), George Crawford (1520 at 165), Vince Peterson (1610 at 181), Roger Estep (1944 at 198), Louie Simmons (1770 at 198), Gary Sanger (1760 at 198), John Black (1725 at 198), Tom Farchione (1860 at 220), and John Florio (1825 at 220)

1978 West Virginia Powerlifter Rankings
WV Powerlifters competing from January 1st, 1978 thru December 31st, 1978
<u>TOP RANKINGS Determined by Total</u>

114 / Name	Squat	Bench Press	Deadlift	Total	Date
Chuck Dunbar	440	281 WR	374	1096*e	8/25/78
Chuck Dunbar	447 AR*	270	370	1087 e	12/10/78
Chuck Dunbar	420*	275*	330	1025*	4/01/78
Chuck Dunbar	415 Y	250	315	980 Y	1/22/78
Cork Hall	270	145	350	765	6/24/78
Cork Hall	200	120	315	635	4/01/78
Scott Wilkenson	170	120	215	505	11/04/78
John Deflorio	145	120	215	480	4/01/78

123	Chuck Dunbar	445	275	330	1050*	5/06/78
		460*	World Record Squat / 4th Attempt			5/06/78
	David Sprouse	275	190	350	815	11/04/78
	Dave McCune	255	180	340	775	4/01/78
	Mike Sarver	260	175	340	775	6/24/78
	Dave Price	250	185	335	770	4/01/78
	Mike Sarver	230	160	325	715	4/01/78
	Dan Palmateer	200	160	295	655	11/04/78

Chuck Dunbar set a World Record Squat on a 4th Attempt at the 1978 Chattanooga Open and another World Record on the Bench Press at the 1978 Senior Nationals

132	Ron Giarletto	360*	200	455*	1015*	4/01/78
	Ron Giarletto	350	200	440	990	10/07/78
	Ed Canjemi	370	195	420	985	11/04/78
	Mike Sarver	290	185	345	820	10/07/78
	David Conaway	235	200	325	760	11/04/78
	David Conaway	250	175	315	740	4/01/78
	Wayne Anderson	225	150	350	725	4/01/78
	Kenny Harmon	240	180	300	720	4/01/78

* - West Virginia State Powerlifting Record

AR – American Record

WR – World Record

Y – YMCA National Powerlifting Record

e – Elite Powerlifting Classification Total

1978 West Virginia Powerlifter Rankings
WV Powerlifters competing from January 1st, 1978 thru December 31st, 1978
TOP RANKINGS Determined by Total

148 / Name	Squat	Bench Press	Deadlift	Total	Date
Bdywt.					
Paul Sutphin (148 ½)	525*Y	330*	570Y	1425*Y e	12/10/78
Paul Sutphin (148)	520*	325	560	1405* e	11/11/78
Paul Sutphin (148 ¾)	490	325	570	1385* e	11/05/78
Paul Sutphin (148 ½)	479	325*	573*	1377* e	7/08/78
Paul Sutphin (148 ¾)	500*	305	555*	1360* e	5/06/78
Paul Sutphin (146 ¾)	485*	300	550*	1335*	4/01/78
Paul Sutphin (148 ¼)	480	300	540	1320	4/29/78
Paul Sutphin (145)	460	275	515*	1250	1/28/78
Paul Sutphin (146 ½)	455	280	510	1245	2/24/78
Paul Sutphin (145 ¼)	450	260	510*	1220	1/22/78
John Priest	450	270	475	1195	4/01/78
Paul Sutphin (146)	435	285	470	1190	1/14/78
Gene Underwood	350	310	450	1110	1/14/78
John Priest	400	245	425	1070	1/14/78
Tim Hill	360	310*	375	1045	4/01/78
Harry Deitzler	300	270	400	970	4/01/78
Mike Fanary	250	230	435	915	1/14/78
Randy Worley	265	225	400	890	1/14/78
165 Jack Wilson	600*	360	645*	1605* e	12/10/78
Jack Wilson	590*	375*	635	1600* e	4/01/78
Jack Wilson	578	374	639	1592 e	8/25/78
Jack Wilson	578	369	639	1587 e	5/21/78
Jack Wilson	565	350	575	1490 e	1/22/78
Don Hundley	515	265	525	1305	10/07/78
Don Hundley	500	270	530	1300	11/05/78
Gene Underwood	420	340	530	1290	4/01/78
Don Hundley	470	265	465	1200	4/01/78
Okey Clevenger	365	255	510	1130	4/01/78
Matt Herrick	375	250	445	1070	4/01/78
Cary Wilson	325	265	400	990	4/01/78
Michael Fanary	325	225	420	970	4/01/78
Al Anderson	385	195	385	965	4/01/78
Gary Park	320	245	375	940	4/01/78

* - West Virginia State Powerlifting Record   e – Elite Powerlifting Classification Total
m – West Virginia State Master's Powerlifting Record   Y – YMCA National Powerlifting Record

1978 West Virginia Powerlifter Rankings
WV Powerlifters competing from January 1st, 1978 thru December 31st, 1978
TOP RANKINGS Determined by Total

181 / Name	Squat	Bench Press	Deadlift	Total	Date
Bill Kyle	545*	380*	560	1485*	12/10/78
Bill Kyle	530	375	565	1470*	4/01/78
Frank Nicholas	540*	375*	550	1465	4/01/78
Gary Clark	505	375	550	1430	4/01/78
Warren Knight	485	305	580*	1370	2/25/78
Warren Knight	470	305	570*	1345	1/21/78
Don Hall	480	280	540	1300	4/01/78
Dave Jeffrey	450	350	500	1300	6/24/78
Bill Kyle	460	345	490	1295	1/14/78
Don Hall	465	280	505	1250	1/14/78
Ross Smith	460	305	470	1235	10/07/78
Emmett Dalrymple	320	265	400	985	4/01/78
Mike Leikari	295	230	415	940	6/24/78
Bill Blankenship	290 m	270 m	330 m	890 m	5/06/78

198	Squat	Bench Press	Deadlift	Total	Date
Roger Estep	769*	490*	685*	1944* e	12/10/78
WR – World Record Squat & Total for Roger Estep					12/10/78
Roger Estep	740*	470	670*	1880* e	4/01/78
Roger Estep	677	479	672	1829 e	8/26/78
Roger Estep	710 Y	485 Y	620	1815 Y e	1/22/78
Roger Estep	722	446	644	1813 e	5/21/78
Scott Tusic	525	380	530	1435	12/10/78
Scott Tusic	500	390	510	1400	4/01/78
Ross Smith	520	325	500	1345	11/05/78
Robert Hill	475	295	550	1320	4/01/78
Warren Knight	450	320	540	1310	1/14/78
Ross Smith	480	320	500	1300	4/01/78
Jim Sharps	425	325	520	1270	1/14/78
Ross Smith	490	305	460	1255	5/06/78
Dave Snyder	425	310	500	1235	4/01/78
Steve Brooks	420	290	500	1210	4/01/78
Dave Snyder	390	305	455	1150	1/14/78
Dan Hall	425	240	480	1145	4/01/78

* - West Virginia State Powerlifting Record
m – West Virginia State Master's Powerlifting Record
Y – YMCA National Meet Record

WR – World Record
e – Elite Powerlifting Classification Total

1978 West Virginia Powerlifter Rankings
WV Powerlifters competing from January 1st, 1978 thru December 31st, 1978
TOP RANKINGS Determined by Total

220 / Name	Squat	Bench Press	Deadlift	Total	Date
Vince White	570	400	480	1450	4/01/78
Vince White	550	415	480	1445	1/22/78
Bob Hill	510	315	600	1425	11/05/78
Ernie Nagy	507 N	385 N	529 N	1421 N	10/29/78
Ernie Nagy	465	380	500	1345	4/01/78
Bob Hill	440	310	590	1340	10/07/78
Ernie Nagy	500	355	480	1335	4/16/78
Brian Tucker	490	270	500	1260	4/01/78
Ross Smith	470	300	455	1225	1/14/78
Tom Jones	375	295	470	1140	4/01/78
Bill Blankenship	275	240	300	815	1/14/78
242 Herb Fitzsimmons	670*m	425m	680*m	1775*m	5/06/78
Mike Wolf	625	500*	645*	1770*	4/01/78
Herb Fitzsimmons	650*	420	610	1680*	1/22/78
Mike Wolf	590	470 Y	600	1660	1/22/78
Nick Busick	605	410	580	1595	10/07/78
Vince White (Bwt@221)	610	420	470	1500	11/05/78
Vince White	580	400	480	1460	12/10/78
Vince White	560	395	460	1415	2/25/78
Jack Anderson	505	350	555	1410	6/24/78
Vince White	520	410	470	1400	1/14/78
Nick Busick	500	370	500	1370	4/16/78
Vince White	550	360	420	1330	6/10/78
Austin Miller	480	280	450	1210	11/05/78
Austin Miller	455	280	445	1180	10/07/78
Austin Miller	430	290	425	1145	5/06/78
Dan Hall	400	230	450	1080	1/14/78
Austin Miller	390	280	405	1075	4/01/78

* - West Virginia State Powerlifting Record

Y – YMCA National Meet Record

m – West Virginia State Master's Powerlifting Record

N – Master's National Powerlifting Championships

1978 West Virginia Powerlifter Rankings
WV Powerlifters competing from January 1st, 1978 thru December 31st, 1978
TOP RANKINGS Determined by Total

275 / Name	Squat	Bench Press	Deadlift	Total	Date
Herb Fitzsimmons	722*	462 m	683	1868*m	7/09/78
Herb Fitzsimmons	650 m	450 m	700*m	1800*m	4/01/78
Herb Fitzsimmons	655*m	425 m	660*m	1740*m	2/25/78
Herb Fitzsimmons	610	425	650	1685	6/10/78
Jim Goodnight	610	465*	600	1675	4/01/78
Herb Fitzsimmons	580*m	400*m	610*m	1590*m	1/14/78
Jack Anderson	600	350	600	1550	11/05/78
Jeff Cook	490	265	605	1360	12/10/78
Jeff Cook	535	240	575	1350	4/01/78
SHW Luke Iams	821*	573*	578	1973*	7/09/78
Luke Iams	810*	550	585	1945*	5/06/78
Luke Iams	804	556*	551	1912	5/21/78
Luke Iams	750	550*	600	1900*	4/01/78
Luke Iams	805 Y *	535*	520	1860*	1/22/78
Luke Iams	750	550	400	1700	12/10/78
Tim Slamick	560	480	425	1465	4/01/78

* - West Virginia State Powerlifting Record

m – WestVirginia State Master's Powerlifting Record

Chapter Fourteen : 1979 – Part One

The year 1979 may have been the best year in Powerlifting for many in the sport, especially for West Virginia. At the beginning of 1979, West Virginia had Top Ranked Powerlifters, two (2) major Powerlifting Meets held annually (West Virginia State Championships and The Mountianeer Open), and a nationally recognized Powerlifting Team, *Luke's Gym* (a.k.a. "The Wild Bunch"). The Powerlifting Team of *Herb's Gym* included National Masters Powerlifting Champions, Herb Fitzsimmons and Don Hundley. Ernie Nagy *(Nagy's Gym)* was also the National Masters Powerlifting Champion and ranked among the best Powerlifters in the USA for the Masters category.

In 1979, the lifting magazines were filled with results, photos, and explicit reports of the most prestigious and exciting events ever to occur on the platform. In order to publicize the official results of a very large number of Powerlifting competitions in America at the end of 1978, *Powerlifting USA* magazine printed two (2) issues for the month of January, 1979. The advertisements in the pages of *Powerlifting USA* magazine were few but the results and the written reports of the contests were thorough. Lifters at nearly every meet produced record-breaking performances that had become the "norm" for Powerlifting competitions from coast to coast in the U.S.A.

In the February, 1979 issue of *Powerlifting USA,* there was an article titled, *"Paul Sutphin."* The story featured a full, two-page report including a training routine. The article appeared three (3) months after the huge story on Luke Iams and the "Wild Bunch." Also featured in the February, 1979 issue of P/L USA, Paul Sutphin was ranked #8 in *The 100 Best Powerlifters of All-Time as of December 31st, 1978*.

Also listed among *The 100 Best Powerlifters of All-Time,* Herb Fitzsimmons ranked 20th in the 275lb. class and 98th in the SuperHeavyWeight's. Roger Estep was #1 at 198, Luke Iams was #23 among the SuperHeavyWeight's, Chuck Dunbar was #2 at 114, and Jack Wilson was #6 at 165. *Finally, Powerlifting was getting the respect that it deserved and individual achievers in the sport of Powerlifting received the respect that they had earned!*

As the month of February, 1979 drew near, it was time for "Friday Night Powerlifting" once again ; the North Carolina Connection : Part VI. The <u>1979 Southern Open Powerlifting Championships</u> were conducted at the Downtown Holiday Inn in Raleigh, North Carolina on the weekend of 2/23/79. At a bodyweight of 148 ¾, I took on Clyde Wright and came up short, even though I made a PR Total of 1435, 6th of All-Time among U.S.A. Lightweight Powerlifters.

Vince White, competing in the 220lb. class at the 1979 Southern Open Powerlifting Championships Totaled 1380 with a 600 Squat. Herb Fitzsimmons won easily in the 275lb. class with a Squat of 725, Bench Press of 420, and a Deadlift of 680 for the winning Total of 1825 at the 1979 Southern Open.

4th Annual WV State Powerlifting Championships

The <u>1979 West Virginia State Powerlifting Championships</u> were held on Sunday April 1st, 1979 in New Martinsville, West Virginia under the direction of West Virginia State Powerlifting Chairman, Luke Iams. A Meet Program for the 1979 West Virginia States, supported by advertisers and sponsors, included the West Virginia State Powerlifting Records and the names of all lifters entered in the contest. A record number of fifty-one (51) lifters competed at the 1979 West Virginia State Powerlifting Championships.

Thanks to Ron Giarletto, a well written and thorough report of the 1979 West Virginia State Powerlifting Championships appeared in the May/1979 issue of *Powerlifting USA* magazine. Accompanying the article in the pages of P/L USA were photos of Luke Iams, Herb Fitzsimmons, and Chuck Dunbar.

Unfortunately, we were not able to set official World Records at the 1979 West Virginia State Powerlifting Championships. At 114, Chuck Dunbar made an easy 480 Squat and 295 Bench Press, both unofficial World Records. However, Dunbar's 1135 Total was a new <u>Official</u> American Record. Chuck Dunbar's Total of 1135 exceeded the minimum standards for ELITE Classification in the 114lb. class by over seventy (70) pounds.

The four (4) tiered strategy for Paul Sutphin at New Martinsville on Sunday April 1st, 1979 included :

a.) An official Total to win the 1979 West Virginia State Powerlifting Championships in the 148lb. class.
b.) A PR Total "greater than or equal to" 1440lbs.
c.) Break at least one (1) new West Virginia State Powerlifting Record
d.) Win the Best Deadlift Award (Swartz Formula) for the first session at the 1979 West Virginia State Powerlifting Championships

Since returning home from the *1979 Southern Open*, I had my sights set on a 600 Deadlift with a plan to achieve the goal, 2.5 kilos at a time. After weighing-in at a bodyweight of exactly 148lbs. on 4/01/79, I finished Squats with a West Virginia State Record of 535lbs. and Benched Pressed 320lbs. Following a first place victory with a PR and State Record Total of 1445 along with a PR/State Record Deadlift of 590, all four (4) goals were accomplished. The 590 Deadlift captured the Best Deadlift Award for the first session of the contest, determined by Swartz Formula.

Don Hundley Totaled 1335 in the 165lb. class on 4/01/79 to win his very first West Virginia State Powerlifting Championship. Dave Jeffrey won the 181lb. class with a West Virginia State Record Total of 1500. The 1500 Total by Dave Jeffrey on 4/01/79 included a West Virginia State Record of 400lbs. in the Bench Press. Frank Nicholas finished 2nd in the 181lb. class with a 1480 Total which included a West Virginia State Record Squat of 560lbs. in the 181lb. class.

Scott Tusic won first place while competing in the 198lb. class. Scott Tusic's winning Total of 1550 in the 198's on 4/01/79 included a 420 Bench Press. Scott's Bench Press of 420lbs. later earned the #32 spot in the P/L USA TOP 100 198's.

Mike Wolf won the 1979 West Virginia State Powerlifting title in the 220lb. class over Ernie Nagy and Charleston's Bob Hill. Mike Wolf was a very strong Bencher, especially in the late 1970's, as he finished with a new West Virginia State Record of 490 to complement his 630 Squat and 660 Deadlift, Totaling an impressive 1780. Mike Wolf's Squat, Deadlift, and Total on 4/01/79 were also new West Virginia State Powerlifting Records in the 220lb. class.

How good was Mike Wolf ? Only four (4) lifters : 1) Mike MacDonald 2) Larry Pacifico 3) Rich Keller 4) Jack Sideris were ranked ahead of Mike Wolf in the Bench Press among the TOP 100 220's. In reference to the P/L USA JUL/79 issue, the TOP 100 220's (Powerlifters competing from July, 1978 through June, 1979), Mike Wolf was tied in the ranking with Jack Sideris for the 4th spot with his 490lb. Bench Press.

On April 1st, 1979 Ernie Nagy was fifty-six (56) years young on the day he Totaled a solid 1455 in the 220lb. class. Ernie Nagy's lifts on 4/01/79 included a Squat of 540, a 385 Bench Press, and a 530 Deadlift. Bob Hill, lifting for *Herb's Gym*, pulled 605 on the Deadlift, Totaled 1445, and placed 3rd in the 220's on 4/01/79 while Nick Busick won the 242lb. class.

In the 275lb. class, it was all Herb Fitzsimmons at the 1979 West Virginia State Powerlifting Championships. On 4/01/79 Herb Totaled a whopping 1920 that included lifts of 740 Squat, 450 Bench Press, and a 730 Deadlift! In the article printed in P/L USA, Ron Giarletto emphasized the fact that Herb was forty-six (46) years old and made reference to Fitzsimmons' lifts as "unbelievable."

The SEP/79 issue of P/L USA featured the TOP 100 for the 275lb. weight class. Based on Herb Fitzsimmons' performance on 4/01/79, Herb's 740 Squat and 1920 Total were ranked 10th. Herb Fitzsimmons Deadlifted 740 three (3) weeks after 4/01/79 in Chattanooga, Tennessee and finished with a ranking of 7th for the TOP 100 Deadlifters in the USA!

Elite Total – Luke Iams

In the Superheavyweight class at the 1979 West Virginia State Powerlifting Championships, Luke Iams won his 4th consecutive West Virginia State Powerlifting Championship and officially Totaled Elite for the first time! Luke's Total of 2080 on 4/01/79 exceeded the minimum requirement for SuperHeavyWeight Elite status by 47lbs. (2088 versus the minimum requirement of 2033). Although Luke missed a 625 Deadlift, which would have given him an even 2100, his 875 Squat, 600 Bench Press, and the 605 Deadlift comprised an impressive Total of 2080, which proved to be his finest hour.

On April 1st, 1979, Luke Iams became the first West Virginian to officially Bench Press 600lbs! Luke's Bench Press of 600 on 4/01/79 was a new West Virginia State Bench Press Record which ranked number two (2) in the Powerlifting USA Top 100 Superheavyweights from October, 1978 through September, 1979. In the same TOP 100 USA Superheavyweight Powerlifters published in the October, 1979 issue of *Powerlifting USA* magazine, the 875 Squat of Luke Iams was ranked number four (4), and Luke's Elite Total of 2080 ranked number six (6).   *Powerlifting USA / October, 1979 Vol. 3, No. 3.*

Even though the members of *Luke's Gym* and the "Wild Bunch" were minus two (2) lifters (Jack Wilson and Roger Estep) from the previous year, the 1979 West Virginia State Powerlifting Championship Team Trophy was again won by *Luke's Gym.* From the fifty-one (51) lifters who entered the 1979 West Virginia State Powerlifting Championships, eleven (11) of the lifters represented *Luke's Gym.* Other teams competing at the 1979 West Virginia State Powerlifting Championships were : *Herb's Gym* of St. Albans, *Nagy's Gym* of Weirton, *Mountaineer Barbell Club* of Parkersburg, *Slamick's Gym* of Fairmont, *Doug's Gym, Fred's Gym,* and the *Presque Isle Powermen.*

Competing as a lightweight and in the first session of lifting, I often had the privilege of being "one of the last men standing" following the Deadlifts. It was standing room only at the 1979 West Virginia State Powerlifting Championships in New Martinsville with spectators crowded into the gymnasium of Magnolia High School. The contest was one of those events which began early in the morning and over at a late hour in the evening. In spite of the fact that we were all competitors, competing for Powerlifting championships, records, and awards, we possessed a mutual respect and admiration for our opponents and each other. We were not just lifters...we had become a family!

1979 West Virginia State Powerlifting Championships
Held Sunday April 1, 1979
Magnolia High School
New Martinsville, West Virginia

Wt. Class/Name	Squat	Bench	Deadlift	Total
114 ½				
Chuck Dunbar	480*	295*	360	1135*
Scott McCune	215	140	270	625
Scott Wilkinson	170	125	215	510
Joan Fruth *Female Athlete*	205	75	215	495
123 ½				
Dave Sprouse	310	220	340	870
Cork Hall	295	150	380	825
132 ¼				
Ron Giarletto	340	215	430	985
Dave Conway	345	215	390	950
148 ¾				
Paul Sutphin	535*	320	590*	1445*
Laney Simone	425	240	490	1155
David Hall	400	265	425	1090
Wayne Anderson	395	200	470	1065
Mike Sarver	350	210	420	980
Chris Hindman	320	185	350	855
165 ¼				
Don Hundley	525	260	550	1335
Dana Bee	445	365	500	1310
Gene Underwood	450	325	535	1310
J. Kilbane	400	230	445	1075
Cary Wilson	375	275	420	1070
Randy Whorley	315	255	375	945
Raymond Hackett	285	200	375	860

* Indicates <u>New</u> Official State Record

Wt. Class/Name	Squat	Bench	Deadlift	Total
181 ¾				
Dave Jeffrey	550	400*	550	1500*
Frank Nicholas	560*	390	530	1480
Don Hall	500	290	535	1325
Jeff Bara	315	295	450	1060
198 ¼				
Scott Tusic	560	420	570	1550
Gary Clark	560	400	555	1515
Ross Smith	540	370	510	1420
Earl Snider	450	335	575	1360
Dan Hall	475	250	545	1270
George McLaughlin	430	340	500	1270
Al Anderson	485	275	510	1270
Russ Stump	370	300	470	1140
Terry Phillips	350	260	400	1010
220 ½				
Mike Wolf	630*	490*	660*	1780*
Ernie Nagy	540	385	530	1455
Bob Hill	520	320	605	1445
Warren Knight	490	345	590	1425
Steve Wilkinson	500	340	525	1365
Dave Snyder	430	310	470	1210
242 ½				
Nick Busick	615	425	600	1640
Jack Anderson	625	375	600	1600
Scott Warman	530	405	665	1600
Austin Miller	470	300	480	1250
275 ½				
Herb Fitzsimmons	740*	450	730*	1920*
Jim Goodnight	685	500*	670	1855
Jeff Cook	490	275	640	1405

* Indicates <u>New</u> Official State Record

Wt. Class/Name	Squat	Bench	Deadlift	Total
Super Hvywt.				
Luke Iams	875*	600*	605	2080*
Tim Slamick	610	430	530	1570
Charles Roberts	425	270	420	1115

Outstanding Lifter 1st Session : Chuck Dunbar
Outstanding Lifter 1st Session : Luke Iams
Best Squat : Chuck Dunbar
Best Bench Press : Luke Iams
Best Deadlift : Paul Sutphin

* Indicates New Official State Record

Herb Fitzsimmons – 1920 Total!

Another chapter in the Tennessee Connection : Part VIII for West Virginia Powerlifting took place at the 1979 Chattanooga Open. The <u>1979 Chattanooga Open Powerlifting Championships</u> were held on April 21st, 1979. Following the 1979 West Virginia States, Herb Fitzsimmons planned to Total between 1900 and 1950 at the 1979 Chattanooga Open.

On 4/21/79 at the <u>1979 Chattanooga Open Powerlifting Championships</u>, Herb Fitzsimmons demonstrated resounding consistency with another 1920 Total in the 275lb. class. Herb Squatted with 730, Bench Pressed 450, and Deadlifted 740! For Herb Fitzsimmons, most of his lifts in the 275lb. class were pending Master's World Records!

In the Spring of 1979, other West Virginia Powerlifters were competing elsewhere in the country and the world. Ernie Nagy turned in a very impressive performance at the 1979 Jerrold Blum Open Powerlifting Championships while Chuck Dunbar <u>Officially</u> broke two (2) World Records with a 479 Squat and a 297 Bench Press on May 4th, 1979 in Hawaii. Although Chuck Dunbar placed 2nd to Japan's Hideaki Inaba on 5/04/79 at the International Powerlifting event, Dunbar's Total in Hawaii was 1140, about ten (10) times bodyweight and seventy-six (76) pounds over the minimum requirement for Elite Classification in the 114lb. class. *Powerlifting USA / May, 1979 Vol. 2, No. 11*

Elite at 165

In a quest to lift heavier poundages, I made the decision to compete in the 165lb. class at the 1979 Chattanooga Open and Total over 1500. At a bodyweight of 165 ¼ (the limit for a Middleweight), I Totaled 1505 with PR's on all lifts : 560 Squat, 350 Bench Press, and a 595 Deadlift. The Total marked the first time I exceeded the 1500lb. barrier which represented 165lb. class Elite Classification prior to 1978. The Total of 1505 was 60lbs. greater than the Total mark set at the West Virginia States twenty (20) days earlier. Following the 1979 Chattanooga Open, the short-term goal was to return to the 148lb. class and repeat the Total of 1505lbs. ; a tough task linked to realistic ambitions.

On Saturday May 5th, 1979 I "put it on the line" again at the <u>Roanoke Valley Open Powerlifting Championships</u> in Roanoke, Virginia. The 1979 Roanoke Open was "Virginia Connection" : Part VI for West Virginia Powerlifting. While making a Squat of 540 and a Bench Press of 345, the Deadlift of 600 was a PR (Personal Record)! Lifting in the 165lb. class, the Elite Total of 1485 was good for 2nd Place while competing against my friend, the North Carolina State Champion, Lloyd Wehunt. Lloyd Wehunt was later inducted into the North Carolina Powerlifting Hall of Fame.

Powerlifting USA / June, 1979 Vol. 2, No. 12

Even though I was not happy with the 2nd Place finish at the 1979 Roanoke Open, the Total of 1485 marked the 2nd time in two (2) weeks that I had achieved Elite Powerlifter Classification in the 165lb. class and, for the first time, made the big 600 Deadlift in official Powerlifting competition. However, what I perceived as a lack-luster performance on May 5th, 1979 prompted me to consider the fact that I should contact Joe Zarella, National Powerlifting Chairman, and rescind my application to be selected to compete in the upcoming North American Powerlifting Championships. Instead, my plan would be to concentrate on returning to the Lightweight division (LW – 148lb. class) and win the Junior Nationals scheduled for July 14th and 15th, 1979 at Los Angeles, California.

As the events during the week of May 7th, 1979 unfolded, I did not have to call Joe Zarella. Instead, Joe telephoned me with the long awaited information stating, "Paul, you have been selected to represent the U.S. Team at the North Americans in the 148lb. class." I replied by presenting Joe with a case scenario of bodyweight, circumstances, etc. Given the facts, I told Joe, "I believe I should respectfully decline the opportunity."

Conversely, Joe Zarella's reply was one of encouragement. Joe's instructions were, "Come with the team and lift in the 165lb. class." So, from that moment on, I was excited about the trip to Canada, even though I was aware of the fact I probably would not win first place as a Middleweight. But, knowing that Herb Fitzsimmons was chosen for the 275lb. class and that Louie Simmons was selected for the 220's, the stage was set for outstanding lifting in Canada on 5/26/79!

The strategy for the 1979 North American Powerlifting Championships was to go "9-for-9" and score valuable placement points for Team U.S.A. Hopefully, the points I would score as a Middleweight would enable us to win a victory over a very tough Canadian Powerlifting Team. On May 25th, 1979 Herb Fitzsimmons and I boarded a flight out of Charleston, West Virginia to Buffalo, New York enroute to Toronto, Canada. The uncertainty of flight reservations, due to a labor dispute among airline personnel, made the situation most interesting.

Herb Fitzsimmons : North American Champion!

The <u>1979 North American Powerlifting Championships</u> were conducted in Hamilton, Ontario, Canada on May 26th, 1979. There were eleven (11) Canadians and eleven (11) members of the U.S.A. Team, making the total number of lifters for the prestigious event at twenty-two (22). Dr. Mauro DiPasquale impressed me as he methodically and strategically beat my partner and competitor, Jack Wilson with a "do-or-die" last attempt Deadlift at 644lbs.! Jack was the defending Champion for the North American Championship event.

Herb Fitzsimmons lifted all alone in the 275's on May 26th, 1979. Herb's Total of 1862 (845 kilos) at the *1979 North American Powerlifting Championships* was the highest Total of the contest. On 5/26/79, Herb Fitzsimmons Squatted 705lbs., Bench Pressed 451lbs., and Deadlifted 705 to become the 1979 North American Powerlifting Champion.

Basically, when I decided to make the trip to the 1979 North American Powerlifting Championships and lift at 165 rather than 148, I was just "along for the ride," even though I posted a PR Total of 1510. At a bodyweight of 163lbs., I made PR's on the Squat, Bench Press, and Total. Lifting in the 165lb. class, the PR Total consisted of a 567 ½ lb. Squat (257.5 kilos), 352 Bench Press (160 kilos), 589 Deadlift (267.5 kilos), for another Elite Total of 1510 (685 kilos).

The 1979 North American Powerlifting Championships in Canada marked the third time I exceeded a Total of Elite at 165 in less than six (6) weeks. The team points that I won by capturing the bronze in the Middleweight class scored valuable points to put the U.S.A. Team "over the top," and enabled us to defeat a very talented and competitive Canadian Powerlifting Team. The USA Team defeated the Canadian Team 116 points to 112 points. So, as an overweight 148lb'er, *I took one for the Team!*

The man with the plan at the 1979 North American Powerlifting Championships was Dr. Fred Hatfield. Fred easily Totaled 1835 at 181 to win the Gold over Canada's Tom Campbell who put together 1758! In summary of the 1979 North American Powerlifting Championships, Louie Simmons easily won the 220's and Dave Keagy was all alone in the SHW (SuperHeavyWeight) class. Jerry Welcher made the trip with Joe Zarella and was the official Coach for the 1979 U.S.A. North American Powerlifting Team.

Chapter Fifteen : 1979 – Part Two

After the *1979 North American Powerlifting Championships*, I was determined that things would turnout different in California and that I would not be denied! My theory was that I had been out-lifted on three (3) specific days at three (3) specific meets by the same number of people in the 165lb. class. If those individuals were going to beat me again, they would have to do what I knew that I could do and what they could not do....*reduce to the 148lb. class and take me on!*

For a Powerlifter, from 1965 through 1978, winning the Junior Nationals was one of the most prestigious victories in the sport of Powerlifting because you could only win once! After a lifter won 1st Place at the Junior Nationals, he could never enter the event again. I was the only representative for all of the Powerlifting Teams in West Virginia Powerlifting at the Nationals in Los Angeles, California on July 14th, 1979. Luke Iams, the 1978 Champion, and Chuck Dunbar, the 1976 Champion, were both ineligible and Herb Fitzsimmons elected not to make the trip. The mission statement : *"No way was I going to travel to the West Coast and lose!"*

The 1979 Junior National Powerlifting Championships were held on July 14th and 15th, 1979 in Los Angeles / Inglewood, California. The official lifting results from the 1979 Junior National Powerlifting Championships represented eighty-five (85) lifters, yet there were 101 lifters listed in the Official Meet Program which cost $1.00. The Meet Director was Glenn Maur of the *Atlantis Athletic Club*.

The lifting venue for the 1979 Junior National Powerlifting Championships was at Loyola Marymount College in Los Angeles, California. Among other things, the official Meet Program contained printed results from all of the previous Junior National Powerlifting Championships, from 1965 through 1978. In the November, 1978 issue of *Powerlifting USA*, an "Open Letter" was published by Meet Director Glen Maur seeking the input from Powerlifters in regard to what they wanted to see in a National contest. As a result, the contest was first class!

When I arrived at the lifting venue on July 14th, someone asked me "Paul, what do you plan to Total?" I replied "Whatever it takes!" That is exactly what happened, nothing more – nothing less! My lifts were 247.5 kilo Squat (545lbs.), 155 kilo Bench Press (341lbs.), 270 kilo Deadlift (595lbs.) for a Total of 672.5 kilos (1482lbs.)! A poundage of 2.5 kilos less on any one of the three lifts would've reduced the required weight that Troy Hicks, the 148lb.World Record Holder in the Deadlift, would have needed to pull to become the 1979 Lightweight Powerlifting Champion.

1979 National Powerlifting Champion!
Junior National Championship Total Record!

On Saturday morning at the official weigh-in for the 1979 Junior National Powerlifting Championships, I weighed 66.8 kilos which converts to 147.26728 pounds. The 1482 Total represented a Total of almost 10lbs. over ten (10) times bodyweight and a _new (Jr.) NATIONAL TOTAL RECORD in the 148lb. class, exceeding the previous Total Record set by John Orsini one year earlier by 15 kilos (33lbs)!_ The 1482 Total Record set by Paul Sutphin in 1979 was not broken until the 1983 Junior Nationals at Charlottesville, Virginia by the Powerlifting legend, Danny Austin.

"Most everyone familiar with the 1978 and 1979 Powerlifting scene in the 148lb. class knew that the battle for the 1979 Junior National title would most likely come down to Paul Sutphin and Troy Hicks, the Lightweight Deadlift World Record Holder."

Iron Man magazine, Volume 39, No. 1 / November, 1979

Unlike the Round System of today, in the System of Rotation, you could "wait your opponent out." Troy Hicks finished with 518 on Squat and missed 529. I sat deep with 534 and again on the 2nd attempt of 545. Unfortunately, an effort to break Rickey Crain's National Squat Record with a 3rd attempt of 556lbs. (252.5 kilos) would not go. Troy Benched 308 on a 2nd attempt before missing 314. I took my first attempt Bench Press with 325, then Benched 336, and finished with a PR Bench Press of 155 kilos (341 lbs.). With a Sub-Total lead of 25 kilos and a bodyweight advantage of 66.8 kilos for Sutphin versus 66.9 kilos for Hicks, I opened the Deadlifts and made a solid pull of 595lbs. I missed a 2nd attempt at 606lbs. and passed on the 3rd attempt.

As I watched from "the sidelines" at the 1979 Junior Nationals, Troy Hicks easily pulled an opening attempt Deadlift of 628lbs.! Troy then called for 300 kilos, a new World Record attempt (the 661lbs. needed for the win) and pulled it above his knees before losing his grip. Troy was unsuccessful with the same weight on his 3rd. I won the Outstanding Lifter Award at the 1979 Junior Nationals and Troy Hicks returned to the 1980 Nationals as a 165lb'er and won the title.

While Troy Hicks and Paul Sutphin were battling for the 1979 Junior National Championship title, Armington Rafael and Roger Gorumba were engaged in a classic battle for the American Bench Press Record in the 148lb. class. Rafael finished with 385 while Gorumba made his 3rd attempt of 407 ¾ and a 4th Attempt of 187.5 kilos that actually weighed out at 410lbs! Armington Rafael Totaled 607.5 kilos (1339) while Roger Gorumba Totaled 605 kilos (1333) and finished with the American Bench Press Record in the 148lb. class with a lift of 410lbs.

*Source : Iron Man magazine, Volume 39, No. 1 / November, 1979*

For the return trip back East, I boarded an airplane in Los Angeles after midnight (Pacific Time Zone) on July 16th, 1979. John Florio along with a few others from Ohio were on board the flight during the early morning hours across the USA. After a brief landing in Cleveland, Ohio the flight to Charleston, West Virginia took less than one (1) hour.

When I arrived at the airport in Charleston, West Virginia on the morning of 7/16/79, I received a "Happy 25th Birthday" greeting from Vince White. Vince drove me directly to the *Charleston Daily Mail* headquarters for a scheduled appointment with a noted Sportswriter. A feature story was published on Wednesday July 18th, 1979 headlined, *"Bluefield Native Sets Records"* and *"Paul Sutphin... Could Pinch Hit for Atlas."*

1979 vs. 2009

To win at Powerlifting, a carefully planned stategy counts. After a Sub-Total from the Squat and the Bench Press comes the Deadlift. No truer words were spoken when uttered by someone, "The contest don't start til' the bar hits the floor!" So, how about the Deadlifts in 2009 versus the Deadlifts of 1979?

While implementing an educational, learning strategy of "Compare and Contrast," review the TOP TEN (10) Deadlifts from the Powerlifting U.S.A. TOP 100 148lb. class listing of 2009 and 2010 and compare the 1979 TOP TEN (10) 148lb. Powerlifters to the 2009 and 2010 listings. The TOP 100 148lb. Powerlifters published in the JAN/2009 issue of Powerlifting USA magazine listed 622 in the #1 spot for the Deadlift among 148lb. Powerlifters : The TOP 100 148lb. Powerlifters published in the FEB/1980 issue of Powerlifting USA *had 645 in the #1 spot.*

The P/L USA TOP 100 (2009) Rankings for 148lb. class Powerlifters included 148lb. Powerlifters who competed from November, 2007 through October, 2008. The 2009 LW 148lb. Deadlift rankings (#1 thru #10 respectively) : #1-622, #2-600, #3-584, #4-576, #5-562, #6-556, #7-540, #8-535, #9-535, and #10-535. The TOP 100 148lb. Powerlifters published in the JAN/2010 issue of Powerlifting USA again had the poundage of 622 in the #1 spot for the Deadlift among 148lb. Powerlifters. The TOP TEN (10) 148lb. Deadlifts for 148lb. Powerlifters who competed from November, 2008 through October, 2009 (#1 thru #10) : #1-622, #2-600, #3-567, #4-556, #5-551, #6-551, #7-551, #8-545, #9-540, and #10-534.

The TOP TEN (10) 148lb. Deadlifts for 148lb. Powerlifters who competed from January, 1979 through December, 1979 included Rickey Crain, Troy Hicks, and Paul Sutphin among others. The TOP 100 148lb. Powerlifters published in the FEB/1980 issue of Powerlifting USA *had 645 in the #1 spot*. The <u>1979 Rankings</u> (#1 thru #10 respectively) were : # 1 – 645 (Rick Crain), #2-644(Troy Hicks), #3-630, #4-610, #5-606, #6-600, #7-600, <u>#8-595 (Paul Sutphin)</u>, #9-595, and #10-580. In summation, the Deadlift training of 1979 = 'S' for Superior!

National Powerlifting Championships
TOP TEN (10) Performance RANKINGS (1965 thru 1979)

114 / Name	Squat	Bench Press	Deadlift	Total	Year
Doug Heath	308	220	424*	953*	1978 W
Joe Steinfield	347	242	358	947	1979 W
Mike Sauers	270	270	363	903	1979
B. Schlegel	325	175	390	890*	1977 W
Ernesto Milian	305*	190	390*	885*	1975 W
Mike Hunnicut	286	242	352	881	1979
Joe Steinfield	281	248	347	876	1978
Chuck Dunbar	345*	230*	280	855	1976 W
Mark Shijo	308	170	374	854	1979
Kevin Meskew	270	187	391	848	1978
123 Dave Moyer	455*	245*	450**	1150*	1965 W
John Redding	440	215	460*	1115	1972 W
Nicholas DeSantis	396	264	440	1102	1978 W
Lee Mumford	457*	275	352	1085	1979 W
Bob Lech	395	255	430	1080	1976 W
Mike Gant	402	248	430	1080	1979
Vince Tolisano	363	275	424	1063	1979
J. Nunez	330	285**	440	1055	1977 W
Gerri Ringi	345	280*	425	1050	1971 W
Monte Mason	385	236	424	1047	1979
132 Ray Verdonck	485*	292	462	1240*	1979 W
Joe Grosson	468*	292	473	1234*	1978 W
Leroy Mabie	400	300	500	1200*	1974 W
Mike Wonyette	429	264	501	1196	1979
Ernest Thayer	385	315*	485	1185*	1973 W
B. Haar	418	303	457	1179	1978
B. Benoit	400	260	510*	1170	1973
Bob Luna	402	314	451	1168	1978
Ian Burgess	385	275	505*	1165*	1971 W
Bob Luna	396	303	462	1162	1979

* Junior National Meet Record   **American Record   W – Winner

National Powerlifting Championships
TOP TEN (10) Performance RANKINGS (1965 thru 1979)

148 / Name	Squat	Bench Press	Deadlift	Total	Year
BW					
Paul Sutphin (147.3)	545	341	595	1482*	1979 W
Troy Hicks	518	308	628*	1455*	1979 2nd
John Orsini	523	347	578	1449*	1978 W
Mike Bridges	515	380*	550	1445*	1977 W
Rickey Crain	550**	310	555	1415*	1975 W
Paul Sutphin	479	325	573	1377	1978 2nd
Dave Kinley	501	358	518	1377	1979 3rd
Mike Elliott	540	303	523	1366	1978
Danny Thompson	501	341	518	1361	1978
Jay Rociglione	512	314	534	1361	1979 4th
Roger Wright	512	303	545	1361	1979 5th
Armington Rafael	451	385	501	1339	1979 6th
Roger Gorumba	451	407	473	1333	1979 7th
		413(actual weight 410)** AR Bench Press!			
165 Paul Aston	567	424	600 ¾	1592*	1979 W
Bill Ellis	606	374	600 ¾	1581	1979 2nd
Byron Wadie	600 ¾	336	633	1570	1978 W
Roger Bell	551	347	622	1521	1978
Ted Mossbarger	556	352	611	1521	1978
Larry Stone	570	370*	570	1510*	1977 W
Mike Zeilinski	595	325	589	1510	1978
George Crawford	605*	350	550	1505*	1971 W
Lloyd Wehunt	534	363	606	1504	1978
Mike Roy	611*	363	529	1504	1979 3rd
181 Dean Becker	633	385	688*	1708*	1979 W
Dennis Wright	650*	440	575	1665*	1974 W
Jim Grudzien	573	413	661	1647*	1978 W
Gary Sanger	584	418	617	1620	1978
Ted Mossbarger	600 ¾	374	633	1609	1979
Martin Joyce	550	355	685*	1590	1976 W
J. Dignan	580	360	650	1590	1976
Paul Woods	525	430	630	1585*	1972 W
Martin Joyce	550	360	675	1585	1972
B. Weber	525	430	630	1585	1974

* Junior National Meet Record   **American Record   W – Winner

National Powerlifting Championships
TOP TEN (10) Performance RANKINGS (1965 thru 1979)

198 / Name	Squat	Bench Press	Deadlift	Total	Year
Jim Cash	661	402	749*	1813*	1978 W
Sam Mangialardi	710*	407	688	1807	1978
Keith Boyer	639	440	677	1758	1979 W
Fred Hatfield	650	407	694	1752	1978
Steve Miller	625	465*	640	1730*	1977 W
Keith Boyer	589	440	683	1714	1978
L. Russell	625	430	655	1710*	1974 W
John Needham	606	446	655	1708	1978
Ed Ravenscroft	625*	460	620	1705*	1973 W
Larry Pacifico	610*	460*	630	1700*	1969 W
Rich Woods	600 ¾	468*	628	1697	1979
220 Dennis Reed	733*	418	733*	1884*	1978 W
Jack Sideris	699	473	688	1862	1978
Danny Moraetes	705	435	699	1840	1979 W
Steve Wilson	640	460	715*	1815*	1977 W
John Florio	705	418	683	1807	1979
Richard Keller	620	485*	675	1780	1977
Danny Moreates	655	440	672	1769	1978
Charlie Perkins	617	446	699	1763	1978
Richard Keller	628	512*	622	1763	1978
Charlie Perkins	611	457	672	1741	1979
242 Hollie Evett	700*	480	725*	1905*	1977 W
R. Scott	670*	510*	700	1880*	1971 W
Mark Dimiduk	716	479	683	1879	1979 W
Ernie Steinkirchner	677 ¾	501	672	1851	1978 W
Randy Wilson	688	462	699	1851	1979
Joe Free	672	457	710	1840	1979
Mike MacDonald	655	540*	640	1835	1972 W
Larry Plumlee	677 ¾	468	677 ¾	1824	1978
Terry McCormick	655	470	690	1815	1973 W
Tom Paulucci	661	462	683	1807	1978
Dan Wohleber	788*	220	733*	1741	1979

* Junior National Meet Record   **American Record   W – Winner

National Powerlifting Championships
TOP TEN (10) Performance RANKINGS (1965 thru 1979)

275_ Name	Squat	Bench Press	Deadlift	Total	Year
Dave Shaw	722 ¾	523	793	2039*	1979 W
		4th Attempt	807*		1979
Bill Kazmaier	749	512	771*	2033*	1978 W
Dave Shaw	760*	507	760	2028	1978
Bennett Clayton	727	485	744	1956	1978
Tom Hardman	677	573*	699	1951	1979
Tom Hardman	622	556*	705	1884	1978
Doug Patterson	716	446	710	1873	1979
Herb Fitzsimmons	722	462	683	1868	1978
Barry Groves	699	490	655	1846	1978
John Hawbaker	699	479	633	1813	1978
(SuperHeavyweights)					
Don Reinhoudt	900*	560*	780*	2240*	1973 W
Doyle Kenady	805	515	730	2050	1974 W
Paul Wrenn	840	440	730	2010	1975 W
Dave Keaggy	771	473	738	1984	1979 W
Luke Iams	821	573	578	1973	1978 W
G. Roberson	730*	505*	735*	1970*	1966 W
T. Smith	700	510	730	1940	1975
T. Smith	700	510	730	1940	1976 W
Russ Fletcher	740*	435	760*	1935	1969 W
Wayne Bouvier	700	530	660	1890	1975

* Junior National Meet Record   **American Record   W – Winner

Training Log #3
Paul Sutphin Workouts

[Actual workouts from the 1979 Roanoke Open (5/05/79) to the 1979 National (Junior) Powerlifting Championships in Los Angeles, California (7/14/79)]

Saturday May 05, 1979
Roanoke Valley Open Powerlifting Contest
@ Roanoke, VA

1. Squat – 540
2. Bench Press – 345
3. Deadlift – 600

TOTAL – 1485 @ 165lb. Bodyweight

Wednesday 5/09/79
1. Squats – 181 ¼ x 5, 253 ½ x 5, 330 ½ x 5, 407 ¾ x 5, 407 ¾ x 5.
   Percentage of Squat max at 570.
2. Bench Press – 132 ¾ x 7, 220 ¼ x 5, 270 x 5, 270 x 5, 270 x 5, 270 x 5, 270 x 5.
   Percentage of Bench Press max at 355.

Saturday 5/12/79
1. Bench Press – 180 x 6, 230 x 5, 250 x 5, 300 x 1, 360 x 1,
   missed 370, 250 x 5, 250 x 5, missed 375, missed 380, missed 380, 250 x 5.
2. Incline Bench Press (shoulder width grip) – 135 x 5, 180 x 5, 200 x 5, 210 x 5,
   220 x 5.
3. Dead Stop Bench Press (5 second pause) 280 x 1, missed 310, missed 310.
4. Standing Triceps Presses (EZ Bar / Close-Grip) 65 x 6, 95 x 6, 115 x 6.
5. Cheating Curls (EZ Bar w/Close Grip) – 115 x 5, 135 x 5, 150 x 5, 160 x 5.

Sunday 5/13/79
1. Squats – 180 x 5, 260 x 5, 330 x 5, 400 x 5, 430 x 5.
2. ¼ Squats – 585 x 4, 635 x 3, 635 x 3, 685 x 3, 685 x 3, 685 x 3.

Monday 5/14/79
1. Power Rack Deadlifts (Conventional Style)
   (5-inches below top of knee) – 225 x 5, 335 x 4, 445 x 3, 515 x 3, 515 x 3.
2. Power Rack Deadlifts
   (5-inches below top of knee)(Wide Stance) – 555 x 3, 605 x 3, missed 650, 650 x 1, 650 x 3, 625 x 5.
3. Bench Press – 135 x 7, 230 x 5, 285 x 5, 285 x 4 (missed 5th rep).

Wednesday 5/16/79 - Squats – 260 x 10, 330 x 5, 400 x 4, 450 x 3, 330 x 10.

Saturday 5/19/79 – Seated Presses – 135 x 5, 185 x 3, 200 x 2, 200 x 2, 200 x 2, 200 x 2.

Sunday 5/20/79
1. Squats (Knee Wraps) – 290 x 5, 380 x 4, 440 x 3, 480 x 2.
2. Bench Press – 180 x 6, 230 x 4, 280 x 3, 320 x 1, 330 x 1.

Monday 5/21/79 Deadlifts (Floor) (Conventional Style) – 180 x 10, 320 x 10, 465 x 7.

Wednesday 5/23/79
1. Seated Press – 180 x 4, 210 x 2.
2. Bench Press – 180 x 5, 205 x 4, 250 x 3, 280 x 2, 280 x 2, 280 x 2, 280 x 2.
3. Incline Benches – 135 x 5, 185 x 3, 185 x 3.

Travel to Hamilton, Ontario – Canada
1979 North American Powerlifting Championships

Saturday May 26, 1979
North American Powerlifting Championships
@ Hamilton, Ontario – CANADA

Squat – 567lbs. (257.5 Kilos)
Bench Press – 352lbs. (160 Kilos)
Deadlift – 589lbs. (267.5 Kilos)

Placed 3rd (Bronze Medal) in the 165lb. (75 Kilo) Class

TOTAL – 1510lbs. (685 Kilos)
163.14 pounds. (74 Kilos) Bodyweight

Sunday 6/03/79 – Bench Press – 135 x 8, 225 x 5, 300 x 2.

Wednesday 6/06/79 @ Herb's Gym in St. Albans, West Virginia
1. Deadlifts (Floor) (Conventional Style) – 245 x 10, 425 x 8, 429 x 10.
2. Squats – 225 x 3,. 405 x 1.
3. Bench Presses – 135 x 5, 225 x 5, 275 x 5, 275 x 5, 275 x 5, 275 x 5, 275 x 4 (missed 5th rep).
4. Seated Presses – 135 x 5, 165 x 5, missed 185, 165 x 4.

Sunday 6/10/79 (Afternoon) – Squats – 180 x 8, 250 x 8, 330 x 5, 400 x 5, 400 x 5.

Sunday 6/10/79 (Evening) – Bench Presses – 180 x 6, 250 x 3, 315 x 2, 280 x 6, 280 x 6.

Monday 6/11/79 [Workout @ local YMCA for the purpose of Deadlifting on Olympic weights with the dimension of 45lb. plates]
1. Deadlifts (Floor)(Conventional Style) – 242 x 10, 402 x 10.
2. Standing Triceps Presses (EZ Bar) Bar (25lbs.) x 8, 65 x 6.
3. Wide Grip Bench Presses – 135 x 10, 231 x 10.

Wednesday 6/13/79 [Workout @ local YMCA once again for the purpose of performing Bench Presses on an Olympic bar. Calculating percentage max on 350lbs.]
1. Bench Presses – 135 x 8, 252 x 4, 297 x 3, 297 x 3, 297 x 3.

Thursday 6/14/79 (Evening)
1. Squats – 250 x 5, 325 x 5, 390 x 5, 410 x 5, 410 x 5.
2. Close-Grip Bench Presses – 230 x 10.

(6/14/79 @ Night)

1. Wide Grip Bench Presses – 235 x 10 !
2. Standing Triceps Presses (Regular Bar) – 95 x 6, 95 x 6, 110 x 6, 120 x 6, 130 x 6.

1. Deadlifts (Floor) (Conventional Style) – 260 x 10, 340 x 5, 420 x 4, 475 x 3, 475 x 3, 480 x 3, 480 x 3.
2. Bent Over One Arm Dumbell Rowing – 55 x 8, 80 x 8, 80 x 8.
3. Cheating Eccentric Curls (EZ) – 120 x 6, 145 x 6, 160 x 5.

Sunday 6/17/79 (Afternoon) –

1. Squats – 180 x 5, 250 x 5, 320 x 5, 390 x 5, 450 x 5, 450 x 5.
2. ¼ Squats – 515 x 5, 585 x 4, 635 x 5, 685 x 5.

Sunday 6/17/79 (Evening)

1. Seated Presses – 135 x 5, 185 x 3, 185 x 3, 185 x 3.
2. Bench Presses – 135 x 6, 205 x 5, 245 x 5, 245 x 5, 245 x 5, 245 x 5
3. Close Grip Bench Presses – 238 x 8 missed 9th rep.
4. Lying Triceps Presses (EZ) – 95 x 6, 120 x 6, 145 x 6, 160 x 5.

Monday 6/18/79

1. Deadlifts (75lb. Plates) (Conventional Style) – 425 x 10.
2. Wide Grip Bench Presses – 240 x 10.
3. Bent Over One Arm Dumbell Rowing – 55 x 8, 80 x 7, 80 x 7, 80 x 7.

Wednesday 6/20/79

1. Squats – 253 x 5, 330 x 5, 391 x 5, 429 x 3.
2. Bench Presses – 132 x 5, 220 x 5, 270 x 5, 297 x 5, 292 x 3.

Sunday 6/24/79

1. Squats – 180 x 5, 250 x 5, 320 x 4, 390 x 3, 430 x3, 470 x 3, 470 x 3, 320 x 10.
2. Seated Presses – 135 x 5, 160 x 4, 185 x 3, 190 x 3.
3. Bench Presses – 135 x 5, 205 x 5, 245 x 5, 245 x 5, 245 x 5, 245 x 5.
4. Lying Triceps Presses (EZ) – 95 x 5, 120 x 5, 150 x 5, 160 x 5.

Monday 6/25/79

Deadlifts (Floor)(Wide Stance) – 180 x 5, 335 x 4, 425 x 3, 495 x 3, 540 x 3, 540 x 3.

Tuesday 6/26/79
1. Bench Presses – 135 x 5, 205 x 5, 255 x 5, 285 x 5, 285 x 5, 285 x 5, 285 x 5.
2. Incline Bench Presses – 135 x 5, 185 x 5, 220 x 1.

Wednesday 6/27/79 - Squats – 180 x 6, 260 x 5, 330 x 5, 390 x 3, 390 x 3, 390 x 3.

Thursday 6/28/79
1. Seated Presses – 135 x 5, 160 x 4, decided not to attempt set with 190.

Friday 6/29/79 – Deadlifts (Floor)(Conventional Style) – 290 x 10, 445 x 2.

Saturday 6/30/79 (Morning) – Seated Presses – 200 x 3.

Saturday 6/30/79 (Afternoon) – Deadlifts (Floor)(Conventional Style) 180 x 10, 440 x 3.

Sunday 7/01/79
1. Squats – 180 x 5, 260 x 5, 330 x 5, 390 x 4, 435 x 3, 475 x 2.
2. ¼ Squats – 585 x 3, 635 x 3.
3. Bench Presses – 135 x 5, 225 x 4, 275 x 3, 305 x 3, 305 x 3, 305 x 3, 305 x 3.

Monday 7/02/79
1. Power Rack Deadlifts (Bar 5 inches Below top of knee)(Conventional Style) 225 x 5, 335 x 4, 445 x 3, 525 x 3, 525 x 3.
2. Power Rack Deadlifts (Bar 5 inches Below top of knee)(Wide Stance) 555 x 3, 555 x 3, 555 x 3.
3. Incline Bench Presses – 135 x 5, 185 x 4, 215 x 3, 230 x 3, 230 x 3, 230 x 3.
4. Lying Triceps Presses (EZ) – 90 x 6, 140 x 5, 165 x 5, 180 x 5.

Wednesday 7/04/79
1. Squats – 260 x 10, 330 x 5, 390 x 4, 445 x 3, 335 x 10.
2. Seated Presses – 135 x 5, 160 x 4, 185 x 3, 205 x 2, 220 x 2.
3. Bench Presses – 135 x 5, 205 x 4, 250 x 3, 250 x 3, 250 x 3, 250 x 3, 250 x 3.

<u>Friday 7/06/79</u>
1. Deadlifts (Floor)(Conventional Style) – 180 x 10, 460 x 10.
2. Incline Bench Presses (Shoulder Width Grip) – 135 x 5, 185 x 4, 3, 200 x 3, 205 x 3, 210 x 3.
3. Lying Triceps Presses (EZ Bar) – 100 x 5, 140 x 5, 5, 190 x 5.
4. Cheating Eccentric Curls (EZ Bar) – 140 x 5, 170 x 5, 180 x 5.

<u>Sunday 7/08/79</u>
1. Squats (Put on Knee Wraps) – 290 x 5, 380 x 4, 440 x 3, 475 x 2, 500 x 2.
2. Bench Presses – 135 x 5, 230 x 4, 290 x 3, 315 x 2, 330 x 2.

<u>Monday 7/09/79</u> – Lying Triceps Presses (EZ Bar) – 120 x 6, 170 x 5, 175 x 5.

<u>Wednesday 7/11/79</u>
1. Squats (Put on Knee Wraps) – 290 x 5, 390 x 3, 420 x 2.
2. Seated Presses – 135 x 5, 160 x 4, 185 x 3, 210 x 2.
3. Bench Presses – 135 x 5, 205 x 4, 255 x 3, 270 x 2, 270 x 2, 270 x 2, 270 x 2.
4. Incline Bench Presses – 135x 5, 185 x 3, 185 x 3.

Saturday July 14, 1979
National Powerlifting Championships
@ Inglewood (Los Angeles, Calfornia

Squat – 545lbs. (247.5 Kilos)
Bench Press – 341lbs. (155 Kilos)
Deadlift – 595lbs. (270 Kilos)

Placed 1st in the 148 ¾ lb. (67.5 Kilo) Class
Won Outstanding Lifter Award for the Lightweight Session
The Total of 1482 broke the Junior National Total Record by 15 Kilos (33lbs.). The old record Total of 1449 ½ (657.5 Kilos) was owned by John Orsini, set in 1978.

TOTAL – 1482 (672.5 Kilos)
147.267 pounds. (66.8 Kilos) Bodyweight

Time Runs Out

Over the years, a number of commentaries have been written about many of the Senior National Powerlifting Championships. My perception of the 1979 Senior Nationals may or may not compliment other published reports. A report from my perspective of what actually happened may support a theory or two of what might have been.

The <u>1979 Senior National Powerlifting Championships</u> in Bay St. Louis, Mississippi on August 18th and 19th, 1979 received major network television coverage from NBC's Sports World. I remember vividly Roger Estep being interviewed following his victory in the 198lb. class. The fact that the lifting venue was in a building where air conditioning had to be "blown in" and that television camera lights generated even more heat inside the perimeter of the platform area, created atmospheric conditions most challenging for all lifters. *Powerlifting USA magazine, Vol. 3, No. 3 / September, 1979*

The 1979 Senior National Powerlifting Championships became known as "Meltdown Mississippi." The meet was indeed a meltdown for Paul Sutphin as I could not stand on my feet for about one (1) hour after failing to lose the final ¾ (three-quarters of a pound) necessary to officially make bodyweight and compete in the 148lb. class. With six (6) minutes remaining in the weigh-in, the Official in charge told me, "Paul, you are eligible to compete at 165 as you have exceeded the Qualifying Total in the Middleweight class." I did not have to think about my decision for more than a few seconds as I replied "No thanks!"

Unfortunately, as a lightweight Powerlifter competing in the 148lb. weight class, my time had run out. The reduction in bodyweight was off schedule the entire week prior to boarding the airplane on the morning of August 17th. Confident that I would lose the weight and, only in the final minutes of the official weigh-in, did I know that any chance for an IPF World title in the 148lb. class had suddenly evaporated. After all, there would be next year and the year after that...in a new weight class. Unfortunately, such achievements are often easier said than done. The question that remained in my mind about "Meltdown Mississippi, 1979", "Was it?" or "Was it not...a missed opportunity?"

In the 1970's, the selective process for lifters to represent the USA in the IPF World Powerlifting Championships (the <u>only</u> World Powerlifting Championships at the time) was done the old fashioned way ; the lifter had to "earn it." In other words, you had to "win your way in." To make a long story short, Clyde Wright won 1st Place in the 148lb. class at the 1979 Senior Nationals. Yet, he was not selected as a USA Team member for the 1979 Worlds in Dayton, Ohio. So, by missing the 148 ¾ bodyweight limit on 8/18/79, did I miss an opportunity to win the Senior National Powerlifting Championships and lift at the 1979 IPF Worlds or simply miss an opportunity to win the Seniors?

Time moved on and so did the lifting on 8/18/79. In spite of the climate conditions, Chuck Dunbar of *Luke's Gym* put together a Squat of 485, Bench Press of 303, and a Deadlift of 363 for a winning Total of 1151 in the 114lb. class for the 1979 Senior National Championship title. Competing in the 165lb. class on 8/18/79 were Mike Bridges and Rickey Crain. Rick Gaugler may have had something for both Bridges and Crain as he had done 1712 at 165 earlier in 1979 which included a 694 Deadlift. Unfortunately, circumstances affected Gaugler as he bombed out on the Deadlift with 677.

In the 198lb class, Roger Estep won over Vince Anello, Jerry Jones, and Jim Cash. Larry Pacifico's legendary strength was demonstrated by a "come from behind" win in the 220lb. class. After the Squats, Pacifico was 3rd behind Dennis Reed and Louie Simmons. Larry took the lead on the Bench with a lift of 529lbs., Deadlifted 722lbs., and captured the 220lb. Senior National title with a Total of 2017!

Lifting in the 220's, Louie Simmons injured his bicep on an opening Deadlift attempt of 677. John Kuc Deadlifted 810 and Totaled 2083 to win the 242's. The story of the 275's was an 887 World Record Squat by Ernie Hackett. Winning the 275lb. class at the 1979 Seniors was Larry Kidney with a 2143 Total and Ernie Hackett followed in 2nd Place with a Total of 2132. Winning the Superheavyweight class was Paul Wrenn with a Total of 2148. Paul Wrenn also had a World Record Squat with a solid lift of 953!

The 1979 Senior Nationals was not one of Luke Iams' best competitions. When the P/L USA OCT/79 published the SHW TOP 100 (October, 1978 through September, 1979), Luke finished 4th in the Squat with 875, 2nd in the Bench Press with 600, and 6th with a TOTAL of 2080. In the Bench Press, only Bill Kazmaier bested Luke with a lift of 617lbs. Luke Iams returned to the 1980 Seniors in Madison, Wisconsin for his final Senior National appearance.

Moving Forward : Looking Back

During the 2nd half of 1979, the sport of Powerlifting continued to grow in the state of West Virginia. The 6th Annual Mountianeer Open Powerlifting Championships were held at Parkersburg, West Virginia on October 13th and 14th, 1979 with ninety-nine (99) lifters. Among lifters who did well at the 1979 Mountianeer Open included Don Hundley, Ross Smith, Bob Hill, and Dave Burkey.

Included among the 1979 Master's Hall of Fame Powerlifters were two (2) West Virginia Powerlifters, according to the official contest report from the 1979 National

Masters Powerlifting Championships held October 28th, 1979 in Weirton, West Virginia. Ernie Nagy, Meet Director of the 1979 National Master's Powerlifting Championships, won the 220lb. class.

Ernie Nagy, along with Herb Fitzsimmons, was nominated for the *Master's Hall of Fame.* Among the winners from West Virginia at the 1979 Master's National Powerlifting Championship event in Weirton, West Virginia were :

1) Don Hundley (1st @ 165)
2) Herb Fitzsimmons (1st @ 275)
3) Bill Blankenship (2nd @ 220)
4) Austin Miller (2nd @ 242)

While setting a number of attainable goals for the upcoming decade of the 1980's, one thing was certain ; I was finished as a competitor in the 148lb. class. After a short layoff, I returned to the annual event in Bristol, Tennessee on December 15th, 1979 ; "The Tennessee Connection : Part IX." A conservative Total of 1410 at a bodyweight of 162 ¾ earned a first place win and the Outstanding Lifter Award.

Chuck Dunbar finished number one (1) in the *Powerlifting USA* TOP 100 in the Squat, Bench, and Total for lifters competing from November, 1978 through October, 1979. As a final evaluation of *"Luke's Gym"*, only Chuck Dunbar would eventually become an IPF World Champion. *NOTE : Chuck Dunbar won the 1984 IPF World Championship, beating the undefeated Ten (10) Time World Powerlifting Champion, Hideaki Inaba from Japan.*

1979 West Virginia Powerlifter Rankings
WV Powerlifters competing from January 1st, 1979 thru December 31st, 1979
TOP RANKINGS Determined by Total

114 / Name	Squat	Bench Press	Deadlift	Total	Date
Chuck Dunbar	485 wr	303 wr	363	1151 e	8/18/79
Chuck Dunbar	484	303	358	1146 e	11/02/79
Chuck Dunbar	479 wr	297 wr	363	1140 e	5/04/79
Chuck Dunbar	480	295	360	1135 e	4/01/79
Scott McCune	215	140	270	625	4/01/79
Scott Wilkinson	170	125	215	510	4/01/79
123 Roger Salser	375	270	400	1045	10/14/79
Roger Salser	390 c	255 c	380 c	1025 c	5/12/79
Roger Salser	370	255	395	1020	4/07/79
Dave Sprouse	310	220	340	870	4/01/79
Cork Hall	295	150	380	825	4/01/79
Dan Palmateer	275	205	320	800	10/14/79
132 Ed Canjemi	400*	220	420	1040*	10/14/79
Dave Conaway	365	220	425	1010	10/14/79
Ron Giarletto	360	215	425	1000	4/08/79
Dave Conaway	360 c	215	420 c	995 c	5/12/79
Ron Giarletto	340	215	430	985	4/01/79
Dave Conway	345	215	390	950	4/01/79
Mike Sarver	320	190	375	885	5/12/79
D. James	240	190	300	730	5/12/79

* - West Virginia State Powerlifting Record

c – West Virginia State Collegiate Powerlifting Record

wr – World Powerlifting Record

nr – National (Junior) Powerlifting Record

e – Elite Powerlifting Classification Total

1979 West Virginia Powerlifter Rankings
WV Powerlifters competing from January 1st, 1979 thru December 31st, 1979
TOP RANKINGS Determined by Total

148 / Name	Squat	Bench Press	Deadlift	Total	Date
Paul Sutphin	545*	341*	595* nr	1482* e	7/14/79
Paul Sutphin	535*	320	590*	1445* e	4/01/79
Paul Sutphin	530*	330	575*	1435* e	2/23/79
Laney Simone	425	240	490	1155	4/01/79
David Hall	400	265	425	1090	4/01/79
Wayne Anderson	395	200	470	1065	4/01/79
David Hall	425	255	375	1055	5/12/79
Mike Sarver	350	210	420	980	4/01/79
Greg Perry	345	225	375	945	10/14/79
Mike Sarver	320	205	385	910	10/14/79
Chris Hindman	320	185	350	855	4/01/79
Scott Phillips	275	185	300	760	10/14/79
165 Paul Sutphin	567	352	589	1510 e	5/26/79
Paul Sutphin	560	350	595	1505 e	4/21/79
Paul Sutphin	540	345	600	1485 e	5/05/79
Paul Sutphin (162 ¾)	535	315	560	1410	12/15/79
Dana Bee	500	370	530	1400	10/14/79
Don Hundley	525 m	260	550 m	1335 m	4/01/79
Don Hundley	s	bp	d	1310	JAN/79
Dana Bee	445	365	500	1310	4/01/79
Gene Underwood	450	325	535	1310	4/01/79
Don Hundley	490	270	535	1295	10/14/79
Don Hundley	501	248	490	1240	10/28/79
J. Kilbane	400	230	445	1075	4/01/79
Cary Wilson	375	275	420	1070	4/01/79
Randy Worley	315	255	375	945	4/01/79
Randy Worley	310	255	375	940	10/14/79
Raymond Hackett	285	200	375	860	4/01/79

* - West Virginia State Powerlifting Record

m – West Virginia State Masters Powerlifting Record

wr – World Powerlifting Record

nr – National (Junior) Powerlifting Record

e – Elite Powerlifting Classification Total

1979 West Virginia Powerlifter Rankings
WV Powerlifters competing from January 1st, 1979 thru December 31st, 1979
TOP RANKINGS Determined by Total

181 / Name	Squat	Bench Press	Deadlift	Total	Date
Dave Jeffrey	550	400*	550	1500*	4/01/79
Frank Nicholas	560*	390	530	1480	4/01/79
Don Hall	500	290	535	1325	4/01/79
Tim McCoy	475	300	525	1300	10/14/79
Don Hall	490	295	500	1285	2/24/79
Don Hall	s	bp	d	1255	JAN/79
Steve Brooks	385	290	500	1175	10/14/79
Cary Wilson	430	280	460	1170	10/14/79
Mike Brown	380	280	405	1065	10/14/79
Jeff Bara	315	295	450	1060	4/01/79
Bob Smith	385	175	400	1060	5/12/79
198 Scott Tusic	560	420	570	1550	4/01/79
Bill Kyle	555	390	605	1550	10/14/79
Gary Clark	560	400	555	1515	4/01/79
Ross Smith	540	370	510	1420	4/01/79
Ross Smith	510	350	515	1375	2/24/79
Ernie Nagy	500	350	505	1355	9/01/79
Earl Snider	450	335	575	1350	4/01/79
Ross Smith	500	350	490	1340	5/05/79
Ernie Nagy (56)	495 nm	345 nm	500 nm	1340 nm	5/13/79
Ross Smith	500	350	470	1320	10/14/79
Ross Smith	s	bp	d	1310	JAN/79
Dan Hall	475	250	545	1275	4/01/79
George McLaughlin	430	340	500	1270	4/01/79
Al Anderson	485	275	510	1270	4/01/79
Mike Leikari	405	255	505 c	1165	5/12/79
Russ Stump	400	300	450	1150	10/14/79
Russ Stump	370	300	470	1140	4/01/79
David Kyle	370	320	425	1115	5/12/79
B. Hommel	405	245	440	1090	5/12/79
Terry Phillips	350	260	400	1010	4/01/79
Chuck McCoy	250	350 c	375	975	5/12/79

* - West Virginia State Powerlifting Record

nm – National Masters Powerlifting Record

c – West Virginia State Collegiate Powerlifting Record

1979 West Virginia Powerlifter Rankings
WV Powerlifters competing from January 1st, 1979 thru December 31st, 1979
TOP RANKINGS Determined by Total

220 / Name	Squat	Bench Press	Deadlift	Total	Date
Mike Wolf	630*	490*	660*	1780*	4/01/79
Vince White	s	bp	d	1515	JAN/79
Ernie Nagy	545	402	529	1476	10/28/79
Ernie Nagy	540	385	530	1455	4/01/79
Bob Hill	520	320	605	1445	4/01/79
Warren Knight	490	345	590	1425	4/01/79
Bob Hill	s	bp	d	1400	JAN/79
Ernie Nagy	525	375	500	1400	4/08/79
Vince White	600	300	480	1380	2/24/79
Bob Hill	525	305	550	1380	5/05/79
Steve Wilkinson	500	340	525	1360	4/01/79
Bob Hill	500	290	570	1360	10/14/79
S. Wilkerson	500	340	500	1340	5/12/79
Dave Kyle	450	365	455	1270	10/14/79
Brian Tucker	490	270	500	1260	4/01/79
Dave Snyder	430	310	470	1210	4/01/79
Bill Blankenship	330	259	341	931	10/28/79
242 Nick Busick	615	425	600	1640	4/01/79
Jack Anderson	625	375	600	1600	4/01/79
Scott Warman	530	405	665	1600	4/01/79
Austin Miller	490	303	462	1256	10/28/79
Austin Miller	470	300	480	1250	4/01/79
Austin Miller	s	bp	d	1115	JAN/79

* - West Virginia State Powerlifting Record

c – West Virginia State Collegiate Powerlifting Record

e – Elite Powerlifting Classification Total

1979 West Virginia Powerlifter Rankings
WV Powerlifters competing from January 1st, 1979 thru December 31st, 1979
TOP RANKINGS Determined by Total

275 / Name	Squat	Bench Press	Deadlift	Total	Date
Herb Fitzsimmons	740*	450	730*	1920*	4/01/79
Herb Fitzsimmons	740	450	740*	1920	4/21/79
Herb Fitzsimmons	735	440	700	1875	5/05/79
Herb Fitzsimmons	705	451	705	1862	5/26/79
Jim Goodnight	685	500*	670	1855	4/01/79
Herb Fitzsimmons	725	420	680	1825	2/24/79
Herb Fitzsimmons	650	402	655	1708	10/28/79
Dave Burkey	540	340	545	1425	10/14/79
Jeff Cook	490	275	640	1405	4/01/79
SHW Luke Iams	875*	600*	605	2080* e	4/01/79
Tim Slamick	610	430	530	1570	4/01/79
Jeff Cook	500 c	265	595 c	1360 c	5/12/79
Charles Roberts	425	270	420	1115	4/01/79

* - West Virginia State Powerlifting Record

c – West Virginia State Collegiate Powerlifting Record

e – Elite Powerlifting Classification Total

Chapter Sixteen : 1980 – 1981

At the end of the 1970's, there were only three (3) ELITE Powerlifters in the state of West Virginia :

1) <u>Chuck Dunbar</u> (1151 Total – 114lb. class)
   Total over "Ten (10) Times Bodyweight"
2) <u>Luke Iams</u> (2080 Total at SuperHeavyWeight)
3) <u>Paul Sutphin</u> – (1482 Total – 148lb. class)
   Total over "Ten (10) Times Bodyweight"
   (1510 – Elite Total / 165lb. class)

With an onslaught of attainable goals for the future, I was optimistic about Powerlifting in the 1980's. As a confident young man, I was of the belief that, unless I died or quit lifting, the revised standards for Powerlifting's Elite Classification Totals in the 165lb. class (1527) and the 181lb. class (1642) would be accomplished in short order.

The 1980's became the decade of change for the sport of Powerlifting. Beginning in 1980, Powerlifting became independent from the Amateur Athletic Union (AAU). Effective January 1st, 1980 the United States Powerlifting Federation (USPF) was the unified governing body for the sport of Powerlifting and the USPF rules for USA competitions were the "laws of the sport." Joe Zarella was the USPF President.

For West Virginia Powerlifting, a major championship in Beckley, West Virginia began the Powerlifting decade of the 1980's. After a New Year's celebration, the 1980 YMCA Nationals scheduled for January 5th were only a few days away. Even though I was not in shape for the event, I was anxious to lift again in a major competition after a few short months of being away from the National Powerlifting scene.

Herb Fitzsimmons : YMCA National Champion!

The <u>1980 YMCA National Powerlifting Championships</u> were held January 5th, 1980 at the Raleigh County YMCA in Beckley, West Virginia. The weather was frigid cold with snow and the lifting was heavy ; too heavy for me as I came up short in the 165lb. class against Ohio lifter, Bill Whittaker. Bill was a tough competitor, a good Squatter and Deadlifter, and coached by my friend, Louie Simmons.

Herb Fitzsimmons won the 1980 YMCA National Powerlifting Championships while competing in the 275lb. weight class. Herb's winning Total at the Y-Nationals on 1/05/80 was 1775lbs. Herb Fitzsimmons Squatted 700, Bench Pressed 435, and Deadlifted 640 for a 1775 Total to become : *YMCA National Powerlifting Champion!*

Herb Fitzsimmons – 1980 YMCA National Powerlifting Champion

The performance of Louie Simmons at the 1980 YMCA National Powerlifting Championships highlighted the 220lb. class. Back from a torn bicep at the 1979 Senior Nationals, Louie Simmons won the 1980 YMCA National Powerlifting Championship title at Beckley, West Virginia with a Total of 1950! Included in the 1950 Total by Louie Simmons on 1/05/80 was a YMCA National Record Squat of 765! Louie also Bench Pressed 480 and Deadlifted 705 on 1/05/80 to win the YMCA National title by fifty (50) pounds over his nearest competitor.

Other notable performances at the 1980 YMCA National Powerlifting Championships on 1/05/80 included West Virginia Powerlifters Dave Talbot, Roger Salser, and Ed Canjemi. Dave Talbot opened up the YMCA Nationals with a winning Total in the 114lb. class. Roger Salser's Deadlift of 415 and Total of 1110 in the 123lb. class were new YMCA National Powerlifting Records.

The Powerlifting Records of Ed Canjemi began with a 450 Squat, 255 Bench Press, and a 465 Deadlift for a winning Total of 1170 in the 132lb. class. Canjemi's Squat and Total were new YMCA National Powerlifting Records. All of Ed Canjemi's lifts at the 1980 YMCA National Powerlifting Championships were new West Virginia State Powerlifting Records in the 132lb. class.

Elite Total - 1535 at 165

Even though the 1980 YMCA Nationals had not gone my way, I was sick of the stress involved with weight reduction and making bodyweight. I told myself, "Forget dieting!" Being physically smaller than my peers most of my life, the 165lb. class was certainly not in the long-term forecast. I recognized an opportunity to compete in the 181lb. class at the 1980 King's Classic scheduled for Charlotte, North Carolina.

The 1st Annual King's Classic Open Powerlifting Championships were held on Saturday January 19th, 1980 @ King's Gym in Charlotte, North Carolina. Weighing in at 176 ¾, I Squatted with 580 and missed 600. After Bench Pressing 360, I failed on three (3) attempts to Deadlift 595. The 1980 King's Classic Powerlifting Meet marked the first time in my competitive Powerlifting career where I had "bombed out" on the Deadlift.

The achievements of the 1970's were history and the first two (2) Powerlifting meets of the new decade told me where I stood among the best. Finishing second after a year like 1979 and "bombing out" was certainly out of character and unacceptable. An overall assessment confirmed that I was not in the best shape for championship lifting and that I probably should give the 165lb. class another try. After much thought, my short-term goals were :

1) Compete in the 1980 West Virginia State Powerlifting Championships at New Martinsville on March 30th, 1980 as a 165lb'er.
2) Win the Middleweight (165lb. class) West Virginia State Powerlifting title
3) Defend the *"Best Deadlift Award"* I had won at the 1979 West Virginia State Powerlifting Championships
4) Exceed the "New Standard" for an Elite Total (1527) in the 165lb. class.

The 5th Annual 1980 West Virginia State Powerlifting Championships were held March 30th, 1980 at Magnolia High School Gymnasium in New Martinsville, West Virginia. Once again, a fine Meet Program was produced, paid for by numerous advertisers, and contained an up-to-date list of the West Virginia State Powerlifting Records. The Meet Director was Luke Iams.

On the morning of March 30th, 1980 at the 5th Annual West Virginia State Powerlifting Championships, I weighed exactly 165lbs. at the official weigh-in. During the first session of lifting, I Squatted with an easy opener, made a solid 2nd attempt at 585 but missed a 3rd attempt at a West Virginia State Record of 610lbs. The Bench Press of 345 was good on a 2nd attempt but 350 stopped me cold. Finishing with a Deadlift of 605lbs. exceeded the minimum requirements for "Modern Elite" in the 165lb. class with a Total of 1535lbs.!

The Deadlifts I made at the 1980 West Virginia State Powerlifting Championships included a 550 opener, a 2nd attempt with 605, and an unsuccessful 3rd attempt at 620lbs. I was very proud of the accomplished goal of winning the Best Deadlift Award for the 2nd consecutive year at the 1980 West Virginia State Powerlifting Championships. A Deadlift of 605lbs. at 165 earned the 21st Spot and the 1535 Total was #17 in the TOP 100 Powerlifters of the 165lb. class (Middleweight / 165lb. USA lifters competing from January, 1980 thru December, 1980).

The report of the 1980 West Virginia State Powerlifting Championships would not be complete without commentary given to the solid lifting of several individuals. Gary Clark won the 181lb. class with a Total of 1560. Scott Tusic won the 1980 West Virginia State Powerlifting title in the 220lb. class with a Total of 1590. Vince White mastered the formula for Powerlifting success with lifts of a 585 Squat, 410 Bench Press, and 475 on the Deadlift for a solid 1470 in the 220lb. weight class. Meanwhile, Luke Iams lifted well at the 1980 West Virginia States and won another West Virginia Powerlifting title in the Superheavyweight class.

Among the performances from the 1980 West Virginia State Powerlifting Championships that live on to this day was the lifting of Chuck Dunbar. The Chuck Dunbar Bench Press of 295 in the 123lb. class remains the Top Bench Press to date in the All-Time West Virginia TOP TEN Powerlifters. Chuck Dunbar had two (2) World Records coming into the 1980 West Virginia States as he had Squatted with 485 and Bench Pressed 303 on an earlier date.

Even though training had went well in preparation for the 1980 West Virginia State Powerlifting Championships, *the lifts that I did not make* would've yielded a Total of 1580! Perhaps it was the fact that I had to lose about five or six pounds to make bodyweight? My mind was made up regarding future competitions and bodyweight reduction...I had enough!

The 1980 Roanoke Open was about five (5) weeks away and I made the decision to skip the 165lb. class and go directly to the 181's ; even if the decision would result in missing the 1980 Senior Nationals as I had made the Qualifying Total for the 165lb.

class. With no regrets, the newfound strength with additional bodyweight was long overdue. As a result of my decision, *March 30ᵗʰ, 1980 was the last day I weighed 165lbs.!*

The New Frontier

It had been only a couple of weeks since the 1980 West Virginia State Powerlifting Championships and I couldn't wait until I was on the platform again. Coming off of a *modern* Elite Total at 165, I decided to compete at the 1980 Roanoke Open in the 181lb. class. The 1979 Roanoke Open became the sixth (6ᵗʰ) Chapter (Part VI) of the "Virginia Connection" to West Virginia Powerlifting. The 1980 Roanoke Open marked the 7ᵗʰ Chapter (Part VII).

The 1980 Roanoke Valley Open Powerlifting Meet was held Saturday May 10ᵗʰ, 1980 at Northside High School in Roanoke, Virginia. At a bodyweight of 177 ½, I won First (1ˢᵗ) Place and the Outstanding Lifter Award for the heavier classes. The attempts made on the Squat included an opener with 580lbs. and a 2ⁿᵈ attempt of 605 before a 3ʳᵈ attempt of 625 was denied by two (2) red lights from the officials.

The Bench Press at the 1980 Roanoke Open was 365lbs. on a 3ʳᵈ attempt while the Deadlifts saw amazing improvement with an easy 3ʳᵈ attempt at 625lbs. When it was all said and done, the kind of success I had been looking for happened in Roanoke, Virginia on May 10ᵗʰ, 1980 as three (3) new West Virginia State Powerlifting Records were broken in the 181lb. class : 605 Squat, 625 Deadlift, and a 1595 Total.

The Virginia Connection, Part VIII : The 1980 Atlantic Coast Open Powerlifting Championships were held August 23ʳᵈ, 1980 in Newport News, Virginia. According to the official results, the 1980 Atlantic Coast Open Powerlifting competition had forty-one (41) lifters. Weighing in at 179 ¼ and competing in the 181lb. weight class, the following achievements and awards were won :

    a.) 1ˢᵗ Place (181lb. class)
    b.) Outstanding Lifter (181 thru Superheavyweight)
    c.) Best Squat Award
    d.) Best Bench Press Award
    e.) Best Deadlift Award
    f.) The "Champion of Champions" Award

On 8/23/80 at Newport News, the 622 ¾ Squat and 380 ¼ Bench Press were solid lifts with strength to spare. Due to a couple of failed Deadlift attempts and the fact that kilo weights were used at the contest, the 1598 Total fell two (2) pounds short of an official Total mark of 1600lbs. The 622 ¾ Squat / 282.5 kilos and the 1598 Total / 725 kilos were both new West Virginia State Powerlifting Records in the 181lb. class. After winning the Atlantic Coast Open Powerlifting Championships, the local newspaper published a photo of Paul Sutphin with a caption which read, "Super Lifter." Meanwhile, the number of people lifting weights for fitness was increasing in both Bluefields, thanks to the newly formed *Bluefield YMCA Weightlifting Club.*

Looking back, *maybe* or *perhaps* I should have entered and competed as a 165lb'er at the 1980 Senior National Powerlifting Championships in Madison, Wisconsin. The 1980 Senior National Powerlifting Championships was televised by NBC. Unfortunately, much of the lifting from the 1980 Senior National Powerlifting Championships was not shown by the television network. Only a few of the lifters from the heavier classes were spotlighted, overshadowed by the unfortunate circumstances linked to the technical bombout of Larry Pacifico.

Powerlifting USA / 2011 Judd Biasotto

1980 - World Powerlifting Records and More!

The <u>1980 World Series of Powerlifting</u> was held April 19th, 1980 at Auburn University in Auburn, Alabama. During the Summer of 1980, the 1980 World Series of Powerlifting was televised. Chuck Dunbar had a World Record Squat of 490 at the 1980 World Series of Powerlifting and won the 114lb. class. Luke Iams placed 3rd in Auburn, Alabama behind the lifting of Doyle Kenady and Paul Wrenn.

The <u>1980 World Powerlifting Championships</u> were held November 7th thru 9th, 1980 in Arlington, Texas. Featured on the cover of the December, 1980 issue of *Powerlifting USA* magazine was Chuck Dunbar. Although Chuck Dunbar placed 2nd, he broke two (2) World Records in the Bench Press (114lb. / 52kg. class). Chuck Dunbar successfully made 308lbs. (140 kilos) on a 3rd attempt. After Chuck's 3rd attempt World Record, he was granted a 4th attempt. Chuck Dunbar successfully Bench Pressed 314lbs. (142.5 kilos) on 4th attempt for a World Bench Press Record in the 114lb. class at the 1980 World Powerlifting Championships on 11/07/80 in Arlington, Texas.

Powerlifting USA magazine / Vol. 4 / No. 6 / December, 1980

The <u>7th Annual Mountianeer Open Powerlifting Championships</u> were held October 19th, 1980 at Mineral Wells, West Virginia. According to the official meet results, the 1980 Mountianeer Open had one-hundred twenty-two (122) lifters. Competing in the 165lb. weight class, Don Hundley won on bodyweight with a Total of 1421 which included a *Masters World Record Deadlift of 606!* A poundage of 606 ¼ lbs. (275 kilos) was the weight Don Hundley needed to pull for the win. The 606 ¼ lbs. was a World Masters Deadlift Record (40-49 Age Group). *Powerlifting USA / Vol. 4 / No. 6 / December, 1980*

Ed Canjemi won the 132lb. class at the 7ᵗʰ Annual Mountianeer Open with a Total of 1168 which included a West Virginia State Record Deadlift of 473lbs. Mike Hundley won first place in the Novice Division / 181lb. class with a Total of 1317. Mike Hundley set three (3) Mountianeer Open Powerlifting Meet Records in the Novice Division which included a 501 Squat, 545 Deadlift, and a 1317 Total.

The 1980 Mountian Empire Powerlifting Meet was held on December 13ᵗʰ, 1980 in Bristol, Tennessee. Weighing 181½, Paul Sutphin made the following lifts on 12/13/80 : 640 Squat, 360 Bench Press, and a 625 Deadlift for a 1625 Total ; seventeen (17) pounds short of the minimum standard for Elite Classification in the 181lb. class.

Bob Coulling, lifting in his first official Powerlifting competition, won 1ˢᵗ Place at Bristol, Tennessee on 12/13/80 while competing in the 220lb. class. The 1555 Total by Bob Coulling at the 1980 Mountian Empire Open included a 610 Squat, 365 Bench Press, and a 580 Deadlift.

The Powerlifting team of *Herb's Gym*, won the Team Award at the 1980 Mountian Empire Powerlifting Meet at Bristol, Tennessee, completing Part X of the "Tennessee Connection." Among the West Virginia Powerlifters who represented *Herb's Gym* at the 1980 Mountian Empire Open Powerlifting Meet were Don Hundley (165), Mike Hundley (181), Paul Sutphin (181), Mike Brown (198), Don Hall (198), Ross Smith (220), Bob Coulling (220), Dan Hall (242), and Herb Fitzsimmons (SHW).

1981 YMCA National Powerlifting Champion!
Elite Total at 181

The New Year (1981) began on a positive note with a YMCA National Powerlifting Championship win at Columbus, Ohio on January 10ᵗʰ, 1981. A Total of 1653lbs., Elite Total at 181, marked the third (3ʳᵈ) weight class for the achievement of Elite Powerlifting Classification for Paul Sutphin. The coach and advisor I chose to assist me at the 1981 YMCA National Powerlifting Championships was none other than, Vince White!

The 1981 YMCA National Powerlifting Championships were held Saturday January 10ᵗʰ, 1981 at the Columbus Central YMCA in downtown Columbus, Ohio. The event was sponsored and conducted by the Columbus Central YMCA Weightlifting Club and sanctioned by the Ohio Association of the A.A.U., Inc. The Meet Director for the 1981 YMCA National Powerlifting Championships was Garry Benford. Qualifying Totals for the 1981 YMCA National Powerlifting Championships were listed on the official entry form as Class I Totals.

Paul Sutphin – 639 SQUAT @ 181 – 1/10/81
<u>1653 Total – Elite Powerlifting Classification at 181</u>!
The 1653 Total on 1/10/81 was Elite by traditional and modern standards.

Training Log #4 : Training for the 1981 YMCA Nationals
Paul Sutphin Workouts
(11/23/80 thru 1/10/81)

<u>Sunday 11/23/80</u>

Bench Presses – 180 x 9, 230 x 4, 300 x 3, 340 x 2, missed 370, Missed 370, missed 370, 340 x 1 (missed 2nd rep).

<u>Monday 11/24/80</u>

1. Deadlifts (100lb. Plates)(Wide Stance) 230 x 10, 380 x 5, 490 x 4, 575 x 3.
2. Close-Grip Benches – 135 x 10, 135 x 6, 260 x 8.

<u>Wednesday 11/26/80</u>

Squats – 230 x 10, 330 x 5, 410 x 4, 495 x 3, 495 x 3, 495 x 3, 495 x 3, 510 x 3, 435 x 10!

Thursday 11/27/80 (Thanksgiving Day)

Bench Presses – 135 x 15, 250 x 4, 320 x 3, 370 x 2, 370 x 2!

Friday 11/28/80 –

1. Deadlifts (Floor) (Conventional Style) – 230 x 10, 490 x 10!
2. Lying Triceps Extensions (EZ Bar) – 130 x 10, 180 x 7.

Sunday 11/30/80

1. Squats – 230 x 10, 330 x 5, 410 x 4, 490 x 3 (w / knee wraps0, 565 x 3 (w / knee wraps).
2. ¼ Squats – 715 x 5, attempted 810, but only stood with weight, attempted 810 again, only stood with weight.
3. Bench Presses – 135 x 12, 230 x 5, 300 x 4, 350 x 3, 350 x 3, 350 x 3, 350 x 3!

Monday 12/01/80

1. Deadlifts (Power Rack)(5 inches below knee)
   230 x 7, 380 x 4, 500 x 3, 600 x 3, 670 x 1 !
2. Seated Presses – 135 x 6, 185 x 5, 210 x 4, 225 x 4.
3. One Arm Rowing – 105 x 8, 105 x 8.
4. Close Grip Bench Presses – 135 x 8, 260 x 8 (missed 9th rep).

Wednesday 12/03/80 Squats – 230 x 10, 330 x 5, 415 x 4, 460 x 10!

Thursday 12/04/80 Bench Presses – 135 x 12, 230 x 5, 300 x 3, 300 x 3, 300 x 3
   (3 second pause after each rep), 300 x 3 (4 sec pause after each rep).

Friday 12/05/80 (1st Session / Early Evening @ Bluefield YMCA)

Deadlifts (Floor)(Conventional Style) – 310 x 10, 500 x 8 !

Friday 12/05/80 (2nd Session @ Home / Night)

1. Seated Presses – 135 x 6, 185 x 4, missed 235.
2. Incline Benches – 135 x 10, 205 x 5 (long pauses).
3. One Arm Rowing – 105 x 10.
4. Lying Triceps Presses (EZ Bar) – 130 x 7, 200 x 5, 200 x 5, 200 x 5.
5. Curls (EZ) – 150 x 8, 200 x 5.

Sunday 12/07/80 – Squats – 230 x 10, 330 x 5, 430 x 4, 520 x 3, 605 x 2.

Monday 12/08/80 – Bench Presses – 135 x 10, 240 x 4, 310 x 3, 360 x 2, 330 x 2.

Tuesday 12/09/80 – Lying Triceps Presses (EZ Bar) – 130 x 7, 220 x 3.

Saturday 12/13/80 – Lifted in the 7th Annual Mountian Empire Open Powerlifting Meet at Bristol, TN. Bodyweight at 181 ½, won 1st Place and the Outstanding Lifter Award. Lifts were 640 SQUAT, 360 BENCH PRESS, 625 DEADLIFT, for a 1625 TOTAL.

Saturday 12/20/80 – Bench Presses – 230 x 10.

Sunday 12/21/80
1. Squats – 230 x 10, 330 x 5, 430 x 4, 510 x 3, 580 x 3.
2. Cambered Bar Bench Presses – 125 x 6, 210 x 5, 260 x 5.
3. Lying Triceps Presses (EZ Bar) – 130 x 10, 160 x 8.

Monday 12/22/80 - Deadlifts (Floor)(100lb. Plates)(Sumo Style)
   230 x 10, 380 x 5, 490 x 4, 585 x 3.

Wednesday 12/24/80 (Christmas Eve)
1. Squats – 230 x 10, 380 x 4.
2. Bench Presses – 230 x 6, 320 x 5.

Thursday 12/25/80 (Christmas Day) –
   Cambered Bar Bench Presses 165 x 6, 235 x 5, 265 x 5.

Friday 12/26/80
   Deadlifts (Floor)(Wide Stance) – 230 x 10, 380 x 5, 515 x 4, missed 600, missed 600.

Saturday 12/27/80 – Bench Presses – 135 x 12, 230 x 5, 300 x 4, 350 x 3, 375 x 2.

Monday 12/29/80
1. Squats – 230 x 10, 340 x 5, 430 x 4, 520 x 3, 610 x 3.

2. ¼ Squats – 800 x 3.
3. Squats – 465 x 10. *A PR for 10 reps.*
4. Lying Triceps Presses (EZ Bar) – 130 x 8, 180 x 6, 205 x 5, 205 x 5.

Friday 1/02/80
1. Bench Presses – 135 x 12, 245 x 5, 315 x 5.
2. Deadlifts (Floor)(Olympic 45lb. Plates) – 135 x 10, 315 x 5, 465 x 4, missed 565.
3. Deadlifts (Floor)(Conventional Style) – 405 x 10.

Monday 1/05/80 - Squats – 230 x 10, 330 x 5, 430 x 4, Put on knee wraps – 510 x 3.

Tuesday 1/06/80
1. Bench Presses – 230 x 6, 230 x 4, 300 x 3, 350 x 2,
   300 x 2(3 second pause between reps),
   320 x 2 (3 second pause between reps).
2. Lying Triceps Presses (EZ Bar) – 130 x 7, 155 x 4, 190 x 3, 210 x 3.
3. Bent Over One Arm Dumbell Rowing w/ Dumbell – 105 x 8.

*Won the YMCA National Powerlifting Championships
with an ELITE Total in the 181lb. Class*

Saturday January 10, 1981
1981 YMCA National Powerlifting Championships
@ Columbus, Ohio

1. Squat – 639 ¾ lbs. (290 Kilos)
2. Bench Press – 385lbs. (175 Kilos)
3. Deadlift – 628lbs. (285 Kilos)

Placed 1ˢᵗ in the 181lb. (82.5 Kilo) Class

TOTAL – 1653lbs. (750 Kilos)
181 ¼ pounds. (82.2 Kilos) Bodyweight

1981 West Virginia State Powerlifting Championships

The 6th Annual West Virginia State Powerlifting Championships were held in New Martinsville, West Virginia on March 28th and 29th, 1981. The 1981 West Virginia State Powerlifting Meet was the first West Virginia State Powerlifting Championship conducted in kilos. For whatever reason, the official meet results of the 1981 West Virginia State Powerlifting Championships were not published in any of the lifting periodicals or newsletters, leaving a number of people highly upset. In lieu of the fact, the official West Virginia State Records broken at the 1981 West Virginia State Powerlifting Championships were confirmed and documented from both days of the contest, allowing for efficient record keeping synonymous to previous years.

The first day of the 1981 West Virginia State Powerlifting Championships included all women competitors and the 114 thru the 165lb. classes for the men. The 2nd Day of the 1981 West Virginia State Powerlifting Championships included the weight classes beginning at 181 thru the SuperHeavyweights. On the first day of the 1981 West Virginia State Powerlifting Championships, Doug Currence entered his first Powerlifting competition while competing in the 148lb. class. At a bodyweight of 148lbs., Doug Currence Squatted with 396, Bench Pressed 297, and Deadlifted 490 for a Total of 1184.

Competing in the 165lb. class, it was "Hundley versus Hundley." Don Hundley won the 1981 West Virginia State Powerlifting Championship in the 165lb. class while his son, Mike Hundley, placed 2nd. The battle for first place came down to the Deadlift with Don (father) pulling nearly 100 pounds more than Mike (son).

Day Two of the 1981 West Virginia State Powerlifting Championships began with the 181lb. class. In the Squat, the nearest competitor finished with a Squat of 562lbs., a weight of 255 kilos. After seeing a majority of red lights for the first and second attempts on my opening Squat of 606lbs. / 275 kilos, I set up with a closer stance and buried the weight to satisfy the judges on the 3rd attempt, rightfully earning three (3) white lights. At a bodyweight of only 178lbs., the lightest lifter in the 181lb. class, I had a lead of 44 pounds / 20 kilos, most of which my opponent would get back on the Bench Press.

Due to a pectoral muscle injury two (2) weeks prior to 3/29/81, I managed a "Close-Grip" Bench Press of only 341 lbs. (155 kilos) while my opponent Bench Pressed 396lbs. (180 kilos). The difference in Sub-Total had me behind by five (5) kilos (11 pounds). When the Deadlifts began, I knew that it would come down to the last lift. My opponent Deadlifted 611 ¾ lbs. (277.5 kilos) on his 2nd attempt. I pulled a Deadlift of 622 ¾ (282.5 kilos) for the first place victory in the 181lb. class.

In the 198lb. class, the lifting of Earl Snider caught the attention of the West Virginia Powerlifting community as Earl Deadlifted 677lbs., thinking he had won. Instead, Earl placed 3rd in a three-way tie for first place. Competing in the 220lb. class and lifting for *Luke's Gym*, Scott Tusic won his 3rd consecutive West Virginia State Powerlifting Championship title. Scott Tusic, at a bodyweight of 203, Squatted with 617, Bench Pressed 424, and Deadlifted 611 for a winning Total of 1653lbs. in the 220lb. class! Scott Tusic's Bench Press of 424 at a bodyweight of 203lbs. won the Best Bench Press Award for the Heavyweight Classes.

In the 275lb. class, Luke Iams narrowly got by Herb Fitzsimmons for the win. Luke Bench Pressed 529 for a new West Virginia State Powerlifting Record in the 275lb. class. Since 1976, *Luke's Gym* had won the West Virginia State Powerlifting Championship Team Award for six (6) consecutive years! The 6th Annual (1981) West Virginia State Powerlifting Championships was the last time *Luke's Gym* sponsored the West Virginia State Powerlifting Championships.

New talent emerged at the 1981 West Virginia State Powerlifting Championships. A couple of weeks following the 1981 West Virginia States in New Martinsville, Bret Russell competed at the 1981 Canton Open Powerlifting Meet in Canton, Ohio. Bret Russell's Total of 1690 in Canton, Ohio on April 18th, 1981 included a 645 Squat, 370 Bench Press, and a 675 Deadlift. Bret Russell's 645 Squat and 675 Deadlift were new West Virginia State Powerlifting Records in the 220lb. class.

Virginia Connection : Part IX

For West Virginia Powerlifting, it was the <u>1981 Roanoke Valley Open Powerlifting Championships</u> on May 30th, 1981 at Roanoke, Virginia. According to the official results, the 1981 Roanoke Valley Open Powerlifting Meet had eighty-one (81) lifters. There were no Sub-divisions at the 1981 Roanoke Valley Open. The 1981 Roanoke Valley Open Powerlifting Meet had one (1) division ; the Open Division.

There were at least fourteen (14) Powerlifters from the state of West Virginia entered at the 1981 Roanoke Valley Open. A Total of nine (9) Powerlifters from West Virginia represented *Herb's Gym*. The Powerlifters representing *Herb's Gym* at the 1981 Roanoke Valley Open Powerlifting Meet were : Don Hundley (165), Doug Currence (165), Vince White (181), Tom Russell (181), Paul Sutphin (198), Ross Smith (198), Bob Coulling (220), Curt Jones (220), and Herb Fitzsimmons (275lb. class).

Competing in a field of twelve (12) lifters on 5/30/81, Don Hundley won an overwhelming first place victory in the 165lb. class. Don Hundley also won the

Outstanding Lifter Award for the lighter classes. At the 1981 Roanoke Valley Open Powerlifting Meet, Don Hundley Squatted 551, Bench Pressed 281, and Deadlifted 600 for a Total of 1433lbs.

Doug Currence, in only his second Powerlifting competition and competing in the 165lb. class for the first time, placed 3rd with lifts of 435 Squat, 281 Bench Press, and a 462 Deadlift for a Total of 1179.

Vince White made one of his rare appearances in the 181lb. class at the 1981 Roanoke Valley Open Powerlifting Meet. Competing in a field of twelve (12) lifters on 5/30/81, Vince White placed 4th in the 181lb. class. At the 1981 Roanoke Valley Open Powerlifting Meet, Vince White Squatted 523, Bench Pressed 341, and Deadlifted 424 for a Total of 1289. Tom Russell placed 6th while competing in the 181lb. class on 5/30/81 with a Total of 1102.

The 1981 Roanoke Valley Open Powerlifting Meet was one of the few times I competed at a Powerlifting competition in the state of Virginia and came away without a first place victory. Based on my training phase at the time, I decided to compete in the 198lb. class for the first time ever. The rationale for the decision was linked to the strategy of "spreading out" the talent of the *Herb's Gym Powerlifting Team.*

The Powerlifting team of *Herb's Gym* had officially entered two (2) lifters in the 181lb. class and one (1) at 198 for the 1981 Roanoke Valley Open Powerlifting. Prior to the entry deadline of the 1981 Roanoke Open, I asked myself, "Which way should I go.? : A 181lb.'er or as a *light* 198?" The best case scenario was to have the maximum of two (2) lifters allowed in each weight class. At a bodyweight of 190 ¾, I entered the 198lb. class at the 1981 Roanoke Open on 5/30/81.

At the end of the day, my decision to compete in the 198lb. class at the 1981 Roanoke Valley Open Powerlifting proved to be a disadvantage to the Powerlifting team of *Herb's Gym.* Bodybuilding star and Powerlifter from North Carolina, Mike Ashley, competed in the 198lb. class. Ashley Squatted 722 and Bench Pressed 407. I fell short of overcoming Ashley's advantage on Sub-Total of 1129 to 997 and finished 3rd with a Total of 1614 in a field of eleven (11) competitors.

Mike Ashley won first place in the 198lb. class at the 1981 Roanoke Open with a Total of 1697. Jackie Cooper of *Roanoke Barbell Club* won 2nd Place with a Total of 1636. Ross Smith of *Herb's Gym* finished 4th while competing in the 198lb. class on 5/30/81 with a Squat of 540, Bench Press of 341, and a Deadlift of 529 for a Total of 1410. Competing in a field of eleven (11) lifters on 5/30/81, Bob Coulling of *Herb's Gym* finished 2nd in the 220lb. class with a Total of 1559. Bob's Total of 1559 included a Squat of 600 and a Deadlift of 600. Novice lifter Curt Jones of *Herb's Gym* finished with a Total of 1184 in the 220lb. class.

After the 1981 Roanoke Open, Herb Fitzsimmons unofficially retired from Powerlifting competition. Herb's lifts at the 1981 Roanoke Open Powerlifting Championships were 683 Squat, 380 Bench Press, and a 661 Deadlift for a Total of 1725. The fact that only two (2) International Referees were present at the 1981 Roanoke Open, Master's World Records could not be officially recognized. When reading the commentary of the 1981 Roanoke Open which accompanied the official contest report printed in the pages of the AUG/81 issue of *Powerlifting USA* magazine, one might perceive that the achievements of Herb Fitzsimmons, Don Hundley, and the Powerlifters from *Herb's Gym* were downplayed. Based on the point scoring of first place (5 points), second place (3 points), and third place (1 point), the *Roanoke Barbell Club* won the Team Award at the 1981 Roanoke Valley Open Powerlifting Championships over *Herb's Gym* by one (1) point.

A Total not much more than 1300 won first place in the 181lb. class at the 1981 Roanoke Open. Based on the logistics, had I competed in the 181lb. class rather than the 198's on 5/30/81, *Herb's Gym* would've won the Team Championship at the 1981 Roanoke Valley Open Powerlifting by a comfortable point margin. Therefore, I take full responsibility for the fact that there is one (1) less first (1st) Place Team Award in the trophy case at *Herb's Gym.*   *Powerlifting USA magazine / Vol. 5 / No. 2 / August, 1981*

Herb Fitzsimmons – Roanoke, Virginia – 5/30/81

October – December, 1981

The 8th Annual (1981) Mountianeer Open Powerlifting Championships were held October 31st and November 1st, 1981 at Mineral Wells, West Virginia. According to published results, there were approximately one-hundred forty-nine (149) lifters at the two (2) day event. The *Mountianeer Barbell Club* won the team championship at the 1981 Mountianeer Open. According to the championship report in the DEC/81 issue of *Powerlifting USA* magazine, there were seven (7) Elite lifters, eighteen (18) lifters met the standards for Master's Classification, while twenty-eight (28) lifters Totaled Class I. Jeff Cook won the Superheavyweight (SHW) class in the Open Division at the 1981 Mountianeer Open with a 1575 Total which included a new West Virginia State Record Deadlift of 677lbs.

The 8th Annual Mountian Empire Open Powerlifting Championships were held Saturday December 5th, 1981 at the Bristol Family YMCA in Bristol, Tennessee. The 1981 Mountian Empire Powerlifting Meet was the Tennessee Connection : Part XI. Bob Coulling improved from his Total of 1555 in 1980 by 105lbs. on 12/05/81, coming in with an impressive mark of 1660lbs.! At the 1981 Mountian Empire Powerlifting Meet at Bristol, Tennessee, Bob Squatted 650, Bench Pressed 370, and Deadlifted 640 for the win in the 220lb. class.

1980-1981 West Virginia Powerlifter Rankings

WV Powerlifters competing from January 1st, 1980 thru December 31st, 1981

TOP RANKINGS Determined by Total

114 / Name	Squat	Bench Press	Deadlift	Total	Date
Chuck Dunbar	507*	308*	374	1190* e	11/07/80
Chuck Dunbar – Bench Press 314 * wr (World Record) 4th attempt					
Chuck Dunbar	490*	286*	369	1146* e	4/19/80
Chuck Dunbar	479	305	363	1146 e	7/12/80
Dave Talbott	275	187	325	787	10/19/80
Scott Wilkinson	240	150	275	665	4/12/80
Dave Talbott	145	140	280	565	1/05/80

123	Squat	Bench Press	Deadlift	Total	Date
Chuck Dunbar	sq	295*	dl	1120*	3/30/80
Roger Salser	415	280*	415*	1110*	1/05/80
Dan Palmateer	325	231	407	964	10/31/81
Cork Hall	255	155	385	795	3/07/81

132	Squat	Bench Press	Deadlift	Total	Date
Ed Canjemi	450 y*	255*	465*	1170 y*	1/05/80
Ed Canjemi	451	242	473*	1168*	10/19/80
Ed Canjemi	451	259	457	1168	10/31/81
Roger Salser	455*	275*	425	1155	4/12/80
Roger Salser	415 c	285*c	425 c	1125 c	4/27/80
Ed Canjemi	440	230	440	1110	4/12/80
Dave Conway	375	225	435	1035	1/05/80
Mark McCoy	400	195	425	1020	5/10/80
Dan Palmateer	325	225	370	920	3/07/81

148	Squat	Bench Press	Deadlift	Total	Date
Doug Currence	396	297	490	1184	3/28/81
Laney Simone	457	231	479	1168	10/19/80
Mark McCoy	479	220	457	1157	5/30/81
Mike Sarver	407	264	479	1151	10/31/81
Mark McCoy	460	215	475	1150	11/22/80
David Hall	425	280	440	1145	1/05/80
Dave Conway	405	230	445	1080	4/12/80
Voltaire Jagdon	374	220	451	1046	10/31/81
Mike Sarver	380	236	424	1041	10/19/80
Fernando Aquilar	330	225	402	958	10/31/81
Scott Phillips	350	205	375	930	1/12/80

e – Elite Powerlifting Classification
* - West Virginia State Powerlifting Record
c – West Virginia State Collegiate Powerlifting Record
y – YMCA National Record
wr – World Record

1980-1981 West Virginia Powerlifter Rankings
WV Powerlifters competing from January 1st, 1980 thru December 31st, 1981
TOP RANKINGS Determined by Total

165 / Name	Squat	Bench Press	Deadlift	Total	Date
Paul Sutphin	585	345	605	1535 e	3/30/80
Paul Sutphin	570	340	560	1470	1/05/80
Don Hundley	573	259	617 wm	1449	1/10/81
Don Hundley	551	281	600	1432	5/30/81
Don Hundley	562	253	606 wm	1421	10/19/80
Dana Bee	520	380*	500	1400	1/05/80
Don Hundley	567	270	540	1377	10/31/81
Don Hundley	535	265	570	1370	11/07/81
Dana Bee	501	347	501	1349	10/19/80
Don Hundley	505	260	535	1300	3/30/80
Gene Underwood	473	330	496	1300	10/31/81
Doug Currence	460	290	485	1235	11/07/81
Greg Perry	462	281	473	1217	10/31/81
Doug Currence	435	281	462	1179	5/30/81
Mark Matson	440	275	440	1157	10/31/81
Randy Worley	402	275	451	1129	10/19/80
Harry Deitzler	315	300	440	1055	3/30/80
Randy Worley	390	250	415	1055	3/30/80
Randy Worley	350	270	420	1040	1/05/80
Randy Worley	370	250	405	1025	1/12/80
Aldo Pucci	303	231	402	936	10/31/81

* - West Virginia State Powerlifting Record

e – Elite Powerlifting Classification

wm – World Master's Record

1980-1981 West Virginia Powerlifter Rankings
WV Powerlifters competing from January 1st, 1980 thru December 31st, 1981
<u>TOP RANKINGS Determined by Total</u>

181 / Name	Squat	Bench Press	Deadlift	Total	Date
Paul Sutphin	639*	385	628*	1653* e	1/10/81
Paul Sutphin	640 u	360	625	1625 u	12/13/80
Paul Sutphin	622*	380	595	1598*	8/23/80
Paul Sutphin	605*	365	625*	1595*	5/10/80
Bill Kyle	600	396	578	1576	10/19/80
Paul Sutphin (178)	606	341	622	1570	3/29/81
Dave Jeffrey (179.5)	562	396	611	1570	3/29/81
Paul Sutphin	610	355	600	1565	12/05/81
Tim McCoy	540	325	555	1420	3/30/80
Dana Bee	500	385	535	1420	3/30/80
Dana Bee	540	370	500	1410	4/12/80
Tim McCoy	545	315	550	1410	5/10/80
Tim McCoy	525	315	550	1390	11/22/81
Don Hall	510	300	560	1370	3/30/80
Mike Hundley	501	286	562	1349	10/31/81
Don Hall	512	292	540	1344	10/19/80
Mike Hundley	501	270	545	1317	10/19/80
Vince White	523	341	424	1289	5/30/81
Don Hall	485	300	500	1285	1/05/80
Carey Wilson	465	300	510	1275	3/30/80
Robert Griffith	440	314	507	1261	10/19/80
Robert Hill	440	270	529	1239	10/31/81
Carey Wilson	440	303	479	1223	10/19/80
Tom Russell	418	303	429	1151	10/31/81
Greg Weaver	430	320	400	1150	6/13/81
Tom Russell	374	297	440	1113	10/19/80
Tom Russell	380	292	429	1102	5/30/81

* - West Virginia State Powerlifting Record

u – Unofficial West Virginia State Powerlifting Record

e – Elite Powerlifting Classification

1980-1981 West Virginia Powerlifter Rankings
WV Powerlifters competing from January 1ˢᵗ, 1980 thru December 31ˢᵗ, 1981
TOP RANKINGS Determined by Total

198 / Name	Squat	Bench Press	Deadlift	Total	Date
Paul Sutphin	617	380	617	1614	5/30/81
Gary Clark	580	400	580	1560	3/30/80
Gary Clark	560	390	580	1530	4/12/80
Gary Clark	570	390	540	1500	1/31/81
Earl Snider	505	355	625	1485	3/30/80
Tony Culp	556	325	540	1421	11/01/81
Buster Whitener	556	325	534	1416	11/01/81
Ross Smith	540	341	529	1410	5/30/81
Bret Russell	518	314	578	1410	10/19/80
Mike Brown	507	325	551	1383	11/01/81
Don Hall	507	314	529	1350	11/01/81
Ken McCoy	515	300	530	1345	11/22/80
Ross Smith	529	341	473	1344	10/19/80
Ken McCoy	501	303	534	1339	5/30/81
Steve Brooks	451	319	540	1311	10/19/80
Mike Brown	485	330	490	1306	5/10/80
Ken McCoy	490	275	530	1295	10/19/80
Greg Weaver	485	341	462	1289	11/01/81
Mike Leikari	410	300	545	1255	6/13/81
Mike Leikari	405	285	540	1230	3/07/81
Mike Leikari	407	292	529	1229	5/30/81
Robert Griffith	440	300	470	1210	4/12/80
Robert Griffith	440	300	445	1185	3/30/80
Mike Leikari	400	275	505	1180	4/12/80
Mike Leikari	390	275	465	1130	1/12/80

* - West Virginia State Powerlifting Record

e – Elite Powerlifting Classification

1980-1981 West Virginia Powerlifter Rankings
WV Powerlifters competing from January 1st, 1980 thru December 31st, 1981
TOP RANKINGS Determined by Total

220 / Name	Squat	Bench Press	Deadlift	Total	Date
Bret Russell	650	380	710	1741	11/01/81
Bret Russell	645*	370	675*	1690	4/18/81
Bret Russell	606	352	711	1669	10/17/81
Bob Coulling	650	370	640	1660	12/05/81
Scott Tusic	617	424	611	1653	3/29/81
Bob Coulling	630	370	640	1640	11/07/81
Bill Fox	565	445	630	1640	11/07/81
Scott Tusic	575	415	600	1590	3/30/80
Bob Coulling	600	358	600	1559	5/30/81
Bob Coulling	610	365	580	1555	12/13/80
Mike Fuscardo	610	370	570	1550	12/05/81
Ernie Nagy	560	415	565	1540	6/13/81
Bill Fox	529	418	584	1532	3/22/81
Bill Fox	530	400	565	1495	11/22/80
Ernie Nagy	540	385	562	1488	4/26/81
Ernie Nagy	550	385	550	1485	3/29/81
Ernie Nagy (Age 58)	501	407	567	1477 wm	10/25/81
Vince White	585	410	475	1470	3/30/80
Bill Fox	515	370	550	1435	6/28/80
Ernie Nagy	523	380	529	1432	5/03/80
Ernie Nagy (Age 57)	473	402	545	1421 wm	10/25/80
Randy Scott	451	407	545	1405	11/01/81
Dave Kyle	535	335	515	1385	4/12/80
Allen Johnson	510	360	505	1375	1/12/80
Allen Johnson	545	355	475	1375	3/30/80
Ernie Nagy	465	370	530	1365	8/30/80
Dan Hall	505	280	575	1360	1/05/80
Bill Fox	465	365	505	1335	1/12/80
Kevin Loy	501	297	534	1333	11/01/81
Mark Modesitt	451	369	462	1283	10/19/80
Dave Snyder	451	303	479	1234	11/01/81
Greg Moodie	450	290	480	1220	6/13/81
Greg Moodie	450	260	480	1190	3/07/81
Curt Jones	402	270	512	1184	5/30/81
Greg Moodie	430	270	470	1170	1/31/81
Greg Moodie	420	270	475	1165	1/12/80
Greg Moodie	420	260	485	1165	3/08/80

* - West Virginia State Powerlifting Record
wm – World Masters and National Masters Powerlifting Champion

1980-1981 West Virginia Powerlifter Rankings
WV Powerlifters competing from January 1st, 1980 thru December 31st, 1981
TOP RANKINGS Determined by Total

242 / Name	Squat	Bench Press	Deadlift	Total	Date
Scott Warman	667	385	667	1719	11/01/81
Al Johnson	628	369	622	1620	5/30/81
Jack Anderson	600	360	600	1560	1/05/80
Dan Bloxton	551	374	633	1559	11/01/81
Jack Anderson	600	350	600	1550	3/30/80
Scott Warman	545	374	595	1515	10/19/80
Dan Hall	551	303	578	1432	11/01/81
Bill McKisic	500	315	565	1380	3/07/81
Dan Hall	510	300	560	1370	3/30/80
Dan Hall	518	292	551	1361	10/19/80
Vince White	520	370	460	1350	1/19/80
Bill McKisic	479	308	562	1350	10/19/80
Dave Kyle	505	335	505	1345	3/30/80
Austin Miller	485	305	485	1275	1/05/80
Austin Miller	500	300	450	1250	4/27/80
Austin Miller	460	300	440	1200	1/19/80
275 Herb Fitzsimmons	685	420	700	1805	1/19/80
Herb Fitzsimmons	700	435	640	1775	1/05/80
Herb Fitzsimmons	683	380	661	1725	5/30/81
Bill McKisic	633	391	644	1669	11/01/81
Denny Cain	650	355	655	1660	6/13/81
Bill McKisic	600	325	600	1526	5/30/81
Jeff Cook	474	292	644	1410	10/19/80
Jim Slider	446	292	462	1201	11/01/81
Jim Slider	391	270	424	1085	10/19/80
Luke Iams	sq	529*	dl	T	3/29/81
SHW Luke Iams	727	529	600	1857	4/19/80
Jeff Cook	551	347	677*	1575	11/01/81
Luke Iams	855	580	d	T	3/30/80

* - West Virginia State Powerlifting Record

wm – World & National Masters Powerlifting Champion (50+ Age Group)

Chapter Seventeen : 1982

The <u>1982 YMCA National Powerlifting Championships</u> were conducted in Columbus, Ohio on January 9th, 1982. Scott Warman Totaled 1895 with a 749 Squat, 424 Bench Press, and a 722 Deadlift in the 242lb. class. With an Elite Total of 1895 in the 242lb. class, Scott Warman became the fourth (4th) West Virginia Powerlifter to Total Elite.

Depending on "What question was asked" or "To whom the question was directed to," supported the following argument : "1981 was a lackluster year for West Virginia Powerlifting." When the events were analyzed, we had come too far to allow regression. Therefore, a change of leadership was on the horizon.

Beginning with the Ohio Connections, the lifters of *Herb's Gym* and the *Holley Strength System* were determined to make 1982 a banner year for the Champions of West Virginia Powerlifting. The <u>1st Annual Muskingum Valley Open Powerlifting Championships</u> were held Sunday February 7th, 1982 in Zanesville, Ohio. The following Powerlifters represented *Herb's Gym* at Zanesville, Ohio on 2/07/82 : Don Hundley (165lb. class), Doug Currence (165), Paul Sutphin (181lb. class), Mike Hundley (181), Tom Russell (181), Don Hall (198lb. class), Jim Duffield (220lb. class), Vince White (220), Ross Smith (242lb. class), and Curt Jones (275lb. class).

Along with a 1495 Total, Don Hundley Deadlifted 650 in the 165lb. class for an unofficial World Record in the Master's Division (Age 45-49 category). Doug Currence put together a strong Total in the 165lb. class of 1305. At a bodyweight of 179 ¾ on 2/07/82 at Zanesville, Paul Sutphin Squatted 650, Bench Pressed 385, made one Deadlift of 585, and Totaled 1620.

Mike Hundley Totaled 1340 on 2/07/82 which included a 555 Deadlift for a 2nd Place finish in the 181lb. class. Tom Russell finished 7th at 181 with 1155. Don Hall finished 5th in the 220lb. class with a Total of 1425 behind Louie Simmons' first place finish at 1900 and Bret Russell's 2nd Place Total of 1810. Jim Duffield finished with a respectable 1355 in the 220lb. weight class.

Vince White was off to a good start in the 220lb. class with a 575lb. Squat and 370 Bench Press but failed to pull the Deadlift. Ross Smith finished 4th Place in the 242lb. class with a 1445 Total. Curt Jones Totaled 1395 in the 275lb. class for a 3rd Place finish. At the end of the day, *Herb's Gym* came away with a 2nd Place Team finish at a very tough Powerlifting competion in Zanesville, Ohio on 2/07/82.

Since the early 1970's, the Bob Moon Memorial Powerlifting Championship represented one of the most prestigious competitions in the sport of Powerlifting. The <u>1982 Bob Moon Memorial Powerlifting Championships</u> were held Saturday and Sunday on February 13th and 14th at Findlay, Ohio.

Competing in the 165lb. class, Don Hundley won first place at the 1982 Bob Moon Memorial with a Total of 1410. Don's lifts included a Squat of 567, Bench Press of 259, and a Deadlift of 584. Hundley's Deadlift of 584lbs. / 265 kilos was a Master's World Record (Age 45-49) in the 165lb. weight class.

Since 1972, one of my goals in Powerlifting was to compete and win at the Bob Moon Memorial Powerlifting Championships. On Saturday February 13th, 1982 the goal was accomplished. Weighing in at 180 ½, I Squatted with 606 ¼, Bench Pressed 358, Deadlifted 622 ¾, and Totaled 1587 for a first place victory in the 181lb. weight class.

In a field of ten (10) competitors, Vince White Totaled 1444 for a 3rd place finish while competing in the 198lb. class at the 1982 Bob Moon Memorial. On 2/13/82, Vince White Squatted 584, Bench Pressed 380, and Deadlifted 479 for a solid Total of 1444, adjudicated by National and Internationally certified officials.

"Setting the Records Straight" : Part I

The 7th Annual (1982) West Virginia State Powerlifting Championships were held Saturday April 24th and Sunday April 25th, 1982 at Fairmont State College in Fairmont, West Virginia. In preparation for a large turnout, the 1982 West Virginia State Powerlifting Championships were scheduled for two (2) days. The 114lb. classes thru the 165lb. weight classes lifted on Saturday April 24th and the 181lb. thru SuperHeavyWeight classes lifted on Sunday April 25th. In contrast to 1981, the 1982 West Virginia State Powerlifting competition was conducted in pounds rather than kilos.

During the Deadlifts of the first session, the pull of 430lbs. by Cork Hall in the 123lb. class replaced the previous mark of 420 owned by Roger Salser. The All-Time West Virginia Deadlift Record by Chuck Mooney of 425 was also broken by Cork Hall on April 24th, 1982. Ed Canjemi won the 1982 West Virginia State Championship in the 148lb. class with a Master Classification Total of 1250lbs. Included in Ed Canjemi's Total of 1250 was a Squat of 520lbs.

On Saturday April 24th, 1982 *Don Hundley "wiped out" the 645lb. Deadlift Record in the 165lb. class!* Don Hundley's West Virginia State Deadlift Record of 650lbs. in the 165lb. class broke the old mark of 645lbs. owned by Jack Wilson. Don Hundley successfully made the 650 Deadlift on a 3rd attempt to win the 1982 West Virginia State Powerlifting Championships in the 165lb. class.

Unfortunately, there was a lobbying effort led by a few individuals which challenged many of the existing West Virginia State Powerlifting Records. Apparently, the origin of the controversy focused on the West Virginia State Powerlifting Records that I had set while winning the *1981 YMCA National Powerlifting Championships* in the 181lb. class.

The argument, *"A YMCA National Powerlifting Championship should not be a contest where West Virginia State Powerlifting Records can be set or broken."* Highly motivated by the attempt to undermine the West Virginia Powerlifting system and eliminate existing Powerlifting Records, I told at least a few people, "I will win tomorrow and set the records again!" When it was all said and done, the "records argument" was laid to rest at the 1982 West Virginia Powerlifting Committee Meeting by a newly elected West Virginia Powerlifting Chairman.

On "Day Two" of the 1982 West Virginia State Powerlifting Championships, I began setting new records in the 181lb. class at a bodyweight of 180 ½. A solid first attempt opener on the Squat was like a warm-up. On a 2nd attempt, I Squatted 630lbs. but the 3rd attempt with an easy 660 was denied by two (2) red lights from the officials. After a 365 Bench Press, I finished the contest with a 630 Deadlift, a new West Virginia State Record in the 181lb. class and a seventh (7th) consecutive West Virginia State Powerlifting Championship with a 1625 Total.

Bret Russell became the fifth (5th) West Virginia Powerlifter to officially Total Elite on 4/25/82. With a Squat of 705, Deadlift of 770, and Total of 1870, Bret Russell became the new owner of three (3) West Virginia State Powerlifting Records in the 220lb. class. With the 1870 Elite Classification Total in the 220lb. class, Bret qualified for the 1982 Senior National Powerlifting Championships.

The Top 100 165lb. class including USA lifters competing from November, 1981 through October, 1982 ranked Don Hundley #9 on the Deadlift with a lift of 650lbs.! The date of the 650lb. Deadlift was 2/07/82. The eight (8) Powerlifters ranked in front of Don Hundley in the TOP 100 165lb. class (11/81 thru 10/82) were familiar names in Powerlifting : #1 Rick Gaugler (716 Deadlift), #2 Rickey Crain (699 Deadlift), #3 Troy Hicks (688 Deadlift), #4 Jim McCarty (683 Deadlift), #5 Mike Feight (677 Deadlift), #6 John Topsogolou (672 Deadlift), #7 Mike Facteau (665 Deadlift), and #8 Jack Welch (655 Deadlift). Don Hundley once again Deadlifted 650lbs. for an official West Virginia State Powerlifting Record on day number one (1) of the 1982 West Virginia State Powerlifting Championships on 4/24/82.

Vince White : West Virginia Powerlifting Chairman

The 1982 West Virginia Powerlifting Committee Meeting was conducted immediately following the Awards Presentation at the West Virginia State Powerlifting Championships on Sunday April 25th, 1982. Herb Fitzsimmons came to the West Virginia State Powerlifting Championships to officiate and cast a ballot representing

Herb's Gym at the meeting of the West Virginia Powerlifting Committee. In addition to Fitzsimmons, other representatives from West Virginia's five (5) registered Powerlifting clubs expressed their concerns and cast their votes. At the end of the day, Vince White was elected West Virginia Powerlifting Chairman on Sunday evening April 25th, 1982.

Under the direction of a new West Virginia Powerlifting Chairman, more Powerlifting meets in the state of West Virginia were placed on the calendar. In 1982, the Teenagers would have their own State Powerlifting Championship. The 1st Annual Parkersburg Open would be held in May at Mineral Wells. Pending the approval for a sanction from the USPF National Office, a <u>Powerlifting Qualifier</u> was tentatively on the agenda for Charleston at the end of May. The 9th Mountianeer Open Powerlifting Championships were set for the month of October and a Powerlifting Meet at Weirton would be held during December, 1982.

The <u>1982 West Virginia State Teenage Powerlifting Championships</u> were held at Parkersburg. In addition to a couple of local lifters, West Virginia Powerlifting Chairman Vince White and myself performed the official's duties. Many West Virginia State Teenage Powerlifting Records were set in one categorical age group (Age 14 thru 19). The 1982 West Virginia Teenage Powerlifting Championship was the first event of its kind due to the fact that all three (3) lifts (SQ-BP-DL) were contested. The teenage Powerlifters of West Virginia set *Official* West Virginia State Powerlifting Records in the Squat, the Bench Press, the Deadlift, and Total at the 1982 West Virginia Teenage Powerlifting Championships.

The <u>1st Annual Parkersburg Open Powerlifting Meet</u> was held May 22nd, 1982 at Mineral Wells, West Virginia. The 1982 Parkersburg Open had fifty-eight (58) lifters. Doug Currence won the 165lb. class with a Total of 1344 and the Outstanding Lifter Award. Don Hall finished 3rd in the 198lb. class with a Total of 1482.

Virginia Connection : Part X

As late as 1982, Powerlifters did not have the option of entering the Senior National Powerlifting Championships without achieving a Qualifying Total. A Qualifying Total in a bonafide USPF sanctioned Powerlifting competition was mandatory prior to the deadline, approximately six (6) weeks before the Senior National Powerlifting Championship event. In most cases, the Qualifying Total was well above the minimum standard for Elite Powerlifter Classification in each weight class. Proof of a lifter's Qualifying Total was a requirement in order for the lifter's entry form to be accepted.

By May of 1982, making the Qualifying Total for the 1982 U.S. Senior National Powerlifting Championships became priority number one (1) for Paul Sutphin. The 1982 Roanoke Centennial Open Powerlifting Championships were held Saturday May 15th, 1982 in Roanoke, Virginia. The turnout for the 1982 Roanoke Open was fifty-eight (58) lifters. Don Hundley, Warren Knight, and Paul Sutphin represented the Powerlifters of West Virginia well with three (3) first place victories and two (2) Outstanding Lifter Awards.

The Qualifying Total of 1670lbs. in the 181lb. class for the 1982 Senior Nationals was achieved by Paul Sutphin at Roanoke, Virginia on 5/15/82 at a bodyweight of 181¾. A Squat of 655, Bench Press of 370, and a Deadlift of 645 comprised a Total of 1670 in the 181lb. weight class. The 1670lb. Total won 1st Place at 181 and the Outstanding Lifter Award at the 1982 Roanoke Open.

For Don Hundley, 1982 was the 2nd consecutive year of winning the Outstanding Lifter Award at the Roanoke Open. Don Hundley pulled a 590 Deadlift to win first place in the 165lb. class on bodyweight with a Total of 1410. Warren Knight won the 220lb. class at the 1982 Roanoke Open with a 1600 Total.

1982 Senior Nationals

The 1982 U. S. Senior National Powerlifting Championships were held Saturday July 10th and Sunday July 11th, 1982 at the Dayton Convention Center in Dayton, Ohio. The Meet Director was Larry Pacifico. Larry Pacifico had won and *has won* more World Titles in Powerlifting than anyone with a bodyweight of over 200lbs. As Director and organizer of the 1982 Senior Nationals, Larry gave Powerlifting and Powerlifters a contest to be remembered for decades.

The 1982 Senior Nationals had it all. The West Virginians in the event included Bret Russell (220), Scott Warman (2nd Place @ 242), and Paul Sutphin (181). The performance of Scott Warman at the 1982 Senior Nationals set the stage for future championship wins. Scott's Squat of 826, Deadlift of 771, and Total of 2039 were new West Virginia State Powerlifting Records in the 242lb. class.

While competing in the 181lb. class at the 1982 Seniors at a bodyweight of 181.43 lbs., I managed an Elite Total of 1653, completing only 5 of 9 attempts. The 1653 Total included a Squat of 650, Bench Press of 380, and a Deadlift of 622. I was mostly content with the Total of 1653 at the 1982 Senior Nationals. As a matter of fact, the 1653 Elite Total made at the 1982 U.S. Senior Nationals would've placed 4th at the 1982 IPF World Powerlifting Championships.

Chillicothe to Lexington

The 1st Annual Southern Ohio Open Powerlifting Meet was held on August 21st and August 22nd, 1982 at Chillicothe, Ohio. Included in the official results, *the 1982 Southern Ohio Open Powerlifting Meet* had one-hundred nineteen (119) lifters. Winning first place in the 181lb. weight class in a field of twelve (12) competitors (Class II & Below Division), Mike Hundley Totaled 1370 which included a 570 Deadlift. Scott Tusic won the 220lb. class with a 1640 Total.

While competing in the 198lb. class at the *1982 Southern Ohio Open Powerlifting Meet*, Vince White tied for first place with a Total of 1440. The Total of 1440 by Vince White at the 1982 Southern Ohio Open included a 570 Squat, 395 Bench Press, and a 475 Deadlift. The 395 Bench Press in the 198lb. class by Vince White on 8/22/82 was a PR for Vince as a Middleheavyweight while competing in an *official Powerlifting competition.*

The 1982 Lexington Open Powerlifting Meet was held on October 9th, 1982 in Lexington, Kentucky. For the first time in over six (6) years, a number of West Virginia Powerlifters returned to Lexington, Kentucky for the Lexington Open. According to the official meet results, the 1982 Lexington Open Powerlifting Meet had fifty (50) lifters. Among the winners, Ross Smith Totaled 1475 in the 198lb. class and tied for first place at the 1982 Lexington Open.

While lifting at Lexington, Kentucky on 10/09/82, Vince White "picked up where he left off" in January, 1976. Vince White broke the Lexington Open Bench Press Record at the 1975 Lexington Open and another Meet Record at the 1976 Lexington Open Powerlifting Championships. While competing in the 220lb. class at the 1982 Lexington Open, Vince White Totaled 1445 with lifts of 565 Squat, 400 Bench Press, and a 480 Deadlift. The Bench Press of 400lbs. by Vince White was a Lexington Open Powerlifting Meet Record and the highest Bench Press of the 1982 Lexington Open Powerlifting Championships conducted on 10/09/82.

9th Annual Mountianeer Open

The 9th Annual Mountianeer Open Powerlifting Championships were held October 30th and 31st, 1982 at Mineral Wells, West Virginia. In reference to the official results published in the December, 1982 issue of *Powerlifting USA* magazine, the 1982 Mountianeer Open Powerlifting Championships had ninety-one (91) lifters. Among the winners were Chuck Mooney (114lb. class), Butch Brown (165lb. class), and Don Hall (220lb. class).

While competing at the 1982 Mountianeer Open, Butch Brown made an Elite Total of 1537lbs. / 697.5 kilos in the 165lb. class. The Elite Total of 1537 by Butch Brown on 10/30/82 included a 584 Squat, 325 Bench Press, and a 628 Deadlift. Butch Brown's Squat, Deadlift, and Total on 10/30/82 were new Mountianeer Open Powerlifting Meet Records in the 165lb. class. The Elite Total of 1537 by Butch Brown at the 1982 Mountianeer Open Powerlifting Championships ranked #29 in the Top 100 165lb. class for USA lifters competing from November, 1981 through October, 1982.

Don Hundley continued to break World Masters Powerlifting Records while competing at the 1982 Mountianeer Open Powerlifting Championships on 10/30/82. While competing in the 165lb. class, Don Hundley broke three (3) World Master's Powerlifting Records with a 573 Squat, 606 Deadlift, and a Total of 1438lbs, specific to the Master's Category (Age 45-49) / 165lb. weight class. For whatever the reason, the 573 Squat, 617 Deadlift, and 1449 Total by Don Hundley from the 1981 YMCA Nationals were not recorded as official Masters Powerlifting Records. On 10/30/82, Don Hundley duplicated the 573 Squat, Deadlifted 606, and Totaled 1438, "Setting the Records Straight."

For the first time ever, Don Hall won first place at the Mountianeer Open Powerlifting Championship on 10/31/82. Don Hall's Total of 1510 while competing in the Open Division of the 220lb. class included a 589 Squat, 347 Bench Press, and a 573 Deadlift. The 1510 Total by Don Hall on 10/31/82 was the highest of all eleven (11) lifters competing in both the Open and Below Class II Divisions of the 220lb. weight class.

1982 : Powerlifting in December

On the weekend of December 11th, 1982 there were two (2) Powerlifting competitions scheduled in two (2) different cities approximately 400 miles apart. The annual event at Bristol, Tennessee just happened to be on the same weekend as the Powerlifting meet in Weirton, West Virginia. In order to avoid a conflict of interest, West Virginia Powerlifting Chairman Vince White and several others from *Herb's Gym* were committed to the event at Weirton. As for Paul Sutphin and a few lifters from the *Bluefield YMCA Weightlifting Club*, it was Powerlifting at Bristol.

The 1982 Mountian Empire Open Powerlifting Meet was held Saturday December 11th, 1982 at Bristol, Tennessee. The 1982 Powerlifting competition at Bristol, Tennessee was the Tennessee Connection : Part XII. The *Bluefield YMCA Weightlifting Club* competed as a Team at the 1982 Mountian Empire Open. Jim Simon, competing in his first Powerlifting competition, finished with a Total of 1265 in the 198lb. class. Jim's Total of 1265 included a Squat of 440, Bench Press of 325, and a Deadlift of 500. Bobby Fox also placed in the 198lb. class with a Total of 1035.

The 1st Annual Body Shop Powerlifting Meet was held December 11th & 12th, 1982 in Weirton, West Virginia. According to the official results, the 1st Annual Body Shop Powerlifting Meet had approximately ninety (90) lifters. A total of three (3) West Virginia State Powerlifting Records were broken. While competing in the 132lb. class, Ed Canjemi Squatted with 465, a new West Virginia State Powerlifting Record. Canjemi's Total of 1175 was also a new West Virginia State Record. Don Hundley won first place in Weirton on 12/11/82 in the 165lb. class with a Total of 1490. Included in the 1490 Total by Don Hundley was a new West Virginia State Record Deadlift of 655lbs. Don Hundley also won the Masters Division and the Outstanding Lifter Award at Weirton, West Virginia on 12/11/82.

1982 West Virginia Powerlifter Rankings
WV Powerlifters competing from January 1st, 1982 thru December 31st, 1982
TOP Performance RANKINGS Determined by Total

114 / Name	Squat	Bench Press	Deadlift	Total	Date
Dave Talbott	314	225	374	914	5/22/82
Dave Talbott	305	225	380	910	4/24/82
Chuck Mooney	281	181	402	865	10/30/82
Rick Casey	242	187	292	721	10/30/82
Sonny Shrader	209	181	253	644	10/30/82
123 Cork Hall	330	190	430*	950	4/24/82
Cork Hall	330	192	402	925	5/22/82
Rick Yates	281	187	352	820	10/30/82
Rick Yates	260	190	330	780	8/21/82
Scott Steele	242	181	286	710	10/30/82
132 Ed Canjemi	475 u	260	480 u	1215 u	10/09/82
Ed Canjemi	465*	240	470	1175*	12/11/82
Dan Palmateer	446	270	407	1124	10/30/82
Dan Palmateer	415	260	425	1100	4/24/82
Maurice Kinzer	363	248	435	1047	8/06/82
Art Williamson	330	195	440	965	12/11/82
Mike Kimball	370	200	390	960	12/11/82
Art Williamson	325	185	405	915	6/26/82
Art Williamson	330	198	305	914	5/22/82
Art Williamson	320	185	365	870	3/13/82
Art Williamson	325	190	350	865	4/24/82
Art Williamson	300	175	345	820	2/07/82

* - West Virginia State Powerlifting Record

u – Unofficial West Virginia State Powerlifting Record

1982 West Virginia Powerlifter Rankings
WV Powerlifters competing from January 1st, 1982 thru December 31st, 1982
<u>TOP RANKINGS</u> Determined by Total

148 / Name	Squat	Bench Press	Deadlift	Total	Date
Ed Canjemi	520	275	455	1250	4/24/82
Don McCartney	465	290	450	1205	12/11/82
Mark McCoy	490	242	468	1201	12/11/82
Mark McCoy	480	235	465	1180	10/09/82
Mark McCoy	450	245	480	1175	4/24/82
Mike Sarver	410	265	480	1155	4/24/82
Mike Sarver	418	270	446	1135	3/19/82
Don McCartney	395	290	455	1135	4/24/82
Mike Sarver	385	275	468	1129	10/30/82
Mike Sarver	374	248	440	1063	5/22/82
Keith Gandee	374	270	402	1047	10/30/82
Scott Phillips	402	203	424	1030	5/22/82
Paul Hickman	265	255	415	935	4/24/82
165 Butch Brown	584	325	628	1537 e	10/30/82
Don Hundley	580	265	650 u	1495	2/07/82
Don Hundley	580	265	650*	1495	4/24/82
Don Hundley	585	250	655*	1490	12/11/82
Butch Brown	555	290	600	1445	4/24/82
Don Hundley	573 wm	259	606 wm	1438 wm	10/30/82
Don Hundley	567	259	584 wm	1410	2/13/82
Don Hundley	550	270	590	1410	5/15/82
Greg Perry	518	303	540	1361	3/19/82
Doug Currence	501	303	540	1344	5/22/82
Doug Currence	485	300	520	1305	2/07/82
Mark Matson	450	305	465	1220	4/24/82
Scott Phillips	470	225	475	1170	12/11/82
Scott Phillips	451	253	451	1157	10/30/82
Paul Hickman	395	270	455	1120	12/11/82

e – Elite Powerlifting Total

wm – World Master's Record Powerlifting Record

* - West Virginia State Powerlifting Record

u – Unofficial West Virginia State Powerlifting Record

1982 West Virginia Powerlifter Rankings
WV Powerlifters competing from January 1st, 1982 thru December 31st, 1982
TOP RANKINGS Determined by Total

181 / Name	Squat	Bench Press	Deadlift	Total	Date
Paul Sutphin	655 u	370	645 u	1670 u e	5/15/82
Paul Sutphin	650*	380	622	1653* e	7/10/82
Paul Sutphin	630 r	365	630*	1625 r	4/25/82
Paul Sutphin	650 u	385	585	1620	2/07/82
Paul Sutphin	606	358	622	1587	2/13/82
Robert Griffith	575	365	645	1585	10/09/82
Robert Griffith	550	350	625	1525	4/25/82
Doug Currence	530	330	590	1450	12/11/82
Don Hall	540	320	525	1385	4/25/82
Greg Perry	523	319	540	1383	10/30/82
Mike Hundley	515	285	570	1370	8/21/82
C. Dave Drennan	468	369	507	1344	5/22/82
Mike Hundley	500	285	555	1340	2/07/82
Doug Currence	490	303	534	1328	10/30/82
Tom Warren	479	358	485	1322	5/22/82
Marshall Moore	485	248	562	1295	5/22/82
Tom Russell	457	325	501	1283	5/22/82
Cary Wilson	473	303	501	1278	10/30/82
Tom Russell	445	310	475	1230	4/25/82
Jerry Pomposelli	460	280	455	1195	12/11/82
Tom Russell	418	319	424	1162	10/30/82
Tom Russell	400	300	455	1155	2/07/82
M. Davis	400	250	450	1100	4/25/82
Aldo Pucci	385	260	420	1065	2/07/82

e – Elite Powerlifting Total

* - West Virginia State Powerlifting Record

r – (Revised) West Virginia State Powerlifting Record

u – West Virginia State Powerlifting Record

1982 West Virginia Powerlifter Rankings
WV Powerlifters competing from January 1st, 1982 thru December 31st, 1982
TOP RANKINGS Determined by Total

198 / Name	Squat	Bench Press	Deadlift	Total	Date
Buster Whitener	600	391	655	1647	10/30/82
Buster Whitener	600	374	644	1620	5/22/82
Buster Whitener	610	370	635	1615	4/25/82
Tony Culp	622	374	600	1597	10/30/82
Gary Clark	610	400	570	1580	3/27/82
Gary Clark	610	390	580	1580	12/12/82
Tony Culp	600	360	585	1545	4/25/82
Dave Drennan	534	424	562	1520	10/30/82
Don Hall	570	340	585	1495	12/12/82
Tony Culp	570	350	565	1485	3/27/82
Don Hall	573	341	567	1482	5/22/82
Ross Smith	560	375	540	1475	10/09/82
Ken McCoy	595	330	540	1466	12/11/82
Ken McCoy	570	330	560	1460	10/09/82
Vince White	584	380	479	1444	2/13/82
Vince White	570	395	475	1440	8/21/82
Don Hall	535	330	560	1425	2/07/82
Rick Dotson	523	341	501	1366	10/31/82
Mike Leikari	435	303	600	1339	5/22/82
Mike Leikari	445	320	555	1320	8/21/82
Jim Simon	440	325	500	1265	12/11/82
Aldo Pucci	450	320	475	1245	12/11/82
Aldo Pucci	451	314	462	1228	10/31/82
Bill Blankenship	410	245	470	1125	4/25/82
Bobby Fox	380	240	415	1035	12/11/82

1982 West Virginia Powerlifter Rankings
WV Powerlifters competing from January 1st, 1982 thru December 31st, 1982
TOP RANKINGS Determined by Total

220 / Name	Squat	Bench Press	Deadlift	Total	Date
Bret Russell (OL)	705*	395	770*	1870* e	4/25/82
Bret Russell	700	400	710	1810	2/07/82
Bret Russell	650	380	755	1785	1/09/82
Bret Russell	650	385	727	1763	7/11/82
Bill Fox	639	451	595	1686	3/20/82
Scott Tusic	600	440	600	1640	8/22/82
Paul Sutphin (199 ¾)	650	355	630	1635	12/11/82
Warren Knight	575	380	645	1600	5/15/82
Randy Scott	550	435	600	1585	3/27/82
Mike Fuscardo	640	360	575	1575	12/12/82
Tim McCoy	633	347	540	1521	12/11/82
Warren Knight	550	350	620	1520	11/20/82
Don Hall	589	347	573	1509	10/31/82
Ernie Nagy	550	400	540	1490	3/27/82
Ernie Nagy (216)	540	385	540	1465	12/12/82
Vince White	580	390	475	1445	4/25/82
Vince White	565	400	480	1445	10/09/82
Ken McCoy	530	285	535	1420	4/25/82
Kevin Loy	534	308	534	1377	5/22/82
Ernie Nagy	490	330	540	1361	9/05/82
Kevin Loy	530	285	535	1350	4/25/82
Greg Moodie	480	300	525	1305	12/12/82
Cary Wilson	500	305	480	1285	12/12/82
Dave Snyder	474	319	490	1283	10/31/82
Greg Moodie	450	300	520	1270	3/13/82
Ernie Nagy (207)	473	308	457	1240	6/13/82
Dave Snyder	440	303	479	1223	5/22/82

* - West Virginia State Powerlifting Record

e – Elite Powerlifting Total

1982 West Virginia Powerlifter Rankings
WV Powerlifters competing from January 1st, 1982 thru December 31st, 1982
TOP RANKINGS Determined by Total

242/ Name	Squat	Bench Press	Deadlift	Total	Date
Scott Warman	826*	440	771*	2039* e	7/11/82
Scott Warman	780 u	435	745 u	1960 u e	3/27/82
Scott Warman	749 u	424	722 u	1895 u e	1/09/82
Bill Fox	690	470	650	1810	12/12/82
Randy Scott	667	485	622	1774	10/31/82
Bill Fox	672	485	611	1769	6/06/82
Bill Fox	665	455	605	1725	5/15/82
Randy Scott	615	455	610	1680	4/25/82
Dan Bloxton	645	385	640	1670	8/22/82
Nick Busick	680	410	580	1670	12/12/82
Nick Busick	650	451	562	1664	10/31/82
Allen Johnson	600	375	590	1565	4/25/82
Bill McKisic	530	350	615	1495	12/12/82
Ross Smith	570	370	505	1445	2/07/82
Mark Modesitt	501	391	501	1394	10/31/82
275 Scott Warman	716	391	672	1780	12/11/82
Dan Hall	610	355	615	1580	12/12/82
Dan Hall	625	330	590	1545	4/25/82
Bill McKisic	562	352	600	1515	5/22/82
Bill McKisic	555	345	600	1500	4/25/82
Curt Jones	500	300	600	1400	4/25/82
Curt Jones	490	325	580	1395	2/07/82
Wayne Lilly	374	292	462	1129	10/31/82
SHW Jeff Cook	622	385	699 u	1708	10/31/82
Jeff Cook	600	358	667	1625	3/20/82
Charles Ashcraft	530	300	480	1310	12/12/82
Luke Iams	600	400	Bombed Out---		4/25/82

* - West Virginia State Powerlifting Record

u – Unofficial West Virginia State Powerlifting Record

e – Elite Powerlifting Classification Total

Chapter Eighteen : 1983

While Vince White and I attended the 1983 YMCA National Powerlifting Championships on the weekend of January 8th, 1983 in Columbus, Ohio, several West Virginia Powerlifters competed at the <u>West Virginia Challenge Cup Powerlifting</u> held Sunday January 9th, 1983 at Beckley, West Virginia. According to the official meet results, the 1983 West Virginia Challenge Cup Powerlifting competition had thirty-two (32) lifters. Among the winners at the 1983 West Virginia Challenge Cup Powerlifting Meet included the following lifters :

Chuck Mooney (114lb. class – 900 Total),
Darrell Devor (123lb. class – 825 Total),
Ed Canjemi (132lb. class – 1235 Total),
Doug Currence (181lb. class – 1455 Total),
Don Hall (198lb. class – 1455 Total),
Jim Simon (220lb. class – 1295 Total), and
Dan Hall (275lb. class – 1545 Total).

For the first time, the 1983 West Virginia State Powerlifting Championship event was scheduled for the Charleston area ; Elkview, West Virginia. Since 1980, the attendance at the West Virginia State Powerlifting Championships had peaked. With a low turnout in 1982, the new location for the 1983 event energized the lifting population with renewed enthusiasm.

From what began in 1976, the "Program" for West Virginia Powerlifting was two-fold : 1) The "Program" in hard-copy was designed, printed, and distributed to all lifters, participants, and spectators at the 1983 West Virginia Powerlifting Championship. 2) The "West Virginia State Powerlifting Program" was moving forward under the direction of a new West Virginia Powerlifting Chairman, Vince White.

An Official State Meet Program was not provided at the 1982 West Virginia State Powerlifting Championships. The Official West Virginia State Powerlifting Championship Meet Program returned in 1983. The 1983 Official West Virginia State Powerlifting Championship Meet Program consisted of a welcome letter from West Virginia's Secretary of State, a list of trivia questions containing facts about West Virginia Powerlifters, a list of the West Virginia State Powerlifting Records, scoring charts, and the official rules for Powerlifting. Also included in the 1983 West Virginia

State Meet Program were the formulas for calculating the Outstanding Lifter Award among male and female Powerlifters.

Not since 1975 in York, Pennsylvania had I attempted to take the National Referee's Exam for Powerlifting. For the purpose of administering Powerlifting's National Referee Examination, Vince White (IPF Category II Referee) provided accommodations and assistance to those individuals willing to study the rules of the sport of Powerlifting. A number of successful candidates participated in a Rules Clinic on Friday evening 3/25/83, took the National Referee's Exam, and earned a passing grade of "greater than or equal to" ninety (90) percent.

Following the process of administering the National Referee's Examination on the eve of the 1983 West Virginia State Powerlifting Championships, Vince White made available to State Powerlifting Referees a circular, yellow badge which read, "West Virginia State Powerlifting Official."

8th WV State Powerlifting Championships

The 8th Annual (1983) West Virginia State Powerlifting Championships were held Saturday March 26th, 1983 at Elkview, West Virginia. The 1983 West Virginia State Powerlifting Championships represented the largest turnout for a West Virginia State Powerlifting Meet with seventy-seven (77) lifters. The Meet Director for the 1983 West Virginia State Powerlifting Championships was Vince White, West Virginia State Powerlifting Chairman.

The "West Virginia State Powerlifting Marathon" would be a good name for the 1983 West Virginia State Powerlifting Championships. Not a disadvantage, in my view. Looking back, the 1983 West Virginia State Powerlifting Championship was one of my favorites for a number of reasons. Given the facts, the 1983 West Virginia State Powerlifting Championships began Saturday 3/26/83(am) and ended on Sunday 3/27/83(am). While lifting at a bodyweight of approximately 192lbs., I took the 644 ¾ Deadlift (292.5 kilos) on 3rd attempt to finish with a 1703 Total for the win in the 198lb. class at about 1:30 a.m., Sunday March 27th, 1983.

There was plenty of action "early on" from the first session of the 1983 West Virginia State Powerlifting Championships. Winning his first West Virginia State Powerlifting title since 1976, Chuck Mooney won the 114lb. class over four (4) competitors. Mooney's PR Deadlift of 429 and Total of 914 gave him a comfortable margin of victory over his nearest competitor.

Roger Salser dominated the 123lb. class for the 1983 West Virginia State Championship victory with a Total of 1030 in a field of six (6) competitors. Cork Hall broke his own Deadlift record mark while competing in the 123lb. class with a lift of 435lbs. Cork Hall's Total on 3/26/83 was 986 for 3rd place.

In the 132lb. class, it was Dan Palmateer winning the 1983 West Virginia State Powerlifting title over Acie Simmons. Acie Simmons Bench Pressed a West Virginia State Record of 336lbs. (152.5 kilos) and put together a Total of 1124 for 2nd Place. Palmateer's lifts included a West Virginia State Deadlift Record in the 132lb. class of 479lbs. and a West Virginia Total Record of 1184.

While competing in the 148llb. class on 3/26/83, Gene Underwood cruised to victory with a 1245 Total over ten (10) competitors. Butch Brown placed first in the 165lb. class with a Total of 1493 which included a 567 Squat, 308 Bench Press, and a 622 Deadlift.

Robert Griffith won the 181lb. class at the 1983 West Virginia States with a 1614 Total and a West Virginia State Record Deadlift of 644lbs. Competing in the 181lb. class, C. Dave Drennan set a new Bench Press Record of 402lbs., while winning 3rd place. Drennan's Total on 3/26/83 was 1471.

Paul Sutphin broke the 1700lb. Total barrier for the first time on March 26th, 1983 and won his eight (8th) West Virginia State Powerlifting Championship title while competing in the 198lb. class. At a bodyweight of 192, Sutphin won the 1983 West Virginia State Powerlifting title over ten (10) competitors. Sutphin's performance at the 1983 West Virginia States represented a West Virginia State Championship win in four (4) different weight classes. The 677 ¾ Squat by Sutphin on 3/26/83 in the 198lb. weight class ranked #38 in the P/L USA TOP 100 Powerlifters for USA lifters competing from December, 1982 through November of 1983.

Bret Russell won the 220lb. class at the 1983 West Virginia State Powerlifting Championship for the 2nd consecutive year. Russell's Total of 1840 captured the "Champion of Champions" Award for the entire contest based on Swartz Formula. Randy Scott won the 242lb. class on 3/26/83 with a Total of 1846. The 1846 Total by Randy Scott included a new West Virginia State Bench Press Record of 227.5 kilos / 501lbs. in the 242lb. class.

Dan Hall won the 1983 West Virginia State Championships in the 275lb. class. Jeff Cook won the SuperHeavyWeight class on 3/26/83 with a Total of 1746 including a new West Virginia State Deadlift Record of 722lbs. Jeff Cook's new Deadlift Record on 3/26/83 broke the old official mark of 677lbs. set in 1981.

When the numbers were "crunched" in determining the 1983 West Virginia State Powerlifting Championship Team Award, the absence of Don Hundley in the 165lb. class cost *Herb's Gym* valuable team points. Powerlifters competing for *Herb's Gym* won victories in the following weight classes : 114, 198, and 275's. Powerlifters competing for the *Mountianeer Barbell Club* won victories in the following weight classes : 123, 132, 165, 181, and 220's. Consequently, the *Mountianeer Barbell Club* won the Team Award at the 1983 West Virginia State Powerlifting Championships.

The 1983 West Virginia State Powerlifting Championships on 3/26/83 had three (3) competitors in the Master's Division. Ernie Nagy proved he was the "Man of Steel" with four (4) new American Powerlifting Records while in the Master's Division (Age 60-64). Ernie Nagy Totaled 1471 while competing in the 220lb. class.

Ernie Nagy's American Master's Record Squat of 523lbs., Bench Press of 407, and Deadlift of 540 equaled the American Record Total of 1471lbs. John Bayliss set four (4) West Virginia State Masters Records while competing in the 148lb. class. Austin Miller won the Master's Division in the 242lb. class with a Total of 1113.

For the 2nd consecutive year, the 1983 West Virginia State Teenage Powerlifting Championships were held in Parkersburg, West Virginia on Saturday April 23rd, 1983. According to the official results, the 1983 West Virginia State Teenage Powerlifting Championships had a total of fifty (50) lifters. For the second consecutive year, Vince White and myself assisted the Meet Directors with the event. A Total of sixteen (16) West Virginia State Teenage Powerlifting Records were broken at the 1983 West Virginia State Teenage Powerlifting Championships.

1983 Parkersburg Open

The <u>1983 Parkersburg Open Powerlifting Championships</u> were held at Mineral Wells, West Virginia on May 28th, 1983. According to the official results, the 1983 Parkersburg Open had approximately sixty (60) lifters. Notable performances at the 1983 Parkersburg Open Powerlifting Championships included another win by Virginia Teenage Powerlifting Champion Darrell Devor in the 123lb. class. In the 132lb. class, Richard Walsh won the Class II & Under Division. Other winners on 5/28/83 included Bret Russell (1st @ 220) and Randy Scott (1st @ 242). Dan Palmateer lifted as Extra Lifter at a bodyweight of 144lbs. and Totaled 1245 in the 148llb. class.

On 5/28/83, the standard for an official Elite Powerlifting Classification required a minimum Total of 1642 in the 181lb. class. However, the Qualifying Total for the 1983 U.S. Senior Nationals was 1714lbs. / 777.5 kilos. It just so happened that the 1714 Total became reality for Paul Sutphin at the 1983 Parkersburg Open Powerlifting Meet. Paul Sutphin was the only West Virginia Powerlifter to qualify for the Senior National Powerlifting Championships in 1983.

The 1714 Elite Total by Paul Sutphin in the 181lb. class at a bodyweight of 177 ½ at the 1983 Parkersburg Open included a 688 ¾ Squat, 380 Bench Press, and a 644 ¾ Deadlift. Going "8 for 8" on 5/28/83, Sutphin's 1714lbs. (777.5 kilos) Total with the 688 ¾ (312.5 kilos) Squat in the 181lb. class exceeded the official West Virginia State Powerlifting Records and captured the victory *along with* the Outstanding Lifter Award.

Paul Sutphin – 688 ¾ Squat
Bodyweight of 177 ½ lbs. / 181lb. Class - 1714 Total – 5/28/83

At the <u>1983 Southwest Open Powerlifting Meet</u> on August 27th, 1983 Paul Sutphin Squatted with 705, Bench Pressed 390, and Deadlifted 655 for a Total of 1750 in the 181lb. class.

Summer of 1983

The <u>1983 National (Junior) Powerlifting Championships</u> were held June 4th and 5th, 1983 at Charlottesville, Virginia. According to the official results, the 1983 Junior Nationals had one-hundred seventy-nine (179) lifters. Officiating at the 1983 National (Junior)

Powerlifting Championships at Charlottesville, Virginia were National Referee Paul Sutphin and International Category II Referee, Vince White.

The Virginia Connection (Part XI) to West Virginia Powerlifting was the 1983 Junior National Powerlifting Championships. Chuck Mooney placed 2nd with a PR Total of 983 while competing in the 114lb. class. Chuck pulled the Deadlift he needed to win 2nd Place by a margin of 2.5 kilos / 5lbs. Chuck Mooney's Deadlift of 205 kilos / 451lbs. was a new West Virginia State Deadlift Record in the 114lb. class.

In a field of eleven (11) lifters in the 132lb. class, the lifting of Dan Palmateer placed 5th with a Total of 1190 on 6/04/83. Competing in the 165lb. class in a field of seventeen (17) competitors, Butch Brown achieved Powerlifting Elite Classification once again with a Total of 1559 for 5th Place at the 1983 Junior National Powerlifting Championships. Butch Brown's 1559 Total included a new West Virginia State Record Deadlift of 661lbs. / 300 kilos in the 165lb. class.

The 1st Annual Southeastern Bench Press Championship was held Saturday June 25th, 1983 at Charleston, West Virginia under the direction of West Virginia State Powerlifting Chairman, Vince White. Vince obtained several sponsors for the event in a successful effort to promote Powerlifting at a recreational facility in the downtown area of Charleston. The event hosted several of West Virginia's Powerlifters for a "Bench Press only" competition.

"The Program : Continued" described not only a printed agenda for the 1983 Southeastern Bench Press Championship but the entire year of 1983 for West Virginia Powerlifting. The "Program" for the event on 6/25/83 was distributed to all lifters and participants in hard copy. The contents of the official meet program included a letter from the Mayor of Charleston, West Virginia and a narrative of "Greetings" from the Parks and Recreation Director. Photos of many local Powerlifters appeared in addition to advertisements from the sponsors of the event.

The 1983 Senior National Powerlifting Championships were held on July 23rd and 24th, 1983 in Austin, Texas. If I could live again during the Summer of 1983, I would do at least a few things different. In other words, I would have avoided the "Bombout" at the 1983 Seniors and at least made a Total for the 181lb. class. Although I treasure the memories of the long drive from Charleston, West Virginia to Austin, Texas with Vince White and two (2) others, I would've taken an airplane rather than drove the 1100 + mile, one-way distance.

When planning the trip, I was of the belief that if I arrived a couple of days before the 181lb. class was scheduled to lift, the situation would be no different than a ride of 200 to 300 miles, as I had done on numerous occasions. Enroute to Austin, Texas, we left Charleston on Wednesday July 20th, drove several hundred miles, and stayed overnight in Arkansas. On Thursday July 21st, we drove the remainder of the distance and arrived in Austin, Texas at approximately 4:00 p.m., Texas time. Vince White and I attended the National Committee Meeting on Friday July 22nd.

Based on journal entries and memory recall from the events of the day, I believe that a Total for Paul Sutphin on 7/23/83 in excess of 1650 was certain. However, during the lifter introductions, while standing among the best, Mike Bridges and Ed Coan, I made a decision. In my mind, it was going to be a Total in excess of 1700 or no Total at all.

After two (2) failed attempts with a Squat of 644 ¾ and a 3rd attempt failure @ 655, the latter situation prevailed and I viewed the remainder of the meet as a spectator. After it was all said and done, the absolute best Total I could've left on the platform would have finished no higher than 4th place. In the aftermath, making a TOTAL should have been first and foremost in my mind at Austin, Texas.

For descriptive details, the weights I attempted as openers on the Squat at the 1983 Senior Nationals ; 644, 644, and 655 actually felt very light. When it came to flexibility, my lower back including the thoracic region refused to cooperate. The feeling could be described as a severely overtrained lower back with no discomfort or pain. Perhaps a much lighter poundage for an opener would have made a difference. Based on the circumstances, a hard lesson was learned.

At the 1983 Senior Nationals, Rick Weil, a topic of conversation among many within the Powerlifting community, competed in the 165lb. class. Rick Weil Totaled an impressive 1708 @ 165 *along with* a 485 Bench Press. Other notable performances were in the 181lb. class. Mike Bridges Totaled 2011 for the win and Ed Coan, weighing 171lbs., Totaled 1857 for second. Vincent Keyhea finished 3rd with 1774.

The first of three (3) Teenage National Powerlifting Championship titles for Darrell Devor began on 8/05/83 in Scottsdale, Arizona. The October, 1983 issue of P/L USA on page 12 said it all in print. "Darrell Devor and Coach Paul Sutphin didn't come up with the lifts they had planned but Darrell managed enough to pull away with the victory, and he appears to have a super career ahead of him." Darrell Devor Totaled 826 to win first place in the 123lb. class on August 5th, 1983 in Scottsdale, Arizona.

Powerlifting USA magazine / October, 1983 / Vol. 7, NO. 4 / page 12.

Before I boarded the plane for Scottsdale, I was determined to visit at least one Powerlifting gym while in Arizona. One of the many Powerlifting Champions that I have admired throughout my Powerlifting career was Jon Cole. A major highlight of the trip to Arizona for the 1983 Teenage National Powerlifting Championships included a visit to Jon Cole's Gym. After observing a lengthy workout by a group of local Powerlifters, *I met one of Powerlifting's greatest legends, Jon Cole.*

The 1st Annual Southwest Virginia Powerlifting Contest at Norton, Virginia was the "Virginia Connection, Part Twelve (Part XII)." Following the 1983 Senior Nationals, I experienced what may be described by some as a "deloading phase." I was the strongest I had ever been on August 27th, 1983. After an overly stressed or overtrained lower back several days after the 1983 Senior Nationals, the training I did between July 25th and August 22nd, 1983 was far less than I had been doing in preparation for the big event in Austin, Texas.

The 1st Annual Southwest Virginia Powerlifting Contest was held August 27th, 1983 at Norton, Virginia with thirty-two (32) lifters. Several weeks prior to the scheduled event at Norton, Virginia I received a special invitation from the Meet Director. Based on the fact that I was going to the 1983 Senior Nationals, I committed to lift only as a "Guest Lifter" at Norton.

At a bodyweight of 181lbs. on 8/27/83, a 705 Squat, 390 Bench Press, and a 655 Deadlift posted a Record Total of 1750! The lifts were ranked among the TOP 100 Lightheavyweights (181 ¾ / 82.5 kg.) for USA lifters competing from November 1982 through October 1983). The 705 Squat was tied for 4th (official ranking of 5th), the 655 Deadlift was #26, and the 1750 Total was ranked #7.

The 1750 Total by Paul Sutphin on 8/27/83 met the minimum requirements for a "Pro" Total in the 181lb. class measured by modern Professional Powerlifting standards. Also, the 1750 Total exceeded the minimum requirements for Elite Powerlifting Classification for the 198lb. weight class. While highlighting the 1750 "TOTAL Package," *along with* the 705 Squat and 655 Deadlift on 8/27/83 was a PR Bench Press of 390lbs. at 181.

Vince White won first place in the 220lb. class at the 1st Annual Southwest Virginia Powerlifting Meet with a Total of 1415. Included in Vince's Total on 8/27/83 was a 600 Squat. Doug Currence won the 181lb. class with a Total of 1520. Chuck Mooney Totaled 975 for the win in the 114lb. class. Darrell Devor Squatted 370, Bench Pressed 205, and Deadlifted 350 for a Total of 925 for a first place win in the 123lb. class.

National Master's Powerlifting

The 1983 National Masters Powerlifting Championships were held October 15th and 16th in Syracuse, New York. The official results were published in the Jan/84 issue of *Powerlifting USA* magazine. Appearing for the first time in Master's Powerlifting competition, Vince White placed 5th in the 198lb. class (40-44 Age Group) out of a field of twelve (12) competitors with an impressive Total of 1444lbs.

At a bodyweight of 195.9lbs. (88.8597 kilos), Vince White's Total of 1444 at the 1983 National Master's included a Squat of 600 ¾ lbs. (272.5 kilos), a Bench Press of 363lbs. (165 kilos), and a 479 Deadlift. Vince White's Squat, Bench Press, and Total were new West Virginia State Masters Powerlifting Records in the 198lb. class (40-49 Age Group). As of 8/31/2013, the Vince White Squat Record in the Master's Division of 600 ¾ lbs. remains standing among the USPF West Virginia Masters Powerlifting Records.

Ernie Nagy was victorious in the 220lb. class (60-64 Age Group) at the 1983 National Master's Powerlifting Championships in Syracuse, New York. Ernie lifted conservatively and Totaled 1383. Ernie Nagy had Totaled a whooping 1471 earlier in the year at the 1983 West Virginia State Powerlifting Championships.

The 10th Annual Mountianeer Open Powerlifting Championships were held on Saturday October 29th and Sunday October 30th, 1983 at the Convention Center Hotel in Huntington, West Virginia. According to the official results, the 1983 Mountianeer Open Powerlifting Championships had one-hundred twenty-six (126) lifters for the two (2) day event.

The lifting of Vince White won the Master's Division at the 1983 Mountianeer Open Powerlifting Championships on 10/29/83 over all competitors. Vince White weighed-in at a bodyweight of 198 and Squatted 606, exceeding his official West Virginia State Record by 2.5 kilos set on 10/15/83. Vince went on to Bench Press 363, and Total 1432 on 10/29/83. The official results of the 1983 Mountianeer Open Powerlifting Championships were published in the JAN'84 issue of *Powerlifting USA* magazine.

While competing at the 1983 Mountianeer Open Powerlifting Championships, Don Hundley won 1st Place in the 165lb. class and the Outstanding Lifter Award with a Total of 1460. Included in Don Hundley's 1460 Total on 10/29/83 *was another American Master's Deadlift Record of 617lbs. / 280 kilos (45-49 Age Group).*

Tennessee Connection : Part XIII

In December of 1983, two (2) teams of West Virginia Powerlifters returned to Bristol, Tennessee. The 1983 Mountian Empire Open Powerlifting Championships were held at the Bristol Family YMCA on December 10th, 1983. According to the official meet results, the 1983 Mountian Empire Powerlifting Meet at Bristol, Tennessee had forty-three (43) lifters. The 1983 Mountian Empire Open Powerlifting Championships became the Tennessee Connection : Part XIII.

While competing in the 181lb. class, Paul Sutphin Totaled 1600 on 12/10/83. Sutphin's lifts at Bristol, Tennessee on December 10th, 1983 included a 610 Squat, 370

Bench Press, and a 620 Deadlift for first place and the Outstanding Lifter Award for the heavyweight classes. For the purpose of helping the local lifters from the Bluefield YMCA, I did not compete as a team member of the *Holley Strength Systems*. Instead, on 12/10/83, Paul Sutphin earned team points for the *Bluefield YMCA Weightlifting Club*.

With a solid team effort while winning the 123, 132, 148, 165, 181, and the 242lb. classes, the *Bluefield YMCA Weightlifting Club* won the team title over the *Holley Strength Systems* at Bristol, Tennessee on 12/10/83. The 220lb. class was won by Ross Smith of *Holley Strength Systems* with a Total of 1590. Beverly Hart, a member of the *Bluefield YMCA Weightlifting Club*, won 1st Place in the Women's Division at the 1983 Mountian Empire Open Powerlifting in Bristol, Tennessee.

Lifting for the *Holley Strength Team* on 12/10/83, Dave Jeffrey won first place in the 198lb. class at the 1983 Bristol, Tennessee Powerlifting competition with a Total of 1595. Vince White was 2nd @ 198 with a 1480 Total. As he had done for over twenty (20) years, Vince White had one of the heaviest lifts of the contest on 12/10/83 with a Bench Press of 380. *Along with* the 380 Bench Press, Vince added a 610 Squat as part of his 1480 Total. Finishing 3rd in the 198lb. class was M. Shawn Byrd with a Total of 1440.

Other members competing on 12/10/83 representing the *Holley Strength Powerlifting Team* were : Don Hall (2nd Place @ 220 – 1560 Total), Dave Snyder (2nd @ 242 – 1315 Total), Mike Nidy (3rd @ 242 – 1305 Total), and Dan Hall (SuperHeavyWeight Class – 2nd Place with a 1745 Total).

Don Hundley : Elite Total at 165

The <u>1983 YMCA National Powerlifting Championships</u> were held on December 17th, 1983 in Columbus, Ohio. As was the case in 1978, there happened to be two (2) YMCA National Powerlifting Championships conducted in the same calendar year. The first Y-Nationals for 1983 was in January and the second Y-Nationals were conducted in December.

The 1983 YMCA National Powerlifting Championships was one of Don Hundley's finest hours. At the 1983 YMCA National Powerlifting Championships, Don Hundley placed 5th with an Elite Total of 1527! The place finished does not always tell the story. Don Hundley Squatted 589, Bench Pressed 292, and Deadlifted 644, for an Elite Total of 1527 in the 165lb. class on 12/17/83.

Don Hundley – 650 Deadlift / 165lb. class
One of the many Deadlifts pulled by Don Hundley
for a Powerlifting Championship win.

1983 West Virginia Powerlifter Rankings
WV Powerlifters competing from January 1st, 1983 thru December 31st, 1983
TOP RANKINGS Determined by Total

114 / Name	Squat	Bench Press	Deadlift	Total	Date
Chuck Mooney	325	209	451*	986	6/04/83
Chuck Mooney	330	215	430	975	8/27/83
Chuck Mooney	281	203	429	914	3/26/83
Chuck Mooney	300	190	410	900	1/09/83
Rick Casey	286	192	319	799	4/23/83
Rick Casey	264	187	314	766	3/26/83
Sonny Shrader	253	209	303	766	4/23/83
Sonny Shrader	248	203	303	755	3/26/83
Scott Steele	231	192	308	733	5/28/83
Sonny Shrader	230	200	270	700	1/09/83
123 Roger Salser	374	281	374	1030	3/26/83
Greg Spencer	341	225	424	992	3/26/83
Cork Hall	352	198	435*	986	3/26/83
Rick Yates	336	209	407	953	3/26/83
Dorian Murphy	341 t	176	402	920 t	4/23/83
Dorian Murphy	330	181	374	885	3/26/83
Greg Spencer	290	185	335	810	1/09/83
Scott Steele	264	198	330	793	3/26/83
Scott Steele	270	203	314	788	4/23/83
Scott Steele	235	185	310	730	1/09/83
132 Ed Canjemi	515 u	260	460	1235 u	1/09/83
Dan Palmateer	468*	281	440	1190*	6/04/83
Dan Palmateer	429	275	479*	1184*	3/26/83
Acie Simmons	402	336*	385	1124	3/26/83
Acie Simmons	400	330	390	1120	12/10/83
Maurice Kinzer	391 t	259 t	440 t	1091 t	4/23/83
Mike Kimball	352	248	374	975	5/28/83
Art Williamson	360	200	405	965	3/12/83
Rick Yates	347	220	374	942	10/29/83
Dwayne Adkins	308	225	380	936	4/23/83
Art Williamson	330	203	402	935	3/26/83
Rick Yates	300	200	370	870	1/09/83
Richard Walsh	292	192	352	837	5/28/83

* - West Virginia State Powerlifting Record

t – West Virginia State Teenage Powerlifting Record

u – Unofficial West Virginia State Powerlifting Record

1983 West Virginia Powerlifter Rankings
WV Powerlifters competing from January 1st, 1983 thru December 31st, 1983
TOP RANKINGS Determined by Total

148 / Name	Squat	Bench Press	Deadlift	Total	Date
Gene Underwood	468	303	479	1251	5/28/83
Gene Underwood	440	297	507	1245	3/26/83
Dan Palmateer (144)	479	286	479	1245	5/28/83
Mark McCoy	518	242	479	1240	3/26/83
Keith Gandee	451	275	451	1179	5/28/83
Mike Sarver	380	270	501	1151	3/26/83
Keith Gandee	402	275	462	1140	3/26/83
Scott Phillips	429	242	468	1140	3/26/83
Kevin McComas	380 t	236	424	1041 t	4/23/83
Shane Carlson	402	236	385	1025	3/26/83
Brian Richards	369	231	413	1014	3/26/83
Steve Lamb	363	225	385	975	4/23/83
Donald Robbins	300	255	400	955	12/10/83
Greg Wilson	314	248	385	947	3/26/83
Jack Hourouras	341	203	402	947	4/23/83
Reese Booth	320	185	400	905	1/09/83
John Bayliss	253*m	214*m	347*m	815*m	3/26/83
165 C. Butch Brown	567	330	661*	1559 e	6/04/83
Don Hundley	589	292	644	1527 e	12/17/83
C. Butch Brown	562	308	622	1493	3/23/83
Don Hundley	578	264	617	1460	10/29/83
Shawn Dixon	501	297	496	1295	3/26/83
Mark Matson	451	325	490	1267	10/29/83
Mark Matson	451	314	485	1250	3/26/83
Tim Bonnett	407	297	523 t	1229 t	4/23/83
Mike Sarver	424	275	507	1206	10/29/83
Mark Davis	435	253	479	1168	3/26/83
Marty Decourcey	396	303	468	1168	10/29/83
Keith Radford	396	281	457	1135	4/23/83
David Patton	457 t	236	435	1129	4/23/83

* - West Virginia State Powerlifting Record
*m – West Virginia State Masters Powerlifting Record
t – West Virginia State Teenage Powerlifting Record
e – Elite Powerlifting Classification Total

1983 West Virginia Powerlifter Rankings
WV Powerlifters competing from January 1ˢᵗ, 1983 thru December 31ˢᵗ, 1983
TOP RANKINGS Determined by Total

181 / Name	Squat	Bench Press	Deadlift	Total	Date
Paul Sutphin	705 u	390	655 u	1750 u e	8/27/83
Paul Sutphin (OL)	688 u	380	644	1714 u e	5/28/83
Robert Griffith	622	347	644*	1614	3/26/83
Paul Sutphin	610	370	620	1600	12/10/83
Doug Currence	573	358	650	1581	12/17/83
Doug Currence	580	340	600	1520	8/27/83
Doug Currence	555	325	625	1505	8/13/83
Doug Currence	551	330	611	1493	3/26/83
Dave Drennan	529	407 u	551	1488	10/29/83
Dave Drennan	529	402*	540	1471	3/26/83
Jim Priest	575	345	550	1470	8/13/83
Doug Currence	545	330	580	1455	1/09/83
Jim Priest	551	352	551	1455	5/28/83
Allen Strathman	567	347	534	1449	3/26/83
Kevin Phillips	501	385	551	1438	10/29/83
Allen Strathman	485	325	515	1325	1/09/83
Jerry Pomposelli	518	314	479	1311	3/26/83
Joey Calisto	457	303	518	1278	3/26/83
Tom Russell	473	314	462	1251	3/26/83
Tom Russell	450	315	460	1225	1/09/83
Tom Russell	435	303	446	1184	10/29/83
Tony Walters	424	281	451	1157	4/23/83
Shawn Manzo	407	225	462	1096	4/23/83
Donnie Napier	369	236	468	1074	4/23/83
Barry England	336	214	402	953	4/23/83

e – Elite Powerlifting Classification Total

* - West Virginia State Powerlifting Record

u – Unofficial West Virginia State Powerlifting Record

OL – Outstanding Lifter Award

1983 West Virginia Powerlifter Rankings
WV Powerlifters competing from January 1st, 1983 thru December 31st, 1983
TOP RANKINGS Determined by Total

198 / Name	Squat	Bench Press	Deadlift	Total	Date
Paul Sutphin	677	380	644	1703	3/26/83
Buster Whitener	611	391	639	1642	3/26/83
Dave Jeffrey	622	407	584	1614	3/26/83
Dave Jeffrey	625	405	580	1610	3/12/83
Dave Jeffrey	610	435	550	1595	12/10/83
Tony Culp	600	385	600	1587	10/29/83
Gary Clark	611	391	573	1577	3/26/83
Don Hall	589	352	562	1504	3/26/83
Vince White	610 u m	380 u m	490	1480 u m	12/10/83
Ken McCoy	584	330	562	1477	3/26/83
Don Hall	550	340	565	1455	1/09/83
Vince White (195.9)	600 m	363 m	479	1444 m	10/15/83
M. Shawn Byrd	510	400	530	1440	12/10/83
Don Hall	545	336	551	1432	10/29/83
Vince White	606 u m	363	462	1432	10/29/83
Cary Wilson	529	314	501	1344	3/26/83
Domenick Manara	490	281	540	1311	3/26/83
Aldo Pucci	485	330 t	485	1300	4/23/83
Myles Hayden	480	270	500	1250	12/10/83
Aldo Pucci	425	300	500	1225	3/12/83
Aldo Pucci	451	314	451	1218	5/28/83
Bobby Fox	440	275	475	1190	12/10/83
Robert Hill	457	281	451	1189	3/26/83
John Hairston	385	297	507	1189	4/23/83
Paul Sutphin	622 *Injury*	363 *@ Y-Nat's*	176	1162	1/08/83
Joe Mather	429	253	473	1157	4/23/83
Bobby Fox	420	270	455	1145	8/27/83
James Calderis	402	281	451	1135	3/26/83
Bobby Fox	402	264	451	1118	5/28/83
Bobby Fox	425	250	425	1100	1/09/83
Mark Hrko	385	240	445	1070	1/09/83

m – West Virginia State Masters Powerlifting Record

u – Unofficial West Virginia State Powerlifting Record

t – West Virginia State Teenage Powerlifting Record

1983 West Virginia Powerlifter Rankings
WV Powerlifters competing from January 1st, 1983 thru December 31st, 1983
TOP RANKINGS Determined by Total

220 / Name	Squat	Bench Press	Deadlift	Total	Date
Bret Russell	716 u	391	760	1868 e	5/28/83
Bret Russell	705	391	744	1840 e	3/26/83
Bret Russell	710 u	405	705	1820	3/12/83
Bret Russell	683	385	727	1796	6/05/83
Mike Fuscardo	683	407	611	1703	10/09/83
Earl Snider	606	396	688	1692	3/26/83
Mike Fuscardo	644	413	622	1681	9/24/83
Bob Coulling	650	358	650	1658	3/26/83
Ross Smith	610	420	560	1590	12/10/83
Tim McCoy	667	347	562	1577	3/26/83
Bret Russell	655	143	771	1570	1/08/83
Ross Smith	600	391	556	1548	10/30/83
Jim Sharps	573	363	573	1510	3/26/83
Marshall Moore	600 t	286	617 t	1504	4/23/83
Don Hall	600	300	600	1500	12/10/83
Greg Jarvie	551	330	606	1487	10/30/83
Ernie Nagy	534	407	540	1482	5/21/83
Ernie Nagy	523 (AR)	407 (AR)	540 (AR)	1471 (AR)	3/26/83
M. Sean Byrd	529	424	518	1471	10/30/83
John Hairston	551	303	600	1455	3/26/83
Don Hall	535	325	565	1425	8/14/83
Vince White	600	365	450	1415	8/27/83
Ernie Nagy (216.4)	485	374	523	1383	10/16/83
John Nicoloudakis	485	374	523	1383	10/30/83
Sam Moore	501	303	578	1383	10/30/83
Vince White	560	350	470	1380	8/14/83
Jim Simon	455	335	505	1295	1/09/83
Steve Forbes	435	325	529	1289	4/23/83

e – Elite Powerlifting Classification Total

* - West Virginia State Powerlifting Record

u – Unofficial West Virginia State Powerlifting Record

AR – American Masters Record

1983 West Virginia Powerlifter Rankings
WV Powerlifters competing from January 1st, 1983 thru December 31st, 1983
TOP RANKINGS Determined by Total

242 / Name	Squat	Bench Press	Deadlift	Total	Date
Randy Scott	733	485	644	1862	5/28/83
Randy Scott	694	501*	650	1846	3/26/83
Dan Bloxton	677	380	705	1763	5/28/83
Dan Bloxton	622	363	672	1658	3/26/83
Mark Modesitt	562	402	540	1504	3/26/83
Joe Lepera	512	380	567	1460	10/30/83
John Hairston	500	305	615	1420	1/09/83
Kevin Loy	551	319	540	1410	3/26/83
Greg Moodie	512	314	573	1399	5/28/83
Wallace Kirk	529	363	501	1394	5/28/83
Mark Olenick	501	347	540	1388	5/28/83
Jim Simon	510	360	515	1385	12/10/83
Jim Simon	501	347	512	1361	3/26/83
Wallace Kirk	479	352	501	1333	3/26/83
Carl Cook	529	325	479	1333	5/28/83
Dave Snyder	496	325	507	1328	10/30/83
Greg Moodie	485	336	501	1322	9/24/83
Dave Snyder	500	325	490	1315	12/10/83
Mike Nidy	460	345	500	1305	12/10/83
Dave Snyder	479	314	490	1284	3/26/83
Tommy Vance	391	248	485	1124	4/23/83
Austin Miller	440	270	402	1113	3/26/83
275 Dan Hall	700	385	660	1745	12/10/83
Dan Hall	667	352	677	1697	3/26/83
Dan Hall	615	360	570	1545	1/09/83

e – Elite Powerlifting Classification Total

* - West Virginia State Powerlifting Record

t – West Virginia State Teenage Powerlifting Record

1983 West Virginia Powerlifter Rankings
WV Powerlifters competing from January 1st, 1983 thru December 31st, 1983
TOP RANKINGS Determined by Total

SHW / Name	Squat	Bench Press	Deadlift	Total	Date
Jeff Cook	650	395	730 u*	1775	8/14/83
Jeff Cook	672	380	699	1752	5/28/83
Jeff Cook	644	380	722*	1746	3/26/83
Troy McNett	479	418	545	1444	3/26/83
Charles Ashcraft	551	325	529	1405	5/28/83
Larry Byrd	429	330	501	1262	3/26/83
Shawne Wilbourne	413 t	270	435	1118 t	4/23/83
Jack Woods	396	292	418	1107	5/28/83
Jack Woods	352	292	402	1047	4/23/83

e – Elite Powerlifting Classification Total

* - West Virginia State Powerlifting Record

t – West Virginia State Teenage Powerlifting Record

u* - Unofficial West Virginia State Powerlifting Record

Chapter Nineteen : 1984

At the end of calendar year 1983, West Virginia Powerlifting Chairman Vince White unveiled an active agenda for Powerlifting in West Virginia. For the first half of 1984, four (4) major Powerlifting events were confirmed with USPF sanctions pending. The *2nd Annual Steel Valley Open* (2/11 & 2/12/84), *1984 West Virginia State Teenage Powerlifting Championships* (3/03/84), *9th Annual West Virginia State Powerlifting Championships* (3/31 & 4/01/84), and the *3rd Annual Parkersburg Open Powerlifting* for May, 1984.

The 2nd Annual Steel Valley Open Powerlifting Championships were held February 11th and 12th, 1984 at Weirton, West Virginia. According to the official meet results published in the May, 1984 issue of *Powerlifting USA* magazine, the 1984 Steel Valley Open had approximately sixty-five (65) lifters.

While competing in the 220lb. class at the 2nd Annual Steel Valley Open, Ernie Nagy Totaled 1455 for the win in the Masters Division. Other winners on 2/11 & 2/12/84 included Art Williamson (132lb. class – 940 Total), Gene Underwood (165lb. class – 1325 Total), Tom Russell (181lb. class– 1220 Total), Scott Tusic (220lb. class – 1630 Total), Dan Hall (275lb. class – 1740 Total), and Chuck Ashcraft (SuperHeavyWeight – 1540 Total).

The 1984 West Virginia State Teenage Powerlifting Championships were held on March 3rd, 1984 at South Charleston, West Virginia with a record turnout for the event. Vince White was the Meet Director. According to the official results, the 1984 West Virginia Teenage Powerlifting Championships had forty-eight (48) lifters.

Competing in the 220lb. class at the 1984 West Virginia Teenage Powerlifting Championships, Michael (Shawn) Byrd became the first West Virginia lifter to break the Teenage American Bench Press Record with a Bench Press of 473lbs. (215 kilos). The 473lb. Bench Press on 3/03/84 was a new American Teenage Powerlifting / Bench Press Record in the 220lb. class (16-17 Age Group).

The 1984 Teenage Powerlifting Team Award was won by the *Princeton Powerlifting Team*. For the 3rd consecutive year the *Princeton Powerlifting Team*, coached by Jack Pack, won the West Virginia State Teenage Powerlifting Team title.

Powerlifting USA magazine / Vol. 7 / No. 10, May, 1984

"Setting the Records Straight" : Part II

The 9th Annual (1984) West Virginia State Powerlifting Championships were held March 31st and April 1st, 1984 at the South Charleston Recreation Center in South Charleston, West Virginia. For the 2nd consecutive year, Vince White was Meet Director of the West Virginia State Powerlifting Championships. The 1984 West Virginia State Powerlifting Championship was a two (2) day, single platform event with over sixty (60) lifters.

The lifting of Don Hundley included new American Records and another Elite Total in the 165lb. class. The 600lb. West Virginia State Squat Record in the 165lb. class by Jack Wilson (Recorded at 605lbs.) was wiped out by Don Hundley at the 1984 West Virginia State Powerlifting Championships with a Master's American Record Squat of 275 kilos / 606 ¼ lbs. Although the 605lb. Squat Record by Jack Wilson was reported to have been set in 1978, the exact date and location of the 605lb. Squat Record remains undocumented. Don Hundley's performance on March 31st, 1984 lives on with the American Record Squat of 606 ¼ lbs. (275 kilos)!

Don Hundley – Squat of 606 ¼ lbs.
American Masters Record / 165lb. class – 3/31/84

Don Hundley's Elite Total of 1537 on 3/31/84 was ranked #33 in the P/L USA TOP 100 Middleweight (165lb. class) Powerlifters for USA lifters competing from September, 1983 through August, 1984. Hundley's 606 ¼ Squat in the 165lb. class at the 1984 West Virginia State Powerlifting Championships ranked #17, and the Deadlift of 302.5 kilos / 666 ¾ lbs. was ranked #8! The 165lb. Powerlifters who ranked in front of Don Hundley in the P/L USA TOP 100 165lb. Powerlifters published in the November, 1984 issue of *Powerlifting USA* magazine were :

#1 John Topsoglou (685 Deadlift),
#2 Troy Hicks (683 Deadlift),
#3 Rickey Crain (672 Deadlift),
#4 H. Hoffman (672 Deadlift),
#5 Gene Bell (672 Deadlift),
#6 Danny Gay (672 Deadlift), and
#7 Jack Welch (670 Deadlift).

While competing in the 220lb. class of the Master's Division (60-64 Age Group) on 3/31/84, Ernie Nagy set four (4) new National Master's Powerlifting Records! After weighing-in at a bodyweight of 216 at the 1984 West Virginia States, American Powerlifting Record number one (1) for Ernie Nagy was a 545 Squat. Ernie went on to Bench Press 413, Deadlift 573, and Total 1532 on 3/31/84 at South Charleston, West Virginia. Vince White, West Virginia State Powerlifting Chairman and IPF Category II Referee, made sure that all of the American Records were accepted by the USPF National Office.

Before spandex suits and custom lifting belts, the minimum standard for an Elite Classification Total for Powerlifters competing in the 198lb. class was 1710. The Elite Classification Totals for 1984 had been updated and the new standard for Elite in the 198lb. class required a minimum Total of 1731 pounds (785 kilos). Over the years, at least two (2) of Powerlifting's historians have acknowledged me for earning Powerlifting's Elite Classification in four (4) weight classes. For technical reasons, I only claim three (3). So the issue may be, "Did I or did I not Total Elite on April 1st, 1984?" The answer may depend on who is asked the question. Which Total represents the minimum standard for Elite in the 198lb. class? A Total of 1710, 1725, or 1731?

There are those who say, *"A Total of 1750 in 1983 and 1741 (later in 1986) as a 181lb'er. exceeded the 1731 minimum standard Total for Elite in the 198lb. class. Conclusively, Elite status was earned in the 198's."* I accept the latter argument. Another argument may support the fact that a lifter must be officially weighed-in and post a

Total in the designated weight class in order to satisfy the requirement for Powerlifting's Elite Classification within that weight class.

While competing in the 198lb. class at the 1984 West Virginia State Powerlifting Championships, I called for a weight on a 2nd attempt Deadlift of 297.5 kilos (655 ¾ lbs.), the exact poundage required for a first place victory. The Deadlift attempt of 655 ¾ (297.5 kilos) was good and the result was another West Virginia State Powerlifting Championship title in the 198lb. class with a Total of 1725lbs.

Going for 2.5 kilos more than I needed for the win in order to achieve an Elite Total in the 198lb. class of 1731 vs. 1725 did not cross my mind. After all, a few years prior to 1984 I had Totaled Elite in the 148, 165, and 181lb. weight classes many times before. Unfortunately, while competing in the 198lb. class, the Total of 1725lbs. (782.5 kilos) fell short of the official minimum requirement for an Elite Total in the 198lb. class for the 1984 time period.

Doug Currence : Elite Total at 181

The battle for the 181lb. class Deadlift record on 4/01/84 took place between Doug Currence and Robert Griffith. Robert Griffith ended up with the record due to the fact that he was the lighter man. While competing for the win in the 181lb. class at the 1984 West Virginia State Powerlifting Championships, both men (Griffith and Currence) called for the same weight of 661lbs. (300 kilos). In the System of Rotation, Doug Currence lifted the weight for the win, yet Bob Griffith had pulled the same weight on the Deadlift. Due to the fact that Robert Griffith officially weighed in as the lighter man on 4/01/84, the West Virginia State Deadlift Record was awarded to him.

Winning the 181lb. class at the 1984 West Virginia State Powerlifting Championships marked the first West Virginia State Championship Powerlifting title for Doug Currence. A Total of 1642 in the 181lb. class made Doug Currence the eighth (8th) West Virginia Powerlifter to achieve the Elite Powerlifting Classification status.

Among the winners in the 220lb. class at the 1984 West Virginia State Powerlifting Championships were Mike Fuscardo (1st – 1714 Total), Tony Culp (2nd – 1647 Total), and Don Hall (3rd – 1625 Total). Bret Russell pulled an 804lb. Deadlift for a new West Virginia State Deadlift Record in the 242lb. class on 4/01/84 to win the 1984 West Virginia State Powerlifting Championship title. The 804 Deadlift by Bret Russell on 4/01/84 ranked #2 in the TOP 100 242lb. Powerlifters competing from January, 1984 to December, 1984. The #2 Deadlift Ranking for Bret Russell was published in the March, 1985 issue of *Powerlifting USA* magazine.

Dan Hall Totaled 1653 to win his 3rd consecutive West Virginia State Powerlifting Championship title in the 275lb. class on 4/01/84. Competing for the very first time at the annual West Virginia State Powerlifting Championship event, John Messinger Totaled 1620 to win 2nd Place in the 275lb. weight class at South Charleston. Jeff Cook won the SuperHeavyWeight's at the 1984 West Virginia State Powerlifting Championships with a Total of 1752 which included a new West Virginia State Deadlift Record of 744 pounds in the SHW's.

The Powerlifting Team of *Herb's Gym* won the 1984 West Virginia State Powerlifting Championship Team Award over the *Mountianeer Barbell Club*. The Powerlifters competing for *Herb's Gym* with first place victories were : Chuck Mooney (114lb. class – 876 Total), Gene Underwood (148lb. class – 1366 Total), Don Hundley (165lb. class – 1537 Elite Total), Doug Currence (181lb. class – 1642 Elite Total), Paul Sutphin (198lb. class – 1725 Total), Dan Hall (275lb. class – 1653 Total).

Other members of the *"Herb's Gym Powerlifting Team"* at the 1984 West Virginia State Powerlifting Championships were : John Bayliss (Masters Division –1003 Total), Bob Hill (181–1245 Total – 3rd), Tom Russell (181 – 1168 Total – 4th), Mike Hundley (198 – 1466 Total – 4th), Don Hall (220 – 1625 Total – 3rd), Ross Smith (220 – 1521 Total – 5th), John Nicoloudakis (242 – 1543 Total – 4th), John Messinger (275 – 1620 Total – 2nd), Mike Nidy (275 – 1482 Total – 3rd), Wayne Lilly (275 -1311 Total – 4th).

Herb's Gym – 4/01/84
1984 West Virginia State Powerlifting Champions

"Setting the Records Straight": Part III

The 1st Annual National High School Powerlifting Championships were held April 27th and April 28th, 1984 at Oklahoma Baptist University in Shawnee, Oklahoma. According to the official results, the 1st Annual National High School Powerlifting Championships had one-hundred (100) lifters and the Meet Director was Rickey Crain. Lifting in the 198lb. class, Sean Byrd Squatted 545lbs. (247.5 kilos), Bench Pressed 407 ¾ (185 kilos), and Deadlifted 512lbs. (232.5 kilos) for the winning Total of 1466lbs. (665 kilos) for a first place win at the first (1984) National High School Powerlifting Championships.

An exerpt from the contest report published in the AUG/84 issue of *Powerlifting USA* magazine : "*90 kg (198lb.) class. This class saw only two competitors, the smallest group, of the competition as several jumped to the 100kg. (220lb. division) in lieu of tackling 'Big Byrd.' As expected, first place went to Michael Byrd of St. Albans, WV with a fine 665kg. (1466) Total.*" The performance of Michael (Sean) Byrd at the 1984 National High School Powerlifting Championships can best be analyzed by the definition of Powerlifting. Powerlifting Championships require a TOTAL of the Squat, the Bench Press, and the Deadlift.

West Virginia State Powerlifting Records were published frequently in the pages of *Powerlifting USA* magazine during the years of 1983 and 1984. The West Virginia State Powerlifting Records were published in the "For The Record" section of the JUN/84 issue of *Powerlifting USA* magazine. The Squat Record of 468 in the 132lb. class actually belonged to Dan Palmateer set on 6/04/83 at the 1983 National (Junior) Powerlifting Championships. The West Virginia State Powerlifting Records set at the 1984 West Virginia State Powerlifting Championships on 3/31/84 and 4/01/84 were not included in the listing that appeared in the June, 1984 issue of P/L USA.

The West Virginia "Power Gym" Directory was the subject of the "For the Record" section in the JUL/84 issue of *Powerlifting USA* magazine. The Power Gym Directory listed a total of thirty-one (31) gyms or YMCA's which catered to Powerlifters. Among the 31 gyms listed : The Body Shop (Weirton), Dave's Gym @ Belle, Fitness World @ Weirton, Jim's Gym @ Paden City, Herb's Gym @ Nitro, Holley Strength Systems @ Charleston, McCoy's Gym @ Mallory, Slamick's Gym @ Fairmont, South Charleston Recreation Center @ South Charleston, Universal Health Club @ Charleston, YMCA @ Wheeling, YMCA @ Bluefield, YMCA @ Charleston, and YMCA @ Clarksburg.

The American Master's Powerlifting Records were published in the "For The Record" section of the July, 1984 issue of *Powerlifting USA* magazine. Included in the 1984 published listings were the records of three (3) West Virginia Powerlifters : Herb

Fitzsimmons, Don Hundley, and Ernie Nagy. Don Hundley and Herb Fitzsimmons both owned three (3) records each. Ernie Nagy had the most with fifteen (15)!

The 1984 Parkersburg Open Powerlifting Championships were held May 26th and May 27th, 1984 at Parkersburg, West Virginia. The 1984 Parkersburg Open had an Open Division and a "Below Class II Division." According to the official results, the 1984 Parkersburg Open had over ninety (90) lifters.

While competing in the 148lb. class at the 1984 Parkersburg Open, Gene Underwood earned Elite Powerlifter Classification with a Total of 1405. The 1405 Total by Gene Underwood on 5/26/84 included a Squat of 518, Bench Press of 336, and a Deadlift of 551 for an Elite Total of 1405! With exception to John Black's Total of 1873 in the 220lb. class, Gene Underwood was the only lifter with an Elite Total at the 1984 Parkersburg Open.

The 1984 Roanoke Open Powerlifting Championships were held May 19th and May 20th, 1984 at Roanoke, Virginia. According to the official results, the 1984 Roanoke Open Powerlifting Championships had approximately seventy-five (75) lifters. Remembering 1981, I put together a Total of 1675 on 5/19/84 and won the 198lb. class over a field of eight (8) competitors. After competing at six (6) Powerlifting competitions at Roanoke, Virginia since 1978, the Virginia Connection : Part XIII was the "Final lift at Roanoke."

Chuck Mooney – Deadlift of 451 @ 114 : Number One Again! Based on the results of the 1983 National (Junior) Powerlifting Championships in Charlottesville, Virginia on 6/04/83, Chuck Mooney was Number One Again! Listed in the TOP 100 Flyweights (114 ½ / 52 kg.) for USA lifters competing from May, 1983 through April, 1984, Chuck Mooney ranked #23 in the Squat with a lift of 325 made on 6/04/83 at the 1983 National Powerlifting Championships held in Charlottesville, Virginia.

Chuck Mooney competed in a Bench Press contest on 6/25/83, lifted 220, and earned the #18 spot in the TOP 100 114's, and the Total from 6/04/83 was #7. How about the Deadlift? Chuck Mooney...not since 1976...achieved number one (1)! The Deadlift of 451lbs. (205 kilos) from the 1983 National Powerlifting Championships in Charlottesville, Virginia finished #1 among the Flyweights (114lb. Powerlifters) in the USA.

The 11th Annual Mountianeer Open Powerlifting Championships were conducted on November 10th and 11th, 1984 at Huntington, West Virginia. According to the official meet results, the 11th Annual Mountianeer Open had one-hundred twenty (120) lifters. While competing in the 198lb. class at the 1984 Mountianeer Open, Sean Byrd Squatted 567, Bench Pressed 451lbs. (205 kilos), and Deadlifted 451 for a Total of 1471 pounds.

Following the 1984 Mountianeer Open, another Teenage American Bench Press Record by M. Sean Byrd was "applied for." Unfortunately, due to the rule changes and guidelines implemented by the West Virginia State Powerlifting Committee, the lift was not recorded as a West Virginia State Teenage Powerlifting Record in the 198lb. class.

Later in 1984, the World Masters Powerlifting Records were published in the November, 1984 issue of *Powerlifting USA* magazine. Don Hundley's Squat Record in the 165lb. class of 265 kilos (584lbs.) stood in the (40-49 Age Group) category of World Masters Powerlifting Records. The 407 ¾ lbs. (185 kilos) Bench Press set by Ernie Nagy in the 220lb. class (60-69 Age Group) stood among the published marks.

A special section in the *Charleston Daily Mail* on Thursday October 4th, 1984 prior to the 1984 National Masters Powerlifting Championships featured an article titled, *"Iron Pumping Brothers" – Frank, Vince White in Master's Powerlifting Championships.* After a near seven (7) year break from Powerlifting, Frank White returned in 1984 for one major championship event ; the 1984 National Masters Powerlifting Championships. The 1984 National Masters Powerlifting Championships were held on October 13th, 1984 in McClean, Virginia. According to the official meet results, the 1984 National Masters Powerlifting Championships had over two-hundred (200) lifters.

In a rare platform appearance at the 1984 National Master's Powerlifting Championships, Frank White Squatted 429lbs. (195 kilos), Bench Pressed 308lbs. (140 kilos), and Deadlifted 418lbs. (190 kilos), for a Total of 1157lbs. (525 kilos). Finishing with a Total of 1157 in the 165lb. class earned Frank White a 5th Place finish in the category (40-44 Age Group). Only the winner of the 165lb. class (40-44 Age Group) Bench Pressed more weight than Frank White at the 1984 National Masters Powerlifting Championships.

The 1984 Mountian Empire Open Powerlifting Meet was held Saturday December 1st, 1984 at the Bristol Family YMCA in Bristol, Tennessee. For Powerlifting at Bristol, 12/01/84 wrote "The Final Chapter" of the "Tennessee Connection" for West Virginia Powerlifting. For Vince White, 12/01/84 was the first time he had competed in the 181lb. class at the annual event at Bristol since 1972. Vince weighed-in lighter than 181lbs. due to a moderate phase of training and posted very respectable lifts at the 1984 Mountian Empire Open in Bristol, Tennessee.

The date of 12/01/84 marked the last appearance for West Virginia Powerlifters for an official Powerlifting competition at Bristol, Tennessee. Paul Sutphin weighed-in less than 185lbs., won first place in the 198lb. class and the Outstanding Lifter Award for a final win at Bristol. In terms of the most weight lifted, John Nicolaudakis made the final Deadlift of 630lbs. at Bristol on 12/01/84 and Totaled 1620lbs.

The 3rd Annual (1984) Steel Valley Open Powerlifting Championships were held on December 15th & 16th, 1984 at Weirton, West Virginia. According to the official results, the 3rd Annual Steel Valley Open Powerlifting Championships conducted on the weekend of 12/15/84 had approximately one-hundred twenty (120) lifters.

An official / unofficial West Virginia State Deadlift Record in the 181lb. class was set by Doug Currence on 12/15/84. While competing in the 181lb. class, Doug Currence Deadlifted 666 ¾ lbs. (302.5 kilos), exceeding the existing record of 661 pounds (300 kilos) owned by Robert Griffith since 4/01/84. Vince White, West Virginia Powerlifting Chairman, recorded the Doug Currence Deadlift Record of 666 ¾ lbs. (302.5 kilos) from the 3rd Annual Steel Valley Open on 12/15/84 as an *official* West Virginia State Powerlifting Record in the 181lb. class.

1984 West Virginia Powerlifter Rankings
WV Powerlifters competing from January 1st, 1984 thru December 31st, 1984
TOP RANKINGS Determined by Total

114 / Name	Squat	Bench Press	Deadlift	Total	Date
Chuck Mooney	292	181	402	876	3/31/84
Rick Casey	275	203	308	787	3/03/84
Rick Casey	292	181	292	766	3/31/84
James Steele	170	132	248	551	3/03/84
123 Scott Steele	292	214	347	854	3/03/84
Scott Steele	303	214	336	854	3/31/84
Sonny Shrader	242	214	314	771	3/03/84
Doug Hicks	242	176	352	771	3/03/84
132 Dan Palmateer	396	225	407	1030	3/31/84
Rick Yates	374	242	407	1025	3/31/84
Dewayne Adkins	330	225	435	990	3/03/84
Art Williamson	340	195	405	940	2/11/84
148 Gene Underwood	518	335	551	1405 e	5/26/84
Gene Underwood	490	325	551	1366	3/31/84
Gene Underwood	480	320	525	1325	2/11/84
Gene Underwood	462	314	523	1300	7/21/84
Art Williamson	462	264	518	1245	12/15/84
Art Williamson	440	242	490	1173	9/22/84
Mike Kimball	440	270	446	1157	12/15/84
Mike Kimball	429	281	418	1129	9/22/84
Donald Robbins	363	292	473	1129	11/10/84
Art Williamson	420	245	460	1125	11/17/84
Don Robbins (BW@143)	340	290	440	1070	8/11/84
Scott Phillips	396	242	424	1063	9/22/84
Ron Lightner	330	314	402	1047	3/31/84
Art Williamson	370	225	440	1035	7/21/84
Reece Booth	385*	203	435	1025	3/03/84
Mike Kimball	369	253	402	1025	5/26/84
Mike Kimball	370	245	400	1015	7/21/84
Don Robbins	303	259	413	975	3/03/84

e – ELITE Powerlifting Classification Total

* - West Virginia State Powerlifting Record

1984 West Virginia Powerlifter Rankings
WV Powerlifters competing from January 1st, 1984 thru December 31st, 1984
TOP RANKINGS Determined by Total

165 / Name	Squat	Bench Press	Deadlift	Total	Date
Don Hundley	606*m	264	667*m	1537*m e	3/31/84
Don Hundley	567	264	644	1477	11/10/84
Gene Underwood	534	358	573	1466	11/10/84
Keith Gandee	490	335	525	1350	8/04/84
Martin DeCoursey	490	319	518	1328	12/15/84
Mark Matson	473	336	512	1322	3/31/84
Martin DeCoursey	501	303	490	1295	3/31/84
Mark Matson	468	341	485	1294	5/26/84
Tony Magnone	468	281	490	1240	12/15/84
A. Killmer	457	286	479	1224	3/31/84
Mike Cyrus	440	264	490	1196	3/03/84
Bill Keefover	462	275	446	1185	3/03/84
Mike Sarver	418	259	501	1179	3/31/84
Frank White	429	308 wm	418	1157	10/13/84
Tony Magnone	420	270	465	1155	2/11/84
John Bayliss	358	275	468	1102	12/15/84
181 Doug Currence	611	369	661	1642 e	4/01/84
Robert Griffith	589	352	661 u	1603	4/01/84
Doug Currence	567	358	667*	1592	12/15/84
John Priest	600	352	562	1515	5/26/84
Doug Currence	540	315	600	1455	8/11/84
Bill Keefover	551	303	485	1339	5/26/84
Robert Hill	446	275	523	1245	4/01/84
Tom Russell	440	305	475	1220	2/11/84
Vince White	455	325	405	1185	12/01/84
Rocky Roach	418	275	490	1184	12/15/84
Tom Russell	418	297	451	1168	4/01/84
Rocky Roach	391	264	473	1129	11/10/84

e – ELITE Powerlifting Classification Total

* - West Virginia State Powerlifting Record

t – Teenage American Powerlifting Record

m – American Master's Powerlifting Record

wm – West Virginia State Masters Powerlifting Record

u – Unofficial West Virginia State Powerlifting Record

1984 West Virginia Powerlifter Rankings
WV Powerlifters competing from January 1st, 1984 thru December 31st, 1984
TOP RANKINGS Determined by Total

198 / Name	Squat	Bench Press	Deadlift	Total	Date
Paul Sutphin	678	391	655	1725	4/01/84
Dave Jeffrey	650	440	633	1725	4/01/84
Paul Sutphin	640	385	650	1675	5/19/84
Steve Uhas	705	320	645	1670	4/14/84
Steve Uhas	683	341	639	1664	4/01/84
Paul Sutphin	650	355	640	1645	8/11/84
Tony Culp	600	374	633	1609	11/11/84
Scott Tusic	606	413	573	1592	5/26/84
Paul Sutphin	600	330	595	1525	12/01/84
Allan Strathman	622	374	523	1521	5/26/84
M. Sean Byrd	567	451 t AR	451	1471	11/11/84
M. Sean Byrd	545 h	407 h	512 h	1466 h	4/28/84
Mike Hundley	575	300	585	1460	2/12/84
Mike Hundley	551	319	584	1455	4/01/84
Michael Brown	523	336	567	1427	5/26/84
Tim Bonnett	468	325	573	1366	5/27/84
Bob Taylor	451	369	523	1344	5/27/84
Chuck Denny	429	303	606	1339	5/26/84
Ed Towle	485	341	512	1339	11/11/84
Chuck Denny	457	297	578	1333	4/01/84
Dan Young	440	341	501	1284	4/01/84
John Hairston	424	303	501	1229	3/03/84
Vince White	485	330	402	1218	11/11/84

* - WV State Powerlifting Record

t – WV State Teenage Powerlifting Record

t AR – Teenage American Powerlifting Record

h – West Virginia High School Powerlifting Record

m – American Master's Powerlifting Record

1984 West Virginia Powerlifter Rankings
WV Powerlifters competing from January 1st, 1984 thru December 31st, 1984
TOP RANKINGS Determined by Total

220 / Name	Squat	Bench Press	Deadlift	Total	Date
Mike Fuscardo	667	418	628	1714	4/01/84
Buster Whitener	600	415	665	1680	1/21/84
Earl Snider	573	391	705	1669	5/27/84
Tony Culp	622	402	622	1647	4/01/84
Scott Tusic	600	430	600	1630	2/12/84
Don Hall	622	380	622	1625	4/01/84
John Nicoloudakis	560	430	630	1620	12/01/84
Don Hall	620	375	610	1605	2/12/84
Don Hall	600	391	611	1603	12/16/84
John Silvey	600	413	578	1592	5/27/84
Paul Rowand	600	413	562	1576	5/27/84
Greg Jarvie	589	347	633	1570	12/16/84
Steve Uhas	660	305	600	1565	2/12/84
M. Sean Byrd	560	460	540	1560	2/12/84
Greg Jarvie	584	341	633	1559	4/01/84
Ross Smith	589	402	529	1521	4/01/84
M. Sean Byrd	529	473*tAR	501	1504	3/03/84
Ernie Nagy	525	390	540	1455	2/12/84
Paul Rowand	540	369	518	1427	3/03/84
Ernie Nagy	485	385	501	1372	10/14/84
William Farmer	460	330	510	1300	8/11/84
Mike Leikari	430	290	555	1275	2/12/84
Stacy Barber	440	341	473	1256	11/11/84

* - West Virginia State Powerlifting Record

*t AR – Teenage American Powerlifting Record

1984 West Virginia Powerlifter Rankings
WV Powerlifters competing from January 1st, 1984 thru December 31st, 1984

TOP RANKINGS Determined by Total

242 / Name	Squat	Bench Press	Deadlift	Total	Date
Bret Russell	722	446	804	1973 e	7/08/84
Bret Russell	705	457	804*	1967 e	4/01/84
Nick Busick	655	501	655	1813	12/16/84
Nick Busick	630	505	550	1685	4/14/84
John Messinger	622	413	633	1669	7/22/84
John Messinger	622	418	622	1664	12/16/84
John Messinger	622	413	622	1658	5/27/84
Mark Olenick	644	391	622	1658	11/11/84
Sam Moore	600	352	661	1614	4/01/84
Mark Olenick	620	390	595	1605	4/14/84
Mark Olenick	589	380	617	1587	4/01/84
Paul Rowand	573	418	562	1554	11/11/84
John Messinger	575	400	570	1545	2/12/84
John Nicoloudakis	529	413	600	1543	4/01/84
Mark Olenick	550	375	600	1525	1/21/84
Marshall Moore	600	308	600	1510	5/27/84
Greg Moodie	556	363	584	1504	5/27/84
Joe Lepera	529	369	584	1482	3/03/84
Mike Nidy	529	374	573	1477	12/16/84
Rocky Martin	530	375	570	1475	12/01/84
John Alderman	540*t	369	562	1471	3/03/84
Greg Moodie	551	347	562	1460	4/01/84
Mike Nidy	530	355	570	1455	12/01/84
Greg Moody	540	365	530	1435	7/21/84
Ernie Nagy	515 m	380 m	515 m	1410 m	1/21/84
Willie Williams	485	369	551	1405	4/01/84
Greg Moodie	520	340	535	1395	2/12/84
Joe Carvelli	510	365	520	1395	3/17/84
Joe Carvelli	525	345	520	1390	2/12/84

e – ELITE Powerlifting Classification Total

* - West Virginia State Powerlifting Record

t – West Virginia State Teenage Powerlifting Record

m – West Virginia State Masters Powerlifting Record

1984 West Virginia Powerlifter Rankings
WV Powerlifters competing from January 1st, 1984 thru December 31st, 1984
TOP RANKINGS Determined by Total

275 / Name	Squat	Bench Press	Deadlift	Total	Date
Nick Busick	705	505	605	1815	11/18/84
Dan Hall	685	390	675	1750	2/12/84
Nick Busick	683	473	551	1708	9/22/84
Dan Hall	655	358	683	1697	12/16/84
John Messinger	611	424	622	1658	11/11/84
Dan Hall	677	358	617	1653	4/01/84
Sam Moore	595	352	694	1642	11/11/84
John Messinger	600	413	606	1620	4/01/84
Greg Moodie	551	380	573	1504	12/16/84
Mike Nidy	573	352	556	1482	4/01/84
Mike Nidy	551	363	562	1476	5/27/84
Jim Goodnight	545	402	501	1449	5/27/84
Chris Veltri	468	429	540	1438	5/27/84
Mike Nidy	520	360	540	1420	2/12/84
Steve Pauley	512	308	523	1344	5/27/84
Wayne Lilly	446	325	540	1311	4/01/84
Steve Pauley	505	285	480	1270	2/12/84
Phil Massinople	446	319	462	1229	4/01/84
SHW Jeff Cook	611	396	744*	1752	4/01/84
Terry Gill	600	402	606	1609	4/01/84
Charles Ashcraft	633	380	584	1598	4/01/84
Tim Slamick	650	347	600	1598	11/11/84
Charles Ashcraft	639	363	562	1565	5/27/84
Troy McNett	529	440	584	1554	4/01/84
Charles Ashcraft	620	350	570	1540	2/12/84
Tim Slamick	633	303	600	1537	5/27/84
Charles Ashcraft	610	360	520	1490	1/21/84

* - West Virginia State Powerlifting Record

Chapter Twenty : Era II Powerlifting Records

All lifting during the Era II time period of Powerlifting met the criteria for the "Single-Ply" Division of Powerlifting, *without* the Bench Press shirt. The weight classes included in Era II (listed in pounds) : 114, 123, 132, 148, 165, 181, 198, 220, 242, 275, and Superheavyweights (SHW). The Era II of Powerlifting began in 1977 with the introduction of the spandex suit, also known as the "Super Suit."

In addition to the spandex lifting suits, the custom-made, suede belts were also available during the Era II of Powerlifting. In addition to wrist wraps, Powerlifters were permitted to wear a knee wrap called the "Superwrap" in official Powerlifting competitions. The supersuits, superwraps, and custom lifting belts gained universal acceptance in the sport of Powerlifting during 1977.

The West Virginia State Powerlifting Records were under the jurisdiction of the West Virginia State Powerlifting Chairman. With the election of a new West Virginia State Powerlifting Chairman on April 25th, 1982, changes were made in regard to breaking an existing West Virginia State Powerlifting Record. Effective May 1st, 1982, West Virginia State Powerlifting Records would only be recognized in officially sanctioned Powerlifting competitions held within the state of West Virginia with exception to the following Powerlifting Championships :

1) Junior National Powerlifting Championships
2) Senior National Powerlifting Championships
3) Women's National Powerlifting Championships
4) Masters National Powerlifting Championships
5) Teenage National Powerlifting Championships
6) World Powerlifting Championships

Additional language was added to the criteria governing West Virginia State Powerlifting Records in 1983. In the Spring of 1983, the West Virginia State Powerlifting Chairman officially made the declaration, "West Virginia State Powerlifting Records will only be set or broken in the West Virginia State Powerlifting Championships, a National Powerlifting Championship, or the World Powerlifting Championships."

An argument could exist between the Powerlifters of Era One (1960 – 1976) and the Powerlifters of Era Two (1977 – 1984) regarding the Bench Press Records. Even though lifters were permitted to use supersuits, custom lifting belts, and superwraps for the wrists and knees during Era Two, the Bench Press during the years of 1977 through 1983 remained "RAW."

Conclusively, it's all about the Powerlifter's TOTAL. Although the Bench Press was virtually unaffected from the use of the supersuit for Squats and Deadlifts, the Totals were higher as a result. The "RAW" Bench Press Records were finalized at the end of Powerlifting's Era II.

Era Two (1977–1984) : West Virginia Powerlifting

Beginning with the 114lb. class, Chuck Dunbar Squatted a World Record of 507lbs. / 230 kilos and Bench Pressed 314lbs. / 142.5 kilos at the 1980 World Powerlifting Championships held in Arlington, Texas. The World Record Bench Press of 314lbs. by Chuck Dunbar at the 1980 World Powerlifting Championships was the result of a fourth Attempt. Chuck Mooney pulled a West Virginia State Record Deadlift of 451lbs. at the National (Junior) Powerlifting Championships on 6/04/83 at Charlottesville, Virginia.

In the 123lb. class, Chuck Dunbar Squatted a World Record of 460lbs. at the 1978 Chattanooga Open Powerlifting Championships on 5/06/78. At the 1980 West Virginia State Powerlifting Championships on 3/30/80, Chuck Dunbar set the Bench Press Record at 295lbs. and Total Record at 1120lbs. Cork Hall owns the West Virginia State Deadlift Record in the 123lb. class with a lift of 435lbs. Cork Hall's record was set at the West Virginia State Powerlifting Championships on 3/26/83.

In the 132lb. class, Ed Canjemi set unofficial marks of a 475 Squat, 480 Deadlift, and a 1215 Total on 10/09/82. Canjemi added to the Squat and Total on 1/09/83 with a Squat of 515 and a Total of 1235lbs. However, Dan Palmateer owns the official Squat Record in the 132lb. class with a lift of 468 and the official Total Record at 1190lbs. Dan Palmateer set the 132lb. West Virginia State Squat and Total Records at the 1983 Junior National Powerlifting Championships in Charlottesville, Virginia. The Bench Press Record of 336lbs. in the 132lb. class is owned by Acie Simmons set at the West Virginia State Powerlifting Championships on 3/26/83.

Dana Bee set the West Virginia State Bench Press Record of 380lbs. while competing in the 165lb. class at the 1980 YMCA National Powerlifting Championships held in Beckley, West Virginia on 1/05/80. Dana Bee broke the existing Bench Press Record of 375 set by Jack Wilson on 4/01/78. Dana Bee's West Virginia State Bench Press Record in the 165lb. class of 380lbs. was not broken until the "Bench Press Shirt" was used after 1985.

Jack Wilson dominated the 165lb. class in West Virginia Powerlifting during his time of residence from January, 1977 until December, 1978. The Total of 1605 made by Jack Wilson on 12/10/78 still stands as the highest Total among West Virginia's Middleweight Powerlifters.

Dave Jeffrey set a new Bench Press Record in the 181lb. class of 400lbs. and Total Record of 1500lbs. while winning the West Virginia State Powerlifting Championships on 4/01/79. Dave Jeffrey broke the existing mark of 375 set by Frank Nicholas on 4/01/78. On 3/26/83, C. Dave Drennan broke the existing Bench Press Record of Dave Jeffrey in the 181lb. class with a lift of 402lbs. / 182.5 kilos at the West Virginia State Powerlifting Championships.

Doug Currence has the West Virginia State Deadlift Record during Era II in the 181lb. class. During 1984, Doug and Robert Griffith traded ownership of the Deadlift Record for the Lightheavyweight (181lb. class) Division. Doug Currence Deadlifted 666 ¾ (rounded to 667) at the 3rd Annual Steel Valley Open on 12/15/84, exceeding the existing mark of 661lbs. lifted by himself and Robert Griffith on 4/01/84 at the West Virginia State Powerlifting Championships. According to news reports, the Deadlift by Doug Currence of 666 ¾ lbs. (302.5 kilos) on 12/15/84 was declared an official West Virginia Powerlifting Record in the 181lb. class by the West Virginia State Powerlifting Chairman.

Roger Estep owns all of the West Virginia State Powerlifting Records for Era II in the 198lb. class. From January, 1977 through December 10th, 1978, Roger Estep set or broke all of the Powerlifting Records for the state of West Virginia while competing at major Powerlifting competitions in the 198lb. weight class. The World Record Squat of 769, Bench Press of 490, Deadlift of 685, and Total of 1944lbs. were set by Roger Estep on 12/10/78 at the YMCA National Powerlifting Championships.

While competing in the 220lb. class at the West Virginia State Powerlifting Championships on 4/25/82, Bret Russell Squatted a West Virginia State Record of 705lbs. and Deadlifted 770lbs. for another West Virginia State Record and achieved Powerlifting Elite Classification with a West Virginia State Record Total of 1870lbs. On 3/12/83, Bret Russell exceeded his official mark with a Squat of 710. On 5/28/83, Bret Russell set another unofficial mark with a Squat of 716 in the 220lb. class and another Elite Total of 1868lbs.

For the 220lb. weight class, Mike Wolf owns the West Virginia State Powerlifting Record in the Bench Press for Era II of Powerlifting. Wolf's Bench Press of 490lbs. on 4/01/79 at the West Virginia State Powerlifting Championships ranks as the highest Bench Press for all West Virginia Powerlifters competing in the 220lb. class from 1960 thru 1984.

In the 242lb. class, Scott Warman owns the West Virginia State Squat and Total Records for Era II of Powerlifting. While competing in the 242lb. class at the 1982

Senior National Powerlifting Championships on 7/11/82, Scott Warman Squatted 826 and Totaled Elite with a mark of 2039lbs. The 826 Squat and 2039 Total are West Virginia State Powerlifting Records in the 242lb. class for the Era II of Powerlifting.

Randy Scott set a new West Virginia State Powerlifting Record in the Bench Press on 3/26/83 with a lift of 501 while competing in the 242lb. class at the 1983 West Virginia State Powerlifting Championships. On 4/01/84, Bret Russell became the first West Virginian to Deadlift over 800lbs. with a West Virginia State Record of 804lbs. in the 242lb. class at the 1984 West Virginia State Powerlifting Championships.

Jim Goodnight Bench Pressed 465 for a West Virginia State Powerlifting Record on 4/01/78 at the West Virginia State Powerlifting Championships while competing in the 275lb. class. On 4/01/79, Jim Goodnight broke his existing record with a new mark of 500lbs. in the 275lb. class for a new West Virginia State Powerlifting Record in the Bench Press. Luke Iams competed for the first time in the 275lb. class at the 1981 West Virginia State Powerlifting Championships on 3/29/81 and set a new West Virginia State Bench Press Record of 529lbs.

While competing in the Superheavyweight class at the 1984 West Virginia State Powerlifting Championships, Jeff Cook Totaled 1752 on 4/01/84 and Deadlifted 744lbs. for the West Virginia State Deadlift Record. The 744 Deadlift by Jeff Cook on 4/01/84 is the number one (1) Deadlift in the Superheavyweight class for the state of West Virginia during the Era II of Powerlifting.

In the SuperHeavyWeight (SHW) class, Luke Iams owns the Squat, Bench Press, and Total Records during the ERA II of Powerlifting. The Elite Total of 2080 by Luke Iams on 4/01/79 included a Squat of 875 and a Bench Press of 600lbs. The 875 Squat, 600 Bench Press, and Total of 2080lbs. by Luke Iams are the West Virginia State Powerlifting Records for the Superheavyweight class during the Era II of Powerlifting. Jeff Cook set new official West Virginia State Deadlift Records on the dates of 11/01/81, 3/26/83, and 4/01/84.

Powerlifting Records : Paul Sutphin – ERA II

In the 148lb. class, Paul Sutphin owns all of the Powerlifting Records set in the Era II of Powerlifting. The 545 Squat, 341 Bench Press, 595 Deadlift, and 1482 Total of "Ten-times Bodyweight" were set at the 1979 National / Junior Powerlifting Championships at Los Angeles, California on July 14th, 1979. The Total of 1482lbs. (672.5 kilos) set on 7/14/79 earned Paul Sutphin the Outstanding Lifter Award at the 1979 Junior Nationals. The 1482 Total was a Junior National Powerlifting Championship Meet Record which was not broken until 6/04/83. All of the records set by Sutphin on 7/14/79 have yet to be broken under the same conditions.

In the 181lb. class, <u>Paul Sutphin</u> owns the Squat and Total Record for the Era II of Powerlifting. On May 15th, 1982 while qualifying for the 1982 Senior Nationals, Paul Squatted 655, an unofficial West Virginia State mark. One (1) year later, Sutphin Squatted 688 ¾ with an Elite Total of 1714 on 5/28/83. The Squat of 688 ¾ and Total of 1714 were not accepted as official West Virginia State Powerlifting Records.

The Squat and Total Records by Sutphin on 5/28/83 were not listed as official West Virginia State Powerlifing Records due to additional criteria implemented by the West Virginia State Powerlifting Committee defining the acceptance of new West Virginia State Powerlifting Records. Effective April 1st, 1983 only lifts from major Powerlifting championships or from the West Virginia State Powerlifting Championships were accepted as official West Virginia State Powerlifting Records.

The conditions for setting or breaking West Virginia State Powerlifting Records were again revisited during the Summer of 1983 by the West Virginia State Powerlifting Chairman and members of the West Virginia Powerlifting Committee. When it was all said and done, the restrictions implemented on 4/01/83 continued. On 8/27/83, a Squat of 705 and a Total of 1750 were rejected as official West Virginia marks for Paul Sutphin.

The 650lbs. (295 kilos) Squat at the 1982 Senior National Powerlifting Championships in the 181lb. class on 7/10/82 stands as the West Virginia State Squat Record for the Era II of Powerlifting. The 705lb. Squat by Paul Sutphin on August 27th, 1983 ranked number forty-nine (49) in the <u>Men's TOP 50 of ALL-TIME / 82.5 kg (181lb.)</u> *as ranked by Herb Glossbrenner.* *Powerlifting USA / Vol. 25 / No. 2 / September, 2001*

While competing at the *1981 YMCA National Powerlifting Championships*, <u>Paul Sutphin</u> put together an Elite Total of 1653 in the 181lb. class. The Record was duplicated by Sutphin at the 1982 Senior National Powerlifting Championships at Dayton, Ohio. The Total of 1653lbs. (750 kilos) stands as the official West Virginia State Powerlifting Record in the 181lb. class for the Era II of Powerlifting.

Powerlifting Records : Don Hundley – ERA II

Don Hundley owns several Powerlifting Records from the Era II of Powerlifting : 1) 606 Squat / 165lb. class 2) 667 Deadlift / 165lb. class. Both the Squat and Deadlift were set by Hundley on 3/31/84 at the 1984 West Virginia State Powerlifting Championships.

During the Era II of Powerlifting, Don Hundley set an unprecedented number of American Masters Powerlifting Records, World Masters Powerlifting Records, and the West Virginia State Records in the 165lb. class. In October of 1977, Don Hundley won the 1977 National Masters Powerlifting Championships while competing in the 165lb. class (Age 40-44) with a 1150 Total.

Don Hundley appeared on the cover of *Powerlifting USA* magazine in November, 1978. Eleven (11) months later, Don won the 1979 National Masters Powerlifting Championships on 10/28/79 in the 165lb. class (40-44 Age Group) with a 1240 Total. One (1) year later, Hundley set a new World Masters Deadlift Record on 10/19/80 with 606lbs. (275 kilos) in the 165lb. class (40-44 Age Group).

Don Hundley pulled a 617 Deadlift at the 1981 YMCA National Powerlifting Championships on 1/10/81 for another Master's World Deadlift Record in the 165lb. class. On 2/07/82, Don Hundley pulled a 650 Deadlift for an unofficial West Virginia State Powerlifting Record. Six (6) days later, Don Hundley pulled 584lbs. (265 kilos) at the 1982 Bob Moon Memorial Powerlifting Championships at Findlay, Ohio on 2/13/82. The 584 Deadlift by Don Hundley on 2/13/82 was a World Masters Powerlifting Record in the 165lb. class. On 4/24/82, Don Hundley won the 1982 West Virginia State Powerlifting Championships in Fairmont. Competing in the 165lb. class, Don pulled another 650lb. Deadlift for the win. Hundley's 650 Deadlift on 4/24/82 was an OFFICIAL West Virginia State Deadlift Record.

While competing in the 165lb. class at the 1982 Mountianeer Open Powerlifting Championships, Don Hundley set three (3) Masters World Powerlifting Records in the Squat, Deadlift, and Total. Hundley's Total of 1438 on 10/30/82 included a 573 Squat and a 606 Deadlift. The Powerlifting Records by Hundley on 10/30/82 were specific to the 165lb. class / Masters Division (45-49 Age Group).

On 12/11/82, Don Hundley broke his own record with a Deadlift of 655 while competing in the 165lb. weight class. Over one (1) year later, Don Hundley joined the category of Elite Powerlifters. While competing in the 165lb. class at the YMCA National Powerlifting Championships on 12/17/83, Don Hundley Totaled Elite for the first time with a Total of 1527lbs.

In the 165lb. class, Don Hundley Squatted 606 ¼ (275 kilos) and Deadlifted 666 ¾ (302.5 kilos) on 3/31/84 while competing at the West Virginia State Powerlifting Championships. Hundley's Squat of 606 and Deadlift of 667 were World and American Masters Powerlifting Records. Don Hundley's Squat of 606 and Deadlift of 667 in the 165lb. class remain standing!

Powerlifting Records : Herb Fitzsimmons – ERA II

The Powerlifting Records by Herb Fitzsimmons during ERA II began in 1977 at the Lynchburg Open on 1/29/77. Herb set the West Virginia State Record in the Squat with a lift of 580lbs. in the 242lb. class. Herb's 580 Squat at Lynchburg, Virginia on 1/29/77 was a West Virginia State Powerlifting Record in both the Open and the Masters Division.

Herb set another West Virginia Squat Record of 580lbs. in the 242lb. class on 4/17/77 along with a Total of 1540lbs. Both the 580 Squat and 1540 Total by Fitzsimmons were official National Masters Powerlifting Records in the 242lb. class. At the 1977 Chattanooga Open, Herb broke the National Masters Squat Record again while competing in the 242lb. class with a Squat of 610lbs. Along with the 610lb. Squat, Herb Deadlifted a new West Virginia State Masters Record of 600lbs. and Totaled a National Masters Record of 1580lbs.

Herb Fitzsimmons continued to break Powerlifting Records in key events with a Deadlift of 630lbs. while competing in the 242lb. class at the 1977 West Virginia State Powerlifting Championships. The 630lb. Deadlift by Fitzsimmons on 5/21/77 was a new Powerlifting Record in the Open and Masters Division.

On 11/06/77 at the 1977 Mountianeer Open Powerlifting Championships, Herb Fitzsimmons set Powerlifting Records in three (3) categories :

1) West Virginia State Powerlifting – Open Division
2) West Virginia State Powerlifting – Masters Division
3) National Powerlifting Records – Masters Division

Herb Fitzsimmons Squatted 635lbs. for a West Virginia State Squat Record in both the Open and Masters Division at the 1977 Mountianeer Open. Herb's Squat on 11/06/77 became the new National Masters Powerlifting Record. Herb Bench Pressed 400lbs. for a new West Virginia State Masters Record in the 242lb. class. The Total of 1640lbs. by Herb on 11/06/77 was also a new West Virginia State Total Record in the Open and Masters Division *along with* a National Masters Total Record.

While competing at the 1977 Mountain Empire Open Powerlifting Meet at Bristol, Tennessee, Herb Fitzsimmons again set Powerlifting Records in two (2) categories. On 12/17/77, Herb officially weighed-in to compete in the SHW (SuperHeavyWeight) class. Herb's Squat at the 1977 Mountian Empire Open Powerlifting meet was 650lbs. for a new West Virginia State Squat Record in the Masters Division.

Along with the Fitzsimmons' Squat of 650lbs. on 12/17/77 came a Bench Press of 400lbs. for a new West Virginia State Record in the Masters Division, SHW class. To end the day, Herb pulled a new West Virginia Deadlift Record of 650lbs. and Totaled 1700. Herb's Deadlift on 12/17/77 was a new West Virginia State Deadlift Record in the SuperHeavyWeight class for the Open Division as well as the Masters category.

For the year 1978, a new weight class was introduced ; the 275lb. (125 kilo) weight class. For Herb Fitzsimmons, eight (8) new West Virginia State Powerlifting Records were set on 1/14/78 at the 1978 Huntington Open Powerlifting Meet. Competing in the 275lb. class as a "warm-up" for the 1978 YMCA Nationals eight (8) days later, Herb Squatted 580, Bench Pressed 400, and Deadlifted 610 for a Total of 1590lbs. Herb's Squat, Bench Press, Deadlift, and Total were all West Virginia State Powerlifting Records for the new 275lb. class in both the Open and Masters Division.

Herb Fitzsimmons set more Powerlifting Records at the YMCA National Powerlifting Championships on the weekend of January 21st, 1978. On Sunday January 22nd, 1978 Herb competed in the 242lb. class and Totaled a West Virginia State Powerlifting Record of 1680lbs. Included in the 1680 Total was another West Virginia State Record Squat of 650lbs.

Another appearance in the 242lb. class for Herb Fitzsimmons during 1978 happened at the Chattanooga Open on 5/06/78. While competing at the 1978 Chattanooga Open Powerlifting Championships, Herb Squatted 670, Bench Pressed 425, and Deadlifted 680 for a Total of 1775. The Squat, Deadlift, and Total on 5/06/78 were all new West Virginia State Powerlifting Records for Herb Fitzsimmons in the Open AND the Masters Division.

Herb Fitzsimmons dominated the 275lb. class in West Virginia Powerlifting from January, 1977 through the entire year of 1980. The Fitzsimmons' chapter of Powerlifting Records in the 275lb. class continued on 2/25/78. At the 1978 Southern Open, Herb set four (4) new West Virginia State Powerlifting Records in the Open Division and four (4) new West Virginia State Powerlifting Records in the Masters Division. Included in the Fitzsimmons' Total Record of 1740 in the 275lb. class on 2/25/78 : A Squat of 655, Bench Press of 425, and a Deadlift of 660.

While competing in the 275lb. class on 4/01/78 at the West Virginia State Powerlifting Championships, Herb Fitzsimmons continued with four (4) new Master's Powerlifting Records and two (2) West Virginia State Powerlifting Records in the Open Division for the Deadlift and Total. Herb's Total Record of 1800 in the 275lb. class on 4/01/78 included a 650 Squat, 450 Bench Press, and a West Virginia State Deadlift Record of 700lbs.

Herb Fitzsimmons broke more records at the 1978 National / Junior Powerlifting Championships on 7/09/78. Competing in the 275lb. class, Herb Squatted 722, Bench Pressed 462, and Deadlifted 683 for a Total of 1868. The Fitzsimmons' Squat, Bench Press, and Total were all new West Virginia State Masters Powerlifting Records in the 275lb. class. The Squat and Total were also new West Virginia State Records in the Open Division.

On February 24th, 1979 Herb Fitzsimmons Totaled 1825 while competing in the 275lb. class. The Total of 1825 by Herb on 2/24/79 included a new West Virginia State Record Squat of 725lbs. At the 1979 West Virginia State Powerlifting Championships on 4/01/79, the 1900 Total barrier was exceeded by Herb with a new West Virginia State Record of 1920lbs. Included in the Fitzsimmons' Record Total of 1920 was a new West Virginia State Squat Record of 740 and a new West Virginia State Deadlift Record in the 275lb. class of 730lbs.!

The final West Virginia State Powerlifting Record in the 275lb. class set by Herb Fitzsimmons occurred on 4/21/79 when he Deadlifted 740! Herb Fitzsimmons' West Virginia State Deadlift Record of 740 was not broken until 3/26/11 at the 2011 West Virginia State Powerlifting Championships.

While competing as a Superheavyweight on 12/17/77, Herb Fitzsimmons set four (4) West Virginia State Masters Records with lifts of a 650 Squat, 400 Bench Press, and a Deadlift of 650 for a Total of 1700. Herb's Deadlift of 650 on 12/17/77 was a new West Virginia State Deadlift Record from 12/17/77 until 11/01/81.

West Virginia's First Elite Powerlifters

The first West Virginia Powerlifters to Total Elite achieved Powerlifting's Elite Classification during the Era II of Powerlifting (1/01/77 thru 12/31/84). The chronological report includes the listing of individuals, #1 thru #13. Specific to West Virginia Powerlifters, eleven (11) men and two (2) women achieved Elite Powerlifting Classification during the years identified as the Era II of Powerlifting. The first West Virginia Powerlifters to achieve Elite Powerlifting Classification determined by USPF / IPF Standards were :

1) Paul Sutphin
2) Chuck Dunbar
3) Luke Iams
4) Scott Warman

5) Bret Russell
6) Butch Brown
7) Don Hundley
8) Doug Currence
9) Gene Underwood

Jack Wilson – Elite Totals @ 165, Roger Estep – Elite Totals @ 198

1) Joan Fruth – *female athlete*
2) Mary Ryan Jeffrey – *female athlete*

The thirteen (13) West Virginia Powerlifters, including Jack Wilson and Roger Estep, made Elite Totals with Single-Ply Gear <u>WITHOUT</u> the Bench Press Shirt. Jack Wilson and Roger Estep had achieved the Elite Powerlifting Classification before arriving in West Virginia at the beginning of 1977. As a resident of West Virginia from January, 1977 thru December, 1978, Jack Wilson Totaled Elite five (5) times and finished with a 1605 Total in the 165lb. class. As a resident of West Virginia from January, 1977 thru December, 1978, Roger Estep Totaled Elite seven (7) times and finished with a 1944 Total in the 198lb. class.

Seventeen (17) Elite Totals
Three Weight Classes : 148, 165, and 181

During the Era II of Powerlifting, <u>Paul Sutphin</u> Totaled Elite eight (8) times as a competitor in the 148lb. class, four (4) times in the 165lb. class, and five (5) times as a Powerlifter in the 181lb. class. Sutphin, while achieving Elite Powerlifting Classification in three (3) weight classes and, on one occasion, exceeded the minimum criteria for Elite in the 198lb. class with a Total of 1750, defined the Elite standard of performance for West Virginia Powerlifting.

While competing in the 148lb. class at the 1978 Chattanooga Open Powerlifting Championships on 5/06/78, Paul Sutphin Totaled Elite for the first time with a 1360 Total in the 148lb. class. Afterward, there were four (4) additional Elite Totals for Sutphin while competing as a lightweight during the year 1978 : 7/08/78 – 1377 Total, 11/05/78 – 1385 Total, 11/11/78 – 1405 Total, and 12/10/78 – 1425 Total. At the 1979 Southern Open on 2/23/79, a Total of 1435 in the 148lb. class scored another Elite

Total for Paul Sutphin. On 4/01/79, Sutphin Totaled 1445 at the West Virginia State Powerlifting Championships.

Paul Sutphin Totaled Elite for the first time in the 165lb. class at the 1979 Chattanooga Open with a 1505 Total on 4/21/79. Two (2) weeks later, another Elite Total for Sutphin was made at the 1979 Roanoke Open on 5/05/79 with a 1485 Total. Three (3) weeks later at the 1979 North American Powerlifting Championships on 5/26/79, Sutphin Totaled Elite in the 165lb. class once again with a Total of 1510 / 685 kilos.

On 7/14/79, the final Elite Total by Paul Sutphin as a lightweight happened at the 1979 Junior National Powerlifting Championships. Paul Sutphin Totaled "Ten-Times Bodyweight" on 7/14/79 with a Total of 1482lbs. and a championship win in the 148lb. class.

While winning the 5th Annual (1980) West Virginia State Powerlifting Championships on 3/30/80, Paul Sutphin exceeded the newly revised standard for Elite Powerlifting Classification with a Total of 1535 while competing in the 165lb. class. Sutphin Totaled Elite in the 181lb. class for the first time with a Total of 1653 on 1/10/81 while winning the YMCA National Powerlifting Championships.

During the year 1982, Sutphin Totaled Elite twice in the 181lb. class with Totals of 1670 and 1653. The 1653 Total by Paul Sutphin happened at the 1982 Senior National Powerlifting Championships. During 1983, there were two (2) Elite Totals in the 181lb. class by Paul Sutphin : 1714 on 5/28/83 and 1750 on 8/27/83.

Elite Performances : "Less than" or "Equal to" Nine (9)

Chuck Dunbar became the 2nd West Virginia Powerlifter to Total Elite. At the 1978 Senior National Powerlifting Championships on 8/25/78, Chuck Dunbar Totaled Elite for the first time with a Total of 1096 while competing in the 114lb. class. At the YMCA National Powerlifting Championships on 12/10/78, Dunbar Totaled 1087, another Elite Total at 114.

During 1979, Chuck Dunbar Totaled Elite at four (4) major Powerlifting competitions : 1135 Total – 4/01/79, 1140 Total – 5/04/79, 1151 Total – 8/18/79, and a 1146 Total – 11/02/79. Before leaving West Virginia, Chuck Dunbar made three (3) Elite Totals in 1980. While competing at the 1980 World Series of Powerlifting in Auburn, Alabama on 4/19/80, Chuck Dunbar Totaled 1146. At the 1980 Senior National Powerlifting Championships on 7/12/80, Dunbar made another Elite Total of 1146. While competing at the 1980 World Powerlifting Championships on 11/07/80, Chuck Dunbar Totaled

1190 while representing the U.S.A. in the 114lb. class. In summation, Chuck Dunbar owns nine (9) Elite performances from 8/25/78 to 11/07/80.

Luke Iams was the third (3rd) West Virginia Powerlifter to Total Elite. On April 1st, 1979 Luke Iams achieved Powerlifting's Elite Classification status with a Total of 2080lbs. while winning the 1979 West Virginia State Powerlifting Championships. The 2080 Total represents the only Elite Total for Luke Iams.

Scott Warman was the fourth (4th) West Virginia Powerlifter to Total Elite. Scott Warman Totaled Elite for the first time with a Total of 1895 on 1/09/82 at the YMCA National Powerlifting Championships while competing in the 242lb. class. At the 1982 Great Lakes Open Powerlifting on 3/27/82, Scott Warman Totaled 1960, another Elite Total in the 242lb. class. On 7/11/82, Scott Warman became the second West Virginia Powerlifter to Total over 2000lbs. at the 1982 Senior National Powerlifting Championships with an Elite Total of 2039lbs.

Bret Russell became the fifth (5th) West Virginia Powerlifter to Total Elite. At the 1982 West Virginia State Powerlifting Championships, Bret Russell won the title in the 220lb. class with an Elite Total of 1870lbs. While competing in the 242lb. class at the 1984 West Virginia State Powerlifting Championships, Bret Russell Totaled 1967lbs. and earned Powerlifting's Elite Classification in the 242lb. class. Later in 1984, while competing in the 242lb. class at the 1984 Senior Nationals on 7/08/84, Bret produced another Elite Total of 1973lbs.

Butch Brown was the sixth (6th) West Virginia Powerlifter to Total Elite. While competing in the 165lb. class at the Mountianeer Open Powerlifting Championships on 10/30/82, Butch Brown Totaled 1537lbs. On 6/04/83 at the National (Junior) Powerlifting Championships, Butch Brown Totaled 1559 for another Elite Total in the 165lb. class.

Don Hundley, the seventh (7th) West Virginia Powerlifter to Total Elite, put together 1527lbs. on 12/17/83 at the 1983 YMCA National Powerlifting Championships while competing in the 165lb. class. Again, at the 1984 West Virginia State Powerlifting Championships on 3/31/84, Don Hundley made an Elite Total of 1537lbs.

Doug Currence became the eighth (8th) West Virginia Powerlifter to Total Elite. While winning the 1984 West Virginia State Powerlifting Championships in the 181lb. class on 4/01/84, Doug Currence achieved the Powerlifter Elite Classification for the first time with a Total of 1642lbs.

Gene Underwood became the ninth (9th) West Virginia Powerlifter to Total Elite. While competing in the 148lb. class at the 1984 Parkersburg Open on 5/26/84, Gene Underwood Totaled 1405 for an Elite Total. Gene was the last West Virginia Powerlifter to Total Elite in the Era II of Powerlifting.

Era II West Virginia Powerlifting Records
WV Powerlifters competing from January 1st, 1977 thru December 31st, 1984
TOP RANKINGS Determined by Total

114 / Name	Squat	Bench Press	Deadlift	Total	Date
Chuck Dunbar	507*	308*wr	374	1190* e	11/07/80
Chuck Dunbar – 314 Bench Press / World Record 4th attempt*					
Chuck Dunbar	485* wr	303* wr	363	1151* e	8/18/79
Chuck Dunbar	485	303	358	1146 e	11/02/79
Chuck Mooney	325	209	451*	986	6/04/83
Dave Talbott	314	225	374	914	5/22/82
123 Chuck Dunbar	sq	295*	dl	1120*	3/30/80
Roger Salser	415	280	415	1110	1/05/80
Chuck Dunbar	445	275	330	1050*	5/06/78
460 (wr) World Record / 4th Attempt					
Greg Spencer	341	225	424	992	3/26/83
Cork Hall	352	198	435*	986	3/26/83
Dan Palmateer	325	231	407	964	10/31/81
Rick Yates	336	209	407	953	3/26/83
Ken Woodell	280	230	410	920	5/21/77
Dorian Murphy	341 t	176	402	920 t	4/23/83
132 Ed Canjemi	515 u	260	460	1235 u	1/09/83
Ed Canjemi	475 u	260	480 u	1215 u	10/09/82
Dan Palmateer	468*	281	440	1190*	6/04/83
Dan Palmateer	429	275	479*	1184*	3/26/83
Roger Salser	455	275	425	1155	4/12/80
Acie Simmons	402	336*	385	1124	3/26/83
Roger Salser	415 c	285*c	425 c	1125 c	4/27/80
Maurice Kinzer	391 t	259 t	440 t	1091 t	4/23/83
Maurice Kinzer	363	248	435	1047	8/06/82
Ron Giarletto	360	200	455	1015	4/01/78

* - West Virginia State Powerlifting Record

c – West Virginia State Collegiate Powerlifting Record

t – West Virginia State Teenage Powerlifting Record

wr – World Powerlifting Record

e – Elite Powerlifting Total

NOTE : The weight of Chuck Dunbar's SQUAT and DEADLIFT on 3/30/80 at the 1980 West Virginia State Powerlifting Championships not available.

Era II West Virginia Powerlifting Records
WV Powerlifters competing from January 1st, 1977 thru December 31st, 1984
TOP RANKINGS Determined by Total

148 / Name	Squat	Bench Press	Deadlift	Total	Date
Paul Sutphin	545*	341*	595*	1482* N e	7/14/79
Paul Sutphin	535*	320	590*	1445* e	4/01/79
Paul Sutphin	530*	330	575*	1435* e	2/23/79
Paul Sutphin	525* Y	330*	570 Y	1425*Y e	12/10/78
Paul Sutphin	520*	325	560	1405* e	11/11/78
Gene Underwood	518	336	551	1405 e	5/26/84
Paul Sutphin	490	325	570	1385* e	11/05/78
Paul Sutphin	479	325*	573*	1377* e	7/08/78
Gene Underwood	490	325	551	1366	3/31/84
Paul Sutphin	500*	305	555*	1360* e	5/06/78
Paul Sutphin	485*	300	550*	1335*	4/01/78
Gene Underwood	480	320	525	1325	2/11/84
Gene Underwood	462	314	523	1300	7/21/84
Paul Sutphin	460	275	515*	1250	1/28/78
Ed Canjemi	520	275	455	1250	4/24/82
Art Williamson	462	264	518	1245	12/15/84
Mark McCoy	518	242	479	1240	3/26/83
Paul Sutphin	450	260	510*	1220	1/22/78
Paul Sutphin	445	265	505*	1215	12/17/77
Don McCartney	465	290	450	1205	12/11/82
John Priest	450	270	475	1195	4/01/78
Doug Currence	396	297	490	1184	3/28/81
Keith Gandee	451	275	451	1179	5/28/83
Art Williamson	440	242	490	1173	9/22/84
Mike Kimball	440	270	446	1157	12/15/84
Mike Sarver	410	265	480	1155	4/24/82

* - West Virginia State Powerlifting Record

N – National Powerlifting Record

Y – YMCA National Powerlifting Record

t – West Virginia Teenage Powerlifting Record

e – Elite Powerlifting Total

Era II West Virginia Powerlifting Records
WV Powerlifters competing from January 1st, 1977 thru December 31st, 1984
TOP RANKINGS Determined by Total

165 / Name	Squat	Bench Press	Deadlift	Total	Date
Jack Wilson	600*	360	645*	1605*e	12/10/78
Butch Brown	567	330	661*	1559 e	6/04/83
Don Hundley	606*nm	264	667*nm	1537 e	3/31/84
Paul Sutphin	585	345	605	1535 e	3/30/80
Don Hundley	589	292	644	1527 e	12/17/83
Paul Sutphin	567	352	589	1510 e	5/26/79
Paul Sutphin	560	350	595	1505 e	4/21/79
Don Hundley	580	265	650 u	1495 +	2/07/82
Don Hundley	580	265	650 u	1495 +	4/24/82
Paul Sutphin	540	345	600	1485 e	5/05/79
Dana Bee	520	380*	500	1400	1/05/80
Frank White	429	308 m	418	1157	10/13/84
181 Paul Sutphin	705* u	390	655 u	1750* u e	8/27/83
Paul Sutphin	688 u	380	644	1714 u e	5/28/83
Paul Sutphin	655 u	370	645 u	1670 u e	5/15/82
Paul Sutphin	639*	385	628*	1653* e	1/10/81
Paul Sutphin	650*	380	622	1653 r e	7/10/82
Doug Currence	611	369	661	1642 e	4/01/84
Paul Sutphin	640 u	360	625	1625 u	12/13/80
Paul Sutphin	630 r	365	630*	1625 r	4/25/82
Paul Sutphin	650 u	385	585	1620	2/07/82
Robert Griffith	622	347	644*	1614	3/26/83
Robert Griffith	589	352	661*	1603	4/01/84
Paul Sutphin	622*	380	595	1598*	8/23/80
Paul Sutphin	605*	365	625*	1595*	5/10/80
Doug Currence	567	358	667 u	1592	12/15/84
Dave Jeffrey	550	400*	550	1500	4/01/79
Dave Drennan	529	407 u	551	1488	10/29/83
Dave Drennan	529	402*	540	1471	3/26/83

* - West Virginia State Powerlifting Record
u – Unofficial West Virginia State Powerlifting Record
r – "Re-set" West Virginia State Powerlifting Record
m – West Virginia Masters Powerlifting Record

nm – National Masters Powerlifting Record
e – Elite Powerlifting Total
+ - Elite Total by 1978 Standards

Era-II West Virginia Powerlifting Records
WV Powerlifters competing from January 1st, 1977 thru December 31st, 1984
TOP RANKINGS Determined by Total

198 / Name	Squat	Bench Press	Deadlift	Total	Date
Roger Estep	769 ½ * WR	490*	685*	1944* WR	12/10/78
Paul Sutphin	677	391	655	1725	4/01/84
Dave Jeffrey	655	440	633	1725	4/01/84
Paul Sutphin	677	380	644	1703	3/26/83
Paul Sutphin	640	385	650	1675	5/19/84
Steve Uhas	705	320	645	1670	4/01/84
Vince White	610 u m	380 u m	490	1480 u m	12/10/83
M. Sean Byrd	567	451* AtR	451	1471	11/11/84
M. Sean Byrd	545 h	407 h	512 h	1466 h	4/28/84
Vince White	584	380	479	1444	2/13/82
Vince White	600 m	363 m	479	1444 m	10/15/83
Vince White	570	395	475	1440	8/21/82
Vince White	606 u m	363	462	1432	10/29/83
220 Bret Russell	705*	395	770*	1870* e	4/25/82
Bret Russell	716 u	391	760	1868* e	5/28/83
Bret Russell	705	391	744	1840 e	3/26/83
Bret Russell	710 u	405	705	1820	3/12/83
Mike Wolf	630	490*	660	1780*	4/01/79
Mike Wolf	605*	470*	625	1700*	11/06/77
Bret Russell	645*	370	675*	1690	4/18/81
M. Sean Byrd	560	460	540	1560	2/12/84
M. Sean Byrd	529	473 tAR	501	1504	3/03/84

* - West Virginia State Powerlifting Record

tAR – American Teenage Powerlifting Record

h – West Virginia State High School Powerlifting Record

u – Unofficial West Virginia State Powerlifting Record

m – West Virginia State Masters Powerlifting Record

nm – National Masters Powerlifting Record

e – Elite Powerlifting Total

Era-II West Virginia Powerlifting Records
WV Powerlifters competing from January 1st, 1977 thru December 31st, 1984
TOP RANKINGS Determined by Total

242 / Name	Squat	Bench Press	Deadlift	Total	Date
Scott Warman	826*	440	771*	2039* e	7/11/82
Bret Russell	722	446	804	1973 e	7/08/84
Bret Russell	705	457	804*	1967 e	4/01/84
Scott Warman	749 u	424	722 u	1895 u e	1/09/82
Randy Scott	733	485	644	1862	5/28/83
Randy Scott	694	501*	650	1846	3/26/83
Nick Busick	655	501	655	1813	12/16/84
Herb Fitzsimmons	670*m	425 m	680*m	1775*m	5/06/78
Mike Wolf	625	500*	645*	1770*	4/01/78
Herb Fitzsimmons	650*	420	610	1680*	1/22/78
John Messinger	622	418	622	1664	12/16/84
Jim Goodnight	550	425*	590	1565	5/21/77
275 Herb Fitzsimmons	740*	450	730*	1920*	4/01/79
Herb Fitzsimmons	740	450	740*	1920	4/21/79
Herb Fitzsimmons	735	440	700	1875	5/05/79
Herb Fitzsimmons	722*m	462* m	683	1868*m	7/09/78
Herb Fitzsimmons	705	451	705	1862	5/26/79
Jim Goodnight	685	500*	670	1855	4/01/79
Herb Fitzsimmons	725*m	420	680*	1825	2/24/79
Herb Fitzsimmons	650 m	450 m	700*m	1800*m	4/01/78
Herb Fitzsimmons	655*m	425 m	660*m	1740*m	2/25/78
Scott Warman	716	391	672	1780	12/11/82
Dan Hall	700	385	660	1745	12/10/83
Jim Goodnight	610	465*	600	1675	4/01/78
Herb Fitzsimmons	580*m	400*m	610*m	1590*m	1/14/78
Luke Iams	sq	529*	dl	T	3/29/81

* - West Virginia State Powerlifting Record

u – Unofficial West Virginia State Powerlifting Record

m – West Virginia State Masters Powerlifting Record

nm – National Masters Powerlifting Record

e – Elite Powerlifting Total

Era-II West Virginia Powerlifting Records
WV Powerlifters competing from January 1st, 1977 thru December 31st, 1984
TOP RANKINGS Determined by Total

SHW / Name	Squat	Bench Press	Deadlift	Total	Date
(SuperHeavyWeights)					
Luke Iams	875*	600*	605	2080* e	4/01/79
Luke Iams	821*	573*	578	1973*	7/09/78
Luke Iams	810*	550	585	1945*	5/06/78
Luke Iams	804	556*	551	1912	5/21/78
Luke Iams	750	550*	600	1900*	4/01/78
Luke Iams	805 Y *	535*	520	1860*	1/22/78
Luke Iams	750*	510*	585	1845*	5/21/77
Jeff Cook	650	395	730 u	1775	8/14/83
Jeff Cook	611	396	744*	1752	4/01/84
Jeff Cook	644	380	722*	1746	3/26/83
Jeff Cook	622	385	699 u	1708	10/31/82
Herb Fitzsimmons	650 m	400 m	650*m	1700 m	12/17/77
Jeff Cook	551	347	677*	1575	11/01/81

* - West Virginia State Powerlifting Record

u – Unofficial West Virginia State Powerlifting Record

m – West Virginia State Masters Powerlifting Record

nm – National Masters Powerlifting Record

e – Elite Powerlifting Total

Chapter Twenty-One : 1985

Era Three of Powerlifting began in 1985. The introduction of the "Bench Press Shirt", the "Twenty-Four (24) Hour Weigh-In" (a.k.a. "Early" Weigh-in), and the implementation of the "Round System" were game changers for the sport of Powerlifting. Many lifters were using the trial version of a Bench Press shirt as early as 1984. A larger number of Powerlifters were experimenting with the new design at the beginning of calendar year 1985. Supportive shirts for the Bench Press, the early weigh-ins, and the Round System immediately enabled lifters to produce higher Powerlifting Totals.

The Junior Division and the Senior Division : The theme of the 10th Annual (1985) West Virginia State Powerlifting Championships. Beginning in 1985, the West Virginia State Powerlifting Committee adopted two (2) divisions for the lifters competing at the West Virginia State Powerlifting Championships. Based on the achievement level and experience of the lifter, there were now two (2) divisions of which would determine the West Virginia State Powerlifting Champion.

The new categorical system which began at the 1985 West Virginia State Powerlifting Championships allowed anyone who had yet to make an official Total in a sanctioned Powerlifting meet of Class I to compete in a separate division, known as the Junior Division. In addition, once a lifter won the Junior Division, he was automatically graduated to the Senior Division for the next West Virginia State Powerlifting Championship and *would not* be eligible to compete in the Junior Division again. Given the fact most lifters did not have much of a chance to beat a few of the defending West Virginia State Powerlifting Champions, the new division (Junior Division) was created to attract beginning Powerlifters.

The 10th Annual (1985) West Virginia State Powerlifting Championships were held on April 13th and April 14th, 1985 at the Waterford Inn in Newell, West Virginia. According to the official meet results, the 1985 West Virginia State Powerlifting Championships had forty-eight (48) lifters. Because 1985 was the first year for the Junior (Under Class I) Division at the West Virginia State Powerlifting Championships, the top Squat, Bench Press, and Deadlift of each weight class were established West Virginia State Junior Division Records.

Beginning with the Senior Division / Open Division of the 1985 West Virginia State Powerlifting Championships, Mike Konnovich qualified for the Teenage Nationals with a Total in the 114lb. class. Dan Palmateer won the 1985 West Virginia State title in the 132lb. class. Art Williamson achieved his Masters Powerlifting Classification in the 148lb. class with a Total of 1300.

Again, at the 10th Annual (1985) West Virginia State Powerlifting Championships, Don Hundley made Powerlifting history with a Master's World Record Squat in the 165lb. class with 277.5 kilos / 611 ¾ lbs.! Official or unofficial, the record stands today!

The 305 kilo / 672lb. West Virginia State Deadlift Record by Doug Currence at a bodyweight of 181 said it all at the West Virginia State Powerlifting Championships. Doug Totaled Elite once again with 1653lbs. at 181 and made a statement to the Powerlifting world that higher Totals and more championship titles were likely.

While competing in the 220lb. class, the Bench Press Record of 512lbs. (232.5 kilos) by Jeff Wright was done with token lifts in the Squat and the Deadlift. The Deadlift Record of 810lbs. by Bret Russell was enough for the win while Nick Busick set a new Bench Press Record of 507lbs. in the 242lb. class.

Holley Strength Team : A "First"

With a roster of only two (2) lifters, the *Holley Strength Systems* won the 1985 Powerlifting Junior Division Team Championship Award. The performance of Dave DeFrehn in the 198lb. class and the winning Total by Mike Nidy in the 242lb. class of the Junior Division provided all of the points the Holley Strength Team would need to take the 1985 Junior Division Team Award home to Charleston. The only first place victories by members of the Holley Strength Powerlifting Team in the Senior / Open Division were won by Don Hundley (165lb. class – 1482 Total) and Doug Currence (181lb. class – Elite Total of 1653lbs.).

Vince White, West Virginia Powerlifting Chairman and Strength Coach for the *Holley Strength System*, had a long-term plan for the group of Novice and Elite Powerlifters who trained at the Holley Powerlifting Gym in Charleston. The Powerlifters, coached by Vince White, had previously represented *Herb's Gym* when competing at the annual West Virginia State Powerlifting Championship competition. Beginning at the 1985 West Virginia State Powerlifting Championships in Newell, West Virginia, the Powerlifting Team led by Vince White officially entered as the *Holley Strength Team.*

For the 3rd time in four (4) years, the West Virginia State Powerlifting Championship Team Award was won by the *Mountianeer Barbell Club.* Only the victory by *Herb's Gym* at the 1984 West Virginia State Powerlifting Championships at South Charleston prevented the *Mountianeer Barbell Club* from winning four (4) consecutive State Powerlifting Team Championship Awards.

The Senior Division Team Award at the 1985 West Virginia State Powerlifting Championships marked the final victory for the *Mountianeer Barbell Club* at the Annual USPF West Virginia State Powerlifting Championship event. From what began in the Junior Division (Class I & Under) at the 1985 West Virginia State Powerlifting Championships, *the Holley Strength Team has won the West Virginia State Powerlifting Team Championship Award in the Senior Division every year since 1986!*

Diversity in Powerlifting

The association of the term "diversity" to the sport of Powerlifting is not singularly related to the cultural or ethnic background of participating athletes. Instead, "diversity," synonymous to the growing number of Powerlifters from 1975 thru 1985, describes the philosophical differences on a number of issues which eventually divided the sport.

In the midst of reality, with rapid growth also comes change. During 1985, due to the growing number of Powerlifters combined with the diversity of the population from the rank and file, the sport of Powerlifting would no longer function within a single, unified governing body. Unfortunate!

In spite of the controversy, the argument of a few maintained, "With diversity comes _additional_ growth" : A theory perpetuated from the belief that many lifters _not_ at the Elite level would be more likely to participate in Powerlifting meets with other lifters at their level of classification. In addition, due to the fallout from philosophical feuds and the option of more than one Powerlifting federation, many athletes felt that since there were other organizations besides the USPF, why not participate?

The APF (American Powerlifting Federation), as a result of the rift at the 1985 National Powerlifting Committee Meeting in Chicago, began promoting Powerlifting competitions in several states. In addition to the APF, another Powerlifting organization had been promoting meets with growing numbers since 1981. In summation, pro or con, the division that took place during the Summer of 1985 forever changed the landscape for the sport of Powerlifting.

12th Annual Mountianeer Open

The 12th Annual Mountianeer Open Powerlifting Championships were held on November 9th and 10th, 1985 at Parkersburg, West Virginia. Spectacular lifting was centerfold at the 1985 Mountianeer Open Powerlifting Championships. Many lifters seized the opportunity to enjoy the "Early Weigh-In," while making weight on Friday evening for Saturday's sessions of lifting. The "Round System" was implemented and well received by a large majority of the lifters.

A cherished memory from the 1985 Mountianeer Open came after succeeding with a weight of 402lbs. (182.5 kilos) on the Bench Press. Afterward, Vince White was the first person to offer congratulations for officially becoming a member of the "400 Bench Press Club." *Along with*...the 402lb. Bench Press was a Squat of 644 ¾ lbs. for a new Mountianeer Open Powerlifting Championship Meet Record and a Deadlift of 650lbs. for an Elite TOTAL of 1697lbs. (770 kilos) in the 181lb. class. During the week of November 11th, 1985 a newspaper headline read, *"Best Lifter : 1985 Mountianeer Open"* and *"Sutphin Wins Mountianeer Title."*

1985 West Virginia Powerlifter Rankings
WV Powerlifters competing from January 1st, 1985 thru December 31st, 1985
TOP RANKINGS Determined by Total

114 / Name	Squat	Bench Press	Deadlift	Total	Date
Mike Konnovich	231	132	264	628	4/13/85
123	*** *No WV Rankings for 1985 @ 123* ***				
132 Dan Palmateer	402	225	429	1058	4/13/85
Rick Yates	352	242	429	1025	4/13/85
Rick Yates	341	236	407	986	5/04/85
Grady Sutton	214	170	275	661	4/13/85
148 Art Williamson	485	286	529	1300	4/13/85
Mike Kimball	462	303	440	1207	4/13/85
Donald Robbins	385	310	485	1180	4/19/85
Bill Rutherford	369	264	451	1085	4/13/85
Scott Phillips	391	220	424	1036	4/13/85
Scott Phillips	400	215	400	1015	7/27/85
Stuart Breeding	380	236	391	1008	12/14/85
Jim Deem	347	248	396	992	11/09/85
Scott Phillips	369	214	402	986	12/14/85
165 Gene Underwood	562	363	578	1504	12/14/85
Gene Underwood	562	369	567	1499	11/09/85
Don Hundley	611 ¾ WR*m	270 m	600	1482	4/13/85
Gene Underwood	570	345	560	1475	7/27/85
Gene Underwood	551	369	551	1471	4/13/85
Gene Underwood	534	363	551	1449	7/20/85
Marty DeCoursey	551	330	523	1405	4/13/85
Artie Williamson	490	300	540	1330	7/27/85
Tony Gerdes	429	303	551	1284	11/09/85
Mike Kimball	450	320	450	1220	7/27/85
Tony Magnone	473	281	473	1229	12/14/85
Reese Booth	451	248	490	1190	4/13/85
Mike Sarver	445	260	480	1185	7/27/85
Tony Gerdes	380	285	485	1150	7/27/85

WR – World Record / Master's Division
* - West Virginia State Powerlifting Record
m – West Virginia State Masters Powerlifting Record

1985 West Virginia Powerlifter Rankings
WV Powerlifters competing from January 1st, 1985 thru December 31st, 1985
TOP RANKINGS Determined by Total

181 / Name	Squat	Bench Press	Deadlift	Total	Date
Paul Sutphin	644	402	650	1697 e	11/09/85
Doug Currence	617	363	672*	1653 e	4/13/85
Paul Sutphin	600	395	620	1615	11/16/85
Doug Currence	606	347	650	1603	6/01/85
Vince White	468	358	396	1223	4/14/85
Rocky Roach	413	281	496	1190	5/04/85
198 M. Shawn Byrd	567	462	600	1631	11/10/85
Dave Jeffrey	622	457	341	1421	4/14/85
Jeff Chambers	501	352	529	1383	11/10/85
Ed Towle	523	330	523	1377	4/14/85
Jeff Chambers	455	340	510	1305	7/28/85
Steve Fuscardo	485	281	534	1300	4/14/85
Dave Defren	413	341	529	1284	4/14/85
Rocky Roach	480	315	475	1270	7/28/85
Jeff Chambers	446	330	451	1228	5/05/85
Vince White	468	358	396	1223	4/14/85
220 Tony Culp	677	402	655	1736	4/14/85
Marshall Moore	633	374	705	1714	12/15/85
Marshall Moore	661	374	661	1697	4/14/85
Marshall Moore	667	358	639	1664	5/05/85
Don Hall	639	374	628	1642	4/14/85
Scott Tusic	610	445	560	1615	7/28/85
Don Hall	617	385	600	1603	5/05/85
John Alderman	573	336	562	1471	4/14/85
Paul Bartley	551	341	562	1455	4/14/85
Rick Knicely	540	310	550	1400	7/28/85
Ernie Nagy	462	385	523	1372 OL	5/12/85
Stacy Barber	479	369	518	1366	4/14/85
Rick Knicely	507	303	540	1350	4/14/85
Bud Simpson	473	330	534	1339	4/14/85
Carl Herald	369	341	468	1179	5/05/85
Jeff Wright	55	512*	253	821	4/14/85

* - West Virginia State Powerlifting Record e – ELITE Powerlifting Total
OL – Outstanding Lifter / Master's Nationals

1985 West Virginia Powerlifter Rankings
WV Powerlifters competing from January 1st, 1985 thru December 31st, 1985
TOP RANKINGS Determined by Total

242 / Name	Squat	Bench Press	Deadlift	Total	Date
Bret Russell	793	462	832	2088 e	11/10/85
Bret Russell	771	473	837	2083 e	12/15/85
Bret Russell	735	475	830	2040 e	3/31/85
Bret Russell	755	468	793	2017 e	6/02/85
Bret Russell	738	457	810*	2006 e	4/14/85
Randy Scott	749	496	699	1945 e	6/02/85
Nick Busick	705	507*	606	1818	4/14/85
John Messinger	688	429	650	1769	11/10/85
John Messinger	672	429	644	1747	7/21/85
Paul Rowand	633	435	617	1686	4/14/85
John Nicoloudakis	606	429	578	1614	4/14/85
Mike Nidy	628	358	628	1614	4/14/85
Jim Goodnight	573	407	551	1532	11/10/85
Stacy Barber	551	380	529	1460	11/10/85
Steve Pauley	479	303	523	1303	5/05/85
275 Randy Scott	744*	501	694	1940	4/14/85
Randy Scott	755	496	683	1934	12/15/85
Sam Moore	688	407	727	1824	4/14/85
Mark Olenick	688	462	650	1802	12/15/85
Dan Hall	722	391	672	1785	4/14/85
John Messinger	667	451	622	1741	4/14/85
Dan Hall	672	380	667	1719	12/15/85
Greg Moodie	600	380	565	1545	7/28/85
Greg Moodie	589	380	567	1537	12/15/85
Greg Moodie	584	374	562	1521	4/14/85
Greg Moodie	589	352	567	1510	11/10/85
Phil Massinople	573	352	556	1482	4/14/85
Bill DeRuise	402	203	451	1057	5/05/85
SHW Stuart Thompson	826	440	705	1973	12/15/85
Jeff Cook	670	430	760*	1860	7/28/85
Stuart Thompson	755	424	677	1857	4/14/85
Jeff Cook	661	424	749	1835	4/14/85
Charles Ashcraft	639	363	584	1587	4/14/85
Charles Ashcraft	620	370	570	1560	7/28/85
Charles Ashcraft	600	380	545	1526	12/15/85

* - West Virginia State Powerlifting Record   e – ELITE Powerlifting Total

Chapter Twenty-Two : 1986

Implementation of the "Round System", the "24-Hour Weigh-In," and a number of extraneous circumstances continued to revolutionize Powerlifting. The year 1986 was the first year following the APF (American Powerlifting Federation) vs. the USPF (United States Powerlifting Federation) and their philosophical divide. For the first time in the history of Powerlifting, there were two (2) (Jr.) Nationals and at least two (2) Senior National Powerlifting Championships during the calendar year of 1986.

In spite of the diversity from within the sport of Powerlifting, the leadership of West Virginia Powerlifting emphasized unity. As a result, unity prevailed in the Mountain State throughout most of the 1980's. During 1986, 1987, and 1988, West Virginia Powerlifters cohesively recognized only one (1) State Powerlifting Champion from one (1) organization for all categories.

In 1983, the West Virginia State Powerlifting Committee changed the rules specific to West Virginia State Powerlifting Records. Only West Virginia State Championship Powerlifting meets or National Championship Powerlifting competitions qualified as contests where West Virginia State Powerlifting Records would be accepted. As a result, the 688 ¾ Squat (181lb. class) from the 1983 Parkersburg Open and the 705 Squat along with the 1750 Total (181lb. class) from the August, 1983 competition in Virginia [*Sutphin Powerlifting Records*] were not recognized as <u>official</u> West Virginia State Powerlifting Records.

Going into 1986, the West Virginia State Powerlifting Records in the 181lb. class were :

<u>650 Squat</u> / 295 kilos (Set @ 1982 Senior Nationals by <u>Paul Sutphin</u>),
<u>402 Bench Press</u> / 182.5 kilos (Set @ 1983 WV States by <u>C. Dave Drennan</u>),
<u>672 Deadlift</u> / 305 kilos (Set @ 1985 WV States by <u>Doug Currence</u>),
<u>1653 Total</u> / 750 kilos (Set @ 1982 Senior Nationals by <u>Paul Sutphin</u>).

The <u>11th Annual West Virginia State Powerlifting Championships</u> were held March 22nd & March 23rd, 1986 in New Martinsville, West Virginia. In acknowledgement of ten (10) years of success, we were home for a Powerlifting reunion, in the town of New Martinsville. On Friday night March 21st, many of us gathered at a local lodging establishment where overnight accommodations had been provided in years past. Present on 3/21/86 at the overnight lodging establishment in New Martinsville on the night before the big event were Allen Smith, Vince White, myself, and several others.

As we were reminiscing, laughing, and predicting what would happen in the next two (2) days, Vince White said to me, "Buddy, this is where we started."

"Setting the Records Straight" : Part IV

Eligibility requirements specific to the residency of an athlete prevented me from competing at the 1985 West Virginia Powerlifting Championship. Due to the frustration I endured for more than a year, I made a declaration to all lifters who were present at the motel in New Martinsville on Friday evening 3/21/86, "Tomorrow, all of the West Virginia State Powerlifting Records in the 181lb. class will be re-written."

By March of 1986, the option of "The 24 hour weigh-in" was practiced by most lifters. Due to a late arrival, I missed the early weigh-in scheduled for Friday evening March 21st. As I had done in all the years before, I officially weighed-in at 179 ½ on the morning of March 22nd, 1986.

Allen Smith began his Powerlifting career at the 1986 West Virginia State Powerlifting Championships with a victory. While competing in the 148lb. class and lifting for *Holley Strength Systems*, Allen Smith won the 1986 West Virginia State Championship title with a Class I Total of 1151. Acie Simmons placed 2nd in the 148lb. class with a Total of 1052 and a new Bench Press Record of 396lbs. (180 kilos).

Lifting in the 165lb. class at the 1986 West Virginia State Powerlifting Championships, Don Hundley sustained a leg injury while Squatting. Hundley, determined to make a Total or die, refused to withdraw from the championship. What was impressive about Don Hundley is that he nearly pulled the Deadlift he needed for the win on only one good leg! The 165lb. class was won by Gene Underwood.

While others were having a good day, I continued to focus on lifting and the Powerlifting Records in the 181lb. class. Following a light opener on Squats and a successful 2nd attempt, the weight of 655 ¾ lbs. (297.5 kilos) for a new West Virginia State Record was loaded on the bar. I Squatted the 655 ¾ with ease, getting three (3) white lights from the officials.

Being the last lifter for the Squats, I realized the flights of lifters had finished in a relatively short period of time. Based on what I experienced in November, 1985 at the Mountianeer Open and during the Squats at the 1986 West Virginia States, *I did not like the Round System!* Given more time, I truly believe I could've Squatted at least 15 kilos (33lbs.) more.

With a new USPF Squat Record on the books, I was determined to revise the Powerlifting Record charts. On the Bench Press, I opened with a lighter weight of 363lbs.

(165 kilos) ; a poundage *I thought* would not present a problem of any kind. Unfortunately, I was called for a technical error by the officials. Taking no chances, I took the weight again and made it, receiving the white lights that were denied on the first "Go Round."

Following the circumstances of the "wasted" first attempt, I had one (1) chance for a shot at the 181lb. Bench Press Record. I needed 185 kilos (407 ¾ lbs.). I called for the weight on my third and final attempt. The weight was pressed solid with power to spare! I still remember the crowd cheering after the completed lift. After acknowledging their support and thanking a number of people, I will never forget storming into the warm-up area, elated and fired up! The story was, after fourteen (14) years of serious lifting, I had officially Bench Pressed over 400lbs., twice in four (4) months....*including a West Virginia State Record of 407 ¾ lbs. (185 kilos) while lifting in the 181lb. class at a bodyweight of 179 ½ ; weighing-in 1½ hours prior to the beginning of the lifting session.*

Although determined, my mindset shifted to the conservative mode after the Bench Press. Being re-directed to task, I owe the West Virginia State Record Deadlift of 677 ¾ lbs. (307.5 kilos) to the decision made by Coach Vince White and others who were present. Actually, I contemplated calling for only 661 pounds (300 kilos) for the 3rd attempt which was all I needed for a PR Deadlift and a new official West Virginia State Record Total in the 181lb. class.

Reminded of what I declared would happen on the night before, the final decision for the 3rd attempt Deadlift was an easy one. Before declaring my 3rd attempt to the Expeditor, I remember Vince White saying, "We're going for the record!" And, so it was. The weight of 307.5 kilos, a new West Virginia State Record Deadlift of 677 ¾ lbs., was given to the Expeditor. The bar was loaded and I pulled the 677 ¾ lbs. / 307.5 kilos Deadlift on the 3rd attempt with power to spare.

The 1986 West Virginia State Powerlifting Championships held at New Martinsville was one of the most memorable : Four (4) New West Virginia State Powerlifting Records at 181! The 1741 lb. Total / 790 kilos (new West Virginia State Total Record in the 181lb. class) was enough for the Outstanding Lifter Award at the 1986 West Virginia State Powerlifting Championships for the 1st Day of lifting.

The Total of 1741 by Paul Sutphin on March 22nd, 1986 earned a P/L USA TOP 100 181lb. class Ranking of #12 in the Oct/86 issue of *Powerlifting USA* magazine. A few of the lifters ranked in front of Sutphin with higher Totals in the 181lb. class were familiar names. Rickey Crain was ranked 11th on Total with 1747, Tom Eiseman (#10 with 1780), and Rick Gaugler was #1 with 2017!

The West Virginia State Record Squat of 655lbs. (297.5 kilos) earned a P/L USA TOP 100 181lb. class Ranking of #27 (tied for 25th) in the Oct/86 issue of *Powerlifting USA* magazine. In the same P/L USA TOP 100 181's, the Bench Press of 407 ¾ lbs. (185 kilos) ranked number 70 (tied for #68). The 677 ¾ lb.(307.5 kilos) Deadlift by Sutphin ranked 14th in the P/L USA TOP 100 181lb. class Powerlifter rankings.

Doug Currence : Elite Total at 198!

On December 10th, 1978 at the 1978-79 YMCA National Powerlifting Championships, Roger Estep Deadlifted 685lbs. while on his way back to Ohio. The 685lb. Deadlift by Roger Estep had been on the books as a West Virginia State Powerlifting Record for seven (7) years and three months. The record fell on Sunday March 23rd, 1986!

The second day of lifting at the 1986 West Virginia State Powerlifting Championships began with the 198lb. class. Doug Currence cruised to victory in the 198lb. class with an Elite Total of 1731lbs. Doug's Elite Total of 1731 on 3/23/86 included a 622 Squat, 418 Bench Press, and a West Virginia State Record Deadlift of 688 ¾ lbs.!

Doug Currence 688 ¾ Deadlift
3/23/86

Doug Currence made Powerlifting history by setting a NEW Deadlift Record of 688 ¾ lbs. (312.5 kilos) on a 2nd attempt. Doug broke the Deadlift Record in the 198lb. class on March 23rd, 1986 and never looked back! As of 9/01/2013, the Doug Currence Deadlift Record of 688 ¾ lbs. / 312.5 kilos in the 198lb. weight class still stands!

Mike Hundley – 3/23/86
600 Squat @ 198

Mike Hundley finished 3rd in the 198lb. class at the 1986 West
Virginia State Powerlifting Championships with a Total of 1510
which included a Squat of 600 ¾ lbs. and a Deadlift of 573.

In the 242lb. class, the Elite Total of 2039lbs. by Bret Russell included a West Virginia State Deadlift Record of 821lbs. Placing second in the 242lb. class was Randy Scott with another Elite Total of 1956 and a new Bench Press Record of 512lbs.

Dan Hall of the *Holley Strength Team* did some impressive lifting to take the West Virginia State Powerlifting Championship title in the 275lb. class with a Total of 1818lbs. Included in the 1818 Total by Dan Hall was a Squat of 727 and a Deadlift of 688lbs.

The Superheavyweight (SHW) class was won by Jeff Cook with a Total of 1868 and a new Deadlift Record of 782lbs. When the second day of lifting was over at the 1986 West Virginia State Powerlifting Championships, the Outstanding Lifter Award went to Bret Russell. In the Senior / Open Division, there were eight (8) new West Virginia State Powerlifting Records set.

Holley Strength Team – Two (2) Team Titles!

The *Holley Strength Systems* won Two (2) Team Titles at the 1986 West Virginia State Powerlifting Championships : Senior Division and Junior Division. The August, 1986 issue of *Powerlifting USA* magazine featured the complete report including a photo of the 1986 West Virginia State Powerlifting Team Champions, The *Holley Strength System Powerlifting Team.*

Holley Strength Powerlifting Team
Open/Senior Division – 3/23/86

<u>Left to Right (Kneeling)</u> : Allen Smith, Vince White (center-3rd from left),
Mike Hundley (Right on end – 5th from left).
<u>Left to Right (Standing)</u> : Paul Sutphin, Doug Currence, John Messinger,
Don Hall (7th from left), Don Hundley (Far right – 8th from left).

312

1986 West Virginia State Powerlifting Championships
Senior Division

Held Saturday and Sunday March 22ⁿᵈ and 23ʳᵈ, 1986
Magnolia High School
New Martinsville, W. VA

Wt. Class/Name	Squat	Bench	Deadlift	Total
114				
Judy Holt female	115	82	187	385
123				
Mary Jeffrey female	380	242	380	1003
123				
Cork Hall	336	170	418	925
132				
Tim Borgia	402	270	429	1102
148				
Allen Smith	440	303	407	1151
Acie Simmons	347	396*	308	1052
Scott Phillips	358	209	402	970
165				
Gene Underwood	545	369	562	1477
Don Hundley	573	253	562	1388
Keith Gandee	507	325	529	1361
Mike Sarver	451	286	490	1229
181				
Paul Sutphin BW 179 ¼	655*	407 ¾*	677 ¾*	1741* e
Tom Russell	451	319	451	1223

Wt. Class/Name	Squat	Bench	Deadlift	Total
198				
Doug Currence	622	418	688*	1731 e
Mike Brown	600	363	589	1554
Mike Hundley	600	336	573	1510
Vince George	501	303	512	1317
220				
Marshall Moore	661	380	699	1741
Scott Tusic	644	451	606	1703
Don Hall	617	385	611	1614
Buster Whitener	655	231	655	1543
242				
Bret Russell	760	457	821*	2039 e
Randy Scott	727	512*	716	1956 e
Carl Cook	606	336	529	1471
275				
Dan Hall	727	402	688	1818
Mark Olenick	688	451	650	1791
Greg Moodie	551	385	573	1510
Super Hvywt.				
Jeff Cook	688	396	782*	1868
Charles Ashcraft	661	391	589	1642

Outstanding Lifter /1st Day – 3/22/86 – Paul Sutphin
Outstanding Lifter / 2nd Day – 3/23/86 – Bret Russell
* - West Virginia State Powerlifting Record

Team Trophy / Senior Division – Holley Strength Systems
Special Award – Vince White

e – Elite Powerlifting Classification Total

1986 West Virginia State Powerlifting Championships
Junior Division / Below Class I

Held Saturday and Sunday March 22nd and 23rd, 1986
Magnolia High School
New Martinsville, W. VA

Wt. Class/Name	Squat	Bench	Deadlift	Total
123				
Mike Emerick	264	165	325	755
Mark Casella	259	176	303	738
Craig Beall	253	137	259	650
132				
Jeff Kirk	336	165	325	826
J. L. Iams	236	165	253	655
148				
Stuart Breeding	435	242	451	1129
Jeff Kilgore	374	259	396	1030
John Burkes	374	214	402	992
Greg Vance	303	225	363	892
Mike Vitrules	303	187	352	843
165				
Tony Gerdes	407	314	523	1245
David Huff	451	286	451	1190
Mark Hughes	457	220	435	1113
Jerry Waltor	352	242	440	1036
Mark Hartzell	358	264	396	1019
Gary Cook	352	214	380	947
Steve Reckenwald	248	181	303	733
181				
Matthew Stuats	501	253	523	1278
Scott Collias	518	275	479	1273
Jamie Robertson	347	209	413	970

Wt. Class/Name	Squat	Bench	Deadlift	Total
198				
Joe Lee	534	396	534	1466
Dave Defren	451	363	600	1416
Jeff Chambers	507	330	534	1372
Rocky Roach	485	308	518	1311
Charles Hahn	485	297	512	1295
Chuck Grindstaff	485	303	407	1195
Brian Bailey	418	281	407	1107
Tom Pratt	341	225	418	986
P. J. Atmadovar	303	236	402	942
220				
Stacy Barber	485	363	523	1372
Don McGregor	523	330	440	1295
Charles Wallace	462	281	507	1251
242				
Wallace Kirk	600	402	556	1559
John Lilly	567	435	556	1559
Steve Pauley	512	341	529	1383
Bobby Fox	501	314	473	1289
Herman Lunsford	429	281	501	1212
Greg Gibson	402	259	507	1168
275				
Wayne Russell	633	341	551	1526
Barry Karnes	485	330	468	1284
Larry McClellan	457	286	507	1251
Charles Trogdon	473	253	485	1212
SuperHeavyWeight				
Jeff Maynard	473	281	468	1223
Roy Proffitt	440	281	330	1052

Team Trophy / Junior Division – Holley Strength Systems

WOMEN'S DIVISION / Malone Formula

Wt. Class/Name	Squat	Bench	Deadlift	Total
Danielle Ray	281	143	259	683
Lora Hager	270	154	330	755
Donna Secreto	242	110	286	639
Maria Ramirez	292	99	270	661
Terri Holstien	214	93	264	573
Lisa Richards	214	99	242	556
Amy Hoffman	55	143	231	429

Training Log #5
Paul Sutphin Workouts

Ten (10) Weeks Prior to the 1986 West Virginia State Powerlifting Championships
Beginning 12/29/85 to 3/22/86

Sunday 12/29/85 – SQUAT – 132 x 5, 220 x 5, 310 x 5, 398 x 5, 398 x 5.

Wednesday 1/01/86 (New Year's Day) – SQUAT – 132 x 6, 255 x 5, 358 x 5, 358 x 5, 358 x 5, 358 x 5, 358 x 5.

Saturday 1/04/86
1. BENCH PRESS – 132 x 8, 220 x 5, 220 x 4, 308 x 3, 341 x 1.
2. Seated Presses – 132 x 8, 176 x 6, 198 x 6.
3. Standing Alternate Dumbell Presses – 3 x 8 w/80lb. Dumbells.
4. Lying Dumbell Flyes – 3 x 12 w/45lb. Dumbells.
5. Bent Over Rowing (w/Dumbell) – 3 x 8 w/80lb. Dumbells.
6. Standing Triceps Extensions (EZ Bar)(Close-Grip) 72 x 10, 82 x 8, 99 x 6.
7. Standing Alternate Dumbell Curls – 3 x 8 w/55lb. Dumbells.

Sunday 1/05/86 – SQUAT – 230 x 5, 380 x 5.

Thursday 1/09/86
1. SQUAT – 254 x 5, 342 x 5, 430 x 5, 491 x 5.
2. BENCH PRESS – 132 x 6, 222 x 5, 310 x 5.
3. DEADLIFTS (Floor)(Wide Stance) – 254 x 5, 342 x 5, 432 x 5, (missed 520).
4. Lying Triceps Presses – 110 x 8, 121 x 8, 132 x 9.
5. Incline Dumbell Presses – 80 x 8, 80 x 7, 80 x 4.
6. Incline Dumbell Flyes – 3 sets of 10 w/45lb. Dumbell.
7. Standing Alternate Dumbell Curls – 55 x 6, 55 x 6, 55 x 6.
8. Wide Grip Chins [Universal Weight Machine] – 1 x 8.

Saturday 1/11/86 - BENCH PRESS – 135 x 8, 135 x 6, 222 x 5, 288 x 5, 288 x 5, 288 x 5, 288 x 5, 288 x 5.

Tuesday 1/14/86 – DEADLIFTS (Floor)(Wide Stance) – 254 x 5, 398 x 5, 453 x 5, 453 x 5, 453 x 5, 453 x 5, 453 x 5.

Thursday 1/16/86 (Session One) – SQUAT – 230 x 5, 380 x 5, 450 x 4, 500 x 5, 555 x 4.

Thursday 1/16/86 (Session Two) – BENCH PRESS – 132 x 8, 132 x 6, 222 x 4, 310 x 3, 310 x 3, 310 x 3, 310 x 3, 354 x 1.

Monday 1/20/86 – BENCH PRESS – 135 x 8, 135 x 6, 225 x 5, 315 x 3, 315 x 3, 315 x 3, 315 x 3, 315 x 5.

Wednesday 1/22/86
1. DEADLIFTS (Floor)(Wide Stance) – 275 x 7, 365 x 5, 455 x 3, 545 x 3, 545 x 3, 545 x 5.
2. DEADLIFTS (Floor)(Conventional Style)(Standing on 5-inch platform) 275 x 6, 365 x 5.
3. Calf Raises (Calf Machine) – 25 x 20, 25 x 20.

Thursday 1/23/86
1. BENCH PRESS – 135 x 8, 135 x 6, 225 x 5, 295 x 5, 295 x 5, 295 x 5, 295 x 5, 295 x 5.
2. Close Grip Curls (Seated on Curl Machine) – 40 x 10, 50 x 10, 50 x 10, 50 x 8, 50 x 5.
3. Seated Triceps Presses (Machine) – 75 x 10, 100 x 10, 125 x 10, 150 x 8, 150 x 8.
4. Seated Triceps Pushouts (Machine) – 100 x 5, 100 x 5.

Sunday 1/26/86 – BENCH PRESS – 140 x 8, 140 x 6, 230 x 5, 285 x 5, 285 x 5, 285 x 5, 285 x 5, 285 x 5.

Monday 1/27/86 - SQUATS – 253 x 6, 430 x 3(knee wraps), 512 x 3(knee wraps), 573 x 2(knee wraps).

Wednesday 1/29/86 – BENCH PRESS – 135 x 8, 135 x 6, 225 x 5, 315 x 3, 335 x 3, 335 x 3, 335 x 3, 335 x 3, 365 x 1.

Saturday 2/01/86
1. DEADLIFTS (Floor)(Wide Stance) – 254 x 6, 398 x 4, 504 x 3.
2. BENCH PRESS – 132 x 9, 132 x 6, 222 x 4, 222 x 3, 310 x 3, 354 x 2, 382 x 1.
3. Lying Bent Arm Dumbell Flyes – 45 x 10, 45 x 10, 45 x 15.
4. Standing Alternate Dumbell Curls – 55 x 6, 65 x 6, 65 x 6.

Monday 2/03/86 – SQUATS – 135 x 8, 225 x 5, 315 x 4, 405 x 3(knee wraps),
495 x 3(Supersuit & knee wraps),
565 x 2(Supersuit & knee wraps), 605 x 2(Supersuit & knee wraps),
645 x 1(Supersuit & knee wraps), 675 x 1 (Supersuit & knee wraps).

Tuesday 2/04/86 – BENCH PRESS – 135 x 8, 135 x 6, 225 x 4, 225 x 3, 275 x 5,
275 x 5, 275 x 5, 275 x 5, 275 x 5.

Thursday 2/06/86 – SQUATS – 135 x 6, 225 x 5, 315 x 4, 405 x 3, 505 x 3 (knee wraps),
505 x 3 (knee wraps).

Saturday 2/08/86 (1st Session) – DEADLIFTS (Power Rack)(5 inches below knee)
230x 5, 380 x 5, 490 x 4, 600 x 3, 650 x 3, 490 x 10.

Saturday 2/08/86 (2nd Session) – BENCH PRESS – 132 x 8, 222 x 4, 222 x 3, 222 x 3,
310 x 3, 354 x 2, 365 x 2, 371 x 2.

Monday 2/10/86
1. SQUATS – 220 x 5, 310 x 4, 430 x 3, 519 x 3(knee wraps), 585 x 3(knee wraps),
607 x 3(supersuit w/knee wraps).
2. BENCH PRESS – 135 x 8, 222 x 4, 222 x 3, 310 x 3, 354 x 1, 310 x 5, 310 x 5,
310 x 5, 310 x 5, 310 x 5.

Thursday 2/13/86 - SQUATS – 140 x 6, 230 x 5, 320 x 5, 400 x 5, 450 x 5.

Saturday 2/15/86 - BENCH PRESS – 130 x 8, 230 x 5, 230 x 4, 300 x 3, 355 x 2, 350 x 3,
350 x 2, 350 x 3, 350 x 3.

Monday 2/17/86 - SQUATS – 135 x 8, 225 x 5, 315 x 4, 405 x 4, 505 x 3 (knee wraps), 405 x 5 (No wraps).

Tuesday 2/18/86 - BENCH PRESS – 140 x 8, 230 x 5, 230 x 4, 320 x 3, 320 x 3, 320 x 3, 320 x 3, 330 x 5.

Saturday 2/22/86
1. BENCH PRESS – 135 x 8, 135 x 5, 222 x 4, 222 x 3, 310 x 3, 310 x 2, 354 x 2, 376 x 1, 398 x 1, 365 x 2.
2. DEADLIFTS (Floor / 100lb. Plates)(Sumo) – 254 x 5, 398 x 4, 488 x 3, 576 x 3, 609 x 4.

Tuesday 2/25/86
1. SQUATS – 135 x 5, 222 x 5, 310 x 4, 398 x 3, 520 x 3(knee wraps), 586 x 2(knee wraps), 637 x 1(knee wraps).
2. ¼ SQUATS – 769 x 3.
3. BENCH PRESS – 135 x 6, 222 x 4, 288 x 3, 288 x 1.
4. Crossovers – 5.5lb. plate in each hand x 50 reps.

Saturday 3/01/86 - DEADLIFTS (Power Rack)(Bar 5 inches below top of knee) 230 x 5, 380 x 4, 490 x 3, 600 x 1.

Sunday 3/02/86 -
1. Standing Dumbell Presses – 75 x 7, 75 x 7, 75 x 8.
2. Lying Dumbell Flyes – 25 x 12, 25 x 15, 25 x 15.
3. Standing Alternate Dumbell Curls – 65 x 6, 65 x 6, 65 x 6.
4. Lying Triceps Presses (EZ Bar) – 90 x 8, 140 x 6, 170 x 6, 190 x 6.
5. Bent Over Rowing – 130 x 8, 130 x 8, 130 x 8.

Tuesday 3/04/86 - SQUATS – 230 x 5, 375 x 4, 475 x 3, 535 x 3 (knee wraps).

Saturday 3/08/86
1. BENCH PRESS – 135 x 8, 135 x 5, 225 x 3, 225 x 2(Bench Press shirt), 315 x 2(Bench shirt), 365 x 1(Bench shirt, 390 x 1(Bench shirt), 410 x 1(Bench shirt), 420 x 1(Bench shirt), elected not to push 425 to lockout in order to avoid potential injury.

2. <u>DEADLIFTS (Floor)(Sumo)</u> – 225 x 5, 315 x 4, 405 x 3, 495 x 3, 575 x 3.

<u>Monday 3/10/86</u>
1. <u>SQUATS</u> – 135 x 5, 225 x 4, 315 x 4, 405 x 3,
    505 x 3(knee wraps), 600 x 2 (supersuit & knee wraps).
2. ¼ <u>Squats</u> – Unnsuccessful w/1st attempt @ 705, then 705 x 1.
    An additional set of Squats (455 x 2, "Raw") following ¼ Squats.
3. <u>Triceps Pressdowns</u> – 100 x 8, 100 x 8, 100 x 8, 100 x 8.
4. <u>Standing Curls (EZ Bar)</u> – 110 x 6, 110 x 6, 130 x 6.
5. <u>Bent Over Rowing (T-Bar)</u> – 90 x 8, 90 x 8, 115 x 8.

<u>Saturday 3/15/86</u>
1. <u>DEADLIFTS (Floor)(Sumo)</u> – 225 x 5, 385 x 4, 475 x 3, 565 x 2.
2. <u>Standing Alternate Dumbell Presses</u> – 65 x 8, 65 x 8,
    Standing DB Presses : VERY strict form 65 x 8, 65 x 8.
3. <u>Lying Dumbell Flyes</u> – 25 x 15, 25 x 15, 25 x 15.
4. <u>Lying Triceps Presses (EZ Bar)</u> – 110 x 6, 160 x 5.
    Did not perform additional sets in order to avoid injury
5. <u>Standing Alternate Dumbell Curls</u> – 55 x 6, 60 x 6, 65 x 6.
6. <u>Flyes on Pec Machine</u> – 50 x 10, 85 x 10.
7. <u>Triceps Pressdowns</u> – 100 x 6, 130 x 6.

<u>Monday 3/17/86</u> - <u>SQUATS</u> – 225 x 5, 365 x 3, 485 x 2, 525 x 2.

Paul Sutphin competed in the <u>1986 West Virginia State Powerlifting Championships</u> held Saturday March 22nd, 1986 at New Martinsville, West Virginia making lifts of :

Bodyweight at morning weigh-in at 179 ½
SQUAT – 655, BENCH PRESS – 407, DEADLIFT – 677, for a TOTAL of 1741.
Four (4) West Virginia State Powerlifting Records
ELITE TOTAL – 181lb. Class

Powerlifting : April – May, 1986

The site of the <u>1986 West Virginia State Collegiate Powerlifting Championships</u> on April 19th, 1986 was the same venue as in 1977 ; Parkersburg Community College. Joe Lee (198), Tom Buzzo (220), and John Lilly (242), all won their respective weight classes and became the 1986 West Virginia Collegiate Powerlifting Champions. Tom Buzzo, Joe Lee, and John Lilly represented the *Concord Power Club*.

Lifting in the 198lb. class on 4/19/86, Joe Lee broke four (4) West Virginia State Collegiate Powerlifting Records. Joey Lee's lifts on 4/19/86 were 551 Squat, 402 Bench Press, 551 Deadlift, for a Total of 1504. Tom Buzzo scored lifts of 451 Squat, 297 Bench Press, 451 Deadlift, for a 1200 Total. Lifting in the 242lb. class, John Lilly also broke four (4) West Virginia State Collegiate Powerlifting Records. John Lilly's lifts on 4/19/86 were 573 Squat, 446 Bench Press, 562 Deadlift, for a Total of 1581.

On Saturday April 26th, 1986 the <u>1986 West Virginia State Teenage Powerlifting Championships</u> were held at Man, West Virginia. The event had forty-one (41) lifters. Donald Robbins won 1st Place in the 148lb. class with lifts of 385 Squat, 360 Bench Press, 485 Deadlift and a Total of 1230.

Scott Collias placed first in the 181lb. class with a 550 Squat, 275 Bench Press, 500 Deadlift, and a 1325 Total. Barry England of the *Concord Power Club* placed 4th in the 181lb. class with a Total of 1165. Steve Banco won the 1986 West Virginia Teenage Powerlifting Championship in the 198lb. class with lifts of 485 Squat, 300 Bench Press, 475 Deadlift, and a 1260 Total. Charles Wallace placed 3rd in the 220lb. class with a 465 Squat, 290 Bench Press, and a 520 Deadlift for a 1275 Total.

The <u>5th Annual Parkersburg Open Powerlifting Championships</u> were held on Saturday May 3rd, 1986 in Parkersburg, West Virginia. According to the official results, the event had over forty (40) lifters. Joe Lee won the 198lb. class with a 1542 Total. In the 220's, it was John Nicoloudakis with a Total of 1642 for first, Don Hall in 2nd Place at 220 with 1631, and Sam Arrington, lifting in his first Powerlifting competition, coming in 3rd Place in the 220's with a 1383 Total.

The lifts made by Sam Arrington on 5/03/86 while competing in the 220lb. class included a 501 Squat, 347 Bench Press, and a 534 Deadlift for a 1383 Total, winning first place at the 1986 Parkersburg Open in the Novice Division. Sam Arrington, along with Tom Jernigan and Dwayne Phillips, were part of the *Concord Power Club* in the early 1970's. All three (3) were Weightlifters and competed in Olympic Weightlifting competitions throughout Virginia and the Eastern Region of the U.S.A. In 1979, Sam Arrington, Tom Jernigan, and Dwayne Phillips were charter members of the *Bluefield YMCA Weightlifting Club.*

Region VI Champion : Victory at Richmond

For the first time since 1976, the right time arrived to return to the Region VI Powerlifting Championships. As it turned out, it was a great day in Fort Knox, Kentucky with new Region VI Powerlifting Records and a Region VI Powerlifting Championship title. The 1986 Region VI Powerlifting Championships became "The Kentucky Connection : Part V."

The <u>1986 Region VI Powerlifting Championships</u> were held June 28th, 1986 at Fort Knox, Kentucky. Lifting in the 181lb. class on an extremely hot day at Fort Knox, the Region VI Powerlifting Championship title was mine with lifts of 622 ¾ Squat, 396 Bench Press, 655 Deadlift, and a Total of 1675. The 622 ¾ Squat, 655 Deadlift, and Total of 1675 represented three (3) new Region VI Powerlifting Championship Records. *Along with* the Region VI Squat, Deadlift, and Total Records, a 396 Bench Press was part of the Elite "TOTAL Package" of 1675lbs. in the 181lb. class on 6/28/86.

"The Virginia Connection," Part Fourteen (Part XIV), took place at Mechanicsville, Virginia on December 6th and 7th, 1986. The <u>Central Virginia Open Powerlifting Championships</u> were held at Gold's Gym in Mechanicsville, Virginia. The spacious facility served as the perfect venue for the two-day, two-platform Powerlifting event. According to the official meet results and contest report from the pages of *Powerlifting USA* magazine, the contest had a total of one-hundred eighteen (118) lifters.

Vince White won the 198lb. class in the Master's Division at Richmond, Virginia on the weekend of 12/06/86 with a Total of 1322. Dan Hall won first place in the 275lb. class with a 1795 Total which included a 705 Squat and a 705 Deadlift. The *Holley Strength Team* won the Team Award at the 1986 Central Virginia Open.

The lifters competing for the *Holley Strength Team* on 12/06 & 12/07/86 were : Allen Smith (2nd Place – 148lb. class), Paul Sutphin (1st Place – 181lb. class), Joe Lee (2nd Place – 198lb. class), Dave Defrenn (198lb. class), Mike Nidy (242lb. class), Steve Pauley (242lb. class), Dan Hall (1st Place – 275lb. class), Vince White (1st Place – Masters Division).

The *Holley Strength Team* missed Don Hundley at Richmond, Virginia on the weekend of December 6th, 1986. Don competed at the YMCA Nationals in Columbus, Ohio on 12/13/86 and set new Powerlifting Records in the Masters Division. On 12/13/86, Don Hundley Squatted 584, Bench Pressed 270, and Deadlifted 622 for a Total of 1477. The 584 Squat and 622 Deadlift by Don Hundley on 12/13/86 were new American Masters Powerlifting Records in the category (50-54 Age Group).

Paul Sutphin – Deadlift of 650lbs.
Richmond, Virginia 12/06/86

Competing in the 181lb. class among a field of thirteen (13) competitors, Paul Sutphin Totaled 1686, an Elite Total in the 181lb. class, for the win. Included in the Elite Total on 12/06/1986 was a Squat of 639, Bench Press of 396, and a Deadlift of 650lbs.

Chapter Twenty-Three : 1987-1989

Published in early lifting magazines on more than one report were two lifters performing the "Two-Man" Deadlift. In the JAN/84 issue of *Powerlifting USA* magazine, it was Ernie Frantz and Ed Coan breaking a record in the "Two-Man" Deadlift. At Fort Knox, Kentucky on January 10th, 1987 it was West Virginians Don Hundley and Doug Currence competing in the "Two-Man Deadlift" competition.

Don Hundley and Doug Currence : First Place in a "Two-Man Deadlift" competition. Just before the "Two Man Deadlift" event, both Hundley and Currence won their weight classes with the following Deadlifts : Don Hundley, lifting in the 181lb. class, Deadlifted 639lbs. for a "blowout" win over six (6) competitors. Doug Currence, lifting in the 198lb. class, pulled 677 ¾ lbs. for the win. Afterward, both men pulled 1153lbs. to win the "Two-Man Deadlift" competition at Fort Knox, Kentucky on 1/10/87.

The 12th Annual West Virginia State Powerlifting Championships were held on April 11th, 1987 at Mineral Wells, West Virginia. The contest had seventy-six (76) lifters and was conducted as a "Two –Platform" event. The August, 1987 issue of *POWERLIFTING USA, Volume 11, Number 1* printed the full report of the 1987 West Virginia State Powerlifting Championships.

For Don Hundley, the 1987 West Virginia State Powerlifting Championships represented six (6) West Virginia State titles! Even though Don Hundley was beaten on the Bench Press by over 100lbs., he dominated all competitors in the 165lb. class. Don's American Record Squatting ability and the owner of one of the top Deadlifts in the nation, "Pound for Pound" (666 ¾ lbs. /302.5 kilos – 165lb. class) "wrote the story" on 4/11/87. As he had done many times before, Don Hundley proved that Sub-Totals in Powerlifting competitions mean nothing until "the bar hits the floor."

While competing in the 165lb. class at the 1987 West Virginia State Powerlifting Championships, Donald Robbins weighed-in at 164½ lbs. and Bench Pressed 185 kilos (407 ¾ lbs.) for a new Teenage American Record (18-19 Age Group) in the 165lb. weight class. The Bench Press of 407 ¾ lbs. / 185 kilos set a new West Virginia State Bench Press Record in the 165lb. class, Open (Senior) Division.

Totaling a conservative 1625lbs. for the win in the 181lb. class, it was West Virginia State Powerlifting Championship number ten (10) for Paul Sutphin. The 198lb. class was won by Doug Currence for the 2nd consecutive year.

In the 220lb. class, Steve Uhas set a new West Virginia State Record in the Squat with a lift of 733lbs. Other notable performances at the 1987 West Virginia State Powerlifting Championships were John Messinger's 1802 Total in the 275lb. class and Mike Nidy's

1681 Total for the win in the 242lb. class. The Outstanding Lifter Award in the Senior Division was won by Randy Scott. The *Holley Strength Systems*, coached by Vince White, won the 1987 West Virginia State Powerlifting Team Championship Award.

For the 2ⁿᵈ consecutive year, the <u>Region VI Powerlifting Championships</u> were conducted in Fort Knox, Kentucky. The 1987 Region VI Powerlifting Championships (Kentucky Connection : Part VI) were held on May 16ᵗʰ & 17ᵗʰ, 1987. Joe Lee won the 1987 Region VI Powerlifting Championships while competing in the 198lb. class. On 5/16/87, Joe Lee Squatted 628, Bench Pressed 424, and Deadlifted 611 for a Total of 1664 in the 198lb. class. John Lilly won the 1987 Region VI Collegiate Powerlifting title in the 242lb. class.

Scott Collias made his first appearance at the 1986 West Virginia State Powerlifting Championships in New Martinsville on 3/22/86. Competing in the 181lb. class / Junior Division, Scott placed 2ⁿᵈ with a Total of 1273 and set two (2) Junior Division Powerlifting Records : A Squat of 518 and a Bench Press of 275.

Five (5) weeks after the 1986 West Virginia State Powerlifting Championships, Scott Collias competed at the 1986 West Virginia State Teenage Powerlifting Championships in Man, West Virginia on 4/26/86. Scott placed first in the 181lb. class in a field of six (6) competitors. Scott Collias' winning Total at the 1986 West Virginia Teenage Powerlifting Championships was a new West Virginia State Teenage Record of 1325 which included a West Virginia State Teenage Squat Record of 550lbs.

At the 1987 West Virginia State Powerlifting Championships on 4/11/87, Scott Collias placed 2ⁿᵈ once again in the Junior Division / 181lb. class. Scott Collias set a new West Virginia State Teenage and Junior Division Record in the Squat with a lift of 250 kilos / 551lbs. Scott qualified for the Teenage National Powerlifting Championships at the 1987 West Virginia State Championships.

On 8/01/87 at the <u>USPF Teenage Nationals</u> held at Allentown, Pennsylvania, Scott Collias placed 4ᵗʰ in the 181lb. class (18-19 Age Group). While taking on very tough competition in the 181lb. class, Scott Collias Squatted 611 ¾, Bench Pressed 325, and Deadlifted 534 for a Total of 1471. Scott's lifts at the 1987 Teenage National Powerlifting Championships were new West Virginia State Teenage Powerlifting Records in the 181lb. class.

1988

A group of lifters from the *Concord Power Club* in Athens, West Virginia adopted the ambitious project of promoting the 1988 West Virginia State Powerlifting Championships. For the benefit of the lifters, the following divisions were included in the 1988 West

Virginia State Powerlifting Championships : Open / Senior Division, Junior (Under Class I) Division, Masters Division, Teenage Division, and the Collegiate Division.

The 13th Annual West Virginia State Powerlifting Championships were held at Concord College in Athens, West Virginia on Saturday March 5th & Sunday March 6th, 1988. The Meet Directors were Tom Buzzo and John Lilly. The 1988 event was conducted in one (1) session per day, single platform. The 1988 West Virginia State Powerlifting Meet was a two (2) day event and hosted a record number of participants with approximately one-hundred five (105) lifters!

Since 1976, Don Hall had competed in every West Virginia State Powerlifting Championship and either finished 2nd or lower. While competing in the Senior (Open Division – 220lb. class), Don Hall Totaled 1499lbs. for the win. The 1499 Total by Don Hall on 3/06/88 included a Squat of 600, Bench Press of 358, and a Deadlift of 540. A big win for Don Hall!

Don Hall
1988 West Virginia State Powerlifting Champion

Matt Cardello set a new Bench Press Record of 413lbs. / 187.5 kilos while competing in the 181lb. class at the 1988 West Virginia State Powerlifting Championships. The Bench Press Record of 413lbs. set by Matt Cardello on 3/05/88 was a new West Virginia State Bench Press Record in the Open / Senior Division and the Collegiate Division in the 181lb. class.

John Lilly won the West Virginia State Collegiate Powerlifting Championships in 1986 and 1987. While competing in the 242lb. class of the Collegiate Division, John Lilly Totaled 1510lbs. for the win which included a new West Virginia Collegiate Bench Press Record of 451 pounds. Fourteen (14) days later on 3/20/88 in Philadelphia, Pennsylvania, John Lilly represented Concord College at the 1988 National Collegiate Powerlifting Championships and placed 3rd with a 1499 Total in the 242lb. class which included lifts of 507 Squat, 435 Bench Press, and a 556 Deadlift.

Randy Scott broke two (2) West Virginia State Powerlifting Records in the Squat and Total while competing in the 275lb. class at the 1988 West Virginia State Powerlifting Championships. The Elite Total of 1967lbs. for a West Virginia State Record included a West Virginia State Record Squat of 749lbs. in the 275lb. class. Randy Scott won the Outstanding Lifter Award in the Open / Senior Division at the 1988 West Virginia State Powerlifting Championships.

For the 3rd consecutive year, the *Holley Strength Systems* won the 1988 West Virginia Powerlifting Team Championship Award. Later in 1988, *Powerlifting USA* magazine published the official results with a complete report of the 1988 West Virginia State Powerlifting Championships.

Scott Collias won the Outstanding Lifter Award among all of the thirty-three (33) Teenage competitiors at the 1988 West Virginia State Powerlifting Championships at Concord College on March 5th and 6th, 1988. Competing in the 198lb. class in a field of five (5) competitors, Scott Collias Totaled 1466 for the first place victory and the Outstanding Lifter Award.

Competing in the 198lb. class in 1988 versus the 181lb. class in 1986 could have placed Scott at a disadvantage in terms of the coefficients for determining the Outstanding Lifter Award ; Yet, the 1466 Total by Collias on 3/06/88 won the award among all of West Virginia's Teenage Powerlifters. In addition to the Outstanding Lifter Award, the 1466 Total by Scott Collias included a new West Virginia State Teenage Squat Record in the 198lb. class with a lift of 606lbs., a Bench Press of 336, and a Deadlift of 523.

Vince White : Masters National Champion!

The <u>APF Master's National Powerlifting Championships</u> were conducted at Barboursville, West Virginia on July 9th & 10th, 1988. The written article of the 1988 APF Master's National Powerlifting Championships, along with a photo of Vince White, appeared in the January, 1989 issue of *Powerlifting USA* magazine. Vince White, while competing for the first time in the 45-49 Age Group, put together a winning Total of 1328 in the 198lb. class which included a Squat of 540 and a Bench Press of 369.

Don Hundley, National Masters Powerlifting Champion, won another National Masters Powerlifting Championship title on 7/09/88 with the APF (American Powerlifting Federation). Don Hundley (50-54 Age Group) set four (4) APF American / World Masters Powerlifting Records while competing in the 165lb. class. Don Hundley's winning Total of 1394 in the 165lb. class consisted of a 551 Squat, 253 Bench Press, and a 589 Deadlift.

Competing in the Teenage Division on 7/10/88 with a win (18-19 Age Group) was Scott Collias with a 1532 Total. Scott Collias Squatted 622, Bench Pressed 352, and Deadlifted 556 for the 1532 Teenage National Powerlifting Championship Total. The lifting of Scott Collias was significant to the West Virginia State Powerlifting Records as nearly all of the Squats, Deadlifts, and Total by Scott Collias were new West Virginia State Teenage Powerlifting Records.

The 1587 Total by Don Hall at the 1988 National Masters Powerlifting Championships included a Squat of 644lbs. / 292.5 kilos for a new West Virginia State Powerlifting Record in the Master's Division / 220lb. class. Austin Miller won the 242lb. class (60-64 Age Group) and John Martin won the SuperHeavyWeight class (40-44 Age Group).

Powerlifting USA magazine / Vol. 12 / No. 6 / JAN/89

Don Hall – 7/10/88
Squat of 644 ¾ lbs. – 220lb. class

1989

The 14th Annual West Virginia State Powerlifting Championships were held in Glenville, West Virginia on Saturday March 11th & Sunday March 12th, 1989. According to the official results, the 1989 West Virginia State Powerlifting Championships had eighty (80) lifters. There were no West Virginia State Powerlifting Records broken in the Senior Division at the 1989 West Virginia State Powerlifting Championships. The contest report for *Powerlifting USA* magazine of the 1989 West Virginia State Powerlifting Championships was written by West Virginia State Powerlifting Chairman, Vince White.

Allen Smith won his fourth (4th) consecutive West Virginia State Powerlifting Championship title while winning the 148lb. class on 3/11/89 with a Total of 1339. Don Hundley won "West Virginia State Powerlifting Championship number seven" on 3/11/89. Doug Currence won his fifth (5th) West Virginia State Powerlifting Championship title on 3/11/89 while competing in the 181lb. class.

Scott Collias, competing in the Collegiate Division, won the West Virginia State Powerlifting title in the 198lb. class in a field of eight (8) competitors. Scott put together a winning Total of 1515 in the 198lb. class with a 600 Squat, 352 Bench Press, and a 562 Deadlift to outlift his nearest competitor by ninety-five (95) pounds.

"Setting the Records Straight": Part V
"Single-Lift" Records

Until the latter part of 1988, Powerlifting competitions offered only the Powerlifting (3-lift) option for lifters. Beginning in 1989, "new rules" defining competitions with only the Bench Press or the Deadlift were written and approved by the USPF National Committee. In addition to Powerlifting Records set in a traditional format of the Squat – Bench Press – Deadlift with a required Total, "Single-Lift Records" would also be recognized by the USPF (United States Powerlifting Federation).

During early September of 1989, Vince White resigned as the West Virginia State Powerlifting Chairman. Vince held the position approximately one (1) week shy of seven (7) years and five (5) months. A few days following Vince's resignation, I was approached by a number of members from the *Holley Strength Team* and elsewhere about filling the huge void as a result of Vince White's resignation. Meanwhile, I received a phone call from the Region VI Powerlifting Chairman on the subject of filling the position left vacant by Vince White's resignation. Making a long story short, effective October 1st, 1989 Paul Sutphin became the West Virginia Powerlifting Chairman…Again!

As West Virginia State Powerlifting Chairman, it was my responsibility to protect, preserve, and correctly maintain the West Virginia State Powerlifting Records! "Single-Lift" extravaganzas, side-show events, etc., would NOT replace the integrity of what had been built for over three (3) decades. Maintenance, preservation, and protection of the existing West Virginia State Powerlifting Records became priority number one (1) regarding the West Virginia State Powerlifting Program and the ultimate survival of Powerlifting.

In response to the USPF ruling regarding "Single-lift Records," Powerlifting Records set in full (3-lift) meets were maintained the same as in years past. However, beginning on October 1st, 1989 a separate list of records were kept for "Single-Lift" competitions. The *existing* Bench Press and Deadlift Records were used as benchmarks for every weight class in the new "Single-Lift" category. Therefore, if a lift recorded from a "Single-Lift" competition did not exceed the existing benchmark, then the lift was not recognized as a West Virginia State "Single-Lift Record."

Powerlifting Records : Women's Division

It wasn't until the late 1970's when a few women in West Virginia chose to demonstrate their talents in the most popular sport of iron, Powerlifting. At the 1979 West Virginia State Powerlifting Championships, Joan Fruth was the only female athlete entered at the competition. In reference to the Official Meet Program of the 1980 West Virginia State Powerlifting Championships, there were no female entries. However, there was at least one (1) Powerlifting competition held in West Virginia during 1979 and 1980 specifically for the Women and Masters Powerlifting competitors.

Listed in the Official Meet Program of the 1981 West Virginia State Powerlifting Championships were five (5) women scheduled to compete on 3/29/81 at New Martinsville. In 1982, there were no female athletes competing at the West Virginia State Powerlifting Championships held in Fairmont. According to the official meet results, a total of three (3) women competed at the 1983 West Virginia State Powerlifting Championships.

In 1983, Beverly Hart won the Women's Division at the Mountianeer Open Powerlifting Championships. As a member of the *Bluefield YMCA Weightlifting Club,* Beverly competed with the Powerlifting team and contributed to the Team

Championship Award won by the *Bluefield YMCA Weightlifting Club* at the 1983 Mountian Empire Open in Bristol, Tennessee.

Beverly Hart won the 1984 West Virginia State Powerlifting Championships on 3/31/84 at South Charleston, West Virginia. According to the official results of the 1984 West Virginia State Powerlifting Championships published in the July, 1984 issue of *Powerlifting USA* magazine, there were a total of six (6) women competing in the Women's Division for the 1984 State Powerlifting title. The 1984 West Virginia State Champion for the Women was determined by the Malone Formula.

Powerlifting USA magazine / Vol. 7 / No. 12 / July, 1984

Published in the MAR/84 issue of *Powerlifting USA* magazine was the first WOMEN'S TOP 20. The lifting of Mary Jeffrey prevailed in the 1980's. Mary was also featured on the cover of the MAR/93 issue of *Powerlifting USA* magazine. According to the official results of the 1985 West Virginia State Powerlifting Championships at Newell, West Virginia only one (1) female athlete competed in the competition. In contrast, at the 1986 West Virginia State Powerlifting Championships, there were nine (9) women competing at New Martinsville on 3/22/86.

In 1987, a record number of eleven (11) women for a West Virginia State Powerlifting Championship lifted at Mineral Wells. Eleven (11) was also the number of female athletes listed in the official results of the 1988 West Virginia State Powerlifting Championships while ten (10) women competed at the 1989 West Virginia State Powerlifting Championships at Glenville.

Women's Division : WV Powerlifter Rankings
WV Female Powerlifters competing from January 1st, 1979 thru December 31st, 1989
Women Powerlifter RANKINGS Determined by Total
Ranking Totals from 1986 thru 1989 include use of the "Bench Press Shirt"

97 / Name	Squat	Bench Press	Deadlift	Total	Date
Joan Fruth	236	132*	286*	655* e	1/29/83
Joan Fruth	242*	115	253	611*	10/19/80
Joan Fruth (WC)	237*	110	259*	606* WC	5/03/80
Joan Fruth (NC)	220	121*	253*	595* NC	1/26/80
Joan Fruth	220	121	242	584	8/06/82
Joan Fruth	225* c	95* c	240* c	560* c	5/12/79
Joan Fruth	187	115	253	556	10/31/81
Joan Fruth	200	90	235	525	10/14/79
Lisa Romanowski	165	77	203	446	3/05/88
105 Joan Fruth	253	143	319	716 e	2/20/82
Sara Jeffrey	181	77	203	462	4/11/87
Debbie Dye	170	90	200	460	12/11/82
Sara Jeffrey	176	82	198	457	6/06/87
Michelle Zirkle	137 c	99 c	181 c	418 c	3/11/89
Sara Jeffrey	165	60	181	408	2/07/87
114 Mary Jeffrey	380	242	380	1003 e	3/22/86
Mary Jeffrey	385* WR	230	385* WR	1000* WR e	2/15/87
Mary Jeffrey	380	225	370	975 e	11/15/86
Mary Jeffrey	369	231	369	970 e	3/08/86
Mary Jeffrey	358	225*AR	352	936	1/26/85
Mary Jeffrey	352	231*AR	352	936	11/01/86
Pam Jeffrey	275	126	286	688	10/31/81
Terry Holstein	220	104	259	584	10/31/87
Marcia Gochenaur	220	105	250	575	5/20/89
Joan Fruth	200	110	250	560	1/05/80
Sara Jeffrey	220	93	220	534	10/31/87
Pam Jeffrey	200	80	245	525	10/14/79
Kathlene Bruch	187 c	115 c	214 c	518 c	3/11/89

* - West Virginia State Women's Powerlifting Record
AR – American Powerlifting Record
WR – APF Women's World Record
e – Women's Elite Powerlifting Classification Total
NC – Women's National Powerlifting Champion
c – West Virginia State Women's Collegiate Powerlifting Record
WC – Women's World Powerlifting Champion

Women's Division : WV Powerlifter Rankings
WV Female Powerlifters competing from January 1st, 1979 thru December 31st, 1989
Women Powerlifter RANKINGS Determined by Total
Ranking Totals from 1986 thru 1989 include use of the "Bench Press Shirt"

123 / Name	Squat	Bench Press	Deadlift	Total	Date
Mary Jeffrey	424*	264*	413*	1102* e	7/16/88
Mary Jeffrey	407 I	253 I	407	1069 I e	1/30/88
Mary Jeffrey	407	253*	390	1052* e	10/31/87
Mary Jeffrey	420 w	236	391	1047 e	7/14/89
Mary Jeffrey wc	369	220	391	981 e	11/13/89
Donna Secreto	281 t	165 t	308	755 t	7/09/88
Donna Secreto	264 t	159 t	314 t	738 t	3/05/88
Donna Secreto	253	154 t	303 t	710	12/05/87
Danielle Ray	275 t	143 t	292 t	710 t	3/08/86
Pam Jeffrey	280	120	305	705	12/11/82
Debbie Lass	253	148	264	667	10/31/87
Lisa Richards	253	121	281	655	4/11/87
Ethel Martin	209 m	121 m	253 m	584 m	3/11/89
132 Debbie Lass	336*	187*	330	854 e	3/05/88
Donna Secreto	286	176	330	793	11/05/89
Maria Ramirez	270	148	286	705	3/11/89
Wendy Thomas	275	115	292	683	11/10/84
Wanda Smith	275	127	264	667	3/05/88
Michelle Helminski	236	115	275	628	10/31/87
Marsha Yates	203	99	264	567	3/11/89
Angela Williamson	220	115	225	562	3/11/89
Terry Holstein	187	104	259	550	5/03/86
Michelle Helminski	198	104	242	545	4/11/87
Terry Holstein	176	88	231	495	11/10/84

* - West Virginia State Women's Powerlifting Record   w – IPF Women's World Powerlifting Record
m – West Virginia State Women's Masters Record   AR – American Powerlifting Record
NC – Women's National Powerlifting Champion   I – IPF Women's World Powerlifting Record
e – Women's Elite Powerlifting Classification Total   WC – Women's World Powerlifting Champion
t – West Virginia State Women's Teenage Powerlifting Record   WR – APF Women's World Record

Women's Division : WV Powerlifter Rankings
WV Female Powerlifters competing from January 1st, 1979 thru December 31st, 1989
Women Powerlifter RANKINGS Determined by Total
Ranking Totals from 1986 thru 1989 include use of the "Bench Press Shirt"

148 / Name	Squat	Bench Press	Deadlift	Total	Date
Earlene Boston	352	143	352	848	3/11/89
Cindy DeHaven	264	198	314	777	4/11/87
Earlene Boston	297	143	319	760	10/31/87
Ladonna Kirk	242	125	319	688	11/05/89
Maria Ramirez	281	104	270	655	11/09/85
Shelley Hager	225	137	275	639	3/05/88
Sandy Reed	220	110	264	595	10/31/81
Lisa Richards	214	99	253	567	11/09/85
165 Beverly Hart	308	165	391*	865	3/05/88
Beverly Hart	303	165	363	832	4/11/87
Earlene Boston	336	148	347	832	3/05/88
Beverly Hart	314	154	363	832	3/11/89
Beverly Hart	303	148	363	815	10/29/83
Beverly Hart	300	155	355	810	5/11/85
Beverly Hart	295	140	365	800	12/10/83
Beverly Hart	295	150	355	800	12/01/84
Beverly Hart	303	148	341	792	3/31/84
Candy Moraczewski	253	143	275	672	4/11/87
Joyce Strictland	270	127	275	672	3/05/88
Maria Yoakum	181	88	214	485	5/28/83
181	*Women's Rankings Not Available for 181lb. Weight Class*				
198 Maria Yoakum	220 m	115 m	270 m	606 m	3/05/88
Maria Yoakum	187	99	225	512	7/09/88
UNL Peg Conley	391	176	369	936	11/05/89

* - West Virginia Women's Powerlifting Record

e – Women's Elite Powerlifting Classification Total

m – West Virginia State Women's Masters Powerlifting Record

In the 1990's, female athletes demonstrated their talents in different weight classes from a number of Powerlifting organizations. In 1991, Marion Smith, competing in the Women's Masters Division, won the West Virginia State Powerlifting Championships at Morgantown with a Squat of 292, Bench Press of 192, and a Deadlift of 336 for a Total of 821.

The official results of the 1992 Junior National Powerlifting Championships (Age 14 thru 23) conducted in Brockton, Massachusetts appeared in the July, 1992 issue of *Powerlifting USA* magazine. According to the official results of the 1992 Junior National Powerlifting Championships held May 1st thru 3rd, 1992, Lori Jeffrey won the 1992 Women's Junior National Championship title while competing in the 48 kilo / 105lb. class / (14-15 Age Group) along with the Outstanding Lifter and the Champion of Champions Award in the Women's Division.

According to the official results of ADFPA Powerlifting during the 1990's, Stephanie Bowling and Tina Mondlak competed in Powerlifting events and held West Virginia State Powerlifting Records in the ADFPA / USA Powerlifting organization. Also included in the published ADFPA Powerlifting Records of the 1990's were the names of Kristal McClellan, Loretta Barron, Marcia Gochenaur, and Linda Hampe

Beginning in 1996, the name of Sue Pack was added to the list of Women's Powerlifting Records. Sue won the Westside Invitational on 2/27/99 while competing in the Women's Masters Division. Sue Pack's lifts at the 1999 Westside Invitational were 250 Squat, 205 Bench Press, and a 310 Deadlift for a Total of 765.

Powerlifting USA magazine / Vol. 22 / No. 10 May, 1999

Sue Pack won the 1999 IPA Nationals and set four (4) IPA Women's Masters World Records in the Amateur Division (55-59 Age Group – 181lb. class) for a 785 Total. Sue Pack won the 1996 USPF National Master's Championships in Dayton, Ohio. A slew of Powerlifting and Bench Press Records were set or broken by Sue Pack in the 21st century. Sue Pack owns several National, American, and World Bench Press Records in the Women's Master's Division. *Powerlifting USA magazine / Vol. 23 / NO. 7 / February, 2000*

Since 1999, Lynne Homan also owns National Records in USPF and USAPL Women's Masters Powerlifting competitions. According to the official meet results of the 1999 APF West Virginia State Powerlifting Championships, Lynne Homan placed 1st in the 148lb. weight class in the Women's Division with a 705 Total. Among the most recent achievements, Lynne Homan placed 2nd in the IPF Women's World Powerlifting Championships at Kileen, Texas in November of 2012.

Powerlifting USA magazine / Vol. 23 / NO. 6 / January, 2000

In the 21st Century, Deb Barnette has won several Women's Powerlifting titles in the Women's Masters Division while competing in the USPF. In 2011, Deb Barnette won the USPF West Virginia State Powerlifting Championship while competing in the Women's Masters Division.

Women's Elite Powerlifter Classification

During the Era II of Powerlifting (1977 thru 1984), only one (2) female athletes achieved Elite Powerlifting Classification among West Virginia's Powerlifters. According to the United States Powerlifting Federation (USPF) Elite Classification Standards for Women, Joan Fruth earned the Women's Powerlifter Elite Classification in both the 97lb. and 105lb. weight classes. According to the official results of the 1982 Women's National Powerlifting Championships held in Auburn, Alabama, Joan Fruth became the first female Powerlifter from West Virginia to achieve Elite Powerlifting Classification.

Powerlifting USA magazine

While competing in the 105lb. weight class at the Women's National Powerlifting Championships on 2/20/82, Joan Fruth Totaled Elite with a Total of 716. According to the official results of the 1983 Women's National Powerlifting Championships at Chicago, Illinois on 1/29/83, Joan Fruth Totaled Elite in the 97lb. weight class with a Total of 655lbs.

Powerlifting USA magazine

During Era II and Era III of Powerlifting, Mary Jeffrey, while winning a multiple number of World Powerlifting Championships in both the 114lb. and 123lb. weight classes, Totaled Elite many times over! During the Era III of Powerlifting, Mary Jeffrey, Debbie Lass, and Lori Jeffrey achieved the Women's Elite Powerlifting Classification.

USPF Standards

ELITE Powerlifting Classification Standards for Women

CLASS	97	105	114	123	132	148	165	181	198	198+
Elite	639	683	733	782	827	909	981	1053	1130	1190
Master	579	623	667	711	749	827	893	959	1025	1080
Class I	518	562	601	639	672	744	805	865	920	970
Class II	463	496	535	568	601	661	706	766	821	865
Class III	402	435	468	496	524	579	623	672	706	755
Class IV	347	375	402	424	452	496	535	573	617	650

https://uspf.com/lifterclassification.htm

Chapter Twenty-Four : Powerlifting in the 1990's

In the first quarter of 1990, diversity continued to integrate the sport of Powerlifting at all levels. For the 2nd consecutive year, multiple Powerlifting federations created what had never been experienced in West Virginia. For the second time, two (2) West Virginia State Powerlifting Championships sanctioned by two (2) different Powerlifting organizations were conducted during the same calendar year.

The 15th Annual USPF West Virginia State Powerlifting Championships were held March 24th, 1990 at Barboursville. The 1990 West Virginia State Championships at Barboursville was the second (2nd) West Virginia State Powerlifting Championship conducted in a hotel. Among the winners were Don Hundley, Allen Smith, Bob Hill, and John Messinger.

Don Hundley won his eighth (8th) West Virginia State Powerlifting Championship title at the 1990 West Virginia State Powerlifting Championships. Allen Smith won the 148lb. class with a 1245 Total for his fifth (5th) consecutive West Virginia State Powerlifting title. Bob Hill won the 1990 West Virginia State Powerlifting Championship in the 198lb. class while competing in the Masters Division.

John Messinger had a great day on 3/24/90 and began what would be the first of eleven (11) USPF West Virginia State Powerlifting Championship titles! John Messinger's winning Total in the 242lb. class on 3/24/90 included lifts of 655 Squat, 402 Bench Press, and a 606 Deadlift for a Total of 1664lbs.

There were no Senior / Open Division Powerlifting Records broken on 3/24/90 at the West Virginia State Powerlifting Championships. The *Holley Strength System* won the 1990 West Virginia Powerlifting Team Award for the fifth (5th) consecutive year. Also, recognition of a Master's Team Champion was awarded to *Universal Health Club* of St. Albans.

In the spirit of unity, the diplomatic solution I had as the USPF West Virginia State Powerlifting Chairman was to go to the 1990 ADFPA West Virginia State Powerlifting Championships in Berkeley Springs as a lifter and win. On May 19th, 1990 John Messinger, Doug Currence, and Paul Sutphin competed at the ADFPA West Virginia State Powerlifting Championships and set new West Virginia State Powerlifting Records. While winning his second (2nd) West Virginia State Powerlifting Championship in two (2) months, John Messinger Squatted 660, Bench Pressed 400, and Deadlifted 620 for the winning Total of 1680 in the 275lb. class on 5/19/90 at Berkeley Springs, West Virginia.

Regarding training and the enthusiasm in 1990 versus the West Virginia Powerlifting Championships of the 1970's and most of the 1980's, there was not much of a comparison. However, like it or not, the stage was set as to how Powerlifting would be for the next decade and beyond. Multiple federations along with *a growing number of people claiming State, National, and...WORLD (?) Powerlifting titles.*

As a veteran Powerlifter, rather than adopt a reclusive lifestyle and refuse to participate in rivaling organizations, I made an important choice : *I chose to "Take it to the competition!"* After winning the 198lb. class at the 1990 ADFPA West Virginia State Powerlifting Championship event, I remember the interview by a West Virginia television station followed by an article in the *Twin State Observer.* The article featured in the section for SPORTS read, *Paul Sutphin : "He's Hard to Beat."*

During the 1990's, most of the existing West Virginia State Powerlifting Records in the Open / Senior Division from the 1970's and 1980's stood throughout the decade. The majority of activity in regard to new Powerlifting Records was specific to the Class I & Under Division (a.k.a., Junior Division), Masters Division, Women's Division, and the newly created Sub-Masters (Age 35-39) Division.

John Messinger
West Virginia State Powerlifting Champion
1996 National Masters Powerlifting Champion

340

On March 24th, 1990 John Messinger won his first West Virginia State Powerlifting Championship. John went on to win ten (10) additional USPF West Virginia State Powerlifting Championships including 1991, 1993, 1994, 1995, 1996, 1997, 1998, 1999, 2000, and 2004. On May 12th, 1996, John won the USPF National Masters Powerlifting Championships in the 275lb. class (40-44 Age Group).

1991-1993

The 16th Annual (1991) USPF West Virginia State Powerlifting Championships were held on March 24th, 1991 at Morgantown, West Virginia. The 1991 USPF West Virginia State Powerlifting Championships had over eighty-five (85) lifters. For the sixth (6th) consecutive year, the *Holley Strength Team* won the 1991 West Virginia State Powerlifting Team Championship Award. In the Men's Open / Senior Division, no records were broken at the 1991 West Virginia State Powerlifting Championships in Morgantown.

After a Squat of 639lbs., John Messinger won the 242lb. class at Morgantown on 3/24/91 with token lifts on the Bench Press and Deadlift due to an injury. Willie Williams won the SuperHeavyWeight (SHW) class and the Outstanding Lifter Award with a Total of 1923. Don Hundley took advantage of the 1991 West Virginia State Powerlifting Championships held in Morgantown to prepare for the upcoming National Masters Powerlifting Championships.

The 1991 USPF Masters and Sub-Masters National Powerlifting Championships were held in Greensboro, North Carolina on May 18th & 19th, 1991. The story of the meet was Don Hundley breaking new Master's World and American Records in the 165lb. class (55-59 Age Group). "Eight (8) New Powerlifting Records" and *Master's World Records* were broken by Don Hundley at the 1991 USPF National Masters Powerlifting Championships.

In Greensboro, North Carolina on the weekend of May 18th & 19th, 1991 the members of the *Holley Strength Team* included : Don Hundley, Don Hall, John Messinger, Vince White, and Paul Sutphin. The addition of the Sub-Masters category at the 1991 National Masters Powerlifting Championships did not set well with the veterans of Masters Powerlifting. Personally, I seen no problem with taking advantage of the added category to win another championship. After winning the Sub-Masters (Age 35-39) in the 198lb. class at Greensboro, a local newspaper wrote, *"Sutphin Wins Fourth Crown."*

The 1991 ADFPA West Virginia State Powerlifting Championships were held on September 28th, 1991 at Berkeley Springs, West Virginia. Among the winners were

Allen Smith (1285 Total – 148), Don Brotherton (1260 Total – 181), and Scott Collias (1420 – 198). Allen Smith and Scott Collias set new West Virginia Powerlifting Records on 9/28/91 at Berkeley Springs.

In 1992, the West Virginia State Powerlifting Championships returned to the Kanawha Valley for the first time since 1984. The 17ᵗʰ Annual (1992) USPF West Virginia State Powerlifting Championships were held at Institute, West Virginia. John Messinger was the Meet Director of the 1992 event with over ninety (90) competitors.

Phil Hile established residency in West Virginia during 1991. Phil Hile occasionally worked out at the *Holley Strength Systems* in South Charleston. While competing at the 18ᵗʰ Annual (1992) West Virginia State Powerlifting Championships, Phil Hile won the 114lb. class with a Total of 1151. Included in the 1151 Total by Phil Hile on 3/14/92 was a new West Virginia State Deadlift Record with a pull of 473lbs., breaking the existing Deadlift Record of 451lbs. owned by Chuck Mooney since 1983. Phil Hile also won the Outstanding Lifter Award for the Senior Division at the 1992 West Virginia State Powerlifting Championships.

Allen Smith Squatted 551lbs. / 250 kilos taken on a 4ᵗʰ attempt for a new West Virginia State Powerlifting Record in the 148lb. class. Allen won the 1992 West Virginia State Powerlifting Championships in the 148lb. class with a Total of 1372lbs. The Squat Record of Allen Smith was one (1) of only two (2) Powerlifting Records broken in the Men's Senior / Open Division at the 1992 West Virginia State Powerlifting Championships.

Don Hundley won his ninth (9ᵗʰ) West Virginia State Powerlifting Championship title competing in the 165lb. class with a Total of 1273lbs. Don won the Open (Senior) Division at the 1992 West Virginia State Powerlifting Championships. The 1273 Total by Don Hundley on 3/14/92 beat all Master's competitors by formula and all Totals in the 165lb. weight class.

Scott Collias won the 198lb. class at the 1992 West Virginia State Powerlifting Championships with a Total of 1559lbs. Scott Collias' 1559 Total on 3/14/92 included a 622 Squat, 363 Bench Press, and a 573 Deadlift. Winning the new category of Sub-Masters at the 1992 West Virginia State Powerlifting Championships were : Greg Jackson (148), Chris Miragliotta (165), Paul Sutphin (198), Butch Schaffer (220), and Phil Geyer (SuperHeavyWeight).

In the Masters Division at the 1992 West Virginia State Powerlifting Championships, Lloyd Arthur won the 198lb. class with a 1252 Total. Gary Clark Totaled 1554 in the Masters for the win in the 220's. Dan Hall won the 1992 West Virginia Master's Powerlifting Championship title in the 275lb. class.

The <u>1992 USPF West Virginia Teenage and Collegiate Powerlifting Championships</u> were held Saturday May 2nd, 1992 at Man, West Virginia. The West Virginia State Teenage and Collegiate Powerlifting Championships on 5/02/92 had thirty-eight (38) lifters. Scott Collias won the 198lb. class and set three (3) new West Virginia State Collegiate Powerlifting Records. Competing in the 242lb. class, Bill Jackson Squatted 660lbs. for a new West Virginia State Collegiate Powerlifting Record. Bill Jackson Bench Pressed 350 and Deadlifted 550 for a winning Total of 1560 in the 242lb. class.

The <u>18th Annual (1993) USPF West Virginia State Powerlifting Championships</u> were held in Parkersburg on March 20th, 1993. Allen Smith won the Outstanding Lifter Award at the 1993 West Virginia State Powerlifting Championships while competing in the 148lb. class with a Total of 1350. Paul Sutphin won the Sub-Masters (Age 35-39) in the 198lb. class with two (2) West Virginia State Powerlifting Records. John Messinger won the 220lb. class while setting four (4) new West Virginia State Powerlifting Records in the Sub-Masters (35-39 Age Group) which included a 1675 Total.

Troy McNett Totaled 1857lbs. to win the SuperHeavyWeight Division at the 1993 West Virginia State Powerlifting Championships. The Total of 1857 by Troy McNett on 3/20/93 included a Squat of 672, Bench Press of 512, and a Deadlift of 672. There were no records broken in the Senior / Open Division at the 1993 West Virginia State Powerlifting Championships. However, there were at least twenty (20) West Virginia State Powerlifting Records in the sub-groups, with at least one (1) from a fourth (4th) attempt. The *Holley Strength Systems* won the 1993 West Virginia State Championship Team Award.

"Setting the Records Straight" : Part VI

The official results and contest report of the 17th Annual USPF (1992) West Virginia State Powerlifting Championships appeared in the July, 1992 issue of *Powerlifting USA* magazine. Included in the text of the article of which I wrote, "Several lifters took advantage of the rule allowing fourth (4th) attempts for the purpose of breaking State Records." From what had begun in 1990, more and more lifters requested and EXPECTED the privilege of being granted a "4th attempt," especially at Single-Lift events.

Although the turnout of lifters was lower at the 1993 West Virginia State Powerlifting Championships in comparison to 1991 and 1992, the fourth (4th) attempt rule was perceived by a large number of the lifters to be an "entitlement" or "bonus" for entering the Powerlifting meet. Since the majority of lifters were entered in the sub-groups (i.e., Women, Sub-Masters, and additional age categories of the Men's Masters, etc.), approximately 40% of the lifters met the criteria for requesting a fourth (4th) attempt for the purpose of setting or breaking a West Virginia State Powerlifting or Single-lift Record. As a result, lifting competitions were extended beyond the normal timeframe, while a number of existing Powerlifting Records set under the required format of "A maximum of three (3) attempts" were compromised under controversial circumstances.

A successful fourth (4th) attempt at any Powerlifting competition will not count in a Powerlifter's Total. Technically, when a lifter is granted a fourth (4th) attempt, which is not included in the lifters' Total, the 4th attempt actually falls into the "Single-lift Category." Effective April 1st, 1993, pending the presence of properly certified officials, fourth (4th) attempts were only granted for the purpose of setting American or World Powerlifting Records.

The 1993 USPF High School National Powerlifting Championships were conducted on April 2nd thru April 4th, 1993 at Beckley, West Virginia. The Meet Director was Coach John H. Lilly. The 1993 USPF High School National Powerlifting Championships hosted High School Powerlifting Teams from several states. The 1993 USPF High School National Powerlifting Championships was the largest National High School Powerlifting Championship ever with over two-hundred sixty (260) lifters.

While competing in the 181lb. class (14-15 Age Group), Brian Critchfield placed first (1st) in a field of eight (8) competitors with a Total of 1146. The Brian Critchfield Total of 1146 on 4/03/93 included a Squat of 424, a Teenage American Bench Press Record of 308lbs, and a Deadlift of 413. Brian Critchfield, granted a fourth (4th) attempt by the Head Referee in Charge (Paul Sutphin), was successful with another Teenage American Record of 319lbs.!

When it came to Powerlifting, "IPF style," Vince White was one of the best. The 1993 IPF Pan American Powerlifting Championships were held September 17th thru 19th, 1993 at Rockville, Maryland. Vince White became the 1993 Pan American Powerlifting Champion while competing in the Masters (Over Age 50) in the 220lb. weight class. Vince White Squatted 545lbs. (247.5kilos), Bench Pressed 347lbs. (157.5 kilos), and pulled a Deadlift of 413 to finish with a Total of 1295lbs.

Doug Currence, John Messinger, and Paul Sutphin set Deadlift Records in the "Single-Lift" category during 1994. All three (3) Powerlifters (Currence, Messinger, and Sutphin) won National Deadlift Championship titles in 1994. From February (94) to April (94), Paul Sutphin won three (3) West Virginia State Championships in the same number of organizations.

The 19th Annual (1994) USPF West Virginia State Powerlifting Championships were held April 2nd, 1994 at Shady Springs, West Virginia. John H. Lilly was Meet Director.

John Messinger won his fourth (4th) USPF West Virginia State Championship in the 242lb. class with a Total of 1658lbs. The John Messinger Total of 1658 on 4/02/94 included a Squat of 622, Bench Press of 413, and a 622 Deadlift. There were no West Virginia State Powerlifting Records broken in the Open (Senior) Division at the 1994 West Virginia State Powerlifting Championships.

On October 31st, 1994 Willie Williams became the first West Virginian to officially Bench Press over 700lbs. Prior to the historical event on October 31st, 1994 at the annual Bench Press competition in St. Albans, West Virginia, Willie Williams won the 1991 West Virginia State Powerlifting Championships in the Superheavyweight class with a Total of 1923lbs.

Willie Williams' Total of 1923 at the 1991 West Virginia State Powerlifting Championships included a Bench Press of 512lbs. Willie Williams increased his PR Total to 1934 at the 1992 West Virginia State Powerlifting Championships which included a Bench Press of 545lbs.

The 20th Annual (1995) USPF West Virginia State Powerlifting Championships were held in Institute, West Virginia on Saturday April 8th, 1995. The Meet Director was John Messinger. John Messinger captured his fifth (5th) USPF West Virginia State Powerlifting title with a new Squat Record in the Masters Division (Age 40-49) of 677 ¾ lbs. while competing in the 242lb. class. John Messinger's winning Total of 1703lbs. at the 1995 West Virginia State Powerlifting Championships also included a Bench Press of 402, and a Deadlift of 622.

There were two (2) West Virginia State Powerlifting Records broken in the Open (Senior Division) at the 1995 West Virginia States : Phil Hile, winner of the 114lb. class, set a new West Virginia State Total Record with 1201lbs. (545 kilos). Dan Lass set a new Bench Press Record of 429lbs. (195 kilos) while competing in the 181lb. class.

Paul Sutphin won the Masters Division (40-49 Age Group) in the 198lb. class. For Paul Sutphin, the 1995 win at the USPF West Virginia State Powerlifting Championships marked the fourteenth (14th) West Virginia State Powerlifting Championship with the USPF. Other winners at the 1995 USPF West Virginia State Powerlifting Championships were Doug Currence (198 – Open / Senior, and Sub-Masters Division), and Don Hall (1st / 220 / Masters (Age 40-49).

In May of 1995, Ernie Nagy passed away at the age of 72. *Powerlifting USA* magazine printed a chronology of Ernie Nagy's accomplishments including many of the major Powerlifting championship wins and records earned by Ernie from 1973 until 1995. According to the 1987 USPF Master's (40+) Powerlifting Classification Standards, Ernie Nagy Totaled Elite while competing in the Masters Division several times.

Powerlifting USA magazine / Vol. 18, No. 12 / July, 1995

John Messinger : National Masters Champion

The 21ˢᵗ Annual (1996) USPF West Virginia State Powerlifting Championships were held on April 20ᵗʰ, 1996 at New Martinsville, West Virginia. Competing in the 198lb. class, Mike Hill was the winner. John Messinger won his sixth (6ᵗʰ) USPF West Virginia State Powerlifting title with a Total of 1681lbs. while competing in the 275lb. class. Included in the Total of 1681 on 4/20/96 by John Messinger was a 622 Squat, 424 Bench Press, and a 633 Deadlift. There were no records broken in the Open / Senior Division at the 1996 West Virginia State Powerlifting Championships.

The 1996 USPF National Masters Powerlifting Championships were held May 10ᵗʰ thru May 12ᵗʰ, 1996 at Dayton, Ohio. While competing in the 275lb. weight class in a field of four (4) competitors (Age 40-44 category), John Messinger won the National Masters Powerlifting Championship title with a Total of 1725lbs. Included in the John Messinger Total on 5/12/96 was a Squat of 661, Bench Press of 435, and a Deadlift of 628lbs.!

Don Hundley won another National Masters Powerlifting Championship title while competing in the 165lb. class / Age 60-64 category. Don's winning Total of 1207lbs. included a Master's World Deadlift Record of 540lbs. Vince White placed 4ᵗʰ while lifting in the 220lb. class / 50-54 Age Group with a Total 1173lbs.

"Setting the Records Straight" : 1997 - 1999

Winning his seventh (7ᵗʰ) USPF West Virginia State Powerlifting Championship title at the 1997 USPF West Virginia States, John Messinger Squatted with 705,   B e n c h Pressed 413, and Deadlifted 600 for a Total of 1719lbs. in the 275lb. class. Competing in the 242lb. class at the 1997 West Virginia State Powerlifting Championships, John Spadafore Squatted with 584, Bench Pressed 402, and Deadlifted 600 for a Total of 1586.

The 1997 ADFPA West Virginia State Powerlifting Championships were held on April 12ᵗʰ, 1997 at Bluefield, West Virginia. Among the winners were : Donald Robbins (165lb. class), Doug Currence (198lb. class), and Paul Sutphin (220lb. class). Donald Robbins set a new ADFPA West Virginia State Powerlifting Record in the Bench Press with a lift of 430lbs. while winning the 165lb. class *along with* a Total of 1300. Doug Currence set West Virginia State Powerlifting Records in the 198lb. class and Paul Sutphin, competing in the Masters (40-44 Age Group) set new West Virginia State Powerlifting Records in the 220lb. class.

On September 20th, 1997 Willie Williams Bench Pressed 720lbs. for a Personal Record and was ranked number one (1) among the TOP 100 Bench Pressers in the USA. Featured in the February, 2004 issue of *Powerlifting USA* magazine, the 720lb. Bench Press by Willie Williams on 9/20/97 ranked #94 in the "Men's All-Time World Bests – Stupendous Benches." The "All-Time World's Best Benches Ranking" was determined by Schwartz Formula and compiled by Herb Glossbrenner.

Powerlifting USA / Vol. 27 / No. 6 / February, 2004

A new wave of Powerlifting emerged across the USA in 1998. New technology regarding supportive gear and innovative training methods enabled lifters to maximize the effectiveness of the Monolift when Squatting. The new methods coupled with the Monolift moved Powerlifting in another direction along with many of the nation's Elite Powerlifters.

The 1998 Westside Invitational Powerlifting Championships were conducted in Columbus, Ohio on February 8th, 1998. The Meet Director was Louie Simmons. On 2/08/98, both Mike Hill and Paul Sutphin received honors for lifting at the event. Mike Hill Totaled Elite by USPF standards in the 220lb. weight class with a Total of 1825lbs. while competing at the 1998 Westside Invitational.

The 23rd Annual (1998) USPF West Virginia State Powerlifting Championships were conducted on March 28th, 1998 at Institute, West Virginia. There were no records broken in the Open / Senior Division at the 1998 USPF West Virginia State Powerlifting Championships. Don Hall won the Masters (50-59) in the 220lb. class with a 1344 Total.

John Messinger won his eighth (8th) USPF West Virginia State Championship title on 3/28/98. With a winning Total in the Master's Division (40-49) and a 1736 Total in the 275lb. class, John Squatted 710, Bench Pressed 424, and Deadlifted 600. Troy McNett won the Submasters (35-39) in the SHW (Superheavyweight) class with a Total of 1879.

The new Powerlifting *Division of Law Enforcement and Fire Fighters* was recognized at the 1998 USPF West Virginia State Powerlifting Championships on 3/28/98. Eligibility requirements were one (1) of two (2) conditions :

1) Resident of the state of West Virginia
2) Employed in the capacity of Law Enforcement in the state of West Virginia.

While competing in the 148lb. class, Danny Akers set four (4) West Virginia State Powerlifting Records in the Law Enforcement Division. On 3/28/98, Danny Akers Squatted 385, Bench Pressed 259, and Deadlifted 473 for a Total of 1117lbs.

From the USPF to the USAPL. On November 28th, 1998, a USAPL Powerlifting / IPF Qualifier Meet was held in New Martinsville, West Virginia. Doug Currence won first place in the 198lb. class while Warren McComas won the 242lb. class. Warren McComas Squatted 672, Bench Pressed 424, and Deadlifted 672 for a winning Total of 1769lbs.

In 1999, Willie Williams won the Arnold Classic in Columbus, Ohio. At the 1999 Arnold Classic, Willie Williams had the highest Bench Press of the day, 705lbs.! On February 26th, 2000 Willie returned to the Arnold Classic, Bench Pressed 705lbs. once again and placed 3rd. Willie Williams' 705 Bench Press on 2/26/2000 earned the #3 spot in the TOP 100 SHW's (SuperHeavyWeights) for Powerlifters competing from April, 1999 through March, 2000. *Powerlifting USA / June, 2000 Vol. 23, NO. 11*

The 24th Annual (1999) USPF West Virginia State Powerlifting Championships were held March 27th, 1999 at Charleston, West Virginia. Competing in the Women's Division, Lynne Homan and Sue Pack dominated their respective categories. While competing in the 275lb. class in the Open / Senior Division and the Junior (Age 20-23) category, Brian Siders set a new Bench Press Record of 534. Brian's Bench Press Record was the only West Virginia State Powerlifting Record broken in the Open / Senior Division at the 1999 West Virginia State Powerlifting Championships.

Brian Siders won the 275lb. class at the 1999 USPF West Virginia State Powerlifting Championships with a Total of 1818. Included in the Total of 1818 by Brian Siders on 3/27/99 was a West Virginia State Junior Division (Age 20-23) Squat Record of 650 and Deadlift Record of 633lbs.

Along with the 650lb. Squat and 633 Deadlift, Brian Siders broke an "18-year old Bench Press Record" with a lift of 534lbs. As verification, the Bench Press Record prior to 3/27/99 was 529lbs. in the 275lb. weight class set by Luke Iams on 3/29/81. The Bench Press of 534lbs. on 3/27/99 by Brian Siders was a new West Virginia State Powerlifting Record in the Open / Senior and Junior Division for the 275lb. class.

John Messinger won his ninth (9th) USPF West Virginia State Powerlifting Championship title at the 1999 USPF West Virginia State Powerlifting Championships. Messinger's Total in the new 308lb. class on 3/27/99 was 1802lbs. John Messinger's lifts on 3/27/99 included a 722 Squat, 451 Bench Press, and a 628 Deadlift. All of John's lifts at the 1999 West Virginia State Powerlifting Championships were new West Virginia State Powerlifting Records for both the Open and Masters Divisions in the new 308lb. weight class recognized by the USPF.

On August 29th, 1999 the APF West Virginia State Powerlifting Championships were conducted at Charleston, West Virginia. The 8/29/99 Powerlifting competition was officially sanctioned by the American Powerlifting Federation. The Meet Director was Mike Hill.

Mike Hill Squatted 775 and won the 220lb. class with an Elite Total of 1930lbs. The Squat and Total by Mike Hill on 8/29/99 were *All-Time West Virginia State Powerlifting Records* and *Official West Virginia State Powerlifting Records in the APF (American Powerlifting Federation)*. Paul Sutphin won the Masters Division (Age 45-49) in the 220lb. class at the 1999 APF West Virginia State Powerlifting Championships. Sutphin's Masters Total Record of 1730lbs. included a West Virginia State Record Squat of 755lbs. in the Masters Division.

Chapter Twenty-Five :
Best USA Powerlifters of the 20th Century

Featured in the February, 2000 issue of *Powerlifting USA* magazine were statistics compiled by Herb Glossbrenner of the *"BEST USA POWERLIFTERS OF THE CENTURY."* In the 148lb. class, <u>Paul Sutphin ranked 5th with a 1482 Total</u>. The *"Best USA Powerlifters of the Century"* Ranking was specific to the 1482 Total in the 148lb. class by Paul Sutphin during the 1970's, a Total of "Ten-Times Bodyweight," and a Junior National Championship Total Record.

Paul Sutphin achieved Powerlifter Elite Classification in three (3) weight classes (148lb. class, 165lb. class, and 181lb. class). For the record, a Total of 1750 and a Total of 1741 (both Totals in the 181lb. class) exceeded the minimum standard for Elite (1731) in the 198lb. class.

Paul Sutphin – 1/10/81
1981 YMCA Nationals - 628 Deadlift @ 181
Elite Total of 1653

Statistical rankings do not define the support system of a Powerlifter. Without Vince White, Don Hundley, Frank White, and Herb Fitzsimmons, the opportunity to achieve at the highest level in the sport of Powerlifting may not have been there for Paul Sutphin. The list, *"The Best Powerlifters of the 20th Century,"* has been amended to include : *Herb Fitzsimmons, Don Hundley, Frank White,* and *Vince White.*

Herb Fitzsimmons and Don Hundley were competing as Master lifters (Age 40 plus) in the Open Division of Powerlifting when both of them were in their late forties. However, with exception to the National Masters Powerlifting Championships, Herb Fitzsimmons and Don Hundley refused to compete in Powerlifting's Masters Division during the 1970's and the 1980's. Both Hundley and Fitzsimmons "applied for" and accepted the Masters Powerlifting Records, yet they refused to enter the Master's Division at local and state Powerlifting competitions. For Hundley and Fitzsimmons, there was only one (1) division for Powerlifting, the OPEN Division.

Herb Fitzsimmons
BEST USA POWERLIFTERS OF THE 20TH CENTURY

The 2004 newspaper article read, *"Survival of the Fittest."* The article was written about Herb Fitzsimmons. Before devoting all training time to the three (3) Powerlifts, Herb was active in Physique and Weightlifting competitions during the 1950's and early 1960's. Herb made a statement to me recently in the form of a question, "Did you know that I was the first "Mr. West Virginia?" Aside from the fact, Herb worked out regularly in 2013.

Charleston Gazette-Mail / February 22, 2004

Herb Fitzsimmons was one of the first athletes in West Virginia to begin competitive Weightlifting. The January – February 1961 issue of *Physical Power* magazine featured an article written about Weightlifting at the Charleston, West Virginia YMCA. Herb Fitzsimmons was pictured in the magazine with exerpts from the article which read, *"Powerful Herb, a football lineman, has been lifting for six years. He has lifts of 270 Clean & Press, 225 Snatch, and a 310 Clean & Jerk."*

Physical POWER / January-February, 1961, page 20-21

During the second half of the 1970's decade, Herb Fitzsimmons was proud of holding National and World Powerlifting Records in the Master's Division (45-49 Age Group). However, Herb Fitzsimmons was most satisfied with the fact that he always competed in the Open Division ...and WON...most of the time! As a result, Herb Fitzsimmons earned respect for his lifting from all lifters at every level.

The philosophy of Herb Fitzsimmons was to "compete often" and "lift heavy." Herb's accomplishments were American and World Master's Powerlifting Records set at nearly every Powerlifting competition he entered. Among the many records set and championships won, Herb was awarded the honor of Powerlifting's "Masters Hall of Fame" in October, 1979.

At the end of calendar year 1981, Herb Fitzsimmons quietly retired from major Powerlifting competition. Twenty-one (21) years later, Herb returned to the 2002 (27th Annual) USPF West Virginia State Powerlifting Championships and won the title in the Masters (70 -74 Age Group) of the 242lb. class, setting a new West Virginia State Bench Press Record of 303lbs. Afterward, Herb made a decision not to pursue additional Powerlifting titles in the 21st century.

Herb Fitzsimmons (1974)

Don Hundley
BEST USA POWERLIFTERS OF THE 20TH CENTURY

In the February, 1987 issue of *Powerlifting USA* magazine, Editor Mike Lambert wrote about the 165lb. class winners at the 1986 YMCA National Powerlifting Championships; *"While Don Hundley didn't come out on top, he was nonetheless remarkable. This man continues, year after year, to handle most respectable poundages, and he is well into the Master's category. Age doesn't effect his lifts or looks negatively."*

In commemoration of the *"Best Powerlifters of the 20th Century,"* Don Hundley was a major influence on my lifting and several others beginning in 1971 and continuing through the 1990's. From 1971 through 1996, Don Hundley made Powerlifting history on numerous occasions. Besides a mentor, Don Hundley has also proven to be a very effective Powerlifting Coach.

Don Hundley once told a news reporter, *"No one can follow my workouts."* The statement ended up in print in a newpaper with statewide circulation. As a matter of fact, *I have followed a version of Don Hundley's Deadlift workout since our introduction in 1972.* Over the years, I have often referenced the Deadlift routine of pulling three (3) times per week as, "The Don Hundley Approach."

As a pre-existing condition before Powerlifting, Don Hundley's shoulder problem restricted his capability to handle extremely heavy poundages in the Bench Press. Given the facts, Don Hundley Totaled Elite more than once and repetitively won major Powerlifting championships with an average Bench Press for a Middleweight. Don Hundley achieved the Elite Classification for Powerlifting on 3/31/84 for the 2nd time with a Total of 1537 in the 165lb. class which included a Bench Press of only 264lbs.

The 1978 photo of Don Hundley on the cover of *Powerlifting USA* magazine was picturesque of a Powerlifter. In support of Hundley's ability to Squat and Deadlift with World Record poundages in the 165lb. class, I told someone in a published interview during 2003, *"Don Hundley is one of the greatest Deadlifters the state (West Virginia) has ever seen."*

At the 1987 West Virginia State Powerlifting Championships, Don Hundley's Deadlift of 628lbs. (285 kilos) at 165lb. bodyweight said it all. On 4/11/87 Don Hundley broke his own existing Deadlift Record from the 1986 YMCA National Powerlifting Championships. Hundley's Deadlift of 622 ¾ lbs. (282.5 kilos) from 12/13/86, along with other Powerlifting Records in the Masters Division (165lb. class), remain as USPF American Master's Deadlift Records (Age 50-54).

Following the 1996 USPF National Masters Powerlifting Championships held at Dayton, Ohio Don Hundley retired from Powerlifting competition. Don told me during an interview on March 26th, 2011, "I never bombed out of a meet." After much research, Don's declaration has been confirmed as a true statement. Very few Powerlifters with tenure can lay claim to the fact that they NEVER bombed out of a lifting event.

Don Hundley – 1/10/81
Deadlift – 1981 YMCA Nationals

Frank White
BEST USA POWERLIFTERS OF THE 20ᵀᴴ CENTURY

Frank White (1974)

Since the 1950's, *Frank White competed in Olympic Weightlifting competitions and became the only West Virginia Weightlifter to hold an American Record in the Clean & Press!* Frank White set the Teenage American Record in the Clean & Press with a lift of 230lbs. in the 148lb. class while competing at the *Teenage National Weightlifting Championships* on June 17ᵗʰ, 1961 in York, Pennsylvania. Several years later, while competing in the 165lb. class, Frank White's official Florida State and Regional Weightlifting Record in the Clean & Press of 275lbs. will forever exist in the archives of Weightlifting.

From the Charleston YMCA as a young teenager to an American Record Holder in the Clean & Press at the age of nineteen (19), Frank White repeatedly broke Weightlifting Records in the Press, Snatch, Clean & Jerk, and Total for the three (3) lifts in Olympic Weightlifting. Following the elimination of the Clean & Press at the end of 1972 from official AAU Weightlifting competitions, Frank White continued to set records in the

Snatch, Clean & Jerk, and *Total of only two (2) lifts in the sport of Olympic Weightlifting.* The Weightlifting Records from the three (3) lift competitions set by Frank White in the 165lb. class remain standing.

Before Powerlifting was recognized by the AAU as an official sport, Frank White was among the first West Virginia lifters to compete and set records in Powerlifting (a.k.a. "Odd lifts"). During the 1950's, 1960's, and 1970's, Physique competitions were held in conjunction with official Weightlifting and Powerlifting competitions. During the 1960's and 1970's, Frank White competed regularly in Physique competition and won a number of titles.

The eligibility criteria for a combined "Six (6) Lift Ranking" extends to athletes who practiced the Olympic Lifts when they were officially three (3) in number. The "Three (3) in number" phrase is a reference to official Olympic Weightlifting competitions which included the Clean & Press, the Snatch, and the Clean & Jerk. In addition, the same athletes eligible for a "Six (6) lift Total" had a resume of Powerlifting in the same weight class.

Frank White is one of the few individuals eligible for a combined "Six (6) Lift Ranking" with the following lifts included : 1) Two-Hands Clean & Press 2) Two-Hands Snatch 3) Clean & Jerk 4) Squat (RAW) 5) Bench Press (RAW) 6) Deadlift (RAW)

The Total by Frank White on the three (3) Olympic lifts on 5/13/67 included a 270 Clean & Press, 210 Snatch, and a 295 Clean & Jerk for a Total of 775 in the 165lb. class. The Total by Frank on the three (3) Olympic lifts on 12/30/67 included a 265 Clean & Press, 205 Snatch, and a 300 Clean & Jerk for a Total of 770, also in the 165lb. class.

With a "RAW" Powerlifting Total of 1260 while competing in the 165lb. class on 11/17/73 combined with the Olympic Lifting Total of 775 on 5/13/67, Frank White owns a "Six (6) Lift Combined Total" of 2035lbs. While competing in the 165lb. weight class, the "RAW" Powerlifting Total of 1255 on 12/08/73 combined with the 770 Weightlifting Total from 12/30/67 equals a Total of 2025lbs.

Chapter Twenty-Six : 21ˢᵗ Century Powerlifting

At the 25ᵗʰ Annual (2000) USPF West Virginia State Powerlifting Championships, a special honor was extended to several of the veterans from West Virginia Powerlifting. On March 25ᵗʰ, 2000, Frank White, Vince White, Don Hundley, Herb Fitzsimmons, Luke Iams, Ernie Nagy, and Don Hall were honored with a Powerlifter's Hall of Fame presentation at the 2000 USPF West Virginia State Powerlifting Championships. Among others to receive recognition were John Bayliss, Bill Kyle, Jack Pack, and Kenny Woodell.

Powerlifting USA magazine Vol. 23, No. 12 / July, 2000

Jim Rubenstein won the Law Enforcement and Firefighters Division at the 2000 West Virginia State Powerlifting Championships with a Total of 1344 in the 220lb. class. Richard Fortson Totaled 1244 in the 181lb. class to capture the Master's Division (Age 45-49). Included in Richard Fortson's Total was a Squat of 440 and a Deadlift of 551. Don Hall was solid as usual while winning the Masters Division in the 220lb. class (Age 50-54) at the 2000 USPF West Virginia State Powerlifting Championships. Don Hall's performance on 3/25/2000 included a 512 Squat, 330 Bench Press, and a 501 Deadlift for a Total of 1344.

John Messinger won his tenth (10ᵗʰ) USPF West Virginia State Powerlifting Championship title on 3/25/2000 with a Total of 1774 while competing in the 275lb. weight class. *Along with* the Total of 1774 by John Messinger was a new West Virginia State Record in the Bench Press (Masters Division 45-49 Age Group) with a lift of 468lbs.

Since 1999, the 308lb. weight class was recognized by the USPF and included in many of the Powerlifting competitions. For the purpose of ranking, lifts made in the 308lb. class are included in the SuperHeavyWeight (SHW) class. While lifting in the 308lb. class on 3/25/2000, Brian Siders Totaled 1917lbs. Siders' 1917 Total on 3/25/2000 included a 683 Squat, 562 Bench Press, and a Deadlift of 672.

There were a number of new West Virginia State Powerlifting Records set on 3/25/2000 in the sub-divisions of Powerlifting. With exception to the 308lb. weight class, there were no West Virginia State Powerlifting Records broken in the Open (Senior) Division at the 2000 USPF West Virginia State Powerlifting Championships.

A major Powerlifting event in West Virginia began in 1999 and continued into the 21ˢᵗ century. Nick Busick teamed up with ESPN for one of Powerlifting's most prestigious events, the Mountaineer Cup. On June 24ᵗʰ and 25ᵗʰ, 2000 Nick Busick was Meet Director of the 2000 USPF Senior National Powerlifting Championships in Chester,

West Virginia in addition to the *"Mountianeer Cup II Powerlifting Tournament."* The winner of the 2000 Mountianeer Cup was Ed Coan with a 2403 Total and $10,000!

Powerlifting USA / Vol. 24, NO. 2

Allen Baria won the 2000 Senior National Powerlifting Championship title in the 242lb. class with an Elite Total of 1978lbs. Allen's lifts were 722 Squat, 600 Bench Press, and a 655 Deadlift. Allen Baria's Bench Press of 600lbs. on 6/24/2000 was a new West Virginia State Powerlifting Record in the 242lb. class, breaking the previous mark of 512 set on March 23rd, 1986 by Randy Scott.

While competing in the <u>Mountianeer Cup II</u> on June 25th, 2000 Brian Siders lifted at a bodyweight of 303lbs. and Totaled 2038 as a Superheavyweight. Brian Squatted 722, Bench Pressed a new West Virginia State Record in the SHW (SuperHeavyWeight) class with a lift of 622lbs., and Deadlifted 694lbs.

On September 9th, 2000 at the <u>APF (American Powerlifting Federation) West Virginia State Powerlifting Championship</u>, a West Virginia Powerlifter's Hall of Fame was recognized. Nominations and selections were confirmed on 9/09/2000. Three (3) months later, two (2) members were honored on December 16th, 2000 for achieving Powerlifting's APF Elite Classification in one (1) or more weight classes : Mike Hill (220lb. class) and Paul Sutphin (181lb. class) were presented with awards. Recognition was also awarded to Donald Robbins (West Virginia State Bench Press Champion 1999 & 2000) for a Bench Press of 555lbs. ("Triple-Bodyweight") in the 181lb. weight class.

Powerlifting USA magazine / Vol. 24, Numbers. 6 & 10 /JAN/2001, MAY/2001

On October 7th, 2000 the United States Powerlifting Federation (USPF) conducted a National Powerlifting Championship for Law Enforcement and Firefighters. The <u>2000 USPF Law/Fire Nationals</u> were conducted on October 7th, 2000 in Nutter Fort, West Virginia. Jim Rubenstein won first place in the 220lb. class with a Total of 1388. Jim Rubenstein's lifts on 10/07/2000 included a Squat of 529, Bench Press of 336, and a Deadlift of 523. The official meet results of the 2000 Law/Fire Powerlifting Nationals were published in the March, 2001 issue of *Powerlifting USA* magazine along with a photograph of the winners.

2001-2005

The <u>2001 APF Mountianeer Barbell Powerlifting Championships</u> were held in South Charleston on February 24th, 2001 with over fifty (50) lifters participating. The Meet Director was Mike Hill. Top performances included a 1900 Total by Chris Young while winning the 220lb. weight class. While winning the Masters Division of the 220lb. class (45-49 Age Group), Paul Sutphin Totaled 1600 which included a 710 Squat.

The 26th Annual (2001) USPF West Virginia State Powerlifting Championships were held March 25th, 2001 at Institute, West Virginia. Both Don Hall and Jim Rubenstein won their age group categories in the Masters Division of the 220lb. class. There were no West Virginia State Powerlifting Records broken in the Open (Senior) Division at the 2001 USPF West Virginia Powerlifting Championships.

Allen Smith won the Sub-Masters Division (Age 35-39) category in the 165lb. class at the 2001 USPF West Virginia State Powerlifting Championships with a 1240 Total. Included in Allen Smith's 1240 Total was a Squat of 501, Bench Press of 330, and a Deadlift of 407.

As a representative of Women's Powerlifting at the 2001 USPF West Virginia State Powerlifting Championships, Sue Pack won the Women's Division while competing in the Women's Masters category with a Total of 733. Carmel Hughes and Sue Pack were inducted into the *USPF Powerlifting Hall of Fame* at the 2001 West Virginia State Powerlifting Championships. A photo of both lifters accepting their awards from Vince White appeared in the JUN/2001 issue of *Powerlifting USA* magazine.

Powerlifting USA magazine / Vol. 24, / NO. 11 / June, 2001, (Pg.65)

On May 19, 2001 Chris Young was recognized as a member of the *APF West Virginia Powerlifting Hall of Fame* for achieving APF Elite Powerlifter Classification at the APF Mountianeer Barbell Powerlifting Championships on 2/24/2001.

Powerlifting USA magazine / Vol. 25 / NO. 10 / May, 2002

For the "Single-Lift Specialists," a trip to Charlottesville, Virginia on June 16th, 2001 and a Championship win at the *USAPL Squat Nationals* made a weekend vacation a memorable affair. Competing in the Masters Division / 220lb. Class (45-49 Age Group), Paul Sutphin won the 2001 National Squat Championships and set a National "Single-lift" Squat Record of 660lbs., which stands today.

The 27th Annual (2002) West Virginia State Powerlifting Championships were held March 23rd, 2002 at Institute, West Virginia. According to the official results, Brian Siders dominated a number of categories. Although Brian scored lifts in the 308lb. class, all of Brian's lifts included in the Elite Total of 2199 are ranked in the SHW (SuperHeavyWeight) class.

On 3/23/2002, Brian Siders Totaled Elite for a West Virginia State Record of 2199lbs. Brian's Squat of 766 and Bench Press of 666 ¾ were new West Virginia State Collegiate Powerlifting Records. Brian's Bench Press of 666 ¾ lbs. (302.5 kilos) was also a new West Virginia State Record in the Open (Senior) Division.

Brian Siders earned his first trip to the <u>IPF World Powerlifting Championships</u> on November 17th, 2002 in Trencin, Slovakia. Brian Totaled Elite with 2171 in the Superheavyweights and finished seventh (7th) in a field of thirteen (13) competitors. Included in Brian Sider's 2171 Elite Total at the 2002 IPF World Powerlifting Championships was a Squat of 804, Bench Press of 606, and a Deadlift of 760lbs.

Troy McNett, a Superheavyweight Powerlifter, passed away during August, 2002. Troy Totaled 1879 on 4/11/87 as a SHW. On 12/17/94 Troy McNett Totaled 1900 which included a 700 Deadlift. The OCT/2002 issue of *Powerlifting USA* was dedicated to Troy McNett.

P/L USA / Vol. 26, / NO. 3 / October, 2002

In February, 2003 the late Richard Fortson received the honor from the APF of West Virginia for induction into the *APF West Virginia Powerlifting Hall of Fame*. The MAY/2003 issue of *Powerlifting USA* was dedicated to Richard Fortson.

P/L USA / Vol. 26, / NO. 10 / May, 2003

The <u>28th Annual (2003) USPF West Virginia State Powerlifting Championships</u> were held March 17th, 2003 at Institute, West Virginia. Don Hall won the Masters Division in the 220lb. class (Age 55-59) with a 1306 Total. Jim Rubenstein won the 242lb. class with a 1366 Total. Mike Highfield won the Masters (Age 55-59) in the 275lb. class with a 1377 Total. There were no West Virginia State Powerlifting Records broken in the Open / Senior Division at the 2003 USPF West Virginia State Powerlifting Championships.

On June 23rd, 2003 Vince White placed 2nd at the <u>USPF National Master's Powerlifting Championships</u> held at Chester, West Virginia. While competing in the 220lb. class (Age 60-64), Vince White's Total included a 336 Bench Press. Winning first place on 6/23/2003 in the 242lb. class (50-54 Age Group), Jim Rubenstein Totaled 1388 with lifts of 501 Squat, 325 Bench Press, and a 562 Deadlift.

The <u>29th Annual (2004) West Virginia State Powerlifting Championships</u> were held on March 27, 2004 at South Charleston, West Virginia. John Messinger set four (4) new West Virginia State Powerlifting Records in the Masters Division (Age 50-54) while competing in the 275lb. class. A Squat of 600 ¾, Bench Press of 402, and Deadlift of 600 ¾ comprised a West Virginia State Masters Total Record of 1603lbs. in the 275lb. class.

Courtney Stanley won the Masters Division (Age 55-59) category in the 242lb. class at the 2004 West Virginia State Powerlifting Championships with lifts of 451 Squat, 363 Bench Press, and a 562 Deadlift for a Total of 1377. There were no West Virginia State Powerlifting Records broken in the Open / Senior Division at the 2004 USPF West Virginia State Powerlifting Championships.

Luke Iams passed away in April of 2004. Luke Iams was the first West Virginia Powerlifter to Squat with over 800lbs. and also the first West Virginia lifter to Bench

Press 600lbs. *Along with* the 600lb. Bench Press of Luke Iams was a Squat of 875 and an Elite Total of 2080. In summary, Luke Iams became the first West Virginian to officially Total over 2000lbs. The AUG/2004 issue of *Powerlifting USA* ran the article titled, "Luke Iams" written by Paul Sutphin.   *P/L USA / Vol. 27/ No. 11 / August, 2004*

The 30th Annual (2005) USPF West Virginia State Powerlifting Championships were held on March 19th, 2005 at South Charleston, West Virginia. Jim Rubenstein won the Masters Division (Age 50-54) in the 220lb. class and set new West Virginia State Powerlifting Records in the category of *Law Enforcement and Fire Fighters.*

There were no West Virginia State Powerlifting Records broken in the Senior (Open) Division at the 2005 USPF West Virginia State Powerlifting Championships. While competing in the Masters Division at the 2005 USPF West Virginia State Powerlifting Championships, Courtney Stanley won the 242lb. class (Age 55-59) with a Total of 1377. The Total of 1377 on 3/19/2005 by Courtney Stanley included a Squat of 485, Bench Press of 341, and a Deadlift of 551.

In June of 2005, Powerlifting suffered another loss with the passing of Roger Estep. Featured in the August/2005 issue of *Powerlifting USA* magazine, the article written by Paul Sutphin highlighted a few of Roger's achievements as a team member of *Luke's Gym* during 1977 and 1978.   *Powerlifting USA / Aug, 2005 / Vol. 28 / No. 11 / Pg. 59.*

While highlighting the achievements of Roger Estep, a two-part series appeared in the pages of Powerlifting USA magazine. Featured in the July/2005 issue of *Powerlifting USA* magazine, the author wrote, "In a small meet in West Virginia, (Roger) "totaled an unheard of poundage of 1945." The Total of 1945 by Roger Estep occurred on 12/10/78 at the *YMCA National Powerlifting Championships* in Ohio. The photo of Estep's World Record Squat was the actual photo from the YMCA Nationals rather than the "Parkersburg YMCA" as indicated in the printed text which appeared below the photo in the July/2005 issue of *Powerlifting USA* magazine.

Powerlifting USA / July, 2005 / Vol. 28 / No. 10, pg. 45.

Brian Siders
IPF World Powerlifting Champion!
"Back-to-Back" 2003–2004

In 2003, Brian Siders won the <u>USAPL Senior National Powerlifting Championships</u> as a SuperHeavyWeight at the age of twenty-four (24). On July 20th, 2003 at Rapid City, South Dakota, Brian Siders weighed 328.26lbs. and made the following lifts : 909 Squat, 672 Bench Press, and a Deadlift of 804 for a winning Total of 2386. At the 2003 USAPL Senior Nationals, Brian won the Outstanding Lifter Award among the Heavyweight Powerlifters. For the 2nd consecutive year, Brian was ready for a serious run at the IPF World Powerlifting Championship title in the Superheavyweight (SHW / 125+ kilo) class.

The <u>2003 IPF (International Powerlifting Federation) Men's World Powerlifting Championships</u> were held November 4th thru November 9th, 2003 at Vejle, Denmark. While representing Team USA and competing as a Superheavyweight, Brian Squatted with 892lbs. (405 kilos), Bench Pressed 699 ¾ lbs. (317.5 kilos), and Deadlifted 793lbs. (360 kilos) for a winning Total of 2386lbs. (1082.5 kilos).

Brian Siders again won the *USAPL Senior National Powerlifting Championships* in 2004. On November 14th, 2004 at the <u>IPF Men's World Powerlifting Championships</u> held in Cape Town, South Africa, Brian successfully defended his IPF World Championship title in the Superheavyweight class. While winning "Back-to-Back" the *IPF World Powerlifting Championship*, Brian Siders Squatted 964, Bench Pressed 744, and Deadlifted 821, for a Total of 2529lbs!

On November 14th, 2004 Brian Siders broke the "twenty-three (23) year-old" World Record Total set by Bill Kazmaier. Sider's World Record Total was 1147.5 kilos (2529lbs.)! In an interview by Dr. Larry Miller published in the December, 2004 issue of *Powerlifting USA* magazine, Brian was quoted as saying, "When I was 17 years old, a friend introduced me to a gym where I still train today. There I met John Messinger and Vince White. They showed me just about everything I know in the sport."

Powerlifting USA / Vol. 28, No. 3 / pg. 10 / December, 2004

"Setting the Records Straight" : Part VII
2006-2009

The 31st Annual (2006) USPF West Virginia State Powerlifting Championships were held March 25th, 2006 at South Charleston, West Virginia. There were no West Virginia State Powerlifting Records set in the Open / Senior Division at the 2006 West Virginia States.

Among the top performances from 3/25/2006 included the lifting of Courtney Stanley in the Masters Division of the 242lb. class (60-64 Age Group). Courtney Stanley Totaled 1548 on 3/25/2006 which included a 578 Squat, 341 Bench Press, and a Deadlift of 628. Jim Rubenstein won the Masters Division and the Law Enforcement and Firefighters Division while competing in the 220lb. class with a 1273 Total.

The 32nd Annual (2007) USPF West Virginia State Powerlifting Championships were held on March 31st, 2007 at South Charleston, West Virginia. Matt McCase won the 220lb. class with a 1696 Total which included a 688 Deadlift. Josh Stottlemire won the Junior / Novice Division in the 220lb. class with a Total of 1592 which included a Bench Press of 462lbs. There were no West Virginia State Powerlifting Records broken in the Open / Senior Division at the 2007 USPF West Virginia State Powerlifting Championships.

The 33rd Annual (2008) USPF West Virginia State Powerlifting Championships were held on March 22nd, 2008 at South Charleston, West Virginia. Allen Baria won the 275lb. class and set a new West Virginia State Record in the Bench Press with a lift of 683lbs. While winning the 275lb. weight class in the Open / Senior Division, Allen Baria Totaled 1675 *along with* the new West Virginia State Bench Press Record of 683lbs. The new West Virginia State Powerlifting / Bench Press Record by Allen Baria on 3/22/2008 replaced the mark of 534lbs. set by Brian Siders at the *1999 USPF West Virginia State Powerlifting Championships.*

While competing in the Teenage Division at the *2008 USPF West Virginia State Powerlifting Championships,* Blake Brooks won the 308lb. class with a Total of 1316. Competing in the Teenage Division (16-17 Age Group), all of Brook's lifts were new West Virginia State Teenage Powerlifting Records *along with* a Bench Press of 402lbs.

Since 1995, Phillip Battle had opened a new "Virginia Connection" to West Virginia Powerlifting. On March 9th, 2008 Phillip Battle of Richmond, Virginia passed away unexpectedly. Phillip Battle won numerous Powerlifting Championship titles while competing in the Teenage, Collegiate, Junior, Amateur, and Open Divisions.

Phillip Battle's Powerlifting accomplishments identified with at least four (4) Powerlifting organizations. Phillip competed in the ADFPA (USAPL), APF, AAU, and the IPA. Phillip won the *2003 IPA World Powerlifting Championships* in the Amateur Division of the 308lb. class with a Total of 1820. Included in the 1820 Total by Phillip Battle on 8/10/2003 was a Squat of 770, Bench Press of 430, and Deadlift of 620. Phillip Battle also won the Virginia State Powerlifting Championship several times.

Powerlifting USA / Vol. 31, NO. 8. / June, 2008

Marty Bavetz earned *Powerlifter Elite Classification* in the 165lb. class with a Total of 1547 on 4/19/08. While competing at the USPF Power Sports & Fitness Expo Powerlifting Meet, Marty's 1547 Elite Total exceeded the minimum standard for Powerlifting's Elite Classification. Chris Young earned *Powerlifter Elite Classification* in the 275lb. class with a Total of 1951 on 11/01/08 at the USPF Regional Powerlifting Championships held in Parkersburg, West Virginia.

The 34th Annual (2009) USPF West Virginia State Powerlifting Championships were held on March 28th, 2009 at South Charleston, West Virginia. The lifting of Marty Bavetz at the 2009 USPF West Virginia State Powerlifting Championships was among the highlights. Competing in the 181lb. class, Marty Bavetz Totaled 1592 for the win. Included in the 1592 Total on 3/28/2009 by Marty was a Squat of 617, Bench Press of 418, and a Deadlift of 556lbs. There were no West Virginia State Powerlifting Records broken at the 2009 USPF West Virginia State Powerlifting Championships.

"Setting the Records Straight" : Part VIII

The ERA III West Virginia Powerlifter Rankings represent top performances from January 1st, 1985 until September 30th, 2013. The *ERA III Powerlifter Rankings* include separate listings for the Single-Ply and Multi-Ply categories. Since 1985, Powerlifting Totals have included the use of a Bench Press shirt. By the end of calendar year 1985, most Powerlifting competitions provided to the lifter the option of a 24-Hour Weigh-In while all Powerlifting meets were governed by the Round System.

During the Era III of Powerlifting in West Virginia, three (3) female athletes achieved Women's *Powerlifter Elite Classification* : Mary Ryan Jeffrey, Debbie Lass, and Lori Jeffrey. In the 114lb. class, Phil Hile made three (3) Elite Totals : A Total of 1151 on 3/14/92 followed by a Total of 1179 on 4/02/94. On 4/08/95, Phil Hile totaled Elite with 1201, a West Virginia State Powerlifting Record.

Rusty Greene joined the ranks of the Elite with a 1405 Total in the 148lb. class on 2/25/95. Allen Smith broke the Squat Record in the 148lb. class with a lift of 551lbs. (250 kilos) on 3/14/92. Allen Smith also won seven (7) consecutive West Virginia State Powerlifting Championships with the USPF from 1986 thru 1992.

Since 3/31/84, the 666 ¾ Deadlift (302.5 kilos) by <u>Don Hundley</u> in the 165lb. class has survived nearly thirty (30) years without a threat to be replaced in the Powerlifting Record books. Beginning in 1985, Don Hundley continued to set new American and World Powerlifting Records in the Masters Division. The 611 ¾ Squat (277.5 kilos) in the 165lb. class by Don Hundley on 4/13/85 remains the number one (1) lift for the *All-Time West Virginia Powerlifter Rankings.*

Along with seventeen (17) Elite Totals from ERA II in three / four weight classes (148, 165, 181, 198-?), <u>Paul Sutphin</u> added four (4) Elite performances in the 181lb. class to the list during the ERA III of Powerlifting. According to the Era II and ERA III Powerlifter Rankings, the Totals of 1750 and 1741 by Sutphin in the 181lb. class rank number one (1) and number two (2) in the *All-Time West Virginia Powerlifter Rankings* for the Single-Ply/Traditional category.

On November 9th, 1985 at the *Mountianeer Open Powerlifting Championships,* <u>Paul Sutphin</u> Totaled Elite with a 1697 Total in the 181lb. class. Sutphin followed with another Elite performance in the 181lb. class on 3/22/86 with a Total of 1741. The Elite Totals in the 181lb. class of 1741, 1697, 1686 (12/06/86), and 1675 (6/28/86) remain at the top of the *ERA III West Virginia Powerlifter Rankings / Single-Ply.* The Deadlift Record of 677 ¾ lbs. (307.5 kilos) in the 181lb. class on 3/22/86 at a bodyweight of 179 ½ lives on.

<u>Marty Bavetz</u> Totaled 1547 for *Elite Powerlifter Classification* in the 165lb. class on 4/19/08 at the *USPF Expo Powerlifting* held in Mineral Wells, West Virginia. Marty Squatted with 600 ¾, Bench Pressed 385, and Deadlifted 562 for an Elite Total of 1547 and the number one (1) spot in the *ERA III West Virginia Single-Ply Powerlifter Rankings.* Approximately eleven (11) months later, <u>Marty Bavetz</u> Totaled 1592 while competing in the 181lb. class at the *2009 USPF West Virginia State Powerlifting Championships.* Marty Bavetz's Total of 1592 in the 181lb. class on 3/28/09 included a 617 Squat and a 418 Bench Press.

<u>Doug Currence</u> Totaled Elite with 1653 in the 181lb. class at the *1985 West Virginia State Powerlifting Championships.* Doug set a new Deadlift Record of 672lbs. (305 kilos) on 4/13/85 and held it for eleven (11) months. <u>Dan Lass</u> owns the Bench Press Record among the *ERA III West Virginia Single-Ply Powerlifter Rankings* with a lift of 429lbs. (195 kilos) set at the *1995 West Virginia State Powerlifting Championships. Along with* the 429 Bench Press in the 181lb. class on 4/08/95, Dan Lass Totaled 1554.

<u>Doug Currence</u> Totaled Elite with 1731 at the *1986 West Virginia State Powerlifting Championships* and Deadlifted 688 ¾ lbs. (312.5 kilos) for a new West Virginia State Record in the 198lb. class. On 8/23/08, <u>Josh Stottlemire</u> Totaled 1647 in the 198lb. class which included a Bench Press of 490 ½ lbs. (222.5 kilos).

Steve Uhas Totaled 1686 at 220 on 4/11/87. Steve Squatted a new West Virginia State Record of 733lbs. (332.5 kilos) at the *1987 West Virginia State Powerlifting Championships* and Deadlifted 600 to go *along with* the 1686 Total. Marshall Moore Totaled 1829 in the 220's with three (3) West Virginia State Collegiate Powerlifting Records on 5/11/86. Marshall Moore's Squat of 705, Deadlift of 716, and Total of 1829 were new West Virginia Collegiate Powerlifting Records in the 220lb. class.

Josh Stottlemire Totaled 1504 in the 220lb. class on 4/03/2010 at the *USPF Ohio Valley Open Powerlifting Championships* at New Martinsville, West Virginia. Included in Josh's 1504 Total was an American Record Bench Press of 622 ¾ lbs. (282.5 kilos). Less than one (1) year later, Josh Bench Pressed a West Virginia State Record of 628lbs. at the *2011 West Virginia State Powerlifting Championships* in the 220lb. class.

Bret Russell continued with Elite Totals in the 242lb. class during ERA III. While competing in the 242lb. class at the *West Virginia State Powerlifting Championships* on 3/23/86, Bret Totaled 2039 for an Elite Total. Less than one (1) month later, Bret Russell broke the 2100lb. barrier in the 242lb. class with another Elite Total mark of 2105. At the *APF Junior National Powerlifting Championships* on 5/11/86, Bret Totaled Elite once again with 2088 while competing in the 242lb. class. The year 1986 ended for Bret at the *YMCA Nationals* on 12/13/86 with another Elite Total of 2110 while competing in the 242lb. class.

Nick Busick Totaled 1818 at the *1985 West Virginia State Powerlifting Championships* and set a new Bench Press Record in the 242lb. class with a lift of 507lbs. Less than one (1) year later, Randy Scott Totaled 1956 for an Elite Total in the 242lb. class at the *1986 West Virginia State Powerlifting Championships. Along with* the 1956 Elite Total by Randy Scott on 3/23/86 was a new West Virginia State Record in the Bench Press at 512lbs.

Allen Baria won the *2000 USPF West Virginia State Powerlifting Championships* in the 242lb. class with a Total of 1873. Allen broke the existing Bench Press Record of Randy Scott with a lift of 584 on 3/25/2000. Three (3) months later, Allen made an Elite Total of 1978 in the 242lb. class at the *Mountianeer Cup / USPF Senior National Powerlifting Championships* held on 6/24/2000. Included in the 1978 Total by Allen Baria on 6/24/2000 was a new West Virginia State Record Bench Press of 600lbs.

Chris Asbury won the 2011 *USAPL West Virginia Powerlifting Championships* in the 242lb. class with a Total of 1686. Included in the 1686 Total by Chris Asbury on 8/06/2011 was a new USAPL American Masters Bench Press Record of 650lbs. (295 kilos) and an *All-Time West Virginia State Bench Press Record* in the 242lb. class.

Bret Russell Totaled Elite with 2040 on 3/31/85 at Zanesville, Ohio for an Elite Total in the 242lb. class. Two (2) weeks later, Bret again Totaled Elite with a Total of 2006 at the *West Virginia State Powerlifting Championships* on 4/14/85. On 6/02/85 at the *1985*

National (Junior) Powerlifting Championships, Bret Russell Totaled 2017 for another Elite Total. Over five (5) years later, while competing in the 275lb. class, Bret Totaled Elite with 2028 at the *1990 Mountianeer Open Powerlifting Championships* on 11/17/90.

Randy Scott competed on 6/02/85 at the *1985 Junior Nationals* in the 275lb. class and Totaled Elite with a Total of 1946. At the *1987 Steel Valley Open Powerlifting Championships* at Weirton, West Virginia Randy Totaled Elite in the 275lb. class with 1973. The 1973 Total by Randy Scott on 2/08/87 was an unofficial West Virginia State Total Record.

Approximately thirteen (13) months later on 3/06/88, Randy Scott competed at the *1988 West Virginia State Powerlifting Championships* and Totaled Elite once again with 1967 in the 275lb. class. The 1967 Total by Randy Scott on 3/06/88 was an official West Virginia State Total Record. Included in the 1967 Elite Total by Randy Scott was a West Virginia State Squat Record of 749lbs. in the 275lb. class.

Chris Young earned *Powerlifter Elite Classification* for the USPF on 11/01/2008 at the *USPF Regional Powerlifting Championships* held at Parkersburg, West Virginia. Chris Young's Elite Total of 1951 included a Bench Press of 584lbs. The Elite Total of 1951 *along with* the 584 Bench Press are *All-Time West Virginia Powerlifting Records* in the 275lb. class for the Masters Division (Age 40-49).

Allen Baria made an Elite Total of 2182 in the 275lb. class on 4/03/2010 at the *Ohio Valley Powerlifting Championships* at New Martinsville, West Virginia. Allen's 2182 Elite Total included a USPF American Record Bench Press of 744lbs. in the 275lb. class. Less than one (1) year later at the *USPF West Virginia State Powerlifting Championships*, Allen Baria Totaled Elite once again in the 275lb. class with a West Virginia State Record Total of 2326! *Along with* the Elite Total of 2326 on 3/26/2011 was a West Virginia State Record Squat of 832 and another *USPF American Record Bench Press* in the 275lb. class with a weight of 749lbs.!

John Messinger : Powerlifting Records

The Powerlifting Records of John Messinger began during ERA I in 1975. On 4/12/1975 at Johnson City, Tennessee John Deadlifted 555 for a new West Virginia State Powerlifting Record in the 220lb. class with a Total of 1390. On 11/01/75, John Messinger Squatted a new West Virginia State Record of 525 in the 220lb. class and Totaled 1420. For the year 1975, John owns the two (2) highest Totals in the 220lb. class and finished number one in the 1975 West Virginia Powerlifter Rankings. The 555lb. Deadlift remains in the archives as a permanently retired mark among the West Virginia State "RAW" Powerlifting Records.

John returned to serious Powerlifting competition in 1984 and finished among the top three (3) Powerlifters in the 1984 West Virginia Powerlifter Rankings for the 242lb. class with Totals of 1669, 1664, and 1658. John also competed in the 275lb. class in 1984 and finished with more Totals among the West Virginia Powerlifter Rankings. John Messinger has several Totals included in the ERA III West Virginia "Single-Ply" Powerlifter Rankings for the 220, 242, 275, and SHW classes.

In 1985, John Messinger placed 2nd at the <u>ADFPA Senior National Powerlifting Championships</u> on 7/21/85 with a Total of 1747 and became one of the first West Virginia Powerlifters to own Powerlifting Records in the organization of the ADFPA/USA Powerlifting.

In 1990, John Messinger began a run of West Virginia State Powerlifting Championship titles with the USPF. John won eleven (11) West Virginia State Powerlifting Championship titles from 1990 through 2004 with the USPF before announcing his retirement from official Powerlifting competition. Since 1991, John has set over fifty (50) West Virginia State Powerlifting Records in the Sub-Masters (Age 35-39) and Masters Divisions (40-44, 45-49, and 50-54 Age Groups) for the following weight classes : 220, 242, 275, 308, and SHW (SuperHeavyWeight).

At the *1996 USPF Masters National Powerlifting Championships* on 5/12/96 in Dayton, Ohio John Messinger won the National Master's Powerlifting Championship title in the 275lb. class (40-44 Age Group) with a 1725 Total.

In addition to Powerlifting Championship wins and Powerlifting Records, John Messinger has served as the USPF West Virginia State Powerlifting Chairman since March, 1994 and the Meet Director of the USPF West Virginia State Powerlifting Championships for the following years : 1992, 1995, 1997, 1998, 1999, 2000, 2001, 2002, 2003, 2004, 2005, 2006, 2007, 2008, 2009, 2010, 2011, 2012, and 2013.

Brian Siders : Powerlifting Records

In the Superheavyweight class (SHW), <u>Brian Siders</u> owns most of the Powerlifting Records during ERA III. An extensive review of the accomplishments by Brian Siders is not difficult for the following reason : Many of the Powerlifting Records owned by Brian Siders are *USAPL American Powerlifting Records* and / or *IPF World Powerlifting Records.*

On 3/28/98, Brian Siders set all new West Virginia State Teenage Powerlifting Records in the 275lb. class in the Squat, Bench Press, and Deadlift included in a Total of 1828. Brian set all new West Virginia Records while competing in the Junior Division (Age 20-23) at the *1999 USPF West Virginia State Powerlifting Championships*. Siders' Total of 1818 on 3/27/99 included a new West Virginia State Bench Press Record of 534lbs. in the 275lb. class.

On 6/25/2000, Brian Siders broke the 2000 Total barrier with a Total of 2038. Included in the 2038 Total was a new West Virginia State Record in the Bench Press of 622lbs. Moving on in 2001, Brian earned *Powerlifter Elite Classification* with a Total of 2150. Brian's Total of 2150 on 3/10/01 at the *2001 USAPL Virginia Open Powerlifting Championships* included an unofficial West Virginia State Bench Press Record in the Superheavyweight class of 640lbs.

In 2002, Brian Siders began breaking records at the *2002 USPF West Virginia State Powerlifting Championships*. On 3/23/2002, Brian set three (3) new West Virginia State Collegiate Powerlifting Records in the Superheavyweight class in the Squat, Bench Press, and Total. *Along with* the 2199 Total by Siders on 3/23/2002 was a new West Virginia State Bench Press Record of 667. Brian's Squat of 766 at the 2002 West Virginia States was a new West Virginia Collegiate Powerlifting Record.

On 6/22/2002 at the *Mountianeer Cup IV*, Brian Siders broke the 2200lb. Total barrier, going 848 Squat, 650 Bench Press, and a new West Virginia State Record Deadlift of 788 for a Total of 2286! Less than one (1) month later, Brian won the *2002 USAPL Senior National Powerlifting Championships*.

Brian Siders continued in 2003 with a victory at the *2003 USAPL Senior National Powerlifting Championships* which included a Squat of 909, Bench Press of 672, and a Deadlift of 804, breaking the 2300 Total Barrier with a mark of 2386 on 7/20/03. Later in 2003, Brian Siders won the first of "back-to-back" IPF World Powerlifting Championship titles on 11/09/03 with a Total of 2386.

During 2004, Brian Siders Totaled 2452 (USAPL Senior Nationals), 2545 (Mountianeer Cup VI), and 2529 (IPF World Powerlifting Championships). In 2005, Brian continued with more championship victories and Elite Totals, winning the *2005 USAPL Senior Nationals* with a Total of 2491 on 5/08/05. On 5/06/06, Brian Totaled 2200 at a *"Raw" Powerlifting Championship*.

At the conclusion of the 2007 calendar year, Brian Siders set a new IPF World Record Total on 12/02/2007 in Scranton, Pennsylvania at the *USAPL American Open Powerlifting Championships* with a Total of 2601. Brian's Total of 2601 included a 959 Squat, 777 Bench Press, and an 865 Deadlift. In 2010, Brian's best Total of 2650 included a Squat of 1019, Bench Press of 799, and a Deadlift of 832.

The multiple performances of Brian Siders in the SuperHeavyWeight (SHW) class from 2001 thru 2010 include nineteen (19) Elite Totals. From 6/24/2001 until 5/15/2010, Brian's Totals range from 2127 to a PR of 2650!

Era III (1/01/1985 – 7/31/2013)

Key to Era III West Virginia Powerlifter Rankings :

1) * - West Virginia State Powerlifting Record.
2) c – West Virginia State Collegiate Powerlifting Record
3) m – West Virginia State Masters Powerlifting Record
4) e – ELITE Powerlifting Total
5) am – American Masters Powerlifting Record
6) j – West Virginia Junior (Age 20-23) Powerlifting Record
7) nm – National Masters Powerlifting Record
8) wm – World Masters Powerlifting Record
9) R – Region VI Powerlifting Record
10) RC – Region VI Powerlifting Champion
11) rw – "RAW" Powerlifting Record / ERA III
12) t – West Virginia State Teenage Powerlifting Record
13) ta – Teenage American Powerlifting Record
14) u – Unofficial West Virginia State Powerlifting Record
15) AR – USPF American Powerlifting Record
16) ar – American Powerlifting Record
17) WC – World Champion!
18) wr – World Powerlifting Record

Era III : WV Powerlifters / Single-Ply
WV Powerlifters competing from January 1st, 1985 thru July 31st, 2013
TOP RANKINGS Determined by Total
Single-Ply, "The Bench Press Shirt," the 24 hour weigh-ins, and the Round System

114 / Name	Squat	Bench Press	Deadlift	Total	Date
Phil Hile	451	286	462	1201 e	4/08/95
Phil Hile	429	275	473	1179 e	4/02/94
Phil Hile	424	253	473*	1151 e	3/14/92
Joe Vukovich	286	220 c	369c	876 c	3/14/92
Mark Sargent	248	264	336	848	8/22/92
Scott Poole	280	190	360	830	2/13/93
Scott Poole	240	210	325	775	5/22/93
Greg York	320	135	305	760	4/21/90
Chris Duckworth	220	176 c	347 c	743 c	4/19/86
Chuck Beal	292 c	143	303	738	4/19/86
Dave Jeffrey, Jr.	265	187	286	738	8/23/08
123 Phil Hile	375	275	450	1100	9/28/91
Cork Hall	336	170	418	925	3/22/86
Dave Jeffrey, Jr.	336	220	358	914	6/19/10
Joe Vukovich	270 c	225 c	352 c	848	3/24/91
Mark Sargent	248	264	336	848	8/22/92
Mike Emerick	303	192	325	820	4/19/86
Mike Emerick	292	181	330	804	5/03/86
Greg York	319	143	308	771	3/14/92
Mike Emerick	264	165	325	755	3/22/86
Chris Duckworth	230	175	345	750	2/28/87
132 Tim Borgia	402	270	429	1102	3/22/86
Rusty Greene	375	210	435	1020	5/02/92
Eddie Walsh	335	270	410	1015	5/20/89
Jeff Kirk	424	192	374	992	2/07/87
Paul Armentrout	300	255	430 c	985	5/02/92
Rick Yates	341	220	407	970	4/11/87
Greg Vance	305	230	405	940	4/26/86
Dorian Murphy	325	200	405	930	4/26/86
Ken Woodell	281	270 m	374 m	925 m	3/20/93
Corey Politino	345	190	365	900	5/22/93

* - West Virginia State Powerlifting Record
c – West Virginia Collegiate Powerlifting Record
m – West Virginia State Masters Powerlifting Record
e – Elite Powerlifter Classification

Era III : WV Powerlifters / Single-Ply
WV Powerlifters competing from January 1st, 1985 thru July31st, 2013
TOP RANKINGS Determined by Total
Single-Ply, "The Bench Press Shirt," the 24 hour weigh-ins, and the Round System

148 / Name	Squat	Bench Press	Deadlift	Total	Date
Rusty Greene	518	303	584	1405 e	2/25/95
Allen Smith	523	347	501	1372	3/14/92
Allen Smith – 551 SQUAT (4th Attempt) 3/14/92 / WV State Squat Record					
Allen Smith	496	336	518	1350	3/20/93
Allen Smith	507	352	507	1344	4/04/92
Allen Smith	512	336	490	1339	3/11/89
Allen Smith	523	319	473	1317	4/02/94
Allen Smith	485	341	485	1311	3/05/88
Allen Smith	501	325	473	1300	10/01/88
Allen Smith	500	325	460	1285	9/28/91
Allen Smith	485	320	475	1280	2/12/94
Rusty Greene	462	275	534	1273	6/24/94
Allen Smith	451	336	468	1255	12/06/86
Allen Smith	518	308	418	1245	3/24/90
Greg Jackson	429	325	490	1245	3/14/92
Rusty Greene	465 t	255	515 t	1235 t	5/22/93
Donald Robbins	385	360 t	485	1230 t	4/26/86
Mike Kimball	462	303	440	1207	4/13/85
Allen Smith	457	319	418	1195	4/11/87
Donald Robbins	385	310	485	1180	4/19/85
Danny Akers	400	280	490	1170	5/30/98
James Turner	429	236	501	1168	3/14/92
Stuart Breeding	462	242	457	1162	8/09/86
Allen Smith	440	303	407	1151	3/22/86
Mike Vitrules	402	253	462	1118	3/24/90
James Turner	407	242	468	1118	3/24/91
Danny Akers	385	259	473	1118	3/28/98
Eddie Walsh	402	286	424	1113	3/24/91
Jim Deem	407	265	429	1102	10/31/87
Jason Osborne	415	240	445	1100	5/02/92
Rick Yates	402	253	435	1091	10/31/87
Scott Phillips	402	231	440	1074	2/07/87
Ty Cook	407	253	402	1063	4/08/89
Acie Simmons	347	396*	308	1052	3/22/86
Chris Bailey	352	303 c	396	1052	3/05/88

* - West Virginia State Powerlifting Record   c – West Virginia State Collegiate Powerlifting Record
t – West Virginia State Teenage Powerlifting Record

Era III : WV Powerlifters / Single-Ply
WV Powerlifters competing from January 1st, 1985 thru July 31st, 2013
TOP RANKINGS Determined by Total
Single-Ply, "The Bench Press Shirt," the 24 hour weigh-ins, and the Round System

165 / Name	Squat	Bench Press	Deadlift	Total	Date
Marty Bavetz	600 ¾	385	562	1547 e	4/19/08
Gene Underwood	562	363	578	1504	12/14/85
Gene Underwood	562	369	567	1499	11/09/85
Gene Underwood	589	374	523	1488	3/05/88
Don Hundley	611 ¾ WR	270	600	1482	4/13/85
Gene Underwood	545	369	562	1477	3/22/86
Don Hundley	584 am	270	622 am	1477	12/13/86
Don Hundley	584	259	628	1471	4/11/87
Gene Underwood	551	358	562	1471	11/01/86
Art Williamsonson	535	340	570	1445	2/25/89
Rusty Greene	523	363	523	1410	3/25/01
Don Hundley	551 wm	253	589 wm	1394 wm	7/09/88
Keith Gandee	535	340	515	1390	4/12/86
Don Hundley	573	253	562	1388	3/22/86
Art Williamson	518	303	562	1383	3/05/88
Allen Smith	540	352	490	1383	3/24/91
Gene Underwood	550	330	500	1380	5/20/89
Keith Gandee	507	325	529	1361	3/22/86
Allen Smith	505	365	490	1360	6/15/96
David Jones	501	303	551	1355	4/02/94
Donald Robbins	429	407* ta	512	1350	4/11/87
Don Hundley (54)	523	236	573	1333	3/24/90
Don Hundley (55)	529	248	540	1317	3/24/91
Don Hundley (55)	507 wm	231	573 wm	1311 wm	5/18/91
Donald Robbins	400	430*	470	1300	4/12/97
Don Hundley	507	231	551	1289	3/11/89
Stuart Breeding	523	259	501	1284	2/07/87
Don Hundley	501	220	540	1262	3/14/92
Don Hundley	512	220	523	1256	4/02/94
Mike Kimball	450	320	450	1220	7/27/85
Don Hundley (60)	462	203	540 nm	1207	5/11/96

* - West Virginia State Powerlifting Record   ta – Teenage American Record
nm – National Masters Powerlifting Record   am – American Masters Powerlifting Record
wm – World Masters Powerlifting Record   e – Elite Powerlifting Total

Era III : WV Powerlifters / Single-Ply
WV Powerlifters competing from January 1st, 1985 thru July31st, 2013
TOP RANKINGS Determined by Total
Single-Ply, "The Bench Press Shirt," the 24 hour weigh-ins, and the Round System

181 / Name	Squat	Bench Press	Deadlift	Total	Date
Paul Sutphin (179 ¼) *	655	407 ¾ *	677 ¾ *	1741* e	3/22/86
Paul Sutphin	644	402	650	1697 e	11/09/85
Paul Sutphin	639	396	650	1686 e	12/06/86
Paul Sutphin	622 R	396	655 R	1675 R e	6/28/86
1675 Total – RC / Region VI Powerlifting Champion					
Doug Currence	617	363	672	1653 e	4/13/85
Paul Sutphin	617	380	628	1625	4/11/87
Dan Lass	615	425*	585	1625	4/23/88
Paul Sutphin	600	395	620	1615	11/16/85
Doug Currence	606	347	650	1603	6/01/85
Gene Underwood	633	402	562	1597	4/11/87
Marty Bavetz	617	418	556	1592	3/28/09
Dan Lass	573	429*	562	1554	4/08/95
Adam Kwitakowski	600 ¾	385	529	1515	3/27/04
Matt Cardello	534	413*c	534	1482 c	3/05/88
David Snodgrass	560	295	625	1480	12/17/94
Scott Collias	611 ¾ t	325	534	1471 t	8/01/87
Doug Burns	545	325	600 ¾	1471	11/17/90
Adam Kwitakowski	562	352	551	1466	3/15/03
Doug Burns	520	315	620	1455	5/19/90
Doug Burns	518	297	633	1449	3/24/90
Doug Currence	540	325	556	1421	12/04/93
Doug Currence	501	347	567	1416	3/20/93
Denver Turner	545	264	600	1410	3/20/93
Matt Cardello	562	363	479	1405	10/31/87
Frank Adkins	545	369	490	1405	3/14/92
Eric Green	518	380	501	1399	3/24/91
Kevin Keyes	490	347	496	1333	4/08/95

* - West Virginia State Powerlifting Record,

e – Elite Classification Total

c – West Virginia State Collegiate Powerlifting Record

t – West Virginia State Teenage Powerlifting Record

R – Region VI Powerlifting Record

RC – Region VI Powerlifting Champion

Era III : WV Powerlifters / Single-Ply
WV Powerlifters competing from January 1st, 1985 thru July31st, 2013
TOP RANKINGS Determined by Total
Single-Ply, "The Bench Press Shirt," the 24 hour weigh-ins, and the Round System

198 / Name	Squat	Bench Press	Deadlift	Total	Date
Doug Currence	622	418	688*	1731 e	3/23/86
Doug Currence	633	407	655	1697	4/11/87
Doug Currence	628	402	667	1697	5/17/86
Joe Lee	628	424	611	1664 RC	5/17/87
Joe Lee	628	407	617	1653	4/11/87
Josh Stottlemire	573	490 ½	584	1647	8/23/08
Doug Currence	589	402	644	1636	11/02/86
Doug Currence	595	391	650	1636	3/28/98
M. Sean Byrd	567	462	600	1631	11/10/85
Joe Lee	622	435	573	1631	12/07/86
Joe Lee	620	420	575	1615	11/16/86
Doug Currence	590	370	655	1615	5/30/98
Doug Currence	590	400	610	1600	6/15/96
Victor Nelson	615	330	650	1595	3/13/94
Doug Currence	589	396	600	1587	11/28/98
Doug Currence	584	380	611	1576	4/08/95
Scott Collias	625 c	370	575 c	1570 c	5/02/92
Victor Nelson	622	325	622	1570	12/05/93
Jeff Chambers	589	369	606	1565	4/11/87
Scott Collias	628 c	358	578 c	1565	8/22/92
Paul Sutphin	660	350	550	1560	12/18/93
Dan Lass	584	402	573	1559	3/06/88
Scott Collias	622 c	363	573 c	1559 c	3/14/92
Mike Brown	600	363	589	1554	3/23/86
Joe Lee	573	407	562	1543	5/03/86
Rando Coyle	600	363	578	1543	3/06/88
Rob Graham	567	391	578	1537	11/22/92
Mike Hundley	600	336	573	1510	3/23/86
Greg Pernell	606	330	529	1466	3/24/90

* - West Virginia State Powerlifting Record

e – ELITE Powerlifting Total

c – West Virginia State Collegiate Powerlifting Record

m – West Virginia State Masters Powerlifting Record

t – West Virginia State Teenage Powerlifting Record

RC – Region VI Powerlifting Champion

Era III : WV Powerlifters / Single-Ply
WV Powerlifters competing from January 1st, 1985 thru July31st, 2013
TOP RANKINGS Determined by Total
Single-Ply, "The Bench Press Shirt," the 24 hour weigh-ins, and the Round System

220 / Name	Squat	Bench Press	Deadlift	Total	Date
Marshall Moore	705 c	407	716 c	1829 c	5/11/86
Keith Zurek	680	445	655	1780	11/06/88
Matt McCase	606	446	705	1758	8/23/08
Marshall Moore	661	380	699	1741	3/23/86
Tony Culp	677	402	655	1736	4/14/85
Doug Currence	633	451	628	1714	5/06/07
Scott Tusic	644	451	606	1703	3/23/86
Paul Sutphin (212)	716 m	374	611	1703 m	11/10/96
Matt McCase	611	402	688	1703	3/31/07
Steve Uhas	733*	352	600	1686	4/11/87
John Messinger	655	402	617	1675	3/20/93
Doug Currence	611	451 m	611 m	1675 m	3/31/07
Andy Meadows	672	429	567	1669	8/22/92
Paul Sutphin	680	370	615	1665	12/14/96
Paul Sutphin (206)	675	380	605	1660	6/15/96
Paul Sutphin	700 m	355	600	1655	10/14/95
Don Hall	639	374	628	1642	4/14/85
John Nicoloudakis	567	429	644	1642	5/03/86
Don Hall	628	391	611	1631	5/03/86
Rando Coyle	622	385	622	1631	3/14/92
Don Hall	617	385	611	1614	3/23/86
Scott Grigsby	628	363	617	1609	3/28/09
Tony Marcum	628	413	562	1603	11/22/92
Dominick Marrara	617	374	606	1598	3/24/90
Bob Taylor	501	451	644	1598	3/24/91
Josh Stottlemire	556	462	573	1592	3/31/07
Don Hall	644 m	341	600	1587	7/10/88
Don Hall	622	380	573	1576	4/11/87
Jack Mayhew	589	429	545	1565	3/24/91
Tom Buzzo	589	363	578	1532	4/11/87
Josh Stottlemire	341	622 ¾ AR	540	1504	4/03/10
Jim Simon	575	415	510	1500	11/16/86
Josh Stottlemire	507	435	551	1493	10/22/06
Benny Farmer	534	396	518	1438	4/02/94

* - West Virginia State Powerlifting Record   m – West Virginia State Masters Record

AR – USPF American Powerlifting Record   e – ELITE Powerlifting Total

c – West Virginia State Collegiate Record

Era III : WV Powerlifters / Single-Ply
WV Powerlifters competing from January 1st, 1985 thru July31st, 2013
TOP RANKINGS Determined by Total
Raw or Single-Ply, "The Bench Press Shirt," the 24 hour weigh-ins, and the Round System

242 / Name	Squat	Bench Press	Deadlift	Total	Date
Bret Russell	804	462	843	2110 e	12/13/86
Bret Russell	820	460	825	2105 e	4/12/86
Bret Russell	810	457	821	2088 e	5/11/86
Bret Russell	760	457	821*	2039 e	3/23/86
Allen Baria	722	600*	655	1978 e	6/24/00
Randy Scott	727	512*	716	1956 e	3/23/86
Maurice Smith	771	501	672	1945	3/08/92
Allen Baria	650	584*	639	1873	3/25/00
Maurice Smith	760	473	633	1868	3/03/91
Maurice Smith	760	501	600	1862	12/05/93
Mark Olenick	711	468	672	1852	3/02/91
Nick Busick	705	507*	606	1818	4/14/85
Doug Currence (Age 51)	683 m	479 m	644 m	1807 m	5/08/11
John Messinger	688	429	650	1769	11/10/85
Doug Currence (Age 52)	667	473	628	1769 WC	10/01/11
Chris Young	661	451	650	1763	4/20/96
John Silvey	672	446	617	1736	7/10/88
Doug Currence	650	480	605	1735	3/08/08
John Silvey	661	451 m	606	1719	3/06/88
John Messinger	677 m	402	622	1703	4/08/95
Keith Rippeto	667	391	644	1703	3/28/98
John Messinger	644	418	622	1686	5/19/91
Chris Asbury	551	650*m	485	1686	8/06/11
Mike Nidy	644	374	661	1681	4/11/87
John Messinger	655	402	606	1664	3/24/90
Andy Meadows	655	435	562	1653 c	7/14/91
Ronnie Harbert	556	534	556	1647	3/19/05
Courtney Stanley (60-64)	584 m	385	650 m	1619 m	6/20/10
John Lilly	573 c	446 c	562 c	1581 c	4/19/86
John Lilly	580 c	425	565	1570	2/28/87
John Lilly	501	451 c	556	1510	3/06/88
Ed Starcher	584	380	534	1499	3/24/90
Ed Starcher	556	369	485	1410	4/08/89
Bret Russell	143	143	859	1145	11/02/86

* - West Virginia State Powerlifting Record
c – West Virginia Collegiate Record
m – West Virginia State Masters Record

t – West Virginia Teenage Record
WC – World Champion!
E – ELITE Powerlifting Total

Era III : WV Powerlifters / Single-Ply
WV Powerlifters competing from January 1st, 1985 thru July31st, 2013
TOP RANKINGS Determined by Total
Single-Ply, "The Bench Press Shirt," the 24 hour weigh-ins, and the Round System

275 / Name	Squat	Bench Press	Deadlift	Total	Date
Allen Baria	832*	749*AR	744*	2326* e	3/26/11
Allen Baria	705	744 AR	733	2182 e	4/03/10
Bret Russell	799 u	479	749 u	2028 e	11/17/90
Mark Olenick	760*c	520 c	700 c	1980*c	4/24/88
Randy Scott	760 u	501	710	1973 u e	2/08/87
Randy Scott	749*	518	699	1967* e	3/05/88
Chris Young (40-49)	700	584 m	667	1951 m e	11/01/08
Randy Scott	749	496	699	1946 e	6/02/85
John James	749	501	650	1900	3/29/97
Mark Olenick	744	485	667	1895	11/01/87
Mark Olenick	727	512	655	1895	3/24/90
Randy Scott	722	507	661	1890	4/11/87
Chris Young (40-49)	650	573	650	1873	4/19/08
Brian Siders	650 t	523 t	655 t	1828 t	3/28/98
Sam Moore	688	407	727	1824	4/14/85
Dan Hall	727	402	688	1818	3/23/86
Brian Siders	650 j	534*c j	633 j	1818 j	3/27/99
Wayne Stewart	710	455	650	1815	5/19/90
John Messinger	683	451	667	1802	4/11/87
Jim Compton	655	496	650	1802	3/25/06
S. Modesitt	617	518	667	1802	3/25/06
Stuart Thompson	733	418	633	1785	2/08/87
John Messinger	705	468 m	600	1774	3/25/00
Wayne Stewart	700	440	620	1760	5/20/89
Andy Meadows	694	473	562	1731	6/25/94
John Messinger	661	435	628	1725	5/12/96
Marion Tennant	622	457	600	1681	4/02/94
Allen Baria	677	683*	314	1675	3/22/08
Booker Stephens	501	424	633	1559	4/27/13
Austen Vickers	556	402	573	1531	3/23/13
Barry Karnes	551 c	380	573	1504 c	4/11/87
Barry Karnes	510 c	360	610 c	1480 c	2/28/87
Bobby Fox	530	325	500	1355	11/16/86
Mark Hrko	479	319	551	1350	3/06/88

* - West Virginia State Powerlifting Record   AR – USPF American Powerlifting Record
u – Unofficial West Virginia Powerlifting Record   c – West Virginia Collegiate Record
j – West Virginia Junior (Age 20-23) Record   t – West Virginia Teenage Record
m – West Virginia State Masters Powerlifting Record   e – ELITE Powerlifting Total

Era III : WV Powerlifters / Single-Ply
WV Powerlifters competing from January 1st, 1985 thru July31st, 2013
TOP RANKINGS Determined by Total
Single-Ply, "The Bench Press Shirt," the 24 hour weigh-ins, and the Round System

SHW / Name	Squat	Bench Press	Deadlift	Total	Date
Brian Siders	1019* ar	799	832	2650*ar e	5/15/10
Brian Siders	959	777	865*	2601*wr e	12/02/07
Brian Siders	987* ar	804*	771	2562* e	6/25/05
Brian Siders	992* ar	744	816	2552 e	6/15/08
Brian Siders WC	964*	744*	821*	2529* e	11/14/04
Brian Siders	942	722	859*	2524 e	7/09/06
Brian Siders	975*	744*	826*	2545* e	8/14/04
Brian Siders	953	771*	766	2491* e	5/08/05
Brian Siders	936*	699	815*	2452* e	7/11/04
Brian Siders	909*	672	804	2386* e	7/20/03
Brian Siders WC	892	699*	793	2386 e	11/09/03
Brian Siders	903*	667	810*	2380* e	6/23/03
Brian Siders	848	650	788*	2286* e	6/22/02
Brian Siders	804	644	793	2243 e	7/14/02
Brian Siders	785 rw	605 rw	810 rw	2200 rw e	5/06/06
Brian Siders	766 c	667* c	766	2199* c e	3/23/02
Brian Siders	804	606	760	2171 e	11/17/02
Brian Siders	780	640 u	730	2150 e	3/10/01
Brian Siders	793	600 ¾	733	2127 e	6/24/01
Brian Siders	722	622*	694	2038	6/25/00
Jeff Cook	749	440	788	1978	2/08/87
Stuart Thompson	793	468	716	1978	3/14/92
Stuart Thompson	826	440	705	1973	12/15/85
Willie Williams	710	545	677	1934	3/14/92
Willie Williams	749	512	661	1923	3/24/91
Jeff Cook	705 c	429	782 c	1918 c	5/11/86
Troy McNett	675	525	700	1900	12/17/94
Mark Olenick	705	501 c	688	1895	3/05/88
Jeff Cook	705	435	738	1879	4/11/87
Troy McNett	705	501	672	1879	3/28/98
John Messinger	722	451	628	1802	3/27/99
Wayne Stewart	670	475	655	1800	9/28/91
Dan Hall	744	385	655	1785	4/11/87

* - West Virginia State Powerlifting Record
t – West Virginia Teenage Powerlifting Record
c – West Virginia State Collegiate Powerlifting Record
WC – IPF World Powerlifting Champion
u – Unofficial West Virginia State Powerlifting Record

wr – World Powerlifting Record
rw – "RAW" Powerlifting Record,
ar – American Powerlifting Record
e – ELITE Powerlifting Total

Chapter Twenty-Seven : Powerlifting in the Modern Era

Coverage of the first Professional Powerlifting events were published in *Powerlifting USA* magazine. Newer designs in supportive gear, the Monolift, and the latest technological advances of steel on the platform elevated Powerlifting to a new level. The JAN/2000 issue of *P/L USA* reported the official results and highlights of the *1999 APF West Virginia State Powerlifting Championships* held in Charleston on August 29th, 1999.

Mike Hill – 805lb. Squat
220lb. class

Mike Hill : Powerlifter / "Pro Elite." Currently, Mike Hill owns Elite Powerlifting Totals in three (3) weight classes : 1) 198lb. class 2) 220lb. class 3) 242lb. class

After the "Modern Era" of Powerlifting began, a few Meet Directors promoted what would later be defined as "Professional" Powerlifting events. Lifting in the Modern Era of Powerlifting with multi-ply supportive gear and the proficient use of a Monolift, Mike Hill refused to consider doing it any other way. After dragging the iron sled with

Mike on a hot evening at Charleston, West Virginia in June of 1997, Mike asked me the question, "I wonder if this is what it takes to be a Champion?"

Beginning in 1997, Mike Hill became a pupil of the most modern training methodology written by Powerlifter/Strength Coach, Louie Simmons of *Westside Barbell*. After six (6) years of serious training, Mike Hill achieved Professional Elite with a 1910 Total in the 198lb. class at the <u>Iron House Classic Powerlifting Championships</u> in Delaware, Ohio on April 12th, 2003.

A brief overview of the early career of Mike Hill reveals the ultimate desire to compete against the absolute best. Getting started, Mike lifted as a teenager in a few local competitions. Mike Hill competed at the *1991 APF Teenage Nationals* (2nd Place), the *1991 ADFPA West Virginia State Powerlifting Championships*, the *1992 USPF West Virginia State Powerlifting Championships*, the *1995 USPF West Virginia State Powerlifting Championships*, and the *1996 USPF West Virginia State Powerlifting Championships*, just to name a few.

Mike Hill won first place in the Class I Division at the 1995 USPF West Virginia State Powerlifting Championships while competing in the 198lb. class. Mike returned to the USPF West Virginia State Powerlifting Championships in April, 1996 and won the title in the Senior / Open Division with a Total of 1510. Mike Hill also won the Bench Press Division at the 1996 West Virginia State Powerlifting Championships.

Although content with winning the USPF West Virginia State Powerlifting Championships on 4/20/96, Mike Hill was not at all satisfied with a Total of 1510 at 198 or any bodyweight. Mike's ideology was, "Why settle for 1510 instead of 1810 or 1900?" In July of 1996, Mike continued to improve with another victory in the 198lb. class. At Ironton, Ohio on 7/06/96, Mike Hill won first place at the <u>Big Iron on the River Powerlifting Championships</u> in the 198lb. class with a 635 Squat, 405 Bench Press, and a 565 Deadlift for a 1605 Total.

The "Road to Elite" was wide open for Mike Hill after shifting into high gear at the end of 1997. Mike posted an 1825 Total in the 220lb. class at the *1998 Westside Invitational* held on February 8th, 1998 in Columbus, Ohio. Prior to 1998, most Powerlifting organizations defined "Elite" by using the USPF Powerlifting Elite Classification Totals as benchmarks. By the same standards, Mike earned his first Elite Total with 1825 in the 220lb. class on 2/08/98 at the Westside Invitational. Included in Mike Hill's Total of 1825 was a 700 Squat, a 500 Bench Press, and a 625 Deadlift.

Mike Hill Placed 2nd in the 220lb. class at the <u>1998 IPA Senior National Powerlifting Championships</u> at Annapolis, Maryland with a Squat of 725, Bench Press of 490, and a Deadlift of 640 for a Total of 1855. Mike's Total of 1855 earned the #11 spot in the P/L USA TOP 100 220's for USA lifters competing from December, 1997 through November, 1998.

Competing at the <u>1999 Westside Invitational</u> on 2/27/99, Mike won the 220lb. class with a Total of 1805, going 680 Squat, 500 Bench Press, and a 625 Deadlift. Later in the year, Mike Hill directed the <u>APF West Virginia State Powerlifting Championships</u> at Charleston, West Virginia on August 29th, 1999. Many lifters from *Westside Barbell* competed at the event while a number of West Virginia's Powerlifters began a chapter of Modern Powerlifting with use of the Monolift and the latest innovations in personal equipment.

On 8/29/99, Mike Hill Totaled Elite at 220 with a 1930 Total at the APF West Virginia State Powerlifting Championships in Charleston. While competing in the 220lb. class, Mike set new APF and *All-Time West Virginia State Powerlifting Records* with a 775 Squat and a 1930 Total. Mike continued to produce Elite Totals throughout 2000, 2001, and 2002. In the year 2003, Mike won the *APF Junior National Powerlifting Championships* in the 198lb. class with an Elite Total of 1865.

Mike Hill has Totaled Elite at least seventeen (17) times since 1999, beginning with the 220lb. class. For the 198lb. class, Mike has six (6) Elite Totals and two (2) *Professional* Elite Totals on record. For the 220lb. class, Mike Hill has eight (8) Elite Totals documented as official record. For the 242lb. class, Mike Totaled Elite one (1) time on 6/16/2001.

Mike Hill
Bench Press

Along with a Professional Elite Total in the 198lb. class at 1900lbs., Mike Hill owns the IPA West Virginia State Bench Press Record in the 198lb. class with 510lbs. In the 220lb. class, Mike Hill has officially Bench Pressed 565 and Totaled 2005lbs.

"Setting the Records Straight" : Part IX
Era III : WV Powerlifter Rankings / Multi-Ply

The TOP Powerlifters listed in the <u>West Virginia Powerlifter Rankings (Multi-Ply)</u> represent the best Powerlifters in West Virginia from July 1st, 1995 through September 30th, 2013. In the 181lb. class, <u>Marty Bavetz</u> has one (1) Elite Total / SPF standards in 2009 at 1745. Marty Totaled Professional Elite with 1815 on 8/20/2010 with lifts of 710 Squat, 500 Bench Press, and a Deadlift of 605. The 500lb. Bench Press in the 181lb. class by Marty Bavetz is an *All-time West Virginia State Bench Press Record* among West Virginia Powerlifters competing in the 181lb. class.

<u>Mike Hill</u> Totaled Professional Elite in the 198lb. class for the first time with a Total of 1900lbs. on 11/15/2002. The 1900 Total by Mike Hill on 11/15/2002 included a Squat of 770, Bench Press of 510, and a Deadlift of 620. The 510lb. Bench Press by Mike Hill on 11/15/02 is an *All-Time West Virginia Bench Press Record for the 198lb. class.* On 4/13/2003, Mike Totaled 1910 for a Professional Elite Total. The Total of 1910 by Mike Hill included an <u>*All-Time West Virginia State Squat Record in the 198lb. class with 805lbs.*</u>

<u>Mike Hill</u> owns eight (8) Elite Totals in the 220lb. class. Mike's Total of 2005 on 8/20/2010 included a Squat of 835, Bench Press of 565, and a Deadlift of 605. The Squat of 835 and Total of 2005 by Mike Hill on 8/10/2010 are *All-Time West Virginia State Powerlifting Records.* The 2000 Total by Mike Hill on 12/05/2009 included a Bench Press of 540. The 540 Bench Press by Mike Hill on 12/05/2009 was the *All-Time West Virginia State Bench Press Record* for the 220lb. class until April, 2010. On 6/16/2001, Mike Hill Totaled 1945 for Elite Powerlifter Classification in the 242lb. class.

<u>Lee Angle</u> Totaled Elite while competing in the 220lb. class on 4/04/2004 with a Total of 1875. On 11/21/2004, Lee Angle Totaled 1950 in the 242lb. class for Elite Powerlifter Classification.

<u>Chris Young</u> Totaled 2015 for Elite in the 242lb. class at the *APF West Virginia State Powerlifting Championships* on 8/29/99. Chris Totaled 1900 for Elite in the 220lb. class on 2/24/2001. On 11/18/2001, Chris Young Totaled 1975 for another Elite Total in the 242lb. class. Chris Totaled 2100 on 5/24/2009 for Elite Powerlifter Classification in the 275lb. class.

Era III : WV Powerlifter Rankings / Multi-Ply
WV Powerlifters competing from July 1st, 1995 thru September 30th, 2013
TOP RANKINGS Determined by Total

181 / Name	Squat	Bench Press	Deadlift	Total	Date
Marty Bavetz	710*	500*	605	1815* e	8/20/10
Marty Bavetz	675	470	600	1745 e	12/05/09
Dave Revels	560	330	560	1450	8/09/03
Dave Revels	500	305	550	1405	4/12/03
198 Mike Hill (197)	805*	475	630	1910 pe	4/13/03
Mike Hill	770	510*	620	1900 pe	11/15/02
Mike Hill	785	475	605	1865 n e	3/15/03
Mike Hill	800	460	605	1865 e	10/27/07
Mike Hill	750	510	605	1860 e	7/20/02
Mike Hill	755	485	600	1840 e	4/01/07
Mike Hill	720	500*	615	1835 e	3/30/02
Mike Hill	700	480	610	1790 e	11/17/01
Titus Russell	805 t	390	570	1765 t e	3/05/11
220 Mike Hill	835*	565	605	2005* e	8/20/10
Mike Hill	820	540*	640	2000* e	12/05/09
Mike Hill	805	525	630	1960* e	12/06/08
Mike Hill	815	520	615	1950 e	5/24/09
Mike Hill	775	510	645	1930* e	8/29/99
Mike Hill	800	530	600	1930 e	11/12/05
Mike Hill	735	515	650	1900 e	2/20/00
Chris Young	750	500	650	1900 e	2/24/01
Mike Hill	760	535*	600	1895 e	11/20/04
Lee Angle	800	440	635	1875 e	4/04/04
Mike Hill	725	490	640	1855	11/01/98
Chris Young	720	480	635	1835	11/19/00
Mike Hill	700	500	625	1825	2/08/98
Chris Young	725	440	660	1825	2/20/00
Lee Angle	750	450	625	1825	11/16/03
Mike Hill	680	500	625	1805	2/28/99
Lee Angle	650	430	615	1695	7/20/02
Lee Angle	650	435	605	1690	11/16/02

* - West Virginia State Powerlifting Record   t – WV Teenage Powerlifting Record
n – National Powerlifting Championship   nc – National Powerlifting Champion
e – Elite Powerlifting Classification Total
pe – Elite Powerlifting Classification Total / Professional Standards

Era III : WV Powerlifter Rankings / Multi-Ply
WV Powerlifters competing from July 1st, 1995 thru September 30th, 2013
TOP RANKINGS Determined by Total

242 / Name		Squat	Bench Press	Deadlift	Total	Date
	Chris Young	785	520	710	2015 e	8/29/1999
	Chris Young	805*	485	685	1975 e	11/18/2001
	Lee Angle	825*	500	625	1950 e	11/21/2004
	Mike Hill	800*	520	625	1945 e	6/16/2001
	Chris Young	745	510	680	1935 e	9/13/1997
	Chris Young	675	460	655	1790	7/08/1996
	Lee Angle	710	450	605	1765	2/24/2001
	Lee Angle	715	415	630	1760	9/09/2000
	Lee Angle	660	390	600	1650	8/29/1999
	Chris French	700	430	505	1635	11/12/2005
	Chris French	715	365	550	1630	4/17/2005
	Lee Angle	700	135	635	1470	3/30/2002
	Tom Keim	505	390	475	1370	9/15/2013
275	Chris Young	800	610	690	2100 e	5/24/2009
	Chris Young	825	510	640	1975	7/20/2002
	Chris Young	800	500	650	1950	11/17/2002
	Chris Young	735	550	665	1950	10/27/2007
	Morris Macklin	650	300	600	1550	8/29/1999
SHW	John Phillips	750	560	725	2035	11/18/2001
	John Phillips	600	500	620	1720	2/24/2001

Professional Elite - RPS Powerlifting @ Allentown, Pennsylvania

198	Josh Stottlemire	730	575*	625	1930 pe	12/03/2011

* - West Virginia State Powerlifting Record

n – National Powerlifting Championships

e – Elite Powerlifting Classification Total

pe – Elite Powerlifting Classification Total / Professional Standards

Era III : WV Powerlifter Rankings / Multi-Ply
WV Powerlifters competing from July 1ˢᵗ, 1995 thru September 30ᵗʰ, 2013
TOP RANKINGS Determined by Total
Masters (Age 40 thru 59)

181 / Name	Squat	Bench Press	Deadlift	Total	Date
Richard Fortson	500	300	550 m	1350	2/24/2001
Richard Fortson	425	200	465	1085	8/29/1999
198					
Paul Sutphin (40)	630 m	340	585 m	1555 m	7/08/1995
Paul Sutphin (56)	600	320	535	1455	6/25/2011
Paul Sutphin (56)	610 m	300	540 m	1450 m	5/07/2011
Richard Fortson	600	300	550	1450	3/30/2002
Richard Fortson	520	250	600	1370	11/17/2001
Richard Fortson	500	300	550	1350	2/24/2001
220					
Paul Sutphin (45)	755 m	385	590	1730 m	8/29/1999
Paul Sutphin (49)	720 Iw	400 Iw	580 Iw	1700 Iw	8/09/2003
Paul Sutphin (48)	705	415 m	570	1690	7/20/2002
Paul Sutphin (42)	685	380	615	1680	10/05/1996
Paul Sutphin (44)	675	390	605	1670	2/08/1998
Paul Sutphin (41)	680	385	600	1665	7/06/1996
Paul Sutphin (42)	670	380	590	1640	7/12/1997
Paul Sutphin (47)	685	370	575	1630	11/18/2001
Paul Sutphin (48)	710	365	540	1615	4/12/2003
Paul Sutphin (46)	725	335	550	1610	5/19/2001
Chris French	680	315	615	1610	4/12/2003
Paul Sutphin (48)	625	420 m	560	1605	11/16/2002
Paul Sutphin (46)	710	340	550	1600	2/24/2001
Chris French	705	330	550	1585	11/16/2003
Chris French	700	320	540	1560	7/20/2002
Chris French	650	320	570	1540	8/09/2003
242					
Chris French	700	430	505	1635	11/12/2005
Chris French	715	365	550	1630	4/17/2005
Chris French	615	365	590	1570	11/18/2001
275					
Chris Young	800 m	610 m	690	2100 m e	5/24/2009

* - West Virginia State Powerlifting Record
m – West Virginia Masters Powerlifting Record / Modern Powerlifting
Iw – IPA Amateur World Powerlifting Record
e - Elite Powerlifting Classification Total / Professional Standards

Era III : WV Powerlifter Rankings / Multi-Ply
WV Powerlifters competing from July 1st, 1995 thru September 30th, 2013
TOP RANKINGS Determined by Total
Masters (Age 50 & Over)

198 / Name	Squat	Bench Press	Deadlift	Total	Date
Paul Sutphin (56)	600	320	535	1455	6/25/2011
Paul Sutphin (56)	610	300	540	1450	5/07/2011
Paul Sutphin (55)	565	305	530	1400	9/05/2009
220 Paul Sutphin (51)	625	365	560	1550	4/01/2006
Paul Sutphin (53)	605	350	505	1460	5/03/2008
Paul Sutphin (59)	600	330	510	1440	9/15/2013
Paul Sutphin (57)	550	300	520	1370	5/05/2012
Paul Sutphin (58)	500	330	530	1360	7/28/2012
Paul Sutphin (59)	455	300	505	1260	7/27/2013

m – West Virginia State Masters Powerlifting Record

Era III : WV Masters Powerlifter Rankings
WV Powerlifters competing from January 1ˢᵗ, 2010 thru July 31ˢᵗ, 2013
RANKINGS Determined by Total
USPF, USAPL, IPF, Single-Ply
Masters (Age 55-59)

198 / Name	Age	Squat	Bench Press	Deadlift	Total	Date
Paul Sutphin	(57)	501*	303*	545*m	1349*m	8/06/2011
Paul Sutphin	(56)	512 m	292	540 m	1344 m	3/26/2011
Paul Sutphin	(55)	507 m	292	534 m	1339	4/10/2010
Paul Sutphin	(57)	485	303	512	1300	3/31/2012
Paul Sutphin	(58)	462	319	518	1300	3/23/2013

* - USAPL West Virginia State Masters Powerlifting Record

m – West Virginia State Masters Powerlifting Record

8/06/2011 – USAPL West Virginia State Powerlifting Championships
4/10/2010, 3/26/2011, 3/31/2012, 3/23/2013 – USPF WV State P/L Championships

Powerlifting : 2010 – 2013

Over thirty-four (34) years had passed since the first official West Virginia State Powerlifting Championship. After winning the 35th Annual USPF West Virginia State Powerlifting Championship on April 10th, 2010 in South Charleston, an alliance with old friends, rivals, and a number of Powerlifters from the "Modern Era" renewed an element of camaraderie that had been missing for quite sometime. Winning the 2010 West Virginia State Championship with a Master's Division Elite Total and breaking the West Virginia State Record in the Deadlift (Age 50-59 Category) was synonymous with "tradition and old times."

On May 15th, 2010, I officiated at the USAPL West Virginia State Powerlifting Championships in the capacity as IPF Category II Referee, HRIC. Following the record-breaking performance of SHW (SuperHeavyWeight) Brian Siders and a Total of 2650, *Four (4) AMERICAN RECORDS* were on the books. Brian Siders became the first West Virginian to Squat 1000lbs. With a 1019lb. Squat to his credit, Brian is among the few men in the world to Squat over 1000lbs., IPF-USA Powerlifting style. The strong set-up by Brian Siders with over ½ ton of steel followed by a Squat executed to perfection was one for the ages!

It had been nearly five (5) years since Brian broke the "800lb. Barrier" on the Bench Press. Along with the 1019lb. Squat and Deadlift of 832, Brian Siders owns a Bench Press of 799lbs. / 362.5 kilos. With a Bench Press of 800lbs., Brian Siders became a member of the "1000lb. Squat Club" on May 15th, 2010 at South Charleston, West Virginia.

The 2010 Power Station Pro / Am Powerlifting Championships were held on August 20th, 2010 in Sharonville, Ohio. Marty Bavetz Totaled Elite once again while competing in the 181lb. class with a *Professional Total of 1815!* Mike Hill competed at the same competition and finished with an Elite Total of 2005 in the 220lb. class.

The 36th Annual (2011) USPF West Virginia State Powerlifting Championships were held on March 26th, 2011 at South Charleston, West Virginia. There were five (5) West Virginia State Powerlifting Records broken in the Open / Senior Division. Josh Stottlemire broke the Bench Press Record in the 220lb. class with a lift of 628lbs. / 285 kilos. Allen Baria Totaled Elite in the 275lb. class on 3/26/2011 and set three (3) new West Virginia State Powerlifting Records in the Squat, Bench Press, and Total. The Elite Total of 2326lbs. by Allen Baria included a Squat of 832lbs., Bench Press of 749lbs., and a Deadlift Record of 744.

Putting together a Total of 1344lbs. in the 198lb. class on 3/26/2011 with a West Virginia State Record Squat of 512lbs. (55-59 Age Group) and another West Virginia

State Record Deadlift of 540lbs. made a productive day for Paul Sutphin. A Master's Elite Total of 1344lbs. in the 198lb. class exceeded the minimum USPF standards for Elite among Masters Powerlifters (55-59 Age Group).

Later in 2011, Paul Sutphin posted victories at the <u>IPA Powerlifting "Championship of the Two Virginias,"</u> the <u>2011 IPA Strength Spectacular</u> at York, Pennsylvania, and the <u>2011 USAPL West Virginia State Powerlifting Championships</u> held at South Charleston. Paul Sutphin set National and State Powerlifting Records while competing in the Masters Division at all four (4) Powerlifting competitions in 2011.

Doug Currence : Powerlifting Records

Doug Currence
Bench Press

Along with the Deadlift Record of 688lbs. and a Squat of 622lbs., Doug Currence Bench Pressed 418lbs. in the 198lb. class to complete the "TOTAL Package" of an *Elite Powerlifting Classification* of 1731 at the 1986 West Virginia State Powerlifting Championships. Twenty-Five (25) years later, Doug Bench Pressed 479lbs. in the 242lb.

class and Totaled 1807, winning a first place victory (50-54 Age Group) at the <u>USAPL Masters National Powerlifting Championship</u> on 5/08/2011 in Atlanta, Georgia.

Doug Currence began Powerlifting in 1980. Shortly after the YMCA National Powerlifting Championships in January, 1981 I stopped at Herb Fitzsimmons' gym in St. Albans, West Virginia for a workout. At that time, West Virginia Powerlifters were preparing for the 1981 West Virginia State Powerlifting Championships. Shortly after the workout began, Herb Fitzsimmons and Vince White introduced me to Doug Currence. As a topic of our first conversation, Doug announced he was training for his first meet, the 1981 West Virginia State Powerlifting Championships on 3/28/81. Doug competed in the 148lb. class at the 1981 West Virginia State Powerlifting Championships and won 2nd place.

Following an intro period of about three (3) years and increasing his training weight from 155lbs. to approximately 180lbs., Doug Currence approached Elite Powerlifting Classification in the 181lb. class. While competing in the 181lb. class on 4/01/84 at the 1984 West Virginia State Powerlifting Championships, Doug Currence Totaled Elite in the 181lb. class with a Total of 1642 and won the West Virginia State Powerlifting Championship.

The Powerlifting Records by Doug Currence began on 4/01/84 at the West Virginia State Powerlifting Championships with a Deadlift of 661lbs. (300 kilos) for a new West Virginia State Deadlift Record. However, the record was short-lived as his competitor, Robert Griffith, also Deadlifted 661 at a lighter bodyweight and was officially awarded the Deadlift Record. Doug reclaimed the West Virginia State Deadlift Record at the Steel Valley Open Powerlifting Meet on 12/15/84 with a lift of 666 ¾ lbs. (302.5 kilos).

Doug Currence won the 1985 West Virginia State Powerlifting Championships in the 181lb. class with an Elite Total of 1653lbs. While winning the 1985 West Virginia State Powerlifting Championships on 4/13/85 at Newell, West Virginia, Doug Currence pulled a new West Virginia State Deadlift Record of 672lbs. (305 kilos) in the 181lb. class.

Eleven (11) months later at the 1986 West Virginia State Powerlifting Championships, Doug broke Roger Estep's West Virginia Deadlift Record with a pull of 688 ¾ lbs. (312.5 kilos). Doug Currence won the 1986 West Virginia State Powerlifting Championships in the 198lb. class with an Elite Total of 1731lbs.

Since 2005, Doug Currence has set several West Virginia State Powerlifting Records in the Master's Division (Age 45-49) and (Age 50-54) while competing in the 220lb. class and the 242lb. class. Doug has also capitalized on the resurgence of "Raw" or "Classic

Powerlifting," while setting numerous "Raw Powerlifting Records," identified as new American "Raw" Powerlifting Records while competing in USAPL (USA Powerlifting) and at least one (1) other organization.

Doug Currence
IPF World Master's Powerlifting Champion

Doug Currence – 667 Squat /302.5 kilos
2011 World Masters Powerlifting Champion!

On October 1st, 2011 Doug Currence became the <u>IPF World Masters Powerlifting Champion</u> while competing in the 231lb. (105 kilo weight class). At the age of fifty-two (52) and at a bodyweight of 230 ½ lbs., Doug Currence posted a winning Total of 1769lbs. (802.5 kilos) to take the *2011 Gold Medal at the IPF World Masters Powerlifting Championships* at St. Catherines, Canada. The 1769 Total by Doug Currence on 10/01/2011 included a Squat of 666 ¾ lbs. (302.5 kilos), Bench Press of 473lbs. (215 kilos), and a Deadlift of 628lbs. (285 kilos).

Athletic Hall of Fame

Paul Sutphin was a student at Bluefield College beginning in the Fall of 1972 and graduated in the Spring of 1977. During that time, Paul competed in a number of Powerlifting competitions including the *1976 National Collegiate Powerlifting Championships* at Ohio University. On Saturday October 15th, 2011, Paul Sutphin was officially inducted into the Bluefield College Athletic Hall of Fame. The Director of Alumni Relations at Bluefield College in 2011 wrote, *"Paul has taken his passion for Weightlifting to a level of significant national acclaim."*

Published in Bluefield College Alumni magazine
Powerlifting USA magazine / Vol. 35, No. 2 / December, 2011

Athletic Hall of Fame
Paul Sutphin

Paul Sutphin Deadlifting 480 for a 1205 Total in the 148lb. class at the 1976 Lexington Open Powerlifting Championships. Paul Totaled 1240 at the National Collegiate Powerlifting Championships.

Powerlifting : Don Hall
Thirty-Eight (38) and Counting...

The record of competing in <u>thirty-eight (38) consecutive</u> West Virginia State Powerlifting Championships is one for "Any" Book of Records. Don Hall has never missed a West Virginia State Powerlifting Championship since 1976. With thirty-eight (38) consecutive years of Powerlifting tradition, Don Hall has represented the *Charleston Barbell Club*, *St. Albans Barbell Club, Herb's Gym,* and the *Holley Strength Systems.*

Don Hall : Powerlifting Chronological Report
Annual Totals from official results of USPF WV State Powerlifting Championships

Year / Class	SQUAT	BENCH	DEADLIFT	TOTAL	PLACE / Division
<u>1976</u> – <u>181</u>	425	265	500	1190	3rd / Open
<u>1977</u> - <u>181</u>	450	275	520	1245	3rd / Open
<u>1978</u> - <u>181</u>	480	280	540	1300	4th / Open
<u>1979</u> - <u>181</u>	500	290	535	1325	3rd / Open
<u>1980</u> - <u>181</u>	510	300	560	1370	3rd / Open
<u>1981</u> – TOTAL 3/29/81 @ the <u>6th Annual WV State Powerlifting Championships</u>					@ New Martinsville
<u>1982</u> - <u>181</u>	540	320	525	1385	3rd / Open
<u>1983</u> - <u>198</u>	589	352	562	1504	5th / Open
<u>1984</u> - <u>220</u>	622	380	622	1625	3rd / Open
<u>1985</u> - <u>220</u>	639	374	628	1642	3rd / Open
<u>1986</u> - <u>220</u>	617	385	611	1614	3rd / Open
<u>1987</u> - <u>220</u>	622	380	573	1576	2nd / Open
<u>1988</u> - <u>220</u>	600	358	540	1499	<u>1st / Open</u>
<u>1989</u> - <u>220</u>	556	325	540	1421	1st / Masters (40+)
<u>1990</u> - <u>220</u>	551	314	490	1355	4th / Open
<u>1991</u> - <u>220</u>	551	319	523	1391	4th / Open
<u>1992</u> – <u>220</u>	562	330	534	1427	2nd / Masters (40+)
<u>1993</u> - <u>220</u>	534	308	507	1350	3rd / Masters (40+)
<u>1994</u> - <u>220</u>	518	303	473	1294	1st / Masters (40+)
<u>1995</u> - <u>220</u>	545	325	501	1372	1st / Masters (40-49)
<u>1996</u> - <u>220</u>	473	281	451	1207	1st / Masters (45-49)

Year / Class	SQUAT	BENCH	DEADLIFT	TOTAL	PLACE / Division
1997 - 220	529	319	501	1349	1st / Masters (45-49)
1998 – 220	518	325	501	1344	1st / Masters (50+)
1999 - 220	551*	325	501	1377	1st / Masters (50-54)
2000 - 220	512	330	501	1344	1st / Masters (50-54)
2001- 220	518	319	501	1339	1st / Masters (50-54)
2002 - 220	463	303	440	1207	1st / Masters (50-54)
2003 - 220	501	303	501	1306	1st / Masters (55-59)
2004 - 198	143	143	143	429	1st / Masters (55-59)
2005 - 220	352	264	385	1001	1st / Masters (55-59)
2006 - 220	402	292	418	1113	1st / Masters (55-59)
2007 - 220	418	297	424	1139	1st / Masters (55-59)
2008 - 198	143	264	308	715	1st / Masters (60-64)
2009 - 198	330	264	363	959	1st / Masters (60-64)
2010 – 198	143	165	303	611	1st / Masters (60-64)
2011- 198	275	209	319	804	1st / Masters (60-64)
2012 – 198	303	214	325	843	1st / Masters (60-64)

38th Annual West Virginia State Powerlifting Championships

@ South Charleston, West Virginia

Year / Class	SQUAT	BENCH	DEADLIFT	TOTAL	PLACE / Division
2013 - 198	303	236	330	869	1st / Masters (65-69)

The 37th Annual (2012) USPF West Virginia State Powerlifting Championships were held March 31st, 2012 at South Charleston, West Virginia. Winners included Doug Currence, Don Hall, and Paul Sutphin. There were no West Virginia State Powerlifting Records broken in the Open / Senior Division at the 2012 USPF West Virginia State Powerlifting Championships. Several weeks after the 2012 USPF West Virginia State Powerlifting Championships, Paul Sutphin won the 2012 RPS Powerlifting "Championship of the Two Virginias" on May 5th, 2012 at Winchester, Virginia for the 2nd consecutive year.

The 38th Annual West Virginia State Powerlifting Championships were held March 23rd, 2013 at South Charleston, West Virginia. Again, winners included Doug Currence, Don Hall, and Paul Sutphin. Don Hall won the Masters (Age 65-69) with four (4) new West Virginia State Powerlifting Records. There were no West Virginia State Powerlifting Records broken in the Open / Senior Division at the 2013 USPF West Virginia State Powerlifting Championships.

Vince White
BEST POWERLIFTERS OF THE 20th CENTURY

Remembering.....

Vince White
Weightlifter, Powerlifter, IPF Category II Referee, Athletes Representative

The passing of Vince White on April 29th, 2013 was a sad day for all of us who knew him as family and a great loss to the sport of Powerlifting. Vince was often referred to as, "The Powerlifter's friend." Vince White held numerous Olympic Weightlifting and Powerlifting Records. Vince was the founder of the *Holley Strength Systems* and a certified IPF (International Powerlifting Federation) Category II Referee from 1982 until

2008. The experience and knowledge of the sport of iron (Weightlifting, Powerlifting, and Bodybuilding) possessed by Vince White contributed to the overall success of the *Charleston Barbell Club* (later known as *Holley Health Club / Holley Strength Systems*).

The Powerlifting Records of Vince White began with the "Odd Lift" events as early as 1960. Vince White ranks number one (1) in the All-Time West Virginia Weightlifter Rankings for the 123lb. class with a Total of 480lbs. Vince is also number one (1) in the West Virginia Powerlifter Rankings for the 198lb. class during the years of 1973, 1974, and 1975. For the year 1978, Vince White is ranked number one (1) among Powerlifters in the 220lb. class in the West Virginia Powerlifter Rankings.

As a teacher and coach of many who chose to learn the iron game, Vince White always modeled the highest level of confidence linked to a mode of discipline essential for winning at Powerlifting. Vince White was elected as the West Virginia State Powerlifting Chairman from April, 1982 until his resignation in September, 1989. Vince was elected by the Powerlifters in the USA as Athlete's Representative for the United States Powerlifting Federation (USPF), more than once.

The year 1983 represented the 25th year of Weightlifting and Powerlifting for Vince White. Long before his 40th birthday, Vince looked forward to competing in the Masters Division of Powerlifting. In the year 1983, Vince became eligible for the Masters Division. At the 1983 National Masters Powerlifting Championships, Vince Totaled 1444lbs. in the 198lb. class. Among the Masters Powerlifting competitors for the state of West Virginia, Vince held the Total Record for the number one (1) spot in the 198lb. class for a period of ten (10) years.

As Athlete's Representative and the West Virginia Powerlifting Chairman, Vince White demonstrated with consistency the highest level of competence essential for recreational and administrative leadership. By 1986, the resume of Vince White documented over twenty-eight (28) years of competitive lifting experience which included a progressive agenda in the best interest of Powerlifting and Powerlifters.

On March 23rd, 1986 a special award was given to Vince White on behalf of the Powerlifters of West Virginia in appreciation for the fine job he had done as the West Virginia Powerlifting Chairman since 1982. In addition to supreme leadership, the character of Vince White, synonymous to honesty and integrity, outlined the rationale for such an award.

On March 25th, 2000 at the 25th Annual USPF West Virginia State Powerlifting Championships, Vince White was officially inducted into the *West Virginia Powerlifting Hall of Fame*. In 2003, Vince placed 2nd at the USPF National Master's Powerlifting Championships on 6/23/2003. While competing in the 220lb. class (Age 60-64), Vince White's Total included a 336lb. Bench Press.

Vince White took great pride in his ability to help lifters perform at a higher level. Vince possessed a wealth of knowledge and often shared what he knew with workout partners and the lifters he coached. Vince was a tough competitor as well as a great strategist. From the analytical approach, if there was a way to win, Vince developed the plan to come out on top. As a testimonial, I have yet to see anyone better.

During a Powerlifting competition, an observational assessment from Vince White was 100% accurate, more often than not. There were hundreds of times when many lifters, including myself, asked Vince one or both of the following questions : "What do you think?" or "What should I take for my next attempt?"

While lifting at the *38th Annual (2013) West Virginia State Powerlifting Championships* on 3/23/2013, Vince White was present for the Deadlifts. After pulling a successful 2nd attempt Deadlift, I asked Vince the question, "What should I take for my 3rd attempt?" Vince made the call…for what would be the last time. After a successful 3rd attempt, as I had done many times for many years, I told Vince, "Thank you!"

Powerlifter Rankings include numbers and achievements made on exact dates at specific locations. Statistically, the support systems complimentary to the same achievements of a lifter are overlooked. Over the years, Vince White was part of the "support system" for many Powerlifters. Not to mention the hundreds of accomplishments by Vince himself,

Vince White ranks among…..

"The BEST POWERLIFTERS OF THE 20th CENTURY!"

"Setting the Records Straight" : Part X

In the second decade of the 21st century, Powerlifting moves on with multiple organizations, single-lift specialists, and lifters with diversified goals. The resurgence of *"Classic Powerlifting"* could be the most popular choice for many novice lifters who have chosen to practice the Powerlifts and compete in official Powerlifting competition. Notwithstanding, *the Powerlifting Records of the 1960's, 1970's, and the early 1980's ARE the Original "RAW" Powerlifting Records.* An athlete's option to measure individual performance without the use of supportive gear is a personal choice. Respectively, I support *"Classic Powerlifting."*

Well into the second decade of the 21st century, Powerlifting moves on with an Elite group of lifters *lifting equipped with Multi-Ply Divisions and the use of supportive gear.* For whatever the reason, the Multi-Ply Division and use of the Monolift have yet to be accepted by a few of the oldest Powerlifting federations. On the upside of the argument, the Monolift, special bars, and the ultimate in supportive gear *are legal in a larger number of Powerlifting organizations.*

Looking back to the 1970's and the 1980's, I would have seized the opportunity to use the Monolift, special bars, and the innovative designs available to Powerlifters today. With much enthusiasm, *I am in full support of Multi-Ply Divisions in Powerlifting and the lifters who choose to compete while using the latest versions of personal equipment.* Therefore, given Powerlifting in the traditional format of the Squat, the Bench Press, and the Deadlift *along with* a required TOTAL, *I am a proponent of Multi-Ply / Professional Powerlifting!*

The lifters of today have the advantage of surfing the net and visiting hundreds of websites for the purpose of obtaining lifting information, Powerlifting routines, workout schedules, and Powerlifting history. In addition, there exists a network of social media which makes it possible for an individual to have hundreds of friends with continuous interaction. Recently, when surfing the internet, I discovered a message posted October 21st, 2006 on a popular Powerlifting website :

"Over at Fortified Iron, posters are trying to come up with all of the Powerlifters who have totaled Elite in three weight classes. Who they've come up with so far : Louie Simmons, Ed Coan, Fred Hatfield, Jim Cash, Larry Pacifico, Mike Bridges, Vince Anello, Paul Sutphin, and Steve Wilson."   *http://www.powerliftingwatch.com/node/3233*

Final Message : May God Bless all Powerlifters!

To be continued...

Paul Sutphin
National Powerlifting Champion
Elite Powerlifter

1979, 1981 YMCA National Powerlifting Champion
Thirty (30) West Virginia State Powerlifting Championship Titles

Dates of Weightlifting Competitions
Beginning 1959 thru 1975

2/14/59 - First Kanawha Valley Open Weightlifting Championships
@ Charleston, West Virginia

2/60 – Second Kanawha Valley Open Weightlifting Championships
@ Charleston, West Virginia

1960 – 1960 Ohio – West Virginia Area Weightlifting Championships
@ Ohio

2/11/61 – Third Kanawha Valley Open Weightlifting Championships
@ Charleston, West Virginia

3/18/61 – Ohio – West Virginia Area Weightlifting Championships
@ Cincinnati, Ohio

4/15/61 – 11th National YMCA Weightlifting Contest
@ Toledo, Ohio

6/03/61 – Wilbur Smith Memorial Weightlifting Championships
@ Pittsburgh, Pennsylvania

6/17/61 – 1961 National Teenage Weightlifting Championships
@ York, Pennsylvania

6/18/61 – 1961 A.M.A. 3rd Annual Steelworkers Open Weightlifting Meet
@ Aliquippa, Pennsylvania

2/24/62 – 4th Annual Kanawha Valley Weightlifting Championships
@ Charleston, West Virginia

3/24/62 – 13th Annual Mr. Capitol District Weightlifting Meet
@ Richmond, Virginia

3/31/62 – Ohio / West Virginia Area Weightlifting Championship
@ Toledo, Ohio

5/11/63 – 1963 National Collegiate Weightlifting Championships
Michigan State University @ East Lansing, Michigan

3/14/64 – 1964 National Collegiate Weightlifting Championships
Michigan State University @ East Lansing, Michigan

5/16/64 – Wilbur Smith Memorial Weightlifting Championships
@ Pittsburgh, Pennsylvania

5/08/65 – 1965 National Collegiate Weightlifting Championships
Michigan State University @ East Lansing, Michigan

4/22/67 – <u>Florida State Weightlifting Championships</u>
   @ Lakeland, Florida

5/13/67 – <u>Region III Weightlifting Championships</u>
   @ Jacksonville Beach, Florida

12/30/67 – <u>10th Annual Tournament of Champions Weightlifting Contest</u>
   @ Jacksonville Beach, Florida

4/06/68 – <u>Florida State Weightlifting Championships</u>
   @ Jacksonville Beach, Florida

3/20/71 – <u>AAU Open Weightlifting Meet</u>
   @ Kittaning, Pennsylvania

4/03/71 – <u>Chesapeake Bay Invitational Weightlifting Contest</u>
   @ Hampton, Virginia

9/18/71 – <u>AMA Open Weightlifting Contest</u>
   @ Pittsburgh, Pennsylvania

11/20/71 – <u>Butler Open Weightlifting Meet</u>
   @ Butler, Pennsylvania

9/16/72 – <u>Open AMA Weightlifting Contest</u>
   @ Pittsburgh, Pennsylvania

4/14/73 – <u>Region III Weightlifting Championships</u>
   @ Savannah, Georgia

4/28/73 – <u>Region IV Weightlifting Championships</u>
   @ St. Petersburg, Florida

9/29/73 – <u>AMA Open Weightlifting Contest</u>
   @ Pittsburgh, Pennsylvania

10/27/73 – <u>Beaver County Weightlifting Championships</u>
   @ Butler, Pennsylvania

Dates of Powerlifting Competitions
Beginning 1/01/1960 thru 9/30/2013

2/06/60 – <u>First Annual West Virginia Power Lift Championships</u>
  @ Charleston, West Virginia

12/17/60 – <u>Second Annual West Virginia Power Lift Championships</u>
  @ Charleston, West Virginia

1/28/61 - <u>Powerlifting / Boy's Club</u>
  @ Pittsburgh, Pennsylvania

1/27/62 – <u>Open Power Meet</u>
  @ Pittsburgh, Pennsylvania

1/26/63 – <u>Annual Power Lift "Odd Lift" Championships</u>
  @ Pittsburgh, Pennsylvania

6/14/63 – <u>Odd-Lift Competition</u>
  @ Benwood, West Virginia

9/05/64 – <u>Powerlifting Tournament of America</u>
  @ York, Pennsylvania

8/65 – <u>1st Annual Junior National Powerlifting Championships</u>

9/04/65 – <u>1st Annual Senior National Powerlifting Championships</u>

12/06/69 – <u>1969 National Collegiate Powerlifting Championships</u>
  Florida State University @ Tallahassee, Florida

12/05/70 – <u>Open Novice Powerlifting Meet</u>
   @ Norristown, Pennsylvania

5/07/71 – <u>Mahoning Valley Powerlifting Championships</u>
   @ Youngstown, Ohio
6/27/71 – <u>3rd Kettering Open Powerlifting</u>
   @ Kettering, Ohio
10/24/71 – <u>1st Annual Miami Valley Open Powerlifting Meet</u>
   @ Franklin, Ohio

2/05/72 - <u>Atlanta Open Powerlifting</u>
   @ Atlanta, Georgia
2/12/72 – <u>Open Powerlifting</u>
   @ Wilmerding, Pennsylvania
3/11/72 – <u>State Correctional Institution Open Powerlifting Meet</u>
   @ Pittsburgh, Pennsylvania
4/22/72 - <u>Tri-State Open Powerlifting</u>
   @ Hopewell, Virginia
7/09/72 – <u>4th Kettering Open Powerlifting Meet</u>
   @ Kettering, Ohio
10/22/72 - <u>2nd Miami Valley Open Powerlifting Meet</u>
   @ Franklin, Ohio
12/09/72 - <u>Open Powerlifting</u>
   @ Bristol, Tennessee

2/10/73 - <u>1973 Open Powerlifting</u>
   @ Youngstown, Ohio
2/24/73 - <u>1st Open Power Meet</u>
   @ Steubenville, Ohio
4/15/73 - <u>Concord Invitational Powerlifting / Concord College</u>
   @ Athens, West Virginia
5/20/73 - <u>1973 (9th Annual) Midwest Open Powerlifting Championships</u>
   @ Cincinnati, Ohio

10/13/73 - 2nd Open Powerlifting Meet

@ Steubenville, Ohio

11/17/73 - 1973 David Stoken Memorial Open Power Meet

@ Munhall, Pennsylvania

12/08/73 - 1973 All-South Powerlifting Championships

@ Durham, North Carolina

1/12/74 – 1st Annual Lexington Open Powerlifting

@ Lexington, Kentucky

2/23/74 – Open Powerlifting Meet

@ Steubenville, Ohio

4/13/74 – 1974 Tri-City Open Powerlifting Meet

@ Hopewell, Virginia

6/28/74 – Powerlifting Meet

@ Parkersburg, West Virginia

10/26/74 – 1st Annual Mountianeer Open (Bench Press Only)

@ Parkersburg, West Virginia

11/16/74 – New Castle Open Powerlifting Meet

@ New Castle, Pennsylvania

12/14/74 – 1974 Mountian Empire Open Powerlifting Championships

@ Bristol, Tennessee

1/18/75 – Lexington Open Powerlifting

@ Lexington, Kentucky

1/75 – YMCA National Powerlifting Championships

3/01/75 – 2nd Annual AAU N.C.S.U. Open Powerlifting (Southern Open)

@ Raleigh, North Carolina

3/08/75 – First Annual Keystone Open / Novice Powerlifting

@ Latrobe, Pennsylvania

4/12/75 – 1st Annual Johnson City Open Powerlifting Meet

@ Johnson City, Tennessee

4/26/75 – Jerrold Blum Open Powerlifting

@ Ambridge, Pennsylvania

4/27/75 – Buckeye Open Powerlifting

@ Bedford Heights, Ohio

5/18/75 – <u>Canton Open Powerlifting</u>
   @ Canton, Ohio
6/07/75 – <u>Mid-Ohio Valley Open Bench Press – Deadlift – Physique Competition</u>
   @ Parkersburg, West Virginia
9/27/75 – <u>Open Powerlifting</u>
   @ Cumberland, Maryland
10/18/75 - <u>Open Powerlifting</u>
   @ Weirton, West Virginia
10/25/75 – <u>2nd Annual Mountianeer Open Bench Press</u>
   @ Parkersburg, WV
11/01/75 – <u>Powerlifting / Huntington YMCA</u>
   @ Huntington, West Virginia
   @ Parkersburg, West Virginia
12/13/75 – <u>Mountian Empire Open Powerlifting</u>
   @ Bristol, Tennessee
1/17/76 – <u>3rd Annual Lexington Open</u>
   @ Lexington, Kentucky
1/25/76 – <u>1976 YMCA National Powerlifting Championships</u>
   @ Ohio
2/14/76 – <u>First Official AAU West Virginia State Powerlifting Championships</u>
   @ New Martinsville, West Virginia
3/27/76 – <u>Great Lakes Powerlifting</u>
   @ Erie, Pennsylvania

4/03/76 – <u>1976 National Collegiate Powerlifting Championships</u>
   Ohio University @ Athens, Ohio
4/17/76 – <u>1976 Buckeye Open Powerlifting</u>
   @ Bedford, Ohio
4/24/76 – <u>1976 Huntington Open Powerlifting Championships</u>
   @ Huntington, WV
5/08/76 – <u>8th Annual (1976) Jerrold S. Blum Memorial Open Power Meet</u>
   @ Ambridge, Pennsylvania
6/12/76 – <u>1976 Region VI Powerlifting Championships</u>
   @ Lexington, Kentucky
7/10 & 7/11/76 – <u>1976 Junior National Powerlifting Championships</u>
   @ Bedford, Ohio

8/07 & 8/08/76 – <u>1976 Teenage National Powerlifting Championships</u>
 @ El Dorado, Arkansas

10/17/76 – <u>1976 Eastern U.S. Powerlifting Championship</u>
 @ Westernport, Maryland

11/06/76 – <u>3rd Annual (1976) Mountianeer Open Powerlifting Championships</u>
 @ Parkersburg, West Virginia

12/11/76 – <u>1976 Mountian Empire Open Powerlifting</u>
 @ Bristol, Tennessee

1/29/77 – <u>1977 Lynchburg Open Powerlifting Championships</u>
 @ Lynchburg, Virginia

3/12/77 – <u>1977 (1st Annual) West Virginia Collegiate Powerlifting Championships</u>
 @ Parkersburg, West Virginia

5/21/77 – <u>1977 (2nd Annual) West Virginia State Powerlifting Championships</u>
 @ New Martinsville, West Virginia

8/20 & 8/21/77 – <u>1977 Senior National Powerlifting Championships</u>
 @ Santa Monica, California

11/06/77 – <u>4th Annual (1977) Mountianeer Open Powerlifting</u>
 @ Parkersburg, West Virginia

11/12/77 – <u>1977 All-South Powerlifting Championships</u>
 @ Durham, North Carolina

12/17/77 – <u>1977 Mountian Empire Open Powerlifting</u>
 @ Bristol, Tennessee

1/14/78 – <u>1978 Huntington Open Powerlifting Meet</u>
 @ Huntington, West Virginia

1/22/78 – <u>1978 YMCA National Powerlifting Championships</u>
 @ Bedford Heights, Ohio

1/28/78 – <u>1978 Lynchburg Open Powerlifting</u>
 @ Lynchburg, Virginia

2/24 & 2/25/78 – <u>1978 Southern Open Powerlifting Championships</u>
 @ Raleigh, North Carolina

4/01/78 – <u>3rd Annual (1978) West Virginia State Powerlifting Championships</u>
 @ New Martinsville, West Virginia

4/16/78 – <u>27th Annual Great Lakes Open</u>

    @ Erie, Pennsylvania

4/29/78 – <u>1978 Roanoke Open Powerlifting</u>

    @ Roanoke, Virginia

5/06/78 – <u>1978 Chattanooga Open Powerlifting Championships</u>

    @ Chattanooga, Tennessee

5/21/78 – <u>1978 North American Powerlifting Championships</u>

6/10/78 – <u>1978 Maryland Open Powerlifting Championships</u>

    @ Cumberland, Maryland

6/24/78 – <u>Novice Powerlifting Meet</u>

    @ New Cumberland, West Virginia

7/08 & 7/09/78 – <u>1978 National (Junior) Powerlifting Championships</u>

    @ North Little Rock, Arkansas

8/25 & 8/26/78 – <u>1978 Senior National Powerlifting Championships</u>

    @ California

10/07/78 – <u>1978 Ohio Valley Open Powerlifting Championships</u>

    @ Weirton, West Virginia

10/29/78 – <u>1978 National Masters Powerlifting Championships</u>

    @ Arlington, Texas

11/04 & 11/05/78 – <u>5th Annual (1978) Mountianeer Open Powerlifting</u>

    @ Parkersburg, West Virginia

11/11/78 – <u>1978 All-South Powerlifting Championships</u>

    @ Durham, North Carolina

12/10/78 – <u>1978 (79) YMCA National Powerlifting Championships</u>

    @ Sandusky, Ohio

1/79 – <u>Mountian Empire Open Powerlifting</u>

    @ Bristol, Tennessee

2/23 & 2/24/79 – <u>1979 Southern Open Powerlifting Championships</u>

    @ Raleigh, North Carolina

3/10/79 – <u>1979 Keystone Open / Novice Powerlifting</u>

    @ Ambridge, Pennsylvania

4/01/79 – <u>4th Annual (1979) West Virginia State Powerlifting Championships</u>

    @ New Martinsville, West Virginia

4/07/79 – <u>1979 Canton Open Powerlifting Championships</u>

    @ Canton, Ohio

4/08/79 – <u>28th Annual (1979) Great Lakes Open Powerlifting</u>
@ Erie, Pennsylvania

4/21/79 – <u>1979 Chattanooga Open Powerlifting Championships</u>
@ Chattanooga, Tennessee

5/04/79 – <u>1979 Hawaii International Powerlifting Championships</u>
@ Hawaii

5/05/79 – <u>1979 Roanoke Open Powerlifting Championships</u>
@ Roanoke, Virginia

5/12/79 – <u>1979 West Virginia State Collegiate Powerlifting Championships</u>
@ Parkersburg, West Virginia

5/12 & 5/13/79 – <u>11th Annual (1979) Jerrold S. Blum Open Powerlifting</u>
@ Ambridge, Pennsylvania

5/26/79 – <u>1979 North American Powerlifting Championships</u>
@ Hamilton, Ontario / Canada

7/14 & 7/15/1979 – <u>1979 National (Junior) Powerlifting Championships</u>
@ Los Angeles (Inglewood), California

8/12/79 – <u>Ohio River Festival Bench Press</u>
@ Ravenswood, West Virginia

8/18 & 8/19/79 – <u>1979 Senior National Powerlifting Powerlifting Championships</u>
@ Bay St. Louis, Mississippi

9/01/79 – <u>1979 Butler Open Powerlifting Meet</u>
@ Butler, Pennsylvania

10/14/79 – <u>6th Annual (1979) Mountianeer Open Powerlifting Championships</u>
@ Mineral Wells, West Virginia

10/28/79 – <u>1979 National Masters Powerlifting Championships</u>
@ Weirton, West Virginia

11/02, 11/03, & 11/04/79 – <u>1979 (9th) World Powerlifting Championships</u>
@ Dayton, Ohio

12/15/79 – 1979 Mountian Empire Open Powerlifting
@ Bristol, Tennessee

1/05/80 – <u>1980 YMCA National Powerlifting Championships</u>
@ Beckley, West Virginia

1/12/80 – <u>1980 WBC Under Class II Powerlifting Meet</u>
@ Washington, Pennsylvania

1/19/80 – <u>1980 King's Classic Powerlifting Championships</u>
  @ Charlotte, North Carolina

3/08/80 - <u>6th Annual (1980) Keystone Open / Below Class II Powerlifting</u>
  @ Ambridge, Pennsylvania

3/30/80 – <u>5th Annual (1980)West Virginia State Powerlifting Championships</u>
  @ New Martinsville, West Virginia

3/30/80 – <u>29th Annual (1980) Great Lakes Open Powerlifting Championships</u>
  @ Erie, Pennsylvania

4/12/80 – <u>1980 Canton Open Powerlifting Championships</u>
  @ Canton, Ohio

4/19/80 – <u>1980 World Series of Powerlifting</u>
  @ Auburn, Alabama

4/27/80 – <u>1980 West Virginia State Collegiate Powerlifting Championships</u>
  @ Huntington, West Virginia

4/27/80 – <u>1980 West Virginia Women's Powerlifting Championships</u>
  @ Huntington, West Virginia

5/03/80 – <u>1980 Eastern Open Powerlifting Meet</u>
  @ Conshohocken, Pennsylvania

5/03 & 5/04/80 – <u>1980 Women's World Powerlifting Championships</u>
  @ Lowell, Massachusetts

5/10/80 – <u>1980 Roanoke Open Powerlifting Championships</u>
  @ Roanoke, Virginia

6/28/80 – <u>1980 Central Virginia Class I Open Powerlifting Championships</u>
  @ Stanardsville, Virginia

7/12 & 7/13/80 – <u>1980 Senior National Powerlifting Championships</u>
  @ Madison, Wisconson

8/23/80 – <u>1980 Atlantic Coast Open Powerlifting Championships</u>
  @ Newport News, Virginia

8/30/80 – <u>1980 Butler Powerlifting Championships</u>
  @ Butler, Pennsylvania

10/19/80 – <u>7th Annual (1980) Mountianeer Open Powerlifting Championships</u>
  @ Mineral Well, West Virginia

10/24 & 10/25/80 – <u>1980 World / National Masters Powerlifting Championships</u>
  @ Victorville, California

11/07 thru 11/09/80 – <u>1980 World Powerlifting Championships</u>
  @ Arlington, Texas

11/22/80 – <u>1980 Charlottesville (Class I) Open Powerlifting</u>
@ Charlottesville, Virginia

12/13/80 – <u>1980 Mountian Empire Open Powerlifting</u>
@ Bristol, Tennessee

1/10/81 – <u>1981 YMCA National Powerlifting Championships</u>
@ Columbus, Ohio

1/31/81 – <u>1981 West Penn Ironmen's Open Powerlifting</u>
@ Pittsburgh, Pennsylvania

3/07/81 – <u>7th Annual (1981) Keystone Open Powerlifting & Below Class II</u>
@ Washington, Pennsylvania

3/21 & 3/22/81 – <u>1981 Virginia State Powerlifting Championships</u>
@ Stanardsville, Virginia

3/28 & 3/29/81 – <u>6th Annual (1981) West Virginia State Powerlifting Championships</u>
@ New Martinsville, West Virginia

3/29/81 – <u>30th Annual (1981) Great Lakes Powerlifting Championships</u>
@ Erie, Pennsylvania

4/18/81 – <u>1981 Canton Open Powerlifting Championships</u>
@ Canton, Ohio

4/26/81 – <u>1981 Eastern Masters Powerlifting Championships</u>
@ Conshohocken, Pennsylvania

5/30/81 – <u>1981 Roanoke Valley Open Powerlifting Championships</u>
@ Roanoke, Virginia

6/13/81 – <u>2nd Annual (1981) Appalachian Open Powerlifting</u>
@ Zanesville, Ohio

7/11 & 7/12/81 – <u>1981 Senior National Powerlifting Championships</u>
@ Corpus Christi, Texas

10/17/81 – <u>1st Annual Dayton Open Powerlifting</u>
@ Dayton, Ohio

10/24 & 10/25/81 - <u>1981 World & National Masters Powerlifting Championships</u>
@ Naperville, Illinois

10/31 & 11/01/81 – <u>8th Annual (1981) Mountianeer Open Powerlifting</u>
@ Mineral Wells, West Virginia

11/07/81 – <u>1981 Virginia Open Powerlifting Championships</u>
@ Stanardsville, Virginia

12/05/81 – <u>1981 Mountian Empire Open Powerlifting</u>
    @ Bristol, Tennessee

12/05/81 – <u>1981 AMA Powerlifting Championships</u>
    @ Slippery Rock, Pennsylvania

1/09/82 – <u>1982 YMCA National Powerlifting Championships</u>
    @ Columbus, Ohio

2/07/82 – <u>1982 Muskingum Valley Open Powerlifting Championships</u>
    @ Zanesville, Ohio

2/13 & 2/14/82 – <u>1982 Bob Moon Memorial Powerlifting Championships</u>
    @ Findlay, Ohio

2/20 & 2/21/82 – <u>1982 Women's National Powerlifting Championships</u>
    @ Auburn, Alabama

3/13/82 – <u>8th Annual (1982) Keystone Open Powerlifting Championships</u>
    @ Washington, Pennsylvania

3/19 & 3/20/82 – <u>1982 National Collegiate Powerlifting Championships</u>
    Marshall University @ Huntington, West Virginia

3/27/82 – <u>31st Annual (1982) Great Lakes Open Powerlifting Championships</u>
    @ Erie, Pennsylvania

4/24 & 4/25/82 – <u>7th Annual (1982) West Virginia State Powerlifting Championships</u>
    @ Fairmont, West Virginia

5/15/82 – <u>1982 Roanoke Centennial Open Powerlifting</u>
    @ Roanoke, Virginia

5/22/82 – <u>1st Annual (1982) Parkersburg Open</u>
    @ Mineral Wells, West Virginia

6/05/82 – <u>1st Annual (1982) West Virginia Teenage Powerlifting Championships</u>
    @ Parkersburg, West Virginia

6/05 & 6/06/82 – <u>1982 National (Junior) Powerlifting Championships</u>
    @ Portland, Oregon

6/13/82 – <u>1982 Eastern Masters Powerlifting Championships</u>
    @ York, Pennsylvania

6/26/82 – <u>3rd Annual (1982) Appalachian Masters Powerlifting</u>
    @ Zanesville, Ohio

7/10 & 7/11/82 – <u>1982 Senior National Powerlifting Championships</u>
    @ Dayton, Ohio

8/06 & 8/07/82 – <u>National Cup Powerlifting Championships</u>
   @ Nashville, Tennessee

8/06, 8/07, & 8/08/82 – <u>1982 Teenage National Powerlifting Championships</u>
   @ Greensburg, Pennsylvania

8/21 & 8/22/82 – <u>1st Annual (1982) Southern Ohio Open Powerlifting</u>
   @ Chillicothe, Ohio

9/04 & 9/05/82 – <u>1982 National Master's Powerlifting Championships</u>
   @ Greensboro, North Carolina

10/09/82 – <u>1982 Lexington Open Powerlifting Meet</u>
   @ Lexington, Kentucky

10/30 & 10/31/82 – <u>9th Annual (1982) Mountianeer Open Powerlifting</u>
   @ Mineral Wells, West Virginia

11/20/82 – <u>1982 Virginia Open Powerlifting Meet</u>
   @ Stanardsville, Virginia

12/10 & 12/11/82 – <u>Western North Carolina Open Powerlifting</u>
   @ Canton, North Carolina

12/11/82 – <u>1982 Mountian Empire Open Powerlifting</u>
   @ Bristol, Tennessee

12/11 & 12/12/82 – <u>1st Annual Body Shop Powerlifting Meet</u>
   @ Weirton, West Virginia

1/08/83 – <u>1983 YMCA National Powerlifting Championships</u>
   @ Columbus, Ohio

1/09/83 – <u>West Virginia Challenge Cup Powerlifting</u>
   @ Beckley, West Virginia

1/29 & 1/30/83 – <u>1983 Women's National Powerlifting Championships</u>
   @ Chicago, Illinois

2/09 & 2/10/83 – <u>1st Annual (1983) Interservice U.S. Military Powerlifting</u>
   @ San Diego, California

3/12/83 – <u>1983 Muskingum Valley Open Powerlifting</u>
   @ Zanesville, Ohio

3/25 & 3/26/83 – <u>1983 National Collegiate Powerlifting Championships</u>
   @ College Station, Texas

3/26/83 – <u>8th Annual (1983) West Virginia State Powerlifting Championships</u>
   @ Elkview, West Virginia

4/23/83 – <u>2nd Annual (1983) West Virginia Teenage Powerlifting Championships</u>
  @ Parkersburg, West Virginia

4/30 & 5/01/83 – <u>1983 Virginia State Powerlifting Championships</u>
  @ Roanoke, Virginia

5/21/83 – <u>Eastern US Masters Powerlifting Championships</u>
  @ Ambridge, Pennsylvania

5/28/83 – <u>2nd Annual (1983) Parkersburg Open Powerlifting Championships</u>
  @ Mineral Wells, West Virginia

6/04 & 6/05/83 – <u>1983 Junior National Powerlifting Championships</u>
  @ Charlottesville, Virginia

6/25/83 – <u>1st Annual Southeastern Bench Press Championships</u>
  @ Charleston, West Virginia

7/23 & 7/24/83 – <u>1983 Senior National Powerlifting Championships</u>
  @ Austin, Texas

8/05, 8/06 & 8/07/83 – <u>1983 Teenage National Powerlifting Championships</u>
  @ Scottsdale, Arizona

8/13 & 8/14/83 – <u>2nd Annual (1983) Southern Ohio Open Powerlifting</u>
  @ Chillicothe, Ohio

8/27/83 – <u>1st Annual (1983) Southwest Virginia Powerlifting</u>
  @ Norton, Virginia

9/03 & 9/04/83 – <u>1983 World Masters Powerlifting Championships</u>
  @ London, Ontario, Canada

9/24/83 – <u>1983 Ambridge VFW Powerlifting Championships</u>
  @ Ambridge, Pennsylvania

10/08 & 10/09/83 – <u>1983 Police and Fire Fighters National Powerlifting</u>
  @ Dayton, Ohio

10/15 & 10/16/83 – <u>1983 National Masters Powerlifting Championships</u>
  @ Syracuse, New York

10/29 & 10/30/83 – <u>10th Annual (1983) Mountianeer Open Powerlifting</u>
  @ Huntington, West Virginia

12/10/83 – <u>1983 Mountian Empire Open Powerlifting</u>
  @ Bristol, Tennessee

12/17/83 – <u>1983 YMCA National Powerlifting Championships</u>
  @ Columbus, Ohio

1/28 & 1/29/84 – <u>1984 Women's National Powerlifting Championships</u>
@ Austin, Texas

2/08 & 2/09/84 – <u>1984 Military Interservice Powerlifting Championship</u>
@ El Toro, California

2/11 & 2/12/84 – <u>2nd Annual Steel Valley Open</u>
@ Weirton, West Virginia

3/03/84 – <u>1984 West Virginia Teenage Powerlifting Championships</u>
@ Charleston, West Virginia

3/17/84 – <u>10th Annual (1984) Keystone Open Powerlifting</u>
@ Washington, Pennsylvania

3/17 & 3/18/84 – <u>1984 Virginia State Powerlifting Championships</u>
@ Stanardsville, Virginia

3/23 & 3/24/84 – <u>1984 National Collegiate Powerlifting Championships</u>
@ Villanova, Pennsylvania

3/31 & 4/01/84 – <u>9th Annual (1984) West Virginia State Powerlifting Championships</u>
@ South Charleston, West Virginia

4/14/84 – <u>33rd Annual (1984) Great Lakes Powerlifting Championships</u>
@ Erie, Pennsylvania

4/27 & 4/28/84 – <u>1984 High School National Powerlifting Championships</u>
@ Shawnee, Oklahoma

5/19 & 5/20/84 – <u>1984 Roanoke Open Powerlifting Championships</u>
@ Roanoke, Virginia

5/26 & 5/27/84 – <u>1984 Parkersburg Open Powerlifting Championships</u>
@ Parkersburg, West Virginia

6/02 & 6/03/84 – <u>1984 Junior National Powerlifting Championships</u>
@ Portland, Maine

7/7 & 7/08/84 – <u>1984 Senior National Powerlifting Championships</u>
@ Dayton, Ohio

7/21/84 – <u>1984 Western PA Class II & Below Open Powerlifting</u>
@ Butler, Pennsylvania

7/21 & 7/22/84 – <u>1984 ADFPA National Powerlifting Championships</u>
@ Rosemont, Illinois

8/04 & 8/05/84 – <u>3rd Annual (1984) Southern Ohio Open</u>
@ Chillicothe, Ohio

8/05/84 – <u>1984 Teenage National Powerlifting Championships</u>
@ Chicago, Illinois

8/11/84 – <u>1984 Southwest Virginia Open Powerlifting</u>
   @ Coeburn, Virginia

9/22/84 – <u>1984 Ambridge VFW Powerlifting Championships</u>
   @ Ambridge, Pennsylvania

9/20 thru 9/23/84 – <u>1984 World Junior / Master's Powerlifting Championships</u>
   @ Perth, Australia

10/13 & 10/14/84 – <u>1984 National Masters Powerlifting Championships</u>
   @ McClean, Virginia

11/10 & 11/11/84 – <u>11th Annual (1984) Mountianeer Open Powerlifting Championships</u>
   @ Huntington, West Virginia

11/17/84 – <u>1984 AMA Powerlifting</u>
   @ Slippery Rock, Pennsylvania

11/18/84 – <u>1984 Hancock County Powerlifting</u>
   @ New Manchester, West Virginia

11/23, 11/24, & 11/25/84 – 1984 (14th) <u>World Powerlifting Championships</u>
   @ Dallas, Texas

12/01/84 – <u>1984 Mountian Empire Powerlifting Championships</u>
   @ Bristol, Tennessee

12/15 & 12/16/84 – <u>3rd Annual Steel Valley Open</u>
   @ Weirton, West Virginia

1/26 & 1/27/85 – <u>1985 Women's National Powerlifting Championships</u>
   @ Boston, Massachusetts

3/03/85 – <u>1985 Hawaii Invitational Powerlifting</u>
   @ Honolulu, Hawaii

3/30 & 3/31/85 – <u>1985 Virginia State Powerlifting Championships</u>
   @ Woodbridge, Virginia

3/31/85 – <u>1985 Muskingum Valley Open Powerlifting</u>
   @ Zanesville, Ohio

4/13 & 4/14/85 – <u>10th Annual (1985) West Virginia State Powerlifting Championships</u>
   @ Newell, West Virginia

4/19/85 – <u>1985 West Virginia State Teenage Powerlifting Championships</u>
   @ Man, West Virginia

5/04 & 5/05/85 – <u>1985 Parkersburg Open Powerlifting Championships</u>
   @ Parkersburg, West Virginia

5/11 & 5/12/85 – <u>1985 National Master's Powerlifting Championships</u>
 @ Dallas, Texas

5/11 & 5/12/85 – <u>1985 ADFPA Women's National Powerlifting Championships</u>
 @ Chicago, Illinois

5/31 thru 6/02/85 – <u>1985 IPF Women's World Powerlifting Championships</u>
 @ Vienna, Austria

6/01 & 6/02/85 – <u>1985 Junior National Powerlifting Championships</u>
 @ Arlington, Virginia

6/28, 6/29 & 6/30/85 – <u>1985 Teenage National Powerlifting Championships</u>
 @ Rockport, Maine

7/20 & 7/21/85 – <u>1985 ADFPA National Powerlifting Championships</u>
 @ Wilkes-Barre, Pennsylvania

7/27 & 7/28/85 – <u>Tri-State Open Powerlifting Meet</u>
 @ Fairmont, West Virginia

11/09 & 11/10/85 – <u>12th Annual Mountianeer Open Powerlifting</u>
 @ Parkersburg, West Virginia

11/16 & 11/17/85 – <u>Eastern USA Open Powerlifting</u>
 @ Charlotte, North Carolina

12/14/85 – <u>1985 YMCA National Powerlifting Championships</u>
 @ Columbus, Ohio

12/14 & 12/15/85 – <u>1985 (4th Annual) Steel Valley Open</u>
 @ Weirton, West Virginia

2/01 & 2/02/86 – <u>USPF Women's National Powerlifting Championships</u>
 @ Salt Lake City, Utah

3/08 & 3/09/86 – <u>APF Women's National Powerlifting Championships</u>
 @ Canton, Ohio

3/22 & 3/23/86 – <u>11th Annual (1986) West Virginia State Powerlifting Championships</u>
 @ New Martinsville, West Virginia

4/12/86 – <u>1986 Buckeye Open Powerlifting Championships</u>
 @ Nelsonville, Ohio

4/19/86 – <u>1986 West Virginia State Collegiate Powerlifting Championships</u>
 @ Parkersburg, West Virginia

4/26/86 – <u>1986 West Virginia State Teenage Powerlifting Championships</u>
 @ Man, West Virginia

5/03/86 – <u>1986 Parkersburg Open Powerlifting Championships</u>
    @ Parkersburg, West Virginia

5/10 & 5/11/86 – <u>1986 A.P.F. National Powerlifting Championships</u>
    @ Philadelphia, Pennsylvania

5/17/86 – <u>Bob Moon Memorial Powerlifting Championships</u>
    @ Findlay, Ohio

6/28 & 6/29/86 – <u>1986 Region VI Powerlifting Championships</u>
    @ Fort Knox, Kentucky

8/09 & 8/10/86 – <u>1986 USPF Teenage National Powerlifting Championships</u>
    @ St. Louis, Missouri

11/01 & 11/02/86 – <u>13th Annual (1986) Mountianeer Open Powerlifting Championships</u>
    @ Parkersburg, West Virginia

11/15 & 11/16/86 – <u>Eastern USA Open Powerlifting Championships</u>
    @ Raleigh, North Carolina

11/15 & 11/16/86 – <u>1986 APF World Powerlifting Championships</u>
    @ Maui, Hawaii

12/06 & 12/07/86 – <u>Central Virginia Open Powerlifting Championships</u>
    @ Mechanicsville, Virginia

12/13/86 – <u>YMCA National Powerlifting Championships</u>
    @ Columbus, Ohio

1/10/87 – <u>Fort Knox Power Classic (Bench Press / Deadlift)</u>
    @ Lexington, Kentucky

1/17 & 1/18/87 – <u>USPF Women's National Powerlifting Championships</u>
    @ San Francisco, California

2/07 & 2/08/87 – <u>1987 Steel Valley Open Powerlifting Championships</u>
    @ Weirton, West Virginia

2/28/87 – <u>1987 West Virginia Collegiate Powerlifting Championships</u>
    @ Concord College – Athens, West Virginia

3/29/87 - <u>1987 APF National Master's Powerlifting Championships</u>
    @ Fort Knox, Kentucky

4/11/87 – <u>12th Annual (1987) West Virginia State Powerlifting Championships</u>
    @ Mineral Wells, West Virginia

5/09 & 5/10/87 – <u>1987 APF Junior National Powerlifting Championships</u>
    @ St. Petersburg, Florida

5/16 & 5/17/87 – <u>1987 USPF National Master's Powerlifting Championships</u>
    @ Irving, Texas

5/16 & 5/17/1987 – <u>1987 Region VI Powerlifting Championships</u>
    @ Lexington, Kentucky

5/31 & 6/01/87 – <u>1987 IPF Women's World Powerlifting Championships</u>
    @ Perth, Australia

6/06 & 6/07/87 – <u>APF Teenage National Boy's & Girl's Powerlifting Championships</u>
    @ Fort Knox, Kentucky

7/25/87 – <u>Lexington ADFPA Power Festival</u>
    @ Lexington, Kentucky

8/01 & 8/02/87 – <u>1987 USPF Teenage National Powerlifting Championships</u>
    @ Allentown, Pennsylvania

10/31 & 11/01/87 – <u>14th Annual (1987) Mountianeer Open Powerlifting</u>
    @ Parkersburg, West Virginia

11/12 thru 11/15/87 – <u>1987 IPF World Powerlifting Championships</u>
    @ Fredrikstad, Norway

11/21 & 11/22/87 – <u>1987 APF World Powerlifting Championships</u>
    @ Dayton, Ohio

11/28/87 – <u>1987 Natural Nationals Powerlifting Regionals</u>
    @ Columbus, Ohio

12/05 & 12/06/87 – <u>1987 APF / WPC World Teen / Jr. / Masters Powerlifting</u>
    @ Ft. Knox, Kentucky

12/12/1987 – <u>YMCA National Powerlifting Championships</u>
    @ Columbus, Ohio

1/30 & 1/31/88 – <u>1988 USPF Women's National Powerlifting Championships</u>
    @ Austin, Texas

2/06 & 2/07/88 – <u>6th Annual (1988) Steel Valley Open Powerlifting Championships</u>
    @ Weirton, West Virginia

2/13 & 2/14/88 – <u>1988 USPF Natural National Powerlifting Championships</u>
    @ Dallas, Texas

3/05 & 3/06/88 – <u>13th Annual (1988) West Virginia State Powerlifting Championships</u>
    @ Athens, West Virginia

3/19 & 3/20/88 – <u>1988 USPF Men's Collegiate National Powerlifting Championships</u>
    @ Philadelphia, Pennsylvania

4/23 & 4/24/88 – <u>1988 APF Junior National Powerlifting Championships</u>
  @ Chicago, Illinois

5/05 & 5/06/88 – <u>1988 IPF Women's World Powerlifting Championships</u>
  @ Brussels, Belgium

5/14 & 5/15/88 – <u>1988 USPF National Masters Powerlifting Championships</u>
  @ Salt Lake City, UT

7/09 & 7/10/88 – <u>1988 APF National Masters & Teenage Powerlifting Championships</u>
  @ Barboursville, West Virginia

7/09/88 – <u>ADFPA Lexington Open Powerlifting Festival</u>
  @ Lexington, Kentucky

7/16 & 7/17/88 – <u>1988 APF Senior National Powerlifting Championships</u>
  @ Columbus, Ohio

10/01 & 10/02/88 – <u>Natural Nationals Regional Powerlifting</u>
  @ Cincinnati, Ohio

11/05 & 11/06/88 – <u>7th Annual (1988) Steel Valley Open Powerlifting Championships</u>
  @ Weirton, West Virginia

11/28/88 – <u>1988 WPC World Powerlifting Championships</u>
  @ Johannesburg, South Africa

2/25/89 – <u>Keystone Open Powerlifting Championships</u>
  @ Ambridge, Pennsylvania

3/11 & 3/12/89 – <u>15th Annual (1989) West Virginia State Powerlifting Championships</u>
  @ Glenville, West Virginia

3/18 & 3/19/89 – <u>ADFPA (7th Annual) Shenandoah Open Powerlifting</u>
  @ Maurtown, Virginia

4/02/89 – <u>Budweiser World Record Breakers Powerlifting Championships</u>
  @ Honolulu, Hawaii

4/08/89 – <u>1989 West Virginia State Teenage Powerlifting Championships</u>
  @ Man, West Virginia

5/13 & 5/14/89 – <u>1989 USPF National Masters Powerlifting Championships</u>
  @ Dallas, Texas

5/20/89 – <u>1989 ADFPA West Virginia State Powerlifting Championships</u>
  @ Berkeley Springs, West Virginia

7/14, 7/15, & 7/16/89 – <u>USPF Men's and Women's National Powerlifting Championships</u>
  @ Las Vegas, Nevada

7/15/89 – <u>APF National Masters & Teenage Powerlifting Championships</u>
 @ Cleveland, Ohio

7/22 & 7/23/89 – <u>APF Men's and Women's Senior National Powerlifting Championships</u>
 @ Columbus, Ohio

7/29 & 7/30/89 – <u>ADFPA Senior National Powerlifting Championships</u>
 @ Wilkes-Barre, Pennsylvania

11/05/89 – <u>1989 Mountianeer Open Powerlifting Championships</u>
 @ Barboursville, West Virginia

11/05/89 – <u>Natural Nationals Powerlifting Regionals</u>
 @ Lexington, Kentucky

11/13 thru 11/17/89 – <u>1989 IPF Men's & Women's World Powerlifting Championships</u>
 @ Sydney, Nova Scotia, Canada

12/01 thru 12/03/89 – <u>1989 WPC World Powerlifting Championships</u>
 @ Stone, England

12/02/89 – <u>1989 YMCA National Powerlifting Championships</u>
 @ Columbus, Ohio

3/24/90 – <u>1990 USPF West Virginia State Powerlifting Championships</u>
 @ Barboursville, West Virginia

4/21/90 – <u>1990 West Virginia State Teenage Powerlifting Championships</u>
 @ Man, West Virginia

5/19/90 – <u>1990 ADFPA West Virginia State Powerlifting Championships</u>
 @ Berkeley Springs, West Virginia

11/17/90 – <u>1990 Mountianeer Open Powerlifting Championships</u>
 @ Parkersburg, West Virginia

2/28 thru 3/03/91 – <u>1991 NASA Natural National Powerlifting Championships</u>
 @ Oklahoma City, Oklahoma

3/24/91 – <u>17th Annual (1991) USPF West Virginia State Powerlifting Championships</u>
 @ Morgantown, West Virginia

5/18 & 5/19/91 – <u>1991 USPF National Masters Powerlifting Championships</u>
 @ High Point, North Carolina

7/13 & 7/14/1991 – <u>APF Teenage Nationals</u>
 @ Charleston, West Virginia

9/28/91 – <u>1991 ADFPA West Virginia State Powerlifting Championships</u>
@ Berkeley Springs, West Virginia

11/09/91 – <u>1991 Mountianeer Open Powerlifting Championships</u>
@ Parkersburg, West Virginia

2/15/92 – <u>West Virginia High School Powerlifting Championships</u>
@ Parkersburg, West Virginia

2/22/92 – <u>USPF Coalfield Conference High School Powerlifting</u>
Shady Spring High School / Shady Spring, West Virginia

3/05 thru 3/08/92 – <u>1992 NASA Natural National Powerlifting Championships</u>
@ Oklahoma City, Oklahoma

3/14/1992 – <u>USPF 1992 National Collegiate Powerlifting Championships</u>
@ Raleigh, North Carolina

3/14/92 – <u>18th Annual (1992)USPF West Virginia State Powerlifting Championships</u>
@ Institute, West Virginia

4/04 & 4/05/92 – <u>ADFPA Powerlifting Nationals</u>
@ Baltimore, Maryland

5/02/92 – <u>USPF West Virginia State Teenage / Collegiate Powerlifting Championships</u>
@ Man, West Virginia

5/01 thru 5/03/92 – <u>USPF (Teenage) Junior National Powerlifting Championships</u>
@ Brockton, Massachusetts

5/16 & 5/17/92 – <u>USPF National Masters Powerlifting Championships</u>
@ Raleigh, North Carolina

5/30 & 5/31/1992 – <u>USPF High School National Powerlifting Championships</u>
@ Port Charlotte, Florida

8/22/1992 – <u>USPF Beast of the East Regional Powerlifting</u>
@ Huntington, West Virginia

11/21 & 22/1992 – <u>1992 Mountianeer Open Powerlifting Championships</u>
@ Parkersburg, West Virginia

2/13/93 – <u>West Virginia High School Powerlifting Championships</u>
@ Shady Spring, West Virginia

3/20/93 – <u>18th Annual (1993) USPF West Virginia State Powerlifting Championships</u>
@ Parkersburg, West Virginia

4/02 thru 4/04/1993 – <u>1993 USPF High School National Powerlifting Championships</u>
   @ Beckley, West Virginia

5/08/1993 – <u>1993 NASA West Virginia State Powerlifting Championships</u>
   @ Fairmont, West Virginia

5/22/1993 – <u>1993 USPF West Virginia State Teenage Powerlifting Championships</u>
   @ Man, West Virginia

9/17 thru 9/19/93 – <u>IPF Powerlifting Championship of the Americas</u>
   @ Rockville, Maryland

12/04 & 12/05/1993 – <u>NASA West Virginia Regional</u>
   @ Fairmont, West Virginia

12/18/1993 – <u>3rd Annual USPF Open Powerlifting</u>
   @ Beckley, West Virginia

2/12/94 – <u>1994 ADFPA West Virginia State Powerlifting Championships</u>
   @ Beckley, West Virginia

3/12 & 3/13/94 – <u>12th Annual ADFPA Shenandoah Open Powerlifting</u>
   @ Woodstock, Virginia

3/19 & 3/20/94 – <u>NASA Powerlifting Natural Nationals</u>
   @ Pittsburgh, Pennsylvania

4/02/94 – <u>19th Annual (1994) USPF West Virginia State Powerlifting Championships</u>
   @ Shady Springs, West Virginia

4/01 thru 4/03/94 – <u>1994 ADFPA Powerlifting Nationals</u>
   @ Baltimore, Maryland

4/30 & 5/01/94 – <u>1994 NASA West Virginia State Powerlifting Championships</u>
   @ Fairmont, West Virginia

5/28 & 5/29/94 – <u>1994 NASA Sub-Masters & Masters National Powerlifting Championships</u>
   @ Nashville, Tennessee

6/22 thru 6/25/94 – <u>12th IPF Junior Worlds Powerlifting Championships</u>
   @ Bali, Indonesia

11/05 & 11/06/94 – <u>NASA West Virginia Powerlifting Regionals</u>
   @ Fairmont, West Virginia

12/17/94 – <u>ADFPA Open Powerlifting</u>
   @ Beckley, West Virginia

2/25/95 – <u>1995 ADFPA West Virginia State Powerlifting Championships</u>
    @ Beckley, West Virginia

2/25/95 – <u>1995 USPF Junior National Powerlifting Championships</u>
    @ Philadelphia, Pennsylvania

4/08/95 – <u>20th Annual (1995) USPF West Virginia State Powerlifting Championships</u>
    @ Institute, West Virginia

4/29 & 4/30/1995 – <u>1995 NASA West Virginia State Powerlifting Championships</u>
    @ Ravenswood, West Virginia

6/17 & 6/18/1995 – <u>NASA Grand Nationals Powerlifting</u>
    @ Cincinnati, Ohio

7/08/1995 – <u>APF Big Iron on the River</u>
    @ Ironton, Ohio

10/14/95 – <u>1995 Ohio State Powerlifting Championships</u>
    @ Chillicothe, Ohio

11/12/95 – <u>NASA West Virginia Regional Powerlifting</u>
    @ Ravenswood, West Virginia

4/13/96 – <u>AAU Virginia State Powerlifting Championships</u>
    @ Ft. Lee, Virginia

4/20/96 – <u>21st Annual (1996) USPF West Virginia State Powerlifting Championships</u>
    @ New Martinsville, West Virginia

4/27 & 4/28/96 – <u>1996 NASA West Virginia State Powerlifting Championships</u>
    @ Ravenwood, West Virginia

5/10 thru 5/12/96 – <u>USPF National Masters Powerlifting Championships</u>
    @ Dayton, Ohio

6/15/96 – <u>ADFPA Invitational Powerlifting</u>
    @ Bluefield, West Virginia

7/06/96 – <u>2nd Annual Big Iron on the River Powerlifting Championships</u>
    @ Ironton, Ohio

10/05/96 – <u>1996 Ohio State Powerlifting Championships</u>
    @ Chillicothe, Ohio

11/10/96 – <u>NASA West Virginia Regional Powerlifting</u>
    @ Ravenswood, West Virginia

12/14/96 – <u>ADFPA Holiday Invitational Powerlifting</u>
   @ Bluefield, West Virginia

3/29/97 – <u>22nd Annual (1997) USPF West Virginia State Powerlifting Championships</u>
   @ Institute, West Virginia

4/12/97 – <u>ADFPA West Virginia State Powerlifting Championships</u>
   @ Bluefield, West Virginia

7/12/97 – <u>APF 3rd Annual "Big Iron on the River" Powerlifting Championships</u>
   @ Ironton, Ohio

9/13/97 – <u>Iron House Classic Powerlifting</u>
   @ Zanesville, Ohio

9/20/97 – <u>Bench Press Invitational</u>
   @ Bluefield, West Virginia

2/08/98 – <u>1998 Westside Invitational Powerlifting Championships</u>
   @ Columbus, Ohio

3/28/98 – <u>23rd Annual (1998) USPF West Virginia State Powerlifting Championships</u>
   @ Institute, West Virginia

5/30/98 – <u>USAPL/ADFPA (1998) West Virginia State Powerlifting Championships</u>
   @ Bluefield, West Virginia

10/30 & 11/01/98 – <u>1998 IPA Senior National Powerlifting Championships</u>
   @ Annapolis, Maryland

11/28/98 – <u>USAPL West Virginia IPF Qualifier</u>
   @ New Martinsville, West Virginia

2/27/99 - <u>1999 Westside Invitational Powerlifting Championships</u>
   @ Ohio

3/27/99 – <u>24th Annual (1999) USPF West Virginia State Powerlifting Championships</u>
   @ Institute, West Virginia

8/29/99 – <u>APF/AMPF 1999 West Virginia State Powerlifting Championships</u>
   @ Charleston, West Virginia

11/19 thru 11/21/99 – <u>IPA National Powerlifting Championships</u>
   @ York, Pennsylvania

2/20/2000 – <u>Westside Invitational Powerlifting</u>
  @ Columbus, Ohio
3/25/2000 – <u>25th Annual (2000) USPF West Virginia State Powerlifting Championships</u>
  @ Institute, West Virginia
6/24 & 25/2000 – <u>USPF Senior National Powerlifting Championships Mountianeer Cup II Powerlifting Tournament</u>
  @ Chester, West Virginia
9/09/2000 – <u>APF West Virginia Powerlifting</u>
  @ South Charleston, West Virginia
11/17 thru 11/19/2000 – <u>IPA Senior National Powerlifting Championships</u>
  @ Columbus, Ohio

2/24/2001 – <u>APF Mountianeer Powerlifting</u>
  @ South Charleston, West Virginia
3/10/2001 – <u>USAPL Virginia Open Powerlifting</u>
  @ Charlottesville, Virginia
3/25/2001 – <u>26th Annual (2001) USPF West Virginia State Powerlifting Championships</u>
  @ Institute, West Virginia
6/16/2001 – <u>USAPL Squat Nationals</u>
  @ Charlottesville, Virginia
6/22 thru 6/24/2001 – <u>Mountianeer Cup III & USPF Senior Nationals</u>
  @ Chester, West Virginia
11/17 & 18/2001 – <u>IPA Senior National Powerlifting Championships</u>
  @ Columbus, Ohio

3/23/2002 – <u>27th Annual (2002) USPF West Virginia State Powerlifting Championships</u>
  @ Institute, West Virginia
3/30/2002 – <u>IPA Mountianeer Powerlifting Championships</u>
  @ Charleston, West Virginia
5/04 & 5/05/2002 – <u>USAPL National Masters Powerlifting Championships</u>
  @ Charlottesville, Virginia
5/10 thru 5/12/2002 – <u>AAU Triple Crown Powerlifting Championships</u>
  @ Richmond, Virginia

6/22/2002 – <u>USPF Senior National Powerlifting Championships</u>
   @ Chester, West Virginia

6/22/2002 – <u>Mountianeer Cup IV</u>
   @ Chester, West Virginia

7/12 thru 7/14/2002 – <u>USAPL Men's Powerlifting Championships</u>
   @ Lincolnwood, Illinois

7/20/2002 – <u>IPA World Cup & Iron House Classic Powerlifting Championships</u>
   @ Zanesville, Ohio

11/13 thru 11/17/2002 – <u>IPF Men's World Powerlifting Championships</u>
   @ Trencin, Slovakia

11/15 thru 11/17/2002 – <u>IPA Senior National Powerlifting Championships</u>
   @ Worthington, Ohio

3/15/2003 – <u>28th Annual (2003) USPF West Virginia State Powerlifting Championships</u>
   @ Institute, West Virginia

3/15/2003 – <u>APF Junior National Powerlifting Championships</u>
   @ Turner, Maine

4/12 & 4/13/2003 – <u>IPA Iron House Classic Powerlifting</u>
   @ Delaware, Ohio

6/23/2003 – <u>USPF Seniors & Masters National Powerlifting Championships</u>
   @ Chester, West Virginia

7/19 & 7/20/2003 – <u>USAPL Men's National Powerlifting Championships</u>
   @ Rapid City, South Dakota

8/08 thru 8/10/2003 – <u>IPA World Powerlifting Championships</u>
   @ Harrisburg, Pennsylvania

11/04 thru 11/09/2003 – <u>IPF Men's World Powerlifting Championships</u>
   @ Vejle, Denmark

11/14 thru 11/16/2003 – <u>IPA Senior National Powerlifting Championships</u>
   @ Harrisburg, Pennsylvania

3/27/2004 – <u>29th Annual (2004) USPF West Virginia State Powerlifting Championships</u>
   @ South Charleston, West Virginia

4/04/2004 – <u>IPA Iron House Classic Powerlifting</u>
   @ Newark, Ohio

7/07 thru 7/11/2004 – <u>USAPL Men's National Powerlifting Championships</u>
    @ Baton Rouge, Louisiana
7/31/2004 – <u>USAPL West Virginia Powerlifting</u>
    @ Wheeling, West Virginia
8/14/2004 – <u>Mountianeer Cup VI</u>
    @ Chester, West Virginia
11/09 thru 11/14/2004 – <u>2004 IPF World Powerlifting Championships</u>
    @ Cape Town, South Africa
11/19 thru 11/21/2004 – <u>IPA Senior National Powerlifting Championships</u>
    @ Shamokin, Pennsylvania

3/19/2005 – <u>30th Annual (2005) USPF West Virginia State Powerlifting Championships</u>
    @ South Charleston, West Virginia
4/16 & 4/17/2005 – <u>IPA Iron House Classic Powerlifting Championships</u>
    @ Newark, Ohio
5/06 thru 5/08/2005 – <u>USAPL Men's National Powerlifting Championships</u>
    @ Killeen, Texas
6/25/2005 – <u>Mountianeer Cup VII</u>
    @ Chester, West Virginia
8/20/2005 – <u>USAPL Virginia State Powerlifting Championships</u>
    @ Charlottesville, Virginia
11/12/2005 – <u>SPF/WBPLA World Championships</u>
    @ Gatlinburg, Tennessee

3/25/2006 – <u>31st Annual (2006) USPF West Virginia State Powerlifting Championships</u>
    @ South Charleston, West Virginia
4/01 & 4/02/2006 – <u>IPA Iron House Classic Powerlifting</u>
    @ Newark, Ohio
5/06/06 – <u>New England Record Breakers</u>
    @ Boston, Massachusetts
5/05 thru 5/07/2006 – <u>USAPL National Masters Powerlifting</u>
    @ Killeen, Texas
7/06 thru 7/09/2006 – <u>USAPL Senior National Powerlifting</u>
    @ Miami, Florida

8/19/2006 – <u>USPF Senior Nationals</u>
  @ Chester, West Virginia
10/22/2006 – <u>USPF Regional Powerlifting</u>
  @ New Martinsville, West Virginia

3/31/2007 – <u>32nd Annual (2007) West Virginia State Powerlifting Championships</u>
  @ South Charleston, West Virginia
3/31 & 4/01/2007 – <u>IPA Iron House Classic Powerlifting Championships</u>
  @ Newark, Ohio
5/04 thru 5/06/2007 – <u>USAPL Masters National Powerlifting Championships</u>
  @ Milwaukee, Wisconsin
10/27/2007 – <u>IPA Iron House Open Powerlifting Championships</u>
  @ Zanesville, Ohio
12/01 & 02/2007 – <u>USAPL American Open Powerlifting Championships</u>
  @ Scranton, Pennsylvania

3/08/2008 – <u>USAPL Virginia Open Powerlifting Championships</u>
  @ Stanardsville, Virginia
3/22/2008 – <u>33rd Annual (2008) USPF West Virginia State Powerlifting Championships</u>
  @ South Charleston, West Virginia
4/19/2008 – <u>USPF Power Sports & Fitness Expo Powerlifting</u>
  @ Mineral Wells, West Virginia
5/03/2008 – <u>IPA Virginia State Powerlifting Championships</u>
  @ Fredericksburg, Virginia
6/12 thru 6/15/2008 – <u>USAPL Men's National Powerlifting Championships</u>
  @ Killeen, Texas
8/23/2008 – <u>USPF American Record Breakers</u>
  @ New Martinsville, West Virginia
11/01/2008 – <u>USPF Regional Powerlifting Championships</u>
  @ Parkersburg, West Virginia

3/28/2009 – <u>34th Annual (2009) USPF West Virginia State Powerlifting Championships</u>
  @ South Charleston, West Virginia

5/23 & 5/24/2009 – <u>SPF National Powerlifting Championships</u>
    @ Nashville, Tennessee

9/05/2009 – <u>SPF "Battle in the Valley" Powerlifting Championships</u>
    @ Salem, Virginia

12/05/2009 – <u>SPF Cell Block Classic Powerlifting</u>
    @ Nashville, Tennessee

4/03/2010 – <u>USPF Ohio Valley Powerlifting Championships</u>
    @ New Martinsville, West Virginia

4/10/2010 – <u>35th Annual (2010) West Virginia State Powerlifting Championships</u>
    @ South Charleston, West Virginia

5/15/2010 – <u>USAPL West Virginia State Powerlifting Championships</u>
    @ South Charleston, West Virginia

6/19 & 6/20/2010 – <u>2010 USPF National Powerlifting Championships</u>
    @ Warwick, Rhode Island

8/20/2010 – <u>SPF Power Station Pro / Am Powerlifting</u>
    @ Sharonville, Ohio

3/05 & 3/06/2011 – <u>SPF Iron Man Classic (2 Day ProAm Event)</u>

3/26/2011 – <u>36th Annual (2011) West Virginia State Powerlifting Championships</u>
    @ South Charleston, West Virginia

5/07/2011 – <u>IPA Championship of the Virginias</u>
    @ Gore, Virginia

5/07 & 5/08/2011 – <u>2011 USAPL National Masters Powerlifting</u>
    @ Atlanta, Georgia

6/25 & 6/26/2011 – <u>IPA Strength Spectacular Powerlifting Championships</u>
    @ York, Pennsylvania

8/06/2011 – <u>USAPL West Virginia State Powerlifting Championships</u>
    @ South Charleston, West Virginia

10/01/2011 – <u>IPF 28th World Men's Masters Powerlifting Championships</u>
    @ St. Catherines, Canada

12/03/2011 – <u>RPS Powerlifting</u>
    @ Allentown, Pennsylvania

3/31/2012 – 37th Annual (2012) USPF West Virginia State Powerlifting Championships
    @ South Charleston, West Virginia

5/05/2012 – RPS (2012) Powerlifting Championships of the Virginias
    @ Winchester, Virginia

7/28/2012 – RPS (2012) Pennsylvania State Powerlifting Championships
    @ Lancaster, Pennsylvania

3/23/2013 – 38th Annual (2013) West Virginia State Powerlifting Championships
    @ South Charleston, West Virginia

4/27/2013 – NASA (2013) West Virginia State Powerlifting Championships
    @ Ravenswood, West Virginia

7/27/2013 – RPS (2013) Pennsylvania State Powerlifting Championships
    @ Lancaster, Pennsylvania

9/15/2013 – APF (2013) Ohio State Powerlifting Championships
    @ Columbus, Ohio

Bibliography / References

Books

AAU Official Handbook 1974-75

Champion of Champions by Larry Pacifico

Guide to Weightlifting Competition by Bob Hoffman

    Copyright 1959 by STRENGTH AND HEALTH PUBLISHING COMPANY

    York, Pennsylvania

Physical POWER / January-February, 1961

    "YMCA Weightlifting in Charleston, West Virginia," Robert A. Rule, Page 20-21.

Weightlifting – AAU Official Rules *Copyright 1971*

Journals

Iron Game History, The Journal of Physical Culture, Volume 8, Number 3, May / June 2004

    http://www.starkcenter.org/iron-game-history/

Weightlifting Journal, Volume 1 / Number 4 / November/December, 1971

Weightlifting Journal, Volume 1 / Number 5 / June, 1972

Weightlifting Journal, Volume 1 / Number 6 / September, 1972

Weightlifting Journal, Volume 1 / Number 7 / January, 1973

Magazines

Iron Man, Volume 38 / Number 1 / November, 1978

Iron Man, Volume 39 / Number 1 / November, 1979

Muscle Builder / Power, Volume 10 / Number 10 / August, 1969

Muscular Development, Volume 7 / Number 6 / June, 1970

    1969 National Collegiate Powerlifting Championships, pg. 66

Muscular Development, November, 1971

Muscular Development / February, 1972

Muscular Development / May, 1972

    "Young Strength Stars" – Paul Sutphin

Muscular Development / February, 1973

Muscular Development / October, 1973

Muscular Development / July–August, 1976

Muscular Development / November – December, 1976

Muscular Development / October, 1980

POWERMAN, Volume 2 / Number 3 / January-February, 1974

1974 YMCA National Powerlifting Championships @ Erie, PA – 1/27/74, pg. 39

Powerlifting News / September, 1972

Powerlifting News / December, 1972

IPF Officers – Charlie Gschwind

220lb. Class – No Wrap Rule – Lifting Sequence Changed

1972 IPF World Championship Results

Powerlifting USA magazine, All Volumes / All issues.

Volume 1 / Number 1 / June, 1977 *thru* Volume 35 / Number 6 / May, 2012

Strength & Health / 1961

1961 Teenage National Weightlifting Championships – Frank White

Strength & Health / January, 1963

"Success Stories" - Vince White

Strength & Health / May-June, 1971

Strength & Health / August, 1971

Strength & Health / June, 1972

Strength & Health / September, 1973

Strength & Health / March, 1974

Newsletters

Charleston, West Virginia YMCA, Volume 10 / Number 2 / June, 1999

National Masters Lifting Newletter / Vol. 1, No. 6., June 5th, 1977

Powerlift Forum, Vol. 1, NO. 3, "Deadlift to Win"

Powerlifting News / January, 1974 thru December, 1976

"The Lifter" by Mike Kennedy

Newspapers

Bluefield Daily Telegraph – Week of April 16th, 1973

"Charleston Club Wins Power Meet"

Bluefield Daily Telegraph – August 6th, 1978

"Sutphin Would Rather Be First"

Charleston Daily Mail – July 11th, 1972

"5-5 : No Weakling"

Charleston Daily Mail – July 18th, 1979
    "Bluefield Native Sets Record"
Charleston Daily Mail – Week of April 11th, 1985
    "Holley Strength Systems"
Charleston Gazette / Mail – February, 1962
Charleston Gazette / Mail – February 22nd, 2004
    "Survival of the Fittest"
Charleston Gazette, March 13th, 1972, *"Weightlifters Gain 5 Trophies"*
Charleston Gazette - June, 1973 / Daily publications.
Charleston Gazette – January, 1976
    "Charleston Weightlifter Sets National Record"
Twin State Observer – June, 1990
    Paul Sutphin : "He's Hard to Beat"

Websites

International Powerlifting Association (IPA)
    http://www.ipapower.com
International Powerlifting Federation (IPF)
    http://www.powerlifting-ipf.com/
Powerlifting's Roots / J.V. Askem
    http://www.marunde-muscle.com/fitness/askem_hist_roots.html
    http://jva.ontariostrongman.ca/PLR.htm
Powerlifting Watch
    http://www.powerliftingwatch.com/
    http://www.powerliftingwatch.com/node/3233
Revolution Powerlifting Syndicate (RPS)
    http://www.rychlakpowersystems.com
Southern Powerlifting Federation (SPF)
    http://www.southernpowerlifting.com
United States Powerlifting Federation
    https://uspfthelegend.com/
World Powerlifting Congress / American Powerlifting Federation (APF)
    http://www.worldpowerliftingcongress.com

Contacts / Interviews

Danny Akers – 12/21/2011

Sam Arrington – 8/22/2011

Lloyd Arthur – 3/26/2011

Mark Chaillet – 5/07/2011, 6/25/2011

Scott Collias – 3/23/2013

Bob Coulling – 9/26/2010, 10/03/2010, 6/29/2011

Rickey Crain – Phone conversations 7/05/2010, 8/12/2010

Doug Currence – 10/30/2010, 1/30/2011, 3/29/2011, 9/11/2011, 12/31/2011, 3/31/2012, 8/26/2012, 3/22/2013, 3/23/2013, 5/03/2013, 5/04/2013

Harry Deitzler – 10/03/2011

Darrell Devor – June, 2009 Interview

Herb Fitzsimmons – 5/23/2011, 6/02/2011, 8/02/2012

Bobby Fox – 8/14/2010

Don Hall – 3/25/2011, 3/26/2011, 3/31/2012, 3/22/2013, 3/23/2013.

Mike Hill – 6/17/2011, 6/25/2011, 5/03/2013

Don Hundley – 3/26/2011, 8/06/2011, 3/31/2012, 3/23/2013, 5/04/2013

Mike Hundley – 3/26/2011, 8/06/2011, 3/31/2012, 5/03/2013

Dave Jeffrey – 7/10/2010

Mike Lambert – Phone conversations : 8/13/2010, 11/23/2011

John Lilly – 3/26/2011

John Messinger – 4/10/2010, 5/15/2010, 3/25/2011, 8/06/2011, 3/20/2012, 3/30/2012, 3/31/2012, 3/22/2013, 3/23/2013, 5/03/2013, 5/04/2013

Gary Moody – 10/23/2010

Chuck Mooney – 3/26/2011, 3/31/2012, 3/23/2013

Dr. Victor Poletajev – Phone interview 2/26/2011

Jim Rubenstein – 5/03/2011, 5/04/2011

Jack Pack – 5/15/2010, 3/26/2011

Sue Pack – 5/15/2010, 3/26/2011

Dwayne Phillips – 12/24/2011

Brian Siders – 5/15/2010, 8/06/2011, 5/04/2013

Louie Simmons – Phone interview 1/01/2010, Interview 10/13/2012

Jim Simon – 2/07/2012

Tim Slamick – 7/21/2011

Allen Smith – 8/06/2011, 5/04/2013

Earl Snider – E-mail 10/21/2011

John Spadafore – 7/21/2011

Eddie Starcher – 3/26/2011

Scott Tusic – E-mails - 12/29/2010, 9/06/2011

Frank White – 3/26/2011, 6/13/2011, 6/17/2011, 8/06/2011, 3/31/2012, 5/22/2012, 3/23/2013.

Vince White – 4/10/2010, 5/15/2010, 3/10/2011, 3/26/2011, 3/29/2011, 4/05/2011, 5/25/2011, 8/27/2011, 11/23/2011, 8/02/2012, 11/21/2012, 3/23/2013

Willie Williams – 8/06/2011

Chris Young – 5/03/2013

About the Author

Paul Sutphin has been Powerlifting in official competition since 1972. While competing in the 148lb. weight class, Paul won the 1979 National (Junior) Powerlifting Championships with a "Ten-times bodyweight Total" of 1482lbs. (672.5 kilos), breaking the Lightweight Junior National Total Record.

By 1981, Sutphin had officially earned *Powerlifter Elite Classification* with Elite Totals in three (3) weight classes (148 – 1482, 165 – 1535, and 181 – 1653) and ranked among the *"Top Ten Lightweight Powerlifters of the 20th Century."* While being the first Powerlifter from West Virginia to Total Elite in multiple weight classes, Paul Sutphin earned National Referee's certification for Powerlifting in 1983 and International (IPF Category II) Referee credentials in 1991.

As an education professional, Paul earned a Bachelor's Degree in Business Administration in May, 1977 and an additional Bachelor's Degree in Teacher Education (2000), majoring in Physical Education and Health Education. Sutphin later earned a Master's Degree in Education (2004), Graduate Certificates in Mathematics (2007 and 2009), and additional endorsements for Secondary Mathematics (2011 and 2013).

On October 15th, 2011 Paul Sutphin was officially inducted into the Bluefield College Sports Hall of Fame in honor of achieving national fame in the sport of Powerlifting. Paul continued to win Powerlifting Championships and set Powerlifting Records in 2012 and 2013.